HOSPITALITY MANAGEMENT ACCOUNTING

HOSPITALITY MANAGEMENT ACCOUNTING

NINTH EDITION

MARTIN G. JAGELS

Contributing Author

CATHERINE E. RALSTON

WILEY

JOHN WILEY & SONS, INC.

Copyright © 2007 by John Wiley & Sons, Inc. All rights reserved.

Published by John Wiley & Sons, Inc., Hoboken, New Jersey
Published simultaneously in Canada

For general information on our other products and services or for technical support, please contact our Customer Care Department within the United States at (800) 762-2974, outside the United States at (317) 572-3993 or fax (317) 572-4002.

Wiley also publishes its books in a variety of electronic formats. Some content that appears in print may not be available in electronic books. For more information about Wiley products, visit our web site at www.wiley.com.

Library of Congress Cataloging-in-Publication Data:

Jagels, Martin G.
    Hospitality management accounting / Martin G. Jagels ; Catherine E. Ralston, contributing author.—9th ed.
        p. cm.
    Includes index.
    ISBN-13: 978-0-471-68789-4
    ISBN-10: 0-471-68789-8 (cloth)
1. Hotels—Accounting. 2. Taverns (Inns)—Accounting. 3. Food Service—Accounting. 4. Managerial accounting. I. Ralston, Catherine E. II. Title.
    HF5586.H75C53 2007
    657′.837—dc22

                                                                2005028314

Printed in the United States of America

CONTENTS

P R E F A C E

Welcome to the **ninth** edition of *Hospitality Management Accounting*. Your studies of the hospitality, tourism, and service industries are taking place during a time of amazing growth and success. Around the world, new operations are being created, while established companies continue to expand their products and services—which, in turn, enhances competition. This increasing growth and competition affects not only hospitality operators, but also the potential customers they seek to serve.

Across the industry, hospitality operators and managers are relying on managerial accounting techniques to help them thrive in this expanding environment. The industry as a whole is becoming more cost and profit conscious, while potential customers are placing increased importance on price, quality, and the level of services they receive. Hospitality industry providers have begun focusing greater attention on increasing their revenue, minimizing costs, and maximizing profit levels, without affecting the quality of service they can provide, relative to the cost of providing those services.

Hospitality Management Accounting continues to evolve with the industry, to give students a solid understanding of how they can use managerial accounting skills in their future careers. This text makes no attempt to cover the detailed concepts and mechanics of financial accounting, or the detailed procedures of bookkeeping. However, Chapter 1 presents a complete review of the basic fundamentals of financial accounting. The scope and content is designed for the student who is taking courses that are related to the managerial aspects of the hospitality industry and are, by their nature, accounting oriented. Although most of the chapters are quite complete, they are not, nor are they meant to be, exhaustive. This book is introductory in nature, and it is hoped that the reader will be prompted to independently explore some of the topics in other books where they are discussed in greater detail.

NEW TO THE NINTH EDITION

- All material, including and especially the exercises and problems, has been thoroughly checked and rechecked to allow for greatest accuracy.
- Chapter 1 has been revised so straight-line, units-of-production, sum-of-the-years'-digits, and double-declining depreciation methods are discussed in detail and consolidated into one chapter.

- In Chapter 2, the section on inventory control methods has been revised to improve conceptual understanding, with greater emphasis placed on perpetual inventory.
- The section on the statement of cash flows is now incorporated into Chapter 10 so its discussion, along with that of working capital, can be examined sequentially.
- Technology concepts, previously in an appendix, are now integrated throughout the book.
- Additional exercises and problems have been added at the end of each chapter to allow students to test their skills and comprehension of the chapter concepts.

ORGANIZATION

The book is designed to give students both a conceptual understanding and a practical use of internal accounting information. The structure and sequence of topics in the book were carefully planned to serve as a basis for developing managerial accounting procedures, quantitative analysis techniques, and reporting concepts. For the ninth edition, all information, procedures, and concepts have been updated.

Chapter 1, "Basic Financial Accounting Review," provides a condensed view of basic financial accounting concepts. Coverage of the fundamental accounting equation has been expanded to improve student understanding and emphasize the equation's purpose, how changes to the equation are developed, recorded, and implemented, and how those changes affect the basic accounting equation. Also included are straight-line, units of production, sum-of-the-year's digits and double-declining depreciation methods. The concept of adjusting entries is discussed in detail, as is the discussion of the accounting cycle of a profit-oriented business.

Chapter 2, "Understanding Financial Statements," emphasizes creating an income statement, statement of ownership equity, and balance sheet. Inventory control methods are presented to improve conceptual understanding, with emphasis on perpetual inventory.

Chapter 3, "Analysis and Interpretation of Financial Statements," uses supporting exhibits to explain comparative balance sheets and comparative income statements.

The discussion of liquidity ratios in Chapter 4, "Ratio Analysis," demonstrates how changes in the current accounts affect the current ratio as well as working capital. The illustrations support the discussion of liquidity and turnover ratios. Credit sales are rapidly changing toward credit card sales from accounts receivable or house accounts, so credit card ratios are discussed in conjunction with accounts receivable.

The text and illustrations in Chapter 6, "The 'Bottom-Up' Approach to Pricing," explains the nature and purpose of this pricing method and how it can be compared to a completed income statement. This chapter emphasizes the techniques used to determine operating income (income before tax) and net income (after tax).

Chapter 8, "The Cost–Volume–Profit Approach to Decisions," emphasizes the relationship between breakeven sales volume and breakeven unit sales. Breakeven is discussed in detail to ensure that students have a clear understanding of this concept before going on to learn how added cost functions are brought in to complete a profit volume analysis.

Chapter 10, "Statement of Cash Flows and Working Capital Analysis," contains a detailed discussion of the statement of cash flows, indirect method, with supporting illustrations. By studying the statement of cash flows and working capital sequentially, students can follow a clear progression through the chapter and see how key operating, financial, and equity accounts are used to develop a statement of cash flows and a working capital analysis. The discussion of working capital analysis stresses the strong link between the statement of cash flows and the working capital analysis.

Although they are not essential components of a managerial accounting course, Chapter 13, "Feasibility Studies—An Introduction," and Chapter 14, "Financial Goals and Information Systems," can be used in class as supplemental chapters at the discretion of the professor.

The exercises and problems have been expanded to further test student assimilation of the material.

FEATURES

The book contains several pedagogical features in every chapter to help students grasp the concepts and techniques presented:

- **Introductions** introduce the key topics that will be presented in the chapter. **Chapter objectives** list the specific skills, procedures, and techniques that students are expected to master after reading the material.
- **Key terms** are in bold within the text so that students can easily familiarize themselves with the language of managerial accounting and develop a working vocabulary.
- **Computer applications** are included at the end of each chapter. They explain how managers and accountants are using computers to process accounting information and improve managerial decision making.
- The **chapter summary** concisely pulls together the many different points covered in the chapter to help trigger students' memories.

- **Discussion questions** ask students to summarize or explain important concepts, procedures, and terminology.
- An **ethics situation** for each chapter challenges students' decision-making abilities and teaches them to look beyond the numbers and consider how accounting information can be used to affect other areas of a hospitality operation.
- **Exercises** have been expanded to tie together concepts from each chapter.
- **Problems** test students' basic accounting skills and the application of concepts. Each chapter has been upgraded.
- The **case** at the end of each chapter presents a business scenario to aid students in understanding managerial accounting applications and developing analysis techniques using realistic business examples. The chapter case problem is tied together with other cases throughout the book and builds on the concepts learned in previous chapters. Thus, each chapter's case will build on or rely on information a student derived in a preceding chapter's case as a starting point or as a source of supplemental information.
- The **glossary** summarizes the key terms presented in the text.

SUPPLEMENTARY MATERIALS

A *Student Workbook and Study Guide* (0-471-68926-2) is available to accompany this text. It contains an outline summary of the key topics in each chapter, a short series of word completion, true/false and multiple-choice questions, short exercises, and comprehensive problems. The word completion, true/false, and multiple-choice questions are oriented toward a conceptual understanding of the chapter material, while the short exercises and comprehensive exercises are practical and application oriented. Solutions to these questions and problems are included after each chapter. Following a three-chapter sequential block, the workbook/study guide contains a three-chapter self-review test, with answers included, so students can gauge their progress through the course.

An *Instructor's Manual* (0-471-78199-1) is also available. It contains detailed solutions to each chapter's exercises, problems, and cases, all of which have been thoroughly checked for accuracy. Alternative math solutions are shown where possible throughout the exercise and problem solutions. Course instructors may select the print version of the *Instructor's Manual* or go to **www.wiley.com/college/jagels** for an electronic version of the *Instructor's Manual* and an electronic true/false and multiple-choice test bank.

WebCT and **Blackboard** online course are available for this book. Visit www.wiley.com/college and click on Technology Solutions for more information, or contact your Wiley representative.

ACKNOWLEDGMENTS

I would like to thank Cathy Ralston of the University of Guelph, in particular, who read every word of the eighth and ninth edition manuscripts and checked the exercises and problems as well as their solutions in the *Instructor's Manual* to help ensure their accuracy.

Additionally, a number of professors and instructors have given suggestions and advice, which aided in the development of the ninth and previous editions. I thank them for taking the time and effort to share their thoughts with me:

Earl R. Arrowood, Bucks County Community College

Herbert F. Brown III, University of South Carolina

Ronald F. Cox, New Mexico State University

Ben K. Goh, Texas Tech University

Karen Greathouse, Western Illinois University

Robert A. McMullin, East Stroudsburg University

John W. Mitchell, Sault College

Susan Reeves, University of South Carolina

John Rousselle, Purdue University

John M. Tarras, Michigan State University

Paul Teehan, Trident Technical College

Thanks to the copyeditor and proofreader of this edition for their assistance. Finally, the editors at John Wiley & Sons, especially Nigar Hale, Julie Kerr, and Scott Amerman, have been especially helpful in bringing the ninth edition to publication.

Martin G. Jagels

CHAPTER 1

BASIC FINANCIAL ACCOUNTING REVIEW

INTRODUCTION

Every profit or nonprofit business entity requires a reliable internal system of accountability. A business accounting system provides this accountability by recording all activities regarding the creation of monetary inflows of sales revenue and monetary outflows of expenses resulting from operating activities. The accounting system provides the financial information needed to evaluate the effectiveness of current and past operations. In addition, the accounting system maintains data required to present reports showing the status of asset resources, creditor liabilities, and ownership equities of the business entity.

In the past, much of the work required to maintain an effective accounting system involved extensive manual effort that was tedious, aggravating, and time consuming. Such systems relied on individual effort to continually record transactions, to add, subtract, summarize, and check for errors. The rapid advancement of computer technology has increased operating speed, data storage, and reliability, accompanied by a significant cost reduction. Inexpensive microcomputers and accounting software programs have advanced to the point where all of the posting, calculations, error checking, and financial reports are provided quickly by the computerized system. The efficiency and cost-effectiveness of accounting computer software allow management to maintain direct personal control of the accounting system.

To effectively understand concepts and analysis techniques discussed within this text, it is essential that the reader have a conceptual as well as a practical understanding of accounting fundamentals. This chapter reviews basic accounting principles, concepts, conventions, and practices. This review should be of particular benefit to the reader who has not taken an introductory accounting course or who has not received accounting training for some time.

CHAPTER OBJECTIVES

After studying this chapter and completing the assigned exercises and problems, the reader should be able to

1. Define and explain the accounting principles and concepts.

2. Explain the conceptual difference between the cash and accrual methods of accounting.

3. Explain the rules of debits and credits and their use as applied to double-entry accounting by increasing or decreasing an account balance of the five basic accounts: **A**ssets, **L**iabilities, **O**wnership **E**quity, **S**ales **R**evenue, and **E**xpenses.

4. Explain the basic balance sheet equation: **A**ssets = **L**iabilities + **O**wnership **E**quity.

5. Explain and demonstrate the difference between journalizing and posting of an accounting transaction.

6. Explain the income statement and its major elements as discussed and applied to the hospitality industry.

7. Complete an unadjusted trial balance, balance sheet, and income statement.

8. Explain and demonstrate end-of-period adjusting entries required by the matching principle.

9. Demonstrate the use of four depreciation methods.

10. Complete an analysis to convert a business entity from cash to an accrual accounting basis.

Financial accounting is concerned with the recording of financial transactions and analyzing the effect of such transactions to assist in the development of business decisions. In addition, financial accounting provides information in the form of balance sheets, income statements, and other financial statements to users outside of businesses that are in some way concerned or affected by the performance of the business—stockholders, creditors, lenders, governmental agencies, and other outside users.

Hospitality management accounting is concerned with providing specialized internal information to managers who are responsible for directing and controlling operations within the hospitality industry. Internal information is the basis for planning alternative short- or long-term courses of action and the decision as to which course of action is selected. Specific detail is provided as to how the selected course of action will be implemented. Managers direct the needed material resources and motivate the human resources needed to carry out a selected course of action. Managers control the implemented course of action to ensure that the plan is being followed and, as necessary, modified to meet the objectives of the selected course of action.

CAREERS IN HOSPITALITY ACCOUNTING

For the student interested in accounting, there are a variety of career opportunities in the hospitality industry. First, there is general accounting, which includes the recording and production of accounting information and/or specialization in a particular area such as food service and beverage cost control. Second, larger organizations might offer careers in the design (or revision) and implementation of accounting systems. A larger organization might also offer careers in budgeting, tax accounting, and auditing that verifies accounting records and reports of individual properties in the chain.

HOSPITALITY ACCOUNTING OVERVIEW

Hospitality business operations, as well as others, are generally identified as having a number of different cyclical sales revenue cycles. First, there is the **daily operating cycle** that applies particularly to restaurant operations where daily sales revenue typically depends on meal periods. Second, there is a **weekly cycle.** On one hand, business travelers normally use hotels, motels, and other hospitality operations during the week and provide little weekend hospitality business. On the other hand, local people most often frequent restaurants on Friday through Sunday more than they do during the week. Third, there is a **seasonal cycle** that depends on vacationers to provide revenue for hospitality operations during vacation months. Fourth, a generalized **business cycle** will exist during recessionary inflationary cycles, and hospitality operations typically experience a major decline in sales revenue.

The various repetitive **accounting cycles** encountered in hospitality operations create unique difficulties in forecasting sales revenue and operating costs. In particular, variable costs (e.g., cost of sales and labor costs) require unique planning procedures that assist in budget forecasting. Since hospitality operations are people-oriented and people-driven, it is more difficult to effectively automate and control hospitality costs than in other nonhospitality business sectors.

Unfortunately, most accounting textbooks and generalized accounting courses emphasize accounting systems using procedures and applications that are applicable to services, retailing, and manufacturing businesses. These types of businesses do not normally require the use of the unique accounting procedures and techniques required by hospitality operations. In manufacturing operations, all costs are generally assigned to products or product lines and identified as direct costs and indirect costs. **Direct costs** include all materials and labor costs that are traceable directly to the product manufactured. **Indirect costs** generally refer to manufacturing or factory overhead, and include such items as administrative salaries, wages and miscellaneous overhead, utilities, interest, taxes, and depreciation. The basic nature of indirect costs presents difficulties isolating specific costs since they are not directly traceable to a particular product. Portions of supporting *indirect costs* are assigned by allocation techniques to each product or product line.

However, a hospitality operation tends to be highly departmentalized with separate operating divisions that provide rooms, food, beverage, banquet, and gift shop services. A hospitality accounting system must allow an independent evaluation of each operating department and its operating divisions. Costs directly traceable to a department or division are identified as direct costs. Typically, the major direct costs include cost of sales (cost of goods sold), salary and wage labor, and specific operating supplies. After direct costs are determined, they are deducted from sales revenue to isolate **contributory income,** which represents the department's or division's contribution to support undistributed indirect costs of the whole operation.

Indirect costs are not easily traceable to a department or division. Generally, no attempt is made at this stage of the evaluation to allocate indirect costs to the department or divisions. Managers review operating results to ensure that contributory income from all departments or divisions is sufficient to cover total indirect costs for the overall hospitality operation and provide excess funds to meet the desired level of profit.

GENERAL FINANCIAL ACCOUNTING TERMS

The objective of this text is to provide managers in the hospitality industry with a working knowledge of how an accounting system develops, maintains, and provides financial information. Managerial analysis is enhanced with an understanding of the information provided by an accounting system. Without management's understanding of the information being provided, management effectiveness will be greatly reduced.

Financial accounting is a common language developed by accountants over time to define the principles, concepts, procedures, and broad rules necessary for management's use in a viable accounting system for making decisions and maintaining an efficient, effective, and profitable business. An **account** is a record in which the current status of each type of asset, liability, owners' equity, sales revenue, and expense is kept. The **balance** is the current status of an account—the amount that is in a particular account at a specific point in time. An accounting system shows detailed information regarding each of the account categories, and it governs recording, reporting, and preparation of financial statements that show the financial condition of a business entity. The **accounting period** is the time period covered by the financial statements.

CASH VERSUS ACCRUAL ACCOUNTING

The cash and accrual basis are the two methods of accounting. The difference between the two methods is how and when sales revenue and expenses are recognized. The **cash basis** of accounting recognizes sales revenue inflows when cash is received and operating expense outflows to generate sales revenue when cash is paid. Simply put, the cash basis recognizes sales revenue and operating expenses only when cash changes hands. The **accrual basis** of accounting recognizes inflows of sales revenue when earned and operating expense outflows to produce sales revenues when incurred; it does not matter when cash is received or paid. Many small operations use the cash basis of accounting for their type of business; no requirement exists to prepare and report their financial position to external users.

The cash basis can be computed as follows:

Beginning cash + Cash sales revenue − Cash payments = Ending cash

There is no basic equation for the accrual basis.

To illustrate cash accounting, we will assume that a new restaurant purchased and sold inventory on a cash basis for two months of operation. A partial income statement prepared on a cash basis for the first two months of operation, assuming monthly sales revenue of $10,000 and total inventories of $8,000 for resale, would show the following:

	Month 1	Month 2
Cash sales revenue	$10,000	$10,000
Cash purchases	(8,000)	-0-
Gross margin (before other expenses)	$ 2,000	$10,000

This method gives a distorted view of the operations over the two months. The combined two-month gross margin (or gross profit) would be $12,000; however, the accrual method will give a more accurate picture of the real situation, a gross margin (before other expenses) of $6,000 each month. In the following accrual example, cost of sales is estimated at 40% of sales revenue. Cost of sales refers to cost of goods sold.

	Month 1	Month 2
Cash sales revenue	$10,000	$10,000
Cash purchases	(4,000)	(4,000)
Gross margin (before other expenses)	$ 6,000	$ 6,000

The examples given are not meant to suggest that the cash basis of accounting is never used. As indicated in the previous discussions, many small businesses find the cash basis appropriate. However, the cash basis is not considered adequate for medium and larger business organizations, which normally use the accrual basis of accounting. The accrual method is used throughout this text, except in cases where cash management supplements the decision-making process. Exceptions to the accrual method will be discussed in Chapter 10, "Statement of Cash Flows and Working Capital Analysis," Chapter 11, "Cash Management," and Chapter 12, "The Investment Decision."

Without a basic knowledge of the accounting system and the information provided, it will be difficult to produce or understand financial reports. The two major financial reports are the balance sheet and income statement.

BALANCE SHEETS AND INCOME STATEMENTS

The **balance sheet** reveals the financial condition of a business entity by showing the status of its assets, liabilities, and ownership equities on the specific ending date of an operating period. The **income statement** reports the economic results of the business entity by matching sales revenue inflows, and expense outflows to show the results of operations—**net income or net loss.** The income statement is generally considered the more important of the two major financial reports. Since it reports the results of operations, it clearly identifies sales revenue inflows and the cost outflows to produce sales revenue. We will discuss the income statement later in this chapter.

The balance sheet provides an easier basis for understanding double-entry accounting, so it will be discussed first. The **accounting equation,** as it is known, consists of three key elements and defines the basic format of the balance sheet. The basic configurations of a balance sheet and an income statement discussed in this chapter are expanded in Chapter 2.

The balance sheet equation is $A = L + OE.$

Assets (A)	Resources of value used by a business entity to create sales revenue, which, in turn, increases assets.
Liabilities (L)	Debt obligations owed to creditors as a result of operations to generate sales revenue; to be paid in the near future with assets. Liabilities represent creditor equity or claims against the assets of the business entity.
Ownership equity (OE)	Ownership equity represents claims to assets of a business entity. There are three basic forms of ownership equity: **1.** Proprietorship—entity financing provided by a sole owner.

2. Partnership—entity financing provided by two or more owners (partners).
3. Corporation—a legal entity incorporated under the laws of a state, separate from its owners.
   - *Capital stock:* Financing provided by stockholders (or shareholders) with ownership represented by shares of corporate stock. Each share of stock represents one ownership claim.
   - *Retained earnings:* Earnings of the corporation that have been kept in the business after dividends are paid.

The equality point indicates an absolute necessity to maintain the same on both sides of the equation. The sum total of the left side of the equation, total assets, *A,* must equal the total sum of the right side of the equation, liabilities, *L,* plus ownership equity, *OE.* When a transaction affects both sides of the equation, equality of the equation must be maintained. One side of the equation cannot increase or decrease without the other side increasing or decreasing by the same amount. If a transaction occurs that affects only one side of the equation, total increases must equal total decreases.

The assets consumed produce sales revenue that become cost of sales and operating expenses. The liabilities and ownership equity elements of the equation represent the claims against assets by creditors (liabilities) and claims against the assets by the ownership (OE). The following describes the balance sheet elements:

ASSETS	=	LIABILITIES	+	OWNERSHIP EQUITY
⇕		⇕		⇕
Resources	=	Creditors' Equity	+	Ownership Equity

Because the balance sheet equation is a simple linear equation, knowing the dollar values of two of the three basic elements allows the value of the missing element to be identified. The following balance sheet equation has values given for all three elements. Then each of the three examples has the value of one element omitted from the equation to show how to find the value of the missing element:

ASSETS	=	LIABILITIES	+	OWNERSHIP EQUITY
⇕		⇕		⇕
$100,000	=	$25,000	+	$75,000

$$[A - L = OE] = \$100{,}000 - \$25{,}000 = \underline{\$\ 75{,}000}$$
$$[A - OE = L] = \$100{,}000 - \$75{,}000 = \underline{\$\ 25{,}000}$$
$$[L + OE = A] = \$\ 25{,}000 + \$75{,}000 = \underline{\$100{,}000}$$

DOUBLE-ENTRY ACCRUAL ACCOUNTING

The analysis of accounting transactions, the recording, posting, adjusting, and reporting economic results and financial condition of a business entity is the heart of **double-entry accrual accounting.**

For an accounting transaction to occur, at least one element of the balance sheet equation or the income statement elements must be created or changed. An exchange between a business entity where services are rendered or goods are sold to an external entity for cash or on credit, or where services are received or goods are purchased creates a transaction. Following the transaction, adjusting entries must be made to adjust the operating accounts of the business entity at the end of an operating period to recognize internal accruals and deferrals. Such transactions will recognize sales revenues earned but not yet received or recorded, and expenses incurred but not yet paid or recorded. To complete the accounting period, a requirement also exists to close the temporary income statement operating accounts (sales revenue and expenses) to bring them to a zero balance and transfer net income or net loss to the capital account(s) or the retained earnings account. Note that this requirement means that an entry is made on both sides of the equation—thus, the name *double-entry accounting.* Adjusting and closing entries will be discussed in detail later in this chapter.

Since no transaction can affect only one account, the balance sheet equation is kept in balance and the equality between both sides of the equation, $A = L + OE,$ is maintained. Each transaction directs the change to be made to each account involved in the transaction. Each directed change will cause an increase or decrease in the stated dollar amount to a specified account. It is important to understand how a journal entry directs such changes to a specific account. This is accomplished through the use of two account columns to receive numerical values that follow the rules of debit and credit entries.

GENERALLY ACCEPTED ACCOUNTING PRINCIPLES

Accounting is not a static system; it is a dynamic process that incorporates **generally accepted accounting principles (GAAP)** that evolve to suit the needs of financial statement readers, such as business managers, equity owners, creditors, and governmental agencies with meaningful, dependable information. The general principles and concepts discussed in this text will include business entity, monetary unit, going concern, cost, time period, conservatism, consistency, materiality, full disclosure, objectivity, and matching principle. In addition, the gain or loss recognition on the disposal of depreciable assets will be discussed.

BUSINESS ENTITY PRINCIPLE

From an accounting, if not from a legal, point of view, the transactions of a **business entity** operating as a proprietorship, partnership, or corporation are considered to be separate and distinct from all personal transactions of its owners. The separation of personal transactions of the owners from the business entity must be maintained, even if the owners work in or for the business entity. Only changes to assets, liabilities, ownership equity, and other transactions of the business entity are entered to the organization's accounting records. The ownership's personal assets, debts, and expenses are not part of the business entity.

MONETARY UNIT PRINCIPLE

The assumption of the **monetary unit principle** is that the primary national monetary unit is used for recording numerical values of business exchanges and operating transactions. The U.S. monetary unit is the dollar. Thus, the accounting function in our case records the *dollar value* of **sales revenue inflows** and **expense outflows** of the business entity during its operations. The monetary unit of the dollar also expresses financial information within the financial statements and reports. Information provided and maintained in the accounting system is recorded in dollars.

GOING CONCERN PRINCIPLE

Under normal circumstances, the **going concern principle** makes the assumption that a business entity will remain in operation indefinitely. This continuity of existence assumes that the cost of business assets will be recovered over time by way of profits that are generated by successful operations. The balance sheet values for long-lived assets such as land, building, and equipment are shown at their actual acquisition cost. Since there is no intention to sell such assets, there is no reason to value them at market value. The original cost of a long-lived physical asset (other than land) is recovered over its useful life using depreciation expense.

COST PRINCIPLE

The assumption made by the monetary concept is tied directly to the **cost principle,** which requires the value of business transactions be recorded at the actual or equivalent *cash cost*. During extended periods of inflation or deflation, comparing income statements for different years becomes difficult, if not meaningless, under the stable dollar assumption. However, some exceptions are made with the valuation of inventories for resale, and also to express certain balance sheet and income statement items in terms of current, rather than historic dollars.

TIME PERIOD PRINCIPLE

The time period principle requires a business entity to complete an analysis to report financial condition and profitability of its business operation over a specific **operating time period.** An ongoing business operates continuously. For example, electrical power in reality flows continuously to the user, yet in theory the flow stops when the service meter reading is recorded. The billing statement says that service for the period technically ended at a certain date, although service continued without interruption. This example relates to a monthly period; however, the theory applies to any time period—daily, weekly, monthly, quarterly, semiannually, or annually. An accounting year is an accounting period of one year. A *fiscal year* is for any 12 consecutive months and does not necessarily coincide with a calendar year that begins on January 1 and ends on December 31 of the same year. In the hospitality business, statements are frequently prepared on a monthly and, in some cases, a weekly basis.

CONSERVATISM PRINCIPLE

A business should never prepare financial statements that will cause balance sheet items such as assets to be overstated or liabilities to be understated, sales revenues to be overstated, or expenses to be understated. Situations might exist where estimates are necessary to determine the inventory values or to decide an appropriate depreciation rate. The inventory valuation should be lower rather than higher. **Conservatism** in this situation increases the cost of sales and decreases the **gross margin** (also called the *gross profit*).

 The costs of long-lived assets (other than land) are systematically recovered through **depreciation expense,** and should be higher rather than lower. Conservatism in this case will increase expenses and, therefore, lower reported operating income; its goal is to avoid overstating operating income. However, caution must be exercised to ensure that conservatism is not taken to the extreme, creating misleading results. For example, restaurant equipment with an estimated five-year life could be fully depreciated in its first year of use. Although this procedure is certainly conservative, it is hardly realistic.

CONSISTENCY PRINCIPLE

The **consistency principle** was established to ensure comparability and consistency of the procedures and techniques used in the preparation of financial statements from one accounting period to the next. For example, the cash basis requires that cash be exchanged before sales revenue or expenses can be recognized, while the accrual basis of accounting requires recognition of sales revenue when earned and expenses when incurred. Switching back and forth between the two would not be consistent, nor would a random change in inventory valuation methods from one period to the next. When changes made are not consistent with the last accounting period, the full disclosure principle, discussed below, requires informing probable and potential readers of the statements of such changes. The disclosure should show the economic effects of the changes on financial results of the current period and the probable economic impact on future periods.

MATERIALITY CONCEPT

Theoretically, items that may affect the decision of a user of financial information are considered important or material, and must be reported in a correct way. The **materiality concept** allows immaterial small dollar amount items to be treated in an expedient although incorrect manner. In the previous discussion of conservatism, an item of restaurant equipment with a five-year life could be fully depreciated in its first year. This technique would be considered overly conservative, particularly if it has a material effect to operating income. Consider the alternatives. First, equipment costing $50,000 with no estimated residual value could be fully depreciated the first year to maximize depreciation expense, thus reducing operating income. Second, the equipment could be systematically depreciated over each year of estimated life, to allocate depreciation expense charges against sales revenue in each year of serviceable life.

	First Alternative, First Year Fully Depreciate $50,000 First Year	Second Alternative, First Year Depreciate $10,000 per Year Five Years
Sales revenue	$500,000	$500,000
Operating expenses	(450,000)	(450,000)
Income before depreciation	$ 50,000	$ 50,000
Depreciation expense	(50,000)	(10,000)
Operating income	$ -0-	$ 40,000

Depreciating equipment systematically each year over the life of the asset provides the most realistic alternative. This technique recovers the cost of a long-lived physical asset by allocating depreciation expense based on the consumption of the benefits received from the asset over five years of use. However, a restaurant might have purchased a supply of letterhead stationery for use over the next five years at a cost of $200. The restaurant could show the total amount of $200 as an expense in the year purchased, opting not to expense the stationery at $40 per year over five years. Operating income would not be materially affected by completely expensing the purchase in year one.

FULL DISCLOSURE PRINCIPLE

Financial statements are primarily concerned with a past period. The **full disclosure principle** states that any future event that may or will occur, and that will have a material economic impact on the financial position of the business, should be disclosed to probable and potential readers of the statements. Such disclosures are most frequently made by footnotes.

For example, a hotel should report the building of a new wing, or the future acquisition of another property. A restaurant facing a lawsuit from a customer who was injured by tripping over a frayed carpet edge should disclose the contingency of the lawsuit. Similarly, if accounting practices of the current financial statements were changed and differ from those previously reported, the changes should be disclosed. Changes from one period to the next that affect current and future business operations should be reported if possible. Changes of this nature include changes made to the method used to determine depreciation expense or to the method of inventory valuation; such changes would increase or decrease the value of ending inventory, cost of sales, gross margin, and net income or loss. All changes disclosed should indicate the dollar effects such disclosures have on financial statements.

OBJECTIVITY PRINCIPLE

This **objectivity principle** requires a transaction to have a basis in fact. Some form of objective evidence or documentation must exist to support a transaction before it can be entered into the accounting records. Such evidence is the receipt for the payment of a guest check or the acceptance of a credit card, or the record of billing a **house account**—account of a hotel guest—that supports earned sales revenue. The accrual basis of accounting recognizes sales revenue when earned, not necessarily when received. Sales revenue is earned when cash is received or when credit is given, thereby creating accounts receivable—a record of the amount expected to be received in the near future. Expenses are incurred when cash is paid or when credit is received, creating an accounts payable on which payment is to be made in the near future.

If payment of a receivable becomes uncollectible, it may be written off as **bad debt** expense (income statement method for income tax purposes). An uncollectible account may also be written off through the creation of an allowance for uncollectable accounts (balance sheet method for financial reporting purposes). The allowance for uncollectible accounts may be established to provide for future bad debts. However, the creation of an allowance account for bad debts (balance sheet method) is an example of an exception to the objectivity concept. The allowance account has no absolute basis in fact because it relates to future events that might or might not occur. However, the allowance account for bad debts is normally based on past historical experience on the percentage of receivables not collected. Evidence of past receivables that were not collected is considered supporting evidence within the bounds of the objectivity concept and the conservatism concept.

MATCHING PRINCIPLE

The **matching principle** reinforces the accrual basis of accounting. Assets are consumed to generate sales revenue inflows while outflows of assets are identified as operating expenses. The matching principle requires that for each accounting period all sales revenues earned must be recognized, whether payment is received or not. It also requires the recognition of all operating expenses incurred, whether paid or not paid during the period. As previously discussed, sales revenue is recognized when earned and operating expenses are recognized when incurred, regardless of when cash is received or paid.

The matching principle also conforms to the timing of the recognition of sales revenue inflows and expense outflows that allow matching of sales revenue to expenses for an accounting period. When a profit-directed operation ends its operating period, it seeks to determine the best estimate of operating results—**net income** or *net loss*. When total sales revenue is greater than total expenses, net income will exist. When total sales revenue is less than total expenses, a net loss will exist. The financial statement that discloses financial results for an accounting period is the income statement. If all sales revenues earned and operating expenses incurred at the end of an operating period are not recognized, the resulting net income or net loss will not provide the most accurate estimate of profit or loss.

If a depreciable asset is disposed of, the total accumulated depreciation charges over its life are deducted from its original cost to find its **book value.** When a long-lived asset is sold, traded, or otherwise disposed of, the book value of the asset is matched against the value received (not original historical cost) to determine if a gain or loss is to be recognized at its disposal.

THE LEDGER ACCOUNT AND DEBIT—CREDIT FUNCTIONS

In a manual accounting system, the **general ledger** maintains separate accounts for each type of accounting transaction. These accounts are identified by name and account number using a standardized format. Ledger accounts are necessary to record transactions on all items reported on the financial statements. The ledger account records each dollar value posted and reports the account balance after each entry is posted. The journal entry is the source of instructions that identifies a specific account by name, the dollar value, and the debit or credit column to be entered. The effect of the **debit** or **credit** entry will *increase* or *decrease* the balance of the account posted, depending on whether the normal balance is a debit- or credit-balanced account. A ledger account page generally uses the following format:

Account Name: _____   *Account No:* _____

Date	*Explanation*	*P/R*	*Debit*	*Credit*	*Balance*

P/R is the posting reference that identifies the journal entry page number that directs posting of an account by name and a dollar amount.

A **modified T account** is a simple format used to aid in understanding account posting. This format shows a continuous balance that eliminates the need to total the debit and credit columns to find the correct balance of an account. The same principle of posting dollar amounts to the *left* or debit column and the *right* or credit column applies whether a manual or computerized system is being used. A modified T format shows the key elements of a ledger account. The use of this format is more than adequate for academic understanding.

Any Account

Left side or *Debit side*	*Right side or* *Credit side*	*Account* *Balance*

RULES OF DEBIT–CREDIT FUNCTIONS AND THEIR EFFECT ON THE BALANCE SHEET ACCOUNTS

Assets are debit-balanced accounts and are increased by debits and decreased by credits. Liabilities and ownership equity accounts are credit-balanced and increased by credits and decreased by debits. The debit–credit rules as applied to the balance sheet equation are summarized as follows:

Assets	**=**	**Liabilities**	**+ Ownership equity**
(Debit-balanced accounts)		**(Credit-balanced accounts)**	
Increased by debits		**Increased by credits**	**Increased by credits**
Decreased by credits		**Decreased by debits**	**Decreased by debits**

RULES OF DEBIT–CREDIT FUNCTIONS AND THEIR EFFECT ON INCOME STATEMENT ACCOUNTS

Sales revenue accounts are credit-balanced accounts; credits increase a credit-balanced account and debits decrease a credit-balanced account. Expense accounts are debit-balanced; debits increase a debit-balanced account and credits decrease a debit-balanced account. The debit–credit rules for income statement accounts are summarized below:

Sales revenue accounts   **Expense accounts**
⇕   ⇕
(Credit-balanced accounts)   **(Debit-balanced accounts)**

THE JOURNAL AND JOURNAL ENTRY

A **journal** includes all accounting transactions and is considered the historical record for a business entity. All transactions must be recorded through a **journal entry** that provides specific instructions in a line-by-line sequence. Each line names a specific account and an amount designated as a debit or credit function to be posted to each named account. Three requirements characterize journal entries:

1. The journal entry must identify at least two accounts.
2. The journal entry must show at least one debit and one credit entry.
3. The sum of the debits and credits must be equal.

Each business transaction must be analyzed to determine the effects of increasing or decreasing an asset, liability, owners' equity item, sales revenue, or expense accounts. It is incorrect to view debits as increases and credits as decreases in the balance of all ledger accounts. All accounts are referred to as being normally debit or credit balanced, based on their classifications. The normal account balances for each of the five types of accounts and their debit–credit relationships as a review are summarized as follows:

Account Category	*Normal Balance*	*Balance Increased by*	*Balance Decreased by*
Assets	Debit	Debits	Credits
Liabilities	Credit	Credits	Debits
Ownership equity	Credit	Credits	Debits
Sales revenue	Credit	Credits	Debits
Operating expenses	Debit	Debits	Credits

Consider the following transaction: A proprietor, Gram Disk, begins a business entity called the Texana Restaurant on May 1, 2006. He makes an initial investment of $100,000 cash to begin operations. The transaction creates the following balance sheet equation:

Assets		Liabilities		Ownership equity
Assets	=	Liabilities	+	Ownership equity
$100,000	=	-0-	+	$100,000

Date	Account Titles	P/R	Debit	Credit
05-01-2006	Cash	101	$100,000	
	Gram Disk, Capital	502		$100,000

P/R: The posting reference identifying the number of the account posted.

Dates and account numbers are used in this exhibit to clarify their use in a typical ledger account format and *will not* be used in future journal entries.

EXHIBIT 1.1

Texana Restaurant Journal Entry to Initiate Accounting System

Exhibit 1.1 shows the journal entry to record the $100,000 initial cash investment.

The journal entry from Exhibit 1.1 is posted as follows:

Cash *(Asset)*

Debit	Credit	Balance
$100,000		$100,000

Gram Disk, Capital *(OE)*

Debit	Credit	Balance
	$100,000	$100,000

On May 5, 2006, Gram Disk purchased a former restaurant building for $150,000, paying $45,000 in cash and assuming a **note payable** for $105,000 balance owed. In addition, he purchased $8,000 of food inventory and $2,000 of beverage inventory for cash. He purchased equipment for $12,000 on short credit (**accounts payable**). These transactions were journalized in a compound entry, which uses more than two accounts. Then they were posted to modified T ledger accounts, as shown in Exhibit 1.2.

As can be seen, six new ledger accounts were created to post operating journal entry 1.

Cash *(Asset)*

Debit	Credit	Balance
$100,000		$100,000
	$55,000	45,000

Food Inventory *(Asset)*

Debit	Credit	Balance
$8,000		$8,000

Beverage Inventory

Debit	Credit	Balance
$2,000		$2,000

Building *(Asset)*

Debit	Credit	Balance
$150,000		$150,000

Equipment *(Asset)*

Debit	Credit	Balance
$12,000		$12,000

Accounts Payable

Debit	Credit	Balance
	$12,000	$12,000

Notes Payable *(Liability)*

Debit	Credit	Balance
	$105,000	$105,000

Gram Disk, Capital *(OE)*

Debit	Credit	Balance
	$100,000	$100,000

Account Titles	Debit	Credit
Food inventory	$ 8,000	
Beverage inventory	2,000	
Building	150,000	
Equipment	12,000	
Accounts payable		$ 12,000
Notes payable		105,000
Cash		55,000

■ **EXHIBIT 1.2**

Texana Restaurant Operating Journal Entry 1

After posting the journal entry, the balance sheet equation and a balance sheet look like this:

Assets   =   Liabilities   +   Ownership Equity
⇕   ⇕   ⇕
$217,000 $117,000 $100,000

Texana Restaurant
Balance Sheet (Interim)
May 5, 2006

Assets		Liabilities and Ownership Equity	
Cash	$ 45,000	Accounts payable	$ 12,000
Food inventory	8,000	Notes payable	105,000
Beverage inventory	2,000	Total liabilities	$117,000
Building	150,000	Ownership Equity:	
Equipment	12,000	Capital, Gram Disk	$100,000
Total Assets	$217,000	Total Liabilities & OE	$217,000

THE INCOME STATEMENT

The income statement equation consists of three basic elements that produce three possible outcomes in for-profit operations:

Sales revenue (*SR*)   Sales revenue is produced from the sale of goods and/or services.

Cost of sales (*CS*)   Cost of sales reflects the cost of inventories purchased for resale that were sold.

When total sales revenue equals the total cost of producing the revenue, **breakeven** is achieved; no profit or loss exists. If total sales revenue exceeds total cost of producing the revenue, **profit** exists. If total sales revenue is less than the total cost of producing the revenue, a **loss** exists. The income statement shows the ending results of operations as of a specific date for a specific period. These outcomes can be described by the following relationships:

Sales revenue = Cost of sales + Expenses; *Breakeven*
Sales revenue > Cost of sales + Expenses; *Net income*
Sales revenue < Cost of sales + Expenses; *Net loss*

These and a few other terms are useful when discussing income statements:

Gross margin (*GM*)   Sales revenue minus cost of sales (also known as gross profit).

Expenses (*E*)   The cost of assets consumed to produce sales revenue. This does not include the cost of inventory consumed.

Breakeven (*BE*)   An economic result of operations when total sales revenue equals total costs; no profit (operating income) or loss will exist.

Operating income (*OI*)   Income before taxes.

Net income (*NI*)   An economic result of operations when total sales revenue is greater than total costs after income taxes.

Net loss (*NL*)   An economic result of operations when total sales revenue is less than total costs.

Note that because gross margin equals sales revenue minus cost of sales, the income statement can be restated this way:

Gross margin − Expenses = Operating income or Operating loss

Sales revenue is earned when cash is received or when credit is extended, creating a receivable. Credit card sales represent the major source of sales revenue made on credit in the hospitality industry today. **Accounts receivable** (or house accounts) continue to be used but represent a small portion of total sales made on credit. Credit card sales create **credit card receivables** on which reimbursement is normally received in an average of one to five operating days, depending on the type of credit card accepted.

Continuing from the preceding May 1 and 5 with the Texana Restaurant transactions, we will look at typical operating transactions regarding sales revenue and operating expenses. Assume during the period May 6 to May 31 that the following additional transactions occurred:

Paid two-year premium on liability and casualty insurance	$ 3,600
Purchased food inventory on account	4,200
Paid employee wages	3,400
Purchased beverage inventory for cash	1,400
Paid employee salaries	1,800
Received and paid May utilities expense	282
Sales revenue for May; $24,280 cash, $620 on credit cards	24,900
Paid miscellaneous expenses for the month	818

To maintain continuity and simplicity, no date or posting reference columns are shown in Exhibit 1.3 and each transaction is journalized separately.

Account Titles	*Debit*	*Credit*
Prepaid insurance	$ 3,600	
Cash		$ 3,600
Food inventory	$ 4,200	
Accounts payable		$ 4,200
Wages expense	$ 3,400	
Cash		$ 3,400
Beverage inventory	$ 1,400	
Cash		$ 1,400
Salaries expense	$ 1,800	
Cash		$ 1,800
Utilities expense	$ 282	
Cash		$ 282
Cash	$24,280	
Credit card receivables	620	
Revenue		$24,900
Miscellaneous expense	$ 818	
Cash		$ 818

■ **EXHIBIT 1.3**
Texana Restaurant Operating Journal Entry 2

The journal entries in Exhibit 1.3 are posted for Texana Restaurant as follows:

General Ledger

Cash (Asset)

Debit	Credit	Balance
$100,000		$100,000
	$55,000	45,000
	3,600	41,400
	3,400	38,000
	1,400	36,600
	1,800	34,800
	282	34,518
24,280		58,798
	818	57,980

Credit Card Receivables

Debit	Credit	Balance
$ 620		$ 620

Prepaid Insurance (Asset)

Debit	Credit	Balance
$ 3,600		$ 3,600

Food Inventory (Asset)

Debit	Credit	Balance
$ 8,000		$ 8,000
4,200		12,200

Beverage Inventory (Asset)

Debit	Credit	Balance
$ 2,000		$ 2,000
1,400		3,400

Building (Asset)

Debit	Credit	Balance
$150,000		$150,000

Equipment (Asset)

Debit	Credit	Balance
$ 12,000		$ 12,000

Accounts Payable (Liability)

Debit	Credit	Balance
	$12,000	$ 12,000
	4,200	16,200

Notes Payable (Liability)

Debit	Credit	Balance
	$105,000	$105,000

Sales Revenue

Debit	Credit	Balance
	$24,900	$ 24,900

Wages Expense

Debit	Credit	Balance
$ 3,400		$ 3,400

Salaries Expense

Debit	Credit	Balance
$ 1,800		$ 1,800

Utilities Expense

Debit	Credit	Balance
$ 282		$ 282

Miscellaneous Expense

Debit	Credit	Balance
$ 818		$ 818

Gram Disk, Capital (OE)

Debit	Credit	Balance
$100,000		$100,000

At this point, it is advantageous to prepare an **unadjusted trial balance.** All accounts with balances are listed in this order:

1. Current assets
2. Fixed assets and contra assets
3. Current liabilities

4. Long-term liabilities

5. Owners' capital

6. Contra capital

7. Sales revenue

8. Expenses

The objective is to confirm that the sum of all debit-balanced accounts is equal to the sum of all credit-balanced accounts. As you will see from the following unadjusted trial balance, the totals of the debits and credits are equal. However, it should not be assumed that everything is necessarily correct. For example, an entry might have been made for the correct amount but posted to the wrong account. Two accounts could be correctly identified with the wrong amount shown in both cases, or a transaction might have been entirely omitted and not journalized.

Such errors are not uncommon in a manual or computerized system; they normally show up in later stages in the accounting process. When a journal entry or posting error is identified, it is corrected by an adjusting journal entry, creating an **adjusted trial balance.**

The unadjusted trial balance for Texana Restaurant accounts is shown in Exhibit 1.4.

END-OF-PERIOD ADJUSTING ENTRIES

Adjusting entries are needed to ensure that information for the income statement and the balance sheet will be as accurate as possible. Generally, an operating period is one year. A calendar year begins on January 1 and ends on December 31 of the same year. In addition to annual periods, many organizations operate on monthly, quarterly, or semiannual operating periods.

At the end of an operating period, **adjustments** are made to recognize all sales revenue earned. This might be sales revenue not yet recorded or sales revenue that was earned but will not be received until sometime in the new accounting period. Adjustment must also be made to recognize expenses not yet recorded or expenses that were incurred in the current period but not expected to be paid until sometime in the new operating period.

Adjusting entries are needed to ensure that correct amounts of sales revenue and expenses are reported in the income statement, and to ensure that the balance sheet reports the proper assets and liabilities. Adjusting entries are also used for items that, by their nature, are normally deferred. These consist of two types of adjustments:

1. *The use or consumption of an asset and recognition of it as an expense.* This type of adjustment typically adjusts supplies, prepaid expenses, and depreciable assets.

Texana Restaurant Unadjusted Trial Balance for the Month Ended May 31, 2006		
Account Titles	*Debit*	*Credit*
Cash	$ 57,980	
Credit card receivables	620	
Prepaid insurance	3,600	
Food inventory	12,200	
Beverage inventory	3,400	
Building	150,000	
Equipment	12,000	
Accounts payable		$ 16,200
Notes payable		105,000
Gram Disk, capital		100,000
Sales revenue		24,900
Wages expense	3,400	
Salaries expense	1,800	
Utilities expense	282	
Miscellaneous expense	818	
Account Totals	$246,100	$246,100

■ **EXHIBIT 1.4**
Sample Trial Balance: Texana Restaurant

2. *The reduction of a liability and recognition of sales revenue.* This adjustment concerns the recognition of unearned revenue as being recognized as earned.

Operating supplies are assets until they are consumed. At the end of a period, the difference between the balance in the supplies ledger account and the value of supplies remaining in inventory represents the amount consumed that needs to be expensed. Assume that a supplies account had a balance of $1,200 at the end of an operating period and that supplies on hand were $400. Thus, $1,200 − $400 = $800 of supplies were used. The adjusting entry is:

Account	Debit	Credit
Supplies expense	$800	
Supplies		$800

All prepaid items such as prepaid rent and prepaid insurance are paid for in advance and are considered to be assets from which benefits will be received over the life of the prepaid. The amount of a prepaid asset to be expensed over its expected life can be expressed in months or years:

Cost of the prepaid / Life (time) = Amount expensed

For example, assume rent was prepaid for the next two years for $24,000. The rent expense for one year would be $12,000 ($24,000 / 2 years), or $1,000 per month ($24,000 / 24 months):

Account	Debit	Credit
Rent expense	$12,000	
Prepaid rent		$12,000

Period-ending monthly adjustments are needed to ensure that financial statements are based on accurate data. The income statement and balance sheet must conform to the principle of matching sales revenues to expenses, and must include those end-of-period adjustments as are necessary to recognize accruals and deferrals.

Accruals represent end-of-period adjustments recognizing sales revenue earned and expenses incurred, with the receipt of payment or the making of payment expected to occur in the next accounting period. **Deferrals** represent end-of-period adjustments to revenues and expenses, and also include adjustments to assets and liabilities to reflect sales revenue earned and expenses incurred. In our continuing example, we will discuss six adjustments: cost of sales, inventory, prepaid expenses, depreciation, wages, and salaries expense.

COST OF SALES AND INVENTORY ADJUSTMENTS

Any business purchasing inventory or producing it for resale will not expect to sell all items available during an accounting period. A restaurant operation will always maintain a minimum food and beverage inventory to take care of current daily and near-future business operations. At the end of an accounting period, the cost of inventory sold is identified as an expense described as **cost of sales (CS).** Ending inventory (EI) not sold will continue to be classi-

Account Titles	Debit	Credit
Cost of sales	$12,200	
Food inventory		$12,200
Food inventory	$ 3,200	
Cost of sales		$ 3,200

■ **EXHIBIT 1.5**
Texana Restaurant Cost of Sales and Food Inventory Adjustment

fied as an asset and is not expensed. Cost of sales (CS) describes cost of goods sold. It is determined easily: Use the beginning inventory (BI), add inventory purchases (P), and deduct inventory not sold. Using previously discussed information for Texana Restaurant, we can calculate cost of sales. Assuming ending food inventory on May 31, 2005, is $3,200, and ending beverage inventory is $1,175, the cost of sales for both product inventory accounts is $11,225.

[Beginning inventory	+	Purchases	−	Ending inventory	=	Cost of sales]
Food: -0-	+	$12,200	−	$3,200	=	$ 9,000
Beverage: -0-	+	$ 3,400	−	$1,175	=	$ 2,225
				Total Net Cost of Sales:		**$11,225**

Several different methods may be used to adjust the inventory for resale accounts to find cost of inventory sold. The *cost of sales method* will be used in this discussion. Normally, the first of two adjustments requires that cost of sales be debited in the amount equal to the balance of the inventory account, followed by crediting to the inventory account equal to its balance. Posting the entry brings the inventory to a zero balance, and in effect transfers the inventory account balance to the cost of sales account. The next adjustment requires the value of ending inventory to be debited to the inventory account and credited to the *cost of sales account,* and the second entry restores the inventory account to the value of the end of the period closing inventory. Adjusting entries for food and beverage inventory accounts are written and posted as shown in Exhibit 1.5.

Posting the adjusting entry will create the cost of sales account, thereby adjusting the food inventory account to the correct ending balance. Study the following posting effects:

Food Inventory *(Asset)*			Cost of Sales *(Expense)*		
Debit	Credit	Balance	Debit	Credit	Balance
$ 8,000		$ 8,000			-0-
4,200		12,200	$ 12,000		$ 12,200
	$ 12,200	-0-		$ 3,200	9,000
3,200		3,200			

Following the same procedures as before, the journal entry adjusts beverage inventory and cost of sales to the correct ending balances when posted, as shown in Exhibit 1.6.

Posting the journal entry adjusts cost of sales and adjusts beverage inventory to the correct ending balance. Study these posting effects:

Beverage Inventory *(Asset)*			Cost of Sales *(Expense)*		
Debit	Credit	Balance	Debit	Credit	Balance
$ 2,000		$ 2,000			-0-
1,400		3,400	$ 12,200		$ 12,000
	$ 3,400	-0-		$ 3,200	9,000
1,175		1,175	3,400		12,400
				1,175	11,225

This text discusses the two inventory control methods commonly used in hospitality operations—periodic and perpetual inventory controls. The **periodic method** is used to continue the discussion of end-of-period adjustments for Texana Restaurant. This method relies on an actual physical count and costing of the inventory over a specific period to determine the cost of sales. Generally, a physical count is conducted weekly to maintain adequate inventory, and cost

Account Titles	Debit	Credit
Cost of sales	$3,400	
Beverage inventory		$3,400
Beverage inventory	$1,175	
Cost of sales		$1,175

EXHIBIT 1.6

Texana Restaurant Cost of Sales and Beverage Inventory Adjustment

evaluation is normally completed monthly. During a given period, there is no record of inventory available for sale on any particular day unless a computerized inventory control system is used with computerized point-of-sale terminals. The periodic method is usually preferred for inventory control when many low-cost items are involved.

The **perpetual method** requires a greater number of records for continuous updating of inventory showing the receipt and sale of each inventory item, and maintaining a running balance of inventory available. Perpetual inventory control is discussed in Chapter 2.

PREPAID EXPENSE ADJUSTMENTS

When expenses are paid in advance for future periods, normally exceeding a month, for such items as rent or insurance, a prepaid asset account is created. The prepaid item names the benefit to be received and consumed as an expense over a specified number of time periods (e.g., months, quarters, or years). In our example, Texana Restaurant paid in advance $3,600 for a two-year insurance policy on May 6. If the prepaid is expensed monthly, insurance expense for the month of May will be $150 per month ($3,600 / 24). The prepaid insurance account will be reduced $150 and the insurance expense account will increase by $150 when the journal entry is posted.

Prepaid cost / life of prepaid = Amount expensed per period
Prepaid / months = $3,600 / 24 = $150 per month

Alternative: Prepaid cost / years = $3,600 / 2 = $1,800 per year, or
$1,800 per year / 12 months = $150 per month

The adjusting journal entry to reduce the prepaid insurance account and recognize one month of insurance expense is shown in Exhibit 1.7.

Posting of the adjusting journal entry creates the insurance expense account and adjusts the prepaid insurance account. Study the posting effects of this adjusting entry shown.

Insurance Expense *(Expense)*			**Prepaid Insurance** *(Asset)*		
Debit	Credit	Balance	Debit	Credit	Balance
$ 150		$ 8,000	$ 3,600		$ 3,600
				$ 150	3,450

WAGES AND SALARIES ACCRUAL ADJUSTMENTS

Payday seldom falls on the last day of the month. It is not unusual for wages and salaries to be earned but not paid by the end of the month. An accrual adjusting entry is made to record payroll expense belonging to the month just

Account Titles	Debit	Credit
Insurance expense	$150	
Prepaid insurance		$150

■ **EXHIBIT 1.7**

Texana Restaurant Prepaid Expense Adjustment

ended. This adjustment ensures that the income statement and balance sheet reflect the correct expense and payroll payable. Continuing the Texana Restaurant discussion, we will assume that two days of wages and salaries were earned but not paid by May 31. The payroll owed consists of wages, $400, and salaries, $480. The adjusting entry is shown in Exhibit 1.8.

An additional account, payroll payable, is created for this transaction. The previous entry is posted as follows:

Wages Expense *(Expense)*			**Salaries Expense** *(Expense)*			**Payroll Payable** *(Liability)*		
Debit	Credit	Balance	Debit	Credit	Balance	Debit	Credit	Balance
$ 3,400		$ 3,400	$ 1,800		$ 1,800		$ 880	$ 880
400		3,800	480		$ 2,280			

DEPRECIATION EXPENSE ADJUSTMENT

Depreciation is the systematic expensing of the cost of a long-lived physical asset (except land) that provides economic benefits in excess of one year. Estimated value recovered at the end of the asset's serviceable life, such as trade-in value, salvage, or scrap value, is referred to as **residual value.**

All long-lived depreciable assets must remain in the accounting records at their historical cost. This requirement precludes the reduction of the depreciable asset's cost when depreciation expense is recognized. It necessitates the cre-

Account Titles	Debit	Credit
Wages expense	$400	
Salaries expense	480	
Payroll payable		$880

■ **EXHIBIT 1.8**

Texana Restaurant Accrued Payroll Expense Adjustment

ation of a special offset account called a **contra asset account** to depreciation expense. The offset account has the task of recording and accumulating all depreciation expense charges that occur over the life of the depreciable long-lived asset. The account is named to identify its purpose and is called **accumulated depreciation.** It has a credit balance. Each depreciable asset has a specific credit-balanced, accumulated depreciation account assigned by name and ledger account number.

The balance of the accumulated depreciation account is used to determine the book value of a depreciable asset in the event the asset is disposed of. The book value is used to determine whether a gain or loss has occurred on the disposal of a depreciable asset. If the value received for the depreciable asset is greater than its book value, a gain is recognized. Conversely, if the value received for the asset is less than its book value, a loss is recognized. Each depreciable asset is shown on the balance sheet as a fixed asset and shows its historical cost minus the balance of its accumulated depreciation account as its book value.

This section discusses four methods of depreciation: straight line, units of production, sum of the years' digits, and double declining balance. Monthly and yearly depreciation will use straight-line depreciation to confirm the amount of monthly depreciation expense used in the continuing development of Texana Restaurant. Units of production, sum of the years' digits, and double declining balance will be discussed using specific assets named to find depreciation expense based units used on a yearly basis.

Straight-Line Depreciation

Straight-line depreciation breaks depreciation expense to be recovered into equal periods, such as months, quarters, half years, or years. Texana Restaurant purchased equipment and a building on May 5, 2006. Straight-line depreciation systematically breaks the amount to be recovered through depreciation expense into equal amounts over its estimated useful life based on given time periods—months, quarters, and years. Straight line is not accelerated over the early years of a depreciable asset's useful life. Straight-line depreciation will be described using the equipment and building based on monthly and yearly periods. Monthly depreciation is used in the continuing illustration for the Texana Restaurant.

Equipment Depreciation Calculation: Purchased equipment for $12,000 that has an 8-year estimated life and no residual value. (Cost − Residual / Life) = Depreciation expense per period:

$$\text{Cost} - \text{Residual / Life} = \$12{,}000 \text{ / } 96 \text{ months}$$
$$= \underline{\$125} \text{ depreciation expense per month}$$

$$\text{Cost} - \text{Residual / Life} = \$12{,}000 \text{ / } 8 \text{ years}$$
$$= \underline{\$1{,}500} \text{ depreciation expense per year}$$

Building Depreciation Calculation: Purchased a building for $150,000 that has a 25-year life and a residual value of $30,000. **(Cost − Residual / Life) = Depreciation expense:**

(Cost − Residual / Life) = Depreciation expense:
$150,000 − $30,000 / 300 months = $400 per month

(Cost − Residual / Life) = Depreciation expense:
$150,000 − 30,000 / 25 years = $4,800 per year

The adjusting journal entry to recognize depreciation expense for the month of May on the equipment and the building at May 31 for Texana Restaurant is shown in Exhibit 1.9, followed by its posting to the ledger accounts.

Depreciation Expense			Accumulated Depr: Equip.			Accumulated Depr: Bldg.		
Debit	Credit	Balance	Debit	Credit	Balance	Debit	Credit	Balance
$ 525		$ 525		$ 125	$ 125		$ 400	$ 400

Units-of-Production Depreciation Method

Units-of-production depreciation shares some of the elements of straight-line depreciation. Cost minus residual remains the numerator, and the denominator again expresses the life of the asset. However, the life of the asset is expressed in units. Miles driven, gallons produced, and hours used are a few examples. Assume that a van was purchased for $29,800 with an estimated residual value of $1,800 based on a life of 140,000 miles. During the month of May, the van recorded 580 miles of use. The depreciation expense is calculated as follows:

(Cost − Residual) / Life in units = Depreciation expense per unit
× Units used = Depreciation expense

($29,800 − $1,800) / 140,000 = $28,000 / 140,000 = $0.20 per mile
$0.20 per mile × 580 = $116 Depreciation expense

Account Titles	Debit	Credit
Depreciation expense	$525	
Accumulated depreciation: Equip.		$125
Accumulated depreciation: Bldg.		400

■ **EXHIBIT 1.9**
Texana Restaurant Depreciation Expense Adjustment

Subsequent months or years of depreciation would be calculated in the same manner by using the depreciation rate per mile multiplied by the miles driven. In a generic sense, both straight-line and units-of-production methods are based on the consumption of a depreciable asset. Time periods is the basis for straight-line depreciation. Units of production uses units as the basis of use or consumption during a time period. The production method estimates the life of the depreciable asset, as does the straight-line method, and is useful for budgeting purposes. Like the straight-line method, units of production provide the ability to create accelerated depreciation expense charges.

Sum-of-the-Years'-Digits Depreciation

Commonly called **SYD, sum-of-the-years'-digits depreciation** is an **accelerated depreciation method** that allows greater amounts of depreciation to be expensed in the early years of a depreciable asset's life. An accelerated method presumes that an asset becomes less and less efficient over its life. Thus, it allows the matching of depreciation to the efficiency loss of the asset over time. SYD determines the amount to be depreciated using a fraction multiplied by the cost minus the residual value. The maximum years of a depreciable asset's life becomes the numerator in the first year and then reduces the numerator by one in each subsequent year of the asset's life. The denominator of the fraction is found by summing the years of an asset's life, or by using an equation.

An example using each method of determining the denominator will be based on equipment, which is purchased for $34,200 with a life of five years and a residual value of $600:

Additive function:

Yr 1 + Yr 2 = 3 + Yr 3 = 6 + Yr 4 = 10 + Yr 5 = $\underline{\underline{15}}$ is the denominator

The additive function can be somewhat cumbersome as the years of life of the depreciable asset increase. Both methods determine the denominator, which represents 100% of the amount to be depreciated. The letter n in the equation represents the number of years in a depreciable asset's life:

$$\frac{n(n+1)}{2} = \frac{5(5+1)}{2} = \frac{5 \times 6}{2} = \frac{30}{2} = \underline{\underline{15}} \text{ is the denominator}$$

The equation to calculate SYD depreciation for each year of the asset's life is:

SYD fraction × Cost − Residual = Depreciation expense

The numerator of the fraction will begin with the maximum years of the asset's life in the first year, minus one for each subsequent year. A five-year SYD depreciation schedule would look like this:

Year	SYD Fraction	×	Cost − Residual	=	Depreciation
1	5/15	×	$33,600	=	$11,200
2	4/15	×	$33,600	=	$ 8,960
3	3/15	×	$33,600	=	$ 6,720
4	2/15	×	$33,600	=	$ 4,480
5	1/15	×	$33,600	=	$ 2,240
	Σ = 15/15, or 1		Total depreciation		$33,600

The SYD depreciation schedule indicates that the depreciation expense is accelerated by expensing larger amounts in the earlier years.

Double-Declining-Balance Depreciation

The **double-declining-balance method,** also called *DDB depreciation,* is the second accelerated method to be discussed. This method doubles the straight-line depreciation rate (1/Years) to find a DDB%. This method, unlike straight line, units of production, and SYD, ignores any type of residual value in the calculation of the depreciation expense. The DDB% is multiplied by book value to determine the amount of depreciation expense.

In the first year, no accumulated depreciation account exists until after the depreciation expense is calculated, journalized, and posted. Thus, in the first year, the book value of an asset using the DDB method is the depreciable assets' cost − accumulated depreciation, which is cost − zero because no previous depreciation expense was recorded. After the first year of DDB depreciation expense is posted, the book value changes to cost − first-year depreciation expense. In subsequent years, book value will decrease each year by the amount of depreciation expense charged in the previous year. Although the DDB method ignores residual values in calculating the yearly depreciation expense, the book value of an asset that is fully depreciated may be greater than, but must not be less than, cost minus residual value if residual value exists.

Assume equipment that had a five-year life and a residual value of $1,000 was purchased for $16,000. The DDB equation is stated next, followed by a discussion of each equation element:

DDB% × Book value = Depreciation expense

- **DDB%** is calculated as 100%, or 1 divided by years of life:

100% / 5 = 20% × 2 = 40%, or 1 / 5 = 20% × 2 = 40%

In other words, the straight-line rate has doubled.

- Alternative: Since **DDB%** doubles the straight-line rate, the numerator can be expressed as follows:

$$100\% \times 2 = 200\%, \text{ or 2 divided by years of life} = 2 / 5 = \underline{40}\%$$

- Book value = Cost − Accumulated depreciation.
- Depreciation expense is DDB% Book × value.

Referring to the previous equipment information, the **DDB** equation and the identification of each of its elements, study the following five-year **DDB** depreciation schedule:

5-Year DDB Depreciation Schedule

Year	DDB%	×	Book Value	=	Depr. Expense	Net Book Value
0						$16,000
1	40%	×	$16,000	=	$ 6,400	9,600
2	40%	×	9,600	=	3,840	5,760
3	40%	×	5,760	=	2,304	3,456
4	40%	×	3,456	=	1,382	2,074
5	40%	×	2,074	=	830	1,244
Total accumulated depreciation (expense)					$14,756	

Cost − Accumulated depreciation: $16,000 − $14,756 = $1,244 Book value

Using the same equipment discussed in the previous example of DDB, cost is $16,000 with a five-year life. Assume its residual value is changed from $1,000 to $1,500. The DDB depreciation schedule previously discussed had a book value of $1,244 at the end of Year 5, but the book value cannot be less than the new $1,500 residual value. Thus, the new residual value will force a reduction in the fifth-year depreciation expense to ensure that the book value after the final depreciation expense charge is not less than residual value. Study the following depreciation schedule extract:

Year	DDB%	×	Book Value	=	Depr. Expense	Net Book Value
4	40%	×	$3,456	=	$ 1,382	$2,074
5	$2,074	−	1,500	=	574	1,500
Total accumulated depreciation (expense)					$14,500	

Cost − Accumulated depreciation: $16,000 − $14,500 = $1,500 Book value

It is apparent that the total depreciation expense changed from $14,756 with a residual value of $1,000, to $14,500 ($16,000 − $1,500) with a new residual value of $1,500. Since the ending book value must be equal to or greater than residual value. The change to the depreciation expense for Year 5 must be $574 ($2,074 − $1,500). The forced change to Year 5's depreciation expense conforms to the rule that the final book value may never be less than the residual value.

CLOSING JOURNAL ENTRIES

The general ledger showing the posted operating and adjusting journal entries is shown for review. The general ledger is the source used to prepare an adjusted trial balance that confirms the ledger accounts are in balance. Study the updated general ledger:

General Ledger

Cash *(Asset)*

Debit	Credit	Balance
$100,000		$100,000
	$55,000	45,000
	3,600	41,400
	3,400	38,000
	1,400	36,600
	1,800	34,800
	282	34,518
24,280		58,798
	818	57,980

Credit Card Receivables *(Asset)*

Debit	Credit	Balance
$ 620		$ 620

Prepaid Insurance *(Asset)*

Debit	Credit	Balance
$ 3,600		$ 3,600
	$ 150	3,450

Food Inventory *(Asset)*

Debit	Credit	Balance
$ 8,000		$ 8,000
4,200		12,200
	$ 12,200	-0-
3,200		3,200

Beverage Inventory *(Asset)*

Debit	Credit	Balance
$ 2,000		$ 2,000
1,400		3,400
	$ 3,400	-0-
1,175		1,175

Building *(Asset)*

Debit	Credit	Balance
$150,000		$150,000

Accumulated Depr: Bldg *(Contra)*

Debit	Credit	Balance
	$ 400	$ 400

Equipment *(Asset)*

Debit	Credit	Balance
$ 12,000		$ 12,000

Accumulated Depr. Equip. *(Contra)*

Debit	Credit	Balance
	$ 125	$ 125

Accounts Payable *(Liability)*		
Debit	Credit	Balance
	$12,000	$ 12,000
	4,200	16,200

Payroll Payable *(Liability)*		
Debit	Credit	Balance
	$ 880	$ 880

Notes Payable *(Liability)*		
Debit	Credit	Balance
	$105,000	$105,000

Sales Revenue *(SR)*		
Debit	Credit	Balance
	$24,900	$ 24,900

Wages Expense *(Expense)*		
Debit	Credit	Balance
$ 3,400		$ 3,400
400		$ 3,800

Salaries Expense *(Expense)*		
Debit	Credit	Balance
$ 1,800		$ 1,800
480		$ 2,280

Utilities Expense *(Expense)*		
Debit	Credit	Balance
$ 282		$ 282

Misc. Expense *(Expense)*		
Debit	Credit	Balance
$ 818		$ 818

Insurance Expense *(Expense)*		
Debit	Credit	Balance
$ 150		$ 150

Depreciation Expense *(Expense)*		
Debit	Credit	Balance
$ 525		$ 525

Cost of Sales *(Expense)*		
Debit	Credit	Balance
$ 12,200		$ 12,200
	$ 3,200	9,000
3,400		12,400
	1,175	11,225

Gram Disk, Capital *(OE)*		
Debit	Credit	Balance
	$100,000	$100,000

Before determining operating income or loss, an adjusted trial balance is prepared by extracting each ledger account by name and balance, after adjustments are posted (see Exhibit 1.10). The purpose is to verify that the Texana Restaurant ledger is in balance.

The income statement in Exhibit 1.11 is prepared for Texana Restaurant from information given in the adjusted trial balance using the following format:

Sales revenue − Cost of sales = Gross margin − Expenses
= Operating income (before tax)

The last step in moving through the accounting cycle is to create closing entries, bringing the temporary accounts balances to zero. Closing the temporary accounts will transfer sales revenue and operating expenses to the **income summary** account. The income summary account receives sales revenue and expenses including cost of sales; its final balance represents operating income or net loss.

Closing the income summary account will transfer operating income or operating loss to the capital account. Operating income exists when total sales rev-

Texana Restaurant Adjusted Trial Balance For the Month Ended May 31, 2006

Account Titles	Debit	Credit
Cash	$ 57,980	
Credit card receivables	620	
Prepaid insurance	3,450	
Food inventory	3,200	
Beverage inventory	1,175	
Building	150,000	
Accumulated depreciation: Building		$ 400
Equipment	12,000	
Accumulated depreciation: Equipment		125
Accounts payable		16,200
Payroll payable		880
Notes payable		105,000
Capital, Gram Disk		100,000
Sales revenue		24,900
Cost of sales	11,225	
Wages expense	3,800	
Salaries expense	2,280	
Utilities expense	282	
Miscellaneous expense	818	
Insurance expense	150	
Depreciation expense	525	
Accounts Totals	$247,505	$247,505

■ **EXHIBIT 1.10**

Sample Trial Balance: Texana Restaurant

Texana Restaurant Income Statement For the Month Ended May 31, 2006

Sales Revenue	$24,900
Less: Cost of sales	(11,225)
Gross margin	$13,675
Operating Expenses	
Wages expense	$3,800
Salaries expense	2,280
Utilities expense	282
Miscellaneous expense	818
Insurance expense	150
Depreciation expense	525
Total expenses	(7,855)
Net Operating Income	$ 5,820

■ **EXHIBIT 1.11**

Sample Income Statement: Texana Restaurant

enue is greater than the cost of sales and the total operating expenses. An operating loss exists when the cost of sales and total operating expenses are greater than sales revenue. Operating income is the income before tax, and will become net income after tax is applied. Consider the possibilities shown in Exhibit 1.12 that may exist after closing the temporary income statement accounts.

The function of the income summary is to transfer income or loss to the capital account. This is shown through an analysis of the summary account:

Income Summary			**Gram Disk, Capital**		
Debit	Credit	Balance	Debit	Credit	Balance
		-0-	$100,000		$100,000
	$24,900	$24,900		$ 5,820	105,820
$19,080		5,820			
5,820		-0-			

Total Sales Revenue $24,900 is closed to Income Summary

Total Operating Expenses $19,080 is closed to Income summary

Total Income Summary balance of SR $24,900 − $19,080 − $5,820 is Closed to the Capital account

Texana Restaurant Closing Journal Entries For the Month Ended May 31, 2006		
Account Titles	*Debit*	*Credit*
Sales revenue	$24,900	
Income summary		$24,900
Income summary	$19,080	
Cost of sales		$11,225
Wages expense		3,800
Salaries expense		2,280
Utilities expense		282
Miscellaneous expense		818
Insurance expense		150
Depreciation expense		525
Income summary	$ 5,820	
Gram Disk, Capital		$ 5,820

■ **EXHIBIT 1.12**

Sample Closing Entries: Texana Restaurant

After **closing entries** are posted from the closing journal entry to the ledger, only permanent balance sheet accounts remain in the Texana Restaurant ledger (see Exhibit 1.13). The **post-closing trial balance** is the source of information needed to prepare a final balance sheet.

From the post-closing trial balance, a final post-closing balance sheet is prepared for Texana Restaurant for the month of May (see Exhibit 1.14).

WORKSHEET

A **worksheet** can be prepared at the end of an accounting period to ensure that all the accounts are in balance and to show all information needed to journalize adjusting and closing entries, and to prepare major financial statements. The sequence of completion of the worksheet begins with an unadjusted trial

Texana Restaurant Post-Closing Trial Balance For the Month Ended May 31, 2006		
Cash	$ 57,980	
Credit card receivables	620	
Prepaid insurance	3,450	
Food inventory	3,200	
Beverage inventory	1,175	
Building	150,000	
Accumulated depreciation: Building		$ 400
Equipment	12,000	
Accumulated depreciation: Equipment		125
Accounts payable		16,200
Payroll payable		880
Notes payable		105,000
Gram Disk, Capital		105,820
Post-Closing Trial Balance Totals	$228,425	$228,425

■ **EXHIBIT 1.13**

Sample Post-Closing Trial Blance: Texana Restaurant

Texana Restaurant Balance Sheet For the Month Ended May 31, 2006			
Assets		**Liabilities and Owners' Equity Liabilities**	
Cash	$ 57,980	Accounts payable	$ 16,200
Credit card receivables	620	Payroll payable	880
Prepaid insurance	3,450	Notes payable	105,000
Food inventory	3,200	Total Liabilities	$122,080
Beverage inventory	1,175		
Building	150,000	**Owners' Equity**	
Accumulated depr.: Building	(400)	Gram Disk, Capital	$100,000
Equipment	12,000	Operating income, May 2006	5,820
Accumulated depr.: Equipment	(125)	Total Owner's Equity	$105,820
Total Assets	$227,900	Total Liabilities and *OE*	$227,900

■ **EXHIBIT 1.14**

Sample Balance Sheet: Texana Restaurant

balance. End-of-period adjustments are made in the adjustment columns and then extended to the adjusted trial balance columns. Each account shown in the adjusted trial balance columns belongs to the income statement or balance sheet columns. Sales revenue, cost of sales, and expense accounts are extended to the income statement. Assets, liabilities, and ownership equity accounts are extended to the balance sheet. The debit–credit balances of each of the five two-column sets must be equal. If any total debit and credit balances of the five two-column sets are not equal, an error has been made, and it must be corrected before continuing completion of the worksheet. If all column sets are balanced correctly, the worksheet is completed if no errors are noted.

All information is shown in the worksheet to journalize adjusting and closing entries, and to prepare the income statement and balance sheet. A worksheet is shown in Exhibit 1.15 to illustrate all operating transactions, adjusting, and closing journal entries, including the income statement and balance sheet for Texana Restaurant.

The following describes the column contents in Exhibit 1.15:

- *Debit–credit column sets 1, 2, and 3:* Unadjusted trial balance, adjustments, and adjusted trial balance column sets verify that total debits are equal to total credits.
- *Debit–credit column set 4:* The income statement column shows a subtotal for total operating expense outflows and total sales revenue inflows. Unless total expenses are equal to total sales revenue (breakeven), the debit–credit subtotals will not be equal. If sales revenue is greater than expenses, the amount of the difference represents operating income. If total expenses exceed total sales revenue, the amount of the difference represents operating loss. The amount-of-the-difference debit or credit is used to bring the balance of the total debit–credit columns into equality.
- *Debit–credit column set 5:* The balance sheet columns show the ending balance of total assets, liabilities, and ownership equity. Operating income increases ownership equity, whereas an operating loss decreases ownership equity. The worksheet shows all information needed to prepare an end-of-period balance sheet.

The accounting cycle can be summarized in these steps:

1. *Perform transactional analysis.* Verify documentation or information such as invoices, sales, and checks to indicate that a journal entry is required.
2. *Journalize.* Record a business transaction in the journal.
3. *Post a journal entry.* Transfer journal instructions to a specific account and in the amount directed.
4. *Prepare an unadjusted trial balance.* List all ledger accounts with balances to confirm the debit-balanced accounts are equal to the credit-balanced accounts.

Account Titles	Unadjusted Trial Debit	Unadjusted Trial Credit	Adjustments Debit	Adjustments Credit	Adjusted Trial Debit	Adjusted Trial Credit	Income Statement Debit	Income Statement Credit	Balance Sheet Debit	Balance Sheet Credit
Cash	$ 57,980				$ 57,980				$ 57,980	
Credit card receivables	620				620				620	
Prepaid insurance	3,600			(c) $ 150	3,450				3,450	
Food inventory	12,200		(a)$3,200	(a)12,200	3,200				3,200	
Beverage inventory	3,400		(b) 1,175	(b) 3,400	1,175				1,175	
Building	150,000				150,000				150,000	
Equipment	12,000				12,000				12,000	
Accounts payable		$ 16,200				$ 16,200				$ 16,200
Notes payable		105,000				105,000				105,000
Capital, Gram Disk		100,000				100,000				100,000
Sales revenue		24,900				24,900		$24,900		
Wages expense	3,400		(e) 400		3,800		$ 3,800			
Salaries expense	1,800		(e) 480		2,280		2,280			
Utilities expense	282				282		282			
Miscellaneous expense	818				818		818			
Unadjusted Trial Balance Totals	$246,100	$246,100								
Cost of sales (goods sold) (and inventories adjustment)			(a)12,200 (b) 3,400	(a) 3,200 (b) 1,175	11,225		11,225			
Insurance expense			(c) 150		150		150			
Depreciation expense			(d) 525		525		525			
Accumulated depreciation: Equip.				(d) 125		125				125
Accumulated depreciation: Bldg.				(d) 400		400				400
Payroll payable				(e) 880						880
Totals			$ 21,530	$ 21,530	$247,505	$247,505	19,080	24,900	$228,425	
Operating Income,							5,820			
Increases Capital							$24,900	$24,900	$228,425	$228,425

Adjustments: (a) Adjusts Cost of Sales. (b) Adjusts Food and Beverage Inventories. (c) Adjusts Prepaid Insurance and Insurance Expense. (d) Adjusts Depreciation Expense and Accumulated Depreciation. (e) Adjusts Wages Expense, Salaries Expense and Payroll Payable.

EXHIBIT 1.15

Texana Restaurant Worksheet For the Month Ended May 31, 2006

5. *Prepare a worksheet (optional).* Record the unadjusted trial balance, record end-of-period adjusting entries, develop adjusted trial balance, and extend appropriate accounts to the income statement and balance sheet columns.

6. *Adjust the ledger accounts.* Journalize and post end-of-period adjustments to the specified accounts. An unadjusted trial balance or a completed worksheet will provide needed information.

7. *Close the temporary accounts.* Journalize and post closing entries to bring the temporary accounts to a zero balance. An adjusted trial balance or a completed worksheet shows needed information.

8. *Prepare a post-closing trial balance.* Take information from the ledger accounts or a post-closing trial balance, or complete a worksheet to show needed information. The post-closing trial balance verifies the accuracy of the adjusting and closing procedures and confirms that all temporary accounts have been closed to a zero balance.

9. *Prepare the income statement.* Take information from the income statement ledger accounts or from a completed worksheet and prepare an income statement in proper format.

10. *Prepare the balance sheet.* Take information from the balance sheet ledger accounts or a post-closing trial balance, or complete a worksheet, and prepare a balance sheet in the proper format.

COMPUTER APPLICATIONS

Throughout this text, manual systems of financial control will be discussed and demonstrated. The materials presented within this text are not intended to impart financial accounting expertise, but to make the reader familiar with certain basic financial accounting concepts, structure, and terminology. An understanding of basic accounting procedures and the managerial applications needed to assist management in the decision-making process is essential.

Today, most hospitality businesses in hotels, motels, food service, and beverage operations are using computers to record, report, and analyze the effectiveness of internal operations and the preparation of financial statements. Computers have, in effect, successfully removed much of the time-consuming drudgery present in a manual accounting system. The use of computers allows the creation of and updating of account ledgers, through journal entries, and provides unadjusted and adjusted trial balances of accounts, a post-closing trial balances, and financial statements.

Thus, it is essential to understand what information is needed as input to a computer system and also understand the output of information the computer is capable of providing. In essence, all of the information provided by manual procedures in the examples and exhibits can automatically be generated with a computer system set-up with a basic office oriented software system. Knowing what an average check is for a food service operation is one thing, but knowing how it is determined gives a greater insight as to how it can be changed. This simple analogy rings true for the great majority of developed ratios, percentages, units, and dollar values that can be generated through computer analysis. Needless to say, software programs are available for specific business operations within the hospitality industry, which can assist in safeguarding the assets, controlling cost, maximizing profit, and providing information to measure the efficiency and productivity of an operation.

SUMMARY

Accounting has been developed to accumulate, maintain, and provide financial information regarding internal business transactions. In this chapter we discussed and used basic accounting principles and procedures common to a manual system. Computerized systems incorporate all of the fundamental accounting principles of the manual system.

A common language has developed from the practice of accounting with its own set of rules or assumptions, commonly called *principles* and *concepts*. It is important to have a good understanding of each of these principles and concepts to be able to interpret financial information correctly. These assumptions include the following:

- Business entity principle
- Monetary unit principle
- Going concern principle
- Cost principle
- Time period principle
- Conservatism principle
- Consistency principle
- Materiality concept
- Full disclosure principle
- Objectivity principle
- Matching principle

Journal entries provide the instructions needed to create and maintain accounts that reflect all transactions of a business entity. A journal entry must, as a minimum, consist of two accounts. There must be at least one debit and one credit entry, and the sum of the debits and credits must be equal.

Ledger accounts are identified by name and are described as being normally either debit- or credit-balanced, based on the category of the account. Each ledger account has two specific columns that are identified to receive numerical values. The left column is identified to receive only debit entries and the right column receives only credit entries. The category of an account will determine if an entry in the left or right column of a ledger account will increase or decrease the balance of an account. The debit–credit rules of whether entries increase or decrease the balance for each category of balance sheet accounts are as follows:

Assets =	**Liabilities** +	**Ownership Equity**
(Debit-balanced accounts)	(Credit-balanced accounts)	
Increased by debits	Increased by credits	Increased by credits
Decreased by credits	Decreased by debits	Decreased by debits

Contra Assets	**Contra Equity**
(Credit-balanced accounts)	(Debit-balanced accounts)
Increased by credits	Increased by debits
Decreased by debits	Decreased by credits

The income statement equation describes the economic results of for-profit operations: net income, net loss, or breakeven. The income statement format is expressed as follows:

Sales revenue − Cost of sales = Gross margin − Expenses
= Operating income or loss
Or: **Gross margin − Expenses = Operating income or loss**

The debit–credit rules of whether entries increase or decrease the balance for each category of income statement accounts are as follows:

Sales Revenue Accounts	**Expense Accounts**
(Credit-balanced accounts)	(Debit-balanced accounts)
Increased by credits	Increased by debits
Decreased by debits	Decreased by credits

Adjusting entries are made at the end of an operating period to recognize sales revenue earned and expenses incurred but not yet recorded. Prepaid expense items are consumed over the life of the prepaid:

Prepaid cost / Life (years, months) = Prepaid expense per period

Depreciation is a method of systematically writing off the cost of long-lived assets (except land) over the life of the asset. Only a portion of the cost is shown as a depreciation expense deduction from income on each period's income statement. Four depreciation methods were discussed:

Straight line: (Cost − Residual) / Life (time) = Depreciation expense per period

Units of Production:
[(Cost − Residual) / Life (units)] × Units used = Depreciation expense

SYD: SYD fraction × (Cost − Residual) = Depreciation expense
DDB: DDB% × (Book value) = Depreciation expense

Each depreciable asset has a separate credit-balanced contra account called *accumulated depreciation.* The contra asset account is used to accumulate all depreciation expense charges over the life of the asset. Historical cost of the asset minus its accumulated depreciation equals the book value of the asset.

D I S C U S S I O N   Q U E S T I O N S

1. Explain the major difference between cash and accrual accounting.

2. In what way can a business manager use accounting information?

3. Using examples, give a short description of five accounting principles or concepts.

4. Explain why a ledger account has only a debit and credit column to receive dollar value entries.

5. Explain if it is possible for a transaction to affect an asset account without also affecting some other asset or a liability or owners' equity account.

6. Why is the rule for debit and credit entries the same for liability and owners' equity accounts?

7. Discuss why the adjusting entries is necessary at the end of each operating period are made before the end-of-period financial statements are prepared.

8. A hotel shows office supplies such as stationery on its balance sheet as a $500 asset, even though to any other hotel these supplies might have a value only as scrap paper. Which accounting principle or concept justifies this?

9. Define the concept of depreciation.

10. What is the purpose of an accumulated depreciation account?

11. Explain the concept of accelerated depreciation discussed in this chapter.

12. Describe the double declining balance and the sum of the years' digits depreciation equations.

13. Describe the straight-line and units-of-production methods of depreciation.

14. Explain how the book value of a depreciable asset is determined.

15. A restaurant has purchased a new electronic point-of-sale register. With adequate maintenance, the machine could last 10 years; however, with the rapid advance of technological improvements, it is expected that a newer

register will be purchased within five years to replace the unit recently purchased. For depreciation purposes, what would be the useful life of the machine? Explain why.

16. Under what circumstances might the individual account balances not be correct even though a trial balance is in balance?

E T H I C S   S I T U A T I O N

A restaurant manager has a contract with the restaurant's owner that he is entitled to eat meals in the restaurant without charge when on duty. The manager lives in a rented apartment above the restaurant with his wife and two children. Generally, the family members eat their meals in the restaurant every day of the week. No sales checks or other records make note of the consumed meals. Discuss the ethics of this situation based on the accounting principles and concepts discussed in this chapter.

E X E R C I S E S

(When an exercise requires a journal entry, use the basic journal entry format shown in the text.)

E1.1 A number of accounting principles and concepts (such as the matching principle) were discussed in this chapter. For each of the following situations, state which principle or concept is involved.

    a. A case of food poisoning occurred in a restaurant. The restaurant is being sued by a number of its customers who were hospitalized. The estimated cost that the restaurant is likely to suffer from this lawsuit is disclosed in a footnote because of the _____ principle.

    b. A hotel has traditionally depreciated its furniture and equipment using the straight-line method. This year, a different depreciation method was used without advising its financial statement readers of this change. As a result, it is violating both the _____ principle and the _____ principle.

    c. A motel's normal payday for employees is every Friday. The year-end occurs on a Monday. The pay earned by employees for those three days is recorded in the motel's accounts because of the _____ principle.

    d. Last year a remote fishing resort purchased a floatplane to fly guests to the resort. The aircraft cost at that time was $150,000. This year, the plane is worth $160,000. However, it continues to be recorded on the books at $150,000 because of the _____ principle and the _____ principle.

e. If a restaurant operator takes home food from the restaurant and uses these products for his or her personal use, this act violates the _____ principle.

f. If a hotel estimated expenses to be higher than they actually might be, this reduces the hotel's profit and conforms to the _____ _____ principle.

g. A hotel purchased a box of 100 pencils for office use. At the end of the month, 90 pencils remain, with a total value of $4.50. The remaining pencils are not included as inventory on the balance sheet because of the _____ concept.

E1.2 Write a short explanation of the following terms:

a. Operating income	**c.** Net income	**e.** Net loss
b. Sales revenue	**d.** Gross margin	**f.** Breakeven

E1.3 Identify the normal balance as debit or credit for each of the following categories of accounts:

Account:	Assets	Liabilities	Ownership Equity	Sales Revenue	Operating Expenses
Balance:	_____	_____	_____	_____	_____

E1.4 Write the abbreviated linear equation for the balance sheet and income statement.

Balance sheet equation _____

Income statement equation _____

E1.5 At the end of an accounting period, it was determined that employee wages of $858 and management salaries of $1,400 have been earned. Journalize the entry to accrue the wages and salaries expense.

E1.6 A restaurant reported the following for the first quarter of Year 2007: Sales revenue (SR) of $420,680, cost of sales (CS) $201,928, and total expenses (E) of $175,170. Find the gross margin (GM) and net income (NI).

E1.7 For the month of March, a restaurant reported a beginning food inventory (BI) of $18,662, ending food inventory (EI) of $16,882, and food purchases (P) for resale was $197,900. What was the cost of food sales (CS) for the month of March?

E1.8 Restaurant had $8,480 supplies on hand at the beginning of April. During the month $11,222 of supplies was purchased. At the end of the month a check of the supplies indicated that $8,104 of supplies was on hand. Determine the amount of supplies used and journalize the adjusting entry.

E1.9 Equipment was purchased for $70,468. The equipment is estimated to have a serviceable life of 8 years and a residual value of $2,500. Using straight-line depreciation, answer the following:

   a. What is the amount of depreciation expense per month and per year?

   b. Give the journal entry to record the depreciation expense for one year.

E1.10 A new van was purchased for $40,000 and was estimated to have a life of 4 years or 110,000 miles; trade-in (residual) value is estimated to be $4,800. In the first year, the van was driven for 27,500 miles.

   a. Use the units-of-production method to determine the depreciation per mile (unit).

   b. What is the total depreciation expense for the first year?

E1.11 Equipment was purchased for $46,400 with an estimated life of 8 years and a residual value of $4,000. What is the depreciation expense for the first year using each of the following separate depreciation methods?

   a. Sum of the years' digits

   b. Double-declining balance

E1.12 A restaurant paid $9,120 cash in advance for liability and casualty insurance for two years of coverage.

   a. Journalize the transaction for the payment.

   b. What is the amount of insurance expense for one year and for one month?

   c. Record the journal entry for six months of insurance expense.

E1.13 Referring to the journal entries you completed for E1.12, (a) and (c), name and post the journal entries using the modified T account format.

Name: Cash			Name: _____			Name: _____		
Debit	Credit	Balance	Debit	Credit	Balance	Debit	Credit	Balance
(Beginning bal.)		$24,000	(Beginning bal.)		$ -0-	(Beginning bal.)		$ -0-

E1.14 A business using the cash basis of accounting cannot locate all of its records for a given month of operations. Beginning cash was $22,260 and ending cash was $18,388. Cash payments of $162,800 were verified from vendor receipts. The amount of cash sales is unknown. Determine unknown cash sales revenue.

E1.15 A restaurant pays $10,800 in advance for six months' building rent and recognizes rental expense every month.

   a. What is the monthly rental expense?

   b. Journalize the monthly adjusting entry.

P R O B L E M S

P1.1 Study the restaurant transactions for the month of March 2006 shown in the following list, and record the necessary journal entries, skipping a line between each entry. Journal entries and modified T ledger accounts can be prepared easily on lined paper following the examples shown in the text. To further simplify the problem, use the following account titles shown by category to prepare modified T accounts:

Balance Sheet Accounts

Assets:	Cash, Credit Card Receivable, Accounts Receivable, Food Inventory, Beverage Inventory, Prepaid Rent, Prepaid Insurance, Supplies, Equipment, and Furnishings.
Liabilities:	Accounts Payable, Note Payable.
Ownership Equity:	Capital.

Income Statement Accounts
   Sales Revenue, Salaries Expense, Wages Expense, and Interest Expense.

a. The owner opened a business account and deposited $60,000 in the bank.

b. The owner borrowed and deposited $30,000 on a note payable to the bank.

c. The owner paid one year of rent in advance on the restaurant space, $18,000 cash.

d. The owner purchased equipment $46,000; $16,000 in cash and the balance on account.

e. Furnishings were purchased for $30,400 cash.

f. The owner purchased $3,200 of food inventory on account and paid $3,800 cash for beverage inventory.

g. The owner purchased supplies for $2,650 cash.

h. The owner purchased $3,800 of food inventory on account.

i. The owner paid $2,700 for a one-year liability and casualty insurance policy.

j. Employees were paid wages of $12,800 and salaries of $2,400.

k. Sales revenue for the first month was $42,800; 90% cash, 8% credit cards, and 2% on accounts receivable.

l. The owner paid $16,600 on accounts payable.

m. The owner paid $8,000 on note payable, plus interest of $960.

Journalize each transaction and then post each transaction to a general ledger; prepare an unadjusted trial balance for the month ended March 31, 2006.

P1.2 A friend has asked you to look at the accounts of his small restaurant and recommend the end-of-period adjusting entries. After viewing the accounts, it was apparent that the following adjusting entries were required. Complete the adjusting journal entries for each of the following items.

a. Wages of $2,877 and salaries of $1,400 have been accrued but not paid.

b. A total of $8,800 of prepaid rent has been consumed.

c. Total depreciation expense of $10,700 must be recognized, consisting of kitchen equipment, $4,900, and furnishings $5,800.

d. A total of $4,000 of prepaid insurance must be expensed.

e. Supplies of $1,218 have been used but not expensed.

f. Interest on a note payable in the amount of $436 must be accrued.

P1.3 The following transactions occurred for a new motel prior to and during the first month of operations. Study the transactions shown below and record necessary journal entries skipping a line between each entry. Journal entries and modified T ledger accounts can be prepared easily on lined paper following the examples shown in the text.

a. The owner invested $250,000 cash deposited in the business bank account.

b. The owner paid $108,000 cash for land.

c. The owner borrowed $300,000 on a mortgage payable at 8% interest.

d. The owner paid $285,400 cash for a building.

e. Equipment was purchased for $48,000, paying $12,000 cash; and the balance owed on a note payable.

f. Furnishings were purchased for $120,000 cash.

g. Linen inventory was purchased for $7,894 cash.

h. Supplies were purchased for $3,200 on account.

i. Vending inventory was purchased for $540 cash.

j. Room sales revenue during the month was $58,740; 98% cash and 2% credit cards.

k. Vending sales revenue from vending machines was $880 cash.

l. Wages of $3,120 cash were paid.

m. The owner paid $3,200 on accounts payable.

n. The owner paid $4,200 on an annual liability and casualty insurance policy.

o. The owner paid $1,600 on the mortgage payable and $1,728 for interest.

After journalizing and posting the operating transactions, journalize the following adjusting entries (Use separate entries for clarity.):

1. Estimated closing value of the linen inventory is $7,220.

2. Wages earned by employees but unpaid are $416.

3. One-twelfth of the prepaid insurance has been consumed.

   4. Interest owing, but not yet paid on the equipment note payable account is 1% of the balance owing at month-end.

   5. Equipment has a 10-year life and a $3,000 residual value; SL depreciation.

   6. Furnishings have an 8-year life and a $7,000 residual value; SL depreciation.

   7. Building has a 20-year life and a $42,000 residual value; SL depreciation.

   8. Supplies used during the first month are $533.

P1.4 Joe Fast started a mobile snack food service on January 2, 2006, investing $15,000 cash deposited in a bank account in the name of "Fast Snacks." He purchased a second-hand, fully equipped truck. Joe operated on the cash basis of accounting, and at year's end, he asks you to help him find his income or loss for the first year of operation. You have determined the following:

   a. He purchased a used $24,000 truck that is depreciable at 20% per year. He paid $12,000 cash and financed $12,000 on a note at 8% interest.

   b. He started the operation with $3,000 cash available.

   c. He has $375 cash on hand and $28,454 cash in the bank at the end of the year.

   d. His receipts for cash purchases of inventory for resale total $30,280.

   e. The value of his ending inventory for resale is $624.

   f. He paid $1,024 cash for all truck operating costs. In addition, he has an unpaid invoice for a recent truck repair in the amount of $280.

   g. He paid $1,280 of interest on the truck loan.

   h. He informed you that he took $1,625 a month for 12 months to use for living and other personal expenses.

You discover Joe kept no record of the cash sales he made during the year. Cash sales revenue must be determined from the information already noted. Show Joe how cash sales were determined and prepare an income statement using accrual accounting to show his operating income for the year.

P1.5 Art Angel operated a small seasonal lake marina, renting boats and selling snacks and beverages. He rents marina space for four months in Year 2006, from May 15 to September 15, for $800 per month. He started the current season with $25,000 in the bank and paid the marina seasonal rent in advance. In May, he bought three new boats for $10,000 each, $15,000 in cash and the balance of $15,000 was financied at 6% simple interest by the boat dealer. The new boats are estimated to have a 10-season life and a residual (trade-in) value of $2,250 each. Straight-line depreciation will be used.

Purchase invoices show he paid $8,754 cash for food and beverage inventory. One unpaid invoice for food in the amount of $137 remains unpaid. No food or beverage inventory remained at season end. Other costs incurred during the season were boat maintenance and fuel costs of $1,822, and casual labor costs, $2,400. On September 14, Art paid the boat dealer $15,000 and $900 interest. In addition, Art said he withdrew $1,800 per month during the season. The season-ending cash balance in the bank is $22,697. No records exist regarding the amount of cash sales; (Task 1).

Cash sales revenue must be determined (Task 2): Set up linear statement using information already noted. Show how you determine the unknown cash sales; (Task 3) and prepare an accrual income statement to show him operating income (before tax) for the period ending 09-15-2006.

C A S E   1

This is the first part of an ongoing case that will appear at the end of most subsequent chapters. It is recommended that you keep case solutions, notes, and other case information in a separate file or binder for quick reference.

Charlie Driver has $35,000 saved and has decided to attend college, taking courses in marketing and retailing. To help pay his tuition and living expenses, he contracted with a mobile catering company as an independent driver. Charlie will run his mobile catering business on a cash basis; he has named his business Charlie's Convenient Catering, or the 3C Company for short. He opened a company bank account with $35,000. He bought a used, fully equipped mobile catering truck for $29,000, and operated from January 4 to December 31, 2005. At the end of the year, Charlie had $28,110 in the bank and $208 in a cash drawer. Invoices show he purchased food, beverages, and supplies inventories for $48,222; ending inventory remaining on the truck was $280. His invoices for truck operating expenses paid in cash total $3,288, and he has one unpaid truck repair invoice for $188. Charlie withdrew $2,400 a month for personal expenses. The truck has a five-year life and a residual value of $4,000, and straight-line depreciation is to be used.

Charlie asks you to help him put together his business information and reconstruct his cash sales. He recorded his daily cash sales in a notebook that cannot be found. Calculate 3C Company's sales revenue and prepare an accrual income statement. Charlie is concerned that he has less cash now than he had when he started. Explain why.

UNDERSTANDING FINANCIAL STATEMENTS

I N T R O D U C T I O N

This chapter discusses the two major financial statements—the balance sheet and the income statement. In hospitality operations, balance sheets are normally prepared for an overall operation, and income statements are prepared by each of the subordinate operating departments or divisions. Two basic classifications of costs, direct and indirect, are incurred in a hospitality operation.

Departmental income statements report **operating costs** that are classified as **direct costs,** which are *directly traceable* to the department. **Indirect costs** are costs that are not easily traceable to a specific department, and are usually undistributed costs. **Undistributed costs** are normally incurred to support the overall facility rather than individual departments and will normally appear on a summary income statement. All costs shown in an income statement will be shown as **cost of sales** and **named expenses.**

Cost of sales was discussed in an example in Chapter 1. Calculating the cost of sales will be expanded in this chapter. Four methods of calculating the value of inventory will be discussed and how to adjust the cost of food and beverages used to arrive at **net cost of sales** will be explained. These adjustments may include interdepartmental transfers, as well as adjustments for employee and promotion meals.

Responsibility accounting will be introduced and discussed for profit and cost centers. Allocation methods used to distribute indirect costs to departments will be discussed, as will the effect that a change to sales mix among departments would have on overall profit.

A sample balance sheet will be illustrated. An account called **retained earnings** is demonstrated as the link between the income statement and balance sheet in a corporate business entity. This section will also discuss the difference between the equity section of a balance sheet for **sole proprietorships, partnerships,** and incorporated business entities.

CHAPTER OBJECTIVES

After studying this chapter and completing the assigned exercises and problems, the reader should be able to

1. Explain the main purpose of the income statement and balance sheet.

2. Explain the value of a uniform system of accounts.

3. Define and explain the difference between a balance sheet and an income statement.

4. Using examples, describe the difference between a direct cost, indirect cost, and undistributed costs (expenses).

5. Calculate the value of ending inventory using each method discussed, and demonstrate possible adjustments to find the net cost of sales.

6. Prepare income statements in proper format.

7. Discuss the concept of responsibility accounting.

8. Explain the effect that a specific change in interdepartmental revenue mix will have on overall operating income (income before tax).

9. List and give an example of each of the six major categories (classifications) of accounts that may appear on a balance sheet.

10. Define, calculate, and explain the purpose of retained earnings.

11. Prepare a balance sheet in proper format and state the two forms of balance sheet presentations. Discuss the importance and limitations of a balance sheet.

UNDERSTANDING FINANCIAL STATEMENTS

Being able to understand **financial statements** does not necessarily mean you must be able to prepare them. However, if you are able to prepare a set of statements, primarily a balance sheet and income statement, then you have the advantage of being able to analyze the information in greater depth and, therefore, use it to enhance the results of a business operation.

There are many internal (various levels of management) and external users, (employees, stockholders, creditors, county, and local and national regulatory agencies) of financial statements. However, the primary emphasis of this text is for use by internal management, from the department head up to general management. Managers at all levels need financial information if they are to make rational decisions for the immediate or near future. The financial statements are sources of required information.

UNIFORM SYSTEM OF ACCOUNTS

Most organizations in the hospitality industry (hotels, motels, resorts, restaurants, and clubs) use the **Uniform System of Accounts** appropriate to their particular segment of the industry. The Hotel Association of New York initiated the original Uniform System of Accounts for Hotels (USAH) in 1925. The system was designed for classifying, organizing, and presenting financial information so that uniformity prevailed and comparison of financial data among hotels was possible.

One of the advantages of accounting uniformity is that information can be collected on a regional or national basis from similar organizations within the hospitality industry. This information can then be reproduced in the form of average figures or statistics. In this way, each organization can compare its results with the averages. This does not mean that individual hotel operators, for example, should be using national hotel average results as a goal for their own organization. Average results are only a standard of comparison, and there are many reasons why the individual organization's results may differ from industry averages. But by making the comparison, determining where differences exist, and subsequently analyzing the causes, an individual operator at least has information with which to make a decision regarding whether corrective action is required within the operator's own organization.

INCOME STATEMENT AND BALANCE SHEET

Although the balance sheet and the income statement are treated separately in this chapter, they should, in practice, be read and analyzed jointly. The relationship between the two financial statements must always be kept in mind. This relationship becomes extremely clear when one compares the definition and objective of each statement.

- *The purpose of the balance sheet* is to provide at a specific point in time a picture of the financial condition of a business entity relative to its assets, liabilities, and ownership equity. By category, each individual account, by name and its numerical balance, is shown at the end of a specific date, which is normally the ending date of an operating period.
- *The purpose of the income statement* is to show economic results of profit-motivated operations of a business over a specific operating period.
- *The ending date of an operating period* indicated in the income statement is normally the specific date of the balance sheet.

An annual operating period may be any 12-month period beginning on any date and ending on any date 12 months later. In addition, a business entity may use an interim reporting period such as weekly, monthly, quarterly, or semiannually.

INCOME STATEMENTS

The balance sheet presentations differ little from one type of hospitality business to another. As well, the presentations are quite similar to most presentations of non–hospitality-business operations. However, this similarity is not true of the income statement.

Most hospitality operations are departmentalized, and the income statement needs to show the operating results department by department as well as for the operation as a whole. Exactly how such an income statement is prepared and presented is dictated by the management needs of each individual establishment. As a result, the income statement for one hotel may be completely different from another, and income statements for other branches of the industry (resorts, chain hotels, small hotels, motels, restaurants, and clubs) will likely be very different from each other because each has to be prepared to reflect operating results that will allow management to make rational decisions about the business's future.

Discussion of the income statement in this chapter will be in general terms only and not limited to any one branch of the hospitality industry. The USAH recommends a long-form income statement, though it is not mandatory.

SALES REVENUE

Sales revenue is defined as an inflow of assets received in exchange for goods or services provided. In a hotel, sales revenue is derived from renting guest rooms, while in a restaurant, revenue is from the sale of food and beverages. Sales revenue is also derived from many other sources such as catering, entertainment, casinos, space rentals, vending machines, and gift shop operations, located on or immediately adjacent to the property. It is not unusual to receive nonoperating revenues, which are classified as "Other income" items in the income statement following operating income (before income tax). Other income items are nonoperating revenues not directly related to the primary purpose of the business, which is the sale of goods and services. Other income includes items such as interest income on certificates of deposit, notes receivable or investment dividends, and potentially franchise or management fees. When such revenue is received, it should be shown following operating income in a classified income statement before taxes are determined.

The accrual accounting method recognizes sales revenue when earned, not necessarily when it is received. Sales revenue is created and recorded to a sales revenue account by receipt of cash or the extension (giving) of credit. The recognition of sales revenue will, in theory, increase ownership equity. In reality, ownership equity will increase or decrease after expenses incurred are matched to revenues (matching principle) earned during an operating period. Ownership equity increases if revenues exceed expenses $(R > E)$; likewise, if revenue is less than expenses $(R < E)$, ownership equity will decrease.

As discussed in Chapter 1, the cash basis of accounting requires that cash change hands for the recognition of revenues and/or expenses; in theory, the capital account increases with the sale of goods or services and decreases as expense items are paid. The remainder of the topics in the text will be discussed based on accrual accounting.

EXPENSES

Expenses are defined as outflow of assets consumed to generate sales revenue. The accrual method of accounting requires that expenses be recorded when incurred, not necessarily when payment is made. Although the recognition of expenses in theory decreases ownership equity, in reality ownership equity will increase or decrease only after expenses incurred are matched to revenues earned at the end of an operating period.

Determining the increase or decrease in ownership equity follows the same revenue minus expense $(R - E)$ functions noted in the preceding revenue discussion. For example, in a restaurant, food inventory is purchased for resale and recorded as an asset; the cost of sales for a food operation is not recognized until it has been determined how much food inventory was used.

DEPARTMENTAL CONTRIBUTORY INCOME

The term **departmental contributory income** is used in this text and shows departmental revenue minus its direct costs to arrive at income before tax.

By matching direct expenses with the various revenue-producing activities of a department, a useful evaluation tool is created. The departmental income statement provides the basis for an effective evaluation of the department's performance over an operating period. In general, the format in condensed form of a departmentalized operation is shown as follows, using random numbers:

Departmental sales revenue	**$580,000**
Less: Departmental expenses (direct costs)	**(464,000)**
Departmental contributory income	**$116,000**

It is essential that the departmental contributory income statement provides maximum detail by showing each sales revenue and expense account to provide the information needed by management to conduct an effective and efficient evaluation.

If departmental managers are given authority and responsibility for their departmental operations, they need to be provided with more accounting information than sales revenue less total expenses. In other words, expenses need to be listed *item by item;* otherwise, department heads will have no knowledge about which expenses are out of line, and where additional controls may need to be implemented to curb those expenditures.

ANSWERS TO QUESTIONS

The income statement can provide answers to some important questions:

- What were sales last month? How does that compare with the month before and with the same month last year?
- Did last month's sales revenue keep pace with the increased cost of food, beverages, labor, and other expenses?
- What was the sales, by department, for the operating period?
- Which department is operating most effectively?
- Is there a limit to maximum potential sales? Have we reached that limit? If so, can we increase sales in the short run by increasing room rates and menu prices, or in the long run by expanding the premises?
- What were the food and beverage cost and gross profit percentages? Did these meet our objectives?
- Were operating costs (such as for labor and supplies) in line with what they should be for the sales level achieved?
- How did the operating results for the period compare with budget forecasts?

The income statement shows the operating results of a business for a period (week, month, quarter, half-year, or year). The amount of detail concerning sales revenue and expenses shown on the income statement depends on the type and size of the hospitality establishment and the needs of management for more or less information.

For example, a typical hotel would prepare departmental income statements for each of its operating departments. Exhibit 2.1 illustrates an income statement for the food department of a small hotel. Similar statements would be prepared for the beverage department and the rooms department. Others would be prepared for any other operating departments large enough to warrant it. Alternatively, other smaller departments could be grouped together into a single income statement. This would include operating areas such as newsstands, gift shops, laundry, telephone, parking, and so on.

In many establishments, it is not possible to show the food department as a separate entity from the beverage department because these two departments work closely together. They have many common costs that cannot accurately be identified as belonging to one or the other. For example, it is difficult to determine when a server is working for the food department and when a server is working for the beverage department if they serve both food and beverages. Because of this, there is only one income statement produced for the food and beverage department. Wherever possible, it is suggested that the sales revenue and expenses for food be kept separate from the revenue and expenses for beverages because in this way the in-

**Hotel Theoretical Departmental Income Statement—
Food Department
For the Year Ending December 31, 0006**

Sales Revenue		
Dining room	$201,600	
Coffee shop	195,900	
Banquets	261,200	
Room service	81,700	
Bar	111,200	
Total Sales Revenue		$851,600
Cost of sales		
Cost of Sales, Food	$319,500	
Less: employee meals	(30,100)	
Net cost of sales food		$289,400
Net cost of sales beverages		33,000
Total Net Cost of Sales		(322,400)
Gross Margin (*profit*)		$529,200
Departmental Operating Expenses		
Salaries and wages	$277,400	
Employee benefits	34,500	
Total payroll and related expenses	$311,900	
China, glassware	7,100	
Cleaning supplies	6,400	
Decorations	2,200	
Guest supplies	6,500	
Laundry	15,500	
Licenses	3,400	
Linen	3,700	
Menus	2,000	
Miscellaneous	800	
Paper supplies	4,900	
Printing, stationery	4,700	
Silver	2,300	
Uniforms	3,100	
Utensils	1,700	
Total Operating Expenses		(376,200)
Departmental Contributory Income (*Loss*)		$153,000

■ **EXHIBIT 2.1**

Sample Departmental Income Statement

come statements are more meaningful. In this text, therefore, food and beverage are shown as separate operating departments, even though it is recognized that, in practice, this may not always be possible. If necessary, the two separate sets of figures can always be added together later to give a combined food and beverage income statement for comparison with other establishments or with industry averages.

As you review the sample departmental income statement in Exhibit 2.1, take particular note of the following: (1) each sales revenue division is identified; (2) the cost of employee meals is deducted from the cost of sales. The cost of employee meals is the actual cost of the food used, and no sales revenue was generated or received from those meals. The term *net food cost* implies that all necessary adjustments to cost of food sales have been made, and represent the actual cost incurred to produce the sales revenue. Cost of employee meals became a part of the employee benefits reported as a departmental expense.

Each department's income statement reports its share of the expenses directly attributable to it, which is the responsibility of the department head to control. These direct costs would include cost of sales (food cost, beverage cost); salaries, wages, and related payroll costs of the employees working in the department; and linen, laundry, and all the various other categories of supplies required to operate the department. The resulting departmental incomes (sales revenue less direct expenses) are sometimes referred to as contributory incomes because they contribute to the indirect, undistributed expenses not charged to the operating departments. The individual departmental contributory incomes are added together to give a combined, total departmental income as demonstrated in Exhibit 2.2. As mentioned earlier, a departmental income statement similar to Exhibit 2.1 would support each departmental income figure.

From the total departmental income figure are deducted what are sometimes referred to as indirect expenses. Indirect expenses are those that are not directly related to the sales revenue-producing activities of the operation. Indirect expenses are broken down into two separate categories: the undistributed operating expenses and the fixed charges. Undistributed operating expenses include costs such as administrative and general, marketing, property operation and maintenance, and energy costs. Other expenses that might be included in this category, in certain establishments, are management fees, franchise fees, and guest entertainment. Most undistributed operating expenses are considered controllable, but not by the operating department heads or managers. They are controllable by and are the responsibility of the general manager. Note that undistributed operating expenses include the cost of salaries and wages of employees involved.

Income before fixed charges is an important line on an income statement because it measures the overall efficiency of the operation's management. The fixed charges are not considered in this evaluation because they are capital costs resulting from owning or renting the property (i.e., from the investment in land and building) and are thus not controllable by the establishment's operating management.

The final levels of expenses, the **fixed charges,** are then deducted. In this category are such expenses as rent, property taxes, insurance, interest, and depreciation. Income tax is then deducted to arrive at the final net income. The net income figure is transferred to the statement of retained earnings and eventually appears on the balance sheet; the transfer will be illustrated later in the chapter.

Hotel Theoretical Income Statement		
For the Year Ending December 31, 0006		
Departmental Income (*Loss*)		
Rooms		$ 782,900
Food		153,000
Beverage		119,100
Miscellaneous income		18,600
Total Departmental Income		$1,073,600
Undistributed Operating Expenses		
Administrative and general	$238,000	
Marketing	66,900	
Property operation and maintenance	102,000	
Energy costs	71,000	(477,900)
Income before Fixed Charges		$ 595,700
Fixed Charges		
Property taxes	$ 98,800	
Insurance	22,400	
Interest	82,400	
Depreciation	160,900	(364,500)
Operating Income (*before tax*)		$ 231,200
Income tax		(114,700)
Net Income		$ 116,500

■ **EXHIBIT 2.2**

Sample Summary Income Statement

Each of the expenses listed in Exhibit 2.2 would have a separate schedule listing all detailed costs making up the total expenses, if warranted by the size of the establishment. For example, the administrative and general expense schedule could show separate cost figures for such items as the following:

- Salary of the general manager and other administrative employees
- Secretarial and general office salaries and workers' wages
- Accountant and accounting office personnel salaries/wages
- Data processing and/or credit office employees' salaries and wages
- Postage and fax expense
- Printing and stationery expense
- Legal expense
- Bad debts and/or collection expenses
- Dues and subscriptions expenses
- Travel expense

Exhibit 2.3 shows another method of income statement presentation. Accompanying this income statement should be separate departmental income

Hotel Theoretical Income Statement
For the Year Ending December 31, 0006

	Net Sales Revenue	Cost of Sales	Payroll & Other Expenses	Operating Expenses	Operating Income
Departmental Income (*Loss*)					
Rooms	$1,150,200		$251,400	$115,900	$ 782,900
Food	851,600	$322,400	311,900	64,300	153,000
Beverage	327,400	106,800	86,300	15,200	119,100
Other income	38,200	10,600	8,700	300	18,600
Operating Department Totals	$2,367,400	$439,800	$658,300	$195,700	$1,073,600
Undistributed Operating Expenses					
Administrative and general			$115,600	$122,400	
Marketing			35,100	31,800	
Property operation & maintenance			52,900	49,100	
Energy costs			15,800	55,200	
Total undistributed operating expenses			$219,400	$258,500	(477,900)
Income before Fixed Charges					$ 595,700
Fixed Charges					
Property taxes				$ 98,800	
Insurance				22,400	
Interest				82,400	
Depreciation				160,900	(364,500)
Operating Income (*before income tax*)					$ 231,200
Income tax					(114,700)
Net Income					$ 116,500

■ **EXHIBIT 2.3**
Alternative Summary Income Statement

statements for each operating department, similar to the one for the food department illustrated in Exhibit 2.1. Also, where necessary, the income statement should be accompanied by schedules giving more detail of the unallocated expenses.

COST OF SALES AND NET COST OF SALES

In Exhibit 2.1, note that net food cost has been deducted from sales revenue to arrive at gross margin (gross profit) before deducting other departmental expenses. To arrive at net food cost and net beverage cost, some calculations are necessary to match up food and beverage sales with cost of the food and beverage **inventory** sold, or to find the net cost of sales incurred to generate those sales. In the first chapter, we discussed methods to determine the monthly cost of sales using the periodic inventory control method. The periodic method relies on a physical count and costing of the inventory to determine the cost of sales. Using the periodic method normally will not provide a record of inventory available for sale on any particular day. The calculation of cost of sales using the periodic method is as follows:

Beginning inventory (*BI*) + Purchases (*P*) = Goods available (*GA*)
− Ending inventory (*EI*) = Cost of sales (*CS*)

However, this equation determines the cost of inventory used. Later in the chapter, the cost of inventory used will be adjusted to the cost of inventory sold.

The control of inventory for sale is important, for a number of reasons:

- If inventories are not known, the possibility exists that inventory may run out and sales will stop. This situation will certainly create customer dissatisfaction.
- If inventories are in excess of projected needs, spoilage may occur, creating an additional cost that could be avoided.
- If inventories are maintained in excess of the amount needed, holding excess inventories will create an additional cost such as space costs, utilities costs, and inventory holding costs.
- If inventories are maintained in excess of the amount needed, the risk of theft is increased and, therefore, the cost of stolen inventory is higher.

Even though the perpetual inventory method requires keeping detailed records, it will provide the daily information needed to achieve excellent inventory control. As Exhibit 2.4 indicates, the perpetual method requires continuous updating, showing the receipt and sale of inventory as it occurs and allows for the maintenance of a daily running balance of inventory available. To verify that the perpetual inventory record is correct, a physical inventory count must be done.

There are several inventory valuation methods, of which we will discuss four. We will use the information in Exhibit 2.4 to illustrate each of the methods.

1. Specific item cost
2. First-in, first-out (FIFO)
3. Last-in, first-out (LIFO)
4. Weighted average cost

Specific Item Cost

The **specific identification** method records the *actual cost* of each item. In Exhibit 2.4(a), 10 items remain in stock at month end. Of these items, two came

| Item Description: Chateau Dupont | | Balance Available | | |
June	Purchase Received	Issued Sales	Units	Cost
01			2	$18.00
02	6		8	$20.00
08		3	5	
12		3	2	
15	10		12	$22.00
20		3	9	
24		3	6	
28	6		12	$19.00
30		2	10	

■ **EXHIBIT 2.4(a)**
Specific Identification Perpetual Control Record

from the purchase of June 2, four from the purchase of June 15, and four from the purchase of June 28. The value of ending inventory (*EI*) on June 30 would be

(2 @ $20)	+	(4 @ $22)	+	(4 @ $19)	= *EI*
$40	+	$88	+	$76	= $204 Total *EI*

The **cost of sales** used would be

$36 Beginning inventory (*BI*) + $454 Purchases (*P*)
   = Goods available (*GA*) − $204 *EI*
   = $286 Cost of sales (*CS*)

This method of inventory valuation is normally used only for **high-cost items,** such as high-cost wines and expensive cuts of meat.

First-in, First-out Method

Commonly referred to as **FIFO,** the **first-in, first-out inventory control procedure** works as the name implies—the first items received are assumed to be the first items sold. Simply put, the oldest items are assumed to be sold first, leaving the newest items in inventory. This method, when practiced, is based on the concept of stock rotation, which is essential with perishable stock and

Item Description: Chateau Dupont			Balance Available
June	Purchase Received	Issued Sales	Units × Cost = Tot. Cost
01	Bal. Fwd.		2 @ $18.00 = $ 36.00
02	6 @ $20.00 = $120.00		2 @ $18.00 = $ 36.00 6 @ $20.00 = $120.00
08		2 @ $18.00 = $ 36.00 1 @ $20.00 = $ 20.00	5 @ $20.00 = $100.00
12		3 @ $20.00 = $ 60.00	2 @ $20.00 = $ 40.00
15	10 @ $22.00 = $220.00		2 @ $20.00 = $ 40.00 10 @ $22.00 = $220.00
20		2 @ $20.00 = $ 40.00 1 @ $22.00 = $ 22.00	9 @ $22.00 = $198.00
24		3 @ $22.00 = $ 66.00	6 @ $22.00 = $132.00
28	6 @ $19.00 = $114.00		6 @ $22.00 = $132.00 6 @ $19.00 = $114.00
30		2 @ $22.00 = $ 44.00	4 @ $22.00 = $ 88.00 6 @ $19.00 = $114.00
Ending	Purchases = $454.00	Cost of sales = $288.00	Ending Inv. = $202.00

■ **EXHIBIT 2.4(b)**

FIFO Perpetual Inventory Control Record

helps ensure that inventory stock is sold before it spoils. As shown in Exhibit 2.4(b), using FIFO, the ending inventory is valued at $202.

The value of ending inventory, cost of sales, and purchases can be verified as follows:

$$\$36 \ (BI) + \$454 \ (P) = \$490 \ (GA) - \$202 \ (EI) = \underline{\$288} \text{ Cost of sales } (CS)$$

FIFO creates tiers of inventory available. The first tier is the oldest, the second tier is the next oldest, and so on. The oldest units are always assumed to be sold first. The sales revenue flow is from top to bottom of the inventory tiers. Any tier is split to account for the number of units sold. Cost of sales is determined at any time by adding the issued sales column. The value of ending inventory is the total cost shown in the final tier of the balance available column. FIFO uses the earliest costs and, in a period of inflationary costs, lowers cost of sales and increases the value of ending inventory.

Item Description: Chateau Dupont			Balance Available
June	**Purchase Received**	**Issued Sales**	**Units × cost = Tot. Cost**
01	Bal. Fwd.		2 @ $18.00 = $ 36.00
02	6 @ $20.00 = $120.00		2 @ $18.00 = $ 36.00 6 @ $20.00 = $120.00
08		3 @ $20.00 = $ 60.00	2 @ $18.00 = $ 36.00 3 @ $20.00 = $ 60.00
12		3 @ $20.00 = $ 60.00	2 @ $18.00 = $ 36.00
15	10 @ $22.00 = $220.00		2 @ $20.00 = $ 40.00 10 @ $22.00 = $220.00
20		3 @ $22.00 = $ 66.00	2 @ $18.00 = $ 36.00 7 @ $22.00 = $154.00
24		3 @ $22.00 = $ 66.00	2 @ $18.00 = $ 36.00 4 @ $22.00 = $ 88.00
28	6 @ $19.00 = $114.00		2 @ $18.00 = $ 36.00 4 @ $22.00 = $ 88.00 4 @ $19.00 = $ 76.00
30		2 @ $19.00 = $ 38.00	2 @ $18.00 = $ 36.00 4 @ $22.00 = $ 88.00 4 @ $19.00 = $ 76.00
Ending	**Purchases = $454.00**	**Cost of sales = $290.00**	**Ending Inv. = $200.00**

■ **EXHIBIT 2.4(c)**
LIFO Perpetual Inventory Control Record

Last-in, First-out Method

Commonly referred to as **LIFO,** the **last-in, first-out inventory control procedure** works as the name implies—the newest or last items received are assumed to be the first items sold, leaving the oldest items in inventory. Simply put, the newest items are assumed to be sold first. LIFO uses the same concept as FIFO. As shown in Exhibit 2.4(c), using LIFO, the ending inventory is valued at $200.

The value of ending inventory, cost of sales, and purchases can be verified as follows:

$$\$36 \ (BI) + \$454 \ (P) = \$490 \ (GA) - \$200 \ (EI) = \underline{\$290} \text{ Cost of sales } (CS)$$

Sales flow is from the bottom to top of the inventory tiers with the LIFO method. Any tier will be split to account for the number of units sold. Cost of sales is determined at any point by adding the issued sales column. The value of ending inventory is the total cost shown in the final tier of the balance-available column.

Use of the LIFO method during inflationary periods will cause an increase to cost of sales and will reduce gross margin. This effect is true because newer inventory purchases will cost more than older inventory purchases. In some cases, this method is favored based on the following logic: If inventory cost is increasing, then generally sales revenues are expected to increase because cost increases are passed on to customers through higher selling prices. Higher costs will be matched to higher revenues, resulting in a lower taxable operating income and lower taxes. LIFO will also reduce the value of inventory for resale and will be lower than if FIFO was used.

This logic can be seen in some respects by viewing the difference in the value of ending inventories when the FIFO and LIFO Exhibits 2.4(a) and 2.4(b) are reviewed.

Weighted Average Cost Method

This method calculates a weighted average for each item of inventory available for sale. Each time additional inventory is received into stock, a new **weighted average cost** is calculated. All items of inventory will be reported at their weighted average cost per unit. With reference to Exhibit 2.4(d), at the beginning of June, there were two items on hand at $18 each, for a total value of $36. On June 2, six additional items at $20 each with a total value of $120 were added into stock. The new cost of the total eight items at weighted average is $19.50 each. The calculation made was as follows:

$$\frac{\text{Total cost of units available } (TC)}{\text{Total units available } (TU)} = \text{Weighted average cost per unit}$$

$$\frac{(2 \times \$18) + (6 \times \$20)}{2 + 6 \text{ units available}} = \text{Weighted average cost per unit}$$

$$\frac{TC}{TU} = \frac{\$156.00}{8 \text{ units}} = \underline{\underline{\$19.50}} \text{ per unit}$$

Similar calculations are required when inventory is added on June 15 and June 28. Review Exhibit 2.4(d) and confirm the weighted average calculations.

The weighted average inventory evaluation method can generally reduce effects of price-cost increases or decreases during a month or for longer operating periods. As shown in Exhibit 2.4(d), the value of ending inventory is $202.90.

Item Description: Chateau Dupont		Balance Available	
June	*Purchase Received*	*Issued Sales*	*Units × Cost = Tot. Cost*
01 Bal. Fwd.		2 @ $18.00 = $ 36.00	
02	6 @ $20.00 = $120.00	[$156 / 8 = $ 19.50]	8 @ $19.50 = $156.00
08		3 @ $19.50 = $ 58.50	5 @ $19.50 = $ 97.50
12		3 @ $19.50 = $ 58.50	2 @ $19.50 = $ 39.00
15	10 @ $22.00 = $220.00	[$259 / 12 = $ 21.58]	12 @ $21.58 = $258.96
20		3 @ $21.58 = $ 64.74	9 @ $21.58 = $194.22
24		3 @ $21.58 = $ 64.74	6 @ $21.58 = $129.48
28	6 @ $19.00 = $114.00	[$243.48 / 12 = $ 20.29]	12 @ $20.29 = $243.48
30		2 @ $20.29 = $ 40.58	10 @ $20.29 = $202.90
Ending	**Purchases = $454.00**	**Cost of sales = $287.06**	**Ending Inv. = $202.90**
	* Adjusted cost of sales: $287.06 + $0.04 = $287.10		

* The weighted average method will normally create rounding errors. In this case, a 4¢ or $0.04 error: The correct cost of sales: (*BI*) $36 + (P) $454 − (*EI*) $202.90 = $287.10. Cost of sales (*CS*) on the control record of $287.06 is adjusted to be $287.10.

■ **EXHIBIT 2.4(d)**
Weighted Average Perpetual Inventory Control Record

Having discussed the four different inventory evaluation methods, we will now compare the results for ending inventory and cost of sales:

Method	Ending Inventory	Cost of Sales
Specific identification	$204.00	$286.00
First-in, first-out	$202.00	$288.00
Last-in, first-out	$200.00	$290.00
Weighted average cost	$202.90	$287.10

Although the differences among the four inventory valuation methods do not appear to be significant, only one item of inventory in stock was evaluated. If a full inventory were evaluated, the differences may well become significant, and might have an effect on the value of the entire inventory, cost of sales, operating income, and taxes. However, if one inventory method is consistently followed, the effect on inventory valuation, cost of sales, and operating income will be consistent.

Finally, note that the FIFO method generally produces a higher net income when cost prices are increasing and a lower net income when cost prices are declining. It is generally the easiest method to use, particularly when the inventory records are manually maintained. For this reason, FIFO is often the preferred method used for food inventories. FIFO is also consistent with the stock rotation required to maintain fresh-food inventories.

When each item has been counted and costs are established, total inventory value can be calculated. The costing of items sounds like a simple process, and is for most items. However, the process can be more difficult for other items. For example, what is the value of a gallon of soup that is being prepared in a kitchen at the time inventory is taken? In such a case, that value (because the soup has many different ingredients in it) might have to be estimated. The accuracy of the final inventory depends on the time taken to value it. There is a trade-off between accuracy and time required. If inventory is not as accurate as it could be, then neither food (and beverage) cost nor net income will be accurate. Normally, however, relatively minor inventory-taking inaccuracies tend to even out over time. Inventory figures for food should be calculated separately from those for alcoholic beverages.

Compared to costing inventory, the cost of purchases can be calculated relatively easily because it is the total amount of food and beverages delivered during the month less any products returned to suppliers for such reasons as unacceptable quality. Invoices recorded in the purchases account during the month can readily provide this figure. To calculate food cost separately from beverage cost, purchase cost for these two areas must also be recorded in separate purchase accounts.

ADJUSTMENTS TO COST OF SALES–FOOD

To date, we have discussed only the calculation of the cost of sales–food. Why is this figure called "cost of sales–food" rather than "net food cost," "cost of food sold," or "food cost"? In many small restaurants, cost of sales–food is the same as net food cost, but in most food and beverage operations it is necessary to adjust cost of sales food before it can be accurately labeled net food cost. Here are some possible adjustments:

■ *Interdepartmental and interdivisional transfers:* For example, in a restaurant with a separate bar operation, items might be purchased and received in the kitchen and recorded as food purchases that are later transferred to the bar for use there. Some examples include fresh cream, eggs, or fruit used in certain cocktails. In the same way, some purchases might be received by the bar (and recorded as beverage purchases) that are later transferred to the kitchen—for example, wine used in cooking. A record of transfers should be maintained so at the end of each month, both food cost and beverage cost can be adjusted to ensure that they are as accurate as possible. The cost of transfers from the food operation to the bar operation would require the cost of sales–food to be adjusted by deducting the cost of the inventory transferred. The opposite effect would be the bar adding the cost of the transfer to adjust the cost of sales–beverage.

■ *Employee meals:* Most food operations allow certain employees, while on duty, to have meals at little or no cost. In such cases, the cost of that food has no relation to sales revenue generated in the normal course of business. Therefore, the cost of employee meals should be deducted from cost of food used. Employee meal cost is then transferred to another expense account. For example, it could be added to the payroll cost as an employee benefit. Note that if employees pay cash for meals but receive a discount from normal menu prices, this sales revenue should be excluded from regular food revenue because it will distort the food cost percentage calculation. It should be transferred to a separate revenue account, such as other income.

■ *Promotional expense:* Restaurants sometimes provide customers with complimentary (free) food and/or beverages. This is a beneficial practice if it is done for good customers who are likely to continue to provide the operation with business. The cost of promotional meals should be handled in the same way as the cost of employee meals. The cost should not be included in the cost of sales–food or the cost of sales–sbeverage because, again, the food and/or beverage cost will be distorted. The cost should be removed from food cost and/or beverage cost and be recorded as advertising or promotion expense. Employees who are authorized to offer promotional items to customers should be instructed always to make out a sales check to record the item's sales revenue value. Some restaurants, for promotional purposes, issue coupons that allow two meals for the price of one. In this case, the value of both meals should still be recorded on the sales check, even though the customer pays for only one meal. From the sales checks, the cost of promotional meals can be calculated by using the operation's normal food cost and/or beverage cost percentage.

RESPONSIBILITY ACCOUNTING

Responsibility accounting is based on the principle that department heads or managers should be held accountable for their performance and the performance of the employees in their department. A hospitality business with several departments, each with the responsibility for controlling its own costs and with its department head accountable for the departmental profit achieved, is practicing what is known as responsibility accounting. There are two objectives for establishing responsibility centers:

1. Allow top-level management to delegate responsibility and authority to department heads so they can achieve departmental operating goals compatible with the overall establishment's goals.
2. Provide top-level management with information (generally of an accounting nature) to measure the performance of each department in achieving its operating goals.

Within a single organization practicing responsibility accounting, departments can be identified as cost centers, sales revenue centers, profit centers, or investment centers. A **cost center** is one that generates no direct revenue (such as the maintenance department). In such a situation, the department manager is held responsible only for the costs incurred.

Some establishments also have sales revenue centers. These departments receive **sales revenue,** but have little or no direct costs associated with their operation. For example, a major resort hotel might lease out a large part of its floor space to retail stores. The rent income provides revenue for the department, all of which is profit.

A **profit center** is one that has costs but also generates sales revenue that is directly related to that department. The rooms department is an example where the manager is responsible for generating revenue from guest room sales. The manager of a profit center should have some control over the sales revenue it can generate. Thus, profit centers are responsible for both maximizing revenue and minimizing expenses, which, in turn, maximize departmental profit. Each profit center manager or department head can then be measured by how well profit was maximized while continuing to maintain customer service levels established by top-level management.

In both cost and profit centers, a key question is, what costs should be assigned to each center? Generally, only those costs that are directly controllable by that center's department head or manager are assigned.

The final type of responsibility center occurs in a large or chain organization with units located in several different towns or cities. Each unit in the organization is given full authority over how it operates and is held responsible for the results of its decisions. In a large organization such as this, each unit is said to be decentralized. Units are sometimes referred to as **investment centers.** Investment centers are measured by the rate of return their general managers achieve on the investment in that center.

TRANSFER PRICING

In some chain organizations, products are transferred from one unit to another. For example, in a multiunit food organization, raw food ingredients might be purchased and processed in a central commissary before distribution to the individual units. A question arises about the cost to be transferred to each unit for the partially or fully processed products. Many different pricing methods are available. It is important that an appropriate pricing method be decided so each unit can be properly measured on its performance.

For example, the transfer price could be the commissary's cost plus a fixed percentage markup to cover its operating costs. Another method might be to base the transfer price on the market price of the products. The market price would be what the receiving unit would have paid if it had purchased the products from an external supplier. In some cases, the market price might be reduced by a fixed percentage to reflect the commissary's lower marketing and distribution costs. Obviously, each user unit would prefer to have the transfer price as low as possible so its costs are lower, and the commissary would prefer to have the transfer price as high as possible to enhance its performance.

■ DISTRIBUTION OF INDIRECT EXPENSES

One controversial issue concerning the income statement is whether the indirect expenses should be distributed to the departments. The problem arises in selecting a rational basis on which to allocate these costs to the operating departments. Some direct expenses might also have to be prorated between two operating departments on some logical basis. For example, an employee in the food department serving food to customers might also be serving them alcoholic beverages. The food department will receive the credit for the food sales revenue, and the beverage department for the beverage sales revenue. However, it would be unfair for either of these two departments to have to bear the full cost of that employee's wages. That cost should be split between the two departments, possibly prorating it on the basis of the sales revenue dollars. Such interdepartmental cost transfers are easily made; they are necessary to have a reasonably correct profit or loss for each operating department for which the appropriate department head is accountable.

One of the arguments in favor of allocating indirect expenses to departments is that, although departmental managers are not responsible for controlling those costs, they should be aware of what portion of them is related to their department since this could have an impact on departmental decision making, such as establishing selling prices at a level that covers all costs and not just direct costs.

When this type of **full-cost accounting** is implemented in a responsibility accounting system, it allows a manager to know the total minimum revenue that must be generated to cover all costs, even though the control of some of those costs is not their responsibility.

Some undistributed indirect expenses can be allocated easily and logically. For example, marketing could be distributed on a revenue ratio basis. However, if a particular advertising campaign had been made specifically for one department, and it was thought that little, if any, benefit would accrue to other departments, then the full cost of that campaign could reasonably be charged to that one department as a direct cost.

In Exhibit 2.3, note that the total marketing expense (payroll & other expenses plus operating expenses) is $66,900. If management wished to charge (allocate) that expense to the operating departments on a revenue ratio basis, the first step is to convert each department's revenue to a percentage of total revenue, as follows (percentage figures are rounded to the whole percentage):

Department	Sales Revenue	Percentage
Rooms	$1,150,200	48.6%
Food	851,600	36.0%
Beverage	327,400	13.8%
Miscellaneous	38,200	1.6%
Total	$2,367,400	100%

The marketing cost can then be allocated as follows:

Department	Total Marketing Expense Share of Cost	Share of Allocated Marketing Expense
Rooms	$66,900 × 48.6% =	$32,513.40
Food	66,900 × 36.0% =	24,084.00
Beverage	66,900 × 13.8% =	9,232.20
Miscellaneous	66,900 × 1.6% =	1,070.40
Total		$66,900.00

The other indirect costs could be distributed by using the same procedure, but on a different basis. For example, total department payroll and related expenses might be an appropriate basis on which to allocate the administrative and general expense. The square foot (or cubic foot) area could be used for allocating property operation and maintenance, as well as energy costs. Alternatively, property operation and maintenance expenses could be allocated directly to the department(s) concerned at the time of invoicing. Property (real estate) taxes may also be allocated to a specific department on a square footage or sales revenue basis. Insurance could be charged on the basis of each department's insurable value relative to the total insurable value. Depreciation on a building might be apportioned on the basis of each department's property value relative to total property value, or, if this is difficult to determine, on the basis of square footage. Depreciation on equipment and furniture could probably easily be prorated on the basis of each department's equipment and furniture cost, or value, relative to total cost or value. Finally, with respect to interest expense, the only logical basis would be on each department's share of the asset value to total asset value at the time the obligation (mortgage, bond, debenture, loan) was incurred. If a department does not have any assets covered by the obligation, then it should bear none of the interest expense.

Once a method of allocating any, or all, of these indirect costs to the operating departments is selected, it should be adhered to consistently so that comparison of income statements of future periods is meaningful. However, remember that comparison with other, similar organizations' income statements may not be meaningful if that organization had not selected the same allocation basis. The resulting departmental income or loss may or may not be more revealing to the individual manager than the more traditional approach, which takes the departmental income statement to the departmental operating income (contributory income) level only.

If indirect expenses are allocated, the department head should still be made responsible only for the income (or loss) before deduction of indirect expenses, since indirect expenses are not normally controllable by the department head. By allocating indirect expenses, top management will be able to determine if each department is making income after all expenses are considered. If any are not, it may be that the allocation of indirect costs is not fair. Alternatively, analysis of such costs might indicate ways in which the costs could be reduced to eliminate any individual departmental losses and increase overall total net income.

Finally, whether or not indirect expenses are allocated to the various operating departments, the resulting net income (bottom line) figure for the entire operation will not differ. As well, the net income for the entire operation will not differ even if the method of allocating indirect expenses to the various departments is changed.

SALES REVENUE MIX EFFECT ON NET INCOME

Even though the allocation of the indirect expenses to the departments does not affect the operation's total net income because total indirect expenses are the same, there is one factor that will affect net income even if there is no change in total indirect expenses or in total revenue. That factor is a change in the revenue mix. In this particular instance, a change in the sales revenue mix is understood to be a change in the revenue volume of the various operating departments.

	Net Sales Revenue	Direct Expense	Departmental Contributory Income	Contributory Income Percentage
Rooms revenue	$1,150,200	$ 367,300	$ 782,900	68.1%
Food revenue	851,600	698,600	153,000	18.0%
Beverage revenue	327,400	208,300	119,100	36.4%
Miscellaneous income	38,200	19,600	18,600	49.7%
Totals	$2,367,400	$1,293,800	$1,073,600	
Total Indirect Expenses			(842,400)	
Operating Income (before tax)			$ 231,200	

■ **EXHIBIT 2.5**

Contributory Income Schedule

	Net Sales Revenue	Direct Expense	Departmental Contributory Income	Contributory Income Percentage
Rooms	$1,250,200	$ 400,100	$ 850,100	68.1%
Food	801,600	657,300	144,300	18.0%
Beverage	277,400	177,500	99,900	36.4%
Miscellaneous income	38,200	19,600	18,600	47.7%
Totals	$2,367,400	$1,254,500	$1,112,900	
Total Indirect Expenses			(842,400)	
Operating Income (before tax)			$ 270,500	

■ **EXHIBIT 2.6**
Contributory Income Schedule for Revised Sales Revenue

In Exhibit 2.5, contributory income percentage figures have been rounded to the nearest whole percentage. The rooms department has the lowest total of direct costs in relation to its revenue, and its departmental income is the highest, at 68 percent of revenue. Expressed differently, this means that, for every dollar increase in room revenue, $0.68 will be available as a contribution to the total indirect costs.

This is important if there is a change in the revenue mix. In Exhibit 2.6, there has been a change. Room revenue has been increased by $100,000, and food and beverage have each decreased by $50,000. There is, therefore, no change in total revenue. It is assumed that the contributory income percentage for each department will stay constant, despite a change in sales revenue volume; this may or may not be the case. Given this assumption, Exhibit 2.6 shows that, even with no change in total revenue or total indirect expenses, there has been an increase in total contributory income and net income of $39,900. If management is aware of the influence each department has on total contributory income and on net income, it could be important for decision making. For example, it could indicate how the marketing budget should best be spent to emphasize the various departments within the organization. Alternatively, if a limited budget were available for building expansion to handle increased business, a study of each department's relative contributory income would help in deciding how to allocate the available funds.

BALANCE SHEETS

The **balance sheet** provides a picture of the financial condition of a business at a specific point in time and, in essence, consists of two major categories: assets and liabilities. Liabilities consists of two elements that have claims to the

Assets

Current Assets		
Cash		$ 27,900
Credit card receivables		2,480
Accounts receivable (net)		20,620
Marketable securities, at cost (Market value $10,500)		10,000
Food inventory	$ 8,200	
Beverage inventory	9,600	
Supplies	2,100	
Prepaid expenses	5,200	25,100
Total Current Assets		$ 86,100
Property, Plant, and Equipment		
Land (at cost)		$ 315,800
Building	$1,432,800	
Less: Accumulated	(356,900)	1,075,900
Equipment	281,025	
Less: Accumulated	(206,475)	74,550
Furniture	$ 93,675	
Less: Accumulated	(68,825)	24,850
Tableware, linen, & uniforms		25,600
Total Property, Plant, and Equipment		1,516,700
Other assets:		
Organization expense		5,800
Total Assets		$1,608,600

Liabilities and Stockholders' Equity

Current Liabilities		
Accounts payable—trade		$ 19,200
Accrued expenses		3,500
Income tax payable		12,300
Deposits and credit balances		500
Current portion, long-term mortgage payable		27,200
Total Current Liabilities		$ 62,700
Liabilities & Stockholders' Equity		
Long-term Liabilities		
Mortgage payable (building)	$840,100	
Less: Current portion payable	(27,200)	
Total Liabilities		$ 875,600
Stockholders' Equity		
Capital Stock: $100 par, 5,000 Authorized, 3,000 shares issued and outstanding		$300,000
Retained Earnings		
Total Liabilities & Stockholders' Equity		$1,608,600

EXHIBIT 2.7

Balance Sheet Ending December 31, 0006

assets: claims of its creditors and claims of its ownership. The balance sheet equation is stated as Assets = Liabilities and Ownership Equity. Several common titles are used to describe the equity of a sole proprietary organization, a partnership, and a corporation. A **sole proprietorship**—a business entity—may use the titles of proprietor's capital, proprietorship equity, proprietorship net worth, or owner's equity. A **partnership**—an unincorporated business owned by two or more individuals—may use the titles of partners' capital, partnership equity, partnership net worth, or owners' equity. A **corporation**—an incorporated, artificial person who protects individual investors (stockholders) from personal liability and continues its existence through easy transfer of stock—may use the title stockholder equity or owners' equity.

The balance sheet can be presented in a horizontal report format or in a vertical report format. Regardless of the format used, total assets must always equal total liabilities and ownership equity.

The left-hand side of a horizontal balance sheet consists of all assets, which must equal the right-hand side of the balance sheet. The right-hand side is composed of two major sections: liabilities and ownership equity. The liabilities are further broken down into short-term and long-term. Owners' equity normally consists of capital(s) and withdrawals accounts. Stockholders' equity generally consists of capital stock and retained earnings accounts. A balance sheet in horizontal report format is shown in Exhibit 2.7.

ASSETS

Assets represent resources of value owned by the business entity such as cash, amounts owed to the business, inventories for resale, equipment, furnishings, building(s) and land. Generally, assets are categorized as current assets, fixed assets, investments, and other assets.

CURRENT ASSETS

Current assets are shown first in the assets section of the balance sheet. Cash will be shown first, followed by assets that will be converted to cash and other assets that are consumed during an operating period of one year or less whichever is longer.

Cash on Hand

The cash account will normally consist of cash on hand to operate the daily in-house activities, undeposited cash receipts, and cash on deposit in its bank. Most business operations should deposit in the bank the total cash receipts from the preceding day. The amount of cash on hand reported in the balance sheet will normally be equivalent to approximately one day's cash receipts, plus any point-of-sale cash drawer or service-staff-operating cash banks.

Cash in the Bank

Cash in the bank should normally be sufficient to pay current debt liabilities as they come due for payment in each operating period. Cash in excess of the amounts needed for payment of current debt should be invested in short-term interest-bearing instruments.

Credit Card Receivables

These represent credit card receivables that have not yet been reimbursed by the credit card company at the end of an operating period. This amount will normally be equal to the amount of sales revenue purchased on credit cards during the last one to three days before the balance sheet date. The rate at which an operation is reimbursed for credit cards will vary, based on the type of card and the issuing credit card company.

Accounts Receivable

Generally, the use of **accounts receivable** is being replaced by credit cards. When accounts receivable are used as a current asset, they represent the extension of credit for rooms, food and beverages to individuals, or companies for which payment was not immediately received. If an account receivable is not paid, and it appears it will not be paid, the account is normally written off as a bad debt expense.

Marketable Securities

Cash that is in excess of operating requirements can be invested in a number of different interest-bearing instruments. One way is to invest excess funds in short-term **marketable securities** until the cash is needed. Normally, this type of current asset is shown at cost. When the market value of such securities is different from their cost on the balance sheet date, the securities' market value should be reported in the balance sheet by a disclosure footnote. If the securities qualify as trading securities, an unrealized gain or loss can be recognized for accounting purposes by comparing their cost to the present market value.

Inventories

Two different categories of **inventories** exist. The first category is **current assets.** To be considered a current asset, inventories must have been purchased for resale (e.g., food, beverage, and supplies inventories). The second category includes glassware, tableware, china, linen, and uniforms, which are noncurrent assets commonly referred to as *other assets* and normally reported following property, plant, and equipment, in the fixed assets section of the balance sheet.

Prepaid Expenses

Prepaid expenses represent the use of cash to obtain benefits that will be consumed with the passage of time. Prepaid insurance premiums, prepaid rent or lease costs, prepaid advertising, prepaid license fees, prepaid taxes, and other such items are classified as current assets. Although prepaid items are not expected to be converted to cash, they replace cash as a current asset until the benefits are received and recognized as expenses.

PROPERTY, PLANT AND EQUIPMENT (OR FIXED ASSETS)

Property, plant and equipment are noncurrent, nonmonetary tangible assets used to support business operations. They are also known as property, plant, and equipment, and are commonly referred to as *capital assets*. Fixed assets are long lived and of a more permanent and physical nature, and are not intended to be sold.

Land, Building, and Furniture and Equipment

These are three major fixed assets common to property, plant and equipment used in the hospitality industry. They are generally shown at their cost, or cost plus any expenditure necessary to put the asset in condition for use (e.g., freight and installation charges for an item of equipment). If any part of the land or a building is not used for the ordinary purposes of the business (e.g., a parcel of land held for investment purposes), it should be shown separately on the balance sheet. On some balance sheets, this section maybe titled fixed assets.

Accumulated Depreciation

The costs of buildings and furniture and equipment are reduced by **accumulated depreciation.** However, land is not depreciated and is always recorded at its original cost. Accumulated depreciation reflects the decline in value of the related asset due to wear and tear, the passage of time, changed economic conditions, or other factors. This traditional method of accounting, which shows the **net book value** (cost minus accumulated depreciation) of the asset, does not necessarily reflect the market value or the replacement value of the asset in question.

OTHER ASSETS

A company might have other assets that do not fit into either current assets or fixed assets. Some of the more common ones are discussed here.

China, Glassware, Silver, Linen, Kitchen Utensils, and Uniforms

This amount is made up from two figures. The estimated value of items in use is added to the cost of those items still new and in storage. Some of the noted items—china, glassware, silver, linen, utensils, and uniforms—may have a high cost and an estimated life of more than five years. When identified as such, these items are recorded at cost less depreciation and are considered as fixed assets. Any of these items may be held in storage until needed and expensed as they are brought into service.

Deposits

If a restaurant lease or another hospitality type of lease is required to make a cash deposit that is refundable at some point in the future, it can be considered an asset. An example of this would be a cash deposit with a utility company or a rental lease deposit; if such a cash deposit is required, this cash is no longer usable and it should be reported under other assets.

Investments

Long-term investments in other companies or in property or plant not connected with the day-to-day running of the business are shown as a separate category of asset. This category does not include short-term investments, such as a separate building that is owned and rented to another organization.

Leasehold Costs or Leasehold Improvements

It is reasonably common for the land or building to be leased. Where a long-term lease is paid in advance, the unexpired portion of this cost should be shown as an asset. Similarly, if improvements are made to a leased building, these **leasehold improvements** are of benefit during the life of the business or the remaining life of the lease, whichever is shorter. The costs should be spread (amortized) over this life. Any unamortized cost should be shown as an asset. The term **amortization** is similar in concept to depreciation, discussed in Chapter 1. Depreciation is generally used in conjunction with tangible assets, such as buildings and furniture and equipment. Amortization is generally used with intangible assets, such as goodwill or deferred expenses.

Deferred Expenses

Deferred expenses are similar to prepaid expenses except that the deferred expense is long-term in nature and is amortized over future years. An example of this might be the discount (prepaid interest) on a mortgage. This discount is amortized annually over the life of the mortgage. Preopening expenses such as advertising that will benefit the operation in future periods would also fit into this category.

TOTAL ASSETS

All of the various assets discussed, when added together, represent the **total assets** of a company, or the total resources available to it.

LIABILITIES

Liabilities represent debts or obligations owed by the business entity. Generally, assets are categorized as current liabilities or long-term liabilities.

CURRENT LIABILITIES

Current liabilities are those debts that must be paid or are expected to be paid within a year. They include the following items.

Accounts Payable–Trade

Accounts payable–trade include the amounts owing to suppliers of food, beverages, and other supplies and services purchased on account or contracted for in the normal day-to-day operation of a hospitality business.

Accrued Expenses

Accrued expenses include those current debts that are not part of accounts payable. This would include unpaid wages or salaries, payroll tax and related deductions, interest owing but not yet paid, rent payable, and other similar expenses.

Income Tax Payable

This is the income tax owed to the government on the company's taxable income.

Deposits and Credit Balances

Advance cash deposits by prospective guests for room reservations or banquet bookings and the accounts of guests staying in a hotel that have credit balances on them. The total of all these items should be shown as a liability because the money is due to the guest until it has been earned.

Current Portion of Long-Term Mortgage

Since, by definition, current liabilities are debts due within one year, the amount of a long-term liability payable within a year should be deducted from the long-term obligation and shown under current liabilities.

LONG-TERM LIABILITIES

Long-term liabilities are those due more than one year after the balance sheet date. Included in this category would be mortgages, bonds, debentures, and notes payable. If there are any long-term loans from stockholders, they also would appear in that section.

OWNERSHIP EQUITY

In general terms, the **ownership equity** section of the balance sheet is the difference between total assets and total liabilities. It represents the equity, or the interest, of the owners in the enterprise. It comprises two main items, capital stock and retained earnings, although other items, such as capital surplus, may appear.

STOCKHOLDERS' EQUITY ACCOUNTS

Capital Stock

Any company that is incorporated, is limited by law to a maximum number of shares it can issue. This limit is known as the authorized number of shares. Shares generally have a par, or stated, value, and this par value, multiplied by the number of shares actually issued up to the authorized quantity, gives the total value of **capital stock.** Most companies issue shares in the form of common stock. However, often balance sheets will have another type of stock, known as **preferred stock.** Preferred stock ranks ahead of common stock, up to certain limits, to receive dividends. Preferred stockholders may have special voting rights, and they rank ahead of common stockholders to receive reimbursement in the event of the company's liquidation.

Paid-in Capital, Excess of Par

Paid-in capital, excess of par is a term that was formerly referred to as capital surplus and represents the amount received by incorporated companies when their stock sold for more than its par value. This term also applies to companies that sold stock at a price exceeding its stated value. The excess amounts received from selling stock for more than its par or stated value appears in the stockholders' equity section of the balance sheet.

Statement of Retained Earnings
For the Year Ending December 31, 0006

Retained earnings January 1, 0006	$192,500
Add: Net income for Year 0006	270,500
	$463,000
Less: Dividends paid	(30,000)
Retained earnings December 31, 0006	$433,000

■ **EXHIBIT 2.8**
Sample Statement of Retained Earnings

Retained Earnings

Retained earnings is the account that records and accumulates all net income and net losses of an incorporated business. In addition, retained earnings is reduced by the value of all cash or stock dividends declared to be paid or issued by the company. A historical record of the success or failure (profit or loss) of a company and the dividends given to stockholders is shown in this account. Retained earnings can only be used to offset dividends, extraordinary losses, and prior period adjustments. Alternately, retained earnings can be retained for capital expansion to provide for the growth of the company. Retained earnings does not represent cash, although it is a critical link to the income statement and balance sheet. Details regarding changes to retained earnings over an accounting period are shown in a statement of retained earnings in Exhibit 2.8.

The detail shown in Exhibit 2.8 can and has been incorporated into the retained earnings section of stockholders' equity rather than simply showing its ending balance at the end of a period of operations. Exhibit 2.9 illustrates the link between the income statement and balance sheet over two successive accounting periods.

Dividends Payable

If dividends had been declared but not yet paid at the balance sheet date, they would be recorded under current liabilities.

PROPRIETORSHIPS AND PARTNERSHIPS

Capital stock is issued only in incorporated business entities. The sole owner of a business is the proprietor, and a partnership will consist of two or more owners. For sole proprietorships and partnerships, the ownership equity section is called a **statement of capital** and is shown as follows:

Beginning capital + Net income (or − Net loss)
− Owner withdrawals = Ending capital

Condensed Balance Sheet
For the Year Ended Dec. 31, 0007

Assets		$305,000
Liabilities		$145,000
Stockholders' Equity:		
Capital Stock	$100,000	
Retained Earnings	60,000	160,000
Total Liabiliites & Stockholders' Equity		$305,000

Condensed Income Statement
For the Year Ending Dec. 31, 0008

Sales Revenue	$590,000
Expenses	(508,000)
Net Income	$ 82,000

Statement of Retained Earnings
For the Year Ending Dec. 31, 0008

Retained Earnings Dec. 31, 0007	$ 60,000
Net Income for year	82,000
Retained Earnings Dec. 31, 0008	$142,000

Balance Sheet for the Year Ending Dec. 31, 0008

Assets		$340,000
Liabilities		$158,000
Stockholders' Equity:		
Capital Stock	$ 100,000	
Retained Earnings	82,000	182,000
		$340,000

■ **EXHIBIT 2.9**
Link between Balance Sheets, Income Statements, and Statements of Retained Earnings for an Incorporated Company

The format of a statement of capital will generally follow the format shown in Exhibit 2.10.

The difference between a *statement of capital* and a *statement of partnership capital* is the use of a separate capital and withdrawal accounts for each partner. Distribution of partnership net income or net loss is based on the part-

Statement of Proprietor's Capital For the Year Ending December 31, 0006	
Owner's capital, January 1, 0006	$492,500
Add: Net income for Year 0006	116,500
	$609,000
Less: Proprietor's withdrawals during year	(72,800)
Owner's capital, December 31, 0006	$536,200

■ **EXHIBIT 2.10**

Sample Statement of Proprietor's Capital

nership agreement. Detail in the statement of partnership capital will generally follow the basic format shown in Exhibit 2.11.

TOTAL LIABILITIES AND STOCKHOLDERS' EQUITY

The total of all the liabilities and stockholders' equity, or capital, accounts should agree with the total asset accounts on the left-hand side of the balance sheet. These liability and equity, or capital, accounts show how the company's resources (assets) are currently financed.

BALANCE SHEET DETAIL

The amount of detail shown on a balance sheet depends on the amount of information desired, the operation's size and complexity, and whether it is a proprietorship, partnership, or incorporated company. For example, one business's

Statement of Partners' Capital For the Year Ending December 31, 0006		
	Partner A	**Partner B**
Partners' capital, January 1, 0006	$240,000	$240,000
Add: Net income for Year 0006	72,750	72,750
	$312,750	$312,750
Less: Partners' withdrawals during year	(52,250)	(52,250)
Partners' capital, December 31, 0006	$260,500	$260,500

■ **EXHIBIT 2.11**

Sample Statement of Partners' Capital

balance sheet might show each type of cash account as a separate item, while another business's balance sheet might combine all the various cash accounts into a single figure.

Some operators want their balance sheets simplified as much as possible because this makes them easier to read at first glance. Where more detail about an account is needed, this might then be shown as an addendum or footnote on an adjoining page. For example, the inventories might be shown in total only on the balance sheet and might be supported by a separate schedule that shows them broken down into separate figures for food, beverages, supplies, and others.

BALANCE SHEET PRESENTATION

The balance sheet in Exhibit 2.7 is indicative of the way many balance sheets are presented, with assets on the left and liabilities and capital on the right. This presentation is known as the horizontal format, or account method, and is most commonly used by small- to medium-sized businesses.

Another common method is the report form. This method is a vertical format rather than horizontal. In the vertical form, the balance sheet is considered to have a top half and a bottom half. The top half is for the assets and the bottom half is for liabilities and owners' equity. The report form is normally used by larger-size business entities.

Importance of Balance Sheet

The balance sheet is important because it can provide information about matters such as the following:

- A business's liquidity, or ability to pay its debts when they have to be paid.
- How much of the operation's profits has been retained in the business to help it expand and/or reduce the amount of outside money (debt) that has to be borrowed.
- The breakdown of assets into current, fixed, and other, with details about the amount of assets within each of these broad categories.
- The business's debt (liabilities) relative to owners' equity. In general, the greater the amount of debt relative to equity, the higher is the operation's financial risk.

Balance Sheet Limitations

There are some aspects of a business that the balance sheet may not disclose. For example:

- *True value.* Because transactions are recorded in the value of the dollar at the time the transaction occurred, the true value of some assets on the balance sheet may not be apparent. Suppose that a hotel owned the land on which the building sits and that land had been purchased several years ago. Because of inflation and demand for limited land, it is likely that the land is worth far more today than was paid for it. This may also be true of some other assets. The balance sheet normally does not show this market value.

■ *Goodwill.* If the operation was purchased from a previous owner who had built up a successful business, and if the new owner paid an amount for that business above the actual market value of the assets, that amount would have been recorded on the balance sheet at the time of purchase as **goodwill.** Goodwill that a business has is normally recorded only at the time a business is transferred from seller to buyer. Therefore, if a business was started from scratch, and has a good location compared to its competitors, and/or a good reputation and faithful clientele, and/or a superior work force with good morale, it is probably worth far more than the balance sheet assets show, simply because the goodwill built up is not reflected on the balance sheet.

■ *Employee investment.* Another value similar to goodwill that is not shown on a business's balance sheet is the investment in its employees. This investment is the time and money spent on recruiting, training, evaluating, and promoting motivated individuals. Obviously, it is difficult to assign a value to these human resources, but nevertheless, they are assets to any hospitality business.

■ *Judgment calls.* Many items recorded on balance sheets are a matter of judgment or estimates. For example, what is the best depreciation method and rate to use, and what is the best of several available methods for valuing inventories? There are no absolute answers to these questions. For this reason, a balance sheet may not reflect the correct value for all assets. If the judgments or estimates used are wrong, then the balance sheet is incorrect.

■ *Changing circumstances.* Balance sheets also reflect the financial position of a business at only one moment in time. However, the business is constantly changing, and, therefore, the information on the balance sheet is constantly changing. These changes will not be shown until another balance sheet is produced a month or more later. If a balance sheet shows a healthy cash position at one time, and a week later most of that cash was spent on new furniture, the balance sheet will reveal nothing about the impending use of most of the cash available.

COMPUTER APPLICATIONS

Using a canned software package that can handle the general ledger, journal entries and the development of an operation's balance sheet and income statement, a company can automatically prepare and print its balance sheet and income statement at the end of each accounting period. Inventory control software can be used to maintain a perpetual inventory, as well as to calculate total inventory value at each period end, and this software can be integrated into the other accounting software. As requisitions are printed, the computer adjusts the storeroom inventory count for period-end stocking and can provide a value for items requisitioned but not yet used in production. For example, if inventory records a #10 can of an item when only half a can is required for production, the computer makes a note of this excess and takes it into account when future requisitions are prepared. A computerized system can also calculate a food cost for the day, based on food produced according to forecast sales revenue. From time to time, normal storeroom inventory reconciliation must be carried out; that is, comparing the physical count of items actually in stock with the computer listing of what should be there according to production usage.

Integrated software packages are available from a number of different vendors for general accounting. Most hospitality organizations are using an integrated accounting system approach for their general ledger, sales revenue, accounts receivable, purchases, accounts payable, payroll, and inventory control. Reservations, registration, and guest accounting can also be integrated into such a system. Today, there are integrated software packages available for computerization of this work.

S U M M A R Y

Financial statements provide information that management needs for rational decision making. Most hotel and food service operations pattern their financial statements along the lines of one of the various types of Uniform System of Accounts available to the industry.

The two main statements in a set of financial statements are the income statement and the balance sheet. The income statement shows the operating results of a business over a period of time, ending on the balance sheet date, whereas the balance sheet gives a picture of the financial position of a business at a particular point in time.

Income statements in the hospitality industry are, wherever possible, departmentalized. In other words, each operating department prepares an income statement. Sales revenue and direct costs are controllable by and are the responsibility of that department.

For most foodservice operations, it is necessary to adjust cost of sales–food used to arrive at a net cost of sales–food figure for an income statement. Such adjustments cover such items as interdepartmental transfers, employee meals, and promotion items.

Many hospitality businesses also use income statements to evaluate responsibility accounting, which is based on the principle that department heads or managers should be held accountable for their performance and the performance of their employees.

Summarized departmental contributory incomes are brought together in a general income statement, and all remaining fixed costs and indirect expenses are deducted to arrive at operating income (before income tax). Although it is possible to allocate and distribute all fixed and undistributed costs to operating departments, the difficulty lies in finding a realistic and practical method of prorating them to the departments.

An important point to remember regarding an income statement reporting on two or more operating departments is the effect a change in sales revenue mix may have across the departments. A given change in the sales revenue in one department may have a completely different effect on operating income than the same amount of revenue change in another department. Since different departments normally have different contributory income percentages, management needs to be alert to possible changes in revenue mix, which can result in changes in operating income. The net income (or net loss) is transferred to the balance sheet by way of a statement of retained earnings, described as follows:

Beginning retained earnings + *NI* (or − *NL*)
− Dividends = Ending retained earnings

The statement of retained earnings will show all items that affect ending retained earnings, or ending retained earnings may be shown on the balance sheet as a consolidated or summarized value. The income statement is the source of information regarding net income or net loss.

If the horizontal or account format is used, the balance sheet has assets on the left side and liabilities and stockholders' equity on the right side. If the report is in a vertical or report format, as follows, assets are reported first and followed by liabilities and stockholders' equity.

ASSETS

Current assets	Cash
	Credit card receivables
	Accounts receivable (net)
	Marketable securities
	Inventories
	Supplies
	Prepaid expenses
Total current assets	*Subtotal dollar value*
Property, plant & equipment	Land
(also called fixed assets)	Building
	Furnishings
	Equipment
	Less: (Accumulated depreciation)
Net property plant & equipment	*Subtotal dollar value*
Other assets	Deferred expenses
	China, glassware, silverware, linen, utensils, and uniforms
	Subtotal dollar value
Total Assets	**Sum total dollar value**

LIABILITIES AND OWNERSHIP EQUITY

Current liabilities	Accounts payable
	Accrued expenses
	Income taxes payable
	Deposits and credit balances
	Current portion of mortgage payable
Total current liablities	*Subtotal dollar value*
Long-term liabilities	Mortgage (or other long-term debt) payables
Total Liabilities	*Subtotal dollar value*
Stockholders' Equity	Capital stock
	Paid-in capital, excess of par
	Retained earnings
Total Ownership Equity:	*Subtotal dollar value*
Total Liabilities and Stockholders' Equity	**Sum total dollar value**

Note that the amount of detail appearing in a balance sheet is a managerial decision. Balance sheets may be shown in a horizontal format A = L + OE or vertical format, as shown in the preceding example. Finally, it is important to remember that a balance sheet has a great number of uses, but it also has a number of limitations. Ownership equity may be called stockholders' equity, proprietors' equity (sole owner) or partners' equity (two or more partners) with capital and withdrawals accounts.

DISCUSSION QUESTIONS

1. Why do managers of a motel or food service operation need financial statements?
2. Of what value is the Uniform System of Accounts?
3. What are the differences between a balance sheet and an income statement?
4. Briefly describe two limitations of a balance sheet.
5. What is departmental contributory income?
6. In a departmental organization, what is the difference between direct expenses and indirect expenses?
7. Explain the term *responsibility accounting* and differentiate a profit center from a cost center.
8. What is the difference between FIFO and LIFO inventory control?
9. State the equation for calculating cost of sales and the net cost of sales.
10. Briefly discuss four types of adjustments that may be necessary to convert cost of sales–food, to net cost of sales–food.

11. Discuss some specific types of indirect expenses and an appropriate method or methods to allocate them to individual operating departments.

12. Why should a change in the sales revenue mix among departments have any effect on net income, even if there is no change in total revenue?

13. For each of the following balance sheet categories, name three accounts and briefly discuss each one:

    a. Current assets

    b. Current liabilities

    c. Fixed assets

14. How do current assets differ from fixed assets?

15. Define *retained earnings* and explain how ending retained earnings is determined.

16. Why are guest deposits and credit balances on customer accounts shown as current liabilities?

17. Explain how the account format of a balance sheet presentation differs from the report format.

18. Discuss the difference between periodic and perpetual inventory control methods.

19. Define and discuss the weighted average method of inventory control.

20. Define the term *paid-in capital, excess of par.*

ETHICS SITUATION

The assistant night manager of a mid-size motor hotel has a number of duties, one of which is to assist in preparing the income statement each month. A new nearby competitive motor hotel is due to open in about six weeks. The assistant night manager has applied for the assistant day manager's position at the new hotel. Its owner told him that he has the job if he provides the owner with income statements of the motor hotel for which he has worked for the past three years. Discuss the ethics of this situation.

EXERCISES

E2.1 A hospitality operation may maintain a number of different inventory accounts. What determines if an inventory account is classified as a current asset or an other asset?

E2.2 What is the key word that defines the difference between direct cost and indirect cost?

E2.3 A new restaurant purchased the following wine during the first month of operations:

March 2: Purchased 12 each 750 ml bottles of M & B wine @ $12.50 each.

March 16: Purchased 24 each 750 ml bottles of M & B wine @ $13.50 each.

March 31: Sold 32 bottles during March @ $26 each.

Determine the value of the ending inventory and cost of sales for M & B for March using the following:

a. First-in, first-out method

b. Last-in, first-out method

c. Weighted average method

E2.4 Identify the missing dollar amounts in the equation shown below:

$$BI \quad + \quad P \quad - \quad EI \quad = \quad CS$$
$$\$38,000 \quad + \quad ? \quad - \quad \$24,000 \quad = \quad \$102,000$$

E2.5 A hospitality operation began with retained earnings of $146,000. During the year, cash dividends of $100,000 were paid to the owners. Net income for the year was $228,000. Answer the following:

a. What is the ending balance of retained earnings?

b. What would be the ending balance of retained earnings if a net loss of $12,200 had been reported rather than the net income?

E2.6 A food department reported sales revenue of $128,800 and direct costs of $68,200 during March. Determine the following:

a. What is the department's contributory income?

b. What is contributory income as a percentage of sales revenue?

E2.7 A department has two operating divisions: Food service with sales revenue of $880,000 and a bar-lounge with sales revenue of $440,840. Calculate the sales revenue of each division as a percentage of total departmental sales revenue.

E2.8 Match each of the terms in the left column with the account categories given in the right column.

a. Total assets − Total liabilities   1. Fixed asset

b. Sales revenue − Total expenses   2. Liabilities

c. Depreciable asset   3. Contributory income

d. Debt owed to creditors   4. Net assets, owners' equity

e. Sales revenue − Direct costs   5. Operating income

E2.9 Indirect, undistributed costs of $14,000 are to be allocated to two departments. Department "1" occupies 54% and department "2" occupies 46% of the total square footage available. Calculate the amount to be allocated to each department based on the square footage method.

E2.10 A department with three operating divisions reported the sales revenues for each of its divisions. Determine the percentage of sales revenue provided by each division:

Rooms division	$1,555,632
Food service division	921,856
Beverage division	403,312
Total sales revenue	$2,880,800

E2.11 A food division had beginning inventory of $4,400, purchases of $8,400, and ending inventory of $2,880 for a given week of operations. Determine the cost of goods available and cost of sales–food for the week.

E2.12 A food division reported cost of sales–food of $198,680. Employees' meals cost $1,225, complimentary meals $142, and transfers in were received from the bar operation with a cost of $82. Determine the net cost of sales.

E2.13 Assume that a food division reported sales revenue of $337,218 and the bar-lounge reported sales revenue of $206,682. Indirect costs of $52,400 are to be allocated to each division on the basis of sales revenue.

a. What is the allocated amount of indirect costs to the food division?

b. What is the allocated amount of indirect costs to the beverage division?

E2.14 Assume the following: beginning retained earnings was $125,000 and ending retained earnings was $150,000. Cash dividends were paid in the amount of $77,000. What was net income for the year?

P R O B L E M S

P2.1 Prepare a food department income statement in proper format for Midlands Restaurant using the following information for the first quarter ended on March 31, 0007 (other income received from leasing excess equipment for one month is not a part of normal operations):

Sales Revenue:

Grill room	$183,200
Coffee garden	82,900
Banquets	294,400
Net food costs	224,200
Salaries and wages expense	176,400
Employee meals expense	18,200
Supplies expense	10,300
Glass and tableware expense	4,300
Laundry and linen expense	13,500
License expense	2,400
Printing expense	4,900
Miscellaneous expense	8,200
Other income	800

P2.2 The Purple Rose Restaurant has the following food cost information for a given month. Calculate the food cost of sales and net food cost of sales for March. The following information is provided:

Food inventory, March 1	$2,782
Food inventory, March 31	2,612
Food purchases, March	9,807
Employee meals cost	219
Promotional meals cost	288

P2.3 Dee's Steak House has separate food and bar operations. Calculate food cost of sales and net food cost of sales for August. The following information is provided:

Food inventory, August 1	$15,357
Food inventory, August 31	12,887
Food purchases, August	47,879
Transfers, bar to the kitchen	68
Employee meals cost	1,828
Promotional meals cost	219
Complimentary meals cost	140
Transfers, kitchen to the bar	128

P2.4 The following information is taken from a perpetual inventory record.

Perpetual Inventory Control Record

Description: M & B Supreme

Date	Purchase Received	Issued Sales	Units	Unit Cost
June 1	Balance forward		3	$11.00
4		2		
6	8		9	$11.50
9		3	6	
12		2	4	
15	6		10	$12.00
18		2	8	
20		3	5	
22	6		11	$12.50
25		2	9	
28		3	6	

For each of the following inventory valuation methods, calculate the value of ending inventory and the cost of sales as of June 30. Use formats of Exhibits 2.4(a), (b), and (c).

a. First-in, first-out method

b. Last-in, first-out method

c. Weighted average method

P2.5 Cindy's Restaurant has three sales revenue departments with direct costs and average monthly figures given in the following information:

Departments	Dining	Banquets	Beverages
Sales revenue	$204,000	$110,000	$92,000
Cost of sales	81,600	41,800	29,440
Wages and salaries cost	65,280	35,200	12,880
Other direct costs	18,360	8,800	1,840

The restaurant also has the following indirect, undistributed costs:

Administrative and general expenses	$12,000
Marketing expenses	10,000
Utilities expense	5,000
Property operation and maintenance	12,120
Depreciation expense	14,000
Insurance expense	4,000

a. Prepare a consolidated departmental contributory income statement showing each of the three divisions side by side for comparison. Do not allocate indirect costs.

b. Allocate the indirect costs to the divisions and prepare a departmental income statement showing each of the three divisions side by side for comparison. Administrative, general, and marketing costs are allocated based on sales revenue. The remaining indirect costs are allocated based on square footage used by each division: Round all percentage calculations to a whole percentage.

Dining 2,400 sq. ft.   Banquet 3,000, sq. ft.   Beverage 600 sq. ft.

c. After allocating the indirect costs, would you consider closing any of the divisions? Why or why not?

P2.6 With reference to the information provided for Cindy's Restaurant in Problem 2.5 (round all percentage calculations to a whole percentage):

a. Calculate the contributory income percentage for each of the three divisions.

b. Using the information in Problem 2.5, calculate the cost of sales, wages and salaries costs, and other direct costs as a percentage of sales revenue for each of the divisions.

c. If there were a shift of $8,000 in sales revenue from the banquet area to the dining room, would you expect the restaurant's overall operating income to increase or decrease? Explain your reasoning to support your answer.

d. Assuming that the shift of $8,000 of sales revenue does occur, total sales revenue will not change. Total indirect, undistributed costs will not change. Cost of sales, wages and salaries costs, and other direct costs must be recalculated for each division to find the new departmental total operating income.

e. After allocating the indirect costs, would you now consider closing any of the divisions? Why or why not?

P2.7 Using the following adjusted trial balance, prepare a balance sheet in vertical report format. Identify each account using specific categories and classifications such as current assets, current liabilities, and so on. After completing the balance sheet, check off each item in the trial balance to ensure each item is shown in the balance sheet.

Accounts	Debit	Credit
Cash	$ 10,109	
Credit card receivables	1,554	
Accounts receivable	1,882	
Inventories	7,225	
Prepaid expenses	2,800	
Land	80,000	
Building	712,800	
Accumulated depreciation: (Building)		$ 186,400
Equipment	119,080	
Accumulated depreciation: (Equipment)		35,625
Furnishings	64,120	
Accumulated depreciation: (Furnishings)		11,875
China and tableware	8,780	
Glassware	2,620	
Accounts payable		5,070
Accrued expenses payable		2,900
Income taxes payable		8,770
Current portion, mortgage payable		13,030
Mortgage payable		406,800
Capital stock		152,000
Retained earnings		188,500
Trial Balance Totals	$1,010,970	$1,010,970

P2.8 George Jarvis purchased a trailer park on January 1, 0007. It is now March 31. George has no accounting training but has kept a record of his cash receipts and cash payments for the three months.

	Cash Receipts	Cash Payments
Jarvis investment for trailer park shares	$100,000	
Land		$168,600
Building		216,000
Office equipment		8,000
Mortgage payable	350,000	
Insurance		4,800
Wages		4,500
Maintenance		400
Office supplies		300
Utilities		900
Property taxes		6,000
Jarvis, salary		10,500
Rental sales revenue	60,000	
Mortgage interest expense		4,667
Mortgage principal payments, Jan. and Feb.		2,000

As Mr. Jarvis's accountant, you discover the following additional information:

a. The building has an estimated life of 20 years and straight-line depreciation is used.

b. The office equipment has a five-year life with a trade-in value of $500.

c. The insurance was prepaid on January 1 for the entire year.

d. The wages are for the maintenance worker who worked but has not yet been paid for five days during the period ending March 31, 0007. The wage is $9.95 per hour and the work day is eight hours.

e. An invoice for grounds maintenance expense of $80 has not yet been paid.

f. There are $100 in office supplies remaining in inventory.

g. The March utility bill has not yet been received. It is estimated to be $400.

h. The property taxes were paid in January for the entire year.

i. A rental tenant whose rent is $200 has not yet paid for March.

j. Included in the $60,000 received for rental income to date is the amount for a tenant who has prepaid for the entire year. The rent is $175 per month.

k. No interest or principal has been paid on the mortgage for March. Interest for March is $2,333. Principal payments for the balance of the year (including March) are $12,000 and should be identified as current mortgage payable. The balance of mortgage payable is $336,000.

l. The income tax is 25% of operating income and is payable in April. Using accrual based accounting, prepare an income statement for the three months ending March 31, 0007, and a balance sheet as of March 31, 0007.

CASE 2

Charlie Driver was pleased with the results of 3C Company's operation in year 2005, especially since he only operated on a part-time basis. In fact, he found the catering business to be not only profitable but also an enjoyable challenge. He decided to continue the 3C Company in year 2006, finish his hospitality and marketing education, and search for a suitable restaurant to acquire and operate.

Near the end of year 2006, Charlie found an 84-seat restaurant that had been closed for several months. It was the type of facility he had been looking for. After locating the owner, he reached an agreement to lease the restaurant for five years beginning January 2007. The lease set the first year rental cost at $24,000 and stipulated a 10% yearly rental increase in each of the remaining four years of the five-year lease. In addition, the owner agreed to allow Charlie to trade in the old equipment and furnishings for whatever he can get for them and to purchase new equipment and furnishings. The equipment and furnishings were traded in on new equipment with a net cost of $171,524 and new furnishings with a net cost of $53,596. The new equipment was estimated to have a 12-year life with a residual value of $6,500. The new furnishings had an estimated 8-year life and a residual value of $2,620.

Charlie realized that for tax purposes and other considerations, he should incorporate a new company as "Charlie's Classic Cuisine" Corporation. We will simplify this name to the 4C Company. With the cash he had saved from operating the 3C Company and from the sale of the truck, Charlie purchased $50,000 of 4C Company's $2.00 par value common stock. Charlie used his reputation and good business record over the past two years to obtain a corporate loan from his bank for $200,000. The loan was to be repaid over the next five years in monthly installments of principal and interest.

Although Charlie hired a bookkeeper, he has asked you, a personal friend, to prepare the 4C Company's year-end financial statements and to discuss the results of his first year of operations with him. You agreed to prepare the year-end statements from a year-ending unadjusted trial balance of accounts provided to you.

To make the necessary adjustments, you are given the following information:

- Inventory figures in the unadjusted trial are for the beginning of Year 2007. The December 31, 2007, year-end inventories are $5,915 for food and $2,211 for beverages.
- Accrued payroll of $2,215 must be recognized as of December 31, 2007.
- Depreciation on equipment and furnishings using the straight-line method must be recognized.
- The bank loan principal to be paid in Year 2008 is $38,260.

Using the unadjusted trial and additional information, complete the adjustments and prepare an income statement and balance sheet in the report format for 4C Company for the year ended December 31, 2007. Use an income tax rate of 22% of operating income (income before tax), which will not be paid until the Year 2008.

The unadjusted trial balance is provided on the following page.

4C Company
Unadjusted Trial Balance
December 31, 2007

Accounts	Debit	Credit
Cash	$ 36,218	
Credit card receivables	13,683	
Accounts receivable	3,421	
Inventories, food	6,128	
Inventories, beverages	3,207	
Prepaid insurance	2,136	
Equipment	171,524	
Furnishings	53,596	
Accounts payable		$ 8,819
Bank loan payable		163,518
Common stock		50,000
Sales revenue, food operations		458,602
Sales revenue, beverage operations		180,509
Purchases, food (net)	181,110	
Purchases, beverages (net)	38,307	
Salaries and wages expense	221,328	
Laundry expense	16,609	
Kitchen fuel expense	7,007	
China and tableware expense	12,214	
Glassware expense	$ 1,605	
Contract cleaning expense	5,906	
Licenses expense	3,205	
Misc. operating expenses	4,101	
Administrative—general expenses	15,432	
Marketing expenses	6,917	
Utilities expense	7,918	
Insurance expense	1,895	
Rental expense	24,000	
Interest expense	23,981	
Unadjusted Trial Balance Totals	$861,448	$861,448

ANALYSIS AND INTERPRETATION OF FINANCIAL STATEMENTS

I N T R O D U C T I O N

The first part of this chapter introduces the reader to the various groups of people who might be interested in analyzing a company's financial statements. However, the rest of the chapter concentrates on the basic analysis of financial statements, with the emphasis on the balance sheet and the income statement.

Comparative horizontal financial statements present information for at least two successive time periods shown side by side. The dollar change and the percentage of change for each item of the financial statement are shown to include totals and subtotals. In essence, a comparative horizontal analysis infers that the use of at least two consecutive financial statements (balance sheets, incomes statements, etc.) are analyzed. A second approach to the analysis of financial statements is **common-size vertical analysis,**

where each item of the statement is converted to a percentage using a significant total. This indicates a vertical analysis that converts dollar values to percentages. The terms *comparative horizontal analysis* and *common-size vertical analysis* will be used to illustrate and discuss the methods in this chapter.

An additional method of income statement analysis that determines average check, average cost, average income per guest, and other sales revenue and cost averages will be illustrated and discussed. Another analysis method, called **trend percentages,** results when the difference in the dollar amount between two periods is divided by the dollar amount of the first period to find the percentage of change. These methods provide additional useful information to management and will be illustrated and discussed.

The implications of price and cost level changes, inflation or deflation, on the operating results of a business are covered in some detail. We will explore how to use a readily available trend index, or to compile an index for a specific business, and how to convert historic figures to current dollar amounts.

CHAPTER OBJECTIVES

After studying this chapter, the reader should be able to

1. Explain some of the aspects that different readers of financial statements are interested in.
2. Describe comparative horizontal analysis and use it for balance sheets and income statements analysis.
3. Describe common-size vertical analysis and use it for balance sheets and income statements analysis.
4. Calculate average sales revenue, average costs, and average income per guest.
5. Calculate trend percentages.
6. Prepare a trend index.
7. Use trend index numbers to convert historic dollars to current dollars.

ANALYSIS AND INTERPRETATION OF FINANCIAL STATEMENTS

Analysis and interpretation of financial statements is the process of looking at the various parts of the financial statements, relating the parts to each other and to the picture as a whole, and determining if any meaningful and useful interpretation can be made out of this analysis.

All readers of financial statements, managers, owners, investors, and creditors are interested in analyzing and interpreting the financial statements. However, what is of great interest to one may be of less interest to another. For example, managers are very concerned about the internal operating efficiency of the organization and will look for indications that things are running smoothly, that operating goals are being met, and that the various departments are being managed as profitably as possible. Stockholders, by contrast, are more interested in the net income and about future earnings and dividend prospects. In many cases, they would not be concerned about or familiar with internal departmental results.

Creditors and investors other than stockholders might be interested in the net income but are even more interested in the debt-paying ability of the company. A company might have good earnings but, because of a shortage of cash, might not be able to meet its debt obligations.

An exhaustive coverage of the analysis and interpretation of financial statements is beyond the scope of this text. Therefore, this discussion will be confined to some of the more fundamental analysis techniques that lend themselves well to the hospitality industry. Also, comment will be confined to the two major financial statements: the balance sheet and the income statement. The analysis techniques illustrated are those that normally would be used by the operation's management.

COMPARATIVE HORIZONTAL ANALYSIS OF BALANCE SHEETS

A basic set of financial statements includes a balance sheet at a specific date and an income statement for the accounting period ended on that date. Some sets of financial statements may include a balance sheet and income statement for both the previous and current accounting periods. When prior and current period statements are provided, changes occurring between the two consecutive years or periods can be seen. However, these changes might not be as obvious as you would expect. It is not easy to mentally compare the differences between two sets of figures, and it is extremely useful to have additional information available for analysis.

One method is to complete a **comparative horizontal analysis** of a balance sheet or an income statement. This technique requires at least two consecutive periods of information. The objective is to find and identify changes that have occurred over an accounting period. The difference in dollar value reported between the two statements for each line item, subtotal, or total of the statement is calculated and identified as a positive or negative dollar value change. The change, positive or negative, is divided by the prior period's dollar amount to determine the percentage change.

Completing the comparative horizontal analysis of any item, subtotal, or total appearing in a financial statement is not the difficult part of a comparative horizontal analysis. The difficult part is understanding what the analysis is telling you. Exhibit 3.1 shows balance sheet information for two successive years, and the identity of each line item, subtotals, and totals for all assets, liabilities, and stockholders' equity is shown. In addition, two extra columns are added for comparative horizontal analysis, one to show the dollar value change and the other to express the percentage of change for each line item reported.

In Exhibit 3.1, the ending balance of the cash account in Year 0006 was $22,900, and in Year 0007, the ending balance was $35,400. The ending balance of prepaid expenses in Year 0006 was $5,200 and the Year 0007 ending balance was $4,900. We can see that the ending cash balance is $12,500 positive or higher than Year 0006, and the ending prepaid expense account is $300

ASSETS	Year 0006	Year 0007	$ Change	Change %
Current Assets				
Cash	$ 22,900	$ 35,400	+ $12,500	+ 54.6%
Accounts receivable	23,100	25,200	+ 2,100	+ 9.1%
Marketable securities	15,000	2,000	− 13,000	− 86.7%
Inventories	19,900	24,700	+ 4,800	+ 24.1%
Prepaid expenses	5,200	4,900	− 300	− 5.8%
Total Current Assets	$ 86,100	$ 92,200	+ $ 6,100	+ 7.1%
Property, Plant and Equipment				
Land	$ 161,800	$ 161,800	-0-	-0-
Building	1,432,800	1,432,800	-0-	-0-
Furniture and equipment	374,700	415,600	+ $40,900	+ 10.9%
China, glass, etc.	25,600	28,400	+ 2,800	+ 10.9%
	$1,994,900	$2,038,600	+ $43,700	+ 2.2%
Less: accumulated depreciation	(632,200)	(722,000)	+(89,800)	+(14.2)%
Total Property, Plant and Equipment	$1,362,700	$1,316,600	− $46,100	− 3.4%
Total Assets	$1,448,800	$1,408,800	− $40,000	− 2.8%
LIABILITIES and				
STOCKHOLDERS' EQUITY				
Current Liabilities				
Accounts payable	$ 19,200	$ 26,500	+ $ 7,300	+ 38.0%
Accrued expenses	3,500	4,100	+ 600	+ 17.1%
Income taxes payable	12,300	10,900	− 1,400	− 11.4%
Deposits and credit balances	500	1,800	+ 1,300	+260.0%
Current portion of mortgage	27,200	25,100	− 2,100	− 7.7%
Total Current Liabilities	$ 62,700	$ 68,400	+ $ 5,700	+ 9.1%
Long-term liability				
Mortgage payable	$ 812,900	$ 787,800	− $25,100	− 3.1%
Total Liabilities	$ 875,600	$ 856,200	− $30,800	− 3.5%
Stockholders' Equity				
Common stock	$ 300,000	$ 300,000	-0-	-0-
Retained earnings	273,200	252,600	− $20,600	− 7.5%
Total Stockholders' Equity	$ 573,200	$ 552,600	− $20,600	− 3.6%
Total Liabilities & Stockholders' Equity	$1,448,800	$1,408,800	− $40,000	− 2.8%

■ **EXHIBIT 3.1**
Comparative Horizontal Analysis Balance Sheets

negative or lower than Year 0007. To calculate the dollar change and the percentage change, use the following equation:

Period 2 − Period 1 = $ Change / Period 1 = Percentage change

The calculation for the cash account and the prepaid expense account is as follows:

Cash Account Analysis
Period 2 − Period 1 = $ Change / Period 1 = Percentage change
$35,400 − $22,900 = +$12,500 / $22,900 = +54.6% (Alignment)

Note: From a calculator, the answer will be a decimal. To state the answer as a percentage, multiply by 100 and round to one position right of decimal. The calculation $12,500 / $22,900 = 0.54585 × 100 will show 54.585. Rounding to the first position right of the decimal, the product is 54.6%.

Prepaid Expense Account Analysis
Period 2 − Period 1 = $ Change / Period 1 = Percentage change
$4,900 − $5,200 = (−$300) / $5,200 = (−5.8%) (Alignment)
[(−$300) / $5,200 = (−0.0576) × 100 = (−5.76) and read as (−5.8%)]

The latter two columns are helpful in pinpointing large changes that have occurred, either dollar amount changes or percentage changes. As well, we are looking for percentage changes in one account that are not of the same magnitude as the percentage changes of the other accounts. In Exhibit 3.1, total current assets have increased by 7.1% and total assets have decreased by 2.8%. However, consider the cash account. The change from Year 0006 to Year 0007 is $12,500. This may or may not be a large change, depending on the size of the hotel. The change becomes obvious when expressed in percentage terms: 54.6% ($12,500 / $22,900). Why has the cash account increased by almost 55% in the past year? However, the marketable securities account has decreased $13,000, or 86.7%. It appears that most of the securities held have been cashed in during the year. Is this conversion for a specific purpose? If not, perhaps we should use some of the cash to reduce accounts payable, which have gone up by $7,300 (38%).

Notice also that the amount of money tied up in inventories has gone up by $4,800. This may not be much in dollars, but it is an increase of 24.1% over the previous year. Has our volume of sales revenue increased sufficiently to justify this increase in inventories? An analysis of change in inventory turnover rates might answer this question. (Chapters 4 and 11 discuss inventory turnover.)

Note that the deposits and credit balances account has gone up by 260%. Has there been a change in the policy concerning deposits required for future bookings or reservations, or is this change indicative of a big increase in guaranteed future business compared to a year ago?

In comparative horizontal analysis, the terms *absolute* and *relative change* are sometimes used. An absolute change shows the dollar change from one period to the next. A relative change is the absolute change expressed as a percentage.

An absolute change may sometimes appear large (for example, $10,000) but when compared to its base figure (e.g., $1,000,000) represents a relative change of only 1%. By the same token, a relative change may seem high (e.g.,

50%) but when compared to its base figure is quite small in absolute terms (for example, a $50 base figure increasing to $75). In terms of the total income statement, this $25 change (even though it shows a relative increase of 50%) is insignificant. Therefore, when analyzing comparative horizontal statements, both the absolute and the relative changes should be looked at, and only those that exceed both acceptable norms should be of concern.

For example, absolute changes of concern might be established at $10,000 and relative changes at 5%, and only those changes that exceed both $10,000 and 5% should be investigated. In this situation, the following changes would not be investigated:

- Above $10,000 but below 5%
- Above 5 percent but below $10,000
- Below $10,000 and below 5%

COMMON-SIZE VERTICAL ANALYSIS OF BALANCE SHEETS

Another technique used to analyze balance sheet information is to convert the statement to a common-size vertical analysis format. This method requires only one period of financial data. **Common size** means that total assets have a value of 100% and the numerical value of each item being converted represents a fractional part of total assets. Since Assets = Liabilities + Ownership Equity and each side of the balance sheet has the same total value, every item in a balance sheet, subtotals, and totals, can be expressed as a percentage of total assets. Exhibit 3.2 shows the common-size (vertical) conversion of the comparative balance sheet shown in Exhibit 3.1. The common-size vertical statement shows that the cash account in Year 0006 is 1.6% of total assets, which was calculated by dividing the cash balance by total assets: $22,900 / $1,448,800. Accounts payable in Year 0006 is 1.3% of total assets: $19,200 / $1,448,800. In Exhibit 3.2, each balance sheet item shown for Year 0006 is divided by total assets of Year 0006. The addition of each item percentage shown for Year 0006 will equal 100%, which is the product of total assets divided by total assets.

Any subset of a balance sheet such as current assets, fixed assets, current liabilities, long-term liabilities, or ownership equity can be converted to a common-size vertical format and analyzed separately. Since each current liability is a part of total current liabilities, a common-size vertical analysis of current liabilities will express each individual current liability as a percentage of total current liabilities. As an example, we will use the current liability accounts in Exhibit 3.2 to express each as a percentage of total current liabilities.

Accounts payable + Accrued expenses + Income taxes payable + Deposits and credit balances + Current portion of mortgage = Current liabilities
$$\$19,200 = n_1 + \$3,500 = n_2 + \$12,300 = n_3 + \$500 = n_4$$
$$+ \ \$27,200 = n_5 = \underline{\$62,700} = \Sigma n$$

	Year Ending December 31		Common Size	
	0006	**0007**	**0006**	**0007**
ASSETS				
Current Assets				
Cash	$ 22,900	$ 35,400	1.6%	2.5%
Accounts receivable	23,100	25,200	1.6%	1.8%
Marketable securities	15,000	2,000	1.0%	0.1%
Inventories	19,900	24,700	1.4%	1.8%
Prepaid expenses	5,200	4,900	0.4%	0.3%
Total Current Assets	$ 86,100	$ 92,200	*5.9%	6.5%
Property, Plant, and Equipment				
Land	$ 161,800	$ 161,800	11.2%	11.5%
Building	1,432,800	1,432,800	98.9%	101.7%
Furniture and equipment	374,700	415,600	25.9%	29.5%
China, glass, etc.	25,600	28,400	1.8%	2.0%
Total Property, Plant and Equipment	$1,994,900	$2,038,600	*137.7%	144.7%
Less: accumulated depreciation	(632,200)	(722,000)	(43.6)%	(51.2%)
Net Property, Plant and Equipment	$1,362,700	$1,316,600	*94.1%	93.5%
Total Assets	$1,448,800	$1,408,800	100%	100%
LIABILITIES and STOCKHOLDERS' EQUITY				
Current Liabilities				
Accounts payable	$ 19,200	$ 26,500	1.3%	1.9%
Accrued expenses	3,500	4,100	0.2%	0.3%
Income taxes payable	12,300	10,900	0.8%	0.8%
Deposits and credit balances	500	1,800	0.0%	0.1%
Current portion of mortgage	27,200	25,100	1.9%	1.8%
Total Current Liabilities	$ 62,700	$ 68,400	* 4.3%	4.9%
Long-term Liability				
Mortgage payable	$ 812,900	$ 787,800	56.1%	55.9%
Total Liabilities	$875,600	$856,200	60.4%	60.8%
Stockholders' Equity				
Common stock	$ 300,000	$ 300,000	20.7%	21.3%
Retained earnings	273,200	252,600	18.9%	17.9%
Total Stockholders' Equity	$ 573,200	$ 552,600	39.6%	39.2%
Total Liabilities & Stockholders' Equity	$1,448,800	$1,408,800	100%	100%

*These items do not add up due to rounding

■ **EXHIBIT 3.2**
Common-Size Vertical Analysis Balance Sheets

The common-size vertical analysis can be described using the equation $n_1 + n_2 + n_3 + \ldots + n_x = \Sigma n$. Each element, n_1, n_2, and n_3 is divided by the sum, Σn, to find its percentage relationship; $n_1 / \Sigma n$ identifies what percentage n_1 is of Σn. Thus,

$$[n_1 / \Sigma n] = \$19{,}200 / \$62{,}700 = 30.6\% \text{ of current liabilities}$$
$$[n_2 / \Sigma n] = \$\ 3{,}500 / \$62{,}700 = \ 5.6\% \text{ of current liabilities}$$
$$[n_3 / \Sigma n] = \$12{,}300 / \$62{,}700 = 19.6\% \text{ of current liabilities}$$
$$[n_4 / \Sigma n] = \$\ \ \ 500 / \$62{,}700 = \ 0.8\% \text{ of current liabilities}$$
$$[n_5 / \Sigma n] = \$27{,}200 / \$62{,}700 = 43.4\% \text{ of current liabilities}$$

Using the same five current liabilities, we can also use a math equation that might be more familiar: $X = \$62{,}700$ **total current liabilities** $[A + B + C + D + E = X]$.

$$A / X = \$19{,}200 / \$62{,}700 = 30.6\%$$
$$B / X = \$\ 3{,}500 / \$62{,}700 = \ 5.6\%$$
$$C / X = \$12{,}300 / \$62{,}700 = 19.6\%$$
$$D / X = \$\ \ \ 500 / \$62{,}700 = \ 0.8\%$$
$$E / X = \$27{,}200 / \$62{,}700 = 43.4\%$$

Regardless of whether you are converting a balance sheet or a subset of assets, liabilities, or ownership equity, the conversion procedure is the same.

The advantage of common-size vertical statements is that they show changes in proportion of individual accounts from one period to the next. For example, the cash account in Year 0006 was 1.6% of total assets. In Year 0007, it was 2.5% of total assets. This change in proportion would normally attract a reader's attention and raise questions. Attention might also be drawn to other accounts where large changes have occurred. The common-size vertical analysis technique is particularly useful when comparing two companies whose size and/or level of business are very different, so other techniques of analysis are not appropriate.

Whether a hotel or food service operation uses comparative horizontal balance sheets or common-sized vertical balance sheets is a matter of choice. Normally, only one or the other would be preferred because both draw the attention of the reader to the relevant accounts where changes have occurred. However, sometimes one technique will identify changes that other techniques did not indicate. Identifying changes should provoke questions, the answers to which may be helpful in running the business more effectively. Attention should be focused on the balance sheet because of the need for effective control or management of a company's assets. However, as a management technique for controlling internal day-to-day operations, comparative income statements are often more useful than comparative balance sheets.

COMPARATIVE HORIZONTAL ANALYSIS OF INCOME STATEMENTS

Exhibit 3.3 shows two consecutive annual income statements for a food department of a hotel. The same method that was used to analyze balance sheets is used for income statements. Line by line, find the numerical value change and divide the change by the prior year to find the percentage of change. For example, dining room sales revenue increased by 10.1% from Year 0006 to Year 0007. The calculation to identify the percentage of change is as follows:

(Sales revenue 0007 − Sales revenue 0006) / Sales revenue 0006 = % Change
($221,900 − $201,600) / $201,600 = % Change
$20,300 / $201,600 = <u>10.1%</u>

The comparative horizontal analysis follows the same procedures to calculate the numerical change of each line item and the percentage that change represents. It does not matter what financial information is being compared, as long as two consecutive operating periods of information are provided. The concept remains:

(Period 2 − Period 1) = $ Change / Period 1 = % Change

The other percentage of change figures are calculated in the same way. Note that within each sales revenue area, except banquets, the sales revenue has increased, but total sales revenue has gone up only 2.1%. The reason for this relatively small increase in total sales revenue is that banquet sales revenue was down 7.7% over the year. Can the reasons be determined? Is the sales department not doing an effective job? Is there a new, competitive operation close by? Are prices too high?

Even with the small total sales revenue increase, departmental income has declined $37,100, or 24.2%. This is a drastic change. With revenue up, all other factors being equal, income should also be up, not down.

All other things are, obviously, not equal, because analysis of costs shows that the majority of them have increased at a greater rate than the revenue increase. To select only one example, the laundry cost has gone up $2,900 over the year, or 18.7%. Are we using more linen than before? Has our supplier increased the cost to us by this percentage? Whatever the reason, corrective action can be taken once the cause is known. Each expense should be analyzed. In this particular illustration, assuming the increased costs were inevitable, perhaps the increased costs have not yet been incorporated into the menu selling prices.

COMMON-SIZE VERTICAL ANALYSIS OF INCOME STATEMENTS

Income statements can also be converted to a common-size vertical analysis format. With the conversion of the income statement, total sales revenue takes the

| | Year Ending December 31 | | Increase or Decrease from Year 0006 to 0007 | |
| | 0006 | 0007 | | |
	Sales Revenue	Sales Revenue	$ Change	% Change
Dining room	$201,600	$221,900	*+$20,300	+ 10.1%
Coffee shop	195,900	201,700	+ 5,800	+ 3.0%
Banquets	261,200	241,100	− 20,100	− 7.7%
Room service	81,700	82,600	+ 900	+ 1.1%
Bar		121,800	+ 10,600	+ 9.5%
Total Sales Revenue	$851,600	$869,100	+$17,500	+ 2.1%
Cost of sales				
Cost of sales, food	$319,500	$335,100	+ 15,600	+ 4.9%
Less: employee meals	(30,100)	(32,500)	+(2,400)	+ (8.0%)
Net cost of sales food	$289,400	$302,600	+ 13,200	+ 4.6%
Net cost of sales beverages	33,000	38,600	+ 5,600	+ 17.0%
Total cost of sales	($322,400)	($341,200)	+ 18,800	+ 5.8%
Gross Margin	$529,200	$527,900	−$ 1,300	− 0.2%
Departmental expenses				
Salaries and wages	$277,400	$304,500	+$27,100	+ 9.8%
Employee benefits*	34,500	37,800	+ 3,300	+ 9.6%
China, glassware	7,100	7,800	+ 700	+ 9.9%
Cleaning supplies	6,400	6,800	+ 400	+ 6.3%
Decorations	2,200	1,800	− 400	− 18.2%
Guest supplies	6,500	7,000	+ 500	+ 7.7%
Laundry	15,500	18,400	+ 2,900	+ 18.7%
Licenses	3,400	3,500	+ 100	+ 2.9%
Linen	3,700	4,200	+ 500	+ 13.5%
Menus	2,000	2,500	+ 500	+ 25.0%
Miscellaneous	800	1,100	+ 300	+ 37.5%
Paper supplies	4,900	5,700	+ 800	+ 16.3%
Printing, stationery	4,700	4,600	− 100	− 2.1%
Silver	2,300	2,100	− 200	− 8.7%
Uniforms	3,100	2,400	− 700	− 22.6%
Utensils	1,700	1,800	+ 100	+ 5.9%
Total expenses	(376,200)	(412,000)	+ 35,800	+ 9.5%
Departmental Income	$153,000	$115,900	−$37,100	− 24.2%

*Employee benefits include employee meals

■ **EXHIBIT 3.3**

Comparative Horizontal Analysis of Income Statements—Food Department

value of 100% and all other items on the income statement are expressed as a fraction of total sales revenue. However, for the cost of sales, the cost of each product is divided by its respective sales revenue. Therefore, the cost of sales–food is divided by food sales revenue. A common-size income statement is illustrated in Exhibit 3.4. For example, in Year 0006 dining room sales revenue was 23.7 percent of total sales revenue and is calculated as follows:

Dining sales revenue / Total sales revenue = % of Total sales revenue
$201,600 / $851,600 = 23.7%

All items except the cost of sales in Exhibit 3.4 are calculated the same way, using $851,600 as the denominator and the individual item as the numerator. Note that the percentage given for gross margin is a nonaccount subtotal and cannot be included to arrive at the 100% total of the other items' percentages. Gross margin (also called *gross profit*) is a derived subtotal representing sales revenue minus cost of sales and does not represent an operating cost, nor does it represent the resulting profit or loss from operations.

Note that if this is a combined food and beverage operation, the net food cost would be total sales revenue for each period minus the beverage sales revenue for each period. Cost of beverages of each period is divided by the beverage sales revenue for each period.

Net cost of sales − food / (Total sales revenue − Beverage sales revenue)
= Food cost %
Year 0006: $289,400 / ($851,600 − $111,200) = $289,400 / $740,400
= 39.1%
Cost of sales beverage / Beverage sales revenue = Beverage cost %
Year 0006: $33,000 / $111,200 = 29.7%

Expense items, except the cost of sales–food and cost of sales–beverages, will also use $851,600 as the denominator for Year 0006. For example, the cost of salaries and wages would be calculated as follows:

Year 0006: $277,400 / $851,600 × 100 = 32.6%

One way of interpreting the common-size income statement information in Year 0006 is to say that, out of every $1.00 of sales revenue, 37.9 cents was for total cost of sales, 32.6 cents was for salaries and wages, 4.1 cents was for employee benefits, and 7.6 cents was for all other operating expenses, leaving only 18.0 cents for income. In Year 0007, this income was down to 13.3 cents out of every $1.00 of sales revenue. Common-size income statements show which items, as a proportion of revenue, have changed enough to require investigation.

For example, one of the causes for the decline to 13.3 cents of departmental income from each dollar of sales revenue in Year 0007 is that the amount spent on total cost of sales has risen from 37.9 cents to 39.3 cents out of each dollar of sales revenue. This 1.4-cent increase might seem insignificant, but if it had not occurred, we would have made $12,167 more income, calculated as follows:

$$\$869,100 \times 1.4\% = \$12,167$$

In the interest of brevity in Exhibit 3.4, a number of expenses have been added together under "other operating" expenses. In Year 0006, this figure is 7.6% of sales revenue, and in Year 0007, 8.0% of sales revenue. This is a relatively small change and might normally be unnoticed. It is small only because several of the individual items that decreased offset many of the individual expense items that increased, thus hiding the facts. In practice, for fuller information it would be best to detail each individual expense and express it as a percentage of revenue.

The income statement illustrated for the food operation was analyzed with both comparative horizontal (Exhibit 3.3) and common-size vertical methods (Exhibit 3.4). Normally, only one or the other would be used. They each draw attention, albeit in a different way, to problem areas requiring investigation, and, if necessary, corrective action. However, sometimes one technique will identify problems that should be investigated that the other technique may not indicate. Therefore, sometimes it is a good idea to complete both a comparative and common-size vertical analysis.

Note again that the common-size vertical analysis method is the more appropriate one to use when comparing two companies whose size or scale of operation is quite different.

There is one other method of horizontal comparative analysis particularly suited to the food operation, and that is to calculate and compare average sales revenue per guest, average cost per guest, and average income per guest information.

AVERAGE CHECK, COST, AND INCOME PER GUEST

Averages for sales revenue and cost functions are another useful tool to help analyze the income statement. When using averages, understanding how to calculate averages is essential. The question is to find the per-guest average—but of what? *What* can be identified as total sales revenue, sales revenue by division, total cost, or cost by category. A per-guest average can be determined using the following concept: sales revenue / guests, cost / guests, or operating income / guests. Exhibit 3.5 shows two consecutive years of sales revenue, associated operating costs, and operating income (income before taxes). Two columns have been added: the first identifies the number of guests served by each sales revenue division and the costs incurred by each major cost category; the second shows the average check and average cost per guest. The averages for several different items in Year 0006 are as follows:

	Year Ending December 31		Year Ending December 31	
	0006	0007	0006	0007
Sales Revenue	*Sales Revenue*	*Sales Revenue*		
Dining room	$201,600	$221,900	23.7%	25.5%
Coffee shop	195,900	201,700	23.0%	23.2%
Banquets	261,200	241,100	30.7%	27.7%
Room service	81,700	82,600	9.6%	9.5%
Bar	111,200	121,800	13.1%	14.0%
Total Sales Revenue		$851,600	$869,100	100%	100%
Cost of sales				
Cost of food used	$319,500	$335,100	43.2%	44.8%
Less: employee meals	(30,100)	(32,500)	(3.5%)	(3.7%)
Net cost of sales food	$289,400	$302,600	39.1%	40.5%
Net cost of sales beverages	33,000	38,600	29.7%	31.7%
Total Cost of Sales	($322,400)	($341,200)	**(37.9%)	**39.3%
Gross Margin	$529,200	$527,900	62.1%	60.7%
Departmental expenses				
Salaries and wages	$277,400	$304,500	32.6%	35.0%
Employee benefits (#)	34,500	37,800	4.1%	4.3%
Other operating expenses	64,300	69,700	7.6%	8.0%
Total expenses	(376,200)	(412,000)	(44.2%)	(47.4%)
Departmental Income	$153,000	$115,900	18.0%	13.3%

\# Employee meals are included in employee benefits.

*These items do not add up due to rounding.

**These items do not add up because they have different denominators.

■ **EXHIBIT 3.4**

Common-Size Vertical Analysis Income Statement—Food Department

Total sales revenue	/	Total guests	=	Avg. total check per guest
$2,554,800	/	215,560	=	$11.85
Dining room sales revenue	/	Total dining room guests	=	Avg. check dining room guest
$604,800	/	35,130	=	$17.22
Net food cost	/	Total guests	=	Avg. food cost per guest
$967,200	/	215,560	=	$4.49
Total cost	/	Total guests	=	Avg. cost per guest
$2,095,800	/	215,560	=	$9.72
Operating income	/	Total guests	=	Avg. operating income per guest
$459,000	/	215,560	=	$2.13

When we analyze the information in Exhibit 3.5, we see that the number of guests served *in* all sales revenue areas increased—except in banquets, where there was a decrease of 9,410 (60,190 – 50,780). This is a decrease of 15.6 percent (9,410 / 60,190, then multiplied by 100). At the same time, in the banquet area the average check per guest increased from $13.02 to $14.24. This is an increase of $1.22 per guest, or 9.4 percent ($1.22 / $13.02, then multiplied by 100). The combination of higher average check (average sales revenue) but reduced numbers of guests meant that banquet sales revenue was $60,300 lower in Year 0007 than in Year 0006. Is this a desirable trend? Is our banquet selling policy causing us to sell higher-priced banquets but not allowing us to sell to as many customers? Has an increase in selling prices driven away a considerable amount of business?

In terms of total average sales revenue per guest for the food operation in Year 0007, we took in 12 cents more per guest ($11.97 − $11.85) but we spent 66 cents more per guest ($10.38 − $9.72), and thus our income per guest declined 53 cents ($2.13 − $1.60). Obviously, our costs per guest have risen much faster than our sales revenue per guest. The individual items of expense,

	Year Ending December 31, 0006			Year Ending December 31, 0007		
	Sales Revenue	Guests	Average Check	Sales Revenue	Guests	Average Check
Department						
Dining room	$ 604,800	35,130	$17.22	$ 665,700	36,210	$18.38
Coffee shop	587,700	71,200	8.25	605,100	78,200	7.74
Banquets	783,600	60,190	13.02	723,300	50,780	14.24
Room service	245,100	16,870	14.53	247,800	17,110	14.48
Bar food sales	333,600	32,170	10.37	365,400	35,490	10.30
Totals	$2,554,800	215,560	$11.85	$2,607,300	217,790	$11.97
	Cost	Guests	Average Cost	Cost	Guests	Average Cost
Operating Costs						
Net cost of sales	$ 967,200	215,560	$ 4.49	$1,023,600	217,790	$ 4.70
Salaries & wages	832,200	215,560	3.86	913,500	217,790	4.19
Employee benefits	103,500	215,560	0.48	113,400	217,790	0.52
Other expenses	192,900	215,560	0.89	209,100	217,790	0.96
Totals	$2,095,800	215,560	$ 9.72	$2,259,600	217,790	$10.38
Operating Income	$ 459,000	215,560	$ 2.13	$ 347,700	217,790	$ 1.60

■ **EXHIBIT 3.5**
Comparative Average Check, Cost, and Operating Income per Guest—Food Department

on a per-guest basis, have all increased, some more than others. They need to be investigated to see whether the trend can be reversed. Alternatively, sales prices might need to be increased to compensate for uncontrollable, increasing costs.

Although Exhibit 3.5 illustrated a food operation, a beverage department could be analyzed equally as well using the same approach. Similarly, a hotel rooms department could be analyzed using number of guests or number of rooms as the unit figure to be divided into sales revenue, costs, or income.

TREND RESULTS

Balance sheet and income statement illustrations discussed to this point have considered only an analysis, and comparison of data between two successive periods. Limiting an analysis to only two periods—weeks, months, or years—can be misleading if an unusual occurrence or factor distorted the results for either of the two periods. Looking at results over a greater number of periods can often be more useful in indicating the direction in which a business is heading. For example, the following shows trend results as a percentage for a cocktail lounge for six successive months:

Month	Sales Revenue	Change in Sales Revenue	Change %
1	$25,000	-0-	-0-
2	30,000	+$5,000	+120.0%
3	33,000	+ 3,000	+ 10.0%
4	35,000	+ 2,000	+ 6.1%
5	36,000	+ 1,000	+ 2.9%
6	36,000	0	0.0%

The trend percentage for the first period is always set to 0%. For the first and subsequent years, the trend percentage is determined as follows until the last year is evaluated:

Current period	− Last period	= $ Change/Last period	= Trend %
$30,000	− $25,000	= $5,000/$25,000	= 20.0%
$33,000	− $30,000	= $3,000/$30,000	= 10.0%
$35,000	− $33,000	= $2,000/$33,000	= 6.1%

Here, the change in sales revenue dollars for each period is calculated by subtracting from each period's sales revenue the sales revenue of the preceding period. The trend percentages are then calculated by dividing each period's change in sales revenue dollar amounts by the sales revenue of the preceding period.

Over a long period of time, trend percentages will show the direction in which a business is going. In our particular case, the trend results indicate that although business has been increasing over the past few periods, it now seems to have leveled off. Has the business reached its maximum potential in sales revenue? Has an economic slowdown occurred? Trend percentages may be useful in such areas as forecasting or budgeting, or in decision making. For example, is it time we spent money on advertising to increase volume?

The particular trend result just illustrated was for a specific item (sales revenue in a bar), but comparison of trend percentages of related items (sales revenue and expenses) can be indicative of problems. For example, the cost of sales (liquor cost) figures for this lounge for the same six periods are as follows:

Period	Liquor Cost
1	$ 7,500
2	9,200
3	10,300
4	10,800
5	11,100
6	11,200

This basic information regarding the liquor costs for six periods can also be evaluated to show a trend expressed as a percentage. We use the basic equation shown to evaluate the trend percentages for sales revenue to evaluate trend percentages for costs:

Month	Liquor Costs	Cost Change	Change %
1	$ 7,500		-0-
2	9,200	$1,700	+22.7%
3	10,300	1,100	+12.0%
4	10,800	500	+ 4.9%
5	11,100	300	+ 2.8%
6	11,200	100	+ 0.9%

These relationships are calculated very quickly, and can provide information in a simple format that shows cost increases, and decreases for specific periods. An example using the basic equation is shown for liquor costs:

Month	Sales Revenue	Change in Sales Revenue	Sales Revenue Change %	Liquor Cost	Change in Cost	Change in Cost %
1	$25,000		-0-	$ 7,500	-0-	-0-
2	30,000	+$5,000	+20.0%	$ 9,200	$1,300	22.7%
3	33,000	+ 3,000	+10.0%	$10,300	$1,100	12.0%
4	35,000	+ 2,000	+ 6.1%	$10,800	$ 500	4.9%
5	36,000	+ 1,000	+ 2.9%	$11,100	$ 300	2.8%
6	36,000	0	0.0%	$11,200	$ 100	0.9%

When we compare the percentage increase in sales revenue with the percentage increase in cost, we see that, in general, the liquor cost is increasing somewhat more quickly than the sales revenue, with the exception of months 4 and 5. We need to investigate why this is occurring. Are there some problems with controlling the use of liquor? Has there been a change in sales revenue mix so we are selling more expensive products? Do we need to increase menu prices to compensate for increased product cost that we cannot do anything about?

TREND INDEX ANALYSIS

An index is calculated by assigning a value of 100 (or 100%) in period one for each item being tabulated, as follows:

Period	Sales Revenue	Sales Revenue Index	Liquor Cost	Liquor Cost Index
1	$25,000	100	$ 7,500	100.0
2	30,000	120	9,200	122.7
3	33,000	132	10,300	137.3
4	35,000	140	10,800	144.0
5	36,000	144	11,100	148.0
6	36,000	144	11,200	149.3

Dividing the dollar amount for each period by the base period dollar amount and multiplying by 100 calculates the trend index for each period. An example is given using two sales revenue periods and two liquor cost periods to calculate the trend index. The trend index number for the first, or base, period is set at 100, and subsequent period index numbers are calculated as follows:

> *(Subsequent period / Base period)* × *100 = Trend index*
>
> *Sales Revenue* *Liquor Cost*
> Period 2: ($30,000 / $25,000) × 100 = 120.0 ($ 9,200 / $7,500) × 100 = 122.7
> Period 5: ($36,000 / $25,000) × 100 = 144.0 ($11,100 / $7,500) × 100 = 148.0

Our completed trend index results show us that the liquor cost has been increasing faster than liquor sales revenue. Expressed another way, sales revenue is up 44% (144 − 100) and liquor cost is up 49% (149 − 100). This is normally an undesirable trend that should be investigated and possibly corrected.

PRICE AND COST LEVEL CHANGES (INFLATION OR DEFLATION)

When comparing operating results, and in particular when analyzing trend figures, the reader must be aware of the effect that changing dollar values have on the results. One hundred pounds of vegetables a few years ago weighed exactly the same as 100 pounds of vegetables today, but the purchase cost was much lower. Prices change over time. In the same way that prices change for us, so, too, do the prices we must charge to customers for rooms, food, beverages, and other services. When comparing income and expense items over a fairly long period, it is necessary to consider the implications of upwardly changing prices or costs (inflation), or the reverse (deflation). Consider a restaurant with the following sales revenue in two successive years:

Year 1 $100,000
Year 2 $105,000

This is a $5,000, or 5% ($5,000 / $100,000), increase in volume. But if restaurant menu prices had been increased over the year by 10% due to inflation, then our Year 2 sales revenue should have been at least $110,000 just to stay even with Year 1's volume. In other words, when we try to compare sales revenue for successive periods in inflationary or deflationary times, as in this case, we are comparing unequal values. Last year's dollar does not have the same value as this year's. What a dollar would buy last year might now require $1.10. Is there a method that will allow us to convert a previous period's dollars into current period dollars so trends can be analyzed more meaningfully? The answer is yes, with the use of index numbers.

The **consumer price index (CPI)** is probably one of the most commonly used and widely understood indexes available. But the government and other organizations produce many other indexes. By selecting an appropriate index, conversion of the previous period's dollars into current year dollars is possible. Consider the following figures showing trend results for a restaurant's sales revenue for the past five years.

Year	Sales Revenue	Sales Revenue Change	Change %
1	$420,000	$ -0-	0.0%
2	450,000	30,000	7.1%
3	465,000	15,000	3.3%
4	485,000	20,000	4.3%
5	510,000	25,000	5.2%

The trend percentages show sales revenue has increased each year, which is generally a favorable trend. But is it reasonable to compare $420,000 of sales revenue in Year 1 to $510,000 of sales revenue in Year 5? By adjusting all past sales revenues to comparable Year 5 dollars, a more realistic picture of our restaurant's sales revenues may emerge. The trend index used to adjust sales revenue would be based on restaurant sales revenue, and we would need to use the trend numbers of the same five-year period for which we wish to adjust our restaurant sales revenue. Let us assume the index numbers were as follows:

Year	Trend Index
1	105
2	112
3	119
4	128
5	142

The equation for converting past period's (historic) dollars to current (real) dollars is as follows:

$$\text{Historic dollars} \times \frac{\text{Index number for current period}}{\text{Index number for historic period}} = \text{Current dollars}$$

The following table shows the trend index numbers used to convert the earlier sales revenue figures into today's current dollars (rounded to the nearest hundreds of dollars).

Year	Trend Index	Historic Sales Revenue	×	Conversion Equation	=	Current Dollars
1	105	$420,000	×	142 / 105	=	$568,000
2	112	450,000	×	142 / 112	=	570,500
3	119	465,000	×	142 / 119	=	554,900
4	128	485,000	×	142 / 128	=	538,000
5	142	510,000	×	142 / 142	=	510,000

The resulting picture is quite different from the unadjusted sales revenue figures. In fact, in current dollars, our annual sales revenue has generally declined from Year 1 to Year 5. This would not normally be a desirable trend.

If restaurant sales revenue trend index numbers were not readily available, an operator could easily compile them by converting the annual average check figure for each of a number of years to an index, giving Year 1 the value of 100. This is illustrated as follows:

Year	Check	*Average Index Trend*
1	$10.20	100.0
2	11.01	107.9
3	12.06	118.2
4	12.63	123.8
5	13.68	134.1

Dividing the average check for each year by the average check for Year 1 and multiplying by 100 calculates the trend index numbers for each year. For example, we can compute the Year 3 and Year 5 index numbers:

$$\text{Year 3: } (\$12.06 \, / \, \$10.20) \times 100 = \underline{\underline{118.24}}$$
$$\text{Year 5: } (\$13.68 \, / \, \$10.20) \times 100 = \underline{\underline{134.12}}$$

If this technique looks familiar, it is. This is the same method used to determine the trend index numbers illustrated in an earlier discussion, and it can also be used for cost functions.

A restaurant creating its own trend index in this way might find it much more accurate because it reflects only what has happened to prices within that restaurant. A national average restaurant trend index might have factors built into it that have no bearing on any one individual operation. Preferably, such an individual trend index should be used only if the size and nature of the operation have not changed during the period under review; otherwise, the results could be misleading.

Once the trend index has been prepared, it can be applied using the equation already demonstrated to convert historic sales revenue to current dollars. A bar could use the same type of homemade trend index using average customer spending. For its room sales revenue, a hotel or motel could use average room rates converted to a trend index.

Costs can be converted in the same way, using an appropriate trend index for the particular expenses or costs under review. For example, a wage trend index would probably be appropriate for adjusting cost of labor. Alternatively, an individual establishment might be able to construct its own trend index for each individual expense, as was just demonstrated for room prices, basing the trend indexes on a cost per guest or cost per room occupied. In fact, complete income statements for past periods can be reconstructed by converting them in their entirety to current period, or current year, dollars.

Such wholesale conversions would probably go beyond the needs of the managers of most hotel or food service operations. However, whether or not a major accounting conversion is used, the implications of price and cost level changes should not be ignored.

The same problems also apply to balance sheets. A balance sheet showing a cash balance on hand of $100,000 in each of two successive years might seem to indicate no change in the cash position. But will $100,000 now buy as much as $100,000 did a year ago? Similarly, the historic cost of land, buildings, and equipment on balance sheets may also be misleading. However, a complete and comprehensive discussion of inflation accounting or current dollar accounting is far beyond the scope of this book.

COMPUTER APPLICATIONS

A properly programmed computerized spreadsheet will allow a manager to answer a what-if question in seconds and print out the results. Indeed, multiple what-if changes can be made at the same time at rapid speed. With a spreadsheet program, a computer can prepare and print out both comparative horizontal and common-size vertical balance sheets and income statements, including the relevant dollar and percentage changes. In addition, spreadsheets have a graphics capability that can provide management with more easily interpreted information about the trend of specific items. These graphs can be presented in various forms, such as bar graphs or pie charts.

Spreadsheets lend themselves not only to budgeting but also to forecasting. For example, a spreadsheet can store in its memory all the various menu items a restaurant offers, including how many of each is sold on average by meal periods and day of the week for each specific month. The availability of information on the basis of past performance could show how many portions of each menu item the kitchen should produce for each meal period each day of the current month. Spreadsheets also lend themselves well to the following applications:

- Scheduling employees for improved labor cost control
- Preparing depreciation schedules
- Calculating percentages given the dollar amounts, for common-size vertical financial statement analysis
- Calculating the sales revenue mix and gross profit figures, given menu items sold and their cost and selling prices
- Converting budgeted income statements (given appropriate ratios) to cash budgets to forecast cash inflows and outflows (see Chapter 11)

- Using net present value and internal rate of return analysis for long-term investments (see Chapter 12)
- Preparing budget variance analyses (see Chapter 9)
- Using cost-volume-profit analysis for various types of decisions (see Chapter 8)

As far as planning and control are concerned, word processing, database, and spreadsheet software are closely related. A computer should be able to pass data from its database application to a spreadsheet, and then pass the results to a word processor for addition of text and final printing of a report. Today, single software packages that include all three of these types of programs, such as Microsoft Office, are available.

S U M M A R Y

Financial statement analysis is a matter of relating the various parts of the statements to each other and to the whole, and then interpreting the results. Different users of financial statements are interested in different sections and specific items. They most likely will have different interpretations of the information being viewed. It is likely that different readers of financial statements may arrive at different conclusions based on the results of their analysis.

Comparative horizontal analysis as demonstrated in this chapter is one technique used to analyze financial statements. This involves putting two consecutive balance sheets or two consecutive income statements side by side and showing the changes in numerical value and the percentage that change represents for each line item, subtotals, and totals. The analysis will conclude with an interpretation of the results. The general equation is as follows:

(Period 2 − Period 1) = $ Change / Period 1 = Change %

Common-size vertical analysis of financial statements requires only one balance sheet or one income statement. A common-size vertical analysis of a balance sheet will express each item, subtotal, and total as a percentage of total assets. A common-size vertical analysis of an income statement will divide each item (except cost of sales), subtotal, and total appearing in the income statement by total sales revenue, which expresses the percentage of each element as a percentage of total sales revenue. Cost of sales is normally divided by its respective sales revenue:

Sales revenue item / Total sales revenue = % of total sales revenue

or

$$\text{Cost item / Total sales revenue} = \text{\% of total sales revenue}$$

and

$$\text{Cost of sales food / Sales revenue food} = \text{\% of food sales revenue}$$

or

$$\text{Cost of sales beverage / Sales revenue beverage}$$
$$= \text{\% of beverage sales revenue}$$

Another useful approach in the evaluation of an income statement is to find the average check per guest for each sales division, cost per guest by items, and operating income (before tax) and net income (after tax) figures on an average per-guest basis.

$$\text{Sales revenue / Guests} = \text{Average sales revenue per guest}$$
$$\text{Cost item / Guests} = \text{Average cost per guest}$$
$$\text{Operating income / Guests} = \text{Average operating income per guest}$$

Trend results are similar to comparative horizontal and common-size vertical statements, except that they show figures for several successive periods, showing the change in dollars and the percentage change from each period to the next:

$$\text{Current period} - \text{Last period} = \text{\$ Change / Last period} = \text{Trend \%}$$

A refinement of the raw trend percentage figures is a trend index. A trend index begins with the assignment of a 100 (or 100%) for the first period, which is the base period, monthly, quarterly, or yearly. Subsequent periods of sales revenue or cost figures are expressed as a percentage of the sales revenue or cost figures used in the first period. Trend index numbers are calculated as follows:

$$\text{(Subsequent period / Base period)} \times 100 = \text{Trend index}$$

When analyzing financial results for two or more successive years, the effects of inflation implications should be considered. To convert previous historical period dollars into current period dollars, an appropriate trend index can be used:

$$\text{Historic dollars} \times \frac{\text{Index number for current period}}{\text{Index number for historic period}} = \text{Current dollars}$$

DISCUSSION QUESTIONS

1. Explain what items a stockholder reading a financial statement might be interested in that are different from the manager of the enterprise.

2. What is comparative horizontal balance sheet analysis?

3. Discuss absolute and relative changes with reference to comparative horizontal financial statement analysis.

4. Why are differences between two comparative horizontal statements frequently better shown in percentages rather than only in dollars?

5. What is the objective of common-size vertical income statements?

6. How is average sales revenue per guest calculated?

7. Why are trend results often more meaningful than a comparison limited to two successive accounting periods?

8. How is a trend index calculated?

9. In inflationary times, why is comparative horizontal analysis and a trend index misleading?

10. What is the equation for converting past historic period dollars to current period dollars?

ETHICS SITUATION

A restaurant manager has received a bonus for each of the past five years based on increases in sales revenue that have averaged about 5% over the previous year. The restaurant owner asked to have the sales revenue figures for the last five years adjusted for inflation and the manager had an accountant adjust the figures. On reviewing the results, the manager notices that sales revenues have remained virtually flat, and in one year, sales revenues actually declined slightly. Before submitting the adjusted figures to the owner, the manager decides to change them to show that sales revenue increases averaged approximately 3% a year. By changing the adjusted figures, the manager hopes to show the owner the annual bonuses were justified. Discuss the ethics of this situation.

EXERCISES

E3.1 A restaurant owner expressed concern about the changes in the cash, credit card receivables, and food and beverage inventories accounts in the months of July and August of the current year. He wants you to show him the dollar changes and the percentage of change for each of these accounts using comparative horizontal analysis.

	July	August
Cash	$ 8,240	$ 6,592
Credit card receivables	1,480	2,398
Food inventories	4,680	6,506
Beverage inventories	2,880	2,448
Total Current Assets	$17,280	$17,944

E3.2 Complete a common-size vertical analysis for the months of July and August using E3.1's data.

E3.3 Complete a common-size vertical analysis of the following condensed income statement.

Condensed Income Statement

Sales revenue	$482,000
Cost of sales	(202,440)
Gross margin	$279,560
Operating expenses	(207,400)
Operating income	$ 72,160

E3.4 A room's operation had an average room rate of $50.00 in the first year, $48.00 in Year 2, and $54.00 in Year 3. Establish a trend index starting with the average room rate for the first year and determine the index numbers for Year 1, Year 2, and Year 3.

E3.5 Based on the following, determine the average check per guest.

	Sales Revenue	Guests
Dining room	$150,080	9,380
Bar–lounge	$ 68,050	5,444

E3.6 Based on the following, determine the average cost of sales revenue per guest.

	Cost of Sales Revenue	Guests
Dining room	$51,522	9,040
Bar–lounge	$38,642	6,222

E3.7 The following comparative current asset information has been extracted from a balance sheet for two successive years. Complete a horizontal analysis for Years 0007 to 0008, and a vertical common-sized analysis for Year 0008. Show the increase (+) or decrease (−) in dollars and the percentage of changes in the horizontal analysis.

Current Assets	Year 0007	Year 0008
Cash	$10,000	$12,000
Credit card receivables	1,000	1,500
Accounts receivable	800	880
Food inventory	11,200	7,840
Prepaid expenses	3,300	4,620
Total Current Assets	$26,300	$26,840

E3.8 The following data from a restaurant operation show a partially completed comparative income statement analysis for two consecutive years. Determine the missing dollar values and the missing percentages; show the plus (+) or negative (−) effects.

			Changes	
	Year 0007	*Year 0008*	*Dollars*	*%*
Sales Revenue	$23,502	$	+1,110	%
Cost of sales revenue	− 9,208	−9,438		+2.5%
Gross Margin	$	$	$	%
Direct costs	−10,202		+1,420	%
Contributory Income	$	$3,552		
Indirect costs	− 2,477			−3.0%
Operating Income	$	$1,149	$	%

E3.9 Sales revenue for a restaurant operation is given for the months of March, April, and May of Year 0007. The index numbers are stated for each month. Convert March, April, and May to current dollars. Round answers to the nearest dollar.

Year 0007	*Sales Revenue*	*Trend Index Number*
March	$48,000	110.0
April	$50,000	112.0
May	$52,000	115.0

P R O B L E M S

P3.1 Present in the proper form a comparative horizontal analysis of the corporate balance sheet shown below. Comment on any items of difference that you consider significant.

Assets	Year 0007	Year 0008
Current Assets		
Cash	$ 11,300	$ 15,400
Credit card receivables	4,500	6,300
Accounts receivable	11,100	18,900
Vending inventories	7,500	8,400
Prepaid expenses	4,200	4,100
Total Current Assets	$ 38,600	$ 53,100
Property Plant & Equipment		
Land	$ 81,200	$ 81,200
Building	758,100	795,300
Furnishings	83,712	93,412
Equipment	90,688	90,688
Accumulated depreciation	(315,500)	(335,800)
Glassware, linen inventories	12,200	15,300
Net Property and Equipment	$710,400	$740,100
Total Assets	$749,000	$793,200
Liabilities & Stockholders' Equity		
Current Liabilities		
Accounts payable	$ 9,200	$ 12,200
Accrued expenses payable	4,150	4,900
Taxes payable	12,150	15,500
Current portion, mortgage payable	13,500	11,200
Total Current Liabilities	$ 39,000	$ 43,800
Long-Term Liabilities		
Mortgage payable	$423,800	$412,300
Total Liabilities	$462,800	$456,100
Stockholders' Equity		
Capital stock	$125,200	$145,200
Retained earnings	161,000	191,900
Total Stockholders' Equity	$286,200	$337,100
Total Liabilities & Stockholders' Equity	$749,000	$793,200

P3.2 Using the information shown in P3.1, complete a common-size vertical balance sheet analysis in proper form for Year 0007 and Year 0008. Comment on any changes you consider significant.

P3.3 The following information has been extracted from a hotel's food department for the months of August and September.

	August		September	
Departmental S. R. Divisions	**S. R.**	**Guests**	**S. R.**	**Guests**
Room service	$ 22,600	927	$ 18,000	756
Dining room	118,500	4,628	95,500	3,765
Bar–lounge	5,500	846	4,100	637
Coffee shop	53,400	9,709	48,700	8,604
Banquets	198,600	6,687	211,500	6,805
Totals	$398,600	22,797	$377,800	20,567

Departmental Divisions	**August**	**September**
Cost of sales	$136,200	$127,800
Wages and salaries expense	107,900	101,500
Employee benefits expense	14,000	14,500
Linen expense	6,400	6,000
China expense	10,600	9,800
Supplies expense	9,800	9,400
Other expense	19,200	17,600
Total operating expenses	$304,100	$286,600
Departmental Operating Income	$ 94,500	$ 91,200

a. For each sales revenue division, calculate the average check per guest for August and September.

b. Calculate the average cost per guest and total average cost for each month.

c. Determine the departmental operating income per guest for each month.

P3.4 A company owns two restaurants in the same town. Operating results for the first three months of the current year for restaurants A and B are as follows:

	Restaurant A		Restaurant B	
Sales revenue		$154,300		$206,100
Cost of sales		− 60,200		− 78,900
Gross margin		$ 94,100		$127,200
Direct Expenses				
Wages expense	$45,600		$70,400	
Supplies expense	12,700		16,800	
Other direct costs	4,500	− 62,800	6,100	− 93,300
Contributory Income		$ 31,300		$ 33,900
Indirect Expenses				
Rent expense	$ 6,500		$ 9,000	
Insurance expense	2,000		3,000	
Other indirect expenses	3,200	− 11,700	3,600	− 15,600
Operating Income		$ 19,600		$ 18,300

The owners of the restaurants are concerned that restaurant B reports higher sales revenue, yet produces a lower operating income than restaurant A. Convert this information into a common-size vertical income statement for each restaurant, and comment on the results.

P3.5 The sales revenue, food cost of sales, and guests served for a small fast-food carryout division of a restaurant for the past six months are given as follows:

Month	Sales Revenue	Cost of Sales, Food	Guests Served
1	$258,200	$ 96,200	10,200
2	274,800	104,300	10,400
3	285,600	110,500	10,300
4	289,400	113,100	10,100
5	298,300	118,900	10,400
6	304,600	123,700	10,500

For each of the six months:

a. Calculate average check and average costs of sales food.

b. Using these averages, calculate a trend index number. Set the trend index for month 1 at 100% (or 100) and complete trend index numbers for the remaining five months.

c. With the index numbers identified, convert sales revenue and cost of sales food from historic to current dollars.

d. Comment on the results of your calculations of the three requirements for the six months.

P3.6 A motel had the following annual sales revenue and average room rate figures for the last five years. During this five-year period there were no changes in the number or type of rooms available and the clientele remained basically the same.

Year	Annual Sales Revenue	Average Room Rate
1	$1,401,429	$75.00
2	$1,429,367	$76.30
3	$1,480,552	$77.60
4	$1,520,700	$78.50
5	$1,553,091	$79.90

a. Prepare room rate trend numbers from the average room rates using 100% (or 100) as the base trend index number for Year 1.

b. Use the room rate index numbers identified to convert the reported annual historic sales revenue to current dollars.

c. After the conversion is completed, comment on the results of your analysis.

P3.7 Two successive monthly income statements for the food department of a motor lodge are shown here. Present the income statements in a comparative horizontal analysis format and comment on any significant differences.

Sales Revenue	August	September
Room service	$ 11,300	$ 9,000
Dining room	75,900	63,700
Bar–lounge	5,500	4,100
Coffee shop	53,400	48,700
Banquets	66,200	70,500
Total Sales Revenue	**$212,300**	**$196,000**
Cost of sales	(68,100)	(63,900)
Gross Margin	**$144,200**	**$132,100**
Operating Expenses		
Wages and salaries	$ 75,800	$ 71,100
Employee benefits	11,400	10,700
Linen and laundry	3,200	3,000
China, glassware, & tableware	5,300	4,900
Miscellaneous operating costs	4,900	4,700
Operating supplies	9,600	8,800
Total Operating Expenses	(110,200)	(103,200)
Departmental Operating Income	**$ 34,000**	**$ 28,900**

P3.8 Using the information presented in P3.7, present in proper format a common-size vertical income statement analysis. Comment on any significant results noted.

P3.9 You have the following information concerning a fast-food restaurant for three consecutive months.

	April		May		June	
Sales Revenue		$120,500		$141,300		$165,900
Cost of sales	$41,500		$51,500		$62,800	
Wages	34,200		42,100		51,900	
Other expenses	22,000	$97,700	25,100	$118,700	29,100	$143,800
Departmental		$22,800		$22,600		$22,100
Income						
Guests served		20,200		24,400		29,900

Convert the consolidated income statements to common size. Use the number of customers to prepare additional analyses. Comment on what is happening in this operation using the information you have calculated.

P3.10 Freddy's Fried Chicken provides the following for the months of April and May:

Sales Revenue	April	May
Sales revenue–food	$199,000	$213,500
Sales revenue–beverages	72,000	74,000
Total Sales Revenue	**$271,000**	**$287,500**
Operating Expenses		
Cost of sales–food	$ 71,500	$ 82,000
Cost of sales–beverage	16,800	19,900
Wages expense	76,000	85,000
Other operating expenses	77,100	82,000
Total expenses	**$241,400**	**$268,900**
Operating Income (BT)	**$ 29,600**	**$ 18,600**

Complete the following:

a. Convert the income statement to common-size vertical analysis.

b. Convert the income statement to a comparative horizontal analysis.

c. With the information given, calculate the average check, cost, and operating income per guest. A total of 20,000 guests were served in April and 22,000 in May, comment on Freddy's operating results for the two months of April and May.

d. Compare the information you received from the common-size vertical analysis and the comparative horizontal analysis.

P3.11 You have the following information about Hotshot Hotel's dining room for the months of October and November. Calculate sales revenue average check, cost of sales, expenses and operating income on a per-guest basis.

Sales Revenue	October	Guests	November	Guests
Sales revenue–food	$ 85,432	2,748	$ 81,718	2,645
Sales revenue–beverages	33,249	2,542	37,555	2,444
Total Sales Revenue	**$118,681**	**5,290**	**$119,273**	**5,089**
Operating Expenses				
Cost of sales–food	$ 32,525	2,748	$ 29,487	2,645
Cost of sales–beverages	10,000	2,542	11,547	2,444
Wages expenses	32,352	5,290	31,081	5,089
Other expenses	21,154	5,290	20,550	5,089
Total operating expenses	**$ 96,031**	**5,290**	**$ 92,665**	**5,089**
Department Operating Income (BT)	**$ 22,650**	**5,290**	**$ 26,608**	**5,089**

Use this information to comment about the dining room's operating results for October and November.

P3.12 You have the following information about the sales revenue, cost of sales, and accounts receivable for six consecutive periods for a small to mid-size catering service. Generally, they are paid by check or cash and also extend 15-day accounts receivable credit to selected organizations.

Period	Food Sales Revenue	Food Cost	Accounts Receivable
1	$210,200	$60,330	$20,020
2	$233,322	$72,275	$24,200
3	$243,821	$81,400	$25,800
4	$253,574	$84,200	$27,400
5	$267,521	$90,768	$31,400
6	$273,406	$93,128	$33,600

For each of the three items, calculate trend percentages. Using the results from this analysis, discuss whether the situation developing for the catering service is desirable.

P3.13 Assume that appropriate general trend index numbers for the catering service sales revenue and its food costs were as follows for the six periods referred to in P3.12.

Period	Sales Revenue Index	Cost Index
1	107	121
2	114	125
3	121	131
4	130	137
5	144	144
6	147	151

Convert the historic dollars of sales revenue and the historic dollars of cost of sales in P3.12 to current dollars and discuss the results.

P3.14 A motel had the following annual sales revenue and average room rate figures for the last five years. During this five-year period, there were no changes in the number or type of rooms available, and the type of clientele remained the same.

Year	Annual Sales Revenue	Average Room Rate
1	$2,205,952	$85.00
2	$2,254,695	$88.60
3	$2,299,526	$89.70
4	$2,334,484	$91.40
5	$2,380,856	$93.80

Prepare index numbers from the average room rates. Use the index numbers identified to convert the annual sales revenue to current dollars. After the conversion is completed, comment on the results of your analysis.

CASE 3

a. With reference to the financial statements prepared for the 4C Company for Year 2007 (see Case 2), prepare a common-size vertical statement. The local restaurant association provided Charlie with statistical data that are applicable for a table service, family-oriented, lunch and dinner restaurant similar to his (see below). The data provide percentage ranges for typical elements of an income statement. Comment on how the operating income (before tax) of the 4C restaurant compares to similar restaurants. Is the comparison valid? Explain.

Sales Revenue	Low (%)		High (%)
Food operations	68.0		84.0
Beverage operations	16.0		33.0
Total Sales Revenue		100%	
Cost of sales, food	30.0%		40.0%
Cost of sales, beverages	17.0%		33.0%
Total Cost of Sales	35.0%		44.0%
Gross Margin	62.0%		71.0%
Operating Expenses			
Wages expense	26.0%		31.0%
Salaries expense	2.0%		6.0%
Employee benefits expense	3.0%		5.0%
Employee meals expense	1.0%		2.0%
Laundry, linen, uniforms expense	1.5%		2.0%
Replacements expense	0.5%		1.0%
Services supplies expense	1.0%		2.0%
Menus, printing expense	0.3%		0.5%
Miscellaneous expense	0.3%		0.5%
Entertainment expense	0.5%		2.0%
Advertising, promotion expense	0.7%		2.5%
Utilities expense	2.0%		4.0%
Administrative expense	3.0%		6.0%
Repairs, maintenance expense	1.0%		2.0%
Rent expense	4.5%		7.0%
Property taxes expense	0.5%		1.5%
Insurance expense	0.8%		1.0%
Interest expense	0.3%		1.0%
Depreciation expense	2.0%		2.8%
Franchise expense (if applicable)	3.0%		8.0%
Total Operating Expenses	*51.5%*		*62.5%*
Operating Income (before tax)	1.5%		12.0%

b. The guest count (covers) for the 4C restaurant for the year was 66,612. Determine the overall average check (sales revenue) for food and beverages. In your opinion, does the average check for food and beverages appear reasonable for a budget-conscious, family-type table service restaurant?

c. Calculate the cost percentages for food cost, beverage cost, and the total cost of sales as a percentage of total sales revenue. How does cost of sales for food, beverages, and the total cost of sales compare to the ranges provided for a restaurant of this type?

d. Given the choice, would it be better to have a higher or lower percentage of beverage sales revenue compared to food sales revenue?

CHAPTER 4

RATIO ANALYSIS

INTRODUCTION

The preceding chapters concentrated on developing a general but solid understanding of accounting principles and concepts and their applications to business transactions. Knowing how an accounting system works internally creates an understanding of the source and specific nature of information needed for the preparation of financial statements. This chapter continues financial statement analysis by discussing significant financial and other various ratios, with the objective of obtaining indirect information about economic actions. Ratio analysis expresses the proportional numerical relationships between figures reported in financial statements and are used to compare current period ratios to prior periods and industry averages. To effectively analyze the different figures, one must know where to look for the information needed to conduct a ratio analysis.

To express the relationship between two values, various commonly used ratios are illustrated. Four general methods of evaluating a ratio or percentage will be discussed: industry figures, external competitive figures, the results of operations from a previous period, and predetermined budgetary standards. Typical ratio analysis techniques commonly used by a business to express the status of its operations, financial, and economic condition, are broken into five major categories: current liquidity ratios, long-term solvency ratios, profitability ratios, activity, and operating ratios.

CHAPTER OBJECTIVES

After studying this chapter, the reader should be able to

1. Explain the differences between creditors, owners, and managers in what they look for in financial statements.
2. Explain why creditors are normally concerned with specific areas of financial statements.

3. List and briefly explain each of the current liquidity ratios discussed and illustrated.

4. Explain the purpose of an analysis of credit card receivables.

5. List and briefly explain each of the solvency ratios.

6. List and briefly describe each of the profitability ratios.

7. List and briefly explain each of the activity ratios.

8. Discuss the importance of inventory turnover ratios.

9. List and describe at least five food and beverage operating ratios.

10. List and describe at least five rooms operating ratios.

11. Explain the meaning of gross margin.

12. Explain the difference between operating income and net income.

13. Define financial leverage and explain why it is used.

RATIO ANALYSIS

Ratio analysis in the simplest terms refers to the comparison of two figures, numerical dollar values or quantity values. Ratio analysis allows an evaluation of balance sheet items in conjunction with some income statement information to determine various relationships between selected items. We have already discussed two basic types of ratio analysis in Chapter 2—comparative horizontal and common-size vertical analysis of balance sheets and income statements. Comparative analysis finds the numerical change and expresses the numerical change as a percentage. Common-size analysis expresses each item as a percentage of total sales revenue for the income statement and total assets for the balance sheet.

Ratios are fractions where the numerator is expressed as a portion of the denominator. They can express relationships as a percentage, a numerical value, or a quantity, or on a per-unit basis. For example, assume sales revenue for a given month was $48,000 and cost of sales was $19,200. If we want to know what cost of sales is as a percentage of sales revenue, the calculation is

Cost of sales / Sales revenue = $19,200 / $48,000 = 40%

If we know total current assets are $5,000 and total current liabilities are $2,000 and we want to find the relationship of total current assets to total current liabilities as of a specific date, two calculations can be made based on the same information:

Total current assets / Total current liabilities = $5,000 / $2,000 = 2.5:1

or

Total current liabilities / Total current assets = $2,000 / $5,000 = <u>40.0%</u>

The first ratio tells us that total current assets are 2.5 times greater than total current liabilities; in essence, there is $2.50 in current assets for each $1.00 of current liabilities. The second ratio expresses total current liabilities as 40% of total current assets. The way a ratio is expressed is dependent on the format that will best describe the relationship between two figures and on the information available.

It is important to remember that when two figures are converted to a ratio, the relationship between the two figures must be realistic, meaningful, and understandable. If we compare cost of sales–food to the sales revenue food produced, the ratio analysis would be realistic, meaningful, and understandable. Certainly this would not be the case if food cost of sales were compared to management salaries, as no useful information is provided.

RATIO COMPARISONS

Ratios are used to help a business entity evaluate financial and economic results of profit-oriented operations over a given accounting period. A ratio standing alone is simply a number and appears to have little value, in that the ratio does not directly show favorable or unfavorable results. For example, a restaurant's food inventory turnover of four times per month may appear good, but until the turnover ratio is compared with some standard, such as the average turnover ratio in the restaurant industry for that type of restaurant, its true value cannot be determined.

For a ratio to have meaning, it must be comparable to a standard or an established base ratio. A standard ratio could be an industry average, but such a standard ratio may be the least valuable. Industry standards are generally developed through information received from hospitality organizations having the same type of activities; however, such establishments may be spread over a large geographic area. Different operating conditions prevail in different locations within the geographical area (e.g., average family income, salaries, hourly pay rates, and cost of living levels, and disposable income). As a result of such economic variances across a geographical area, there may not be one operation that is just like the *average operation* from which the standard ratios are determined. Industry averages are good for telling a manager if the operation is in the ballpark with the industry, but should not be used as the operation's standard.

Another method of ratio comparison may use comparable ratios from similar competitive organizations. Obtaining competitive ratios may prove difficult, if not impossible. If competitive ratios are available and they differ when compared to the ratios of your operation, which ratios are better? There are many reasons that may explain the differences in individual ratios between competitors.

A better technique is to compare current operating period ratios with previous operating period ratios. For example, how does the current room occupancy ratio or seat turnover ratio compare with the same ratio from the previous month, or the previous year? What is the trend? Is room occupancy or seat turnover increasing, or is room occupancy or seat turnover decreasing? How do you determine if the difference in the ratio is appropriate or inappropriate? Even with limited exposure, one soon discovers that a hospitality business operates in a dynamic and rapidly changing environment. Therefore, comparison of current period ratios to past period ratios may be like comparing copper to gold.

The best method of ratio comparison is to evaluate current period ratios to predetermined standards for that operating period. The predetermined standard should consider both internal and external factors affecting the operation. Internal factors might include the composition of sales revenue (cash versus credit sales), fixed and variable costs, internal operating policies, changes in operating procedures, and many other similar operating variables. External factors might include general economic conditions and what the competition is doing.

Periodic predetermined operating standards can be used to develop operating plans to assist in developing the annual operating budget (forecasted income statement). The operating budget can be broken down into monthly or quarterly operating periods, which are adjusted for seasonal variations. Operating budgets should project future operations based not only on past operating results but also on current operating results. Budgeting is an important and time-sensitive management skill and is discussed in depth in Chapter 9.

USERS OF RATIOS

Generally, three broad groups of people are interested in the evaluation of ratios: internal operating management, current and potential creditors, and the organization's owners. A proprietorship has one owner, a partnership has two or more owners, and a corporation normally has a number of owners called stockholders or shareholders.

Management has the responsibility of safeguarding the assets, controlling costs, and maximizing profit for the business operation. Ratio evaluation is a major technique used by management to monitor the operation's performance against predetermined standards to determine if the operating budget objectives are being achieved. Certain ratios are used to evaluate the effectiveness of day-to-day operations, to assess its current liquidity position, and to assess other economic positions that define certain objectives to satisfy owners as well as creditors. A number of different ratios used by management to evaluate whether the performance objectives are being achieved are discussed in this chapter.

Creditors of a business operation have an equity claim to the assets of the operation that is shown as the liabilities element of the basic balance sheet equation $A = L + OE$. Creditors loan money or extend trade credit to the business operation. As such, creditors are normally interested in certain ratios that may indicate the level of safety of their loaned funds or trade credit. In addition, existing and potential creditors use certain ratios to estimate their potential risk of future loans that the business operation may need. In some cases, a creditor may require the borrower to maintain a specified level of working capital; that is, a specific level of current assets greater than current liabilities.

Last but not least, the ownership of a business operation can use certain ratios to measure such items as their return on investment or the risk level of their investment, or to estimate the probability of success of future operations.

In many cases, members of the three groups interested in the evaluation of ratios will not agree on what a particular ratio means. This is to be expected because each group interprets the ratio from a different perspective.

RATIO CATEGORIES

Ratio analysis will be discussed in the following five major categories using information from Exhibit 4.1, annual balance sheets for Years 0006 and 0007, and Exhibit 4.2, condensed income statement for the year ended December 31, 0007:

1. *Current liquidity ratios.* The primary purpose of **liquidity ratios** is to identify the relationship between current assets and current liabilities; thus, liquidity ratios provide the basis for an evaluation of the ability of a company to meet its current obligations. Liquidity ratios that provide a direct analysis of current and quick assets in relation to current liabilities are the **current ratio** (or the **working capital ratio**) and the **quick ratio** (or **acid test ratio**). The analysis of credit sales revenue provides an analysis of the average time that elapses between the creation and collection of current receivables. Typical ratios concerning receivables are the credit card receivables turnover; credit card receivables as a percentage of net credit sales; credit cards average collection period; accounts receivable turnover; accounts receivable as a percentage of net credit sales; and accounts receivable average collection period.

2. *Profitability ratios.* Resources and assets are made available to management to conduct sales-revenue-generating operations, and the profitability ratios show management's effectiveness in using the resources (assets) during operating periods. Profitability ratios to be discussed are return on assets, profit to sales ratio, return on ownership equity, return on total investment, and earnings per share.

3. *Long-term solvency ratios.* These ratios are also called *net worth ratios,* and they measure a company's ability to meet its long-term debt repayment responsibilities. Included are ratios that describe total assets to total liabilities, total liabilities to total assets, total liabilities to total ownership equity, cash flow from operating activities to total liabilities, cash flow from operating activities to interest, and the number of times interest is earned.

4. *Activity ratios.* Activity or turnover ratios indicate how well the managers are using assets. The inventory turnover ratio shows the relationship between inventories held for resale and the cost of sales over an operating period. In

Balance Sheets for the Years Ending December 31, 0006 and 0007

	Year 0006	Year 0007
Assets		
Current Assets		
Cash	$ 19,500	$ 30,400
Credit card receivables	8,807	10,208
Accounts receivable	5,983	6,882
Marketable securities	15,400	2,000
Inventories	12,880	14,700
Prepaid expenses	10,800	14,900
Total Current Assets	$ 73,370	$ 79,090
Property, Plant & Equipment		
Land	$ 60,500	$ 60,500
Building	828,400	884,400
Equipment	114,900	157,900
Furnishings	75,730	81,110
Net: Accumulated depreciation	(330,100)	(422,000)
China, glass, silver, & linen	16,600	18,300
Total Property, Plant & Equipment	$766,030	$780,210
Total Assets	$839,400	$859,300
Liabilities & Stockholders' Equity		
Current Liabilities		
Accounts payable	$ 19,200	$ 16,500
Accrued expenses payable	4,200	5,000
Taxes payable	12,400	20,900
Current mortgage payable	26,900	26,000
Total Current Liabilities	$ 62,700	$68,400
Long-term liabilities		
Mortgage payable	$512,800	$486,800
Total Liabilities	$575,500	$555,200
Stockholders' Equity		
Common stock ($5 par; 40,000 shares issued & OS)	$200,000	$200,000
Retained earnings	63,900	104,100
Total Stockholders' Equity	$263,900	$304,100
Total Liabilities & Stockholders' Equity	$839,400	$859,300

■ **EXHIBIT 4.1**

Annual Balance Sheets

addition, the average days of inventory for resale on hand can be determined. Working capital turnover measures the effectiveness of using working capital, and fixed asset turnover measures the effectiveness of using fixed assets.

5. *Operating ratios.* The final category to be discussed includes analysis of items that are oriented primarily to food, beverage, and rooms operations. Operat-

Condensed Income Statement (Year Ended December 31, 0007)		
Sales Revenue		
Sales revenue*		$1,175,200
Cost of Sales		(394,800)
Gross Margin		$ 780,400
Direct Operating Expenses		
Payroll expenses	$305,100	
Other expenses	117,300	
Total Direct Operating Expenses		(422,400)
Operating Income		$ 358,000
Undistributed Operating Expenses		
Administrative and general expenses	$ 60,280	
Marketing expenses	17,088	
Property operation and maintenance	27,222	
Energy expenses	21,100	
Total Undistributed Operating Expense		(125,690)
Fixed Expenses		
Income before fixed expenses		$ 232,310
Property taxes	$ 43,334	
Insurance expense	11,750	
Depreciation expense	82,064	
Total Fixed Expenses		(137,148)
Income Before Interest and Income Tax		$ 95,162
Interest expense		(26,044)
Income before Income Tax		$ 69,118
Income Tax (@ 30%)		(20,735)
Net Income		$ 48,383

*Total sales revenue on average consisted of 26% cash sales, 64% credit card sales, and 10% accounts receivable.

■ **EXHIBIT 4.2**
Sample Condensed Income Statement

ing ratios are generally summarized of the manager's daily or weekly report. This chapter concludes with a discussion on financial leverage, or, simply put, the use of debt to obtain capital. Basically, there are two sources of obtaining operating capital—assuming long-term debt or increasing ownership equity by selling additional ownership rights. **Financial leverage** is the term used to describe the use of debt, rather than equity, financing to increase the return on ownership equity.

Ratios are categorized only for convenience. For example, some people might classify working capital turnover as a current liquidity ratio, whereas in this chapter it is included among the activity ratios. It is important to understand the ratio's meaning and how a ratio can be interpreted, rather than its category.

This analysis requires determining the reasons that caused the value ratio to not be other than what was expected. Individual ratios normally provide information about one aspect of a business operation, whereas the analysis and interpretation of several ratios jointly will yield a more comprehensive view of a business operation than a single ratio or financial statements alone.

CURRENT LIQUIDITY RATIOS

Current liquidity ratios, sometimes just called *liquidity ratios,* indicate the ability of an operation to meet its short-term obligations for the repayment of debt without difficulty. A business's operating income statement may show operating income (before taxes) or a net income (after taxes) without the business operation having the ability to pay its current liabilities, let alone its long-term debt obligations. This situation is discussed and demonstrated in Chapter 11, which discusses cash management. In particular, the reader is referred to the section on cash conservation and working capital management discussed in that chapter. At this point, we will turn our attention to some of the current liquidity ratios that indicate the effectiveness of working capital management. **Working capital** is the difference between current assets and current liabilities ($CA - CL$).

CURRENT RATIO

The most commonly used ratio to express current liquidity is the current ratio. This ratio shows the ability of an operation to pay its short-term debts, which are classified as current liabilities:

Current assets / Current liabilities = <u>Current ratio</u>

The calculation for Year 0006 in Exhibit 4.1 is

$$\frac{\textbf{Current assets}}{\textbf{Current liabilities}} = \frac{\$73,370}{\$62,700} = \underline{\underline{\textbf{1.17:1}}}$$

The calculation for Year 0007 is

$$\frac{\textbf{Current assets}}{\textbf{Current liabilities}} = \frac{\$79,090}{\$68,400} = \underline{\underline{\textbf{1.16:1}}}$$

The ratio for Year 0007 from Exhibit 4.1 shows $1.16 of current assets is available for every $1.00 of current short-term debt (current liabilities). In general, a rule of thumb exists that current assets should exceed current liabilities on a ratio of two to one, which implies $2.00 of current assets exists for each $1.00 of current liabilities. However, this general rule was set to provide a safety margin for operations that normally have a portion of their current assets tied up in inventories (e.g., manufacturing operations and other processing operations). In the hospitality industry, the largest inventories held by a hotel and motel operation are in the form of guest rooms available for sale, and these are included under building, which is a part of fixed assets as property, plant, and equipment. The only current inventories (inventories for resale) held for resale by hotel–motel operations are for food and beverage services, and these current inventories represent a rather small portion of current assets.

Therefore, hotels can operate with a current ratio of 1.5 or less; motels and restaurants have shown that they can operate on a current ratio of less than 1 to 1. For each individual hospitality operation, a minimum ratio must be determined. The minimum ratio will be one that does not create a short-term liquidity problem or sacrifice profitability. Money tied up in working capital is money that is not being used to earn income.

Creditors and potential creditors prefer to see a high ratio of current assets to liabilities, since it provides a positive indicator of a business operation's capability to repay its debt obligations. Many creditors require a minimum current ratio before funds are loaned or credit is extended. Once a loan or credit is extended, the creditor may require that a minimum current ratio be maintained. If a minimum current ratio is required and the current ratio falls below the required level, the creditor might demand immediate payment in full on any balance outstanding.

The opposite is true for owners, who normally prefer a low ratio of current assets to current liabilities, since a high ratio may indicate that more money is tied up in working capital and is not being used efficiently. Owners might be concerned that on-hand inventories for resale might exceed anticipated needs and, as such, will increase the cost of holding inventory. Owners might also be concerned that receivables are not being collected as quickly as they should be. Management of the operation must try to maintain a current ratio that is acceptable to both ownership and creditors—a task not easily achieved.

It is possible to change the current ratio to make it appear better than it really is. Exhibit 4.3 presents the current asset and current liability sections for Year 0006 of the balance sheet shown in Exhibit 4.1. If $20,000 in cash were used just prior to the end of an accounting period to reduce accounts payable by $10,000 and taxes payable were also reduced by $10,000, the adjustment shown in Exhibit 4.4 will create a higher current ratio.

The comparable current ratios would be as follows:

Exhibit 4.3: CA / CL = $79,090 / $68,400 = <u>1.16:1</u>

Exhibit 4.4: CA / CL = $59,090 / $48,400 = <u>1.22:1</u>

In this case, the change is small and not very significant, but in other cases, the change may be large and have a significant effect on disguising the sta-

Current Assets		Current Liabilities	
Cash	$30,400		
Credit card receivables	10,208		
Accounts receivable	6,882	Accounts payable	$16,500
Marketable securities	2,000	Accrued expenses	5,000
Inventories	14,700	Taxes payable	20,900
Prepaid expenses	14,900	Current mortgage payable	26,000
	$79,090		$68,400
Working Capital: CA − CL = $79,090 − $68,400 = $10,690			

■ **EXHIBIT 4.3**
Current Balance Sheet Section for Year 0007

tus of working capital. When the current ratio is changed in this manner, the working capital does not change. This form of manipulation is referred to as window dressing. However, if accounts payable of $15,000 were due, there would be no harm in paying them off in the manner illustrated. Reducing the payables to improve the current ratio makes good sense if the business anticipates the need for short-term financing in the immediate future. Other reasonable methods of window dressing includes borrowing a long-term payable or obtaining additional ownership investments. Another option would be to sell physical property, plant, and equipment assets that are no longer needed to convert them to cash.

Current Assets		Current Liabilities	
Cash	$10,400		
Credit card receivables	10,208		
Accounts receivable	6,882	Accounts payable	$ 6,500
Marketable securities	2,000	Accrued expenses	5,000
Inventories	14,700	Taxes payable	10,900
Prepaid expenses	14,900	Current mortgage payable	26,000
	$59,090		$48,400
Working Capital: CA − CL = $59,090 − $48,400 = $10,690			

■ **EXHIBIT 4.4**
Current Balance Sheet Sections Modified for Year 0007

Current Assets	Year 0006		Year 0007	
	Amount	Percent	Amount	Percent
Cash	$19,500	26.6%	$30,400	38.4%
Credit card receivables	8,807	12.0%	10,208	12.9%
Accounts receivable	5,983	8.2%	6,882	8.7%
Marketable securities	15,400	21.0%	2,000	2.5%
Inventories	12,880	17.6%	14,700	18.6%
Prepaid expenses	10,800	14.7%	14,900	18.8%
	$73,370	*100%	$79,090	*100%

*Items do not add up due to rounding

■ **EXHIBIT 4.5**
Changes in the Proportion of Current Assets

COMPOSITION OF CURRENT ASSETS

We can assess the change in the current liquidity of the operation by using common-size vertical analysis on the current assets using the techniques discussed in Chapter 3. Any subset of a financial statement such as total current assets can be analyzed to show the percentage relationship of each item within the subset.

The current asset sections of Exhibit 4.1 for Years 0006 and 0007 are shown in Exhibit 4.5 in a common-size vertical analysis format. The exhibit shows the change in the proportion of the current assets over a two-year period.

Exhibit 4.5 shows that cash as a percentage of total current assets changed from 26.6% in Year 0006 ($19,500 / $73,370) to 38.9% ($29,400 / $79,090) in Year 0007. However, the most liquid current assets of cash, receivables, and marketable securities have decreased in total from 67.8% (26.6% + 12.0% + 8.2% + 21.0%) in Year 0006, to 62.5% (38.4% + 12.9% + 8.7% + 2.5%) in Year 0007. The cash position has improved, but the total of the four most liquid assets has declined by 5.2%. The major item causing the decline was selling the marketable securities during Year 0006 to reduce current liabilities and increase the current ratio. These most liquid current assets are often classified as **quick assets.**

QUICK RATIO (ACID TEST RATIO)

The quick ratio, also called the acid test ratio, uses an extreme view of liquidity since it only uses current assets that can be readily converted to cash if the need should arise. Current assets that are considered readily convertible to cash are called quick assets and will not include current assets such as inventories, prepaid expenses, and other nonliquid assets. The quick ratio is calculated using the current asset and current liability information shown in Exhibit 4.1.

The quick ratio for Year 0006:

$$\frac{\textbf{Cash + Credit card receivables + Accounts receivable + Marketable securities}}{\textbf{Total current liabilities}}$$

$$\frac{\$19,500 + \$8,807 + \$5,983 + \$15,400}{\$62,700} = \frac{\$49,690}{\$62,700} = \underline{\underline{0.79{:}1}}$$

The quick ratio for Year 0007:

$$\frac{\$30,400 + \$10,208 + \$6,882 + \$2,000}{\$68,400} = \frac{\$49,490}{\$68,400} = \underline{\underline{0.72{:}1}}$$

An alternative method to find the quick ratio is expressed as follows:

$$\text{Quick ratio} = \frac{\text{Total current assets} - \text{Inventories} - \text{Prepaid expenses}}{\text{Current liabilities}}$$

Quick ratio, Year 0007: $79,090 − $14,700 − $14,900

$$= \$49,490\ /\ \$68,400 = \underline{\underline{0.72{:}1}}$$

The quick ratio for Year 0006 is 0.79:1, showing there is $0.79 of quick assets for every $1.00 of current liabilities. In Year 0007, the quick ratio has dropped to 0.72:1, showing only $0.72 of quick assets for every $1.00 of current liabilities. This tells us that the most liquid current assets are below a dollar-to-dollar ratio, which is generally considered as the low end of the safety range for the quick ratio. These low quick ratios indicate a large value of nonliquid current assets that normally consist of inventories for resale and prepaid expenses. Prepaid expenses are nonliquid since prepaid expenses are consumed over the period of time they provide benefits and generally cannot be converted to cash. However, removing inventories for resale in the hotel, food, and beverage industry may be questionable, since inventories of food and beverages turn over in days rather than months as they do in manufacturing businesses. Since inventories for resale are turned over quickly and converted to sales revenue that is recognized as cash and receivables that will be collected as cash within days—or at the most within a week or so, it might be appropriate to include inventories for resale as liquid assets.

The exclusion of inventories may be valid in some industries, where the nature of their business requires inventory availability for periods of months or more. Since the major difference in the current and quick ratios is inventory, some hospitality operations such as a motel without a food or beverage operation may see little variance between the two ratios.

Creditors, owners, and managers analyze and interpret the quick ratio the same way they analyze and interpret the current ratio. Creditors still prefer to see a high ratio, owners prefer a low ratio, and management must continue to maintain a balance between the creditors' and owners' viewpoints.

RECEIVABLE RATIOS

To provide the most accurate evaluation on an annual, monthly, quarterly, or semi-annual basis total sales revenue should be broken into three components: cash, credit card receivables, and accounts receivable from sales revenue. To correctly calculate receivable ratios, at least two successive periods of data is required.

Managers should know how much their sales revenues cash, accounts receivable, and credit card receivables are because they will have to record each of these in the appropriate accounts so they know how much they have to collect.

The most accurate method of determining a receivable ratio is one that evaluates each individual receivable in relation to the type of credit sales revenue produced. If credit card receivables and accounts receivables are not maintained by subsidiary accounts within the total sales revenue figure, the second best alternative is to maintain total sales that are shown to consist of cash plus credit sales. This alternative will skew receivable ratios, because reported credit sales will consist of two different components—credit cards and accounts receivable. The next alternative is to simply use total sales revenue to evaluate receivable ratios; however, the skewing of the ratios will increase because total sales revenue will not show any categories for credit sales. The last but worst alternative is to rely on past historical percentages of credit sales by category to evaluate receivable ratios. The ever-present danger in using historical information is that the ratio of current cash to credit sales may have changed.

Credit card sales are the major portion of sales revenue in the hospitality industry today and should not be ignored as a current receivable to be evaluated. Normally, major large hospitality organizations are computerized with fully automated accounting systems that are capable of immediately accessing any ratios they choose to review. However, this is not particularly true for smaller operations that may not have the online computerized resources of a larger organization. **Credit card sales revenue** is a near-cash transaction due to quick reimbursement by the credit card company. Collections of credit card receivables normally range from 1.0 to 3.0 operating days on average. Depending on the volume of credit card sales and the efficiency of credit card companies, the turnover rate for credit card receivables on average may vary from 243 to 122 times per 12-month operating period.

The collection period varies with the type of card. As well, larger hospitality operations that are tied electronically online with a card-clearing center are reimbursed at the time of sale or on the same day that the credit card sale is made. In general, the discount of 1.5 to 5.0% is charged by credit card companies; the average is 3.25%. The variances in the discount rate may depend on the volume of credit card sales, the size and type of organization, and/or a negotiated rate. The discount rates charged and the average credit card collection period are two major items affecting cash flows.

If customers use **debit cards** to pay for their purchases, the customers' bank accounts are charged at the time of the sale and the money is transferred directly to the operation's bank account. The nature and speed of the reimbursement classifies the use of a debit card as a cash sales transaction.

Although credit card use continues to increase and the use of accounts receivable (trade credit) continues to decrease, accounts receivable will continue to be used in private clubs, for corporate organizations, for special food and beverage functions (banquets), and in other hospitality areas where the use of accounts receivable is considered appropriate.

As discussed earlier, if accounts receivable is calculated based on total sales revenue, the ratio is skewed because total sales revenue is used rather than accounts receivable credit sales revenue. The skewing effect has continued because of failure to recognize the increase of credit card sales revenue that has added a second component to credit sales. This skewing effect, if unnoticed, may increase steadily for years, and the manager may not notice that collection periods are too long.

As the percentage of credit card sales revenue increase, the range is 55 to 65% of total credit sales; the average 60% of total credit sales. It would be prudent to integrate credit card sales revenue under the general classification of accounts receivable. In general, credit card receivables can be integrated into the accounts receivable classification by using subsidiary accounts receivables, which identify each credit card accepted by name—Visa, MasterCard, and so on. The same technique of using subsidiary accounts to identify a person or company that has been extended trade credit should be in place.

The following sections discuss and illustrate the basic methods used (except historical data) to determine various ratios applicable to credit receivables. We will begin with credit card receivables, followed by accounts receivable. The discussion of credit card receivables as a separate classification of credit sales revenue is designed to stress the importance and effect of this classification of credit sales revenue. The potential skewing effects of an operating receivable ratio will become apparent, as each receivable ratio is discussed for credit card sales, accounts receivable credit sales revenue, total credit sales, and total sales revenue. Although receivable ratios may be evaluated on an annual, semiannual, quarterly, or monthly basis, only the annual basis is discussed and illustrated.

CREDIT CARD RECEIVABLES RATIOS

Credit card receivables ratios will be discussed as a percentage of total credit card sales revenue, total credit sales revenue, and total sales revenue. The ratios will be discussed in the following sequence:

1. Credit card receivables ratios based on credit card sales revenue, total credit sales revenue, and total sales revenue
2. Credit card receivables turnover ratios
3. Credit card receivables average collection periods

The information used to calculate each of the following ratios is extracted from Exhibit 4.1 and Exhibit 4.2. Total sales revenue is $1,175,200 with cash sales of 26%, or $305,552, credit card sales revenue of 64%, or $752,128, and accounts receivable sales revenue of 10%, or $117,520.

Credit Card Receivables as a Percentage of Credit Card Sales Revenue, Total Credit Sales Revenue, and Total Sales Revenue

This ratio will show the relationship of credit card receivables to credit card sales revenue, which is the most accurate method:

(Beginning credit card receivables + Ending credit card receivables) / 2 = Average credit card receivables

$$(\$8,807 + \$10,208) / 2 = \$19,015 / 2 = \underline{\$9,508}$$

The calculation: $\dfrac{\text{Average credit card receivables}}{\text{Total credit card sales revenue}} = \dfrac{\$9,508}{\$752,128} = \underline{\underline{1.3\%}}$

This ratio defines credit card receivables remaining uncollected on a given day of operations; it averages only 1.3% of total credit card sales revenue. In addition, this low percentage of average credit card receivables indicates an apparent short collection period for credit card receivables. In our example, credit card sales revenue represents 64% of total credit sales revenue; thus, $0.64 of each dollar of sales revenue is generated through credit card sales. This method also allows the determination of monthly average credit card receivables for a seasonal operation.

The equation to show only the relationship of average credit card receivables and accounts receivable as a percentage of total credit sales using information in Exhibit 4.2:

**Total sales revenue × (Credit card sales revenue %
+ Accounts receivable sales %) = Total credit sales**

**The calculation: $1,175,200 × (64% + 10%)
= $1,175,200 × 74% = $869,648**

**Average credit card receivables / Total credit sales revenue
$9,508 / $869,648 = 1.1%**

By combining all credit sales revenue regardless of category into a single sum of total credit sales revenue, the original estimate of credit card receivables has decreased from 1.3% of total credit card sales revenue to 1.1% of total credit sales because of the inclusion of accounts receivable sales revenue of $117,520. However, the example showing credit card receivables as a percentage of total credit sales revenue fails to recognize that credit card sales revenue is $0.64 per dollar of total sales revenue.

By not discriminating the differences between credit card sales revenue and accounts receivable sales revenue, the skewing effect is further amplified, which prevents the determination of an accurate estimate of all categories of receivables created by total credit sales revenue.

The ultimate skewing of credit card receivables occurs when any reference to credit sales revenue is omitted from the calculation. The ratio to express credit card receivables as a percentage of total sales revenue, which excludes both forms of credit sales revenue, is

Average credit card receivables / Total sales revenue =
9,508 / 1,175,200 = 0.8%

In this calculation, the sources of credit sales revenue that total 74% of sales revenue (64% credit card sales and 10% of accounts receivable sales) have been eliminated. The percentage of credit card receivables and accounts receivable based on total credit sales revenue or total sales revenue is less accurate and less meaningful. *Use of average credit card receivables as a percentage of credit card sales revenue* rather than total credit sales revenue or total sales revenue provides the most accurate and meaningful results.

Credit Card Receivables Turnover Ratios

The turnover ratio expresses the relationship of credit card sales revenue to average credit card receivables and is the inverse of the previous ratio. The **credit card receivables turnover ratio** describes the average number of times during an annual operating period that the repetitive cycle of earning credit card sales revenue and their reimbursement occurred. As with the ratio previously discussed, the operating period can be changed to monthly, quarterly, or annually to calculate this ratio. The ratio doesn't change for monthly, quarterly, or annual calculations; just the figure changes. The equation is in the box on the following page.

The skewing continues and is easily apparent. The calculated turnover ratio for credit card receivables is 79.1 times per year; however, if total credit sales revenue or total sales revenue were used, the turnover ratio increases to 91.5 times per year and 123.6 times per year, respectively. The average credit card collection period will convert the annual turnover ratios from times per year to the number of days for the average collection of credit card receivables.

Credit card turnover ratio = Total credit card sales revenue
/ Average credit card receivables

The calculation: $\dfrac{\text{Total credit card sales revenue}}{\text{Average credit card receivables}}$

$$= \dfrac{(\$1,175,200 \times 64\%) = \$752,128}{\$9,508} = \underline{79.1} \text{ times}$$

If only total credit sales revenue is available, the equation is modified to:

Total credit sales revenue / Average credit card receivables

The calculation: $\dfrac{\text{Total credit sales revenue}}{\text{Average credit card receivables}}$

$$= \dfrac{(1,175,200 \times 74\%) = \$869,648}{\$9,508} = \underline{\underline{91.5}} \text{ times}$$

If only total sales revenue is available, the equation is modified to:

Total sales revenue / Average credit card receivables

The calculation: $\dfrac{\text{Total sales revenue}}{\text{Average credit card receivables}}$

$$= \dfrac{\$1,175,200}{\$9,508} = \underline{\underline{123.6}} \text{ times}$$

Average Credit Card Collection Period

This ratio uses the credit card turnover ratio to create an understandable correlation to the repetitive cycle of credit card sales revenue and the collection of credit card receivables over an operating period in days. In essence, this collection ratio tells us the average number of days it is taking to collect on credit card receivables.

The equation to calculate the annual average credit card collection period, when credit card sales revenue is used is as follows:

Collection period = 365 days / Credit card receivables turnover ratio

To calculate the average credit card collection period for a month or a quarter, the equation is

Days in the period / Credit card receivables turnover ratio for the period

$$\text{The annual calculation: } \frac{365}{79.1} = \underline{\underline{4.6}} \text{ days}$$

Comparing the average collection period based on total credit sales revenue and total sales revenue shows the skewing effect:

Based on total credit sales revenue:

$$\text{The calculation: } \frac{365 \text{ days}}{\text{Credit card turnover ratio}} = \frac{365}{91.5} = \underline{\underline{4.0}} \text{ days}$$

Based on total sales revenue:

$$\text{The calculation: } \frac{365 \text{ days}}{\text{Credit card turnover ratio}} = \frac{365}{123.6} = \underline{\underline{3.0}} \text{ days}$$

Another method to calculate the annual credit card receivables collection period is

(Average credit card receivables / Total credit card sales revenue) $\times$ 365 days

$$\text{The calculation: } (\$9,508 / \$752,128) = 1.44\% \times 365 = \underline{\underline{4.6}} \text{ days}$$

The credit card collection period indicates the average number of days to collect credit card receivables from credit card companies. As discussed earlier, the collection period on average ranges from 1.0 to 3.0 days and should average 2.0 days. It is wise to set up subsidiary accounts for each card company that will identify which companies are not paying within the average of 2.0 days. It is wise to determine the average days taken by each credit card accepted. It would not be unusual to find that at least one credit card company is taking from 6 to 10 days to reimburse.

ACCOUNTS RECEIVABLE RATIOS

Although accounts receivable is decreasing due to increasing use of credit cards, they will continue to be used. Our discussion of accounts receivable ratios will follow the same approach used for credit card ratios. The skewing effect shown for credit card receivables will also apply to accounts receivable; however, they will not be illustrated in depth for accounts receivable. The three basic ratios that analyze accounts receivable use average accounts receivable and accounts receivable sales revenue:

1. Accounts receivable as a percentage of accounts receivable credit sales revenue
2. Accounts receivable turnover
3. Accounts receivable average collection period

Accounts Receivable as a Percentage of Accounts Receivable Credit Sales Revenue

This ratio is best expressed as accounts receivable as a percentage of accounts receivable credit sales revenue. Normally, this ratio provides information for an annual operating period, but it can also be used for monthly, quarterly, and semiannual periods to evaluate accounts receivable. If cash and credit card sales and accounts receivable credit sales revenue are not maintained separately within the total sales revenue figure, a historical percentage of credit sales revenue to total sales revenue may be used. However, use of historical information is a last alternative because historical information may easily produce inaccurate results since the relationship between cash, credit card sales revenue, and accounts receivable sales revenue may have changed. Thus, the ratios will produce the best and most accurate evaluation of average accounts receivable if accounts receivable credit sales revenue is used.

The values in Exhibit 4.1 and Exhibit 4.2 are used in the discussion of accounts receivable ratios. The equation to find accounts receivable as a percentage of accounts receivable credit sales revenue is

(Beginning accounts receivable + Ending accounts receivable) / 2
= Average accounts receivable

($5,983 + $6,882) / 2 = $12,865 / 2 = $6,433

The calculation: $\dfrac{\text{Average accounts receivables}}{\text{Accounts receivable credit sales revenue}} = \dfrac{\$6,433}{\$117,520} = 5.5\%$

The ratio tells us that over the year an average of 5.5% of accounts receivable credit sales revenue was in the form of accounts receivable during any given day of operations. In a drive-in, cash-only operation, this ratio would obviously be zero%. If a private club permits only internal charge transactions with members being billed monthly, accounts receivable as a percentage of sales revenue could range from 12 to 20%. In a typical hotel or restaurant operation, some customers will pay cash, the majority will pay by credit card, and a few customers may have access to a house account or accounts receivable. While credit card use may easily represent 40 to 65% of total sales revenue, house accounts or accounts receivable could represent 10 to 15% of total sales revenue.

These figures represent industry averages, but an organization should be most concerned with information regarding existing trends within its own operation, not a comparison with industry averages.

The procedure discussed on an annual basis uses the beginning accounts receivable plus the ending accounts receivable, divided by 2. Earlier, we discussed the best method for a seasonal operation with highly fluctuating sales revenue. Adding each month's accounts receivable and dividing by 12 months may best calculate the annual average accounts receivable. Average accounts receivable can also be calculated on a monthly, quarterly, or semiannual basis. Although far from being the best method, an annual ratio could be calculated using total credit sales revenue or total sales revenue rather than accounts receivable credit sales revenue. If one of these methods is used, the ratios will be skewed and will not produce the best results, as shown next. Use of total credit sales revenue or total sales revenue should be avoided if at all possible.

Average accounts receivable / Total credit sales revenue

$$= \textbf{Average accts. rec. \%}$$

$$\frac{\$6,433}{\$869,648} = \underline{\underline{\textbf{0.8\%}}}$$

Average accounts receivable / Total sales revenue

$$\frac{\$6,433}{\$1,175,200} = \underline{\underline{\textbf{0.5\%}}}$$

In a cash-only operation, it is obvious that accounts receivable would not exist. However, for a private club that permits only credit charge transactions, billing each member at the month-end, the accounts receivable as a percentage of sales revenue may be as high as 10% to 15%. Updated industry averages exist, but what is most important is the trend of the figures within hospitality operations. The use of either total credit sales revenue or total sales revenue will show the percentage of credit card receivables on any given day of operations over the operating year. However, the use of credit sales rather than total sales provides the best and most accurate results.

Note the calculation of average accounts receivable uses the same basic method that was used to find average credit card receivables—beginning accounts receivable plus ending accounts receivable divided by 2. Also note that using the information in Exhibits 4.1 and 4.2, you can only calculate the accounts receivable ratios for Year 0007.

Accounts Receivable Turnover

The **accounts receivable turnover** ratio equation reverses the previous equation:

Accounts receivable turnover ratio = Total accounts receivable

credit sales revenue / Average accounts receivable

The calculation:

$$\frac{\textbf{Total accounts receivable credit sales revenue}}{\textbf{Average accounts receivable}} = \frac{\$117,520}{\$6,433} = \underline{\underline{\textbf{18.3 times}}}$$

Depending on the volume of accounts receivable, credit sales revenue, and the efficiency of accounts receivable collections, this turnover ratio could vary from 10 to 30 times a year. If this ratio used total credit sales or total sales, the ratio would be highly skewed, as demonstrated earlier. Although it might be difficult to conceptualize the meaning of times per year, this ratio is necessary to calculate an average collection period in days.

Accounts Receivable Average Collection Period

The **accounts receivable average collection period** is the number of days the average receivable remains unpaid. It is calculated as follows:

Accounts receivable average collection period = Days in the period /
Accounts receivable turnover ratio for the period

The annual calculation:

$$\frac{\textbf{365 days}}{\textbf{Accounts receivable turnover ratio}} = \frac{\textbf{365}}{\textbf{18.3}} = \underline{\underline{\textbf{19.9 days}}}$$

The lower the collection period, the more efficient the ability to collect accounts receivable within the business operation. An operation that extends 30-day accounts receivable credit could expect to see an average collection period of 30 to 35 days. An operation extending 15-day accounts receivable credit could see an average collection period of 15 to 20 days. However, if the collection period is 10 days or more beyond the number of days of credit granted, the operation should become concerned and should review its credit collection procedures and reevaluate its credit policies.

To reiterate, the discussion of credit card receivables has emphasized the use of credit card receivable sales revenue rather than total credit or total revenue to produce the best and most accurate results. Examples were shown where total credit sales revenue and total sales revenue replaced credit card and accounts receivable sales revenues. This resulted in skewed ratios, and the skewing was obvious. This skewing will also occur with accounts receivables ratios.

In general, owners and creditors prefer to see a low average collection period or a high turnover ratio on all credit receivables. On the other hand, management prefers a higher average collection period and a lower turnover period as long as the ratios are within or close to the number of days allowed.

LONG-TERM SOLVENCY RATIOS

Solvency ratios are sometimes referred to as **net worth ratios.** Solvency is defined as total tangible assets—that is, total assets excluding nontangible items such as goodwill, less total liabilities. In other words, solvency is usually the same as total stockholders' equity (assuming no intangible assets). Total assets in any business can be financed primarily by either assuming debt (liabilities) or through ownership equity (shares and retained earnings). Solvency ratios show the balance between these two methods of financing. There are three main solvency ratios, each showing this balance in a different way:

1. Total assets to total liabilities ratio
2. Total liabilities to total assets ratio
3. Total liabilities to total stockholders' equity ratio

We need three figures from each year's balance sheet to calculate these ratios.

$A = L + OE$	*Year 0006*	*Year 0007*
Total assets	$839,400	$859,300
Total liabilities	575,500	555,200
Total equity	263,900	304,100

TOTAL ASSETS TO TOTAL LIABILITIES RATIO

The total assets to total liabilities ratio is

Total assets / Total liabilities

$$\text{The calculation, Year 0006: } \frac{\$839,400}{\$575,500} = \underline{\underline{1.46:1}}$$

$$\text{The calculation, Year 0007: } \frac{\$859,300}{\$555,200} = \underline{\underline{1.55:1}}$$

This ratio tells us that in Year 0006 there is $1.46 of assets for each $1.00 of liabilities (debt). Creditors prefer to see this ratio as high as possible; that is, as high as 2:1 or more. The higher the ratio, the more security they have. They want to be assured that they will recover the full amount owed them in the event of bankruptcy or liquidation of the business. If the ratio sinks below 1:1, it could mean that if bankruptcy occurred, they might not recover the full amount owed them. In bankruptcy cases, the value of assets decreases rapidly. This is known as **asset shrinkage;** it occurs because the value of many of the productive assets declines when those assets are not employed in a going concern. In the situation illustrated, note that in Year 0007 the ratio improves (from the point of view of the creditors) to $1.55 for each dollar of debt liabilities.

The total assets to total liabilities ratio is traditionally based on assets at their book value. If a hotel or food service operation includes its land and buildings at book value in this calculation, the ratio could be misleading. Land and buildings frequently appreciate (increase in value) over time. Therefore, a total assets to total liabilities ratio based on the **book value** of assets showing a result as low as 1:1 may not be as bad as it seems from the creditors' point of view. If assets were used at fair market or replacement value, the ratio would probably improve and then show a comfortable **margin of safety.**

TOTAL LIABILITIES TO TOTAL ASSETS RATIO

The total liabilities to total assets ratio is the reverse of the total assets to total liabilities ratio. These figures are extracted from Exhibit 4.1.

$$\textbf{Total liabilities / Total assets}$$

$$\text{The calculation, Year 0006: } \frac{\$575,500}{\$839,400} = \underline{\underline{0.69:1}}$$

$$\text{The calculation, Year 0007: } \frac{\$555,200}{\$859,300} = \underline{\underline{0.65:1}}$$

This ratio tells us that in Year 0006, $1.00 of assets was financed by debt of $0.69 (the balance of $0.31 was financed by equity). In Year 0007, each $1.00 of assets was financed by $0.65 of debt and $0.35 of equity. Traditionally, the hospitality industry has been financed in a range between $0.60 to $0.90 of debt and $0.10 to $0.40 of equity. As debt financing reaches the higher number ($0.90 out of each $1.00), it becomes more and more difficult to raise money by debt. The risk is higher for the lender; therefore, potential money lenders are more difficult to find. Again, this ratio is based on assets at book value. If fair market or replacement value of assets were used (assuming that this value is higher than book value), then the ratio would decline and would perhaps more realistically present the true situation.

TOTAL LIABILITIES TO TOTAL EQUITY RATIO

Sometimes known as the **debt to equity ratio,** the total liabilities to total equity ratio figures are extracted from Exhibit 4.1.

$$\textbf{Total liabilities / Total equity}$$

$$\text{The calculation, Year 0006: } \frac{\$575,500}{\$263,900} = \underline{\underline{2.18:1}}$$

$$\text{The calculation, Year 0007: } \frac{\$555,200}{\$304,100} = \underline{\underline{1.83:1}}$$

This ratio tells us that in Year 0006, for each $1.00 the stockholders have invested, the creditors have invested $2.18. In Year 0007, the comparable figures are stockholders $1.00 and creditors $1.83. The higher the creditors' investment for each $1.00 of stockholders' investment, the higher is the risk for the creditor. In such circumstances, if a hotel or food service operation wished to expand, debt financing would be more difficult to obtain and interest rates would be higher.

The risk situation can perhaps be explained with some simple figures. Total assets equal total liabilities plus owners' equity. Assume total assets are $100,000, total liabilities are $50,000, and owners' equity is $50,000.

$$\textbf{Debt to equity ratio} = \frac{\textbf{Total liabilities}}{\textbf{Total equity}} = \frac{\textbf{\$50,000}}{\textbf{\$50,000}}$$
$$= \underline{\underline{\textbf{1:1}}} \textbf{ (or \$1.00 of liabilities to \$1.00 of equity)}$$

Under these circumstances, total assets of $100,000 could decline by 50%, to $50,000, before the creditors would be running a serious risk. Assume, with the same total assets of $100,000, that total liabilities are $65,000 and ownership equity $35,000.

$$\textbf{Debt to equity ratio} = \frac{\textbf{Total liabilities}}{\textbf{Total equity}} = \frac{\textbf{\$65,000}}{\textbf{\$35,000}}$$
$$= \underline{\underline{\textbf{1.86:1}}} \textbf{ (or \$1.86 of liabilities to \$1.00 of equity)}$$

With this higher debt to equity ratio, the assets could only decline 35% (as opposed to 50%) in value, from $100,000 to $65,000, before the creditors would be facing a difficult situation. This is much riskier from the creditors' point of view.

Therefore, although the creditors prefer not to have the debt to equity ratio too high, the hotel or food service owner often finds it more profitable to have it as high as possible. A high debt to equity ratio is known as having high financial leverage or trading on the equity. Financial leverage will be discussed in a later section of this chapter.

NUMBER OF TIMES INTEREST EARNED

Another way of looking at the margin of safety in meeting debt interest payments is to calculate the number of times per year interest is earned:

$$\textbf{Times interest earned} = \frac{\textbf{Income before interest and income tax}}{\textbf{Interest expense}}$$

$$\textbf{The calculation, Year 0007: \$95,162 / \$26,044} = \underline{\underline{\textbf{3.65}}} \textbf{ times}$$

The number of times interest earned ratio is considered satisfactory if interest is earned two or more times a year. Creditors, owners, and management all like

to see this ratio as high as possible. To creditors, a high number indicates a reduction of their risk and shows that the establishment will be able to meet its
regular loan interest payments when due. To owners, a high number is also desirable, particularly if the establishment has a high debt to equity ratio. Therefore, management also prefers a high ratio because it pleases each of the other
two groups. Note, however, that if this ratio is extremely high it might indicate
that financial leverage is not being maximized.

PROFITABILITY RATIOS

The main objective of most hospitality operations is to generate a profit. In a
partnership or proprietorship, the owner(s) can withdraw profit from the business
entity to increase personal net worth, or profit can be left in the business to expand
it. In an incorporated company, the profit can be paid out in dividends or be retained in the business to expand it, increase the profits further, or improve the value
of the owners' equity investment in the company. Creditors of a company also like
to see increases in the business's profit, because the higher the profits, the less the
risk is to them as lenders. Therefore, one of the main tasks of management is to
ensure continued profitability of the enterprise. Profitability ratios are most often
used to measure management's effectiveness in achieving profitability.

Caution needs to be exercised in the use of the word **profitability.** A company might have a net income on its income statement, and this net income, expressed as a percentage of sales revenue, might seem acceptable. However, the
relationship between this net income and other items (e.g., the amount of money
invested by stockholders) may not be acceptable or sufficiently profitable.

The figures used in the discussion of the following profitability ratios are
extracted from Exhibit 4.1 and Exhibit 4.2.

GROSS RETURN ON ASSETS

The **gross return on assets** ratio (also known as return on assets) measures the
effectiveness of management's use of the organization's assets:

Return on assets = Income before interest and income tax
/ Total average assets

$$\text{Total average assets} = (\$839,400 + \$859,300) / 2$$
$$= \$1,698,700 / 2 = \underline{\$849,350}$$

$$\text{Return on assets} = \$95,162 / \$849,350 = \underline{11.2\%}$$

If the figures fluctuated widely during the year because of such factors as
the purchase and sale of long-term assets, and if monthly figures were avail-

able, the average should be calculated by adding each of the monthly figures and dividing by 12.

Interest and income tax are added back to net income in the equation to compare the resulting percentage (in our case, 11.2%) to the current market interest rate. For instance, if in our example, an expansion of the building were contemplated and the money could be borrowed at a 10% interest rate, one could assume that the new asset would earn a rate of return of 11.2% and it would be better than the 10% interest rule. Although small, this would leave 1.2% to increase the business's income before income tax.

NET RETURN ON ASSETS

The *gross return on assets* calculation measures management's effectiveness in its use of assets and is also useful in assessing the likelihood of obtaining more debt financing for expansion. The **net return on assets,** by contrast, evaluates the advisability of seeking equity, as opposed to debt financing. Using information from Exhibits 4.1 and 4.2, we can calculate net return on assets:

Net return on assets = Net income after income tax / Total average assets

The calculation: $48,383 / $849,350 = 5.7%

Since cash dividends or cash withdrawals are payable from net income earnings after tax, financing a building with stockholders' equity (or capital) would not lead to a very good dividend yield for stockholders. Based on current results, assets are yielding a net return of only 5.7%, and stockholders (or proprietary owners) would most likely assume that the new assets would earn the same net rate of return as the old assets. This might be a poor assumption, since the old assets are at book (depreciated) value. If the calculation were made on assets at their replacement or market value, the rate could well drop below 5.7%. Under these circumstances, management would have to improve its performance considerably to convince stockholders (or proprietary owners) to invest more money for an expansion.

NET INCOME TO SALES REVENUE RATIO

The **net income to sales revenue ratio** (also known as the **profit margin**) measures management's overall effectiveness in generating sales and controlling expenses:

Profit margin = Net income after income tax / Sales revenue

The calculation: $48,383 / $1,175,200 = 4.1%

This means that, out of each $1.00 of sales revenue, we had 4.1 cents net income. In absolute terms, this might not be very meaningful, because it does not truly reflect the profitability of the firm. Consider the following two cases, using assumed values:

	Case A	*Case B*
Sales revenue	$100,000	$100,000
Net income	5,000	10,000
Net income to revenue ratio	5.0%	10.0%

With the same sales revenue, it seems that Case B is a better situation. In Case B, the organization is producing twice as much net income, in absolute terms, as is the organization in Case A ($10,000 to $5,000). This doubling of net income is supported by the net income to sales revenue ratio (10.0% to 5.0%). If these were two similar firms, or two branches of the same firm, these figures would indicate the relative effectiveness of the management of each in controlling costs and generating a satisfactory level of net income. However, to determine the profitability of Case A to Case B, we need to relate the net income to the investment to find the return on owners' equity (ROE):

	Case A	*Case B*
Sales revenue	$100,000	$100,000
Net income	5,000	10,000
Net income to sales revenue ratio	5%	10%
Owners' equity	$40,000	$80,000
Profitability (ROE)	$\dfrac{\$5,000}{\$40,000} = 12.5\%$	$\dfrac{\$10,000}{\$80,000} = 12.5\%$

As can now be seen, despite the wide difference in net income and net income to sales revenue ratio, there is no difference between the two organizations as far as profitability as measured by ROE is concerned: they are both equally good, returning 12.5% on owners' equity.

RETURN ON OWNERS' EQUITY

There are many equations and definitions for return on investment. Should we use (1) income before income tax, (2) income before interest and income tax, or (3) net income after tax? Is the investment (A) the book value of assets, (B) the replacement or market value of the assets, (C) the total investment of debt and equity, or (D) only the stockholders' equity? Perhaps the most useful definition of return on investment is to use net income after income tax—since dividends can only be paid out of after-tax profits—and relate that net income to the stockholders' investment. It is to this group of people, the stockholders or owners, that operating management is primarily responsible.

Return on stockholders' equity = Net income after income tax
/ Average stockholders' equity

Average stockholders' equity: ($263,900 + $304,100) / 2
= $568,000 / 2 = $284,000

The calculation: $48,383 / $284,000 = 17%

This percentage shows the effectiveness of management's use of equity funds, and at 17.0% is highly satisfactory. How high should it be? This is a matter of personal opinion. If an investor could put money either into the bank at an 8% interest rate or into a hotel investment at 10% but with more risk involved, the current investment (17.0% return) might be the best option, with the bank being the next best choice. Even though the hotel investment has a higher return, it is riskier, so is likely the least attractive option.

If the business had issued both preferred and common stock, the return on stockholders' equity equation can be modified, with the numerator becoming net income less preferred dividends and the denominator becoming average common stockholders' equity. To the common stockholders, preferred stock is a form of debt on which a fixed dividend rate must be paid. To the extent that borrowing from preferred stockholders enhances profits and the added profits exceed the fixed rate of dividends paid to preferred stockholders, the additional earnings accruing to the common stockholders will be improved.

OTHER PROFITABILITY RATIOS

Other measures of profitability include annual earnings per share (EPS), dividend rate per share, and book value per share. Such ratios are of most concern to those buying and selling publicly traded stock on the open market and are of less concern to the internal management of the firm. However, management is held accountable by stockholders for producing a net income satisfactory to them, and the **earnings per share** ratio is frequently used to measure net income. The earnings per share ratio is also important because it tends to dictate the value of the shares in the market and indicates the desirability of purchasing the stock of the company to a potential purchaser. Assume there are 40,000 shares outstanding at both the beginning and the end of the year.

EPS = Net income after income tax
/ Average number of common shares outstanding

The average number of shares outstanding is:

(Beginning common shares + Ending common shares) / 2 was 40,000

$$\text{Then EPS} = \frac{\$48,383}{40,000} = \underline{\underline{\$1.21}}$$

If both common and preferred stock have been issued, this equation has to be modified. The numerator will be net income (after tax) less preferred dividends. The denominator will be average number of common shares outstanding.

Note that earnings per share can be increased over time by not paying out all earnings as dividends to shareholders. By retaining all net income and by not paying dividends, the increases to retained earnings can be reinvested to expand the business. Therefore, the number of shares outstanding will be held constant and future profits (earnings) will be increased.

CREDITORS, OWNERS, AND MANAGEMENT

In general, all three groups (creditors, owners, and management) interested in financial ratios prefer to see profitability ratios high and growing rather than low and stable. Creditors will be interested in a ratio such as return on assets, particularly if it is increasing, because this indicates management's effectiveness in its use of all assets and reduces the creditors' risk.

However, the ratio of most interest to owners is return on their equity investment, because they can easily compare this ratio with the return they might receive from alternative investments. In publicly traded companies, if equity investors are not satisfied with their return, they can remove their investment by selling their shares in the stock market and purchasing shares in more profitable companies. If many equity investors with large shareholdings do this, it will depress the market price of the shares. In turn, this will make it more difficult for the company to raise capital money when needed in the future because there will be a reluctance by potential investors to buy the new shares. Stock market investors often measure the value of a share by its **price/earnings ratio,** calculated as follows:

$$\text{P/E} = \frac{\textbf{Market price per share}}{\textbf{Earnings per share}}$$

If the market price of the shares were $10.00, our price/earnings ratio would be computed as follows:

$$\text{P/E} = \frac{\$10.00}{\$1.21} = \underline{\underline{8.26 \text{ times}}}$$

The price/earnings ratio for any specific hospitality company's shares is affected by how buyers and sellers of those shares perceive the stability and/or trend of earnings, the potential growth of earnings, and the risk of investing in those shares.

Management's task is to maintain all profitability ratios at as high a level as possible so that both creditors and owners (investors) are satisfied. The level of that satisfaction in this regard will measure management's effectiveness.

ACTIVITY RATIOS

Activity ratios (sometimes known as **turnover** or efficiency ratios) are calculated to determine the activity of certain classes of assets, such as inventories for resale, working capital, and long-term assets. The ratios express the number of times that an activity (turnover) is occurring during a certain period and can help in measuring management's effectiveness in using and controlling these assets.

INVENTORY TURNOVER RATIO

Inventory turnover ratios are discussed in some detail in the section on cash conservation and working capital management in Chapter 11. For our purpose, only the basic turnover ratio and the subsequent ratio to determine the number of day's inventory is held will be discussed at this point.

Inventory turnover = Cost of sales for the period
                            / Average inventory during the period

Inventory turnover can be determined on a monthly, quarterly, semiannual, or yearly basis. We will assume the following information regarding inventory for the month of March 2008 is as follows:

> **Food inventory on March 1:**   **$ 8,434**
> **Food inventory on March 31:**   **$ 6,870**
> **Cost of sales for March:**   **$55,700**
> **Average inventory = ($8,434 + $6,870) / 2 = $15,304 / 2 = $7,652**
> **The calculation: $55,700 / $7,652 = 7.3 times during March**

INVENTORY HOLDING PERIOD (AVERAGE DAYS FOR INVENTORY TO TURN OVER)

The inventory turnover ratio expresses the number of times during a given period that inventory is theoretically brought to zero. A further analysis will establish the number of days it takes the inventory to turn over during a given period. Using the preceding inventory ratio for March 2008, the equation to convert inventory turnover to days is

$$\frac{\textbf{Operating days for the period}}{\textbf{Inventory turnover ratio for the period}}$$

The calculation: 31 days / 7.3 times = <u>4.25</u> days

Food and beverage inventories will vary based on the geographical area and the size of the city or towns within a given geographical area. Food turnover on average will normally vary between two and four times a month. Beverage turnover varies from one to four times per month. Individual operations should determine in each case the turnover rate appropriate to the area in which the establishment operates (since there are major exceptions to these guidelines), and then watch for deviations from those rates. The turnover rate of 4.25 days is quite fast compared to the standard just stated. However, if this is a fast-food operation in a chain, this turnover rate would be typical.

WORKING CAPITAL TURNOVER

The working capital turnover ratio is a measure of the effectiveness of the use of working capital. **Working capital** is current assets less current liabilities. Our balance sheet (Exhibit 4.1) gives us the following:

	Year 0006	*Year 0007*
Current assets	$73,370	$79,090
Current liabilities	(62,700)	(68,400)
Working capital	$10,670	$10,690

Working capital turnover = Total sales revenue

/ Average working capital

[Average working capital = ($10,670 + $10,690) / 2

= $21,360 / 2 = <u>$10,680</u>]

The calculation: $1,175,200 / $10,680 = <u>110.0</u> times

The ratio calculated based on data from Exhibit 4.1 is rather high. However, this ratio can vary widely, based on geographical locations. In general, the rapidly increased use of credit cards relative to accounts receivable has had the effect of increasing working capital turnover ratios. Normally, the ratio may be as low as 12 times per year (for a restaurant) or as high as 50 times or more a year (for a hotel).

A hospitality operation should probably try to find its most appropriate level of working capital and then compare future performance with this optimum level. Too much working capital (that is, too low a turnover ratio) means ineffective use of funds. Too little working capital (indicated by too high a turnover ratio) may lead to cash difficulties if sales revenue begins to decline.

Note also that, all other factors being equal, the higher the working capital turnover ratio, the lower will be the current ratio. This means that if an establishment has little or no credit sales revenue and a very low level of inventory (e.g., a motel doing cash-only business), it will have both a low current ratio and a high working capital turnover. Thus, with reference to the earlier section on the current ratio, creditors prefer a low working capital turnover, owners prefer a high turnover, and management tries to maintain a reasonable balance between the two extremes to maximize profits by reducing the amount of money tied up in current assets, while maintaining sufficient liquidity to take care of unanticipated emergencies requiring cash.

FIXED ASSET TURNOVER

The **fixed asset turnover** ratio assesses the effectiveness of the use of fixed assets in generating sales revenue. Exhibit 4.1 provides the figures.

$$\text{Fixed asset turnover = Total sales revenue / Total average fixed assets}$$

$$\text{Total average fixed assets} = (\$766{,}030 + \$780{,}210) / 2$$
$$= \$1{,}546{,}240 / 2 = \underline{\$773{,}120}$$

$$\text{The calculation: } \$1{,}175{,}200 / \$773{,}120 = \underline{1.52} \text{ times}$$

In the hotel industry, this turnover rate could vary from as low as 1.5 to as high as 2.0 or more times per year. In the food service industry, a restaurant could have a turnover of 4 to 5 times a year, assuming it is in rented premises. The reason the turnover rate is lower for a hotel is that it has, relatively speaking, a much higher investment in public space (lobbies, corridors) and in guest rooms (the capacity of which cannot be changed in the short run) than does a restaurant. A restaurant can increase its fixed asset turnover rate by increasing the number of seats or, if the demand is there, serving more customers during each meal period.

A high fixed asset turnover ratio indicates management's effectiveness in its use of fixed assets, whereas a low ratio indicates either that management is not effective or that some of those assets should be disposed of to increase the ratio. All groups (creditors, owners, and management) like to see the ratio as high as possible. One problem with this ratio, however, is that the older the assets are (and the more accumulated depreciation there is), the lower is their net book value. This automatically tends to increase the fixed asset turnover ratio. In addition, the use of an accelerated depreciation method hastens this process. Thus, management should resist the temptation to continue to use old and inefficient fixed assets and/or to use an accelerated depreciation method to create a high fixed asset turnover.

One of the uses of this ratio is in evaluating new projects. If the current turnover for a restaurant is 4, and a new project costing $250,000 is going to generate $750,000 in sales revenue, giving a turnover of only 3 ($750,000 divided by $250,000), then the new project may not be acceptable or sufficiently profitable.

OPERATING RATIOS

There are a number of other sales revenue and cost analysis techniques and tools available apart from those already mentioned. These are **operating ratios**— key business ratios that are often calculated daily. Some of the more common ones are discussed briefly in the next section. Caution must be exercised in their use. It is not only important to select the appropriate analysis tool, it is also important to remember that the information provided from the use of these techniques may only indicate that a problem exists. The solution to the problem is entirely in the hands of management.

FOOD AND BEVERAGE OPERATIONS

Food and/or Beverage Cost Percentage

This is expressed as a percentage of the related sales revenue as illustrated and discussed in the previous chapter using Exhibit 3.4. The cost percentages can be compared with a standard or predetermined cost percentage established as a goal in the forecasted operating budget. Any major deviations from standard to actual cost percentages should be investigated.

Labor Cost Percentage

Labor cost includes employee benefits and is expressed as a percentage of the related sales revenue. With reference to Exhibit 3.4, in Year 0006 and Year 0007, we can calculate the labor cost percentage as follows:

Labor cost percentage = (Salaries and wages + Employee benefits) / Total sales revenue

Year 0006: ($277,400 + $34,500) / $851,600
= $311,900 / $851,600 = 36.6%

Year 0007: ($304,500 + $37,800) / $869,100
= $342,300 / $869,100 = 39.4%

As with food and beverage cost percentages, labor cost percentages can be compared with established standard cost percentages. Again, large differences between standard and actual cost percentages should be investigated.

Dollars of Sales Revenue

This ratio may be expressed in per-employee terms on a per-meal period, per-day period, per-week period, or per-month period. For example, if a restaurant had sales revenue for a meal period of $1,200, and 100 guests were served by eight employees, the average dollars of sales revenue per server for a given meal period would be

Meal period sales revenue / Meal period servers

= $1,200 / 8 = $150 sales revenue per server

The average number of guests served per server:

(Guests served / Number of servers) = 100 / 8 = 12.5 guests per server

These ratios are used primarily to assess employee productivity against a standard or to determine any upward or downward trend in productivity.

Average Food and/or Beverage Check by Meal Period and by Sales Revenue Area

The method of calculating the average check was explained in Chapter 3. The trend of this figure is important, but it can also be used to determine, for example, the effect that a change in menu item(s) may have on an average customer's spending.

Seat Turnover by Meal Period or by Day

Seat turnover is calculated by dividing total guests served during a meal period or a day by the number of seats the restaurant has. For example, if a restaurant had 40 seats and 100 guests were served during a given meal period, the seat turnover for that meal period would be calculated as follows:

Seat turnover = 100 guests / 40 seats = 2.5

A high turnover is generally preferable to a low one, as long as the customers are receiving good service and not being rushed. The trend of turnovers should be analyzed. A declining trend may indicate a lowering of service or may indicate that high prices or low-quality food are keeping customers away.

Daily, Weekly, Monthly, or Annual Sales Revenue Dollars per Available Seat

Sales revenue per seat is calculated by dividing revenue for the period by the number of seats the restaurant has. For example, if a 125-seat restaurant had monthly revenue of $250,000, monthly revenue per seat is

(Monthly sales revenue / Total seats) = $250,000 / 125

= **$2,000** sales revenue per seat

The trend of this figure can be revealing. It might also be useful to compare it with the results for similar types of establishments. However, if the guest buys a drink for $4.00 instead of a food item for $8.00, you are likely better off to sell the food item because the dollar contribution margin is higher although the percent contribution margin is lower.

Percentage of Beverage Sales Revenue to Food Sales Revenue

For example, a restaurant had total monthly sales revenue of $85,160, of which food was $68,950 and beverages were $16,210. Beverages are 23.5% of food revenue, calculated as follows:

(Beverage sales revenue / Food sales revenue)

= **$16,210 / $68,950** = **23.5%**

Since beverage sales revenue is generally more profitable than food sales revenue, sales efforts should be directed toward promoting beverage revenue (wine with meals, for example) to increase the ratio.

Percentage of Beverage Sales Revenue and/or Food Revenue to Rooms Sales Revenue

This would apply to a hotel. The calculation is similar to the percentage to sales revenue example shown for the previous ratio. In this case, the room sales revenue becomes the denominator, and the numerator is either food or beverage sales revenue. A change in the revenue sales mix among departments (as indicated by a change in the percentages) can be important because some departments are more profitable than others. Advertising dollars are often more beneficially spent, from a cost/benefit point of view, on departments or areas with the highest gross margin or profitability before operating expenses.

ROOMS DEPARTMENT IN A HOTEL OR MOTEL

Average Rate per Occupied Room

The **average room rate** may be calculated on a daily, a monthly, or an annual basis by dividing sales revenue by rooms occupied for the specific period. For example, if a hotel had total room sales revenue for a given night of $7,200 from 80 rooms occupied, the average daily rate per occupied room is

Average rate per occupied room

= **(Daily room revenue / Daily rooms occupied)** = **$7,200 / 80** = **$90**

If this ratio is to be calculated on a monthly or annual basis, we use the same equation as shown for a daily room rate, substituting monthly or annual figures for the daily numbers. The trend of this figure is important. It can be influenced upward by directing sales efforts into selling higher-priced rooms rather than lower-priced ones, by increasing the rate of double occupancy, or by altering other factors.

Sales Revenue per Available Room (REVPAR)

A hotel's occupancy percentage and average room rate have traditionally been the tools used to measure the rooms department's performance. By themselves, each of these tools has limited value. For example, Hotel A with 200 rooms might have an average occupancy rate of 80% and an average daily room rate of $70, while Hotel B, also with 200 rooms, has an average occupancy rate of 70% and an average daily room rate of $85. All other things being equal, which is the better performing hotel? The answer to this question is difficult to determine without knowing the room sales **revenue per available room** (usually abbreviated to **REVPAR**), calculated as follows:

REVPAR = (Total rooms revenue / Total rooms available)

Hotel A: (200 × 80% × $70 × 365) / (200 × 365)
$$= \$4,088,000 / 73,000 = \underline{\underline{\$56.00}}$$

Hotel B: (200 × 70% × $85 × 365) / (200 × 365)
$$= \$4,343,500 / 73,000 = \underline{\underline{\$59.50}}$$

Or an alternative calculation may be used, following a simplified equation:

REVPAR = (Occupancy percentage × Average room rate)

Using these figures, the relative performance of the two hotels measured in terms of REVPAR is as follows:

Hotel A: 80% × $70 = $56.00
Hotel B: 70% × $85 = $59.50

For measuring performance, REVPAR is thus an improvement over either occupancy percentage or average room rate.

Occupancy Percentage and/or Double Occupancy

A hotel's **occupancy percentage** may be calculated on a daily, weekly, monthly, or annual basis. This ratio is calculated by dividing the rooms occupied during a stated period by the total rooms available during the stated period (rooms available times days in the stated period). For example, if this hotel had 110 rooms, occupancy for a given night is calculated as follows:

Occupancy percentage = (Rooms occupied daily /
Rooms available daily) = 80 / 110 = 72.7%

Double occupancy is based on the rooms sold, not the rooms available. The double occupancy percentage is the percentage of rooms occupied by more than one person. For example, if 80 rooms were occupied on a given night and 20 rooms were occupied by more than one person, the double occupancy rate would be calculated as follows:

Double occupancy rate = (Rooms double occupied daily /
Rooms occupied daily) = 20 / 80 = 25.0%

Double occupancy is sometimes expressed by calculating the average number of people per room occupied (total number of guests for a period divided by total rooms occupied during that period). For example, if 100 guests occupied 80 of the rooms available, the double occupancy rate would be as follows:

Double occupancy rate = (Room guests daily / Rooms occupied daily)
= 100 / 80 = 1.25 average guests per room

Double occupancy is usually higher for resort hotels (catering to families) than for transient hotels (catering primarily to the business person traveling alone).

Obviously, high occupancy and a high double occupancy are both desirable because this indicates greater use of the room's facilities and also potentially greater use of food and beverage facilities by guest room occupants. Therefore, the trend of this information is important.

Note that, when an occupancy percentage is calculated for a period such as a week, it does not mean that the occupancy was the same every night of the week. For example, a hotel could have an average occupancy of 70% for a week and an occupancy rate of more than 90% per night from Monday to Friday but a very low occupancy percentage at the weekend.

Labor Cost Percentage

This percentage is expressed as a percentage of room sales revenue in the same way as was illustrated in the preceding discussion of labor cost percentage for food and beverage operations. It is compared with an established standard.

Number of Rooms Cleaned

This may be calculated in two ways: as rooms per housekeeper per day or dollars of room sales revenue per front desk clerk per day, week, or month. Both productivity measures are calculated in a similar way to the productivity measures illustrated in labor cost percentage for food and beverage operations. These productivity measures can be compared against a standard or used to detect undesirable trends.

Annual Sales Revenue per Available Room

This figure is obtained by dividing annual revenue by the rooms in the establishment. The trend of this figure is important, but it is also useful to compare it with results from similar types of hotels or motels.

Undistributed Cost Dollars per Available Room per Year

Undistributed costs include such expenses as administrative and general, marketing, property operation and maintenance, and energy costs. To determine the ratio, the total annual cost of each undistributed item is divided by the rooms in the establishment. Trends are again important, and comparison with similar establishments' results can be revealing.

MANAGER'S DAILY REPORT

Many of the operating statistics that are useful for analyzing the ongoing progress of an establishment can be calculated on a day-to-day basis. In this way, the success level of the establishment can be monitored daily. Trends, favorable or unfavorable, can be detected while they are occurring, rather than too late for effective action to be taken. Exhibit 4.6 illustrates a sample of a typical **manager's daily report** that would be useful in a small hotel operation. A food operation's operating statistics might be summarized as shown in Exhibit 4.7. Each establishment's management should decide which operating statistics are most useful for getting a daily overview and, subsequently, should prepare a form that will allow these statistics to be summarized quickly each day.

INTERNAL AND EXTERNAL COMPARISONS

Up to this point, only internal comparisons and trends of selected information have been emphasized. A change in selected internal information over time is probably the most meaningful method of seeking out problem areas so that any necessary corrective action can be taken. Nevertheless, external comparisons and trends should not be ignored. Many industrywide external trends are avail-

Day _____ Date _____ Weather _____

	Today	Month to Date	Forecast Month to Date	Last Month to Date	Last Year Month to Date
Rooms					
Food					
Beverage					
Telephone/telegram					
Valet					
Laundry					
Other					
Total revenue					

Statistics

	Today	Month to Date	Forecast Month to Date	Last Month to Date	Last Year Month to Date	Bank Report	
Total rooms occup.						Balance yesterday	
Comps. & house use						Receipts	
Vacant rooms						Disbursements	
Total rooms avail.						Balance today	
Average room rate							
% of occupancy						Accounts Receivable	
No. of doubles						Balance yesterday	
% of double occup.						Charges	
% of food cost						Credits	
% of beverage cost						Balance today	

Payroll and Related Expenses

	Today		Forecast Month to Date		Last Month to Date		Last Year to Date		Month to Date	
	Amount	%	Amount	%	Amount	%	Amount	%	Amount	%
Room										
Food and beverage										
Overhead depts.										

■ **EXHIBIT 4.6**
Hotel Manager's Daily Report

Day _____	Date _____				Weather _____						
	Number of Covers					**Average Check**					
				Totals		*Average Today*			*Check to Date*		
Meals Served:	*Breakfast*	*Lunch*	*Dinner*	*Today*	*to Date*	*Breakfast*	*Lunch*	*Dinner*	*Breakfast*	*Lunch*	*Dinner*
Dining room											
Coffee shop											
Room service											
Banquet											
TOTAL											

■ **EXHIBIT 4.7**
Food Service Daily Report

able that can be useful for comparison with internal results. However, trying to change internal results so they match external industry averages should be done with caution. Industry averages are only that—averages. An average industry figure might not be typical of any specific hotel or food service operation. The management needs to understand why its operation is different from the average operation and what effect that should have on the operation's ratios.

CONCLUDING COMMENTS ON RATIO ANALYSIS

To summarize this discussion of ratios, note these points:

■ *Financial ratios are generally produced from historical accounting information.* As a result, some accounting numbers reflect historic costs rather than present values. An example is a building's cost recorded on the balance sheet at its original purchase price and offset by accumulated depreciation to produce net book value. A ratio based on total assets (such as return on assets) may show a result that is more than acceptable. If it were based on the current replacement cost of those assets, however, it would produce a much more realistic ratio that can then be compared with alternative investments. For this same reason, this type of ratio cannot be readily compared with the ratio for other hospitality companies because they may have purchased their assets at different times or at different costs, and may have used different depreciation methods.

- *Many of the guidelines or rules of thumb given in this chapter on ratio analysis have assumed ownership of all assets.* If assets—particularly land, building, furniture, and equipment—are leased rather than owned, these industry-quoted guidelines must be used with caution. Indeed, rules of thumb should always be used with great care, because every organization that is part of the hospitality industry has unique features. This leads to the next comment.

- *Ratios are only of value when the information related and numbers are compared.* On one hand, for example, the current ratio compares current assets with current liabilities. This is a meaningful comparison. On the other hand, if current assets are compared to owners' equity, this ratio has little value because there is no direct relationship between the two numbers.

- *Although external comparisons of an operation's ratios with industry averages or other similar hotels or food operations are interesting, what is probably of more value is comparing the trend of the operation's ratios over time.* For example, if the working capital turnover ratio is constantly increasing over the years, with little change in sales revenue, this might be more indicative of a problem than the fact that the ratio is different from the industry average.

- *Selectivity is important.* This chapter has tried to include all the ratios that could be useful to a hospitality enterprise. There is no suggestion that a particular operator should use all of them. One should use those that are of benefit in evaluating the results of a business in relation to its objectives.

- *Ratios should not be an end in themselves.* An objective of a company might be to have the happiest stockholders in the world. Emphasis might then be placed solely on increasing net income to the point where the stockholders will see an incredibly large return on their investment. However, the end result might be that, to achieve this, selling prices have been set so high, and expenses cut so low, that the business collapses.

- *Finally, ratios by themselves cure no problems but only indicate possible problems.* For example, the trend of the accounts receivable ratio might show that the time that it is taking to collect the average accounts receivable is becoming longer. That is all the ratio shows. It is only management's analysis of this problem to discover the causes that can correct this deteriorating situation.

FINANCIAL LEVERAGE

Earlier in this chapter, the concept of financial leverage, or trading on the equity, was introduced. To illustrate this, consider the case of a new restaurant that is to be opened at a cost of $250,000 for furnishings, equipment, and working capital. The owners have the cash available, but they are considering not using all their own money. Instead, they wish to compare their relative return on equity if they use either all their own money (100% equity financing) or if they use 50% equity and borrow the other 50% (debt financing) at a 10% interest rate. Regardless of which method they use, sales revenue will be the same, as will all operating costs. With either choice, they will have $50,000 income before interest and taxes. There is no interest expense with the 100% equity financing option. With some debt financing, interest will have to be paid. However, interest expense is tax deductible. Assuming a tax rate of 40% on taxable income, Exhibit 4.8 compares operating results and the return on equity (ROE) based on the initial equity investment.

In Exhibit 4.8, not only do the owners make a better return on their initial investment under Option B (18.0% versus 12.0%), but they also still have $125,000 in cash they can invest in a second venture. In this case, if a 50/50 debt to equity ratio is more profitable than 100% equity financing, would not an 80/20 debt to equity ratio be even more profitable? In other words, what would be the return on initial investment if the owners used only $50,000 of their own money and borrowed the remaining $200,000 required at 10%? Exhibit 4.9 shows the result of this more highly leveraged situation.

Under Option C, Exhibit 4.9, our return on the initial investment has now increased to 36.0%, and we have $200,000 cash still on hand—enough for four more similar restaurant ventures. The advantages of financial leverage are obvious: The higher the debt to equity ratio, the higher will be the owners' return on equity. However, this only holds true if income before interest and income tax is greater than the interest to be paid on the debt. The higher the debt, the higher the risk.

	Option A	Option B
Investment required	$250,000	$250,000
Equity financing	$250,000	$125,000
Debt financing	0	@ 10% $125,000
Income before interest and income tax	$ 50,000	$ 50,000
Interest expense	0	(12,500)
Income before income tax	$ 50,000	$ 37,500
Income tax (@ 40%)	(20,000)	(15,000)
Net income	$ 30,000	$ 22,500
Return on equity	$\dfrac{\$30,000}{\$250,000} = 12.0\%$	$\dfrac{\$22,500}{\$125,000} = 18.0\%$

■ **EXHIBIT 4.8**
Effect of Leverage on ROI

	Option C
Investment required	$250,000
Equity financing	$ 50,000
Debt financing	@ 10% $200,000
Income before interest and income tax	$ 50,000
Interest expense	(20,000)
Income before income tax	$ 30,000
Income tax (@ 40%)	(12,000)
Net income	$ 18,000
Return on equity ($18,000 / $50,000)	36.0%

■ **EXHIBIT 4.9**
Effect of High Leverage on ROI

If income declines, the more highly leveraged a company is, the sooner it will be in financial difficulty. In Option B (relatively low leverage), income before interest and income tax could decline from $50,000 to $12,500 before net income would be zero. In Option C (relatively high leverage), income before interest and income tax could only decline from $50,000 to $20,000 before net income would be zero.

COMPUTER APPLICATIONS

Because most of the ratios discussed in this chapter result from an operation's income statement and balance sheet, if a computer with the appropriate software is used to produce these statements, the ratios can automatically be produced.

In addition to the period-end ratios, a computer allowing the information about the operation's daily operations is also capable of calculating the desired daily operating ratios and can produce a print out of the daily report. For example, if a hotel's night audit is computerized, ratios such as occupancy, double occupancy, average room rate, and sales revenue per available room are automatically calculated.

Restaurants can also keep track of sales, daily purchases, usage, and sales of food—daily and period-to-date food cost is automatically calculated.

Further, if an operation's payroll is computerized and linked to a computerized time clock, each employee's pay rate can be applied to daily hours worked, and total daily labor cost can be calculated by the system. If each day's sales revenues are entered for a department, a daily labor cost percentage can be calculated for cost control purposes.

S U M M A R Y

A number of different ways of expressing ratios were discussed in this chapter, as were four methods of evaluating a ratio: industry averages, competitors' figures, the operation's results from a previous period, and a predetermined standard for the operation. Current liquidity ratios measure a company's ability to meet its short-term obligations. Some of the more common liquidity ratios follow:

1. Current ratio:

$$\frac{\textbf{Current assets}}{\textbf{Current liabilities}}$$

2. Quick (acid test) ratio:

$$\frac{\textbf{Cash + Credit card receivables + Accounts receivable + Marketable securities}}{\textbf{Total current liabilities}}$$

$$or \quad \frac{\textbf{Total current assets − Inventories for resale − Prepaid expenses}}{\textbf{Current liabilities}}$$

3. Credit card receivables as a percentage of credit card sales revenue:

$$\frac{\textbf{Average credit card receivables}}{\textbf{Total credit card sales revenue}}$$

4. Credit card receivables turnover:

$$\frac{\textbf{Total credit card sales revenue}}{\textbf{Average credit card receivables}}$$

5. Average credit cards collection period:

$$\frac{\textbf{Days in the period}}{\textbf{Credit card turnover ratio for the period}}$$

6. Accounts receivable as a percentage of accounts receivable credit sales revenue:

$$\frac{\textbf{Average accounts receivable}}{\textbf{Total accounts receivable credit sales revenue}}$$

7. Accounts receivable turnover:

$$\frac{\textbf{Total accounts receivable credit sales revenue}}{\textbf{Average accounts receivable}}$$

8. Accounts receivable average collection period:

$$\frac{\textbf{Days in the period}}{\textbf{Accounts receivable turnover ratio for the period}}$$

Another useful technique is to complete a common-size analysis of current assets. Total current assets are 100%, and each item of current assets is expressed as a proportion of 100%. By comparing two or more consecutive periods, such an analysis can indicate a change in liquidity due to a change in the proportions of each current asset relative to total current assets.

Long-term solvency ratios, sometimes called net worth ratios, measure a company's ability to meet its long-term credit obligations:

1. Total assets to total liabilities ratio: $\dfrac{\textbf{Total assets}}{\textbf{Total liabilities}}$

2. Total liabilities to total assets ratio: $\dfrac{\textbf{Total liabilities}}{\textbf{Total assets}}$

3. Total liabilities to total equity ratio: $\dfrac{\textbf{Total liabilities}}{\textbf{Total stockholders' equity}}$

4. Times interest earned ratio: $\dfrac{\textbf{Income before interest and income tax}}{\textbf{Interest expense}}$

Profitability ratios provide information that can be used to measure the effectiveness of management's use of the assets (resources) available to conduct operations:

1. Gross return on assets: $\dfrac{\textbf{Income before interest and income tax}}{\textbf{Total average assets}}$

2. Net return on assets: $\dfrac{\textbf{Net income after tax}}{\textbf{Total average assets}}$

3. Net income to sales revenue ratio: $\dfrac{\textbf{Net income after income tax}}{\textbf{Sales revenue}}$

4. Return on stockholders' equity: $\dfrac{\textbf{Net income after income tax}}{\textbf{Average stockholders' equity}}$

5. Earnings per share: $\dfrac{\textbf{Net income after income tax}}{\textbf{Average number of shares outstanding}}$

6. Price/earnings ratio: $\dfrac{\textbf{Market price per share}}{\textbf{Earnings per share}}$

Turnover ratios include the following:

1. Inventory turnover ratio: $\dfrac{\textbf{Cost of sales for the period}}{\textbf{Average inventory for the period}}$

2. Inventory holding period: $\dfrac{\textbf{Operating days in the period}}{\textbf{Inventory turnover ratio for the period}}$

3. Working capital turnover ratio: $\dfrac{\textbf{Sales revenue}}{\textbf{Average working capital}}$

4. Fixed asset turnover ratio: $\dfrac{\textbf{Sales revenue}}{\textbf{Total average fixed assets}}$

Many individual operating ratios are available for food and beverage operations and for rooms operations in a motel or hotel. Ratios should be selected for which are the most appropriate for the operation being analyzed and evaluated. A daily manager's report is normally prepared to record information and statistics that management requires.

Although internal comparisons and analysis are most useful, there are a great many industrywide statistics published for different hospitality organizations. External data and information should not be overlooked to assist in comparing of internal results. Comparison of appropriate external statistics to a complete internal analysis can provide insight into the effectiveness of the internal management.

The reader is cautioned to use ratio analysis with care and not to use general rules of thumb as necessarily being the norm for all businesses. What is most valuable is not how an individual operation's ratios differ from similar external operations, but how the internal results are changing over time. Selection and discretion in using the right ratio for the right occasion should be exercised. Ratios should not become an end in themselves.

Finally, ratios cannot solve problems; they only identify possible problems that only management's evaluation and corrective action can resolve.

This chapter concluded with some comments on the concept of financial leverage, or trading on the equity. Financial leverage is obtained by using debt rather than equity investment to finance an enterprise. As long as operating income before interest is greater than the interest expense, the owners' return on equity will be higher. However, a too highly leveraged company may quickly be in financial trouble if operating income before interest begins to decline.

D I S C U S S I O N   Q U E S T I O N S

1. Describe the three ways in which a ratio can be expressed.
2. List and briefly discuss the four bases on which a ratio can be compared.
3. Which three groups are the main users of financial ratios?
4. What is the value in calculating a current ratio? Contrast how creditors and owners view this ratio.
5. Why can a hotel, motel, or restaurant usually operate with a current ratio considerably lower than other types of businesses, such as manufacturing companies?
6. Why is maintaining a current ratio that is too high not a good business practice?
7. Explain why the calculation of a credit card receivables average collection period is a meaningful statistic.
8. Define the term *profitability.*
9. Why is a high total asset to total liabilities ratio desired by creditors?
10. Why can the book values of assets be misleading when used in the total assets to total liabilities ratio, or the total liabilities to total assets ratio?
11. State the equation for the credit card turnover ratio.
12. Explain the gross return on assets ratio measure. What value is it to a potential creditor?
13. How does the net return on assets ratio differ from the gross return on assets ratio, and why is its calculation valuable?
14. Discuss the purpose of a quick ratio.
15. What does the return on stockholders' equity measure?
16. State how sales revenue per available room is calculated.
17. Discuss the term *financial leverage,* or *trading on the equity.*
18. List four possible operating ratios that could be used in a food operation.
19. List and discuss three operating ratios that could be used in a rooms operation.
20. What is the advantage of calculating the inventory holding period in days?

E T H I C S   S I T U A T I O N

A hotel manager wishes to borrow additional funds from his bank early in the next year. The manager knows the bank manager uses the hotel's current ratio as a major factor in the decision process in making a loan. The manager also knows that the bank manager likes to see a current ratio that is considerably higher than that for a typical hotel. On December 31, the manager instructs his accountant to make up journal entries on that date to record the sale of all of the hotel's marketable securities and the use of the cash proceeds to reduce accounts payable (even though none were actually sold). In this way, the December 31 balance sheet will show a current ratio much higher than it actually is. The accountant was also instructed to reverse the journal entries on January 1. Discuss the ethics of this situation.

EXERCISES

E4.1 A restaurant reported the following current assets: cash $11,200, credit card receivables $808, accounts receivable $260, food inventory $4,482, and prepaid expenses, $1,220. Current liabilities total $6,912. Answer the following:

a. Calculate the current ratio.

b. Calculate the quick ratio (acid test ratio).

E4.2 Referring to information in P4.1 calculate working capital and describe what it means.

E4.3 On March 31, a restaurant reported credit card sales revenue of $48,560. Credit card receivables began with a balance of $1,444 and ended the month with a balance of $1,220. Answer the following:

a. What is the average of credit card receivables?

b. What does credit card receivables represent as a percentage of total credit card sales revenue?

E4.4 The following is an extract of restaurant and beverage operation for two months of operations:

	Month 1	Month 2
Cash	$12,205	$14,695
Credit card receivables	2,781	2,957
Accounts receivable	463	269
Total Quick Assets	$15,449	$17,921

Complete a common-size vertical analysis of quick assets for both months and comment on the changes to quick assets. Round final answers to the nearest tenth of a percentile.

E4.5 Total current assets reported for an operation were $87,200 and total current liabilities were $64,400. Determine working capital for the period and define its structure and purpose.

E4.6 You are given the ending working capital for two consecutive years: Year 1 is $20,800, and Year 2 is $30,520. Sales revenue for Year 2 is $1,078,444. Calculate the working capital turnover ratio.

E4.7 A restaurant and beverage operation reported the following for the operating month of March, which had 27 operating days.

Food service inventory:	March 1	March 31	Cost of Sales
	$7,312	$5,628	$38,820

For the month of March, calculate the food inventory turnover ratio and inventory holding period in days that it takes for food inventory to turn over.

E4.8 Information showing total assets and total liabilities for two consecutive operating years is given below:

	Year 0006	Year 0007
Total assets	$482,200	$506,320
Total liabilities	$330,252	$347,290

Calculate the total assets to total liabilities ratio for both years and comment on the change. Do any additional analysis you need so you can comment on these figures.

E4.9 Assume you were given information regarding current ratios for three consecutive years. Can you determine the general condition of liquidity without calculating working capital? If the following ratios apply to a restaurant, would the ratio for Year 8 be considered adequate? Explain your answers to the questions.

	Year 6	Year 7	Year 8
Current ratio	1.46:1	1.40:1	1.30:1

E4.10 Prepare a comparative horizontal analysis of the change in each current asset account from Year 6 to Year 7. Express each change in dollars and the percentage each change represents. Comment on each change that exceeds 10%. What, if anything, would you do as a manager?

Current Assets	Year 1	Year 2
Cash	$12,892	$14,580
Credit card receivables	2,700	3,460
Accounts receivable	530	150
Food inventories	4,280	4,366
Beverage inventories	1,850	1,702
Prepaid expenses	1,400	1,610
Total Current Assets	$23,652	$25,868

P R O B L E M S

P4.1 A small restaurant reported the following current assets at year's end: Cash $2,440, credit card receivables $1,402, accounts receivable $440, food inventories $2,680, prepaid insurance $1,200, and prepaid rent $1,500. Current liabilities were $3,426. (a) Complete a common-size vertical analysis of current assets. (b) Calculate the current and quick ratios.

P4.2 You are provided with the following information regarding current assets and current liabilities of a restaurant operation for two successive years.

Current Assets	Year 0006	Year 0007
Cash	$12,778	$17,765
Credit card receivables	2,442	2,815
Accounts receivable	580	420
Marketable securities	12,000	16,000
Inventories	6,100	7,100
Prepaid expenses	2,400	2,600
Total Current Assets	$36,300	$46,700

Current Liabilities	Year 0006	Year 0007
Accounts payable	$ 10,410	$12,400
Accrued expenses payable	3,760	6,200
Taxes payable	6,800	8,400
Interest payable	500	800
Current mortgage payable	11,200	9,900
Total Current Liabilities	$32,670	$37,700

Calculate the following for Years 0006 and 0007.

a. Working capital

b. Current ratio

c. Quick ratio

Sales revenue for Year 0007 is $544,800. The composition of sales revenue is cash 36%, credit card sales revenue 61.5%, and accounts receivable credit sales revenue of 2.5%. For Year 0007, calculate the following:

d. Credit card receivables as a percentage of credit card sales revenue

e. Credit card receivables turnover ratio

f. Credit card average collection period

g. Accounts receivable as a percentage of accounts receivable credit sales revenue

h. Accounts receivable turnover ratio

i. Accounts receivable average collection period

j. Cost of sales was $212,472; calculate cost of sales as a percentage of sales revenue

k. Comment on what these ratios tell you about the restaurant.

P4.3 With reference to the information in P4.2, use a common-size vertical analysis to determine the composition of current assets and current liabilities for Years 0006 and 0007. Discuss the results.

P4.4 A fire occurred in a friend's restaurant overnight on December 31, 0007, and the friend has asked for your help. Although many accounting records were lost, some were recovered. With the recovered records and information obtained from outside sources, you believe a balance sheet can be reconstructed for the period ending on the date of the fire. Your friend provided the following information:

■ The forecasted current ratio as of December 31, 0007, was 1.25 to 1.

■ Balance sheets for the previous three years indicated that current assets on average represented 25% of total assets.

■ The bank reported the year-end bank balance was $976. It was estimated that $1,500 in the restaurant's safe was destroyed during the fire.

■ The bank also indicated that it is owed $23,000 on a long-term note, and the current amount due in Year 0007 is $3,444.

■ The value of ending inventories was $4,945.

■ Restaurant suppliers indicated that in total they were owed $3,420 at the close of business on December 31, 0007.

■ All employees were paid up to and including the night of the fire.

Calculate the following:

a. Total current assets

b. Credit card receivables, assuming current assets consisted only of cash, credit card receivables, and inventories

c. Total assets

d. Prepare a balance sheet as of December 31, 0007, to give to your friend.

P4.5 You have the following information taken from the balance sheets for two successive years for a hotel operation.

	Year 0006	*Year 0007*
Total assets	$422,200	$406,700
Total liabilities	312,400	325,500
Total stockholders' equity	109,800	81,200

For each year, calculate:

a. Total assets to total liabilities ratio

b. Total liabilities to total assets ratio

c. Total liabilities to total equity ratio

Discuss the changes that have taken place over the two-year period from the viewpoint of an investor who has been asked to loan the hotel money for expansion.

P4.6 In addition to the information given in P4.5, an income statement for the hotel for Year 0007 is available:

Sales revenue	$851,800
Operating costs	(796,900)
Operating income, before interest and tax	$ 54,900
Less: Interest	(26,100)
Income before tax	$ 28,800
Less: Income tax	(7,200)
Net Income	$ 21,600

For Year 0007, calculate the following:

a. Gross return on assets

b. Net return on assets

c. Number of times interest is earned; discuss acceptability

d. Net income to sales revenue ratio; discuss hotel profitability

e. Return on stockholders' equity; discuss hotel profitability

P4.7 You have the following information from a restaurant operation:

Balance Sheets, December 31		
Assets	**Year 0007**	**Year 0008**
Cash	$ 9,100	$ 14,200
Credit card receivables	4,920	6,240
Accounts receivable	5,280	6,160
Food inventory	14,600	13,900
Prepaid expenses	3,800	4,500
Land	32,000	32,000
Building	315,800	323,200
Equipment	66,640	73,200
Furnishings	16,660	18,300
Accumulated depreciation	(113,700)	(124,500)
Total Assets	$335,100	$367,200

Liabilities & Stockholders' Equity	Year 0007	Year 0008
Accounts payable	$ 16,700	$ 12,500
Bank note payable	4,900	3,600
Income tax payable	12,500	12,600
Accrued expenses payable	7,100	7,500
Mortgage payable (current)	10,400	12,100
Long-term mortgage payable	192,000	180,900
Common stock	10,000	10,000
Retained earnings	101,500	128,000
Liabilities & Stockholders' Equity	$335,100	$367,200

Income Statement (Condensed)
For the Year Ending December 31, 0008

Sales revenue*		$742,600
Cost of sales	$301,900	
Operating expenses	381,200	
Total Operating Costs		(683,100)
Operating income, before interest and tax		$ 59,500
Interest expense		(19,400)
Income before tax		$ 40,100
Income tax		(12,600)
Net Income		$ 27,500

*Sales revenue consisted of 26% cash, 62% credit cards, and 12% accounts receivable.

From the information given, calculate the following:

a. Working capital for Years 0007 and 0008

b. Current ratio for Years 0007 and 0008

c. Quick ratio (Acid test ratio) for Years 0007 and 0008

d. Credit card receivables as a percentage of credit card sales revenue for Year 0008

e. Credit card receivables turnover ratio based on credit card sales revenue for Year 0008

f. Credit card receivables average collection period ratio, based on credit card sales revenue for Year 0008

g. Accounts receivable as a percentage of accounts receivable credit sales revenue for Year 0008

h. Accounts receivable turnover ratio based on accounts receivable credit sales revenue for Year 0008

i. Accounts receivable average collection period based on accounts receivable credit sales revenue for Year 0008

j. Total assets to total liabilities for Years 0007 and 0008

k. Total liabilities to total assets for Years 0007 and 0008

l. Total liabilities to stockholders' equity for Years 0007 and 0008

m. Net return on total assets for Year 0008

n. Number of times interest is earned for Year 0008

o. Net income to total sales revenue ratio for Year 0008

p. Return on stockholders' equity for Year 0008

q. Food inventory turnover ratio for Year 0008

r. Property, plant, and equipment (fixed assets) turnover ratio for Year 0008

Comment on any of the calculated ratios that appear unusually high or low or totally out of range of what is considered acceptable.

P4.8 The owners of a cocktail bar have the following annual income statement information:

Annual sales revenue	$210,000
Cost of sales (30% of sales revenue)	63,000
Payroll expense	50,000
Other operating expenses	20,000
Direct expenses (charges including depreciation)	40,000

The owners are considering new furnishings for the bar at an estimated cost of $20,000 using their own funds. They anticipate the new furnishings will bring in additional customers, and their sales revenue will increase by 10% above their current level. The new furnishings are estimated to have a five-year life with no residual value. The new furnishings will be depreciated using straight-line depreciation.

To provide service to the additional customers, more staff would be hired at an additional cost of $125 per week. Other operating costs will increase by $1,400 per year. There will be no increase to direct (fixed) charges other than depreciation expense. The income tax rate will remain at 25%. The owners will go ahead with the project only if the return on their $20,000 investment is 15% per year or more in the first year.

a. Should they make the $20,000 investment in new furnishings?

b. If they had the alternative of using only $10,000 of their own funds and borrowing the other $10,000 at 10% interest, would the decision change?

P4.9 A restaurant has the following statistical information calculated from its financial statements for the past three years:

	Year 0006	*Year 0007*	*Year 0008*
Current ratio	1.04:1	1.25:1	1.40:1
Credit card turnover ratio	70 times	64 times	61 times
Accounts receivable turnover	18 times	24 times	31 times
Food inventory turnover ratio	37 times	28 times	22 times
Total liabilities to total equity	2.75:1	2.4:1	1.95:1
Return on stockholders' equity	9.7%	9.5%	8.7%
Annual sales revenue	$875,400	$881,900	$879,300

Using this information, answer each of the following questions and explain your answer. A simple yes, no, more, less, or maybe won't do!

a. Are current assets in relation to current liabilities increasing or decreasing?

b. Is the restaurant becoming more or less efficient in the collection of its credit card receivables?

c. Is the restaurant becoming more or less efficient in the collection of its accounts receivable?

d. Over the three-year period, has more or less money been tied up in food inventory?

e. With the stockholders' viewpoint in mind, is profitability improving or not improving?

f. If the restaurant needed to borrow capital through long-term debt, would it be easier to find a lender now than three years ago?

g. Has the restaurant been using leverage to the advantage of the stockholders over the three-year period?

P4.10 A restaurant has the following statistical information calculated from its financial statements for the past three years:

	Year 0006	*Year 0007*	*Year 0008*
Current ratio	1.24:1	1.18:1	1.05:1
Credit card turnover ratio	91 times	93 times	98 times
Accounts receivable turnover	14 times	24 times	31 times
Food inventory turnover ratio	38 times	44 times	48 times
Total liabilities to total equity	1.94:1	2.52:1	2.95:1
Return on stockholders' equity	7.7%	9.6%	9.9%
Annual sales revenue	$880,000	$882,500	$872,300

Using this information, answer each of the following questions and explain your answer. A simple yes, no, more, less, or maybe won't do! A comment is required in each case.

a. Are current assets in relation to current liabilities increasing or decreasing?

b. Is the restaurant becoming more or less efficient in the collection of its credit card receivables?

c. Is the restaurant becoming more or less efficient in the collection of its accounts receivable?

d. Over the three-year period, has more or less money been tied up in food inventory?

e. With the stockholders' viewpoint in mind, is profitability improving or not improving?

f. If the restaurant needed to borrow capital through long-term debt, would it be easier to find a lender now than three years ago?

g. Has the restaurant been using leverage to the advantage of the stockholders over the three-year period?

P4.11 A Resort Hotel has 75 guest rooms and a small dining room with 40 seats. The hotel recorded the following information for the month of March.

- Room revenue was $91,108.
- A total of 1,798 rooms were occupied.
- A total of 3,417 guests are using the 1,798 rooms occupied.
- Dining room food revenue was $45,209.
- Dining room beverage revenue was $14,810.
- The dining room serviced a total of 3,720 guests.
- Cost of sales–food was $18,904.
- Cost of sales–beverage was $4,805.
- Guest rooms labor costs were $21,867.
- Dining room labor costs were $15,011.

Calculate the following for the Resort Hotel:

1. Average rate per room occupied

2. Rooms occupancy percentage

3. Room double occupancy percentage

4. Food cost percentage

5. Beverage cost percentage

6. Rooms labor cost percentage

7. Dining room labor cost percentage

8. Total average check, dining room

9. Dining room average daily seat turnover

10. Average monthly revenue per dining room seat

11. Beverage sales revenue to food sales revenue percentage

12. Beverage sales revenue to room sales revenue percentage

13. Total dining sales revenue to rooms' sales revenue percentage

P4.12 Owners of a catering company also own a number of relatively small coffee shops, one of which shows excellent potential to increase its sales revenue. Selected annual operating figures follow:

Annual sales revenue	$370,000
Cost of sales (38% of sales revenue)	140,600
Payroll expense	103,600
Other operating expenses	74,000

Based on the potential of increasing sales revenue, the owners are seriously considering a 10-year lease on an adjoining property, which requires a full 10-year upfront payment of $97,000. New equipment at a cost of $20,000 would have to be purchased. The equipment is estimated to have a 10-year life and no residual value. An additional investment in food inventory of $1,500 would be required.

Sales revenue is estimated to increase by 20% above the current level, and the cost of sales is expected to remain at the current cost of sales percentage. Payroll costs are expected to increase by $160 per week and other costs by $150 per week. A minimum 15% pretax investment return is wanted by the owners.

1. Should the investment be made?

2. As an alternative, the owners are considering borrowing $60,000 of the required investment at a 10% interest rate. Would the decision change if debt financing were obtained rather than the owners using their funds?

CASE 4

With reference to the 4C Company's unadjusted trial balance, balance sheet, and income statement (Case 2) for the year ending December 31, 0007, calculate each of the following. (This is the first year of 4C Company's operation. When averages are called for but only beginning numbers are available, use the ending numbers shown in Case 2 financial statements.)

a. Working capital

b. Current ratio

c. Quick ratio

d. Credit card receivables average collection period (Credit card sales revenue is 60% of total sales revenue.)

e. Accounts receivable average collection period (Accounts receivable is 10% of total sales revenue.)

f. Net return on assets

g. Net income to total sales revenue ratio

h. Return on stockholders' equity

i. Food inventory turnover ratio

j. Beverage inventory turnover ratio

k. Cost of sales, food percentage

l. Cost of sales, beverage percentage

   1. To conserve cash during the first year of operation, Mr. Driver limited his salary to $1,500 per month. Explain whether the funds being withdrawn as a salary are considered as a deductible operating expense to the 4C Company.

   2. Prepare a short discussion of each calculated ratio, which you believe may be unsatisfactory, and explain why.

   3. It appears that 4C has a good liquid cash position, and Mr. Driver is considering using $20,000 of 4C cash to redeem some of his shares of common stock before the final financial statements of the current year are prepared. He asks for your opinion. Recalculate any of the preceding ratios that will be affected by the repurchase of the stock and discuss the effects if the stock repurchase is made.

INTERNAL CONTROL

I N T R O D U C T I O N

This chapter explains the objectives of internal control and discusses some of the reasons why internal control for hospitality operations is more difficult than for some other businesses.

Principles and procedures of internal control—such as implementing controls as preventative procedures, having an effective philosophy of control, and monitoring the control system—are discussed and illustrated in sufficient detail to clarify their purpose in the following areas:

- Establishing written control procedures and employment responsibilities to include selection and training of employees
- Maintaining adequate records and separating record keeping, asset control, limiting access to assets, conducting surprise checks, and dividing the responsibility for related transactions
- Rotating jobs, using machines for control, establishing standards, evaluating reports, using forms and reports, bonding employees, and requiring mandatory vacations
- Using external audits, providing audit trails, numbering all control documents, and ensuring continuous system review
- Controlling product inventory purchased for resale and the use of documents to aid in the control of product purchases
- Setting specific controls required for cash receipts and cash disbursements, including the use of a voucher system, a bank reconciliation, and the control of cash disbursements
- Setting and evaluating performance standards with reference to the control over product cost of sales

The chapter concludes by listing various methods of loss or fraud that could occur in such areas as delivery and receipt of merchandise, cash funds, accounts payable and payroll, food and beverage sales revenue, and in the front office of a hotel or motel.

CHAPTER OBJECTIVES

After studying this chapter, the reader should be able to

1. Define the purpose of internal control.
2. Briefly describe the two basic requirements for good internal control.
3. Briefly discuss some of the basic principles of good internal control, such as defining job responsibilities, separating record keeping from control of assets, and dividing responsibilities for related tasks.
4. Explain how lapping can be used for fraudulent purposes.
5. List and briefly discuss each of the five control documents used to control purchases.
6. List and discuss the proper procedures for product storage and inventory control.
7. Describe how a petty cash fund operates.
8. Explain briefly how control can be established over cash receipts and cash disbursements.
9. List the procedures necessary to control payroll disbursements.
10. Complete a bank reconciliation.
11. Calculate a standard food or beverage cost from given information.

INTERNAL CONTROL

This text discusses management accounting and management control systems. Management uses the information provided by management accounting to make decisions and implement procedures to safeguard assets, control costs, increase sales revenue, and maximize profitability. The information provided must be accurate and current to assist managers in carrying out their responsibilities. Effective and efficient internal control policies and procedures apply to all facets of an establishment's operations, from purchases through sales. It includes control of and accountability for cash receipts, cash disbursements, and the many other assets an organization uses to conduct operations.

In a small, owner-operated business, such as an independent restaurant or small motel, very few internal controls are required because the control is carried out by the owner who is usually always present and who handles all the cash coming in and the payments going out.

In larger establishments, one-person control is not feasible. In fact, in larger organizations it is necessary to organize operations into various departments and

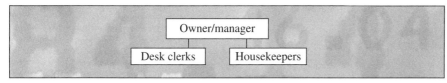

■ **EXHIBIT 5.1**
Organization Chart for 50-room Motel.
Source: M. Coltman, 1989. *Cost Control for the Hospitality Industry.* New York: John Wiley & Sons, Inc.

to draw up a plan of the organization, or an **organization chart.** Indeed, the organization chart itself is the foundation of a good internal control system. It establishes lines of communication and levels of authority and responsibility.

Organization charts for various types and sizes of hospitality establishments are illustrated in Exhibits 5.1 through 5.5. In large establishments, as the organization charts show, lines of authority, responsibility, and communication become more complex. Therefore, the internal control system in a large establishment will also be more complex.

A system of **internal control** encompasses the following two broad requirements:

1. *Methods and procedures for the employees in the various job categories to follow.* Such procedures ensure that employees follow management policies, achieve operational efficiency, and protect assets from waste, theft, or fraud. Assets are defined as cash, credit card receivables, accounts receivable, inventory, equipment, buildings, and land. The types of safeguards needed include the use of safes for holding large sums of cash, the use of locked storerooms for inventories of food and beverage, restricted access to locations where cash and products are stored, and maintenance of all equipment in efficient working order.

2. *Reliable forms and reports that will measure employee efficiency and effectiveness and lead to problem identification.* These reports provide information, usually of an accounting or financial nature, that, when analyzed, will identify any

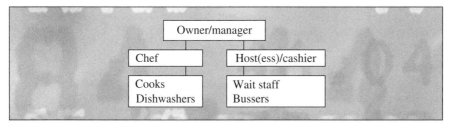

■ **EXHIBIT 5.2**
Organization Chart for 120-seat Coffee Shop
Source: M. Coltman, 1989. *Cost Control for the Hospitality Industry.* New York: John Wiley & Sons, Inc.

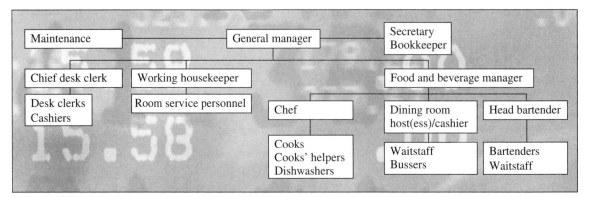

■ **EXHIBIT 5.3**

Organization Chart for 150-room Motor Lodge with 100-seat Dining Room and 80-seat Cocktail Lounge

Source: M. Coltman, 1989. *Cost Control for the Hospitality Industry.* New York: John Wiley & Sons, Inc.

problem areas that exist. This information must be accurate and timely if it is to be useful. It must also be cost effective. In other words, the benefits (cost savings) of an internal control system must be greater than the cost of its implementation and continuation. Information produced must also be useful. If the information is invalid and cannot be used, then effort and money have been wasted.

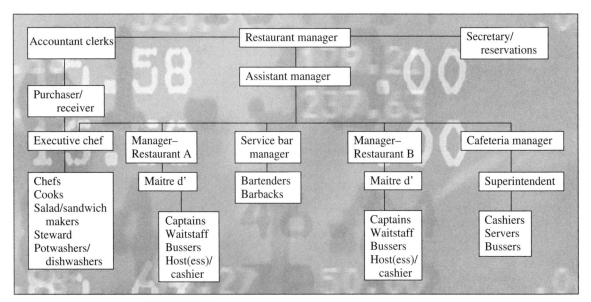

■ **EXHIBIT 5.4**

Organization Chart for a Restaurant Complex

Source: M. Coltman, 1989. *Cost Control for the Hospitality Industry.* New York: John Wiley & Sons, Inc.

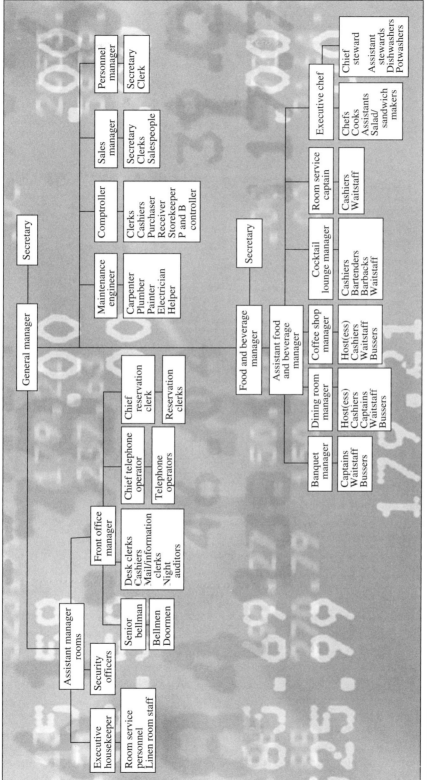

EXHIBIT 5.5

Organization Chart for a Very Large Hotel with Full Facilities

Source: M. Coltman, 1989. *Cost Control for the Hospitality Industry.* New York: John Wiley & Sons, Inc.

It may seem that these two major requirements are in conflict. For example, the procedures used to store and safeguard food products and the paperwork required to obtain those products from storage may be so cumbersome that employees in departments (such as the dining room) that need those products do not bother to replenish depleted stocks. As a result, the operation's efficiency is reduced and sales revenue may be lost. Alternatively, if employees complete all paperwork requirements to ensure they always have sufficient products on hand, the added labor cost may exceed potential losses of products from theft or waste.

Although in this chapter we shall be viewing internal control primarily from an accounting point of view, control is not limited to financial matters. For example, an establishment's personnel policies are part of the system of internal control. A company's policies on such matters as employee skill upgrading and education are important because they are eventually reflected in the company's financial results.

PROBLEMS UNIQUE TO THE HOSPITALITY INDUSTRY

Although most businesses have many shared problems relating to internal control, the hospitality business has some unique problems that often complicate and make more difficult the implementation of total control. This section discusses some of these characteristics.

BUSINESS SIZE

Just about every hospitality operation (even if the individual property is part of a large international chain) can be described as a small business. It is generally more difficult for a small business to have as comprehensive a control system as a large business.

CASH TRANSACTIONS

Even though an increasingly large percentage of hospitality industry customers today use credit cards to pay for their transactions, and this trend continues, many others still pay cash, particularly in restaurants and beverage outlets. This means that there is a fair amount of cash accumulating in sales departments each day, making it easy for some of this cash to "disappear." To further complicate cash handling and its control, many hospitality operations have some departments operating around the clock.

INVENTORY PRODUCTS

Even though the assets in inventory for most hospitality operations are only a small proportion of total assets, many individual products in those inventories (such as bottles of quality wine and expensive containers of food products) are valuable to dishonest employees, who might be tempted to remove them from the establishment for personal consumption or even to sell them for personal gain.

HIGH EMPLOYEE TURNOVER

The industry is characterized by a much higher employee turnover rate than most other businesses. This means that employees often do not receive the training they need because they are often skilled, nor do they have the same loyalty to the operation that long-time employees often develop.

PRINCIPLES OF INTERNAL CONTROL

Some of the basic principles that provide a solid foundation for a good internal control system are discussed in this section.

ESTABLISH PREVENTATIVE PROCEDURES

Internal control procedures need to be preventative. In other words, they should be established so that they minimize and/or prevent theft. This is much more effective than suffering losses from theft or fraud and having a system that detects the culprits only after the event.

ESTABLISH MANAGEMENT SUPERVISION

The majority of employees are honest by nature, but because of a poor internal control system, or, worse still, the complete absence of any controls some employees will yield to temptation and become dishonest. If management does not care, why should the employees?

Control systems, by themselves, do not solve all problems. The implementation of a control system does not remove from management the necessity to observe constantly the effectiveness of the system using supervision. A control system does not prevent fraud or theft; but the system may point out that it is happening. Also, some forms of fraud or theft may never be discovered, even with an excellent control system. **Collusion** (two or more employees working together for dishonest purposes) may go undetected for long periods. The important fact to remember is that no system of control can be perfect. An effective manager will always be alert to this fact.

MONITOR CONTROL SYSTEMS

Any system of control must also be monitored to ensure that it is continuing to provide the desired information. The system must therefore be flexible enough to be changed to suit different needs. If a reporting form needs to be changed, then it should be changed. If a form becomes redundant, then it should be scrapped entirely or replaced by one that is more suitable. To have employees' complete forms that no one subsequently looks at is a costly exercise, and employees quickly become disillusioned when there seems to be no purpose to what they are asked to do. As well, employees may take advantage of management's disinterest and steal from the operation.

INSTITUTE AN EMPLOYEE SELECTION AND TRAINING SYSTEM

Important aspects of effective internal control are employee competence, trustworthiness, and training. This means having a good system of screening job applicants, selecting employees, and providing employee orientation, on-the-job training, and periodic evaluation. Supervisory personnel must also be competent, with skills in maintaining the operation's standards, motivating the employees they supervise, preparing staffing schedules, maintaining employee morale (to reduce the cost of employee turnover), and implementing procedures to control labor and other costs. A poor supervisor will fail to extract the full potential from employees and will thus add to the operation's cost.

ESTABLISH RESPONSIBILITIES

One of the prerequisites for good internal control is to clearly define the responsibilities for tasks. This goes beyond designing an organization chart. For example, in the case of deliveries of food to a hotel, who will do the receiving? Will it be the chef, the storekeeper, a person whose sole function is to be the receiver, or anybody who happens to be close to the receiving door when a delivery arrives? Once the designated person is established, that person must be given a list of receiving procedures, preferably in writing, so if errors or discrepancies arise, that person can be held accountable.

PREPARE WRITTEN PROCEDURES

As mentioned, once procedures have been established for each area and for each job category where control is needed, these procedures should be put into writing. In this way, employees will know what the policy and procedures are. Written procedures are particularly important in the hospitality industry, where employee turnover is relatively high and continuous employee training to support the system of internal control is necessary.

It is impossible in this chapter to establish procedures that will fit every possible situation in the hospitality industry because of the wide variety of types, sizes, and styles of operation. Even in two establishments of similar nature and size, the procedures for any specific control area may differ due to management policy, type of customer, layout of the establishment, or numerous other reasons.

However, for illustrative purposes only, the following might be the way a written set of procedures could be prepared for the receiver in a food operation:

1. *Count each item* that can be counted (number of cases or number of individual items).
2. *Weigh each item* that is delivered by weight (such as meat).
3. *Check the count or weight figures* against the count or weight figure on the invoice accompanying the delivery.
4. *Check the quality* of the items that are delivered.
5. If purchase specifications were prepared and sent to the supplier, *check the quality* against these specifications.
6. *Spot check case goods* to ensure that they are full and that all items in the case are of the same quality.
7. *Check invoice prices* against prices quoted on the market quotation sheet.
8. *If goods were delivered without an invoice,* prepare a memorandum invoice listing the name of supplier, date of delivery, count or weight of items, and, from the market quotation sheet, price of the items.
9. *If goods are short-shipped or if quality is unacceptable,* prepare a credit memorandum invoice listing items missing or returned and obtain the delivery driver's signature acknowledging that the driver is returning with the noted items or that they were short-shipped. Staple the credit memorandum to the original invoice.
10. *Store all items* in the proper controlled storage locations as soon after delivery as possible.
11. *Send all invoices and credit memoranda to the accounting office* so that extensions and totals can be checked and then be recorded.

As another example, the following could be a set of procedures for front-office staff of a hotel or motel for the handling of credit cards:

1. When the guest checks in, ask whether payment will be by credit card, by check, or some other method.
2. If it is to be by credit card, ask to see the card.
3. Verify that the card is one acceptable to this hotel (such as Visa, Master Card, and American Express).
4. If acceptable, check the date on the card to make sure it has not expired.
5. Scan the credit card number for approval.
6. As you return the card, remind the guest to see the front office cashier before departing to verify the accuracy of the account and sign the credit card voucher for the charge.
7. Before filing the folio with the cashier, check the credit card number to make sure it is not on the credit card company's cancellation list. If it is, advise the front office manager of the situation.
8. Initial the credit card number on the folio to show that approval has been obtained or the card has been checked against the cancellation list and is not listed.

9. When the guest checks out, review the guest account to ensure that the credit card number has been initialed.
10. If it has not been, check the cancellation list and advise the front office manager if it is listed. Do not return the card to the guest.
11. If not listed, complete the appropriate credit card company voucher, either electronically or using the manual imprinter.
12. Have the guest sign the voucher. Check the voucher signature against the credit card signature.
13. Return the credit card to the guest with his/her copy of the voucher.

MAINTAIN ADEQUATE RECORDS

Another important consideration for good internal control is to have good written records. For example, for food deliveries there should be, at the very least, a written record on a daily order sheet of what is to be delivered, from which suppliers, and at what prices. In this way, the designated receiver can check invoices that accompany the delivered goods against the actual goods and against the order form. The larger the establishment, the more written records are necessary. For example, a market quotation sheet could be used so a responsible person can be designated to obtain quotes from two or more suppliers before any orders are placed. Without good records, employees will be less concerned about doing a good job, and theft and fraud are more likely to occur. The forms, reports, and other records that are part of the internal control system will depend entirely on the size and type of establishment.

SEPARATE RECORD KEEPING AND CONTROL OF ASSETS

One of the most important principles of good internal control is to separate the functions of recording information about assets and the actual control of the assets. Consider the accounts of the guests who have left a hotel and have charged their accounts to a credit card or company account. Such accounts are assets—accounts receivable—and in some hotels are left in the front office until payment is made. These accounts are known as city ledger accounts. Checks received in payment are given to the front office cashier, who then records the payments on the accounts. These checks, along with other cash and checks received from departing guests are turned in as part of the total remittance at the end of the cashier's shift. As long as the cashier is honest, there is nothing wrong with this procedure!

A dishonest cashier could, however, practice a procedure known as **lapping.** Mr. X left the hotel, and his account for $175 is one of the accounts receivable. When he receives his statement at month's end, he sends in his check for $175. The cashier does not record the payment on Mr. X's account. Instead, the check is simply put in the cash drawer and the cashier removes $175 for personal use. The cashier's remittance at the end of the shift will balance, but

Mr. X's account will still show an outstanding balance of $175. When Ms. Y, who has an account in the city ledger for $285, sends in her payment, the cashier records $175 as a payment on Mr. X's account, puts the $285 check in the cash drawer, and removes a further $110 in cash for personal use. A few days later, Mr. Z's payment of $350 on his city ledger account is received. The cashier records $285 on Ms. Y's account, puts the $350 check in the cash drawer and takes out $65 more in cash. This lapping of accounts will eventually snowball to the point where the cashier can no longer cover a particular account and the fraud will be discovered. However, the outstanding account may be so large that the misappropriated cash cannot be recovered from the dishonest cashier.

To aid in preventing this type of loss, the separation of cash receiving and recording on accounts should be instituted. Checks or cash received in the mail in payment for city ledger accounts could be kept in the accounting office for direct deposit to the bank. The front office cashier is simply given a list of account names and amounts received, and the appropriate accounts can be credited without the cashier handling any money. This procedure may not, however, prevent collusion between the person in the accounting office and the cashier.

The separation of asset control and asset recording does not pertain only to cash. For example, food and beverage inventories maintained in a storeroom may be controlled (received and issued) by a storekeeper, but it is often a good idea to have the records of what is in the storeroom (e.g., perpetual inventory cards) maintained by some other person.

LIMIT ACCESS TO ASSETS

The number of employees who have access to assets such as cash and inventory should be limited. The larger the number of employees with access, the greater is the potential for loss from theft or fraud. In the same way, the amount of cash and inventory should be kept to a minimum. This requires a balancing act, because cashiers need to have enough cash to make change and the store's departments need sufficient inventory so they are not continually running out of products and are unable to satisfy customer demand. Also, control procedures for access to those assets should not be so cumbersome that they severely restrict efficient operations.

CONDUCT SURPRISE CHECKS

Surprise checks such as counting cash or taking inventory should be carried out at unusual times. Two principles are involved here: First, the person conducting surprise checks should always be independent of the part of the operation being checked. In other words, the person who normally takes the month-end storeroom inventory should not be the person who makes the surprise check. Second, such surprise checks should be carried out frequently enough that they become routine, but not scheduled in a predictable pattern.

DIVIDE THE RESPONSIBILITY FOR RELATED TRANSACTIONS

Responsibility for related transactions should be separated so the work of one person is verified by the work of another. This is not to suggest duplication of work—that would be costly—but to have two tasks that must be carried out for control reasons done by two separate employees. This procedure keeps one person from having too much control over assets and may prevent their theft.

For example, many restaurants record items sold and their prices on handwritten sales checks. These checks, when the customers pay, are then inserted in a cash register that prints the total amount paid on the sales check, and on a continuous audit tape. At the end of the shift or the day the machine is cleared, the total sales revenue is printed on the audit tape, which is then removed by the accounting department. The total cash turned in should agree with the total sales on the audit tape. But even if there is agreement, there is no guarantee that the audit tape figure is correct. Overrings or underrings could occur, or a sales check might have been rung up more than once or not rung up at all, or might have been rung up without being inserted in the register. If the same transaction was rung up twice, the cash would be short and the overring would identify the cash shortage. However, if a cash transaction is not rung up, a cash overage would exist, which could be stolen by the cashier.

Because of all these possibilities, further control over sales checks is needed. First, the prices, extensions, and additions of all sales checks should be verified (if time does not allow this daily, then it should be done on a spot-check basis). Then the sequence of numbers of sales checks turned in should be verified to make sure there are no missing sales checks. Finally, an adding machine listing of sales checks should be made. Assuming no errors were made on this adding machine listing, the total on this listing should be reconciled against the cash turned in. If no cashier errors were made, the register audit tape will also agree with the adding machine listing.

A person other than the cashier and server should verify the sales checks for prices, extensions, additions, and other changes to ensure that there are no missing sales checks. This person should also prepare the adding machine tape. In this way the responsibility for sales revenue control is divided, and one person verifies the work of another. The cost of the second person's time conducting the verification will normally be more than recovered in increased net income as a result of reduction of losses from undiscovered errors.

EXPLAIN THE REASONS

Employees who carry out internal control functions should have the reasons they are asked to perform these tasks explained to them. For example, in the previous section it was suggested that a second person verify the work of the cashier. The losses that can occur from servers making errors in pricing items on sales checks, in multiplying prices by quantities, and in totaling sales checks could add up to many dollars. So could losses from missing sales checks where cash was received from the customer, but a dishonest server or cashier kept the cash and destroyed the sales check. The importance of minimizing these losses should be explained to the employee doing the task.

ROTATE JOBS

Wherever possible, jobs should be rotated. This may be difficult to do in a small establishment with few employees. In a larger operation, cashiers could be moved from one department to another from time to time, or accounting office employees could have their jobs rotated every few months. Employees who know they are not going to be doing the same job for a long time will be less likely to be dishonest. The possibilities of collusion are also reduced because the same two employees will not work together for a long time. Job rotation also has another advantage in that it prevents employees from becoming bored from constantly carrying out the same tasks. It also builds flexibility into job assignments and will give the employees a better understanding of how the various jobs relate to each other.

USE MACHINES

Whenever possible, machines should be used. Although machines cannot prevent all possibilities of theft or fraud, they can vastly reduce these possibilities. The installation of a machine may also reduce labor cost if an employee is no longer required to perform a task manually. Such machines include front office billing/audit equipment, restaurant and bar cash registers and/or point-of-sale systems (POS), and mechanical or electronic drink-dispensing bar equipment. For example, an electronic POS will eliminate many of the losses from the types of errors mentioned earlier. Also, the saving in labor (because the manual verifications will no longer be required) will contribute toward the cost of the equipment.

SET STANDARDS AND EVALUATE RESULTS

One of the requirements of a good internal control system is not only to control the obvious visible items, such as cash or inventory, but also to have a reporting system that indicates whether all aspects of the business are operating properly.

For example, one of the many benchmarks used in the food industry to measure the effectiveness of the manager is the **food cost percentage.** Management needs to know whether the food cost percentage actually achieved is close to the standard cost desired. Therefore, the manager must have a standard to which the actual cost information will be compared.

Once procedures have been established and the various employees have been given detailed written guidelines about how to perform tasks, standards of performance should be established. Later in this chapter, we shall see how cost control standards can be established and actual results evaluated.

DESIGN FORMS AND REPORTS

To evaluate results, forms and reports to provide information about all aspects of the business need to be designed. Properly designed forms or reports will provide management with the information it needs to determine whether standards are being met and to make decisions that will improve the standards, increase performance, and ultimately produce higher profits. The manager's daily report, shown earlier in Exhibit 4.6, is one type of form.

Another set of standards derives from budgets and budget reports that allow actual results to be compared with those budgeted. Budgets are discussed in Chapter 9.

BOND EMPLOYEES

Consideration should be given to bonding employees. For example, fidelity bonds protect the operation from losses incurred by employee dishonesty because the establishment is reimbursed up to the face value of the insurance policy for the loss suffered.

INSIST ON MANDATORY VACATIONS

Vacations should be mandatory, particularly for employees who have control of assets. Employees inclined to be dishonest may be discouraged from theft or fraud if they know that during their vacation some other person will have control of those assets and that, if theft or fraud has occurred, it may be discovered during this vacation. Even if theft or fraud has not occurred, the new person doing the job may discover weaknesses in the control system that were not previously apparent. Additional preventative controls can then be implemented.

CREATE AN AUDIT TRAIL

Most good internal control systems are based on having an **audit trail** that documents each transaction from the time that it was initiated through source documents (such as purchase orders or sales checks) and defined procedures through to the final recording of the transaction in the operation's general ledger. A good audit trail allows each transaction, where necessary, to be tracked again from start to finish.

CONTROL DOCUMENTS

Wherever possible, all documents, such as sales checks, requisitions, and purchase orders, should be preprinted with sequential numbers. In this way, individual documents can be tracked and accounted for. Numbering is particularly important for sales revenue control forms, such as sales checks.

When numbered documents are issued, the individual receiving the documents should be required to sign for them to establish responsibility and accountability for the documents.

The accounting department should oversee all documents, even though they are actually used by employees in other departments. In other words, they should be designed, ordered, stored, issued, and have their usage controlled by the accounting office. It is also the accounting office's responsibility to periodically check the sequence of all numbered documents to ensure that none are missing.

INSTITUTE COMPANY AUDITS

One of management's major responsibilities in internal control is constant supervision and review of the system. An **internal audit** is an appraisal of the operating and accounting controls of an organization to ensure that internal control procedures are being followed and assets are adequately safeguarded.

The internal audit is necessary for two reasons: (1) The system becomes obsolete as business conditions change; and (2) Without continuous oversight, the control system can collapse. For example, one of the important control techniques in a food service operation is to ensure each day that there are no missing, prenumbered checks on which sales revenue are recorded. If an employee (after having served food and beverages, presented the sales check, and collected the cash) retains both the sales check and the cash and is subsequently not questioned about this, he or she will realize that the control system is not working effectively. The employee is then free to continue to hold back sales checks and pocket cash.

In small operations, the supervision and review of the internal control system is the responsibility of the general manager. In larger establishments, with accounting departments, the supervision and review responsibility is turned over to the employees in that department. In very large companies, internal auditing teams will be established. They will be responsible for appraising the effectiveness of the operating and accounting controls, and for verifying the reliability of forms, records, reports, and other supporting documentation to ensure that internal control policies and procedures are being followed and assets are adequately safeguarded. All companies, regardless of size, should undergo periodic **external audits.** An external audit is conducted by an objective, outside firm of auditors who are certified public accountants (CPAs). Although the CPA firm cannot guarantee that fraud or theft has not occurred, it is more likely to discover potential or actual abuses.

CONTROL OF PURCHASES

To understand the necessity for control of purchases, assume that in a restaurant operation, every employee had the authority to buy food for resale and that there were no control procedures or forms in use. In such a situation, there would be absolute confusion concerning what had been ordered and received. In addition, there would be duplications, mistakes, over-and-short shipments, payments for items not received, and constant opportunities for dishonest employees to commit theft or fraud.

In order to have control over purchasing, it is necessary to divide the responsibilities among several individuals or departments. Coordination over the various purchasing tasks is achieved using five basic documents:

1. Purchase requisition
2. Purchase order
3. Invoice
4. Receiving report
5. Invoice approval form or stamp

Each of these is discussed in turn in the following sections.

PURCHASE REQUISITION

In making purchases in large, multidepartment operations, the employees of the purchasing department cannot constantly be aware of the supply and service needs of the various operating departments. Generally, the responsibility for having an adequate supply of items in each department is delegated to each department manager. However, the department managers should not be allowed to deal directly with suppliers, since control of purchasing could not then be coordinated. In order to have this control over purchases and the liabilities (accounts payable) that result, purchasing must be centralized. Each department or division manager should be responsible to initiate supply requirements to the responsible purchaser, or the purchasing department. Supply requirements are

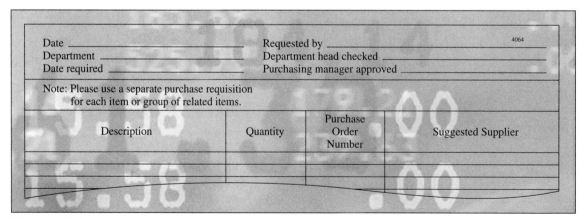

■ **EXHIBIT 5.6**

Sample Purchase Requisition

initiated by use of a **purchase requisition,** prepared in triplicate. The original and duplicate are sent to the purchaser or purchasing department and the third copy is retained by the department head for later checking. A sample requisition is illustrated in Exhibit 5.6.

The purchasing department's role is to make sure that supplies, equipment, and services are available to the operation in appropriate in quantities, at the right price, and at a minimum cost to meet desired standards. Generally, those responsible for purchasing have the authority to commit the establishment's funds for buying required goods or services. Sometimes a maximum dollar amount for any individual purchase may be established beyond which a higher level of authority is required before proceeding with the purchase. Those responsible for purchasing may have authority to question individual purchase requisitions with reference to the particular need or the stipulated specifications.

PURCHASE ORDER

A **purchase order** is a form prepared by the purchasing department authorizing a supplier to deliver needed goods and services to the establishment. A sample purchase order is illustrated in Exhibit 5.7. Generally, four copies are prepared—one for the supplier, one for the department initiating the purchase requisition (this advises them that the required items have been ordered), one

FRANKLYN HOTEL 1260 South St., Manchester Telephone: (261)434-5734			
PURCHASE ORDER (The purchase order number must appear on all invoices, bills of lading, or correspondence relating to this purchase. Invoice must accompany shipment.)			653
Department _____ Purchase order date _____ To supplier:	Purchase requisition # _____ Delivery date: _____		
Description		Quantity	Price
Purchasing manager's signature _____			

■ EXHIBIT 5.7

Sample Purchase Order

that remains with the purchasing department, and the fourth, with a copy of the purchase requisition attached, sent for control purposes to the accounting department. For control purposes it is also a good idea to record the purchase order number on the purchase requisition, and to record the purchase requisition number on the purchase order.

In many cases in the hospitality industry, particularly where it involves day-to-day food and supplies ordering, a system of purchase orders is just not practical because most orders are placed at short notice and by telephone. In such cases, special procedures and forms will prevail. For example, an operation may have a list of approved suppliers from whom it can purchase supplies. If it wants to purchase from a supplier who is not on the list, it must seek approval from the purchasing department before it places an order.

INVOICE

The third document in the system of purchasing control is the **invoice.** An invoice is prepared by the supplier and is simply an itemized listing of the goods or services to be received from the supplier. Generally, in the hospitality industry suppliers are asked to have the priced and totaled invoice accompany the shipped goods, since this aids the receiving department in the receiving process. However, for control purposes it's a good idea to have the supplier also send a copy of the invoice directly to the establishment's accounting office.

RECEIVING REPORT

The **receiving report** is used to verify that the goods being received are the goods requested and should be checked item by item against the invoice. The person or persons responsible for receiving should weigh products purchased by weight, should count cased goods, and confirm that each case is full. As discussed in item 9 of the preceding section on preparing written procedures, prepare a credit memorandum listing the items missing or returned. Obtain the delivery driver's signature acknowledging he or she is returning with the noted items. Staple the credit memorandum to the original invoice. A sample receiving report for food and beverages is illustrated in Exhibit 5.8 for multidepartment organizations. A report such as this should be completed daily and sent at the end of each day with accompanying invoices to the accounting office.

INVOICE APPROVAL FORM OR STAMP

When the accounting department receives the receiving report, it can match it with a copy of the original purchase requisition, a copy of the purchase order, and the related invoice(s). All the relevant information can be compared and verified. The invoice prices should be compared to the prices quoted and

Daily Record of Purchases and Issues

Hotel _____

Dept. _____   Date _____ 20 _____ Day of Week _____

Purchases			Stock to Storeroom				Bar				
1	2	3	4	5	6	7	8	9	10	11	12
Name of Item	Amount of Invoice	Direct Issues to Kitchen	Meat, Fish and Poultry	Staples	Fruits & Vegetables	Dairy Products	Liquor	Beer	Wine	Mixed Ingred	Cartage
A Today's Purchases											
B Balance Forward from Yesterday											
C Total to Date This Month											

13	14	15	16	17	18	19	20	21	22	23	24	25
					Direct Issues							
	Meat	Fish	Poultry	Fruits	Veget.	Dairy Products	Bakery Products	Staples	Coffee	Butter	Eggs	Food Cost 14 to 24
Direct Les.												
Stores Les.												
Total Les.												
Fwd. Bal.												
Total M D												
I Begining Inventory Last Month End												
J Stock to Store Room C4 to 7										5c		
K Store Room Issues E 14 to 24										21 to 25		
L (I + J = K) Balance on Hand												
M Physical Inventory												
N (L + or - M) Adjustment $												
O (N% to M) Adjustment %												
P (Sales/M) Inventory Turnover												

■ **EXHIBIT 5.8**

Sample Receiving Report

Purchase order number	
Requisition checked	
Purchase order checked	
Receiving report checked	
Invoice prices checked	
Invoice calculations checked	
Approved for payment	
Invoice paid	

■ EXHIBIT 5.9

Sample Invoice Approval and Paid Form

recorded on the purchase order. Finally, the invoice should be checked for arithmetical errors. If everything is in order, the accounting department can approve the invoice for payment; stamping it or attaching a form to it can do this. An outline of this **invoice approval stamp** or **form** is illustrated in Exhibit 5.9. Initials or signatures should be put in the appropriate places to indicate that all the proper checks have been completed.

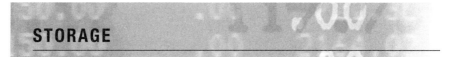

STORAGE

The following practices should be used for product storage:

■ Immediately after goods have been delivered and all receiving checks performed, they should be moved to storage areas or sent directly to the departments that requested them. Proper storage facilities (such as refrigerated areas for perishable food products) should be used.

■ Storage areas should be locked when the storekeeper is not present. Access to storerooms should be limited to the storekeeper and other authorized employees.

■ Storekeepers should not maintain or have access to formal inventory records, nor should accounting department employees who maintain those records have access to storerooms except to take inventories.

■ Inventory counts of stored products should be taken periodically by accounting office employees and compared to perpetual inventory cards (if used). A perpetual inventory card should be maintained for each separate item in stock. It has recorded on it, for each item, quantities received in and quantities issued from the storeroom to provide a running balance of what should be in inventory.

Item _____	Supplier _____	Tel. # _____
Minimum _____	Supplier _____	Tel. # _____
Maximum _____	Supplier _____	Tel. # _____

Date	In	Out	Balance	Requisition Cost Information

■ **EXHIBIT 5.10**

Sample Perpetual Inventory Card

A sample perpetual inventory card is illustrated in Exhibit 5.10. The in-column figures are taken from the invoices delivered with the goods. The figures in the out column are recorded from the storeroom requisitions completed by departments requiring items from storage. A sample requisition is illustrated in Exhibit 5.11.

Blank storeroom requisitions should only be made available, preferably in duplicate, to those authorized to sign them. The original storeroom requisition listing the items and quantities required is delivered to the storekeeper. The person initiating the storeroom requisition checks the quantities received from the storeroom and keeps the duplicate copies. Issuing each department with blank storeroom requisitions of a different color aids in department identification.

The best procedure for taking inventory is to make two accounting office employees responsible. One completes the actual physical count; the other com-

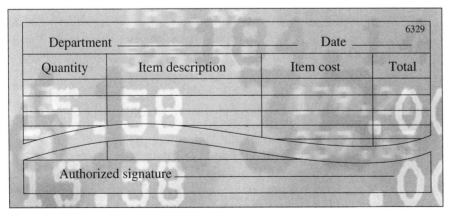

■ **EXHIBIT 5.11**

Sample Storeroom Requisition

pares this with the perpetual inventory card figure and then records the actual count on an inventory sheet.

- If there are any significant differences that cannot be reconciled between the inventory count and what should be in inventory according to perpetual inventory cards, the differences should be investigated to determine the cause. In this way, new procedures to help prevent future differences can be implemented.
- To aid an inventory count, preprinted inventory sheets that list items in the same order as they are located on storeroom shelves should be used.

CASH RECEIPTS

Good cash handling and control procedures are not only important to the business owner or manager but also to the employees involved, because a good system will allow them to prove that they have handled their responsibilities correctly and honestly.

In hotels and restaurants, cash is received in payment for food, beverages, and services at several places in the operation. Each position handling cash (restaurants and/or bar cashiers, front office cashiers, general cashier in the accounting office) needs definite procedures to ensure that all cash due to the business is properly received, recorded, and deposited in the bank. The procedures vary from one operation to another because of differences in use of equipment, number of employees involved, whether credit is extended to customers or guests, and for numerous other possible reasons.

In restaurants, bars, and other sales revenue outlets, each cash sale should be rung up on a cash register or a POS system at the time of the sale. Each cash register should have a locked-in tape that prints the amount of each sale. Those ringing up sales revenue should not have access to this tape (another example of separation of assets and the recording thereof). The accounting office should remove the tape at the end of a shift or each day. In the accounting office, an individual other than the person who collected and handled the cash should record the daily cash register readings. In this way, the tape forms the basis for the entry in the accounting records, and that entry can be verified against the records of the person who handles cash remittances. This prevents the person handling the cash from removing cash and changing the accounting records.

Control over cash received by mail in payment for accounts receivable was discussed earlier in this chapter. In addition, when checks are received in payment for those accounts, a deposit stamp should immediately endorse them with a statement such as "For deposit only to the ABC Hotel's account number 3459."

An important aspect to controlling losses from uncollectable accounts is to age them periodically. This should be done monthly. (Aging of accounts is discussed in Chapter 11.)

If any accounts receivable are to be written off as uncollectable, the general manager or a delegated responsible person who does not handle cash or have any access to recording amounts received on accounts receivable should authorize the write-off. When it is apparent that someone is delinquent in paying an account, all collection efforts should be carefully documented before the final decision to write off the uncollectable amount is made.

All cash receipts should be deposited intact each day in the bank. The business should keep a deposit slip stamped by the bank. This is a form of receipt showing how much was deposited each day. If all cash received is deposited daily, no one who handles cash will be tempted to "borrow" cash for a few days for personal use. It also ensures that no payments are made in cash on invoices. If this were allowed, a dishonest employee could make out a false invoice and collect cash for it.

Employees who handle cash (and other assets, such as inventories) should be bonded. In this way losses are less likely to occur because the employee knows he or she will have to answer to the insurance company.

CASH DISBURSEMENTS

To handle minor cash disbursements, a petty cash fund should be established. Initially, the fund should be established with sufficient cash to handle approximately one month's transactions. The responsibility for accountability and administration of the fund should be controlled by one person. The amount of cash placed into the fund is called the *fund limit* and is accounted for at least monthly. A receipt, invoice, voucher, or memorandum explaining the purpose of each disbursement must support payments from the fund. The receipt, invoice, voucher, or memoranda should be noted as paid in such a manner as to preclude reuse.

Accountability of the fund is summarized as follows:

Fund limit = Cash (coin and currency on hand) + Receipts

Random spot checks of the fund should be made to ensure that the amount of cash on hand in the petty cash fund, plus the receipts, invoices, and so on, equal the limit of the fund. No IOUs or postdated checks should be allowed. The fund is replenished as required to bring the fund back to its limit by exchanging cash for the receipts, invoices, and so on.

All other disbursements should be made by check and should be supported by an approved invoice. All checks should be prenumbered sequentially and should be used in sequence. The person who prepared checks in payment of invoices should not be the person who has authority to sign checks. Preferably, two authorized signatures should be required on checks, and invoices should be canceled in some way when they are paid so they cannot be paid twice. Those authorized to sign checks should not be allowed to prepare them or control the supply of unused (blank) checks. Only those who prepare (but do not sign) checks should have access to blank checks. Any checks spoiled in preparation should be voided in some way so that they cannot be reused. Voided checks must be kept. Used checks should be audited to ensure that all numbered checks are accounted for.

It is advisable to use a check protector to print amounts on checks, because this generally prevents anyone from altering the amounts.

If a mechanical check-signing machine is used, the key that allows this machine to operate should be in the hands of the employee authorized to use it. If the machine keeps a sequential count of the number of checks processed through it, someone in authority should maintain a separate count of the number of blank checks used and reconcile this periodically with the machine count. Once the checks have been signed, manually or mechanically, they should not subsequently be available to the person who prepared them. They should immediately be mailed to suppliers, or distributed by another employer or manager to employees in the case of payroll checks.

Some larger hotels and restaurants control check disbursements using a voucher system. With a **voucher system,** the procedures for control of purchases outlined earlier in this chapter are assumed to be in effect. When the invoice receives approval for payment (see Exhibit 5.9), a final document called a voucher is prepared. Vouchers are numbered in sequence and summarize some of the information from the other documents. There is also space on the voucher for recording the date of payment and the number of the check used in payment of the voucher. The supporting documents are attached to the voucher. When the voucher is to be paid, it is given to the person who prepares the checks. The person or persons who eventually signs the checks then knows the transaction is an authentic one because the check is accompanied by a voucher and the voucher has attached to it the purchase requisition and purchase order, the receiving report showing goods received, and the invoice, which has been checked for accuracy. There is little likelihood of fraud, unless all the documents were stolen and authorized signatures forged, or unless there is collusion.

PAYROLL

The procedures for cash disbursements discussed so far are intended to control purchases made externally. Since labor cost is such a high proportion of operating costs, equal care must be taken to ensure that proper control is exercised over this internal cost. Payroll checks should be written on a different bank account than that used for general disbursement checks, and the preparation and signing of payroll checks should be supported by a sound internal control system so that only properly authorized labor is paid for.

In addition, the following internal control procedures should be in effect for payroll:

- Only the general manager, a department head, or the personnel department (in a large hotel) should authorize the hiring or replacement of an employee and approve a salary or wage rate. The person or persons with this authority should have nothing to do with payroll check preparation.
- After an employee is hired, any subsequent pay rate increase should be authorized and approved on a change in rate of pay form, such as that illustrated in Exhibit 5.12.
- Procedures should be implemented for recording hours worked for hourly paid employees and for reporting them to the person who prepares payroll checks. In some establishments, hours worked are recorded by a time clock. The employee's department head should approve time clock cards before they are forwarded to the payroll department.
- Alternatively, the department head should not refer to the time cards, but should instead record on a separate form each employee's starting and finishing hours for each day of the pay period. In such a case, the payroll department should then compare the department head's record with each employee's time card and investigate any serious differences by discussing the situation with the employee and the department head.
- No overtime hours should be paid without approval by the employee's department head. An overtime approval form is illustrated in Exhibit 5.13.
- From time to time, an authorized accounting office employee should spot-check all payroll sheets to verify that hours worked, pay rates, and gross and net pay calculations are accurate.
- All payments for work performed should be made by check. Check usage control procedures should be the same as outlined earlier, in the section on cash disbursements.
- A separate payroll bank account should be maintained with sufficient funds transferred to it each payday to cover all payroll checks issued.

Employee	_____
Position	_____
Current pay rate	_____
New pay rate	_____
Effect date	_____
Signatures	_____
Department head	_____
Manager	_____

■ **EXHIBIT 5.12**

Authorization for Change in Rate of Pay

Date _____	Department _____
Employee _____	
Position _____	
Overtime hours _____	Overtime rate _____
Reason _____	
Department head signature _____	

EXHIBIT 5.13
Overtime Authorization Form

- Employees independent of each other should handle payroll check preparation and check distribution. Payroll checks should be handed to employees or mailed to the employees' home address. They should not be left for employees to pick up.
- Any paychecks that cannot be distributed to employees should be turned over to the chief accountant or to some other delegated person who has no responsibility for payroll check preparation. That person should hold employee checks until they are picked up by the employees.
- In small hospitality operations, each employee generally picks up checks from the payroll office. In larger establishments, department heads often receive, sign for, and distribute checks to their department's employees. In such cases, employees are often known either to the payroll office employee(s) or to the department heads.
- For further control in some large establishments, an employee of the accounting or audit office is delegated to ensure that an employee actually exists for each check prepared and issued. Because that employee might not be able to identify that each person receiving a paycheck is actually an employee, each person receiving a check is required to sign for it on a form that lists all current employees according to personnel office records. Some operations take this control one step further by ensuring that the employee's signature for the check compares with the one on that employee's initial job application form.
- Wherever possible, avoid paying wages in cash because a dishonest department head can easily forge cash wage forms. Alternatively, department heads may get around full-time staffing restrictions by employing part-time employees and authorizing cash payments to them.

However, it is recognized that sometimes payment of cash wages cannot be avoided. For example, banquet employees are often hired as needed for each separate function, and it would be unfair to make an employee who has worked for only a few hours during a pay period wait until the end of the pay period before being paid by check. Indeed, in many hospitality operations such employees are paid at the end of each function by check or, more often, by cash. In the latter case, each employee should be required to sign a banquet cash-payment form, indicating that the pay (less any necessary deductions) has been received.

Similarly, cash wage advances should be avoided unless a real hardship case is evident. Employees given wage advances often find that it makes their situation more difficult (because they will receive less than the normal pay amount on the regular pay day). Most requests for wage advances are made by employees who have a track record of advance-pay requests.

BANK RECONCILIATION

An essential control procedure in an effective internal control system is a monthly bank reconciliation. **Bank reconciliation** is a most effective tool for the management of money. The person completing the bank reconciliation compares the bank statement balance to the check register (or checkbook) and adjusts both the bank statement and the check register to the same total closing balance. The check register (checkbook) is an important tool that records all cash payments. Each month, the operation should receive a bank statement from the organization's bank providing essential items of information, which at a minimum should include the following:

- Deposits made, amount, and date
- The amount and date of each check paid, by check number
- Amounts added to the bank account and why they were added
- Amounts deducted by the bank from the business's account and why each was deducted
- Checks paid and canceled, returned for the business's records and information

The essence of the bank statement reconciliation is to bring the reported bank statement balance into equality with the check register balance (Exhibit 5.14). Adjustments are made to the reported bank balance by adding or deducting information shown in the check register but not yet handled by the bank. Typically, bank omissions will be deposits made but not shown and checks issued but not cashed by the bank. The bank statement will inform the business of additions and deductions made from the business's checking account that are not known until shown on the bank statement.

To ensure control of cash, the person who controls cash should not control the reconciliation. There are four steps in the bank reconciliation:

1. Review information in the bank statement, noting the date and balance reported by the bank, which will be reconciled to the check register (checkbook).

2. Review the company's records of deposits and compare bank deposits made to those shown as received by the bank. Deposits made but not shown on the bank statement are deposits to be added to the bank statement balance.
3. Review the checks cashed and returned by the bank to the checks written per the check register. All checks issued but not cashed by the bank are noted and classified as *outstanding* and deducted from the reported bank statement balance. Any errors made by the bank should be reported to the bank for correction.
4. Note the balance of the check register and use information regarding additions and/or deductions to the company bank account that are not known until receipt of the bank statement. Adjust the check register (or checkbook).

To illustrate how the bank reconciliation is carried out, the following example is provided:

Reported bank statement balance	$4,442
Check register (checkbook) balance	$5,012
Deposits in transit	$1,206
Outstanding checks: #2820 @ $284	
#2828 @ $138	
#2832 @ $332	$ 754
Interest earned on checking account	$ 42
NSF* check	$ 125
NSF* check charges	$ 15
Bank service charges	$ 20

*NSF refers to a deposited check that was not cashed due to insufficient funds in the account of the maker.

Example reconciliation is shown as follows:

Bank Statement Reconciliation

Bank statement balance	$4,442	Check register balance		$5,012
Add: Deposits in transit	1,206	Add: Account interest		42
Subtotal	$5,648	Subtotal		$5,054
Deduct: Outstanding checks		Deductions:		
#2820 @ $284		NSF check	$125	
#2828 @ 138		NSF check charge	15	
#2832 @ 332	(754)	Service charges	20	(160)
Reconciled Balance	$4,894	Reconciled Balance		$4,894

A separate reconciliation should be conducted on each individual bank account maintained by a business. Exhibit 5.14 is a sample format.

Company X
Bank Reconciliation
For the Month of October 0006

Cash Account Balance	$ xxxxx
ADD	
Items not recorded	
Interest earned	
Errors made in the books	
Loan payments received but not recorded	
Items collected by the bank	
Subtotal	(a) $ amount
DEDUCT	
Items not recorded	
Errors made in the books	
Service charges not recorded	
Subtotal	(b) $ amount
Total Adjustments	(a–b) $ amount
Adjusted Cash Account Balance	**
Bank Statement Balance	$ yyyyy
ADD	
Deposits in transit (outstanding)	
Errors made by the bank	
Subtotal	(c) $ amount
DEDUCT	
Outstanding checks	
Errors made in the books	
Subtotal	(d) $ amount
Total Adjustments	(c–d) $ amount
Adjusted Bank Statement Balance	$ amount**

**These two figures must be the same and, therefore, the bank account has been reconciled
with the general ledger.

■ **EXHIBIT 5.14**

Bank Reconciliation Sample Format

BANKING TRENDS AND ELECTRONIC
FUND TRANSFERS (EFT)

Many business operations and financial organizations are now using and
continue to develop additional ways to use **electronic funds transfer (EFT).**
The EFT techniques speed up receipt and disbursements of funds, reduce costs,
and enhance control to help prevent theft.

The trend for banks and other financial organizations is to hold canceled checks (safekeeping) for a specific time period, normally 90 days or less. The canceled checks are then copied to microfilm and then destroyed. The EFT procedure significantly reduces costs for the financial institutions, hospitality operations, and individuals as well.

Electronic funds transfer of payroll deposits to a bank will automatically transfer paychecks and deposit them to the employees' bank account if authorized by the employees. Employees who do not authorize EFT would draw normal payroll checks. The acceptence of debit cards used to pay for sales revenue purchases or for provided services is another example of EFT. The use of debit cards for services or sales revenue purchases are automatically deducted from the purchaser's bank account and added to the operation's bank account.

CASHIER'S DEPARTMENT

To reduce the possibility of fraud, the head cashier and other employees in that department should not have the responsibility for doing or overseeing any of the following:

- Preparing or mailing invoices or month-end statements to customers who owe the establishment money
- Recording any amounts in, or have any access to any accounts receivable records
- Authorizing rebates, allowances, or any other reductions to any accounts receivable
- Writing off any account as uncollectable
- Preparing checks or other forms of cash disbursement
- Reconciling bank accounts

ESTABLISHING COST STANDARDS

One of the requirements of a good internal control system is not only to control the obvious visible items, such as cash or inventory, but also to have a reporting system that indicates whether all aspects of the business are operating properly and according to desired standards.

For example, one of the benchmarks used in the food service industry to measure the effectiveness of the business is the food cost percentage. Management needs to know if the food cost percentage actually achieved is close to the standard desired.

If proper procedures are established for receiving, storing, issuing, and producing menu items, they are useful for good internal control. To improve the situation further, standard recipes for all menu items should be established, standard portion sizes determined, and menu items individually costed. The individual menu items' standard costs would be revised, when necessary, to reflect changes in prices of ingredients used in the recipes or changes in the recipes or the portion sizes. Therefore, these costs should be current and should not be estimated or based on some past situation that no longer reflects the current situation. Selling prices can then be determined to give a fair markup over cost and to offer the customer a competitive price.

A form, such as that illustrated in Exhibit 5.15, can then be used to record information about the individual menu items' costs and selling prices. The quantities sold figures are the quantities actually sold of each particular menu item during the past week. This information can be obtained by taking a tally from all the sales checks used that week. Alternatively, it can be obtained from electronic sales register records. The total standard cost column is a multiplication of the menu item cost and the quantity sold figures. The total standard sales revenue are calculated by multiplying the *menu item selling price* by the *quantity sold figures.*

Menu Item	Menu Item		Quantity Sold	Total Standard Cost	Total Standard Sales Revenue	Cost Percentage
	Cost	Selling Price				
1	$ 4.00	$ 6.50	486	$ 1,944.00	$ 3,159.00	61.5%
2	2.10	6.00	1,997	4,193.70	11,982.00	35.0
3	1.25	2.75	1,810	2,262.50	4,977.50	45.5
4	1.50	5.50	939	1,408.50	5,164.50	27.3
5	0.75	2.00	602	451.50	1,204.00	37.5
TOTALS				$10,260.20	$26,487.00	

$$\textit{Standard cost percentage} = \frac{\text{Total standard cost}}{\text{Total standard sales revenue}} = \frac{10{,}260.20}{26{,}487.00} \times 100 = \underline{\underline{38.7\%}}$$

$$\textit{Actual cost percentage} = \frac{\text{Total actual cost}}{\text{Total actual sales revenue}} = \frac{}{} \times 100 \quad = \underline{\underline{}}$$

$$\text{Difference} \quad \underline{\underline{}}$$

■ **EXHIBIT 5.15**

Partially Completed Standard vs. Actual Cost Form—Week 1

Menu Item	Menu Item		Quantity Sold	Total Standard Cost	Total Standard Sales Revenue	Cost Percentage
	Cost	Selling Price				
1	$ 4.00	$ 6.50	486	$ 1,944.00	$ 3,159.00	61.5%
2	2.10	6.00	1,997	4,193.70	11,982.00	35.0
3	1.25	2.75	1,810	2,262.50	4,977.50	45.5
4	1.50	5.50	939	1,408.50	5,164.50	27.3
5	0.75	2.00	602	451.50	1,204.00	37.5
TOTALS				$10,260.20	$26,487.00	

$$\text{Standard cost percentage} = \frac{\text{Total standard cost}}{\text{Total standard sales revenue}} = \frac{10,260.20}{26,487.00} \times 100 = 38.7\%$$

$$\text{Actual cost percentage} = \frac{\text{Total actual cost}}{\text{Total actual sales revenue}} = \frac{10,281.40}{26,487.00} \times 100 = 38.8\%$$

Difference   0.1%

■ **EXHIBIT 5.16**
Completed Standard vs. Actual Cost Form—Week 1

The final column of Exhibit 5.16 shows the individual standard cost percentage for each menu item. This information is useful when analyzing the food cost results. A standard cost represents what the cost is expected to be using projected conditions. For example, a change in the sales revenue mix can affect the food cost percentage. If the operation sells more of a menu item with a higher cost percentage, the overall cost percentage will also increase. The individual menu items' standard cost percentage information might also be useful when deciding which items to add to or delete from a menu or to promote. However, a menu item's cost percentage is not the only point to be considered; if a menu item with a higher cost percentage also has a higher dollar contribution margin than an item with a lower cost percentage, the operation might be better off with the menu item that has the higher cost percentage.

The overall standard cost percentage can be calculated using information from the total standard cost and total standard sales revenue columns, as illustrated in Exhibit 5.15. Finally, the actual cost percentage should be calculated, as illustrated in Exhibit 5.16. The information for actual cost is taken from the accounting records and from actual physical inventories using the general equation: Beginning of the period inventory + Purchases − End of the period inventory = Cost of goods sold (actual cost of food used). As discussed in Chapter 2, the actual food used might have to be adjusted for interdepartmental transfers during the period and for employee meals. Actual sales would normally be the same as standard sales. A difference between the two might occur if selling prices were recorded incorrectly on the sales checks or on the sales register or POS system.

The difference between the standard and actual food cost percentages can then be recorded. A difference can be expected because the standard is based on what the cost should be if everything goes perfectly. Such perfection seldom exists. Management must decide what difference will be tolerated before an investigation is carried out to determine the cause.

Exhibit 5.17 shows the completed form for the following week. Note that the figures for both the standard and actual percentages have changed. The reason is that different quantities of the various menu items offered have been sold and the ratio of what has been sold among the various menu items has changed (i.e., there has been a change in the sales revenue mix).

Therefore, it is to be expected that the total standard cost and sales revenue figures, as well as actual cost and sales revenue figures (and the related percentages), will change. With this analysis technique, management can now monitor the situation in an ongoing way. However, note that there has been no change in the cost percentage of any individual menu item.

Even though calculating a weekly standard cost seems like a lot of work, it can be readily computerized. As long as menu item cost and selling prices do

Menu Item	Menu Item		Quantity Sold	Total Standard Cost	Total Standard Sales Revenue	Cost Percentage
	Cost	Selling Price				
1	$ 4.00	$ 6.50	502	$ 2,008.00	$ 3,263.00	61.5%
2	2.10	6.00	1,724	3,620.40	10,344.00	35.0
3	1.25	2.75	1,828	2,285.00	5,027.00	45.5
4	1.50	5.50	759	1,138.50	4,174.50	27.3
5	0.75	2.00	742	556.50	1,484.00	37.5
TOTALS				$9,608.40	$24,292.50	

$$\text{Standard cost percentage} = \frac{\text{Total standard cost}}{\text{Total standard sales revenue}} = \frac{9,608.40}{24,292.50} \times 100 = \underline{\underline{39.6\%}}$$

$$\text{Actual cost percentage} = \frac{\text{Total actual cost}}{\text{Total actual sales revenue}} = \frac{9,816.70}{24,292.50} \times 100 = \underline{\underline{40.4\%}}$$

$$\text{Difference} \qquad \overline{0.8\%}$$

■ **EXHIBIT 5.17**

Completed Standard vs. Actual Cost Form—Week 2

not change, the only information that has to be entered each week is the quantity figure of each item sold, and in most operations today these figures are readily available from point-of-sale terminals. A spreadsheet can be used to carry out all of the remaining calculations.

Although the discussion and illustrations in this section have been related to food, the same technique can be used for alcoholic beverage sales revenue.

There are many other techniques applicable for control for food cost, beverage cost, labor cost, labor productivity, and so on. Because of the complex nature of complete internal control, it is impossible in this chapter to describe and illustrate all of them. Furthermore, most of these techniques have to be developed for or adapted to each establishment with its unique operating problems. Suffice it to say that good internal control would not be complete without such monitoring techniques.

METHODS OF COMMITTING THEFT OR FRAUD

The remainder of this chapter will be devoted to the ways in which theft or fraud have occurred in hospitality industry enterprises. These lists are not exhaustive; they include the more common ways in which misappropriations of assets have occurred. The lists can never be complete because, regardless of the improvements made to internal control systems, there is always a method of circumventing the control system, particularly if there is collusion between employees.

DELIVERIES

Suppliers or delivery drivers can use various methods to defraud a hotel or restaurant when they observe that the internal control procedures for receiving are not being used. They include:

- Invoice for high-quality merchandise when poor quality has been delivered.
- Put correct-quality items on the top of a box or case with substandard items underneath.
- Open boxes or cases, remove some of the items, reseal the boxes or cases, and charge for full ones.
- Deliver less than the invoiced weight of meat and other such items.
- Use padding or excess moisture in items priced by weight.
- Put delivered items directly into storage areas and charge for more than was actually delivered.
- Take back unacceptable merchandise without issuing an appropriate credit invoice.

RECEIVING AND INVENTORY

The people working in and around receiving and storage areas, if not properly controlled, could defraud by doing any of these:

- Work with a delivery driver approving invoices for deliveries not actually made to the establishment. The driver and the receiver could split the proceeds.
- Work with a supplier approving invoices for high-quality merchandise when poor-quality merchandise has been delivered. The driver and the receiver could split the proceeds.
- Pocket items and walk out with them at the end of the shift.
- Use garbage cans to smuggle items out the back door.
- Remove items from a controlled storeroom and change inventory records to hide the theft.

CASH FUNDS

Cash funds include general reserve cash under the control of the head cashier, the petty cash fund, and banks or change funds established for front office or food and beverage cashiers for making change. People handling cash can cheat by doing any of these:

- Remove cash and show it as a shortage.
- Use personal expenditure receipts and record them as expenses for business purposes.
- Remove cash for personal use and cover it with an IOU or postdated check.
- Under-add cash sheet columns and remove cash.
- Sell combinations to safes.
- Fail to record cash sales (income) received from sundry sales, such as vending machines, empty returnable bottles, and old grease from the kitchen.
- Remove cash and adjust the register readings or voiding sales.

ACCOUNTS PAYABLE AND PAYROLL

The person(s) handling accounts payable and/or payroll can practice fraud by doing any of these:

- Set up a dummy company and make out checks on false invoices in the name of this company.
- Work in collusion with a supplier and have the supplier send padded or dummy invoices directly to the accounts payable clerk.
- Make out checks for invoices already paid and cash the checks for personal use.

- Pad payroll with fictitious employee(s) and collect the wages for the fictitious employee(s).
- Pad gross pay amount on one or more employee(s) checks in collusion with the employee(s) by paying more hours than the employee(s) worked or paying a higher rate of pay than the employee(s) was entitled to.
- Carry employee(s) on the payroll beyond termination date.

FOOD AND BEVERAGE SALES REVENUE

For good sales revenue control, a system of sales checks and duplicates should be established (although there are exceptions; e.g., a cafeteria). Even with sales checks, servers or cashiers could practice the following:

- Obtain food and beverages from the kitchen or bar without recording items on original sales check; these items would be for personal consumption.
- Working in collusion with the kitchen, obtain food and beverages without recording the sale, and collect cash from the customer.
- Collect cash from the customer without a sales check and do not record the sale.
- Collect cash from the customer with a sales check already presented to another customer and do not record the sale.
- Collect cash from the customer with a correct sales check, destroy the check, and do not record the sale.
- Over-add the sales check, collect from the customer, and then change the total of the check to correct amount.
- Purposely under-add the sales check or neglect to include an item on it to influence a bigger tip.
- Collect cash with the correct sales check and record the sales check as canceled or void.
- Collect cash with the correct sales check and record it as a charge, with a false signature, to a room number or credit card number.
- Use sales checks obtained elsewhere to collect from customers and do not record the sale.
- Do not return a customer's credit card after the sale is complete, and subsequently use this stolen card to convert cash sales revenue to charge sales using a false signature.
- Since the customer in the preceding situation will eventually discover his or her card is missing and report it to the credit card company, exchange this stolen card after a few days with one from another customer (since customers seldom check to see if they are getting the correct card back); this can prolong the fraud for a long time.
- Collect the credit card from the customer for an authentic charge transaction, but before returning the card to the customer, run off additional

blank charge vouchers with this card through the imprinter and subsequently use the vouchers to convert cash sales to charge ones.

- Collect cash but record sale as a *customer walkout.* One should always be alert to actual walkouts (both intentional and unintentional) in all sales revenue areas.

BAR SALES REVENUE

In bars where the bartender also handles cash, one needs to be even more alert to the possibilities for fraud. In particular, watch for collections of toothpicks, matches, or coins the bartender is using to keep track of underpoured drinks or drinks sold but not recorded so that the bartender knows how much cash to remove when the bar is closed. Watch also for these scams:

- *Underpour drinks* (assume by one-eighth ounce on a one-ounce drink). For every eighth drink sold, do not record the sale, and pocket the cash. Using shot glasses with clear nail polish in the bottom or other measuring devices brought in personally that are smaller than the establishment's standard is one way to hide this.
- *Overpour drinks* (and underpour others to compensate) to influence a bigger tip.
- Bring in personally purchased bottles, selling their contents, and do not record sales revenue.
- Do not record sales from individual drinks until sufficient to add up to a full bottle, then record the sale as a full-bottle sale (which usually has a lower markup) and keep the difference in cash.
- Sell drinks, keep the cash, and record the drinks as spilled or complimentary.
- Dilute liquor and pocket the cash from the extra sales.
- Substitute a low-quality brand for a high-quality brand requested and paid for by customer, pocketing the difference in cash.

FRONT OFFICE

The front office area can also be a source of extra income for dishonest employees. A dishonest desk clerk could practice these tricks:

- Register a late-arriving guest who is also checking out early, collecting in advance. Destroy the registration card and fail to record the sales revenue on a guest account or folio. This may require collusion between the desk clerk and the housekeeper who cleans the room.
- Keep cash from day-rate guests under circumstances similar to those in the previous situation.

- Register the guest, collect the advance, and subsequently cancel the registration card and blank guest folio as a *did not stay*. Again, this may require collusion between the desk clerk and the housekeeper.
- Charge a high rate on the guest's copy of the account and record a lower rate on the hotel's copy where the accounting system is a manual one.
- Change the hotel's copy of the account to a lower amount after the guest has paid and is gone.
- Make a false allowance/rebate voucher with a forged signature after a guest has paid and is gone and use this voucher to authenticate a reduction of the hotel's copy of the guest folio.
- Create false paid-outs for fictitious purchases for the hotel or use personal expenditure receipts to justify the payout.
- Charge cash-paid guest accounts to corporate accounts.
- Use credit cards from authentic charge sales to convert a cash sale to a charge sale subsequently. (See previous examples under Food and Beverage Revenue.)
- Lap payments received on city ledger accounts (see earlier section in this chapter where this was discussed).
- Collect cash from a city ledger account thought to be uncollectible, pocket the cash, and write the account off as a bad debt.
- Collect cash from a city ledger account previously considered as being a bad debt and not recording the cash credit to the account.
- Record the guest account as a *skip* (a guest who intentionally leaves without paying) after the guest has actually paid the account.
- Receive deposits for room reservations in advance of the guest's arrival and fail to set up a folio in advance with the deposit credited.
- In collusion with the guest, do not charge for an extra person in the room in order to receive a tip.
- Sell deposit box or room keys to thieves or burglars.

Here is what a major hotel company had to say in a recent annual report about its internal control system:

> The Company maintains a system of internal control over financial reporting, which is designed to provide reasonable assurance to the Company's management and board of directors regarding the preparation of reliable financial statements. The system includes a documented organizational structure and division of responsibility, established policies and procedures, which are communicated throughout the Company, and the selection, training, and development of employees. Internal auditors monitor the operation of the internal control system and report findings and recommendations to management and the board of directors, and corrective actions are taken to control deficiencies and other opportunities for improving the system if and as they are identified.

There are inherent limitations in the effectiveness of any system of internal control, including the possibility of human error and the circumvention or overriding of controls. If employees conspire with someone else to steal from the corporation, it is very difficult to establish a control system that will prevent the theft and allow for efficient operations. Accordingly, even an effective internal control system can provide only reasonable assurance with respect to financial statement preparation. Furthermore, the effectiveness of an internal control system can change with circumstances.

COMPUTER APPLICATIONS

Word processing software allows management to easily produce internal control policies and procedure manuals for each new employee. When policies and/or procedures change, manuals can be revised and new copies distributed to all affected employees.

As noted earlier, computers can also be used for many aspects of internal control, such as preparing and issuing purchase orders, managing inventory, recording cash, and payroll preparation. Security can also be enhanced. For example, the person recording cash payments received in the mail can access the cash account to make the necessary entries but will not be able to access the accounts receivable account, and vice versa. Computerized (POS) systems can be used to reduce theft in food and beverage operations. The wait staff should only be able to receive food and beverage items after the products requested are entered into the POS system. The wait staff is then responsible for the collection of sales revenue from the guests, because the amount to be collected is already in the POS system.

In particular, a *spreadsheet program* can be used for producing the daily receiving report and completing all the calculations necessary for preparation of a standard versus actual cost form, as illustrated in Exhibits 5.15, 5.16, and 5.17.

SUMMARY

An important aspect of any business is safeguarding its assets. A good internal control system will accomplish this and will provide management with information on which to base business decisions. The internal control system should include methods and procedures for the employees to follow, and reliable forms and reports to provide the required information. With any internal control system, it is important to realize that the system may not prevent all forms of loss or dishonesty. If collusion is occurring, it is sometimes difficult to detect.

Once established, the control system needs to be monitored from time to time to ensure it is working well and continuing to provide valid and timely information. It is important to establish clear responsibilities for the various jobs to be performed so that a specific employee can be held accountable for errors or losses. Employees who are given responsibility should also be provided with detailed written procedures about how to perform their functions.

Written records (forms or reports) should be established to help employees carry out their jobs and to document information. A major principle of good internal control is to separate, whenever possible, record keeping and the actual control of the assets. For example, the person who handles cash should not be the same person who makes entries in the accounting records; otherwise it would be too easy to remove cash and alter the accounting records to hide the theft. By separating the two functions, collusion would then be required to hide theft. Similarly, wherever possible, the responsibility for related transactions should be divided so that the work of one employee will also check on the work of another. This does not mean to suggest that another person should duplicate the work of one person.

Employees should have their work explained to them so that they understand why they are doing specific tasks. In this way, the job should have more meaning to them. Job rotation is also a good idea.

One way to reduce the possibilities of fraud is to employ machines to do certain tasks that improve internal control; this may also lead to a labor cost-saving. Other principles of internal control are to limit access to assets, to carry out surprise checks at unusual times, to bond employees, to make vacations mandatory, to use external audits and provide audit trails, and to number all control documents.

Finally, any system of internal control requires constant supervision and review by management to guard against the system becoming obsolete. A major area requiring a good system of internal control is purchasing. This can be accomplished using five basic documents: a purchase requisition, a purchase order, an invoice, a receiving report, and an invoice approval stamp or form. Special procedures must be established for those handling cash, such as the cashiers at the various sales outlets, the front office cashier in a hotel, and the general cashier in the accounting office. Cash is the most liquid of assets, and without complete control can disappear too easily if employees are dishonest. Employees who are handling cash should be bonded.

Precautionary procedures for the handling of checks must be instituted and a bank reconciliation should be performed once a month. Standards of performance should be established and results evaluated so that management can determine if standards are being met and so that decisions can be made that will improve standards, increase performance, and ultimately produce higher profits.

DISCUSSION QUESTIONS

1. What are the two basic requirements for an internal control system?
2. Define *collusion,* and explain why you think it is difficult to detect.
3. Why is it necessary to define responsibility for particular jobs?

4. Explain what *separation of record keeping from control of assets* means, and why you would use it.

5. Explain how lapping works.

6. What does the term *division of responsibilities* mean?

7. List the five documents or forms used for control of purchases. Briefly explain the use of any two of these documents.

8. List and briefly discuss appropriate procedures for control over product storage and explain how perpetual inventory cards can be used in inventory control.

9. Why should all cash receipts be deposited intact each day in the bank?

10. Describe how a petty cash fund is established.

11. In paying invoices by check, how can control be established?

12. List the special procedures that are necessary for control of payroll and distribution of paychecks.

13. Explain the reasons why payment of cash wages should be avoided.

14. The balance of a company's check register normally will not agree with the bank statement balance prior to reconciliation. Why?

15. List the steps to reconcile the bank statement balance to the check register balance.

E T H I C S   S I T U A T I O N

A restaurant manager recently decided to change wine suppliers and switch to a supplier whose owner is a good friend. The first purchase order was for 15 cases (each containing 12 bottles) of various wines. When the manager arrived home that night, she found an unsolicited case of wine at the house provided free by the supplier. She decided not to tell the restaurant's owner and to keep the free case for herself. Discuss the ethics of this situation.

E X E R C I S E S

E5.1   Define the major objective of internal control.

E5.2   Define the purpose of a petty cash fund.

E5.3   Explain the difference between a purchase order and a purchase requisition.

E5.4   A petty cash fund with a $200 limit had receipts of $152 and cash (coin and currency) of $43. Explain the status of the fund.

E5.5   Explain the purpose of a bank reconciliation.

E5.6   Explain the purpose of standard cost control.

E5.7 Identify to what standard food cost percentage is compared.

E5.8 Assuming total standard cost is $18,282 and total standard sales revenue is $48,487, determine the standard cost percentage.

E5.9 Assuming total actual cost is $18,480 and total actual sales revenue is $48,487, determine the actual cost percentage.

E5.10 Assume the same person handles all cash and checks received in payment of an account. Explain how lapping works. Using the following information showing the day in August each payment was received; determine the amount lapped on each day. Comment on how lapping can be prevented.

Customer Name	*Amount of Check*	*Date Payment Received*
Arnold	$ 51.40	2
Sayers	62.11	4
Carter	101.10	7
Tuney	110.90	12
Lossie	141.20	14
Martie	162.75	17
Buddy	172.83	22
Smithe	185.22	27
Brown	202.90	30

PROBLEMS

P5.1 A motel has established a petty cash fund of $100 that is controlled by the day shift desk clerk. During October, the following disbursements supported by receipts or memoranda were made from the fund. Calculate the amount of the reimbursement check to the fund at the end of October 0006.

October	2	$13.51	flowers for a VIP guest
	2	4.30	postage stamps
	5	15.28	cleaning supplies
	7	7.11	freight on delivery of linen
	8	1.58	office supplies
	15	11.50	postage stamps
	16	5.00	refund to guest
	20	12.00	replacement light bulbs
	22	0.48	postage due
	28	3.75	cutting new keys
	31	6.45	gas for the lawnmower

In the same establishment, the following disbursements were made from the petty cash fund in November 0006:

November	1	$ 3.07	office supplies
	4	14.20	flowers for lobby
	7	1.30	office supplies
	7	12.00	casual wages to cut the lawn
	10	0.32	postage due
	13	11.50	postage stamps (no receipt)
	14	4.60	COD parcel for owner
	18	11.00	taxi cost for owner
	21	3.26	collect telegram
	24	4.02	freight on linen delivery
	24	1.16	office supplies
	29	10.50	postage stamps (note there was no receipt for this)
	30	1.16	stamps

The desk clerk has added these items and requests a reimbursement check for $86.09. A count of the cash by the manager shows there is $1.91 still in the fund, plus an IOU from the clerk for $12.00. What comments do you have about the petty cash fund for November 0006?

P5.2 Tavara's Tavern reconciles its bank statement monthly. At the beginning of July, it found the following concerning the June reconciliation: The bank balance on the bank statement was $4,810, and the bank balance according to the tavern's records was $5,112. Checks #306 in the amount of $27, #309 in the amount of $108, and #311 in the amount of $87 were still unpaid by the bank at June 30. At the end of June, the bank had added to the tavern's bank account an amount of $38 for interest earned on a separate savings account it has at the bank and had deducted $8 for a service charge. A deposit made by the tavern on June 30 in the amount of $554 did not appear on the bank's statement. Prepare Tavara's bank reconciliation for June 30, 0006.

P5.3 A hotel company reconciles its bank statement monthly. At the beginning of November, it found the following concerning the October reconciliation: The bank balance on the bank statement was $3,506, and the bank balance according to the company records was $4,740. Checks #3581 and #3650 in the amounts of $298 and $402, respectively, were still unpaid by the bank. The bank had credited (added) to the company's bank statement an amount of $356, which the company had earned from a separate savings account it has at the bank. The bank had also debited the bank statement wrongly with a check in the amount of $20 that had not been drawn by the hotel company. There was a $4 service charge on the bank statement. The October 31 deposit of $2,266 had not been recorded as received by the bank on the statement. Prepare the company's bank reconciliation for October 0007.

P5.4 A restaurant reconciles its bank statement monthly. The August 31 reconciliation showed the following: The restaurant's bank balance is $4,112 and the bank statement balance is $2,760. Deposits in transit August 30, $456, and August 31, $1,212, have not yet been recorded by the bank. Checks #167 for $61, #169 for $30, and #175 for $172 are outstanding. The bank statement showed a service charge of $6 and an interest credit amount of $61. A check received by the restaurant in payment of a customer's meal for $11, and deposited in the bank on August 25, was debited back to the bank statement on August 31 with the notation that there was not sufficient money in the customer's bank account to pay the check. In verifying the bank's record of daily deposits against the restaurant's records, it is discovered that the bank statement deposit of August 11 shows $1,212 while the company records show $1,221. Further checking shows the bank statement figure is the correct one. Prepare a bank reconciliation for August 0007.

P5.5 The bookkeeper who has worked for a small hotel for more than 30 years is retiring. Because he was such a reliable employee, he was given more and more responsibility over the years and did virtually all of the work, such as keeping all the accounting records, approving invoices for payment, preparing checks, and, in the absence of the hotel's owner, signing checks that needed to be sent to suppliers. His daily duties included collecting the cash at the end of the day from the front office and restaurant, clearing the machine tapes, counting and verifying cash against tapes, depositing the cash in the bank, and making the necessary entries in the hotel's bookkeeping records. At month-end he would do the bank reconciliation. The hotel's owner realizes that she cannot hire and train someone to take over all the responsibilities of the retiring bookkeeper and that it would not be desirable for internal control purposes to do so. She knows that she will have to assume some of the retiring employee's duties. She is busy already, since, as well as generally managing the hotel she does all the ordering of food supplies for the restaurant and all the ordering and receiving of bar supplies.

From an internal control point of view, discuss which of the retiring bookkeeper's responsibilities the owner should take over while, at the same time, minimizing the amount of time this would require.

P5.6 The owner of Charlene's Restaurant believes that her food cost is higher than it should be. Charlene thinks that the problem might be in the receiving area and/or the dining area because she says she has good control over food in storage and production. She has asked you to see what you can determine. By observation, you notice that when drivers make deliveries, they obtain a signature from any restaurant employee who happens to be near the receiving dock in the absence of the receiver or storekeeper. Deliveries are then left at the receiving dock until the goods received can be moved to a storage area. Sometimes invoices are left with food containers; at other times, no documentation is left. It is assumed that suppliers will mail the missing invoices to Charlene's office.

In the dining area you notice that the servers do not use printed sales checks to record customers' orders but simply note orders on scratch pads. They then tell the cooks what they need, and they pick up and deliver food to the customers. When the customers wish to pay, the servers jot down the total amount due on the scratch pad page, present the page to the customer, collect the cash, and put it into a cash drawer. No sales revenue was recorded in the cash register. "Used" scratch pad pages are placed in a box beside the cash drawer.

In both receiving and dining areas, outline the possible problems that current procedures create and suggest to Charlene practices that would probably solve the problems.

P5.7 A restaurant has been in operation for the past five years and has successfully increased its sales revenue each year. One of the reasons is that in the third year the owner began extending credit to local businesspeople who regularly used the restaurant. They were allowed to sign their sales checks and were then sent an invoice at each month-end. The owner is concerned that this credit policy may have led to increases in losses from bad debts (uncollectable accounts receivable) that were not justified by increases in sales revenue. The restaurant operates at a 60% gross margin ratio, and other operating expenses (not including bad debts) are 50% of sales revenue. Following are the credit sales revenue and bad debt figures for the past five years:

Year	Credit Sales Revenue	Bad Debts
1	$160,000	$ 960
2	180,000	900
3	240,000	3,840
4	300,000	4,500
5	360,000	5,400

In a columnar schedule for each year, record the credit sales revenue, cost of sales, gross margin, and operating expenses. In addition, in a second columnar schedule for each year, record income before bad debts (uncollectable accounts receivable), bad debts, operating income, and the bad debts as a percentage of credit sales revenue. Write a brief report to the owner with particular reference to control over bad debt losses and the restaurant's credit policy.

P5.8 A small hotel has an outside accountant prepare an income statement after the end of each month. For the last three months the amount shown as bad debts had increased considerably over any previous month. The owner asked the accountant to verify the authenticity of all accounts receivable written off as bad debts over the last three months. The accountant discovered that a number of accounts in large amounts had in fact been paid, and the persons contacted had canceled checks endorsed with the hotel's stamp to prove this. About three months ago a new hotel bookkeeper was hired to carry out all record keeping and also act as cashier, receiving and depositing the cash from the front office cashier and handling and depositing payments on accounts receivable received by mail. As the hotel's outside accountant, explain to the owner what you think has been happening and suggest how the problem can be resolved so that the same situation does not occur again.

P5.9 At some of the banquets held in a hotel, the bar is operated on a cash basis. All drinks are the same price. Banquet customers buy drink tickets from a cashier at the door. The customers then present the tickets to the bartender to obtain drinks. The bartender will not serve any drink without a ticket. As each ticket is presented, it is torn in half by the bartender to prevent its reuse. Torn tickets are subsequently discarded. At the end of the function the amount of drinks sold, calculated by taking an inventory of liquor still in bottles and deducting from the opening inventory, is compared with the cash taken in by the cashier and with the number of tickets sold.

To cut costs, the hotel is considering eliminating the cashier's position and the sale of tickets. The customers will pay the bartender directly for the drinks. From an internal control point of view, what comments do you have about this proposal?

P5.10 A fast-food restaurant features only three entree items on its menu with the following cost and selling prices:

Item	Cost	Selling Price
1	$2.20	$6.80
2	3.25	8.80
3	3.75	9.85

a. For each item calculate the food cost percentage.

b. If 50 of each item are sold each day, what will the standard food cost percentage be? What is the contribution margin in dollars?

c. If only 25 each of Items 1 and 3 sold and 100 of Item 2, what effect will this have on the standard cost percentage? What is the contribution margin in dollars?

d. Comment on the results of this analysis.

P5.11 The sales records for a coffee shop that has only six items on its menu show the following quantities sold during the month of January. Item standard cost and selling prices are also indicated.

Item	Cost	Selling Price	Quantity Sold
1	$2.50	$6.00	654
2	1.80	4.60	2,195
3	2.30	7.00	1,110
4	1.80	5.30	990
5	2.25	5.00	295
6	2.80	8.00	259

Actual cost of sales for the month of January was $11,885. Actual sales revenue for the month of January was $30,880.

a. Calculate the standard cost percentage and the actual cost percentage for January.

b. Compare the results. If you were the dining room manager, explain why you would or would not be satisfied with the results.

P5.12 A fast-food restaurant uses a standard cost approach to aid in controlling its food cost. The following are the standard cost, selling prices, and quantities sold of each of the five items featured on the menu during a particular week:

Item	Standard Cost	Selling Price	Quantity Sold
1	$1.80	$3.95	260
2	2.10	4.95	411
3	4.20	8.95	174
4	3.05	6.95	319
5	1.40	3.95	522

Total actual cost for the week was $3,804.10 and total actual sales revenue was $8,873.40.

a. Calculate total standard (food) cost, total standard sales revenue, and cost of sales percentages. Comment on the results.

b. The following week, with no change in menu or standard cost and selling prices, there was a change in the sales mix. Although quantities sold of Items 2, 3, and 5 were virtually the same, many more of Item 4 and many less of Item 1 were sold. As a result of this, would you expect the overall standard cost percentage to increase or decrease? Explain your answer.

CASE 5

a. The 4C Company restaurant has 84 seats, which is not large. For this reason, it does not have a large number of people on the payroll. Charlie has been handling the general manager's responsibilities and has a good friend working half a day, five days a week, to take care of such matters as bank deposits, preparing accounts payable and payroll checks, and all other routine office and bookkeeping work.

Charlie is not concerned about the honesty of the person, but he has learned from courses that he has taken that there is a need for any company, however small, to have some internal controls. Write a short report to Charlie pointing out three specific areas where you believe controls might need to be implemented. For each of the three areas, advise Charlie what might happen if a dishonest bookkeeper were hired and how internal control can be implemented to prevent dishonesty.

b. From his experience in the mobile catering company, Charlie had learned the value of standard cost control. In that business he purchased most of his food items proportioned and wrapped, and portion sizes were always the same. Food cost was easy to control, because each day an inventory count of each item he carried, plus the quantity purchased of that item that day, less the quantity still in inventory at the day's end, gave him a figure that, when multiplied by the selling price of the item, produced the standard sales revenue that he should have. When this was done for all food items, he could then compare his total standard food revenue each day with the actual revenue to make sure there were no differences. In this situation he was in complete control of the entire operation.

In the 4C Company's restaurant, because food dishes are produced in its own kitchen, it is not feasible to operate and control costs and sales revenue as with the 3C Company. The restaurant operates with eight main entree items on its menu, plus three soups and four desserts. These are changed seasonally. Coffee is free if an entree is ordered; otherwise, there is a charge. Explain as briefly as possible to Charlie the steps that could be implemented to have a system of standard food cost and sales revenue control. What about the problem that some people have free coffee while others pay, and the fact that customers have to pay for items such as milk and soft drinks?

CHAPTER 6

THE BOTTOM-UP APPROACH TO PRICING

I N T R O D U C T I O N

This chapter introduces various pricing methods that are used in the hospitality industry and points out the need for current, tactical, and long-range pricing methods. In this chapter we discuss in detail the concept of considering net income after tax as a cost in the process of determining product-selling prices. Using net income after tax as a cost is illustrated for a restaurant operation by way of forecasting the average check that will cover all the operation's costs including net income after tax. The illustration continues by showing how an average check per meal period is determined.

This chapter also introduces the subject of pricing individual menu items, and the possible difficulties that may be encountered. The relationship that exists between the sales revenue mix, the average check, and gross margin is discussed, as well as the topics of seat turnover and integrated pricing.

Menu engineering, using a technique of menu analysis that focuses on the contribution margin (gross margin) of each menu item, combined with its popularity, which is measured by customer demand, is discussed.

The chapter continues with a discussion of the use of net income after tax as a cost for a rooms operation. The same techniques used to determine the required average check in a restaurant operation apply to calculating the required average room rate for a hotel or motel operation.

We also look at the approach used to convert an overall average room rate into an average single and double room rate. A method of determining average room rates, based on the square footage of each type of room, is shown. The relationship between room rates and room occupancy is also discussed.

Room-rate discounting and the use of an equation to calculate the equivalent occupancy necessary to maintain total sales revenue (less marginal costs) constant if the rack rate is discounted is illustrated. We look at the use of a potential average room rate as a measuring device, and the establishment of discounted room rates for various market segments. Other pricing considerations such as an organization's objectives, elasticity of demand, cost structure, and competition are also discussed.

This chapter concludes with a section on yield management that matches customers' purchase patterns with their demand for guest rooms. This technique allows ownership to derive a future occupancy forecast with greater accuracy to meet the objective of maximizing room sales revenues.

CHAPTER OBJECTIVES

After studying this chapter, the reader should be able to

1. Discuss the advantages and disadvantages of various traditional pricing methods used in the hospitality industry and understand the difference between long-range and tactical pricing.

2. Explain the concept of using net income after tax as a cost.

3. Calculate total annual revenue required for a restaurant operation to cover all forecasted costs including net income after tax and convert the annual revenue to an average check amount.

4. Use existing information to calculate an average check per meal period and explain the effect that sales revenue mix of the various menu items will have on the average check.

5. Discuss the considerations to be kept in mind when pricing a menu item and calculate seat turnover figures. Also discuss integrated pricing for a restaurant.

6. Complete a menu engineering worksheet and discuss how to adjust the menu to respond to the results.

7. Calculate an average room rate to cover all forecasted costs, including net income after tax, and convert the average rate to an average single and average double rate.

8. Calculate room rates based on the square footage of a room.

9. Discuss room rate discounting and calculate occupancy percentage for a discount grid. Calculate a potential average room rate and discounted rates for various market segments.

10. Discuss some of the important considerations in pricing, such as the objectives of an organization, elasticity of demand, cost structure, and competition.

THE BOTTOM-UP APPROACH TO PRICING

Generally, **pricing theory** suggests that a hospitality operation should price its rooms and its food and beverage menu items to control costs and maximize profit, while at the same time offering guests an appropriate value for their money. The reasoning behind the pricing theory is that owners should be provided with a satisfactory return on investment if the products being sold are properly priced.

The method used to price products will, to a degree, dictate whether financial goals will be achieved. If prices are too high, customers will come to believe they are not receiving adequate value for their money and seek other sources to provide the product and services. On the other hand, if prices are too low, sales revenue potential is not maximized. In either event, profits can be expected to be lower than they should be.

As will be seen, hospitality operators establish price structures using a number of different methods, each with their advantages and disadvantages.

INTUITIVE METHOD

The intuitive method requires no real knowledge of the business or research into costs, profits, prices, competition, or the market. The operator just assumes that the prices established are the right ones because customers are willing to pay them. This method has no advantages. Its main disadvantage is that the prices charged are unrelated to profits.

RULE-OF-THUMB METHOD

Rule-of-thumb methods (such as a restaurant should price its menu items at 2.5 times food cost to achieve a 40% cost of sales) may have had validity at one time but should not be relied on in today's highly competitive environment because they pay no attention to the marketplace (competition, value for money, and so forth).

TRIAL-AND-ERROR METHOD

With the trial-and-error method, prices are changed up and down to see what effect they have on sales revenue and profits. When profit is apparently maximized, prices are established at that level. However, this method ignores the fact that there are many other variables (such as general economic conditions, seasonality of demand, and competition) that affect sales revenues and profits apart from prices. What appears to be the optimum pricing level might later be affected by these other factors. This method can also be confusing to customers during the price-testing period.

PRICE-CUTTING METHOD

Price cutting occurs when prices are reduced below those of the competition. This can be a risky method if it ignores costs, because if variable costs are higher than prices, profits will be eroded. Some restaurant operators set their food menu prices below costs on the risky assumption they will more than make up the losses by profits on alcoholic beverage sales revenue. To use this method, selling additional products must more than compensate for the reduction in prices. If the extra business gained is simply taken away from competitors, they will also be forced to reduce their prices, and a price war may result.

HIGH PRICE METHOD

Another pricing method is to deliberately charge more than competitors and use product differentiation, emphasizing such factors as quality, which many customers equate with price. If this strategy is not used carefully, however, it can encourage customers to move elsewhere when they realize that high price and high quality are not synonymous.

COMPETITIVE METHOD

Competitive pricing means matching prices to those of the competition and then differentiating in such areas as location, atmosphere, and other non-price factors. When there is one dominant operator in the market that generally takes the lead in establishing prices, and its close competitors matching increases and decreases, this method is then referred to as the follow-the-leader method. Competitive pricing tends to ensure there is no price-cutting and resulting reduction in profits. In other words, there is market price stability. This might be a useful method in the short run. However, if competitive pricing is used without knowledge of the differences that exist (in such matters as product, costs, and services) between one establishment and another, then this method can be risky.

MARKUP METHOD

In restaurants, **markup** is the difference between the cost of an item and its selling price. The markup method is used, for example, when a restaurant's traditional food cost percentage (as it appears on past income statements) is applied to determine the price of any new menu items offered. For example, if traditionally the restaurant has been operating at a 40% food cost, any new menu items offered would be priced so that they also result in a 40% food cost. The major problem with this method is that it assumes that 40% is the correct food cost for the restaurant to achieve its desired profit.

USING THE RIGHT METHOD

Many of the pricing methods just reviewed are commonly used because operators understand them and find them easy to implement. Unfortunately, if the establishment is not operating as efficiently as it should, these methods simply tend to perpetuate the situation, and sales revenue and profits will not be maximized. Owners or managers who use these methods are not fully in control of their operations and are probably failing to use their income statements and other financial accounting information to guide them in improving their operating results.

Pricing is a tool that can be used effectively to improve profitability. The dilemma is often a matter of finding the balance between prices and profits. In other words, prices should only be established after considering their effect on profits. For example, a restaurant can lower its prices to attract more customers, but if those prices are lowered to the point that they do not cover the costs of serving those extra customers, profits will decline rather than increase.

LONG-RUN OR STRATEGIC PRICING

Over the long run, price is determined in the marketplace as a result of supply and demand. When prices are established to compete in that marketplace, they must be set with the establishment's overall long-term financial objectives in mind. A typical objective could be any one of the following:

- To maximize sales revenue
- To maximize return on owners' investment
- To maximize profitability
- To maximize business growth in a new operation
- To maintain or increase market share for an established operation

A clearly thought-out pricing strategy will stem from the financial objective or objectives of the business, as well as recognize that these objectives might change over the long run.

TACTICAL PRICING

In addition to a long-run pricing strategy, a hospitality operation needs short-run, or tactical, pricing policies to take advantage of situations that arise from day to day. These situations might include any of the following:

- Reacting to short-run changes in price made by competitors
- Adjusting prices because of a new competitor
- Knowing how large a discount to offer group business while still making a profit
- Knowing how much to increase prices to compensate for an increase in costs

- Knowing how much to increase price to compensate for renovations made to premises
- Adjusting prices to reach a new market segment
- Knowing how to discount prices in the off-season to attract business
- Offering special promotional prices

Many of the remaining chapters in this book are concerned with using accounting-oriented approaches to provide managers with information to help them make decisions about operating cost activities of the operation and to maximize net income and return on investment. However, it is equally important to control sales revenue—that is, to control the prices that are established for the products and services offered. Since there is a relationship between prices charged and total sales revenue, prices will affect the general financial results, such as the ability to cover all operating costs and provide a net income that yields an acceptable return on investment. Price levels also affect such matters as budgeting, working capital, cash management, and capital investment decisions—all of which will be discussed in later chapters.

The traditional method of looking at an income statement is from the top down—that is, by calculating sales revenue and the costs associated with that sales revenue in order to determine if there is a net income. A different approach might be to start with the net income that is required, calculate costs, and determine what sales revenue is required and what prices are to be charged to achieve the desired net income. This bottom-up approach assumes that net income is a cost of doing business, which indeed it is. If a mortgage company lends money at a particular interest rate to a hotel or food service operation, the interest expense is considered to be a cost. The mortgage company is an investor. Another group of investors are the owners of the company (either stockholders or unincorporated individuals). They also expect interest on their investment of money and/or time, except that their interest is called net income. Therefore, net income is just another type of cost. This concept, and the bottom-up approach to calculating sales revenue, can be useful in deciding prices.

RESTAURANT PRICING

In general, various components of the income statement can be expressed as a percentage of total sales revenue or as identifiable (known) dollar values. We know that a common-size vertical analysis will allow us to express every element of an income statement as a percentage of total sales revenue. Known dollar values will consist of costs that are considered fixed or repetitive costs that can be estimated with accuracy. The following example illustrates how total sales revenue is required to cover the variable costs and estimated known dollar value costs and to provide operating income (before tax). Breakeven total sales revenue exists when sales revenue is equal to the total operating costs; thus, there is no profit or loss. The example uses typical restaurant variable cost percentages and a selected few of the typical cost classifications that are fixed or can be estimated with a great deal of accuracy:

Sales revenue		@100%
Total cost of sales (a variable % of total sales revenue)		@ 38%
Labor costs (a variable % of total sales revenue)		@ 25%
Operating costs (a variable % of total sales revenue)		@ 17%
Income before fixed costs		@ 80%
Known Operating Costs		
Management salaries	$38,000	
Administrative expenses	18,000	
Depreciation expense	24,000 } 20%	
Utilities expense	6,500	
Property taxes expense	4,500	
Total known costs		$91,000
Operating Income		$ -0-

This income statement shows sales revenue as 100%. Other variable costs are identified as a percentage of sales revenue. In this case, cost of sales, labor costs, and other operating costs are 80% of total sales revenue. Known, nonvariable operating costs have been isolated to be $91,000, or 20% of sales revenue (100% − 80%); thus, sales revenue can be found by dividing known costs by the percentage it represents of sales revenue:

Total sales revenue = $91,000 / 20% = $455,000

Having found sales revenue, each variable cost element can be converted to dollars and an income statement can be created.

Sales revenue		$455,000
Total cost of sales, food (38% × $455,000)		(172,900)
Labor costs (25% × $455,000)		(113,750)
Operating costs (17% × $455,000)		(77,350)
Gross margin		$ 91,000
Known Operating Costs		
Management salaries	$38,000	
Administrative expenses	18,000	
Depreciation expense	24,000 } 20%	
Utilities expense	6,500	
Property taxes expense	4,500	
Total known costs		$91,000
Operating Income		$ -0-

Building on the techniques of the previous example, the concept of treating net income after tax as a cost will be demonstrated. Let us now consider a 100-seat restaurant whose owner wants to know what sales revenue must be in the coming year. Knowing the total sales revenue objective for the next year allows the calculation of the necessary average check needed to meet the objective for the next year of operation. Information about costs and cost percentages

Net income after tax:	A 20% after-tax return on a $220,000 investment in furnishings and equipment is wanted
Income tax rate:	36% of operating income (before tax)
Depreciation rate:	10% of $220,000, the book value of furnishings and equipment

Annual costs

Rent expense	$42,000	
Insurance and license expense	5,400	
Utilities and maintenance expense	6,800	Total $92,000
Administration, office and phone expenses	12,200	
Management salary	25,600	

Variable costs
Cost of sales–food, averages 37% of total revenue.
Labor cost percentage averages 27% of total revenue.
Other variable operating costs averages 15% of total revenue.

Return on owner investment:

Net Income after tax = Investment of $220,000 × 20% = $44,000

Calculation of operating income and tax:

$$\frac{\text{NI after tax}}{1 - \text{Tax rate}} = \text{Operating income before tax}$$

$$\frac{\text{NI after tax}}{1 - \text{Tax rate}} = \frac{\$44,000}{1 - 0.36} = \frac{\$44,000}{0.64} = \$68,750$$

Tax = Operating income before tax − NI after tax

Tax = $68,750 − $44,000 = $24,750

Alternative calculation of income tax:

Operating income (before tax) × Tax rate = Tax
$68,750 × 36% = $24,750 NI after tax

■ **EXHIBIT 6.1**
Projected Restaurant Costs for Next Year

Sales revenue	$Unknown	100%
Cost of sales, food		(37%)
Labor cost		(27%)
Operating costs		(15%)
Total variable cost percentages		79%
Management salary	$ 25,600	
Administration and office expenses	12,200	
Utilities and maintenance expenses	6,800	
Insurance and license expense	5,400	
Rent expense	42,000	
Depreciation expense ($220,000 × 10%)	22,000	
Income tax	24,750	
Net income	44,000	
Total	$182,750 =	21%
Total Costs as a Percentage of Sales Revenue		100%

■ **EXHIBIT 6.2**

Projected Restaurant Income Statement for Next Year (Incomplete)

shown in Exhibit 6.1 will be evaluated and incorporated into an income statement using the preceding discussion format in Exhibit 6.2, and a condensed income statement is shown in Exhibit 6.3.

An alternative calculation of income tax is to apply the tax rate to the operating income before tax as follows:

Operating income (before tax) × Tax rate = Tax: $68,750 × 36% = $2,750

Assuming cost projections are accurate, total annual sales revenue of $870,238 is required to yield a 20% after-tax return on the owners' investment next year. Now we can look at total sales revenue of $870,238 in relation to the individual customer. The relationship to total sales revenue is the average check.

Sales revenue ($182,750 / 21%)	$870,238
Cost of sales food, labor and other variable costs ($870,238 × 79%)	(687,488)
Contributory income	$182,750
Total operating costs	(114,000)
Operating income (before tax)	$ 68,750
Income tax	(24,750)
Net Income	$ 44,000

■ **EXHIBIT 6.3**

Condensed Restaurant Income Statement for Next Year (Complete)

The **average check** will tell us the average amount each customer will spend in the restaurant over the next year to meet our required total sales revenue objective. Assuming the restaurant is open 6 days per week for 52 weeks, operations will be conducted for 312 days (6×52). Also assume the average seat turnover is two times per day during the next annual operating year. The equation to calculate the average check is as follows:

$$\text{Average check} = \frac{\textbf{Total annaul sales revenue}}{\textbf{Seats} \times \textbf{Seat turnover} \times \textbf{Operating days}}$$

$$= \frac{\$870{,}238}{100 \times 2 \times 312} = \frac{\$870{,}238}{62{,}400} = \underline{\underline{\$13.95}}$$

If we believe faster service can be implemented, it is possible to increase seat turnover from 2 to 2.5 times per day, which, in turn, would decrease the average check from $13.95 to $11.16:

$$\text{Average check} = \frac{\$870{,}238}{100 \times 2.5 \times 312} = \frac{\$870{,}238}{78{,}000} = \underline{\underline{\$11.16}}$$

Regardless of the amount of the average check, it does not tell us what each menu item should be priced at. The average check indicates what each customer on average is expected to spend. It gives us an idea of what the pricing structure of the menu should be with a balance of prices—on average, some higher and some lower.

The average check also provides a barometer that allows an evaluation of whether we are achieving the net income objective as the year progresses. If actual spending per customer is less than the level required and all other items such as seat turnover and operating costs have not changed, then we know something must be done to correct the potential net income shortfall.

If seat turnover must be improved, then selling prices may have to be raised, costs may have to be decreased, or a combination of these changes may be required. The average check discussed to this point represents an average for all meal periods combined. The next section will discuss average check per meal period.

AVERAGE CHECK BY MEAL PERIOD

Most restaurants serving more than one meal period per day will have an average check that is different for each meal period. As a general rule, the average check will increase from breakfast to lunch and increase again from lunch to dinner. Because there is a variance in the average check per meal period, it would be extremely useful to determine the average check for each meal period to supplement the total daily average check information.

To determine the average check per meal period, it is necessary to know what percentage of total sales revenue and the seat turnover each meal period is generating. In an ongoing operation, historical records can provide the necessary information; however, a new restaurant will be dependent on management forecasting to obtain the information needed. As an example, we will assume a restaurant has 100 seats and serves lunch and dinner 6 days per week, or 312 days annually. Records indicate that 40% of total revenue is from the lunch period, with a 2.5 seat turnover, and 60% of total revenue is from the dinner period with a 1.5 seat turnover. To determine the average check per meal period, we will use $870,238 as total sales revenue, using the same equation to find the average check, modified to finding the average check per meal period:

Average check per meal period

$$= \frac{\textbf{Meal period sales revenue (\%)} \times \textbf{Total sales revenue}}{\textbf{Seats} \times \textbf{Meal period seat turnover} \times \textbf{Operating days}}$$

The calculation of the average lunch check is:

$$\frac{40\% \times \$870,238}{100 \times 2.5 \times 312} = \frac{\$348,095}{78,000} = \$4.46$$

The calculation of the average dinner check is:

$$\frac{60\% \times \$870,238}{100 \times 1.5 \times 312} = \frac{\$522,143}{46,800} = \$11.16$$

The accuracy of the average checks determined for both meal periods is verified as follows:

<u>**Lunch:**</u>
100 seats × 2.5 turnover × $ 4.46 average check × 312 days = $347,880

<u>**Dinner:**</u>
100 seats × 1.5 turnover × $11.16 average check × 312 days = $522,288
Total sales revenue = $870,168

Our original estimated annual sales revenue was $870,238, and the estimated annual sales revenue using the calculated average meal period checks is ($870,238 − $870,168)—$70 less due to rounding of the average checks to the closest cent.

PRICING MENU ITEMS

One of the more common methods used to determine the selling price of menu items uses a cost percentage. The cost of each menu item is derived from costing the specific ingredients of each menu item to identify a **standard cost** (what the cost should be) for each menu item. This pricing method can be calculated two different ways to find a selling price based on a cost percentage. As an example, we know from Exhibit 6.2 that 37% was the variable food cost of sales as a percentage of sales revenue. To illustrate the use of a 37% cost percentage, both methods will be used to set a selling price on a menu item with a cost of $4.00, as follows:

$$\frac{\textbf{Menu item cost}}{\textbf{Cost \%}} = \frac{\$4.00}{37\%} = \underline{\underline{\$10.81}} \textbf{ Selling price}$$

or $\qquad$ **Menu item cost** $\times (1 / 37\%) = \$4.00 \times 2.7 = \underline{\underline{\$10.80}}$ **Selling price**

Although the use of a cost percentage is easy to understand and use, it might not be practical to apply the same division or multiplication factors across the board for all menu items. When determining selling prices, the market being serviced must be considered, as well as what potential customers are willing to pay for certain menu items, and what other competitive operations are charging for the same menu item. Setting menu selling prices that are influenced by customers and competitive prices can become a juggling act, causing some selling prices to be set at a cost percentage higher and others lower than the average cost of sales percentage.

The variety of items people choose from the menu is known as the **sales revenue mix.** In menu pricing, it is a good idea to keep the likely sales mixes in mind since the average check, and ultimately net income, can be influenced by a change in the sales mix. Consider the following table, which shows a sales mix for a fast-food restaurant giving an average check of $4.66:

Menu Item	*Quantity Sold*	*Selling Price*	*Total Revenue*
1	25	$3.00	$ 75.00
2	75	4.00	300.00
3	50	5.00	250.00
4	60	5.00	300.00
5	40	6.00	240.00
Totals	250		$1,165.00

$$\textbf{Average check: } \frac{\$1,165.00}{250} = \underline{\underline{\$4.66}}$$

Let us assume that, by promotion or other means, the sales revenue mix was changed; 25 people no longer select menu item #2, five guests switch to menu item #1, and the other 20 guests choose menu item #4. The new sales mix is shown below, with a new higher average check of $4.72. The higher average check would normally result in a higher gross margin, higher operating income, and higher sales revenue.

Menu Item	Quantity Sold	Selling Price	Total Revenue
1	30	$3.00	$ 90.00
2	50	4.00	200.00
3	50	5.00	250.00
4	80	5.00	400.00
5	40	6.00	240.00
Totals	250		$1,180.00

$$\text{Average check: } \frac{\$1,180}{250} = \$4.72$$

The change in sales revenue mixes between the two sales-mix examples shows an increase in sales revenue of $15. However, it might be more meaningful to see how a changed sales mix affects gross margin rather than average check. Consider the previous two sales results, but with three new columns added—food cost of each menu item, gross margin for each item, and total gross margin for each item. Total gross margin replaces total revenue.

Menu Item	Quantity Sold	Food Cost	Selling Price	Gross Margin	Total Gross Margin
1	25	$1.50	$3.00	$1.50	$ 37.50
2	75	1.75	4.00	2.25	168.75
3	50	2.00	5.00	3.00	150.00
4	60	2.00	5.00	3.00	180.00
5	40	2.50	6.00	3.50	140.00
				Total Gross Margin	$676.25
1	30	1.50	$3.00	$1.50	$ 45.00
2	50	1.75	4.00	2.25	112.50
3	50	2.00	5.00	3.00	150.00
4	80	2.00	5.00	3.00	240.00
5	40	2.50	6.00	3.50	140.00
				Total Gross Margin	$687.50

In this situation, the changed sales revenue mix has resulted in an additional gross margin of $11.25, and, all other things being equal (labor and other direct costs), this will result in the same increase in operating income.

MENU ENGINEERING

Another method of menu analysis is known as **menu engineering.** The term and concept of menu engineering were first introduced in a book by Michael L. Kasavana and Donald J. Smith called *Menu Engineering—A Practical Guide to Menu Analysis* (Lansing, MI: Hospitality Publications, 1982).

To use menu engineering, a worksheet such as that illustrated in Exhibit 6.4 is used. A separate worksheet needs to be used for each meal period, and for each meal period a separate worksheet has to be used for each menu category, such as appetizers, entrees, and desserts. The reason for this is that menu engineering uses each menu item's contribution margin (or gross margin) in the analysis. Wide variations in contribution margin can arise between, for example, appetizers and entree items, and if those contribution margins were compared, no meaningful analysis would be achieved.

Menu engineering focuses on the contribution margin (or gross margin) of each menu item and combined with its popularity or customer demand. Menu engineering ignores the food cost percentage since the contribution margin is assessed in dollars, not percentages. The contribution margin is defined as high or low when compared to the average contribution margin for all items sold. For example, if the average contribution is $6.50 for all items, an item with a contribution margin of $5.50 is considered to be low, whereas an item with a contribution margin of $7.00 is considered to be high.

Similarly, each item's popularity is also defined as either high or low by comparing its sales revenue mix percentage to the average sales mix percentage; that is, the quantity sold of each menu item as a percentage of the total quantity sold of all menu items.

A completed menu engineering worksheet is shown in Exhibit 6.5. A summary of each column or box on this exhibit follows:

Column A—Menu item name: Lists all the items in the menu category being analyzed.

Column B—Number sold (MM): MM stands for menu mix (sales revenue mix). This column records the quantity of each menu item sold for the period being analyzed, with the total of all items sold recorded at the bottom of the column in Box N.

Column C—Menu mix %: Converts the number sold of each menu item from column B into a percentage of all items sold. The quantity sold of each item is divided by the total of all items sold, then multiplied by 100. For example, for the first item on the menu, the calculation is

$$\frac{331}{2,873} \times 100 = \underline{\underline{11.5\%}}$$

Column D—Item food cost: Lists the food cost for each menu item.

Restaurant: _____   Date: _____

                                                               Meal Period: _____

(A) Menu Item Name	(B) Number Sold (MM)	(C) Menu Mix %	(D) Item Food Cost	(E) Item Selling Price	(F) Item CM (E − D)	(G) Menu Costs (D × B)	(H) Menu Revenues (E × B)	(L) Menu CM (F × B)	(P) CM Category	(R) MM% Category	(S) Menu Item Classification	(T) Profit Factor
Column Totals:	N					I = ΣG	J = ΣH	M = ΣL				

Additional Computations:

$K = I / J$ $O = M / N$ $Q = (100 / Items)(70\%)$

EXHIBIT 6.4

Blank Menu Engineering Worksheet

Restaurant: _Pavilion_

Date: _July 1, 0003_
Meal Period: _Dinner_

(A) Menu Item Name	(B) Number Sold (MM)	(C) Menu Mix %	(D) Item Food Cost	(E) Item Selling Price	(F) Item CM (E − D)	(G) Menu Costs (D × B)	(H) Menu Revenues (E × B)	(L) Menu CM (F × B)	(P) CM Category	(R) MM% Category	(S) Menu Item Classification	(T) Profit Factor
Steak 8 oz.	331	11.5	5.50	12.95	7.45	1,821	4,286	2,466	L	H	plowhorse	1.10
Steak 10 oz.	295	10.3	6.80	15.95	9.15	2,006	4,705	2,699	H	H	star	1.21
Chicken breast	320	11.1	3.25	7.95	4.70	1,040	2,544	1,504	L	H	plowhorse	0.67
Veal neptune	175	6.1	5.75	12.45	6.70	1,006	2,179	1,173	L	L	dog	0.52
Prime rib	452	15.7	5.95	16.95	11.00	2,689	7,661	4,972	H	H	star	2.22
Lamb chops	307	10.7	5.70	12.95	7.25	1,750	3,976	2,226	L	H	plowhorse	1.00
Fried shrimp	254	8.8	4.20	10.95	6.75	1,067	2,781	1,715	L	H	plowhorse	0.77
Sole filet	314	10.9	5.05	12.45	7.40	1,586	3,909	2,324	L	H	plowhorse	1.04
Crab legs	246	8.6	6.10	13.95	7.85	1,501	3,432	1,931	H	H	star	0.86
Salmon steak	179	6.2	4.95	12.45	7.50	886	2,229	1,343	L	L	dog	0.60
Column Totals:	**N** 2,873					**I = ΣG** 15,352	**J = ΣH** 37,702	**M = ΣL** 22,353				

Additional Computations:

$K = I / J$ → 40.7%

$J = \Sigma H$ 37,702
$M = \Sigma L$ 22,353

$O = M / N$ → $7.78

Average CM = M / Menu Items:
$22,353 / 10 = $2,235

$Q = (100 / \text{Items})(70\%)$
$100 / 10 \times 70\% = 7.0\%$

EXHIBIT 6.5
Completed Menu Engineering Worksheet

Column E—Item selling price: Lists the selling price of each menu item.

Column F—Item CM (E–D): Records the CM (contribution margin) of each menu item by deducting its food cost (column D) from its selling price (column E). The contribution margin is the amount of money obtained from each item sold to cover all other costs and the profit desired by the operation.

Column G—Menu costs (D × B): Lists the total cost for each menu item sold. It is calculated by multiplying the number sold of each menu item (column B) by its food cost (column D). The dollar amounts in this column of the worksheet have been rounded to the nearest dollar for the sake of simplicity.

Column H—Menu revenues (E × B): Lists the total sales or revenue for each menu item sold. It is calculated by multiplying the number sold of each menu item (column B) by its selling price (column E). The dollar amounts in this column have also been rounded to the nearest dollar for the sake of simplicity.

Box I: Records the total cost of all menu items sold and is the total of column G.

Box J: Records the total sales revenue generated from all menu items sold and is the total of column H.

Box K = I / J: Used if the overall food cost percentage for the period is desired. It is calculated by dividing the box I total by the box J total and multiplying by 100.

Column L—Menu CM (F × B): Records the total contribution margin (gross profit) for each menu item. It is obtained by multiplying the quantity sold figure (column B) by the contribution margin figure (column F). Alternatively, it can be calculated by deducting the total food cost for each item (column G) from its total sales revenue (column H). Again, the dollar amounts in this column have been rounded to the nearest dollar for the sake of simplicity.

Box M: Records the total of column L.

Box N: As previously stated, box N records the total of column B.

Box O = M / N: Records the average contribution margin for all items sold. It is obtained by dividing the total contribution margin (box M) by the total number of items sold (box N). The resulting figure in this box is compared to the contribution margin of each individual menu item to determine if its contribution margin is higher or lower than the average contribution margin.

Column P—CM category: Records either an H (for high) or an L (for low) after that item's individual contribution margin is compared with the average contribution margin in box O. If it is higher than the average, an H is recorded; if lower than the average, an L is recorded. For example, the first menu item has a contribution margin of $7.45 in column F, which is lower than the average of $7.78 in box O, so an L is recorded in column P.

Box Q = (100/items) (70%): Records the average popularity of all menu items. In Exhibit 6.5 there are 10 items on the menu, so average popularity is 100% divided by 10 = 10%. (*Note:* If there were only 5 items on the menu, average popularity would be 100% divided by 5 = 20%, and if there were 20 items on the menu, average popularity would be 100% divided by 20 = 5%.)

In our case, the average popularity of each item should be 10% of all items sold. However, Kasavana and Smith state that it is unreasonable in practice to expect that every menu item will achieve this minimum level of sales and suggest, based on their experience, that the minimum popularity of each menu item should be only 70% of the average popularity number. In our situation, this would be 7% (70% × 10%).

Column R—MM% category: Records either an H (for high) or an L (for low). These categories are made by comparing each menu item's menu mix percentage (from column C) with the average of 7% from box Q. If the figure from column C is higher than the average, an H is recorded; and if it is less than average, an L is recorded. For example, the first menu item shows 11.5% in column C, and this is higher than 7% in box Q, so an H is shown in column R.

Column S—Menu item classification: Lists each menu item in one of four categories. There are four possible combinations of letters in columns P and R: HH, LH, HL, and LL. Using the terminology of Kasavana and Smith, the categories are star, plowhorse, puzzle, and dog.

- *Stars* are items with both higher than average contribution margin and higher than average popularity; that is, HH items.
- *Plowhorses* have lower than average contribution margin but higher than average popularity; that is, LH items.
- *Puzzles* have higher than average contribution margin but lower than average popularity; that is, HL items.
- *Dogs* have both lower than average contribution margin and lower than average popularity; that is, LL items.

These categories will be discussed in more detail later in the chapter.

Column T—Profit factor: Compares each item's total contribution margin to the average contribution margin for each item. The profit factor is calculated in two steps:

1. *Divide the menu's total contribution margin by the number of items on the menu to obtain the average contribution margin per menu item.* In our case, the total contribution margin of $22,353 from box M is divided by 10 menu items for an average contribution margin of $2,235.

2. *Divide each item's total contribution margin by the average contribution margin to arrive at the profit factor.* For example, in Exhibit 6.5, the first menu item shows a total contribution margin of $2,466 in column L. This figure divided by the average of $2,235 from step 1, results in a profit factor of 1.10, which is recorded in column T.

It is wrong to assume that if an item has a very high profit factor this is good. Because of the way in which profit factors are calculated, the average of all profit factors is 1.0. This means that any profit factors higher than 1.0 have to be balanced by other profit factors lower than 1.0. In other words, the higher some items' profit factors are, the lower others will be.

Thus, the menu will not be a balanced menu, which it would be if all menu items differ only slightly from the average of 1.0. Items that have very high profit factors have to be offset by items with very low profit factors. The operating expenditures for the very low profit factor menu items are generally considered as being wasted. Such expenditures are for purchasing, receiving, storing, issuing, preparation, and service. However, this point of view is far from correct from a marketing point of view. It is important not to lose sight of this; the variance and availability of a balanced menu is not insignificant from the viewpoint of customers.

Stars

Stars are menu items that the restaurant manager would prefer to sell whenever possible. These items should be left on the menu unless there is a good reason to remove them. However, do not be misled by the profitability of the stars if the menu is unbalanced, as indicated by the profit factors showing that too much of the total contribution margin is derived from too few of the menu items. The total contribution margin should be spread more equitably over all menu items or maximized even further by eliminating the low-contribution margin items.

Stars should also be located in the most favorable position on the menu so they continue to be stars. Also, because of their relative popularity, the prices of such items can often be raised without affecting that popularity, thus increasing profits. Generally, stars are the least price-sensitive (most inelastic, in economic terms, discussed later in this chapter) items on the menu. Prices of these items should never be reduced because the quantity sold will likely not be affected but total contribution margin will be reduced. By contrast, if star prices are increased, demand will be affected very little and total contribution margin will increase. However, if the demand for stars is more elastic, a price reduction might considerably increase sales revenue (and profits) for these items.

Finally, since stars are the most popular and profitable items on the menu, quality control in their preparation and service is extremely important.

Plowhorses

Plowhorses are items that, though popular with customers, provide a low contribution margin per item. They should generally be kept on the menu, but the restaurant manager should try to increase their contribution margin without affecting demand. Raising their prices is one way to do this. Another way is to review the recipes and purchase specifications with the objective of decreasing the cost of ingredients or reducing the portion size. Alternatively, the contribution margin can be increased by repackaging the item with a side item, and then repricing the package upward. If contribution margin cannot be increased, plowhorses should be relegated to a less favorable position on the menu. Because plowhorses have a low contribution margin, lowering their prices is not a good idea because this will reduce the overall total contribution margin. Favoring these items through improved menu location or server suggestion is also not a good idea because those items will simply take business away from more profitable menu items.

The profit factors (from column T of the worksheet) are very important with plowhorses. Some items can, by the high quantity sold, account for a significant portion of the total contribution margin and, thus, profits. They must be analyzed very carefully.

Puzzles

Puzzles have a higher than average contribution margin but lower than average popularity. They are profitable items but do not sell well. Possible reasons for not selling well are that their prices are too high, their quality is not satisfactory, or that they are just not suited to the restaurant's customers. They should generally be kept on the menu, but the restaurant manager should try to increase demand for them by renaming them, making their menu descriptions more appealing, or relocating them to a more favorable position on the menu. Another alternative is to reduce the price, particularly if the item has a relatively high contribution margin and an elastic demand. In other words, sales revenue should be encouraged because such items may be facing price resistance from customers. However, do not reduce the price too much, since this can take business away from the stars and will reduce the contribution margin.

In some cases the price of a puzzle item can be raised, if it is very popular only with a few customers whose demand is inelastic. Increased prices will not affect the demand from these customers, but total contribution margin will increase.

If a puzzle item remains truly unpopular, it should be removed from the menu and replaced by one that a customer survey shows would be much more popular.

Dogs

Dogs have lower than average contribution margin and lower than average popularity. From the restaurant operator's point of view, these are generally the least desirable items to have on the menu. If their contribution margin and/or popularity cannot be increased, these items should generally be replaced on the menu with new and more popular items that also have a higher contribution margin.

However, sometimes there might be a good reason to retain a dog on the menu. If a dog is popular with a few regular customers, it might be a mistake to take it off the menu. In this case, a price increase might be considered so it shifts into the puzzle category. Alternatively, over time its popularity may increase, shifting it to the plowhorse category.

Recap of Menu Engineering

Menu engineering concentrates on three variables: customer demand (that is, how many customers eat in the restaurant), analysis of the menu items' sales revenue mix to determine the popularity of individual menu items, and item contribution margin (the difference between an item's selling price and its food cost). A menu that provides the highest overall contribution margin is considered the most desirable, and overall food cost percent is not a consideration.

Note that any changes made to a menu as a result of menu engineering should be reviewed after a suitable period of time. If a revised menu produces no more total contribution margin than before, then nothing has been achieved. Total contribution margin can be generally improved by emphasizing the stars to customers, reducing the number of puzzles, and eliminating the dogs.

Finally, a problem with menu engineering is that it is oriented toward maximizing item contribution margin. High contribution margin items usually have not only the highest prices, but also the highest food cost percentage. Higher prices can also decrease customer demand and, therefore, profit. However, menu engineering works well when sales revenues are increasing at a good pace, although that is often not the case for many restaurants. Also, below a certain volume of sales, a particular menu item may provide a contribution margin that seems satisfactory but does not cover its total cost.

Because of all the variables that different menu items have, they must be offered with different prices and different markups. Gross profit dollars will vary from menu item to menu item, food cost percentage by itself may not be a meaningful guide in determining selling prices, and the sales mix must be kept in mind. Menu pricing can be a complex task for management.

The comments made in this section on setting food menu selling prices are equally as valid for establishing beer, wine, and liquor prices in a beverage operation.

INTEGRATED PRICING

In pricing food and alcoholic beverages, the manager should also keep **integrated pricing** in mind. This simply means that products should not be priced independently of each other. This is particularly true if the beverage operation is closely integrated with the food operation: that is, the customers eating in the dining area are the ones who provide most of the business for the beverage operation. In such cases, food and beverage prices should complement each other to achieve profit objectives. Generally, in such a situation, the more food that is sold, the higher beverage sales will be (a concept known as derived demand) and vice versa.

SEAT TURNOVER

Earlier in this chapter, it was stated that one way to offset a declining average check, or average customer spending, is to increase customer counts, or **seat turnover.** Let us look at a case concerning two different restaurants, each with 200 seats.

	Restaurant A		Restaurant B	
	Customers	*Seat Turnover*	*Customers*	*Seat Turnover*
Sunday	200	1.00	350	1.75
Monday	250	1.25	350	1.75
Tuesday	350	1.75	350	1.75
Wednesday	350	1.75	350	1.75
Thursday	450	2.25	350	1.75
Friday	550	2.75	450	2.25
Saturday	650	3.25	600	3.00
Week totals:	2,800	14.00	2,800	14.00

Average Daily Customers:

$$\text{Weekly customers, Restaurant A: } \frac{2,800}{\text{Operating days} \quad 7} = 400 \text{ guests per day}$$

$$\text{Weekly customers, Restaurant B: } \frac{2,800}{\text{Operating days} \quad 7} = 400 \text{ guests per day}$$

Average Daily Turnover:

$$\text{Weekly turnover, Restaurant A: } \frac{14}{\text{Operating days} \quad 7} = 2 \text{ turnovers per day}$$

$$\text{Weekly turnover, Restaurant B: } \frac{14}{\text{Operating days} \quad 7} = 2 \text{ turnovers per day}$$

Although the number of customers per week (2,800) and the weekly turnover per week (14) are the same for both restaurants, the daily distribution of customers during the week is quite different. This type of analysis can be helpful in decisions concerning staffing and advertising as well as seeing where increasing the seat turnover to maintain total sales revenue and protect net income might be considered.

ROOM RATES

The approach illustrated earlier in this chapter for determining a required average restaurant check can also be used for calculating **room rates.** Hotel or motel rooms are, however, a different type of commodity from restaurant seats. Restaurant seats can be increased in the short run if you are not already at the maximum capacity allotted by the operation's licenses and the fire code to take care of high demand. Alternatively, service in a restaurant can be speeded up and seat turnover increased to accommodate peak demand periods.

The same cannot be done with guest rooms in a hotel or motel. Room supply cannot be increased in the short run and the number of rooms available is fixed, and turnover cannot be increased. Apart from selling rooms during the day for meetings or similar uses, the normal turnover rate of a room is once per 24-hour period. In a hotel, only 100 persons can occupy 100 single beds in each 24 hours. In a restaurant, 100, 200, or even 300 persons or more can occupy 100 seats, if the demand is there, during a meal period or day.

One other factor to be considered is that if sales revenue for a room on a particular night is not obtained, that revenue is gone forever. Room revenue and the fixed cost of providing rooms cannot be recovered if a room is not sold. This differs from food and beverage operations. If food and beverage inventories are purchased by the restaurant and not sold on a particular day, they can be stored for short periods and sold later, and the cost is recoverable. Thus, in determining price we must emphasize the importance of having room rates that permit the fixed costs of providing the space to be recovered and that maximize the occupancy level of the rooms.

THE DOLLAR PER THOUSAND METHOD

A method developed many years ago for setting an appropriate room rate is the $1 per $1,000 approach. Since the greatest cost in a hotel or motel property is the investment in building (from 60% to 70% of total investment), it was argued that there should be a fairly direct relationship between the cost of the building and the room rate. From this developed the rule of thumb that for each $1,000 in building cost per room, $1 of room rate should be charged in order for the investment to be profitable. In other words, if a 100-room hotel had a building cost of $4,000,000, its average cost of construction per room is as follows:

$$\text{Average cost of construction} = \frac{\$4,000,000}{100} = \underline{\underline{\$40,000}} \text{ per room}$$

Then, for each $1,000 of construction cost per room, there should be $1 of room rate:

$$\text{Average room rate} = \frac{\$40,000}{\$1,000} = 40 \times \$1 = \underline{\underline{\$40.00}}$$

This rule of thumb worked under certain circumstances and assumptions. Some of these assumptions were that the hotel was a relatively large one (several hundred rooms), that there was sufficient rent from shops and stores in the building to pay for interest and real estate taxes, that other departments (food, beverages, and so on) were contributing income to the overall hotel operation, and that the average year-round occupancy was 70%. These assumptions are all quite specific. Consider the following two small hotel operations: Hotel A, which has no public facilities, and Hotel B, with a more spacious lobby and a dining room/coffee shop and banquet rooms.

	Hotel A	*Hotel B*
Building cost	$2,400,000	$3,120,000
Number of rooms	50	50
Cost per room	$40,000	$52,000
Room rate at $1 per $1,000	$40	$52

Assuming the two properties were in the same competitive market and the $1 per $1,000 rule of thumb was used, Hotel B would find itself at a distinct disadvantage to Hotel A. However, these two competitive properties are, of course, not in the same competitive market because Hotel A has no public facilities.

The $1 per $1,000 rule also leaves room rates tied to historical construction costs and ignores current costs, including current financing costs. The bottom-up approach to room rates overcomes the pitfalls inherent in the $1 per $1,000 method. This bottom-up approach to room pricing is frequently referred to as the **Hubbart formula,** which was developed some years ago for the American Hotel and Motel Association.

THE BOTTOM-UP APPROACH

The bottom-up approach to room rates is quite similar to that discussed earlier in determining the average check required in a restaurant. We will use the facts illustrated in Exhibit 6.6. The motel has 50 rooms. Note that the cost projections, even though based on information from historical income statements, have been projected to take care of anticipated increases for next year. The total net cost of operating next year to be covered by the rooms department is $529,167 as shown in Exhibit 6.7.

Net income required	10% after-tax on investment of $550,000 = <u>$55,000</u>
Income tax	40% tax rate
Depreciation	Present book value-building $1,200,000—depreciation rate 5% = $60,000
	Present book value furniture and equipment $150,000—depreciation rate 20% = $30,000
Interest	Present mortgage payable is $750,000 ($75,000 × 10%)
Property taxes and insurance	$30,000 ⎤
Administrative and general	$47,000 ⎟
Marketing	$25,000 ⎬ Total $151,000
Utilities	$17,000 ⎟
Repairs and maintenance	$32,000 ⎦
Rooms department operating costs	$137,000 a year for wages, linen, laundry, and supplies, based on past income statements at a 70% occupancy
Coffee shop contributory income	$15,500 a year at 70% rooms occupancy

■ **EXHIBIT 6.6**
Motel Cost Projections for Next Year

Assuming the motel will continue to operate at 70% occupancy, it will sell the following number of rooms per year:

Rooms available	×	**Occupancy %**	×	**365**	=	**Rooms sold**
50	×	70%	×	365	=	12,775 rooms

Rooms department operating costs		$137,000
Total overhead costs		151,000
Interest		75,000
Depreciation		
Building	$60,000	
Furniture and equipment	<u>30,000</u>	90,000
Income tax		36,667
Net income required		<u>55,000</u>
Total costs		$544,667
Less coffee shop contributory income		(15,500)
Total net costs to be covered by revenue in rooms department		<u>$529,167</u>

■ **EXHIBIT 6.7**
Motel Total Cost Projections of Operating Next Year

Therefore, the average room rate will have to be:

$$\frac{\textbf{Sales revenue required}}{\textbf{Rooms to be sold}} = \frac{\$529,167}{12,775} = \$41.42 \textbf{ average room rate}$$

Note that this figure, $41.42, is only the *average* room rate and is not necessarily the rate for any specific room. Most large hotels have a variety of sizes and types of rooms, each type having a rate for single occupancy and a higher rate for double occupancy. Motels, even if they have only one size and type of room, have a single rate and a double rate for it.

Where there are multiple types of rooms and multiple rates, the calculated average rate can only be a guide as to what the actual rate for each specific type of room will be. Size of room, decor, and view will be some of the factors to consider in arriving at a balance of rates that will both be fair and allow the resulting average rate to work out to the required figure.

Another factor to consider is the double occupancy rooms rate. A room that is occupied by two persons usually has a higher rate than the same room occupied by one person. The higher the proportion of double occupancies, the higher will be the resulting average rates. In our example, a safe way to assure that we achieve at least a $41.42 average would be to make that the minimum single rate for any room. Any rooms we then sell that have a higher single rate, or any rooms sold at the double occupancy rate, would guarantee that our average rate will end up higher than $41.42. Unfortunately, competition and customer resistance may preclude this approach.

In a simple motel situation, with only one standard type of room and all rooms having the same single or double rate, is there a method of calculating what these rates should be? The answer is yes—as long as we decide what the spread will be between the single rate and the double, and as long as we have a good idea of the double occupancy percentage.

CALCULATING SINGLE AND DOUBLE RATES

To illustrate this, we will use the information about our 50-room motel. We know that $41.42 is the average rate required to cover all costs and give us the return on investment we want. Average occupancy is 70% and we know from past experience the **double occupancy rate** is 40%. To determine the rates, we pick a spread of $10 between the single and the double rates. To clarify, the method of determining a double occupancy percentage is shown as follows:

50 rooms × 70% × 365 × 140% = <u>17,885</u> total guests

The double occupancy rate is calculated as follows:	
Total number of guests during year	17,885
Less number of rooms occupied	(12,775)
Equals number of rooms double occupied	<u>5,110</u>

$$\text{Double occupancy rate} = \frac{5,110}{12,775} \times 100 = \underline{\underline{40\%}}$$

A motel double occupancy rate of 40% tells us that two or more people occupied 40% of all rooms sold. If our 50-room motel has a 70% occupancy rate on a typical night, we would have

$70\% \times 50 = 35$ rooms occupied of which
$40\% \times 35 = 14$ will be double occupied, and
$35 - 14 = 21$ will be single occupied

Total rooms sales revenue = 35 rooms $\times$ \$41.42 average rate = $\underline{\underline{\$1,450}}$

The question now is, at what rates can we sell 21 single rooms and 14 double rooms (at a price \$10 higher than the singles) so that total rooms sales revenue is $\underline{\underline{\$1,450}}$? Arithmetically, we solve as follows (with x the unknown single rate):

$$21x + 14(x + \$10) = \$1,450$$
$$21x + 14x + \$140 = \$1,450$$
$$35x = \$1,450 - \$140$$
$$35x = \$1,310$$
$$x = \$1,310 / 35$$
$$x = \underline{\underline{\$37.43}}$$

Therefore, our single rate is \$37.43 and our double rate is \$47.43 (\$37.43 + \$10.00). Let us prove the correctness of these rates:

21 singles $\times$ \$37.43 = \$ 786.00
14 doubles $\times$ \$47.43 = $\underline{\quad 664.00}$
35 rooms $\times$ \$41.42 = $\underline{\underline{\$1,450. 00}}$

The primary purpose of the boxed equations is to find the single room rate and to clarify the removal of the double room's times the spread from day rooms sales revenue. As a result, an alternative linear equation may be used to calculate the single room rate:

$$\frac{\$1,450 - (14 \times \$10)}{35} = \frac{\$1,450 - \$140}{35} = \frac{\$1,310}{35} = \$37.43 \text{ Single room rate}$$

These, then, would be the rates under the given circumstances. They are the rates that, given the correctness of our assumptions about next year, we should be charging. They might not be the rates we do charge. Competition, customer resistance, or age of the property may oblige us to reduce them, in which case we will end up with a smaller return on investment than desired. However, newer establishments in the area with higher construction and operating costs and higher rates, and with customers willing to pay the higher rates, might allow us to increase our rates above our calculated required ones. In this case, we will have a higher return on investment than required.

In trying to determine appropriate room rates, the following factors tend to decrease the average rate:

- Family rates
- Commercial discounts
- Travel agent commissions (unless accounted for separately)
- Convention or group rates
- Special company or government rates
- Weekly or monthly special rates

Extra charges for three or more persons in a room would increase the average double room rate. In addition, special events within the service area might increase room demand beyond the availability of rooms.

ROOM RATES BASED ON ROOM SIZE

One other possible way of determining average rates for different size rooms is to use a room's square footage. Let us suppose our motel had two different sizes of rooms: 30 rooms are 220 square feet (including room entranceway, bathroom, and closet areas) and the other 20 rooms are 180 square feet. The demand for each size of room is about equal. Total square footage available for rental:

$$
\begin{array}{ll}
\textbf{30} \times \textbf{220 sq. ft.} = & \textbf{6,600} \\
\textbf{20} \times \textbf{180 sq. ft.} = & \underline{\textbf{3,600}} \\
\textbf{Total sq. ft.} & \underline{\underline{\textbf{10,200}}}
\end{array}
$$

Assume we are running at a 70% average occupancy. Therefore, each night we expect to sell a total of 35 rooms:

$$
\textbf{70\%} \times \textbf{10,200} = \underline{\underline{\textbf{7,140}}} \textbf{ square feet}
$$

Since we must take in $1,450 a night, on average, to give us the required net income, each square foot sold should produce this sales revenue:

$$
\textbf{Daily rooms revenue: } \frac{\$1,450}{7,140} = \underline{\underline{\$0.203}}
$$

Therefore, the average rate that should be charged for our small and large rooms is:

Small room 180 sq. ft. × $0.203 = $36.54

Large room 220 sq. ft. × $0.203 = $44.66

We can check the accuracy of these figures. Since there are 20 small rooms and 30 large rooms, 14 small (20 × 70%) rooms and 21 (30 × 70%) large rooms will be sold per day.

14 small × $36.54 = $ 511.56
21 large × $44.66 = 937.86
Total revenue per night* = $1,449.42

*Total rooms revenue was rounded earlier
to $1,450. The difference between $1,450
and $1,449.42 is $0.58 and is due to rounding.

Note that these average rates for the small and the large size of room must still be converted into single and double rates for each size, using the method illustrated earlier in this chapter.

AVERAGE OCCUPANCY

Earlier in this chapter, it was demonstrated how an analysis of restaurant seat turnover might indicate where the turnover could be increased. A parallel situation could exist with average room rates and occupancies. Refer to the following:

	Hotel A	*Hotel B*
Saturday	45%	65%
Sunday	45	65
Monday	75	75
Tuesday	95	75
Wednesday	95	85
Thursday	95	85
Friday	75	75
	525%	525%
Average	$\dfrac{525\%}{7} = 75\%$	$\dfrac{525\%}{7} = 75\%$

Both hotels have the same average occupancies, but the analysis by day shows a different picture for each. Hotel A has low occupancy during weekends and very high occupancy during the week. An advertising campaign directed toward bringing in weekend guests would benefit the rooms department and, no doubt, other departments in the hotel. On the other hand, Hotel B has a relatively high weekend business and good, but not high, occupancy during the week. Its advertising should be geared not just toward weekend promotions but also toward improving midweek occupancy.

ROOM RATE DISCOUNTING

Room rate discounting is the practice of reducing prices below the rack rate. The **rack rate** is defined as the maximum rate that will be quoted for a room. Discounting rates for some rooms on any night prevents the hotel from achieving its maximum potential average room rate and maximum potential total sales revenue for that night. Rooms are typically discounted for different groups, such as convention delegates or corporate and government travelers who are regular customers of the hotel. The discounts given are a normal cost of business to maintain occupancy levels, and the reduced room revenue is often compensated for by extra profits achieved from those room guests patronizing the hotel's food and beverage facilities.

Generally a hotel's variable costs for each occupied room are relatively low compared to the room rate and a considerable increase in operating income results from selling each additional room. For example, if the rack rate for a room is $99, and variable cost is $9, $90 of additional net income is obtained from selling each extra room that would otherwise stay unoccupied. Theoretically, this hotel could reduce the rate to $10 (let us say) and still make $1 of additional net income. This does not imply that selling all rooms for $10 would be a good long-term decision. In the long term, only those rooms that would otherwise not be sold should have their rates discounted. Before doing any discounting, a hotel should sell all the rooms it can at its highest rate to those customers who are the least price sensitive. When this is achieved, rates should be discounted to obtain business from those who are more sensitive to prices, and should be discounted further to those who are the most sensitive to prices.

Traditionally, hotels did not operate this way, particularly city hotels that cater to the business traveler whose demand for rooms is primarily during the week, with little or no demand for rooms on weekends. Hotels have reasoned that by offering companies a discounted rate they would obtain more of that company's business, increase market share, and increase profits. As competitive hotels do the same thing to retain their market share, corporate rates are further reduced by all hotels, and nobody wins. Further, these discounted rates are being offered to the market segment that is the least price sensitive, because the corporate guest is not very concerned about the price of the room since the company pays the bill. However, the corporation may select the hotel their employees can use based on room rates.

The negative effect of this strategy of discounting the corporate rate is often combined with the policy of selling as many rooms as possible to that market segment (in order to retain that business), even when those rooms could be sold at higher rates to other market segments. Therefore, the marketing departments of hotels should use caution when discounting hotel rooms to corporate clients.

DISCOUNT GRID

In reviewing room rates and deciding on the discounts to be offered, it is useful to prepare a **discount grid.** This grid in Exhibit 6.8 shows the impact of various room rate discounts on total room sales revenue.

To prepare the grid, the marginal (variable) costs of selling each additional room must be known. Normally, marginal costs occur only in the housekeeping department because no extra costs are incurred in the reservations or front office departments to sell an extra room. Housekeeping costs include such items as employee time to clean the room, cost of linen laundering, cost of guest supplies (soap, shampoo, and similar items), and additional utility costs for lighting and heating or air conditioning. For most hotels, marginal costs are easy to determine.

Let us assume that a 110-room hotel's marginal cost for renting each additional room is $10. We can calculate the equivalent occupancy needed to hold total sales revenue less marginal costs constant if the rack rate is discounted.

$$\frac{\text{Equivalent}}{\text{occupancy}} = \frac{\text{Original}}{\text{occupancy}} \times \frac{\text{Rack rate} - \text{Marginal cost}}{[\text{Rack rate} \times (1 - \text{Discount percentage})] - \text{Marginal cost}}$$

New Occupancy Level Necessary to Maintain the Same Current Profitability if an $80 Rack Rate* with a Marginal Cost of $10 Is Discounted

	Discount			
Occupancy	*5%*	*10%*	*15%*	*20%*
70%	74.2%	79.1%	84.7%	91.0%
65%	68.9%	73.5%	78.7%	84.5%
60%	63.6%	67.8%	72.6%	78.0%
55%	58.3%	62.2%	66.6%	71.5%
50%	53.0%	56.5%	60.5%	65.0%

*This discount grid serves only for an $80 rack rate.

EXHIBIT 6.8
Discount Grid

Assume that all the hotel's rooms have the same rack rate of $80 and that the hotel currently operates at 70% occupancy. If rates were discounted by 10%, the equivalent occupancy required (using the equation) would be:

$$70\% \times \frac{\$80 - \$10}{[\$80 \times (1 - 10\%)] - \$10}$$

$$= 70\% \times \frac{\$70}{(\$80 \times 90\%) - \$10}$$

$$= 70\% \times \frac{\$70}{\$72 - \$10}$$

$$= 70\% \times \frac{\$70}{\$62}$$

$$= 70\% \times 1.13 = \underline{\underline{79.1\%}}$$

This can be proved. Nightly room revenue before discounting is:

70% occupancy $\times$ 110 rooms $\times$ $80 rack rate = $\underline{\$6,160}$

Total marginal costs = 70% occupancy $\times$ 110 rooms $\times$ $10 = $\underline{\$770}$

Net discounted rooms revenue = $6,160 − $770 = $\underline{\$5,390}$

After discounting, nightly revenue at 79.1% occupancy will be:

79.1% occupancy $\times$ 110 rooms $\times$ $72 rate = $\underline{\$6,265}$

Total marginal costs = 79.1% occupancy $\times$ 110 rooms $\times$ $10 = $\underline{\$870}$

Net discounted rooms revenue = $6,265 − $870 = $\underline{\$5,395}$

In other words, net revenue (total sales revenue less marginal costs) is the same as before. The small difference is due to rounding.

Similar calculations can be made for various occupancy levels and discount percentages, and the results can be tabulated in a grid such as that in Exhibit 6.8. Once this has been done, the grid shows the equivalent occupancy that must be achieved to maintain room sales revenue (less marginal costs) at a stipulated level as discounts are increased or decreased. Thus, the grid allows management to make sensible pricing decisions.

For example, the grid shows that if the hotel discounts room rates by 15% and its current occupancy is 70%, the equivalent occupancy after discounting would have to be 84.7%. In our 110-room hotel, this means that, on average, an additional 16.2 rooms would have to be sold per night. If advertising is used to sell the extra 16.2 rooms, this cost must be considered, as would any additional sales revenue that the added guests might provide in the food and beverage departments. In other words, the grid should be used only as an aid in decision making and not be the only criterion.

POTENTIAL AVERAGE ROOM RATE

The potential average room rate is defined as the average rate that would result if all rooms occupied overnight were sold at the rack rate without a discount.

To this point, we have stated that the rack rate is the maximum rate that will be charged for a room. But in fact, most hotels have two or more rack rates for each room. There may be a rack rate for single occupancy, a rack rate for double occupancy, and even a rack rate for occupancy by three or more. How can a potential average room rate be determined in such a situation?

If a hotel sold all its rooms at single occupancy, its potential average rack rate would be the average rate if all rooms were single occupied. If the hotel sold all its rooms at double occupancy, its potential average rate would be the average rate if all rooms were double occupied. For most hotels, neither of these extremes is likely. For most properties on a typical night, some rooms will be single occupied and others will be double occupied. A further complication is that there may be different types of rooms, whose single or double rack rates are different. For example, some rooms might be suites, and some might be pool-side. Thus, the potential average rate must be calculated by taking the hotel's normal sales revenue mix into consideration.

To illustrate, assume that if all of a 90-room hotel's various rooms were each occupied by one person (single occupancy) at the maximum single occupancy rack rate, total sales revenue would be $6,750. Potential minimum average rate is therefore

$$\frac{\$6,750}{90} = \underline{\underline{\$75}}$$

However, if all 90 rooms were double occupied at the maximum double occupancy rack rate, total sales revenue would be $7,650. Potential maximum average rate is therefore

$$\frac{\$7,650}{90} = \underline{\underline{\$85}}$$

(Note that if the hotel has suites or special rooms at higher rates, these can be included in the maximum potential double rate.)

The difference between $85 and $75 is known as the *rate spread*. If this hotel's percentage of double occupancy were 40% (i.e., 40% of all rooms occupied are occupied by two people), the potential average room rate can be calculated as follows:

**Potential average room rate
= Potential average single rate + (Double occupancy % × Rate spread)**

In our case, this results in a potential average room rate of

$$\$75 + (40\% \times \$10.00) = \$75 + \$4 = \underline{\underline{\$79}}$$

COMPARING ACTUAL AVERAGE TO POTENTIAL AVERAGE

Once the potential average room rate has been calculated, the hotel can compare its actual rate to this potential each day or each period. There may be occasions when the actual rate will be higher than the potential. This could occur when the double occupancy rate exceeds the normal 40% and/or if additional charges are made for a third person in a room and/or if front desk employees are doing a good job of selling the most expensive rooms first.

In other cases, the actual average rate will be below the potential rate and can be measured by dividing it by the potential rate and converting to a percentage to arrive at the average rate ratio. For example, if the actual rate achieved during a particular week were $69, the percentage would be

$$\frac{\$69}{\$79} \times 100 = \underline{\underline{87.3\%}}$$

This means the hotel achieved only 87.3% of its potential average rate. This could occur because the double occupancy ratio fell below normal or because the front desk employees did a poor job and sold the lower-priced rooms first. Alternatively, all other factors being equal, it means that rack rates had been discounted 12.7% on average.

ROOM RATES FOR EACH MARKET SEGMENT

With reference to the $79 potential average room rate calculated earlier, it is possible to calculate the room rate for each type of market (market segment) with which the hotel deals. Suppose we have the following information for each of three segments:

Market Segment	Annual Room Nights	Percentage	Rack Rate (%)
Business travelers	5,110	40%	100%
Conference groups	4,471	35%	90%
Tour groups	3,194	25%	80%
	12,775	100%	

The percentage column figures show how much of total business each segment produces. For example, business travelers constitute 40% (5,110 / 12,775 $\times$ 100) of total room nights. The rack rate column tells us the percentage of the rack rate that we are going to charge customers in that market segment. For example, business travelers are going to pay 100% of the rack rate (and receive no discount), whereas conference groups will be charged 90% of the rack rate (or receive a 10% discount), and tour groups 80% of the rack rate (or receive a 20% discount). What must those rates be to ensure that we continue to achieve a $79 average room rate?

We must first calculate what the new potential average rack rate is going to be for the business travelers who receive no discount. We know that it will be higher than before because some segments are going to receive a discounted rate, and thus the new rack rate must increase to compensate for these discounts. The calculation is made by weighting the discount percentage for each market segment and, at the same time, taking into account the percentage of business that each market segment generates, as follows:

$$\frac{\$79}{(40\% \times 100\%) + (35\% \times 90\%) + (25\% \times 80\%)}$$

Note that, in each set of parentheses in the denominator, the first figure represents the portion of the business provided by that segment and the second represents the rack rate percentage for that segment. For example, in the first set of figures the business travelers provide 40% of the business at the full rack rate. Following through on the calculations, we have the following:

$$\frac{\$79}{40\% + 31.5\% + 20\%} = \frac{\$79}{91.\ 5\%} = \underline{\underline{\$86.34}}$$

The discounted rates for the other segments are as follows:

Conference groups	$86.34 $\times$ 90% = $\underline{\underline{\$77.71}}$
Tour groups	$86.34 $\times$ 80% = $\underline{\underline{\$69.07}}$

We can prove that these rates will generate the sales revenue required to yield our desired potential average room rate:

Market Segment	*Room Nights*	$\times$	*Average Rate*	$=$	*Total Sales Revenue*
Business travelers	5,110	$\times$	$86.34	$=$	$ 441,197
Conference groups	4,471	$\times$	77.71	$=$	347,441
Tour groups	3,194	$\times$	69.07	$=$	220,610
Totals	12,775				$1,009,248

OTHER PRICING CONSIDERATIONS

The method demonstrated in this chapter for determining meal selling prices and room rates to ensure an adequate return on investments has its shortcomings. So does the markup (also called cost-plus pricing) method used in conjunction with establishing food and beverage prices relative to the cost of food and beverage ingredients. Both the return on investment and markup methods are simple and easy to use, but because of their simplicity, they ignore many other factors that must be taken into consideration in establishing prices. For that reason, return on investment and markup pricing should be used as reference points only and should not be the only determinants in setting final prices.

In addition, assumptions are made about room occupancy rates (in a hotel situation) and seat turnover (in a restaurant situation). However, adjustments can be made to prices during the actual period when it is seen that room's occupancy and/or seat turnovers differ from those used in the initial calculations.

Unfortunately, the revised decisions may be the reverse of those that should be made under the circumstances. To illustrate, consider the situation of a hotel that had based its average room rate of $79 for next year on a predicted occupancy of 70%. During the year, it is seen that actual occupancy is closer to 65%, and, therefore, the average room rate is revised upward to compensate so that the desired profit (operating income) will still be achieved.

However, when you consider a typical business situation, a price increase will often result in a further decrease in demand for rooms, reducing occupancy still further. In normal economic situations (i.e., when all other things are equal), the correct thing to do to stimulate demand is to lower prices as demand decreases. Then, if demand increases, net income should remain about the same.

If wrong decisions are made as a result of blindly using a bottom-up pricing method and empty hotel rooms and empty restaurant seats (and thus, reduced profit) will probably result. Similarly, there may be missed profit opportunities because prices could be raised above those calculated using the markup method when market conditions are such that customers are prepared to pay those higher prices.

Markup pricing can work during periods of low inflation (as long as economic activity is not declining at the same time) and when there is not an oversupply of hotel rooms or restaurant seats (that is, when it is not a particularly competitive situation). However, it is rare for this situation to prevail, and for that reason many hotels have begun to employ more sophisticated methods that systematically take into consideration all the relevant factors that should be considered in the pricing decision. One of these less simplistic approaches is yield management that is discussed later in the chapter.

Some of the other considerations in pricing are discussed in the following sections.

ELASTICITY OF DEMAND

Elasticity of demand is related to the responsiveness of demand for a product or service when prices are changed. A large change in demand resulting from a small change in prices is referred to as elastic demand. A small change in demand following a large change in prices is referred to as inelastic demand. The following is an equation for calculating the elasticity of demand:

$$\text{Elasticity of demand} = \frac{\text{Change in quantity demanded / Base quantity demanded}}{\text{Change in price / Base price}}$$

For example, suppose a hotel sold 2,000 rooms during the past month at an average rate of $70. For the following month the room rate was increased by $7 to $77. As a result, during the next month 1,900 rooms were sold—a decrease of 100. Placing these numbers in the equation, we have the following:

$$\text{Elasticity of demand} = \frac{100 / 2,000}{\$7 / \$70} = \frac{.05}{.10} = \underline{\underline{0.5}}$$

If the calculations show that the elasticity of demand is less than 1, then the demand is said to be inelastic. If the result is more than 1, then demand is elastic. In our case, demand is inelastic because even though the price increase caused fewer rooms to be sold, total revenue nevertheless increased.

Month 1: **2,000 rooms × $70 = $140,000**

Month 2: **1,900 rooms × $77 = $146,300**

Thus, the easiest way to test whether demand is elastic or inelastic is to note what happens to total sales revenue when prices are changed. If demand is elastic, a decline in price will result in an increase in total sales revenue because, even though a lower price is being received per unit, enough additional units are now being sold to more than compensate for the lower price.

A generalization is that, if demand is elastic, a change in price will cause total sales revenue to change in the opposite direction. If demand is inelastic, a price decline *will cause total sales revenue to fall.* The small increase in units sold that occurs will not be sufficient to offset the decline in sales revenue per unit. Again, one can generalize and say that, if demand is inelastic, a change in price will cause total sales revenue to change in the same direction.

One of the factors that influence elasticity of demand is the availability of substitutes. Generally, hospitality businesses that charge the highest prices are able to do so because there is little substitution possible. An elite hotel with little competition can charge higher room rates, since its customers expect to pay higher rates and can afford to do so and generally would not move to a lower-priced, less luxurious hotel if room rates were increased. Demand is inelastic.

However, a restaurant that is one of many in a particular neighborhood catering to the family trade would probably lose considerable business if it raised its menu prices out of line with its competitors. Its trade is very elastic, its price-conscious customers would simply take their business to another restaurant. Alternatively, a high-average-check restaurant will probably find less customer resistance to an increase in menu prices. In general, one can say, therefore, that the lower the income of a business's customers, the more elastic is their demand, and vice versa.

Closely related to income levels are the habits of a business's customers. The more habit prone the customers are, the less likely are they to resist some upward change in prices, since customers tend to have brand loyalties to hotels and restaurants, just as they have with other products they buy. Enterprises that need to count on repeat business must be very conscious of the effect that price changes may have on that loyalty. Note, also, that the demand for a product or service tends to be more elastic as the time under consideration increases. Even though customers are creatures of habit and do develop loyalties, those habits and loyalties can change over time.

Each separate hospitality enterprise must, therefore, be aware of the elasticity of demand of the market in which it operates and of the loyalty of its customers. In other words, it must have a market-oriented approach to pricing. This market orientation is particularly important in short-run decision making, such as offering reduced weekend and off-season room rates to help increase occupancy, or special food and beverage prices during slow periods. These reduced rates or prices are particularly appropriate where demand is highly elastic.

COST STRUCTURE

The specific cost structure of a business is also a major factor influencing pricing decisions. Cost structure in this context means the breakdown of costs into fixed and variable ones. Fixed costs are those that normally do not change in the short run, such as a manager's salary or insurance expense. Variable costs are those that increase or decrease, depending on sales volume. An example is food cost.

A business with high fixed costs relative to variable ones will likely have less stable profits as the volume of sales revenue increases or decreases. In such a situation, having the right prices for the market becomes increasingly important. In the short run, any price in excess of the variable cost will produce a contribution to fixed costs and net income, and the lower the variable costs, the wider is the range of possible prices. For example, if the variable (or marginal) costs (such as housekeeping wages, and linen and laundry expense) to sell an extra room are $10, and that room normally sells for $95, any price between $10 and $95 will contribute to offsetting fixed costs and increasing net income. In such a situation, those who establish prices have at their discretion a wide range of possibilities for imaginative marketing and pricing to bring in extra business and maximize sales revenue and profits (operating income).

Note that this concept of variable (or marginal) costing is only valid in the short run. Over the long run, prices must be established so that all costs (both fixed and variable) are covered in order to produce a long-run net income.

The subject of fixed and variable costs is covered in some depth in Chapter 7, "Cost Management," and Chapter 8, "The Cost–Volume–Profit Approach to Decisions." In particular, in Chapter 8, the use of the breakeven equation is demonstrated in conjunction with the effect a change in room rates has on volume and profits.

COMPETITION

A hospitality enterprise's competitive situation is also critical in pricing. Very few hospitality businesses are in a monopolistic situation—although some are, such as a restaurant operator who has the only concession at an airport.

Where there is a monopolistic or near monopolistic situation, the operator has greater flexibility in determining prices and may indeed tend to charge more than is reasonably fair. However, in these situations the customer still has the freedom to buy or not buy a meal or drink, or to stay fewer nights in that accommodation. Also, in a monopolistic situation where high prices prevail, new entrepreneurs are soon attracted to offer competition.

In a more competitive, but not completely competitive, situation, there often exists an oligopoly. In an *oligopoly,* there tends to be one major or dominant business and several smaller competitive businesses. The dominant business is often the price leader. When the price leader's prices are raised or lowered, the prices of the other businesses are raised or lowered in tandem. An oligopolistic situation could arise in a resort area where there is one major resort hotel, surrounded by several other motels catering to customers with a slightly lower income level.

However, most hospitality enterprises are in a purely competitive situation where the demand for the goods and services of any one establishment is highly sensitive to the prices charged. In such situations there is little difference, from a price point of view, between one establishment and the next. Where there is close competition, competitive pricing will often prevail without thought to other considerations. For example, an operator practicing competitive pricing may fail to recognize that his or her particular product or service is superior in some ways to that of competitors and could command a higher price without reducing demand.

In a highly competitive situation, an astute operator will look at the strengths and weaknesses of his or her own situation, as well as those of the competitors. In analyzing strengths and weaknesses, operators should try to differentiate themselves and their products and services from their competitors'. The establishments that are most successful in differentiation have more freedom in establishing their prices. This differentiation can be in such matters as ambience and atmosphere, decor, location, view, and similar factors. Indeed, with differentiation, psychological pricing may be practiced. With psychological pricing, the prices are established according to what the customer expects to pay for the different goods or services offered. The greater the differentiation, the higher prices can be set. For example, this situation prevails in fashionable restaurants and exclusive resorts, where a particular market niche has been created. At this point, a monopolistic or near monopolistic situation may again prevail.

In summary, then, there is no one method of establishing prices for all hospitality enterprises. Each establishment will have somewhat different long-run pricing strategies related to its overall objectives and will adopt appropriate short-run pricing policies depending on its cost structure and market situation.

YIELD MANAGEMENT

The hospitality industry has recently adopted a practice called **yield management.** Using calculated yield statistics and basic principles of supply and demand, managers seek to allocate services to patrons in such a way as to maximize sales revenue.

The main goal of the rooms department in many hotels is to sell hotel rooms to increase the occupancy percentage. Management's objective is to maximize the sales revenue (or yield) from the rooms available. Unfortunately, many of the methods used to measure a hotel's marketing effort do not generate sales decisions that maximize sales revenue. Traditionally, marketing effort has been judged in terms of either the occupancy percentage or the average room rate achieved.

The problem with occupancy percentage is that it does not show whether sales revenue is being maximized. For example, a hotel may be 100% occupied, but many of those room occupants might be paying less than the maximum (rack) rate for the room. In other words, managers whose performance is measured by room occupancy are tempted to increase occupancy at the expense of room rate.

Other managers are judged by the average room rate. Again, the average room rate can be increased by refusing to sell any rooms at less than the rack rate, turning away potential customers who are unwilling to pay this rate. Average room rate will be maximized at the expense of occupancy. Average room rate can be slightly more meaningful if it is expressed as a ratio of the maximum potential average rate, as discussed in an earlier section of this chapter, but by itself, it does not provide a complete picture.

Instead of focusing on a high occupancy or a high average rate, a better measure of a manager's performance is the **yield statistic:**

$$\text{Yield} = \frac{\text{Actual sales revenue}}{\text{Potential sales revenue}} \times 100$$

Potential sales revenue is defined as the room sales that would be generated if 100% occupancy was achieved and each room was sold at its maximum rack rate. For example, if a hotel has 150 rooms, each of which has a maximum rack rate of $100, potential sales revenue is $150 \times \$100 = \$15,000$. If actual sales revenue on a particular night is $10,000, then yield is

$$\frac{\$10,000}{\$15,000} \times 100 = \underline{\underline{66.7\%}}$$

Yield thus combines two factors: the number of rooms available (inventory) and room pricing. Room inventory management is concerned with how many rooms are made available to each market segment and its demand for rooms. Pricing management is concerned with the room rate quoted to each of these market segments.

Note that there can be different combinations of room rates and occupancies that achieve the same yield percentage. For example, consider the following three situations that show various combinations that generate the same actual sales revenue, and thus the same yield percentage:

Case A   **100 rooms occupied × $100.00 average rate = $10,000**

Case B   **120 rooms occupied × $ 83.33 average rate = $10,000**

Case C   **140 rooms occupied × $ 71.43 average rate = $10,000**

In each of these three situations, if potential sales revenue was $15,000, the yield will be the same: 66.7%. However, even though each of these situations is equal insofar as total sales revenue and yield percentage are concerned, they may not be equal in terms of other factors. On one hand, in Cases B and C there are more rooms occupied than in Case A; thus, there will be additional housekeeping and energy costs. On the other hand, Cases B and C also mean more guests in the hotel who are likely to patronize and increase sales revenue in food and beverage areas. Further, if those additional customers are first-time guests of the hotel and leave with a favorable impression, they are likely to be repeat customers and will provide positive word-of-mouth advertising, thus increasing future sales revenue.

Finally, note that because the yield statistic is a combination of occupancy percentage and average room rate, it can also be calculated by multiplying the actual occupancy percentage by the average rate ratio. The average rate ratio is the actual average rate expressed as a percentage of the average maximum potential rate. In our 150-room hotel, the maximum average potential rate is $100 ($15,000 potential maximum rooms sales revenue divided by 150 rooms). Yields for the three cases can be calculated as follows:

$$\text{Yield} = \frac{\text{Rooms occupied}}{\text{Potential rooms}} = \frac{\text{Average rate}}{\text{Maximum rack rate}}$$

Case A:
$$\frac{100}{150} \times \frac{\$100}{\$100}$$

$$= 66.7\% \text{ occupancy} \times 1.0 \text{ average rate ratio}$$

$$= \underline{66.7\%} \text{ yield}$$

Case B:
$$\frac{120}{150} \times \frac{\$83.33}{\$100}$$

$$= 80\% \text{ occupancy} \times 0.8333 \text{ average rate ratio}$$

$$= \underline{66.7\%} \text{ yield}$$

Case C:
$$\frac{140}{150} \times \frac{\$71.43}{\$100}$$

$$= 93.33\% \text{ occupancy} \times 0.7143 \text{ average rate ratio}$$

$$= \underline{66.7\%} \text{ yield}$$

Even though the occupancy percentage and the average rate ratio by themselves do not provide complete information, by multiplying them together to provide the yield percentage, a single integrated statistic is produced that is much more meaningful and is a more consistent measure of a hotel's performance.

The objective of yield management is to maximize hotel room sales revenue by using basic economic principles to allocate the right type of room to the right type of guest at a price the guest is prepared to pay. The concept of maximizing sales revenue is not new. Indeed, hotel managers have always known that during slow periods they can increase the demand for rooms by looking at the number of reservations they already have for future periods and then reducing the prices of still-available rooms to stimulate further demand. Conversely, during high-demand periods when occupancy will be at or near 100%, they can increase room rates, knowing that customers are prepared to pay higher rates in order to guarantee a reservation. Most hotel operators have traditionally used this concept of supply and demand in their pricing.

When a hotel's sales manager contracts with a conference group at a room rate lower than that for transient guests, the manager is practicing a form of yield management. Similarly, offering lower transient rates on weekends than during the week is another form of yield management, as is refusing to discount any rates below the rack rate during the peak vacation period. However, it is important for management to go beyond these ad hoc room rate pricing methods to obtain the full benefits of yield management. For example, it has been a common practice for hotels to stop accepting reservations for those days when reservations have reached a certain level. As a result of subsequent cancellations and no shows, empty rooms result. These *spoiled* rooms could have been filled if extra reservations had been taken. A good yield management system can track the level of these spoiled rooms and indicate when extra reservations should be accepted, thus increasing room sales revenue and increasing guest satisfaction because customers who would otherwise have their reservations declined are able to stay at their hotel of choice. A computerized yield management system can also indicate how much additional sales revenue was produced as a result of management decisions based on yield management.

Traditionally, many hotels have quoted a rate (usually the highest, or rack rate) to inquiring customers and have then reduced this quoted rate (sometimes several times) as the customer shows resistance. Hotels that practice this will end up with a declining average rate because of the high number of rooms sold at a discount. This strategy has little to do with rational yield management. In addition, there will be increasing customer dissatisfaction, as guests realize that by offering further resistance they could have obtained an even lower rate.

COMPUTER APPLICATIONS

Computerized spreadsheet software programs can be extremely useful in making pricing decisions because they can rapidly perform the calculations in what-if situations that would take hours to produce if done manually.

For example, a variety of room rates can be entered in the computer, along with an assumed occupancy percentage for each separate room rate. For each room rate and occupancy percentage, the expected level of variable expenses can also be entered. The computer can then calculate the total sales revenue and anticipated departmental profit (operating income) for each possible situation to provide management with information about which average room rate is the most profitable. More sophisticated programs can also predict what effect each room rate and occupancy level will have on other departments, such as food and beverage.

A spreadsheet program can also easily handle the calculations necessary for such things as average checks, seat turnovers, menu gross profit, the Hubbart formula, and a discount grid, as illustrated in Exhibit 6.8.

Spreadsheets or special menu engineering software packages can be used to eliminate the extensive time necessary to produce the worksheets manually. Only each item's cost, selling price, and menu mix have to be entered, and all of the remaining calculations are automatically performed and printed out.

Finally, as mentioned earlier in this chapter, there are special yield management software packages that can be used to implement a yield management system.

SUMMARY

This chapter introduced the reader to various pricing methods that have been used in the hospitality industry. It pointed out the need for both long-range and tactical pricing approaches. The usual way of looking at an income statement is to deduct costs from sales revenue, and call any excess of sales revenue over costs net income. However, if net income (after tax) is considered as a cost, it can then be budgeted for like any other cost; and the required sales revenue that must be realized to cover all costs, including net income after tax, can be calculated in advance each month, quarter, or year.

Once it has been calculated for a restaurant, this figure permits us to calculate average check or average customer spending. This is calculated as follows:

$$\text{Average check} = \frac{\text{Total annaul sales revenue}}{\text{Seats} \times \text{Seat turnover} \times \text{Operating days}}$$

The overall average check can be further broken down by meal period by using the following equation:

Average check meal period

$$= \frac{\text{Meal period sales revenue (\%)} \times \text{Total sales revenue}}{\text{Seats} \times \text{Meal period seat turnover} \times \text{Operating days}}$$

The average check is only an average and not the price of every item on the menu. Menu pricing of individual items can be a complex problem for management, requiring consideration of a great number of factors. Factors considered include the menu price ranges needed to accommodate clientele; gross margin of different menu items; and pricing of the competition. It is important to evaluate the influence the menu sales revenue mix can have on the average check as well as the effect on gross margin and net income.

The effect that seat turnovers can have on total sales revenue should never be ignored. Increasing seat turnover can compensate for a declining average check.

Menu engineering is a method of menu analysis that combines each menu item's contribution margin (gross profit) with its popularity or the demand for that item by the restaurant's customers. Menu items are then classified into one of four categories—stars, plowhorses, puzzles, and dogs—and decisions can be made about how to change the menu.

The average room rate required for a hotel or motel to cover all costs, including net income, can be calculated in a way similar to the calculation of an average check for a restaurant:

$$\text{Average room rate} = \frac{\text{Total sales revenue}}{\text{Rooms} \times \text{Occupancy\%} \times \text{Operating days}}$$

The average room rate, like the average check, is only an average and not necessarily the rate for any classification of rooms. Normally, the average room rate is broken down into an average rate for single rooms and average rate for double rooms. Room rates are also calculated based on the square footage of rooms with different sizes. Total room sales revenue is a combination of average room rate and actual room occupancy. Therefore, one should keep in mind the occupancy of rooms by day of the week, because declining room rate can be compensated for by increasing room occupancy, and vice versa.

In room rate discounting, an equation can be used to calculate the equivalent occupancy needed to hold total sales revenue less marginal costs constant if the rack rate is discounted. The equation to calculate the equivalent occupancy is as follows:

$$\frac{\text{Equivalent}}{\text{occupancy}} = \frac{\text{Original}}{\text{occupancy}} \times \frac{\text{Rack rate} - \text{Marginal cost}}{[\text{Rack rate} \times (1 - \text{Discount percentage})] - \text{Marginal cost}}$$

A potential average room rate can be compared with the actual average. Once a potential average rate has been calculated, it can be used to establish discounted room rates for various market segments.

Note that both the return on investment (bottom-up) method and the markup method of establishing prices should be used primarily as reference points in establishing actual prices. There are several other considerations to keep in mind. For example, prices must be established to meet the organization's long-run objectives. In addition, factors such as the elasticity of demand, the business's cost structure (breakdown between fixed and variable costs), and the competitive environment in which it operates are all very important.

Most hotels measure their rooms department's effectiveness by using either occupancy percentage or average rate, both of which have shortcomings. An alternative is to use the yield statistic, which is a combination of occupancy percentage and average rate. The chapter concluded with a section on yield management, a method of matching customers' purchase patterns and their demand for guest rooms to derive more precise occupancy forecasts, with the objective of maximizing room sales revenue.

DISCUSSION QUESTIONS

1. Discuss the advantages and disadvantages of the three traditional pricing methods used by the hospitality industry.

2. Differentiate long-run from tactical pricing and list four events that might necessitate tactical pricing.

3. Explain why net income (after tax) can be treated as another cost of running a business operation.

4. Explain how forecasted (budgeted) sales revenue for a hospitality operation can be used to determine an average check and an average room.

5. If an average check was established to support a specific level of total sales revenue in a restaurant and the seat turnover rate becomes too low to support the desired total sales revenue, explain how the seat turnover needs to be changed.

6. Define the term *sales revenue mix* and explain what influence it can have on an average check.

7. What factors would a restaurant manager need to consider when establishing individual menu item prices?

8. Explain why you do or do not think that the food cost percentage figure is important in menu pricing.

9. In menu engineering, what are the two main factors about each menu item that are considered?

10. In menu engineering, state what dogs are.

11. Why is loss of sales revenue from hotel rooms not occupied on a given day more of a problem than loss of sales revenue from customers who did not show up in a restaurant on a given day?

12. Explain briefly how a motel's average room rate can be calculated or projected by using the bottom-up approach.

13. If a hotel has an average room rate of $75, explain why every customer staying in the hotel will not pay this average rate.

14. Describe how a double occupancy percentage for rooms is calculated.

15. Of what value might it be to calculate hotel room occupancy by day of the week, or seat turnover in a restaurant by day of the week, rather than using an average weekly figure?

16. Define the terms *rack rate* and *potential average room rate*.

17. Define elasticity of demand and, using figures of your own choosing, show how a reduction in a hotel's average room rate and the resulting change in total sales revenue would indicate an inelastic demand situation.

18. State the equation for calculating elasticity of demand.

19. What implications does the breakdown of a business's costs into fixed and variable ones have on the pricing decision?

20. Discuss the concept of product and/or service differentiation in a restaurant situation.

E T H I C S   S I T U A T I O N

A hotel manager has set a rack rate for all rooms in the hotel of $149 for next year. Corporations, conventions, and conference groups were advised that early next year the rack rate charged could be reduced to a lower rate of $99, and the potential reduction will depend on the volume of business they provide. Travel agencies, which book a large number of hotel reservations for independent travelers, were advised that room rate discounts are available for $139, $129, and $119, with restrictions. The travel agencies were also advised that rooms booked at the $149 rate would increase their commission to 15%, rather than the normal 10% for a discounted rate reservation. Individuals that telephone the hotel directly for a reservation are first quoted the $149 rate; however, employees booking reservations have been trained to lower this rate to $139, $129, and $119, but never lower than $119. In addition, room-booking employees are required to advise potential guests of the restrictions that apply at each rate level. Discuss the ethics of this situation.

E X E R C I S E S

E6.1 Determine the operating income necessary to yield a net after-tax income of $56,000 using a current tax rate of 30%.

E6.2 Using information given in E6.1, identify the amount of income tax to be paid.

E6.3 If the total fixed and other identified operating costs are estimated to be $174,600 and all variable costs total 82% of total sales revenue, what is estimated total sales revenue?

E6.4 Average sales revenue of a restaurant with 90 seats for a month with a seat turnover of 2.7 and 26 operating days is $64,760. Determine the average check for the month.

E6.5 Using information from E6.4, determine the effect on the average check if seat turnover decreases from 2.7 to 2.0 times per day.

E6.6 A restaurant with 100 seats, serving both lunch and dinner 6 days per week, reported total annual sales revenue of $998,000. Dinner generates 68% of total sales revenue, with a seat turnover of 1.75. What is the average check for dinner?

E6.7 A rooms operation reported a total of 18,760 rooms sold, with a total of 23,450 guests in the previous year. What was the double occupancy rate?

E6.8 A small motel operation with 50 rooms has an average yearly occupancy rate of 74%. The forecasted sales revenue for the coming year is $842,712. What is the average room rate expected to be?

E6.9 Assume a rooms operation had 45 each, 220-square-foot rooms, and 25 each, 160-square-foot rooms with an average 70% occupancy for both types of rooms. Room sales revenue per day of $2,390 is required. Determine the rate to charge for each square foot.

E6.10 Using the following information, determine the average single and double room rates:

Average rooms sold per day: 60

Average rooms double occupied: 24

Spread wanted between single and double room rates: $12.00

Average daily revenue: $2,988

P R O B L E M S

P6.1 You have the following projections about the costs in a family restaurant for next year:

Net income required: 22% after income tax on the owner's present investment of $80,000, income tax rate is 28%.

Depreciation: Present book value (consolidated) of furniture and equipment is $76,000, depreciation rate is 20%.

Interest: Interest on a loan outstanding of $35,000 is 8%.

Known Costs		*Variable Costs*
Insurance	$ 3,000	Food cost, 38% of sales revenue
License	2,500	Wage cost, 34% of sales revenue
Utilities	8,400	Other costs, 12% of sales revenue
Maintenance	3,600	
Administration	9,800	
Salaries	41,600	

a. What sales revenue would the restaurant have to achieve next year in order to acquire the desired net income after tax?

b. What is the required average check needed to achieve the annual sales revenue objective if the restaurant is open 365 days, had 60 seats, and had an average seat turnover of 2.5 times per day?

P6.2 A 25-room budget motel expects its occupancy next year to be 80%. The owners' investment is $402,800. They want an after-tax return on their investment of 15%. Tax rate is 25%.

- Interest on a long-term mortgage is 10%. Present balance outstanding is $806,400.
- Depreciation rate on the building is 10% of the present book value of $700,200. Depreciation on the furnishings and equipment is at 20% of the consolidated present book value of $150,400.
- Other known fixed costs total $141,800 a year.
- At 80% occupancy rate the motel's operating expenses, wages, supplies, and laundry, etc. are calculated to be $55,400 a year.
- The motel has other income from vending machines of $5,210 a year.

   a. To cover all costs and produce the required net income after tax, what should the motel's average room rate be next year?

   b. If the motel operates at 30% double occupancy and has an $8.00 spread between its single and double rates, what will the single and double room rates be? Assume only one common room size, all with the same rates.

P6.3 A restaurant has 90 seats. Total annual sales revenue for next year is projected to be $975,000. The restaurant is open 52 weeks a year and serves breakfast and lunch 6 days a week. Dinner is served 7 days a week. Seat turnover per day is anticipated to be 1.2 times for breakfast, 1.25 times for lunch, and 1.20 times for dinner. Sales revenue is derived at 20% from breakfast, 30% from lunch, and 50% from dinner. Calculate the restaurant's average check by meal period.

P6.4 A 140-seat dining room had a weekly customer count by meal period and day:

	Lunch	*Dinner*
Sunday	Closed	180
Monday	160	110
Tuesday	170	112
Wednesday	175	108
Thursday	160	120
Friday	180	210
Saturday	50	250

   a. For each meal period and for each day of the week calculate the seat turnover.

   b. Calculate the average number of customers per day and the average seat turnover for the week for each meal period.

c. List some of the ways in which the information in parts a and b would be useful to the restaurant manager or owner.

P6.5 You have the following information about Beech Tree Café's lunch menu with 10 entrées:

	Number Sold (MM)	Menu Item Food Cost	Menu Item Selling Price
1. Corn beef on rye	328	$1.35	$5.95
2. Salmon salad sandwich	288	1.18	5.50
3. Club sandwich	420	1.36	5.95
4. Egg and tomato sandwich	192	0.76	4.95
5. Roast beef and lettuce sandwich	164	1.05	6.95
6. Chicken wings	236	2.21	8.95
7. Hot dog and fries	152	0.84	4.50
8. Hamburger and fries	536	0.97	6.50
9. Cheeseburger and fries	312	1.12	6.95
10. Veggie burger and salad	185	1.85	6.95

Complete a menu engineering worksheet using the information given above. Exhibits 6.4 and 6.5 can be used as a guide. Discuss how you would adjust the menu.

P6.6 An owner invested $180,000 in a new family-style restaurant, of which $160,000 was immediately used to purchase equipment and $20,000 was retained for working cash. Estimates for the first year of business are as follows:

■ Menu selling prices to be established to give a markup of 150% over cost of food sold
■ Variable wages, 28% of sales revenue
■ Fixed wages, $51,600
■ Other variable costs, 7% of sales revenue
■ Rent, $36,000
■ Insurance, $4,800
■ Depreciation on equipment, 20%
■ Return on investment desired, 12%
■ Income tax rate, 30%

The restaurant has 60 seats and is open 5 days a week for lunch and dinner only. Lunch sales revenue is expected to be 40% of total volume with 2 seat turnovers. Dinner revenue will be 60% of total volume, with 1.25 turnovers.

Calculate the average check per meal period that will cover all costs, including desired return on investment.

P6.7 You have been given the following information about a hotel for the next year. The hotel has 40 rooms and expected occupancy rate of 70%. Rooms department, operating expenses, wages, supplies, laundry, and so on is 27% of room sales revenue.

a. Calculate the hotel's average room rate for next year.

b. If the hotel operated at 30% double occupancy and management wanted a $15 spread between the single and double room rates, what would these rates be?

Administrative and general	$ 38,300
Marketing	28,900
Energy costs	35,100
Repairs and maintenance	28,800
Property taxes	17,600
Insurance	4,800
Telephone department operating loss	(9,700)
Contributory income, food and beverage departments	103,200
First mortgage, at 8% interest, present balance	601,000
Second mortgage, at 12% interest, present balance	402,000
Ownership equity (after-tax return of 15% is expected)	280,000
Book value of fixed assets before depreciation charges:	
Land	250,000
Building	1,860,000
Furniture and equipment (combined)	382,000
Depreciation rate on building	5%
Depreciation rate on furniture and equipment (combined)	20%
Income tax rate	25%

P6.8 A motel has 30 rooms and expects 70% occupancy next year. The owners' investment is presently $520,000, and they expect a 12% after-tax annual return on their investment. The motel is in a 24% tax bracket. The motel is carrying two mortgages: the first mortgage in the amount of $359,000 at a 10% interest rate and the second mortgage in the amount of $140,000 at a 14% interest rate. Present book value of the building is $632,000, and depreciation rate is 5%. Present combined book value of furniture and equipment is $117,000, and the combined depreciation rate is 20%. Indirect costs are $44,800 and direct costs are $59,300. The motel also receives an additional $12,000 a year leasing out its restaurant.

a. Calculate the motel's required average room rate to cover all expenses and provide the owners with their desired return on investment.

b. Calculate the average single and double room rates, assuming a 60% double occupancy and a $12 difference between singles and doubles.

P6.9 A 45-room resort hotel has three sizes of rooms, as follows:

- 15 singles at 150 square feet each
- 15 doubles at 220 square feet each
- 15 suites at 380 square feet each

Occupancy is 80%. Demand for each type of room is about equal. The projected total sales revenue from rooms next year is $912,500. If average room rate were to be based solely on room size, what would the average room rate for each type of room be next year?

P6.10 The Resolute Resort hotel currently operates at 75% occupancy, using a rack rate for all rooms of $60 and a marginal cost per room sold of $8. Calculate the occupancy figures for discount grid using discount percentages of 5%, 10%, 15%, and 20%.

P6.11 Motley Motel's potential average room rate is calculated to be $62. Assume that this motel had three market segments. Vacation travelers use 75% of the room nights and are charged 100% of the rack rate. Business travelers use 15% of the room nights and are charged 90% of the rack rate. Sports teams account for 10% of the room nights and are charged 80% of the rack rate.

a. Calculate the room rate by market segment.

b. Prove that your calculations are correct, assuming that total annual room nights are 7,300.

P6.12 The Inviting Inn has 500 available guest rooms. For a certain week next month, the anticipated transient demand for rooms is as follows:

Monday	200
Tuesday	200
Wednesday	200
Thursday	200
Friday	100
Saturday	50
Sunday	50

The Inviting Inn also has committed the following number of rooms for group sales during the same week:

Monday	200
Tuesday	200
Wednesday	300
Thursday	300
Friday	100
Saturday	100
Sunday	100

The inn has the possibility of booking another group of 100 rooms for the nights of Tuesday, Wednesday, Thursday, and Friday of that week at a discounted rate of $60 per room. The inn's rack rate for transient guests is $80, and its marginal cost per room sold is $15.

a. Assuming the new group is booked, calculate the additional net sales revenue (gross sales revenue less marginal costs) to the inn.

b. What factors, other than net sales revenue, might you consider before committing to this new group sale?

C A S E   6

In the case at the end of Chapter 3, you calculated the average food and beverage check for the 4C Company's 84-seat restaurant in Year 2007. The restaurant was open for 52 weeks, 6 days a week for lunch, and 5 days a week for dinner. An analysis of sales checks indicated that the average turnover was 1.5 times for lunch and 1.25 times for dinner. Lunch contributes about 45% of total sales revenue and dinner contributes 55%. Total beverage sales revenue is 20% at lunch and 80% at dinner.

a. Calculate the average lunch and average dinner checks for food and beverages. This information will be used in a later case.

b. Suggest to Charlie a number of ways in which he could attempt to raise the average check and the total food and beverage sales revenues for Year 2008.

c. In part b, one of the ways might be to substitute, on the food menu, items with a low selling price for items with a high selling price. Write a short report to Charlie about the effect this might have on the restaurant's guests, its food cost percentage, and its gross margin and net income.

CHAPTER 7

COST MANAGEMENT

INTRODUCTION

This chapter introduces and describes various costs that exist in a business operation, including direct costs, indirect costs, controllable and noncontrollable costs, joint costs, discretionary costs, relevant and nonrelevant costs, sunk costs, opportunity costs, fixed costs, variable costs, semifixed or semivariable costs, and standard costs.

The chapter continues by showing how to allocate indirect costs to departments and the potential difficulties this may create. It illustrates how to use relevant costs to assist in determining which piece of equipment to buy.

Fixed and variable costs are discussed in relation to their use in the management decision process; that is, whether to accept or reject an offered price for services to be rendered. The evaluation of fixed and variable costs is illustrated in three additional problems: deciding whether to close during an off-season period; deciding which business to buy; and deciding whether to accept a fixed or variable lease on a facility.

Having illustrated how important understanding fixed and variable cost relationships are in the decision process, the chapter concludes with an illustration of how semifixed or semivariable costs can be separated into their fixed and variable elements.

CHAPTER OBJECTIVES

After studying this chapter, the reader should be able to:

1. Briefly define and give examples of some of the major types of costs, such as direct and indirect costs, fixed and variable costs, and discretionary costs.
2. Prorate indirect costs to sales revenue departments and make decisions based on the results.
3. Use relevant costs to help determine which piece of equipment to buy.

4. Use knowledge about fixed and variable costs for a variety of different business decisions, such as whether to close during the off-season.

5. Define the term *operating leverage* and explain its advantages and disadvantages.

6. Explain and use each of the following three methods to separate semifixed or semivariable costs into their fixed and variable elements: high–low calculation, multipoint graph, and regression analysis.

COST MANAGEMENT

Most of the sales revenue in a hotel or food service enterprise is consumed by costs: as much as 90 cents or more of each sales revenue dollar may be used to pay for costs. Therefore, cost management is important. Budgeting costs and cost analysis is one way to control and manage costs to improve net income. Another way to improve net income is to cut costs, without regard to the consequences. The latter course of action may not be wise. Perhaps a better way is to look at each cost (expense) and see how it contributes toward net income. If advertising cost leads to higher net income than would be the case if we did not advertise, then it would not pay to cut the advertising expense.

One of the ways to better manage costs is to understand that there are many types of costs. If one can recognize the type of cost that is being considered, then better decisions can be made. Some of the most common types of cost are defined in the following sections.

TYPES OF COST

DIRECT COST

A **direct cost** is one that is traceable to and is the responsibility of a particular operating department or division. Most direct costs are variable by nature and will increase or decrease in direct relation to increases and decreases in sales revenue. For this reason, direct costs tend to be controllable by, and the responsibility of, the department or division manager to which they are charged. Examples of these types of costs are cost of sales–food and –beverages, wages and salaries, operating supplies and services, and linen and laundry.

INDIRECT COST

An **indirect cost** is one that cannot be identified with and is not traceable to a particular operating department or division, and thus, cannot be charged to any specific department or division. General building maintenance could only be charged to various departments or divisions (such as rooms, food, or beverage) with difficulty. Even if this difficulty could be overcome, it must still be recognized that indirect costs cannot normally be considered the responsibility of operating departments' or divisions' managers. Indirect costs are frequently referred to as **undistributed costs** (also referred to as overhead costs).

CONTROLLABLE AND NONCONTROLLABLE COSTS

If a cost is *controllable,* the manager can influence the amount spent. For example, the kitchen manager can influence the amount spent on food. However, it is unlikely the kitchen manager can influence the amount spent on rent, especially in the short term. The mistake is often made of calling direct costs **controllable costs** and indirect costs **noncontrollable costs.** It is true that direct costs are generally more easily controlled than indirect costs, but in the long run all costs are controllable by someone at some time.

JOINT COST

A **joint cost** is one that is shared by, and thus is the responsibility of, two or more departments or areas. A dining room server who serves both food and beverage is an example. The server's wages are a joint cost and should be charged (in proportion to sales revenue, or by some other appropriate method) partly to the food department and the remainder to the beverage department. Most indirect costs are also joint costs. The problem is to find a rational basis for separating the cost and charging part of it to each department.

DISCRETIONARY COST

This is a cost that may or may not be incurred based on the decision of a particular person, usually the general manager. Nonemergency maintenance is an example of a **discretionary cost.** The building exterior could be painted this year, or the painting could be postponed until next year. Either way, sales revenue should not be affected. The general manager has the choice; thus, it is a discretionary cost. Note that a discretionary cost is only discretionary in the short run. For example, the building will have to be painted at some time in order to maintain its appearance.

RELEVANT AND NONRELEVANT COSTS

A **relevant cost** is a cost that affects a decision. To be relevant, a cost must be in the future and different between alternatives. For example, a restaurant is considering replacing its mechanical cash register with an electronic one. The relevant costs would be the cost of the new register (less any trade-in of the old one), the cost of training employees on the new equipment, and any change in maintenance and material supply costs on the new machine. As long as no change is necessary in the number of servers required, the restaurant's labor cost would not be a relevant cost. It would make no difference to the decision.

SUNK COST

A **sunk cost** is a cost already incurred and about which nothing can be done. It cannot affect any future decisions. For example, if the same restaurant had spent $250 for an employee to study the relative merits of using mechanical or electronic registers, the $250 is a sunk cost. It cannot make any difference to the decision, and should not be included in any assessment of the costs of the registers.

OPPORTUNITY COST

An **opportunity cost** is the cost of not doing something. An organization can invest its surplus cash in marketable securities at 10%, or leave the money in the bank at 6%. If it buys marketable securities, its opportunity cost is 6%. Another way to look at it is to say that it is making 10% on the investment, less the opportunity cost of 6%; therefore, the net gain is a 4% interest rate.

FIXED COST

Fixed costs are not expected to change in the short run of an operating period of a year or less, and will not vary with increases or decreases in sales revenue. Examples include management salaries, fire insurance expense, rent paid on a square-foot basis, or the committed cost of an advertising campaign. Over the long run fixed costs can, of course, change, but in the short run they are not expected to change. If a fixed cost should change over the short run, the change would normally result only from a decision of specific top management.

VARIABLE COST

A **variable cost** is one that changes in direct proportion to a change in sales revenue. Very few costs are strictly linear, but two that are (with only a slight possibility that they will not always fit this strict definition) are the cost of sales of food and beverages. The more food and beverages sold, the more costs will be incurred. If sales revenues are zero, no food or beverage costs are incurred.

SEMIFIXED OR SEMIVARIABLE COSTS

Most costs do not fit neatly into the fixed or the variable category—they have an element of fixed cost and an element of variable cost. As well, they are not always variable directly to sales revenues on a straight-line basis. Such costs would include payroll, maintenance, and utilities. To make some useful decisions, it is advantageous to break down these **semifixed** or **semivariable costs** into their two elements: fixed or variable. Ways of doing this will be discussed later in this chapter.

STANDARD COST

A **standard cost** is what the cost should be for a given volume or level of sales. We saw some uses of such standards in Chapter 5. Other uses would be in pricing decisions (Chapter 6), in budgeting (Chapter 9), and in expansion planning (Chapter 13). Standard costs need to be developed by each establishment because there are many factors that influence standard costs and that differ from one establishment to another.

Let us look at some of the ways in which an analysis of the type(s) of cost(s) with which we are dealing would help us make a better decision.

ALLOCATING INDIRECT COSTS TO SALES REVENUE AREAS

One of the difficulties in allocating indirect costs is determining the correct basis to be used to apportion indirect costs to each sales revenue department or division. Some of the methods that could be used were discussed in Chapter 2. If the allocation of indirect costs is made using an incorrect basis, then incorrect decisions could be made. If the correct allocation basis were used, then presumably the incorrect decisions would not be made.

Consider the following restaurant complex that has two main sales revenue outlets, a dining room and a snack bar. Sales revenue and direct costs for each sales area and indirect costs that have not been distributed are shown as follows for a typical month; an average monthly operating income for the total operation is $12,000.

	Dining Room	*Snack Bar*	*Total*
Sales revenue	$105,000	$45,000	$150,000
Direct costs	(75,000)	(39,000)	(114,000)
Contributory income	$ 30,000	$ 6,000	$ 36,000
Indirect costs			(24,000)
Operating income			$ 12,000

Management believes the $24,000 of total indirect costs should be allocated to the two operating departments using sales revenue as the basis to allocate the indirect costs. Summing total sales revenue and dividing each operating department's sales revenue by total sales revenue determines the allocation percentages. In other words, the dining room provides 70% ($105,000 / $150,000) of sales revenue and the snack bar provides 30% ($45,000 / $150,000) of sales revenue. The new monthly statement of operating income is:

	Dining Room	Snack Bar	Total
Sales revenue	$105,000	$45,000	$150,000
Direct costs	(75,000)	(39,000)	(114,000)
Contributory income	$ 30,000	$ 6,000	$ 36,000
Indirect costs	(16,800)	(7,200)	(24,000)
Operating income	$ 13,200	($ 1,200)	$ 12,000

This shows that, by distributing indirect costs on the basis of *sales revenue,* the snack bar is losing $1,200 a month. Management of the restaurant complex has an opportunity to lease out the snack bar, as is, for $750 a month rent. The new operator will pay for the indirect costs of the snack bar (such as administration, advertising, utilities, maintenance). The remaining indirect costs were evaluated to be $19,350, all of which must be assumed by the dining room. This seems to be a good offer. A $750 profit appears better than an $1,200 loss, or is it? The following is the new dining room monthly statement of operating income:

Sales revenue	$105,000
Direct costs	(75,000)
Contributory income	$ 30,000
Indirect costs	(19,350)
Income before rent	$ 10,650
Rental income	750
Operating income	$ 11,400

These figures indicate that the dining room's operating income, including rental income, is only $11,400. Earlier it was calculated to have been $13,200 without any rental income. Overall, operating income has decreased $1,800 ($13,200 − $11,400). Obviously, the mistake was made in allocating indirect costs to the dining room and the snack bar on the basis of sales revenue and then making a decision based on this allocation. A more careful assessment of indirect costs should have been made, with allocation made on a more logical basis. If this had been done (with the information we now have about the dining room's indirect costs), the real situation would have been as follows, which shows that both sales departments combined were, in fact, making an operating income:

	Dining Room	*Snack Bar*	*Total*
Sales revenue	$105,000	$45,000	$150,000
Direct costs	(75,000)	(39,000)	(114,000)
Contributory income	$ 30,000	$ 6,000	$ 36,000
Indirect costs	(19,350)	(4,650)	(24,000)
Operating income	$ 10,650	$ 1,350	$ 12,000

This shows that renting out the snack bar that currently provides operating income of $1,350 a month for $750 a month would reduce operating income by $600. To look at it another way, the $750 rental income is the opportunity cost of not renting out the snack bar, but since it is less than the $1,350 now being made, it can be ignored.

WHICH PIECE OF EQUIPMENT SHOULD WE BUY?

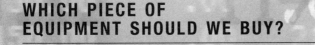

One of the ongoing decisions all managers face is that of choosing between alternatives. Which items do we offer on a menu, which person should we hire, how should we spend the advertising budget? One area of decision making where the knowledge of costs is helpful is that of selecting a piece of equipment. The following might be a typical situation.

A motel owner has asked his accountant to research the photocopier equipment available from vendors, and to recommend the two best equipment alternatives. The motel owner will then decide which item of equipment to purchase. The fee charged for the accountant's research was $500. The accountant's report produced the following information:

	Equipment A	*Equipment B*
New equipment, cash cost	$10,000	$ 8,000
Estimated economic life	5 years	5 years
Equipment residual values	$ 1,000	$ 800
Installation cost	$ 225	$ 200
Initial training cost	$ 500	$ 450
Annual maintenance (for 5 years)	$ 400	$ 300
Annual cost of forms (for 5 years)	$ 650	$ 750
Annual wage cost	$22,500	$22,500

The $500 fee is a "sunk" cost and will be paid regardless of the decision—even if a decision is made not to buy either piece of equipment. To make a decision, the motel owner must sort out the relevant information. Costs of the alternatives being evaluated are considered *relevant costs* if they are different; costs that are the same in the alternatives being evaluated are considered as *irrelevant costs.*

In this example, unique initial first-year costs consist of the new equipment costs, initial training costs, and initial installation costs; all three costs are relevant since they are different. Individual recurring inclusive costs for Years 1–5 consist of maintenance costs and the cost of forms, which are relevant since they are different. In addition, the residual value of each alternative being evaluated, if different, is relevant and deducted to arrive at total recurring costs for Years 1–5. Any cost function that is the same for each alternative being evaluated is considered irrelevant. For example, the annual wage cost is irrelevant because the cost is the same for both items being considered. Annual depreciation expense (cost − residual value) is a non-cash expense and is treated as irrelevant if the residual values are different and considered as relevant. An example of this technique using the information as discussed follows:

	Equipment A	*Equipment B*
Unique Costs, First Year		
Initial equipment cost	$10,000	$ 8,000
Initial installation cost	225	200
Initial training cost	500	450
First-year Costs	$10,725	$ 8,650
Recurring Inclusive Costs Years 1–10		
Maintenance ($400 × 10) & ($300 × 10)	$ 4,000	$ 3,000
Cost of forms ($650 × 10) & ($750 × 10)	$ 6,500	$ 7,500
Less: Equipment residual values	(1,000)	(800)
Total recurring inclusive costs Yrs. 1–10	$ 9,500	$ 9,700
Total First-year Costs	$10,725	$ 8,650
Total First-year & Recurring Cost	$20,225	$18,350

In this example, the total 5-year costs for Equipment B is $1,875 less than the total cost for Equipment A. The following example shows an alternative technique that arrives at the same total costs for items A and B in the previous example. This alternative does not use the initial cost of the assets being evaluated, and residual values are used only to calculate each item's depreciation expense (cost − residual value), which is shown as a recurring cost for items A and B. Generally, the first technique provides a better review of cash costs. However, either method can be used, and one should use the technique that is simpler to understand.

	Equipment A	Equipment B
Unique Costs, First Year		
Initial installation costs	225	200
Initial training costs	500	450
First-year Costs	$ 725	$ 650
Recurring Inclusive Costs Years 1–10		
Depreciation ($10,000 − $1,000) ($8,000 − $800)	$ 9,000	$ 7,200
Maintenance ($400 × 10) & ($300 × 10)	$ 4,000	$ 3,000
Cost of forms ($650 × 10) & ($750 × 10)	$ 6,500	$ 7,500
Total recurring inclusive costs Yrs. 1–10	$19,500	$17,700
Total First-year Costs	$ 725	$ 650
Total First-year & Recurring Cost	$20,225	$18,350

Certain assumptions have been made: that one can forecast costs for 5 to 10 years, and that the costs as originally estimated are accurate. In the final decision, costs might not be the only factor to be considered. A more comprehensive look at the investment decision will be taken in Chapter 12.

CAN WE SELL BELOW TOTAL COST?

The obvious answer to a question of "selling below cost" is dependent on whether the person responding to the question understands the nature of fixed and variable costs. In general, the answer would be, "Not unless you plan to go broke." However, before the question can be answered intelligently, we should first answer *which* cost. The best answer would be: "If variable costs are covered and a contribution toward fixed costs is made, selling below total cost can be considered."

Consider a catering company that rents its facilities for $80,000 per year and has additional annual fixed costs for management salaries, insurance, depreciation charges on furnishings and equipment, and other fixed costs of $66,000. The total fixed costs would be $146,000, or an average of $400 per day.

$$\text{Fixed costs / 365 days} = \$146,000 / 365 = \underline{\underline{\$400}}$$

The catering company and its facilities can handle only one function per day, and it operates with a variable cost of 60% of total sales revenue. The company was approached by an organization wanting to sponsor a lunch for 60 people next week, but it can only pay $10.00 per person. Normally, this catering company would not consider handling a group luncheon this small; however, on this occasion the catering company does not see any likelihood of booking a function in the next few days. If the catering company accepts this function, its income situation will be as follows:

Sales revenue (60 people × $10 each)	**$600.00**
Less: Variable costs (60% × $600)	**(360.00)**
Contribution margin	**$240.00**
Less: Fixed costs	**(400.00)**
Operating loss	**($160.00)**

On the surface, the net loss appears unfavorable; however, considering we incur the $400 fixed cost whether we accept the function or not, we see a different perspective of accepting the function. By selling below the total cost of $760 ($360 + $400), we offset $240 of the $400 of fixed costs that would be incurred with or without the function. In the short run, as long as sales revenue exceeds variable costs and contributes toward fixed costs, it is beneficial to accept the business.

SHOULD WE CLOSE DURING THE OFF-SEASON?

The same reasoning as in the previous case can be applied to a seasonal operation in answering the question of staying open or closing during the off-season. Consider the case of a motel that has this income statement:

Sales revenue	**$390,000**
Operating expenses	**(330,000)**
Operating income	**$ 60,000**

The owner decided to make an analysis of sales revenue and costs by the month and found that for 10 months the operation was making money and for 2 months he was losing money. Variable costs were 20% of sales revenue; total fixed costs were $252,000, or $21,000 a month. The following summarizes his findings:

	10 months	*2 months*	*Total*
Sales revenue	$375,000	$15,000	$390,000
Variable costs	$ 75,000	$ 3,000	$ 78,000
Fixed costs	210,000	42,000	252,000
Total operating costs	$285,000	$45,000	$330,000
Operating income	$ 90,000	($30,000)	$ 60,000

The owner's analysis seems to indicate that he should close to eliminate the $30,000 loss during the 2-month loss period. But if the operation closes, the fixed costs for the 2 months ($42,000) will have to be paid out of the 10 months' net operating income, and $90,000 (10 months net income) less 2 months' fixed costs of $42,000 will reduce the annual net operating income to $48,000 from its current $60,000. If the owner does not want a reduction in annual net operating income, he should not close.

In such a situation, other factors might reinforce the decision to stay open. For example, there could be sizable additional close-down and start-up costs that would have to be included in the calculation of the cost of closing. Also, would key employees return after being laid off? Is there a large enough pool of skilled labor available and willing to work on a seasonal basis only? Would there be recurring training time (and costs) at the start of each new season? Is there a group of regular guests that might not return if the motel was closed for two months? These are some of the types of questions that would have to be answered before any final decision to close was made.

WHICH BUSINESS SHOULD WE BUY?

Just as a business manager has to make choices between alternatives on a day-to-day basis, so, too, does an entrepreneur going into business or expanding an existing business. Let us look at one such situation.

A restaurant chain is eager to expand. It has an opportunity to take over one of two similar existing restaurants. The two restaurants are close to each other, they have the same type of clientele and size of operation, and the asking price is the same for each. They are also similar in that each is taking in $1,000,000 in sales revenue a year, and each has a net operating income of $100,000 a year. With only this information it is difficult to make a decision as to which would be the more profitable investment. But a cost analysis as shown in Exhibit 7.1 reveals differences.

Although the sales revenue and net operating income are the same for each restaurant, the structure of their costs is different, and this will affect the decision of which one could be more profitable. The restaurant chain that wishes to take over either A or B is optimistic about the future. It believes that, without any change in fixed costs, it can increase annual sales revenue by 10%. What effects will this have on the net operating income of A and B? Net operating income will not increase for each restaurant by the same amount. Restaurant A has variable costs of 50%. This means that, out of each dollar of additional sales revenue, it will have variable expenses of $0.50 and a net operating income of $0.50 (fixed costs do not increase). Restaurant B has variable costs of 30%, or $0.30 out of each sales revenue dollar, leaving a net income of $0.70 from each dollar of extra sales revenue (again, fixed costs do not change).

	Restaurant A		Restaurant B	
Sales revenue	$1,000,000	100.0%	$1,000,000	100.0%
Variable costs	$ 500,000	50.0%	$ 300,000	30.0%
Fixed costs	400,000	40.0%	600,000	60.0%
Total costs	$ 900,000	90.0%	$ 900,000	90.0%
Net income	$ 100,000	10.0%	$ 100,000	10.0%

■ **EXHIBIT 7.1**
Statements Showing Differences in Cost Structure

Assuming a 10% increase in sales revenue and no new fixed costs, the income statements of the two restaurants have been recalculated in Exhibit 7.2. Note that Restaurant A has an increased net operating income of $50,000 (to $150,000), but Restaurant B has increased net operating income by $70,000 (to $170,000). In this situation, Restaurant B would be the better investment.

A company that has high fixed costs relative to variable costs is said to have *high* **operating leverage.** From a net operating income point of view, it will do better in times of rising sales revenue than will a company with *low* operating leverage (low fixed costs relative to variable costs). A company with low fixed costs will be better off when sales revenue starts to decline. Exhibit 7.3 illustrates this, under the assumptions that our two restaurants are going to have a decline in sales revenue of 10% from the present $1,000,000 level and that there will be no change in fixed costs. Exhibit 7.3 shows that, with declining sales revenue, Restaurant A will have higher net operating income than Restaurant B.

In fact, if sales revenue declines far enough, Restaurant B will be in financial difficulty long before Restaurant A. If the breakeven point were calculated (the breakeven point is that level of sales revenue at which there will be neither net operating income nor loss), Restaurant A could have a decrease in sales rev-

	Restaurant A		Restaurant B	
Sales revenue	$1,100,000	100.0%	$1,100,000	100.0%
Variable costs	$ 550,000	50.0%	$ 330,000	30.0%
Fixed costs	400,000	36.4%	600,000	54.5%
Total costs	$ 950,000	86.4%	$ 930,000	84.5%
Net income	$ 150,000	13.6%	$ 170,000	15.5%

■ **EXHIBIT 7.2**
Effect of Increased Sales Revenue on Costs and Net Income

	Restaurant A		Restaurant B	
Sales revenue	$900,000	100.0%	$900,000	100.0%
Variable costs	$450,000	50.0%	$270,000	30.0%
Fixed costs	400,000	44.4%	600,000	66.7%
Total costs	$850,000	94.4%	$870,000	96.7%
Net income	$ 50,000	5.6%	$ 30,000	3.3%

■ **EXHIBIT 7.3**

Effect of Decreased Sales Revenue on Costs and Net Income

enue of $800,000, while Restaurant B would be in difficulty at $857,143. This is illustrated in Exhibit 7.4.

One could determine the breakeven level of sales revenue by trial and error, but there is a formula for quickly calculating this level. The formula, and a more in-depth discussion of fixed and variable costs and how an awareness of this structure can be of great value in many types of business decisions, is called cost–volume–profit (CVP) analysis and is covered in Chapter 8.

PAYING A FIXED OR A VARIABLE LEASE

Another situation where fixed and variable cost knowledge can be very useful is in comparing the alternative of a fixed cost lease versus a variable cost lease, based on a percentage of sales. For example, consider the case of a restaurant that has an opportunity to pay a fixed rent for its premises of $5,000 a month ($60,000 a year) or a variable rent of 6% of its sales revenue. Before

	Restaurant A		Restaurant B	
Sales revenue	$800,000	100.0%	$857,143	100.0%
Variable costs	$400,000	50.0%	$257,143	30.0%
Fixed costs	400,000	50.0%	600,000	70.0%
Total costs	$800,000	100.0%	$857,143	100.0%
Normal income	-0-	-0-	-0-	-0-

■ **EXHIBIT 7.4**

Breakeven Sales Revenue Level Depends on Cost Structure

making the decision, the restaurant's management needs to first determine the breakeven point of sales revenue at which the fixed rental payment for a year would be identical to the variable rent. The equation for this is

$$\textbf{Fixed cost lease = Variable cost lease}$$

Or it can be restated as

$$\textbf{Annual breakeven sales revenue} = \frac{\textbf{Fixed cost lease}}{\textbf{Variable cost lease}}$$

Inserting the figures, we can determine the sales revenue level as follows:

$$\textbf{\$1,000,000} = \frac{\textbf{\$60,000}}{\textbf{6\%}}$$

In other words, at $1,000,000 of sales revenue it makes no difference whether the restaurant paid a fixed rent of $60,000 or a variable rent of 6% of sales revenue. At this level of sales, management would be indifferent, and it is often referred to as the *indifference point.*

If management expected sales revenue to exceed $1,000,000, it would select a fixed-rental arrangement. If sales revenue were expected to be below $1,000,000, it would be better off selecting the percentage-of-sales arrangement.

SEPARATING COSTS INTO FIXED AND VARIABLE ELEMENTS

Once costs have been categorized into fixed or variable elements, valuable information is available for use in decision making. Some costs are easy to identify as definitely fixed or definitely variable. The semifixed or semivariable types of costs must be broken down into the two separate elements.

A number of different methods are available for breaking down these semivariable costs into their fixed and variable components, some more sophisticated (and thus usually more accurate) than others. Three will be discussed:

1. High–low method
2. Multipoint graph method
3. Regression analysis method

To set the stage, we will use the income statement of the Model Motel for a year's period (see Exhibit 7.5). The Model Motel is a no-frills, 70-unit budget operation without food or beverage facilities. It operates at 59.9% occupancy

Sales revenue	$612,000
Operating Expenses	
Employee wages expense	$241,600
Management salary expense	40,000
Laundry, linen, and guest supplies expenses	77,400
Advertising expense	15,000
Maintenance expense	34,600
Utilities expense	36,200
Office/telephone expense	8,000
Insurance expense	9,200
Interest expense	16,600
Property taxes expense	40,200
Depreciation expense	70,000
Total Operating Expenses	(588,800)
Operating Income	$ 23,200

■ **EXHIBIT 7.5**

Model Motel Income Statement without a Cost Breakdown

and, as a result of good cost controls, is able to keep its average room rate down to $40.00. Last year it sold 15,300 rooms for a sales revenue of $612,000.

The first step is to list the expenses by category (fixed, variable, semivariable). The owner's or manager's past experience about the costs of the Model Motel, or the past year's accounting records, will be helpful in creating this list.

The figures in the fixed column (see Exhibit 7.6) are those that do not change during the year with a change in sales volume (number of rooms sold). A fixed

	Fixed	*Variable*	*Semivariable*
Employee wages			$241,600
Management salary	$40,000		
Laundry, linen, and guest supplies		$77,400	
Advertising	15,000		
Maintenance			34,600
Utilities			36,200
Office/Telephone			8,000
Insurance	9,200		
Interest	16,600		
Property taxes	40,200		
Depreciation	70,000		

■ **EXHIBIT 7.6**

Costs Allocated as Fixed, Variable, and Semivariable

cost may change from year to year (e.g., insurance rates may change or management may decide to vary the amount spent on insurance), but such changes are not directly related to, or caused by, the number of guests accommodated. The items in the variable column are the costs that are the direct result of guests using the facilities (if there are no guests or customers, there will be no cost for laundry, linen, and guest supplies).

As occupancy levels increase or decrease, the variable costs will also increase or decrease proportionally. The figures in the semivariable column are those we must separate into their fixed and variable components.

To demonstrate the three methods of breaking down a semivariable cost, we will use the wages cost of $241,600. Since much of the wage cost is related to the number of rooms sold, we need a month-by-month breakdown of the sales revenue for each month and the related wage cost for each month. This information could be broken down by week, but there should be sufficient accuracy for all practical purposes with a monthly analysis. The sales and labor cost breakdown is given in Exhibit 7.7. Note that the sales column figures are in numbers of units sold. This column could have been expressed in dollars of sales revenue without it affecting our results (as long as the average room rate of $40.00 had been relatively consistent during the year).

HIGH–LOW METHOD

The **high–low method** is also called the maximum–minimum method. It has three steps. With reference to Exhibit 7.7, note that the month of August is

	Units (Rooms) Sold	Wage Costs
January (low month)	500	$ 14,400
February	1,000	15,800
March	1,300	19,800
April	1,200	21,600
May	1,400	24,400
June	1,500	24,200
July	2,100	26,200
August (high month)	2,100	26,400
September	1,500	23,600
October	1,000	15,200
November	1,000	14,800
December	700	15,200
Totals	15,300	$241,600

■ EXHIBIT 7.7

Analysis of Units Sold and Wage Costs by Month

the high month, which identifies it as the month with the highest units sold and the highest wage costs. In contrast, January is the low month, and shows that units sold and wage costs at their lowest for the year. To use this method, the change in costs that has occurred between the high and low months depends on the change in sales volume (the delta symbol Δ represents change).

Step 1: Deduct the low figure from the high figure of each unit and cost categories:

	Units (Rooms) Sold	*Wage Costs*
August (high)	2,100	$26,400
January (low)	(500)	(14,400)
Change	Δ $1,600	Δ $12,000

Step 2: Divide the change in wage costs by the change in units sold:

$$\frac{\Delta\ \text{Costs}}{\Delta\ \text{Units}} = \frac{\$12,000}{1,600} = \$7.50 \text{ Variable cost (VC) per unit sold}$$

Step 3: Use the VC per unit answer from Step 2 to calculate the fixed cost element:

Total wage costs for August (high)	$26,400
Variable cost (2,100 units sold × $7.50 a unit) =	(15,750)
Fixed cost	$10,650

Using the same procedures, the low wage costs and low units sold, and the variable cost per unit, the same fixed cost can be found:

Total wage costs for January (low)	$14,400
Variable cost (500 units sold × $7.50 a unit) =	(3,750)
Fixed cost	$10,650

Instead of using units and wage costs to determine variable costs of units sold, sales revenue could be used equally as well to separate wages costs into its fixed and variable elements. This method determines the variable cost per dollar of sales revenue:

Step 1: Deduct the low figure from the high figure for each sales revenue and cost catagories:

	Units Sold		Average Rate		Total Sales Revenue	Wage Costs
August (high)	2,100	×	$40.00	=	$84,000	$26,400
January (low)	500	×	40.00	=	(20,000)	(14,400)
Change					Δ $64,000	Δ $12,000

Step 2: Use the change in sales revenue and wage costs from Step 1 to find the variable cost per dollar of sales revenue:

$$\frac{\Delta \text{ Costs}}{\Delta \text{ Sales}} = \frac{\$12,000}{64,600} = \underline{\$0.1875} \text{ per dollar of sales revenue}$$

Step 3: Use the VC per dollar of sales answer from Step 2 to calculate the fixed cost element:

Total wage costs for August (high)	$26,400
Variable cost ($84,000 sales revenue × $0.1875) =	(15,750)
Fixed cost	$10,650

As was the case with using low units, we can use the low wage costs, low sales revenue, and variable cost per dollar of sales revenue and the same fixed costs can be found:

Total wage costs for January (low)	$14,400
Variable cost ($20,000 sales revenue × $0.1875) =	(3,750)
Fixed cost	$10,650

*[Alternative: VC is also (500 units sold × $7.50) = $3,750]

The calculated fixed cost is $10,650 a month, or 12 × $10,650 = $127,800 a year.

With reference to Exhibit 7.6, we can now separate our total annual wage cost into its fixed and variable elements:

Total annual wages	**$241,600**
Fixed costs	(**127,800**)
Variable costs	**$113,800**

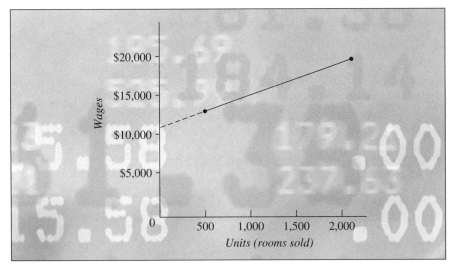

■ **EXHIBIT 7.8**
Maximum–Minimum Figure

The calculation of the monthly fixed cost figure has been illustrated by arithmetical means. The high–low figures could equally as well have been plotted on a graph, as illustrated in Exhibit 7.8, and the fixed cost read from where the dotted line intersects the vertical axis. If the graph is accurately drawn, the same monthly figure of approximately $10,600 is obtained.

The high–low method is quick and simple. It uses only two sets of figures. Unfortunately, either one or both of these sets of figures may not be typical of the relationship between sales revenue and costs for the year (e.g., a one-time bonus may have been paid during one of the months selected). Other, perhaps less dramatic, distortions may be built into the figures.

These distortions can be eliminated, as long as one is aware of them, by adjusting the raw figures. Alternatively, standard costs rather than actual costs could be used for the low and high sales months.

An alternate method to the high–low method that will show any monthly distortions in individual figures is to plot the cost and sales figures for each of the 12 operating months (or any number of months in an operating period) on a graph. As well, the graph will show if the information is linear. If it is not linear, then you cannot use these methods to separate a semivariable cost into its fixed and variable components.

MULTIPOINT GRAPH METHOD

Exhibit 7.9 illustrates a **multipoint graph** for our sales in units and our wage cost for each of the 12 months. Sales revenue and costs were taken from Exhibit 7.7. The graph illustrated is for two variables, sales and wages. In this case, wages are

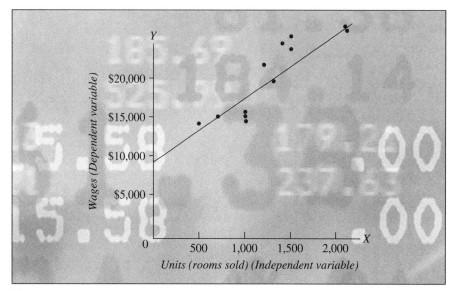

■ **EXHIBIT 7.9**
Scatter Graph

given the name **dependent variable** and are plotted on the vertical axis. Wages are dependent on sales because they vary with sales. Sales, therefore, are the **independent variable.** The independent variable is plotted on the horizontal axis. After plotting each of the 12 points, we have what is known as a scatter graph—a series of points scattered around a line that has been drawn through them. A straight line must be drawn.

There is no limit to how many straight lines could be drawn through the points. The line we want is the one that, to our eye, seems to fit best. Each individual doing this exercise would probably view the line in a slightly different position, but most people with a reasonably good eye would come up with a line that, for all practical purposes, is close enough. The line should be drawn so that it is continued to the left until it intersects the vertical axis (the dependent variable). The intersect point reading is our fixed cost (wages, in this case). Note that, in Exhibit 7.9, our fixed cost reading is approximately $9,000. This is the monthly cost. Converted to annual cost, it is $9,000 × 12 = $108,000.

Our total annual wage cost would then be broken down this way:

Fixed wages cost	**$108,000**
Variable wages cost	**$133,600**
Total wages cost	**$241,600**

Note that, in drawing graphs for the purpose discussed, the point at which the vertical and horizontal axes intersect should be given a reading of 0. The figures along each axis should then be plotted to scale from the (0, 0) intercept.

The straight line on a scatter graph can be drawn by eye, and for most purposes will give us a fixed cost reading that is good enough. However, the question arises as to whether there is one best method that provides the most accurate answers related to the graph or the high–low methods. The answer is yes; the most accurate method is known as regression analysis.

REGRESSION ANALYSIS METHOD

With regression analysis there is no need to draw a graph, plot points, and draw a line through them. The objective in drawing the line is to find out where the line intersects the vertical axis so we can read, at that intersection point, what the fixed costs are. Once we know the fixed costs, we can then easily calculate the variable costs (total costs − fixed costs = variable costs). In **regression analysis** a number of equations have been developed for different purposes. One of the equations allows us to calculate the fixed costs directly, without a graph.

Before the equation is used, we have to take the units (rooms) sold and the wage cost information from Exhibit 7.7 and develop it a little further, as has been done in Exhibit 7.10. In Exhibit 7.10 the units (rooms) sold column has been given the symbol X (X is for the independent variable). The wage cost column (the dependent variable) has been given the symbol Y. Two new columns have been added: XY (which is X multiplied by Y) and X^2 (which is X multiplied by X). Now we can find fixed costs:

$$\text{Fixed costs} = \frac{(\Sigma Y)(\Sigma X^2) - (\Sigma X)(\Sigma XY)}{n(\Sigma X^2) - (\Sigma X)^2}$$

Month	Units (Rooms) Sold X	Wage Costs Y	XY $(X \times Y)$	X^2 $(X \times X)$
January	500	$ 14,400	$ 7,200,000	250,000
February	1,000	15,800	15,800,000	1,000,000
March	1,300	19,800	25,740,000	1,690,000
April	1,200	21,600	25,920,000	1,440,000
May	1,400	24,400	34,160,000	1,960,000
June	1,500	24,200	36,300,000	2,250,000
July	2,100	26,200	55,020,000	4,410,000
August	2,100	26,400	55,440,000	4,410,000
September	1,500	23,600	35,400,000	2,250,000
October	1,000	15,200	15,200,000	1,000,000
November	1,000	14,800	14,800,000	1,000,000
December	700	15,200	10,640,000	490,000
Totals	15,300	241,600	331,620,000	22,150,000

EXHIBIT 7.10

Calculation of Regression Analysis Data

Two new symbols have been introduced in this equation: Σ means the sum of, or the column total figure, and n is the number of periods, in our case 12 (months). The technique shown in Exhibit 7.10 allows us to use the column numerical totals of X, Y, XY, and X^2 by replacing the symbols in the above equation:

$$\text{Fixed costs} = \frac{(\$241,600)(22,150,000) - (15,300)(331,620,000)}{12(22,150,000) - (15,300)(15,300)}$$

$$= \frac{\$5,351,440,000,000 - \$5,073,786,000,000}{265,800,000 - 234,090,000}$$

$$= \frac{\$277,654,000,000}{31,710,000}$$

$$= \$8,756.04 \text{ a month}$$

Our answer could be rounded to $8,800 a month, which gives us a total annual fixed cost of

$$\$8,800 \times 12 = \$105,600$$

COMPARISON OF RESULTS

Let us compare the results of our fixed/variable breakdown of the Model Motel's annual wage cost using each of the three methods described. The results are tabulated as follows:

	Fixed	*Variable*	*Total*
High–low method	$127,800	$113,800	$241,600
Multipoint graph method	108,000	133,600	241,600
Regression analysis method	105,600	136,000	241,600

In practice, only one of the three methods would be used. We know that regression analysis is the most accurate. It can be calculated using a programmed calculator or spreadsheet software that will carry out all the necessary calculations very quickly. One method can be used to spot-check on the results of either of the other two methods.

Multipoint graph results are fairly close to the regression analysis figures, which seems to imply that, if the graph is well drawn, we should have accurate enough results for all practical purposes. The high–low method results are about 21.0% different from what the regression analysis tells us the most correct result should be. Therefore, the high–low method should be used with caution and

	Fixed	*Variable*
Employee wages	$105,600	$136,000
Management salary	40,000	
Laundry, linen, and guest supplies		77,400
Advertising	15,000	
Maintenance	30,800	3,800
Utilities	28,400	7,800
Office/telephone	7,000	1,000
Insurance	9,200	
Interest	16,600	
Property taxes	40,200	
Depreciation	70,000	
Totals	$362,800	$226,000

■ **EXHIBIT 7.11**

Final Cost Allocation by Fixed or Variable Costs

only if the two periods selected are typical of all periods. However, this might be difficult to determine.

Once a method has been selected, it should be applied consistently to all semivariable expenses. With reference to our Model Motel's cost figures in Exhibit 7.6, so far we have analyzed the semivariable wage cost. Similarly, we need to analyze the three other semivariable costs: maintenance, utilities, and office/telephone. Let us assume we have done so using regression analysis; our completed cost analysis gives us the fixed and variable costs shown in Exhibit 7.11.

ALTERNATIVE METHOD

As an alternative to separating semivariable costs by individual expense, the situation can be simplified by first adding together all semivariable costs, then applying one of the three methods outlined in this section to separate only the total into its fixed and variable elements. This considerably reduces the time and effort involved. However, it might reduce the accuracy of the results. In many cases, however, this reduced accuracy might still be satisfactory for making decisions.

In Chapter 8, we shall see how we can use this cost breakdown information for decision making concerning many aspects of our motel operation. Even though a motel situation has been used, the same type of analysis can be carried out equally well for a restaurant or a department in a hotel. In a hotel, the difficulty may be in allocating the overhead costs in an equitable manner to the individual departments.

COMPUTER APPLICATIONS

A spreadsheet program can be used to apply most of the concepts discussed in this chapter. The formula for each concept (such as regression analysis) has to be entered into the program only once, and it will automatically calculate the results for each situation. A computer spreadsheet can also be used to carry out the calculations necessary to separate costs into their fixed and variable elements, using all three methods outlined in this chapter.

SUMMARY

One way of increasing net income in a business is to increase sales revenue. Another way is to control costs. To do this, one must understand that there are different types of costs.

A direct cost is one that is the responsibility of, and is controllable by, a department head or department manager. An indirect cost, sometimes called an overhead cost, is not normally charged to an individual department. If such costs are broken down by department and allocated to the departmental income statement, the resulting departmental profit or loss figure must be interpreted with great care.

All costs are controllable costs at some time by someone, whether they are direct or indirect costs; it is only the level of control responsibility of a cost that changes whether a cost is controllable or noncontrollable.

A joint cost is one that is shared by two or more departments, or by the organization as a whole. A joint cost could be a direct one (such as wages) or an indirect one (such as building maintenance). A discretionary cost is one that can be incurred if a particular person, generally the manager, decides to spend the money. A relevant cost is one that needs to be considered when making a specific decision. If a cost makes no difference to the decision, then it is not relevant.

A sunk cost is a past cost that is not relevant to current decisions. The initial expenditure on a piece of equipment bought five years ago that will be traded in is a sunk cost insofar as the decision to buy a new machine today is concerned.

An opportunity cost is the income forgone by not doing something. A motel could run its own restaurant at a profit, or lease it out. If it runs the restaurant itself, the loss of rent income is an opportunity cost. However, the motel owner would happily endure this opportunity cost if net income from running the operation were greater than any potential rent income.

A standard cost is what a cost should be for a given level of sales revenue or volume of business. The final three types of cost discussed in this chapter were fixed costs, variable costs, and semifixed or semivariable costs. Fixed costs are costs that do not change in the short run, regardless of the volume of sales revenue (the general manager's annual salary is an example). Variable costs are those that do vary in the short run and do so in direct proportion to sales revenue (food and liquor costs are two good examples of variable costs). Most costs, however, do not fall neatly into either the fixed or the variable category; they are semifixed or semivariable costs. To make useful decisions concerning fixed and variable costs and their effect on net income at various levels of sales, the semicosts must be divided into their fixed and variable elements. Three methods were used to illustrate how this can be done.

1. The high–low method, although quick and easy to use, may give misleading results if the high and low sales periods selected are not truly representative of the costs in all periods.
2. The multipoint graph eliminates the possible problem built into the high–low method. The graph is subject to some element of personal judgment, but in most cases will give results that are close enough for most decision-making purposes.
3. Regression analysis, which is the most accurate method, involves quite a number of calculations and can probably best be used as a spot check on the results of using one of the other two methods.

DISCUSSION QUESTIONS

1. Differentiate between a direct cost and an indirect cost.
2. Define *discretionary cost* and give two examples (other than those given in the text).
3. Differentiate between a fixed cost and a variable cost and give an example of each that is not in the text.
4. Why are some costs known as semifixed or semivariable?
5. Why might it be unwise to allocate an indirect cost to various departments on the basis of each department's sales revenue to total sales revenue?
6. What do you think might be the relevant costs to consider in deciding which one of a number of different vacuum cleaner models to buy for housekeeping purposes?
7. Explain why you think it sometimes makes sense to sell below total cost.
8. Define the term *high operating leverage* and explain why, in times of increasing sales revenue, it is more profitable to have high rather than low operating leverage.
9. With figures of your own choosing, illustrate how the high–low calculation method can be used to separate the fixed and variable elements of a cost.

10. Explain why the high–low method may not be a good method to use to separate the fixed and variable portions of a cost.

11. Give a brief explanation of how to prepare a graph when using the multipoint graph method for separating the fixed and variable elements of a cost.

ETHICS SITUATION

A hotel owner decides that to control costs he cannot offer employees a raise next year. However, employees are not told that the hotel's manager has been offered a 15% increase in salary if the manager can convince the employees that the no-pay-raise policy is justified. The manager has agreed to do this and accept his raise. Discuss the ethics of this situation.

EXERCISES

E7.1 If sales revenue is $6,800 and variable costs are $2,856, what is the variable cost percentage?

E7.2 If sales revenue was $48,840 and variable costs were 43%, what is the dollar contribution margin?

E7.3 You were asked to cater a buffet for 70 people at $18 per person. Your variable costs average 68%, and fixed costs are $100 per day. Determine your contribution margin and operating income. Should you accept the proposal?

E7.4 You have decided to allocate $12,000 of indirect costs to your café and bar operations based on square footage used. The café occupies 2,200 square feet and the bar occupies 580 square feet. How much of the $12,000 of indirect costs will be allocated to the café?

E7.5 Given the following information, determine variable cost per guest, and the total fixed costs, using both the high and low data to confirm your calculations. High guests were 18,000 and the low guests were 12,000 and the high and low labor costs were $25,500 and $18,000, respectively.

E7.6 Given the following information, determine variable cost per dollar of sales revenue and the total fixed costs, using both the high and low data to confirm your calculations. The high total sales revenue was $28,000 and the low sales revenue was $23,000. The high and low operating costs were $20,000 and $17,000, respectively.

E7.7 A catering service has been asked to provide a lunch buffet the next day for 40 people at a set price of $10.50 per person; no function has been booked for the next two days. The catering service has fixed costs of $150 a day, or $54,750 per operating year, and it operates with a variable cost of 65% of sales revenue. Calculate the operating income from the function and justify your decision to accept or not accept the booking.

E7.8 Assume you have a restaurant operation and the property owner has offered a 5-year fixed lease rental of $42,000 per year or variable lease rental of 10% of your sales revenue. Your current sales revenue in the new year is projected to be $505,000. Find the indifference point (the breakeven point of sales revenue at which the fixed rent and variable rent for a year are the same). Explain which alternative you would accept.

E7.9 Assume a restaurant owner is showing a positive operating income in 9 of 12 months of operation and is considering whether to close during 3 months of the off-season. Given the information below, do you recommend he close or stay open the last 3 months?

	9 months	*3 months*	*Total*
Sales revenue	$378,000	$22,000	$400,000
Variable costs	$283,500	$16,500	300,000
Fixed costs	45,000	15,000	60,000
Total costs	$328,500	$31,500	$360,000
Operating income	$ 49,500	($ 9,500)	$ 40,000

PROBLEMS

P7.1 You are planning to purchase a range and have to make a choice among the following three models of the same type of equipment:

	Model 1	*Model 2*	*Model 3*
Cash cost	$ 5,000	$ 5,500	$ 5,300
Estimate life	5 years	5 years	5 years
Trade-in value at end of life	$ 1,000	$ 1,200	$ 800
Cash from sale of old machine	$ 200	$ 200	$ 200
Installation of new machine	$ 80	$ 120	$ 100
Initial training cost in Year 1	$ 350	$ 300	$ 325
Annual maintenance contract	$ 275	$ 300	$ 250
Annual cost of supplies	$ 175	$ 225	$ 200
Annual wage costs of employees	$32,000	$32,000	$32,000

Using the concept of relevant costs over the five-year period, which model would be the best investment? (*Note:* In your calculations, ignore any costs that are not relevant.)

P7.2 The fixed cost of the banquet department of a hotel is $350 a day. A customer selected a menu for 100 persons that would have a food cost of $6.50 per person, a variable wage cost of $2.75 per person, and other variable costs of $1.25 per person.

a. Calculate the total cost per person if this banquet were booked.

b. What should be the total selling price (sales revenue) and the price per person if a 20% operating income on sales revenue is wanted?

c. The customer does not want to pay more than $13.75 per person for this function. She is a good customer; she has booked many functions in the banquet room in the past and is expected to do so in the future. The function is three days from now, and there is no likelihood you will be able to book the room for any other function. Explain why you would, or would not, accept the $13.75 per-person price.

(*Note:* Assume that the hotel has only one banquet room.)

P7.3 You have the following annual information about a restaurant complex consisting of three departments:

Contributory Income Statement	Dining Room	Coffee Shop	Lounge	Total
Sales revenue	$194,800	$135,800	$152,800	$483,400
Direct costs	(154,400)	(128,000)	(124,600)	(407,000)
Contributory income	$ 40,400	$ 7,800	$ 28,200	$ 76,400
Indirect costs				(52,000)
Operating income				$ 24,400

The owner wants to allocate indirect costs quarterly to each department based on square footage to get a better picture of how each department is doing.

Dining room	2,200 sq. ft.
Coffee shop	840 sq. ft.
Lounge	960 sq. ft.

a. Allocate the indirect costs as indicated.

b. The owner has an offer from the souvenir store operator who is willing to rent the coffee shop space for $9,600 a year. Advise the owner whether to accept the offer.

c. Before making a final decision, the owner of the restaurant decides to evaluate the changes to indirect costs if the coffee shop space is rented.

Indirect Costs	Present Costs	Costs if Coffee Shop Rented
Administrative and general	$14,100	$13,200
Advertising and promotion	9,800	9,000
Utilities	4,500	4,100
Repairs and maintenance	4,200	3,800
Insurance	3,600	3,100
Interest	5,400	5,400
Depreciation	10,400	7,100

If the coffee shop is not operated, it is estimated that lounge sales revenue will decline by $11,700 a year and lounge direct costs will go down by $8,100. Dining room sales revenue and direct costs will not be affected. Should the owner accept the offer to rent out the coffee shop?

P7.4 You have the following income statements for each of the four quarters of a restaurant operation:

	1st Qtr.	2nd Qtr.	3rd Qtr.	4th Qtr.
Sales revenue	$86,400	$97,000	$89,400	$46,400
Cost of sales	(32,800)	(35,900)	(33,100)	(18,100)
Gross Margin	$53,600	$61,100	$56,300	$28,300
Operating Expenses				
Wages & salaries expense	$32,000	$35,900	$33,100	$17,800
Supplies expense	1,900	2,200	1,970	1,100
Advertising expense	900	900	900	600
Utilities expense	2,600	2,900	2,680	2,400
Maintenance expense	450	450	400	400
Insurance expense	1,200	1,200	1,200	1,200
Interest expense	750	750	750	750
Depreciation expense	700	700	700	700
Rent expense	6,000	6,000	6,000	6,000
Total operating expenses	$46,500	$51,000	$47,700	$30,950
Operating income (loss)	$ 7,100	$10,100	$ 8,600	($ 2,650)

The owner is contemplating closing the restaurant in the fourth quarter in order to eliminate the loss and take a three-month vacation. The owner has asked for your help, and after an analysis of the fourth-quarter expenses, you determine the following:

- *Wages and salaries expense:* $3,000 is a fixed cost of key personnel who would be kept on the payroll even if the operation were closed for three months.
- *Supplies expense:* Cost varies directly with sales revenue; none of the supplies costs are fixed.
- *Advertising expense:* Half of the cost is fixed; the rest of the cost is variable.
- *Utilities expense:* Even if closed for three months, the restaurant will still require some heating; this is expected to cost $100 a month.
- *Maintenance expense:* Some light maintenance work could be done during the closed period; estimated cost is $200.
- *Insurance expense:* Insurance cost will be reduced 60% if closed for three months.
- *Interest expense:* Will still have to be paid, even if closed.
- *Depreciation expense:* With less customer traffic and reduced wear and tear on equipment, there would be a 75% reduction in depreciation expense for the fourth quarter.
- *Rent expense:* This is an annual expense of $24,000 that must be paid, regardless of whether the restaurant is open or closed.

Explain what advice you would give the owner.

P7.5 A company owns three motels in a ski resort area. Although there is some business during the summer months, the company finds it very difficult to staff the three operations during this period and is contemplating closing one of the three motels. The sales revenue and breakdown of costs during this period are as follows:

	Motel A	*Motel B*	*Motel C*
Sales revenue	$265,000	$325,000	$425,000
Variable costs	160,000	150,000	135,000
Fixed costs	110,000	167,000	260,000

a. Assuming one of the motels must be closed and that its closing will have no effect on the sales revenue of the other two, explain which motel should be closed and why.

b. Would your answer be the same if sales revenue remained the same and the variable and fixed costs changed as follows?

	Motel A	*Motel B*	*Motel C*
Sales revenue	$265,000	$325,000	$425,000
Variable costs	100,000	167,000	250,000
Fixed costs	110,000	113,000	112,000

P7.6 Two entrepreneurs are contemplating purchasing one of two similar competitive motels and have asked for your advice. Present sales revenue of each motel is $550,000 per year. Jack's motel has annual variable costs of 55% of sales revenue and fixed costs of $212,500; Jock's motel has annual variable costs of 60% of sales revenue and fixed costs of $185,000. The entrepreneurs think that, if they purchased Jack's motel, they could save $12,000 a year on interest expense (a fixed cost). Alternatively, if they purchased Jock's motel, they could improve staff scheduling to the point that the wage saving would reduce total variable cost to 54%. In the case of purchasing either operation, they think that sales revenue can be increased by 25% a year. Calculate the present net income of each motel. Then, given these assumptions, advise the entrepreneurs which one they should buy, including any cautionary comments.

P7.7 Stella's Steak House has been operating for the past 10 years, and Stella has to negotiate her lease on the premises for the next 5 years. Her options are to pay a fixed monthly rent of $2,800 or to pay a variable monthly rent of 8% of her sales revenue. Over the next 5 years she anticipates her sales to average $525,000 per year.

a. What is Stella's indifference point on an annual sales revenue basis?

b. Which option should she choose? Explain.

P7.8 A hotel wishes to analyze its electricity cost in its rooms department in terms of fixed and variable elements. Monthly income statements show that during its busiest and slowest months, cost and rooms occupied information is as follows:

	Rooms Cost	*Rooms Sold*
Busiest	$4,080	2,800
Slowest	3,100	1,400

Use the high–low method to calculate the following:

a. Variable cost per room occupied

b. Total variable cost for the busiest and the slowest month

c. Total fixed cost per month

P7.9 You have the following information from the records of a restaurant:

	Sales Revenue	Wage Costs
January	$ 11,200	$ 5,300
February	13,000	6,100
March	14,900	6,200
April	19,100	7,000
May	22,000	9,000
June	24,200	9,600
July	26,300	9,700
August	27,400	10,100
September	23,500	8,300
October	20,100	7,600
November	18,200	8,000
December	16,000	7,100
Totals	$235,900	$94,000

Use the high–low method to calculate total fixed cost and total variable cost for the year.

P7.10 Complete a regression analysis to determine total annual fixed and variable costs using the sales revenue and wage costs shown in P7.9. Compare regression analysis results with the results obtained in P7.9, and comment about the results between the two different methods used to find total annual fixed and variable costs.

P7.11 A restaurant has the following 12-month record of sales revenue and wage costs:

	Sales Revenue	Wage Costs
January	$24,900	$11,300
February	24,200	11,100
March	25,600	11,200
April	24,200	11,400
May	34,000	13,200
June	46,200	18,600
July	53,300	21,600
August	44,000	16,100
September	34,200	15,100
October	30,400	12,800
November	28,200	11,200
December	27,000	13,000

Adjustments to the base information shown: Included in the July wages is a lump-sum retroactive wage increase of $1,800, which would not normally be part of the July wage cost. Also, in December, the restaurant catered a special Christmas function that brought in $3,400 in sales revenue, and cost the restaurant an additional $900 in wages. The December wage figure also included $1,400 in Christmas bonuses to the staff. Use the high–low method to calculate the restaurant's monthly fixed wage costs.

C A S E   7

Charlie is thinking of spending $3,000 more in Year 2008 on advertising (part of marketing expense). Because of his marketing courses, he believes he can design appealing advertisements to be placed in local newspapers and aimed at the business luncheon trade. He estimates that if the ads are placed, they will bring in 15 more people at lunch each day.

The average check for the additional lunch guests would be the same as that calculated in Case 6. Use a 52-week year and the days open from Case 6. Assume that the food and beverage total cost of sales percentages will be the same as in Year 2007. (This percentage was calculated in Case 3.)

To serve the extra guests, a new employee will have to be hired at lunch for four hours. Hourly rate of pay including fringe benefits (a free meal while on duty, vacation pay, and so on) will be $5.42 an hour. The following variable expenses will remain at the same percentage to sales revenue as they were in Year 2007 (see Case 3):

- Laundry
- China and tableware
- Glassware
- Other operating expenses

All other expenses are assumed to be fixed and are unaffected by the increased volume of business. Prepare calculations to show whether the $3,000 should be spent. Refer to the income statement for the 4C Company's restaurant for Year 2007.

THE COST–VOLUME–PROFIT APPROACH TO DECISIONS

I N T R O D U C T I O N

This chapter introduces the Cost–Volume–Profit (CVP) method, which can assist management in evaluating current and future events regarding sales revenue inflows and cost outflows. A number of basic questions will be identified and discussed using examples to explain CVP analysis.

A graphical explanation and presentation of CVP is then given, showing how the breakeven level of sales revenue can be determined and how the level of operating income (profit) for a particular volume of sales can be arrived at.

Before discussing and illustrating the CVP equation (which eliminates the need for a graph), several specific key assumptions and limitations inherent in the CVP approach will be addressed. The equation can be used to determine the breakeven level of sales revenue, the sales revenue needed to cover a new fixed cost, the additional sales revenue required to cover a changed variable cost, or multiple changes in costs. The CVP answers can be obtained in sales revenue dollars or sales of units, such as rooms sold or guests served.

The CVP equation can also be used to determine the effect that a change in selling prices will have on operating results to determine the additional sales volume required to cover a loss, or to analyze a new investment.

This chapter illustrates how the CVP equation can be used to handle various situations concerning joint costs in multiple-department organizations and concludes with a discussion on incorporating income tax in the CVP calculation.

CHAPTER OBJECTIVES

After studying this chapter, the reader should be able to

1. Briefly discuss the assumptions and limitations inherent in CVP analysis.
2. Identify and discuss the various functions shown in a graph of sales levels, and fixed and variable costs.
3. State the CVP equation used to determine the sales revenue level in dollars and the equation used to determine the sales level in units.
4. Demonstrate by example how the CVP equations are used to determine breakeven sales revenue in dollars and in units.
5. Demonstrate by example how the CVP equations are used to determine sales revenue volume in dollars and sales quantity in units.
6. Explain the term *contribution margin* and the format of a contribution margin income statement.
7. Discuss how operating income before tax and net income (after tax) can be used in the CVP equation.
8. Discuss the use of CVP analysis to solve problems concerning joint fixed costs in a multiple-department organization.

THE CVP APPROACH TO DECISIONS

Managers of hotels, motels, restaurants, and beverage operations, as well as other hospitality operations providing general goods and services, ask questions such as these:

- What will my operating income be at a specified level of sales revenue?
- What is the amount of additional sales revenue needed to cover the cost of expansion and still provide the wanted level of operating income?
- What effect will a change of selling prices have on my operating income?
- What effect will a change in the variable cost of sales have on my operating income?
- What increase in sales revenue is necessary to cover the cost of a wage increase and still provide the wanted levels of operating income?

These are but a few of many questions, which cannot be answered simply from a traditional income statement. They are, however, easily answered using

CVP analysis. To use the CVP method, costs must be separated into variable and fixed components. They are then used to make informed and rational decisions. However, before the CVP approach can be used, the assumptions and limitations inherent in the CVP method must be clearly understood.

CVP ASSUMPTIONS AND LIMITATIONS

The following assumptions and limitations are built into CVP analysis:

- CVP analysis assumes all costs can be broken into variable and fixed elements with a reasonable level of accuracy.
- CVP assumes that identified fixed costs will remain unchanged during the period affected by the decision being made.
- CVP assumes that variable costs will increase or decrease in a consistent linear relationship with sales revenue during the period being evaluated.
- CVP is limited to specific situations, operating divisions, or departments. Great caution should be used concerning decisions for the entire organization when multiple divisions and departments contribute to overall income. In such cases, it may be appropriate to evaluate sales revenue mix (discussed in Chapter 6).
- CVP assumes that economic and other conditions will remain relatively stable during the period being evaluated. During a highly inflationary period, it might be difficult to forecast sales revenue, selling prices, and cost functions more than a month in advance. Certainly it would be risky to use CVP analysis for the next year.

Thus, CVP analysis produces only estimates to assist management in the decision process. CVP analysis relies on accounting information and mathematical computations, which may indicate that a certain decision is appropriate. However, that decision does not consider customer and employee relations or social and potential environmental impact concerns.

BREAKEVEN ANALYSIS

Before we begin our discussion of CVP analysis, we must become familiar with the basic analysis method upon which it is based. CVP analysis is a logical expansion of breakeven analysis. The objective of using the **breakeven equation** is to find the sales revenue level in dollars or units necessary to cover all operating costs and produce operating income resulting in no profit or loss. We use capital letters to designate their identity in each of the two basic breakeven equations: breakeven sales and breakeven units.

The Breakeven Sales Revenue Equation (BESR)

$$\frac{\text{Fixed costs}}{1 - (\text{Variable cost} / \text{Sales revenue})} = \frac{\text{Fixed costs}}{1 - \text{Variable cost}\ \%} = \frac{\text{Fixed costs}}{\text{Contribution margin}\ \%} = BESR$$

Abbreviations	Breakeven Sales Equation
Breakeven sales revenue = *BESR* Fixed cost = *FC** Sales revenue = *SR* Variable cost = *VC* Variable cost % = *VC/SR* 100% of sales = 1 Contribution margin = 1 − *VC*%	Breakeven sales = $\dfrac{FC}{1 - (VC/SR)}$ $= \dfrac{FC}{1 - VC\%}$ $= \dfrac{FC}{CM\%} = BESR$

*Fixed cost is usually spelled out but is occasionally abbreviated **FC** in this chapter.

Example A: Fixed costs (**FC**) are $128,000, sales revenue (**SR**) is $240,000, and variable costs (**VC**) are $187,200. What is breakeven sales revenue?

$$\frac{FC}{1 - VC/SR} = \frac{FC}{1 - VC\%} = \frac{FC}{CM\%} = BESR$$

$$\frac{\$128,000}{1 - (\$187,200 / \$240,000)} = \frac{\$128,000}{1 - 78\%} = \frac{\$128,000}{22\%} = \$581,818.18 \cong \underline{\underline{\$581,818}}$$

Breakeven Units Equation

$$\frac{FC}{SP_u - VC_u} = \frac{FC}{\text{Contribution margin}_u} = BE_u$$

Abbreviations	Breakeven Units Equation
Breakeven sales units = BE_u Selling price = SP_u Variable cost per unit = VC_u Variable cost % = VC_u / SP_u Sales price per unit = SP_u Contribution margin = $SP_u - VC_u$	Breakeven units = $\dfrac{FC}{SP_u - VC_u}$ $= \dfrac{FC}{CM_u} = BE_u$

Example B: Let us assume fixed costs (FC) = \$128,000, variable costs (VC) = \$187,200 on sales of \$240,000, and the average selling price of the units sold is \$20 each. Find breakeven sales in units.

$$\frac{FC}{SP_u - VC_u} = \frac{FC}{CM_u} = BE_u$$

$$\frac{\$128,000}{\$20.00 - \$15.60} = \frac{\$128,000}{\$4.40} = 29,090.90 \cong \underline{\underline{29,091}} \; BE_u$$

Four interesting relationships can be seen in these two equations. Referring to breakeven Examples A and B, we can observe that variable cost, sales revenue, and units of sales are tied together with respect to breakeven sales revenue volume in dollars, and breakeven sales in units.

First, if we had known the average selling price per unit in Example A, where we found breakeven sales revenue, we could have also found breakeven units:

$$BESR \,/\, SP_u = BE_u = \$581,818.18 \,/\, \$20.00 = 29,090.90 \cong \underline{\underline{29,091 \; BE_u}}$$

Note that any time breakeven sales revenue in dollars and average selling price are being used to convert to sales in units, the entire decimal function (the decimal amount before rounding) must be used to complete the conversion. The same requirement exists when breakeven sales in units are being converted to breakeven sales revenue in dollars.

Second, the reverse is also true—having found breakeven units and knowing the selling price, we can find breakeven sales revenue (BE units must be used before rounding):

$$29,090.90 \times \$20.00 = \underline{\underline{\$581,818}} \; BESR$$

Third, since the relationship between sales revenue, unit selling price, variable cost as a percentage of sales, and the variable cost per unit is based on one set of data, we could have found the breakeven sales by using the base data shown in Example "B."

$$\frac{FC}{1 - VC_u \,/\, SP_u} = \frac{\$128,000}{1 - (\$15.60 \,/\, \$20.00)} = \frac{\$128,000}{1 - 78\%} = \frac{\$128,000}{22\%} = \underline{\underline{\$581,818}}$$

Fourth, if you have the total variable costs, total sales revenue, and know the average unit-selling price, the variable cost per unit can also be found:

VC = \$187,200, SR = \$240,000, and average unit selling price is \$20.00

\$187,200 / \$240,000 = 78%, thus, \$20 × 78% = \$15.60 = VC_u

It is important to note that final dollar answers are rounded to the dollar and final percentage answers are rounded to one tenth of a percent. Rounding of dollar or percentage answers cannot be made to the numerical figures or percentages when moving from sales units to sales revenues or sales revenues to sales units. To preclude any difficulty in rounding a decimal, use the same technique referred to in Chapter 3.

As you will soon see, the elements described in the calculation of breakeven sales revenue or breakeven unit sales are used time and time again in completing a CVP analysis.

In this chapter, for the most part, we will use information developed in Chapter 7 concerning the Model Motel's room sales revenue (Exhibit 7.5), fixed costs, and variable costs. Exhibit 8.1 provides the necessary information needed for a breakeven or CVP analysis.

In many cases, CVP analysis is presented in the form of a **contribution margin income statement** to check the validity of the CVP calculations.

Normally, details of variable and fixed costs, item by item, are shown directly on the income statement or supporting schedule. The contribution to fixed costs is typically referred to as the **contribution margin.** The **contribution margin** is sales revenue minus the cost of sales, which can also be expressed as a percentage of sales revenue. There may be other variable costs, which are not classified as cost of sales. Such variable costs will relate directly to expense

Room sales revenue (15,300 units @ $40 average room rate)		$612,000
Variable cost of sales	$226,000	
Fixed costs	362,800	
Total operating costs		(588,800)
Operating income (BT)		$ 23,200

Other Information:
a. 70 Rooms (units)
b. Average room rate = $40.00

c. Occupancy rate: $\dfrac{15,300}{70 \times 365} = \dfrac{15,300}{25,550} = 59.9\% = 60\%$

d. Average occupancy = 60% × 70 rooms (units) = 42 units per night

e. Variable cost per room occupied = $\dfrac{\$226,000}{15,300} = \$14.77$

f. Variable cost as a % of room sales revenue: $\dfrac{\$226,000}{\$612,000} = 36.9\%$

■ **EXHIBIT 8.1**

Information Required for a BE or CVP Analysis

items shown in the operating expense (wages expense, employee benefits, etc.) section of an income statement.

The contribution margin income statement is also used to answer questions concerning operating income when actual operating data does not agree with the forecasted sales level. The following contribution margin income statement uses the income statement information from Exhibit 8.1.

Contribution Margin Income Statement	
Room sales revenue	$612,000
Less: Variable cost	(226,000)
Contribution margin	$386,000
Less: Fixed costs	(362,800)
Operating income	$ 23,200

On the income statement for a large organization with a number of departments, sales revenue and cost of sales may be shown for each department, and/or a combined contribution margin for all departments may be shown. Total fixed costs of the organization are then deducted to arrive at operating income, or income before tax. The contribution margin will be discussed later in this chapter.

Before we proceed further, let us look at a graphical presentation taken from the information shown in Exhibit 8.1, from the standpoint of breakeven analysis. The same procedures are followed if a graphical presentation is made for a CVP analysis.

GRAPHICAL PRESENTATION

Generally, three steps are used to prepare a graph for breakeven or CVP analysis. To prepare a graph, sales revenue and dollar costs are shown on the vertical axis and sales in units are shown on the horizontal axis. See Exhibit 8.2 for an example.

Step 1. Using information from Exhibit 8.1, draw the fixed cost line by inserting a horizontal line from the vertical axis across the graph. The fixed cost line will originate on the vertical axis at a point representing $362,800, as shown in Exhibit 8.2.

Step 2. Draw the total cost line. Mark $588,800 on the vertical axis above the fixed cost line. Mark 15,300 units on the horizontal axis. Next, plot a point on the graph that is directly across from $588,800 *and* directly above 15,300. This is point *A* in Exhibit 8.3. From the point on the vertical axis where fixed costs intersect, point *B*, extend a line to intercept point *A*, as shown in Exhibit 8.3. This is a total cost line.

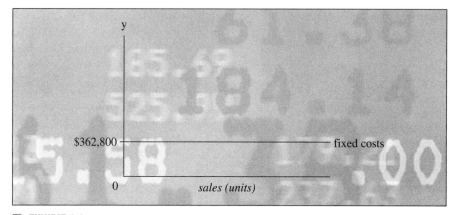

■ **EXHIBIT 8.2**
Fixed Cost Line

Step 3. Draw the sales revenue line. Mark a point on the vertical axis that represents $612,000 sales revenue. Plot a point on the graph opposite $612,000 and above the point that represents 15,300 sales units. This is point *C* in Exhibit 8.4. Connect the intersection of the vertical and horizontal lines (at 0) to the point you just plotted. Point *D*, where the total cost line intersects the sales revenue line, is the breakeven point. Any sales revenue level below the breakeven point shows a loss, and any level above the breakeven point shows operating income (profit before tax).

Exhibit 8.5 shows a completed graph drawn to scale. (Exhibits 8.2, 8.3, and 8.4 are for illustration only; they were not drawn to scale.) This allows us to read certain information with better accuracy. The breakeven point is defined

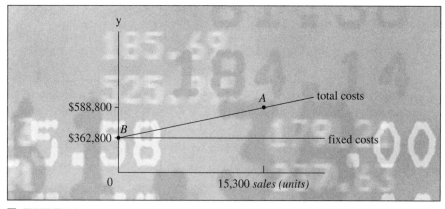

■ **EXHIBIT 8.3**
Total Cost Line

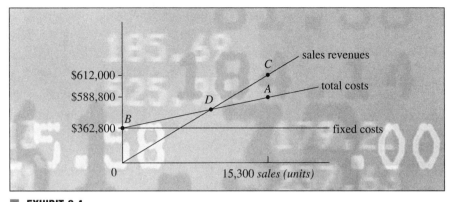

■ **EXHIBIT 8.4**
Sales Revenue and Costs

as the point where the sales revenue line intersects with the total cost line; dotted horizontal and vertical lines aid in defining the intersection at point *D*. The dotted lines also allow us to estimate the total sales revenue and sales units with reasonable accuracy. Using information from Exhibit 8.5, breakeven is approximately $576,000 of sales revenue and 14,400 units.

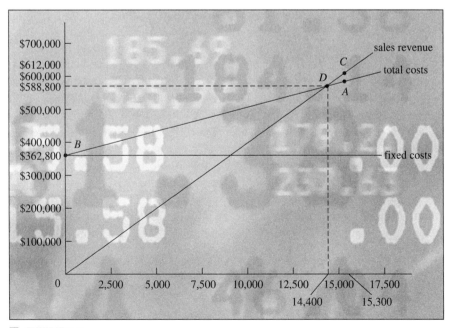

■ **EXHIBIT 8.5**
Estimating Breakeven

Graphs may be accurate enough to give us an acceptable answer and excellent tools to visually depict the information shown. However, structuring a graph can be time consuming. This is especially true if a number of changes are needed to bring the graph up to date as a result of changing costs. Are graphs the best tool to estimate breakeven or required sales in dollars or units? If you are knowledgeable about breakeven and CVP equations, graphs can be used. Let us see how accurate the breakeven point is when using a contribution margin income statement based on Exhibit 8.1.

Room sales revenue at breakeven	$576,000
Cost of sales (36.9% × $576,000)	(212,544)
Contribution margin	$363,456
Less: Fixed costs	(362,800)
Operating income (before tax)	$ 656

Using the contribution margin method, a $656 operating income is shown. Using the breakeven equation, the breakeven would be:

$$\frac{\textbf{Fixed costs}}{1 - VC\%} = \frac{\textbf{\$362,800}}{1 - 36.9\%} = \frac{\textbf{\$362,800}}{63.1\%} = \textbf{\$574,960}$$

In the final analysis, the breakeven equation will provide the most accurate estimate of breakeven. If sales revenue falls below $574,960, the Model Motel will begin losing money. Other questions that pertain to changing costs, room sales revenue, or sales units can be answered more accurately and in less time using the breakeven equation.

Before moving to a discussion of CVP analysis, a comment is required regarding other income an operation may be receiving, and how it should be treated during CVP analysis. We will assume the Model Motel has a coffee shop that is being leased out for $10,000 per year. The $10,000 received is other income and should not be included with regular sales revenue because it is a fixed inflow. The easiest and most acceptable solution is to deduct the lease income from fixed costs. If the motel wants to break even, the lease payment reduces the amount of money it must earn to pay for fixed costs. Therefore, fixed costs would be reduced from $362,800 to $352,800. This is the calculation after fixed costs are reduced by $10,000 of other revenue, using the information from Exhibit 8.1:

$$\frac{\textbf{Fixed costs}}{1 - VC\%} = \frac{\textbf{\$352,800}}{1 - 36.9\%} = \frac{\textbf{\$352,800}}{63.1\%} = \textbf{\$559,113 Breakeven}$$

The contribution margin income statement confirms the calculation.

Neither the variable cost percentage nor the contribution percentage changes, but the calculation produces a different breakeven.

Sales revenue at breakeven	$559,113
Cost of sales (36.9% × $559,113)	(206,313)
Contribution margin	$352,800
Less: Fixed costs	(362,800)
Operating loss	($ 10,000)
Other income	$ 10,000
Total income (before taxes)	-0-

CVP FORMULA

CVP analysis is a logical extension of breakeven analysis. Additional costs can be added to the numerator of the CVP equations in addition to the normal fixed cost. These additional costs are evaluated relative to the contribution margin to determine the sales revenue level necessary to cover the costs. As was the case with breakeven analysis, CVP uses two similar equations—CVP sales revenue and CVP sales units:

$$\text{Required sales (in dollars or units)} = \frac{\text{Fixed costs} + \text{Operating income (BT)} + \text{New fixed costs}}{\text{Contribution margin percentage or units}}$$

It is necessary to identify the term to include potential added cost items. **Operating income (*OI*)** identifies operating income before tax. This identification is used on income statements and contribution margin income statements and in general discussion to indicate income before tax. **Profit before tax** is another trend also substituted for operating income. Operating income defines income *before tax* (BT):

Operating income (BT) = Sales revenue − Cost of sales
= Gross margin − Operating expenses

Operating income (BT) − Tax = Net income (AT)

We will discuss changes that can be made to the elements of the CVP equation. These include changes to the variable cost percentages, fixed costs, unit variable costs, and unit selling prices. There can also be multiple changes in the elements of the equation.

Using the information from Exhibit 8.1, we begin with CVP breakeven analysis by using the same figures we used earlier in the discussions of graphs.

$$\frac{\text{Fixed costs} + \text{Zero net income}}{1 - VC\%} = \frac{\text{Fixed costs} + \text{Zero}}{CM\%} = BESR$$

$$\frac{\$362,800 + 0}{1 - 36.9\%} = \frac{\$362,800}{63.1\%} = \underline{\underline{\$574,960}}\ BESR$$

We can use either a percentage or decimal figures in the denominator. It is important to remember that data being used to forecast breakeven and CVP sales are generally estimates, and breakeven sales is a best estimate.

■ AT WHAT LEVEL OF ROOM SALES REVENUE WILL OPERATING INCOME BE $39,000?

This CVP question is answered quickly using the CVP equation:

$$\text{Required sales revenue} = \frac{\$362,800 + \$39,000}{1 - 36.9\%}$$

$$= \frac{\$401,800}{63.1\%}$$

$$= \underline{\underline{\$636,767}}$$

■ BY HOW MUCH MUST ROOM SALES REVENUE INCREASE TO COVER A NEW FIXED COST?

Normally, if fixed costs increase and no change is made in selling prices, profits can be expected to decline by the amount of the additional fixed cost. We can then ask the question: How much must sales revenue increase to compensate for a fixed cost increase and not decrease operating income? A simple answer is that sales revenue has to go up by the same amount as the fixed cost increases. But this is not correct, because to increase sales revenue (with no increase in selling prices) we have to sell more units; if we sell more units, our variable costs (such as wages and guest supplies) are going to increase. By trial and error, we could arrive at a solution, but our equation will solve this kind of question quickly:

$$\text{Required sales revenue} = \frac{\text{Old } FC + \text{New } FC + OI}{1 - VC\%}$$

Suppose we wish to increase our advertising by $5,000 per year. What additional room sales revenue level must be generated to provide $5,000 of added cost and maintain the operating income at the current level of $24,400? First, we can find the new required room sales revenue and subtract the original room sales revenue from it to determine the required increase in room sales revenue.

$$\textbf{Required sales revenue} = \frac{\$362,800 + \$5,000 + \$23,200}{1 - 36.9\%}$$

$$= \frac{\$391,000}{63.1\%}$$

$$= \$619,651$$

We can verify the calculation by using a contribution margin income statement:

Room sales revenue	$619,651
Variable costs ($621,553 × 36.9%)	(228,651)
Contribution margin	$391,000
Less: Fixed costs ($362,800 + $5,000)	(367,800)
Operating income (before tax)	$ 23,200

The solution tells us room sales revenue should be $619,651 to provide for the fixed cost, the added cost, and operating income. The room sales level increased by $7,651 from the previous level of $612,000. To find the number of additional rooms that must be sold, we use the average room rate of $40 from Exhibit 8.1 and divide the increase by the average room rate:

Increase in room sales revenue / Average room rate = Additional rooms
$7,651 / $40 = 191.3, or 192 rooms per year

Since we can't sell a part of a room, it is suggested we round a partial room up rather than down, from 191.3 to 191 rooms. If we divide the 209 additional rooms by 365 operating days, a little less than one additional room per day must be sold. If more than 192 rooms can be sold, not only will we pay for the advertising cost and the additional variable cost per room occupied, but we will also increase operating income.

In the problem just discussed, we worked the solution by evaluating additional room sales revenue required, which was then converted to rooms to be sold. We could have answered this question working directly with room data. Let us see how this happens.

Variable cost per unit is $14.77 (see Exhibit 8.1) and average sale per unit (average room rate) is $40.

$$\textbf{Variable cost \%} = \frac{\$14.77}{\$40.00} = 0.3693 \times 100 = 36.9\%$$

Included in the $14.77 variable cost per unit is the cost of the wages of a housekeeper to clean the unit. Suppose the hourly wage rate for housekeepers (including all benefits) is $8.00 an hour, and a housekeeper takes half an hour to clean a room. Therefore, $4.00 of the $14.77 variable cost per room sold is for wages and benefits. Let us assume a 20% increase in housekeepers' wages:

$$\$4.00 + (20\% \times \$4.00) = \$4.00 + \$0.80 = \underline{\underline{\$4.80}}$$

or
$$\$4.00 \times 1.20\% = \underline{\underline{\$4.80}}$$

Alternatively, we could say that our variable cost per unit is going to go up by $0.80 and will now be

$$\$14.77 + \$0.80 = \underline{\underline{\$15.57}}$$

But if our variable cost per unit is now $15.57 and there is no change in the average room rate, our variable cost percentage will no longer be the same as before:

$$\frac{\$15.57}{\$40.00} = 0.3893 \times 100 = \underline{\underline{38.9\%}}$$

We can now use this to answer the question: What must my new level of room sales revenue be if my other fixed costs do not change, my profit must not drop, but housekeepers' wages are going to increase by 20%?

$$\textbf{Required room sales revenue} = \frac{FC + OI}{1 - VC\%}$$

$$= \frac{\$362,800 + \$23,200}{1 - 38.9\%}$$

$$= \frac{\$387,200}{61.1\%}$$

$$= \underline{\underline{\$631,751}}$$

Again, we'll use the contribution margin income statement to verify the answer:

Room sales revenue	$631,751
Variable costs ($633,715 × 38.9%)	(245,751)
Contribution margin	$386,000
Less: Fixed costs	(362,800)
Operating income (before tax)	$ 23,200

WHAT ABOUT MULTIPLE CHANGES?

So far, only single changes have been considered. Multiple changes can be handled in the same way with no difficulties. For example, let us assume we are going to spend $5,000 more on advertising, that our housekeepers are to get a 20% wage increase, and we now want our operating income to be $40,000 rather than $23,200. What must our revenue level be? Combining all these changes into one equation we have the following:

$$\text{Required room sales revenue} = \frac{FC + New\ FC + OI}{1 - VC\%}$$

$$= \frac{\$362,800 + \$5,000 + \$40,000}{1 - 38.9\%}$$

$$= \frac{\$407,800}{61.1\%}$$

$$= \underline{\underline{\$667,430}}$$

And the verification is this:

Room sales revenue	$667,430
Variable costs ($667,430 × 38.9%)	(259,630)
Contribution margin	$407,800
Less: Fixed costs	(367,800)
Operating income (before tax)	$ 40,000

HOW CAN WE CONVERT THE ROOM SALES REVENUE LEVEL DIRECTLY INTO UNITS?

In the equation used so far, the denominator has been as follows:

100% − Variables costs as % of room sales revenue

The resulting net figure in the denominator is referred to as the contribution margin. In other words, if room sales revenues is 100% and variable costs are 38.9%, then 61.1% of room sales revenue is available as the contribution toward fixed costs and profit. The 61.1% figure is the contribution margin percentage.

The contribution margin can be expressed as a dollar amount, rather than as a percentage figure. For example, the Model Motel's average room rate is $40, and the variable costs (assuming an increase in housekeepers' wages) total $15.57 per room; therefore, the contribution margin is $24.43. In fact, our general equation for the sales level (either room sales revenue or units) can be simplified like this:

$$\text{Required sales units} = \frac{\text{Fixed costs} + \text{Operating income}}{\text{Contribution margin u}}$$

$$= \frac{FC + OI}{SP_u - VC_u}$$

The contribution margin is an important figure for any hospitality operation's manager to know because it shows how much of the sale of each item is available to cover fixed costs and provide income (profit before tax).

We have been using the CVP equation where the contribution margin in the denominator is expressed as a percentage. The required room sales revenue level we have calculated has been expressed in room sales revenue dollars. If we use the previous equation and express the contribution margin in dollars, we shall have a room sales level expressed in units. Let us test this using information from the problem in the preceding section where we have increased advertising by $5,000, wanted an increased operating income, and increased the housekeepers' wages.

$$\text{Required sales level (units)} = \frac{FC + OI}{SP_u - VC_u} = \frac{FC + OI}{CM_u}$$

$$\text{Required sales level (units)} = \frac{\$362{,}800 + \$5{,}000 + \$40{,}000}{\$40.00 - \$15.57}$$

$$= \frac{\$407{,}800}{\$24.43}$$

$$= \underline{\underline{16{,}693}} \text{ rooms}$$

The reason we might want the solution in units is that in the case of a motel or hotel, it might be useful to have the required room sales revenue level converted to an occupancy percentage. This can be quickly calculated if we know the room sales level in units.

From Exhibit 8.1 we know that our current occupancy level for the 70-room Model Motel is 60%. This was calculated by dividing units used by units available.

To cover our changed fixed and variable costs and the new operating income level, we have to sell 16,693 units a year, which is an occupancy of 65.3%:

$$\frac{16{,}693}{70 \times 365} = \frac{16{,}693}{25{,}550} = 0.6533 \times 100 = \underline{\underline{65.3\%}}$$

IF ROOM RATES ARE CHANGED, WHAT WILL BE THE EFFECT ON ROOMS SOLD?

The contribution margin expressed in dollars is also used in answering questions concerning a change in selling prices. For example, assume fixed costs are $367,800 ($362,800 + $5,000), operating income required is $40,000, and variable costs are $15.57 per room used (with increased housekeeping wages). Then what will our occupancy have to be to offset a 10% reduction in selling prices? Our new average rate will be $36 ($40 − 90%) instead of $40:

$$\textbf{Required sales revenue level (in units)} = \frac{\$367,800 + \$40,000}{\$36.00 - \$15.57}$$

$$= \frac{\$407,800}{\$20.43}$$

$$= \underline{\underline{\textbf{19,961}}} \textbf{ units}$$

Occupancy will therefore have to be 78.1%:

$$\frac{19,961}{70 \times 365} = \frac{19,961}{25,550} = 0.781 \times 100 = \underline{\underline{78.1\%}}$$

In other words, to compensate for a 10% ($40 − $4) cut in average room rate, our occupancy will have to jump from 65.3% to 78.1%. Expressed another way, we could say that we are going to have to sell 9 more rooms per night on average (12.8% × 70 rooms available) to pay for a decrease in average room rate of 10%.

We could have arrived at the same result using the contribution margin expressed in percentages. In fact, it is sometimes necessary to do it this way when we have sales revenue figures or results that cannot be converted to a unit basis. The equation in this case is a little lengthier:

$$\frac{\textbf{Required}}{\textbf{sales}} = \frac{FC + OI \textbf{ desired}}{100\% - \left(\dfrac{\textbf{Present variable cost }\%}{100\% \pm \textbf{Proposed percentage change in prices}} \right)}$$

We will use the same figures we have been using: Fixed cost is $367,800, profit desired is $40,000, variable costs are 38.9%, and a proposed rate decrease is 10%. Substituting in the equation, we have the following:

$$\textbf{Required sales revenue} = \frac{\$367,800 + \$40,000}{100\% - \left(\dfrac{38.9\%}{100\% - 10\%} \right)}$$

$$= \frac{\$407,800}{100\% - \left(\dfrac{38.9\%}{90\%} \right)}$$

$$= \frac{\$407,800}{100\% - 43.2\%}$$

$$= \frac{\$407,800}{56.8\%}$$

$$= \underline{\underline{\$717,958}}$$

In terms of number of units to be sold, this is

$$\frac{\$717,958}{\$36 \text{ (new rate)}} = \underline{\underline{19,943}}$$

This answer of 19,943 units differs slightly from the answer obtained by using the earlier method (19,961), but the difference is caused solely by some slight rounding up to full units and rounding of percentages to the tenth of a percent in our calculations.

HOW DOES THE EQUATION WORK IF WE HAVE A LOSS?

So far we have looked at the CVP equation in breakeven or profitable situations only. It can also be used to answer questions concerning a loss position. For example, using the original cost information, suppose the Model Motel were in the following situation:

Room sales revenue	$559,100 ($559,100 / $40 = 13,978 units)
Variable costs (36.9% × $559,100)	$206,308
Fixed costs	362,800
Total costs	$569,108
Loss	($ 10,008)

The question is: What amount of additional sales revenue must be achieved to eliminate the loss? The answer is to divide the amount of the loss by the contribution margin; using percentage figures for dollar answers, or using dollar figures if we want the answer in units:

	Dollar Sales Revenue		**Unit Sales**
Extra sales revenue required =	$\dfrac{\$10,008}{100\% - 36.9\%}$	*or*	$\dfrac{\$10,000}{\$40.00 - \$14.77}$
=	$\dfrac{\$10,008}{63.1\%}$	*or*	$\dfrac{\$10,008}{\$25.23}$
=	$\underline{\underline{\$15,861}}$	*or*	397 units at $40

If we wanted to calculate the additional volume required to eliminate the loss and give a profit of $15,000, the numerator becomes the amount of the loss plus the profit desired:

$$\text{Sales level required} = \frac{\$10,000 + \$15,000}{100\% - 36.9\%} \quad or \quad \frac{\$10,000 + \$15,000}{\$40.00 - \$14.77}$$

$$= \frac{\$25,008}{63.1\%} \quad or \quad \frac{\$25,000}{\$25.23}$$

$$= \underline{\underline{\$39,632}} \quad or \quad \underline{\underline{991 \text{ units at } \$40}}$$

Is the calculated answer correct? This can be confirmed by completing a contribution margin income statement:

Contribution Margin Income Statement

Total sales revenue ($559,100 + $39,632)	$598,732
Variable costs (36.9% × $598,732)	(220,932)
Contribution margin	$377,800
Fixed costs	(362,800)
Operating income (profit)	$ 15,000

WHAT ABOUT A NEW INVESTMENT?

The CVP equation has been used so far to illustrate how historical information from accounting records can be used to make decisions about the future. CVP analysis is equally valid when we have no past accounting information to help us. In such a case, the fixed and variable costs have to be estimated in the best possible way. Suppose the Model Motel was considering renting the adjacent premises and converting the space into a 50-seat coffee shop to better serve the needs of its motel customers. The owner of the motel and the accountant have developed the cost projections shown in Exhibit 8.6. With this information we can answer the question: What must the minimum sales revenue be to earn the return on investment desired? This can be answered by using the basic CVP equation:

$$\text{Required sales revenue level} = \frac{\text{Fixed expenses} + \text{Return on investment (profit)}}{100\% - \text{Variable cost }\%}$$

$$= \frac{\$85,600 + \$30,150}{100\% - 55\%}$$

$$= \frac{\$115,750}{45\%}$$

$$= \underline{\underline{\$257,222}}$$

Investment required for remodeling and for equipment and furniture, table settings, inventories, and other preopening items	$201,000
Estimated annual fixed costs:	
Rent	$ 15,000
Depreciation of furniture and equipment	10,400
Basic labor cost for supervision, food preparation, and service	48,400
Insurance, telephone, utilities, advertising	11,800
Total Annual Fixed Costs	$ 85,600
Variable operating costs will be kept to these levels relative to sales revenue	
Variable cost percentage, food	35%
Variable cost percentage, labor	15%
Variable cost percentage, other items	5%
Total variable operating costs as a percentage of sales revenue	55%
Return on investment required (15% on initial investment of $201,000)	$ 30,150

■ **EXHIBIT 8.6**
Investment and Cost Data for Proposed Coffee Shop

Assuming the estimates of costs are reasonably accurate, the owner of the Model Motel would have to decide whether the projected required sales revenue of $257,222 could be attained from motel customers and other potential customers in the area. If the volume could be reached, then the new venture would be profitable.

Once in business with the new restaurant, decisions about the coffee shop can then be made using CVP analysis in the same way as was demonstrated for the motel operation. Coffee shop sales revenue can also be handled on a per unit basis. In this case, the unit is the customer and the average check is the measure of the per unit, or customer. For example, at a sales level of $257,222 and an average check of $13.30, the number of customers (units) is

$$\frac{\$257,222}{\$13.30} = \underline{\underline{19,340}} \text{ Customers (units)}$$

WHAT ABOUT JOINT COSTS?

In the problems handled to date, the fixed costs have been identified with a single operation (a motel) or department (the restaurant), and this identification has been easy. What happens in the case of joint costs if, for example, a restaurant has a food department and beverage department? Some of the costs involved will be joint costs shared by the entire operation. In such a case, as long as the variable costs can be identified for each department, CVP analysis can still be

	Food Department		Beverage Department	
Sales revenue (monthly)	$150,000	100%	$50,000	100%
Variable costs	(75,000)	50%	(20,000)	40%
Contribution margin	$ 75,000	50%	$30,000	60%
Total contribution margin		$105,000		
Fixed costs		(85,000)		
Operating income		$ 20,000		

Total combined contribution margin $105,000 ($75,000 + $30,000)

■ **EXHIBIT 8.7**
Operation with Joint Fixed Costs

useful. The fixed costs and the fixed portion of semifixed costs can still be handled in a joint manner.

Let us consider the large restaurant in Exhibit 8.7. Because each of the two departments has a different percentage of variable costs, and therefore a different percentage of contribution margin, a given sales revenue increase for one department will affect operating income in a way different from the same given sales revenue increase in the other department. Consider a $15,000 sales increase in each of the two departments in Exhibit 8.7. Assuming no change in fixed cost, the effect on profit will be as follows:

	Food Department		Beverage Department	
Sales revenue increase	$15,000		$15,000	
Variable costs	(8,250)	(55%)	(6,000)	(40%)
Operating income increase	$ 6,750		$ 9,000	

If a sales revenue increase is desired, it is likely to come from both departments, not just one. Therefore, this is a problem of sales revenue mix. The problem does not, however, prevent us from using our CVP analysis.

Let us suppose the restaurant wanted a $5,000 increase in operating income, with no change in the fixed costs or in the variable cost percentages. Under these circumstances, there are three ways to obtain the extra operating income: an increase in food sales revenue only, an increase in beverage sales revenue only, or (what is more likely to happen in practice) a combined increase in food and beverage revenue.

Increase in Food Sales Revenue Only

In the case of increasing food sales revenue only, the solution is arrived at with the basic CVP equation:

$$\text{Required food sales revenue} = \frac{\text{Operating income increase}}{100\% - \text{Variable food cost \% to food revenue}}$$

$$= \frac{\text{Operating income increase}}{\text{Food contribution margin \%}}$$

$$= \frac{\$5,000}{50\%}$$

$$= \underline{\underline{\$10,000}}$$

Increase in Beverage Sales Revenue Only

The approach is exactly the same as for a food sales revenue increase only, except that we substitute the beverage contribution margin percentage for the food contribution margin percentage.

$$\text{Beverage revenue} = \frac{\$5,000}{60\%}$$

$$= \underline{\underline{\$8,333}}$$

Combined Increase in Food and Beverage Revenue

Since food sales revenue (FSR) increases have a different effect on operating income (profit) than beverage sales revenue (BSR) increases, it is necessary to calculate how much combined total sales revenue must increase. An anticipated sales mix ratio of food sales revenue to total revenue and a ratio of beverage sales revenue to total revenue must be specified. Let us suppose that any combined sales revenue increases will be in the ratio of 75% for food and 25% for beverage. (Since the restaurant currently sells 75% food and 25% beverages, any combined sales revenue increases will likely be the same ratio of 75% food and 25% beverages.) Our equation for solving this type of revenue mix problem follows:

$$\begin{array}{c}\text{Combined} \\ \text{required} \\ \text{sales revenue}\end{array} = \frac{\text{Operating income increase}}{(FSR\% \times \text{Food } CM\%) + (BSR\% \times \text{Beverage } CM\%)}$$

$$= \frac{\$5,000}{(75\% \times 45\%) + (25\% \times 60\%)}$$

$$= \frac{\$5,000}{33.8\% + 15\%}$$

$$= \frac{\$5,000}{48.8\%}$$

$$= \underline{\$10,246}$$

It should be noted that the 52.5% contribution margin in this illustration is a weighted-average contribution margin based on the sales revenue mix of food and beverage operations. We can easily check the accuracy of the answer obtained:

(Format changes only)	*Food Department*	*Beverage Department*
Sales revenue	75% × $10,246 = $7,685	25% × $10,246 = $2,562
Variable costs	50% × $7,685 = (4,227)	40% × $2,562 = (1,025)
Contribution to operating income	$3,458	$1,537
Combined operating income	$3,458 + $1,637 = $4,995	

Compound Changes

Compound changes can be made with no difficulty. With reference to Exhibit 8.7, let us ask the following question: What total sales revenue level would we need if we wanted an operating income of $25,000, if fixed costs increased to $87,000, and if the sales revenue ratio changed to 70% for food and 30% for beverage? There is no change in the contribution margin percentages. The solution:

$$\textbf{Total sales revenue} = \frac{\$87,000 + \$25,000}{(70\% \times 45\%) + (30\% \times 60\%)}$$

$$= \frac{\$112,000}{(31.5\% + 18.0)}$$

$$= \frac{\$112,000}{49.5\%}$$

$$= \underline{\$226,263}$$

To confirm whether this is the correct answer, we can prepare a new condensed income statement for the restaurant, as in Exhibit 8.7.

	Food Department	*Beverage Department*
Sales revenue	70% × $226,263 = $158,384	30% × $226,263 = $67,879
Less: Variable costs	50% × $158,384 = (87,111)	40% × $ 67,879 = (27,152)
Contribution margin	$ 71,273	$40,727
Combined contribution margins	$112,000	
Less: Fixed costs	(87,000)	
Operating income	$ 25,000	

INCOME TAXES

To this point in the discussion of CVP analysis, the effect of income taxes has been ignored. Obviously, at the breakeven level of sales revenue there are no tax implications because there is no operating income (profit). Also, with a proprietorship or partnership the organization pays no income taxes. Any operating income is deemed to be paid out to the owner(s), who then pay income tax on those profits at personal tax rates.

An incorporated company that has a taxable operating income must, however, consider the tax implications when using CVP for decisions. Unfortunately, income tax is neither a fixed cost nor a variable cost dependent on sales revenue. Taxes vary with operating income before tax and thus require special treatment in CVP analysis. This requires adjusting the CVP equation, substituting the term operating income desired.

Consider the figures used earlier in this chapter, where the Model Motel's income desired was $39,000 and the room sales revenue required to achieve this were calculated to be $636,767. Assume now that the motel is in a 45% tax bracket. What sales are required to achieve a $39,000 after-tax profit? The $39,000 can be converted to a before-tax figure as follows, and as we learned in Chapter 6:

Operating income increase = Net income (AT) / (1 − Tax rate)

$$= \frac{\$39,000}{1 - 45\%}$$

$$= \frac{\$39,000}{55\%}$$

$$= \$70,909$$

Operating income − NI (AT) = Tax *or* Operating income × Tax rate = Tax
Tax = $70,909 − $39,000 = $31,909 *or* $70,909 × 45% = $31,909

Thus, if the motel with $362,800 of fixed cost and variable costs of 36.9% of room sales revenue and a net income (after tax) of $39,000, the operating income would have to be $70,909, and the tax equation would be used as shown in the preceding:

$$\textbf{Required sales revenue} = \frac{\textbf{Fixed cost} + (\textbf{Net income (AT) / 1} - \textbf{Tax rate})}{\textbf{Contribution margin \%}}$$

$$= \frac{\$362,800 + [\$39,000 / (1 - 45\%)]}{1 - 36.9\%}$$

$$= \frac{\$362,800 + \$70,909}{63.1\%}$$

$$= \frac{\$433,709}{63.1\%}$$

$$= \underline{\$687,336} \textbf{ Sales revenue}$$

The validity of calculating room sales revenue, which covers all costs to include a specific amount of income after tax, can be verified as shown in a contribution margin income statement format (variable costs of 36.9% and fixed costs of $362,800 came from Exhibit 8.1):

Room sales revenue	$687,336
Variable costs ($687,336 × 36.9%)	(253,627)
Contribution margin	$433,709
Fixed costs	(362,800)
Operating income	70,909
Tax ($70,909 × 45%)	(31,909)
Net income	$ 39,000

CONCLUDING COMMENTS

We have seen only a few of the ways in which the CVP approach and the CVP equations can provide useful information for decision making. However, the mathematical answers arrived at are only as accurate as are the cost breakdowns used and the forecasts about changing costs and sales revenue levels. The results of CVP analysis are not guaranteed because uncertainty about the future can never be eliminated. However, uncertainty is reduced using CVP analysis, and without it decisions made might be nothing more than guesses. Finally, the reader is cautioned to refer again to the assumptions and limitations about CVP analysis listed at the beginning of this chapter.

COMPUTER APPLICATIONS

A spreadsheet program lends itself extremely well to performing the calculations for each of the equations or formulas discussed in this chapter. For example, the breakeven equation has to be entered only once into the program; for each given level of fixed and variable costs, the breakeven sales revenue level can then be calculated, as can the total revenue required to achieve a desired profit. The results of one department can also be combined with those of others to indicate the effect on the overall net income of the operation. For example, if each additional occupied room generated an extra $20 of food and beverage sales, this can be built into the spreadsheet program. Spreadsheet programs also have a graphics capability, which some managers often find more helpful than numbers alone.

SUMMARY

CVP analysis is a method of using knowledge about the level of fixed and variable costs in a business to help in making certain business decisions. The CVP approach must be used only with full knowledge about the assumptions and limitations inherent in it.

Information about sales revenue, costs, and profits can be presented in a graphical form. Graphs are easy to prepare, and the information wanted can be read quickly. Graphs, however, are not very flexible when a variety of possible changes are to be introduced. In such cases, an arithmetical approach using the CVP formula is much handier:

$$\textbf{Required sales revenue} = \frac{\textbf{Fixed costs + Operating income}}{\textbf{1 − Variable cost \%}}$$

If we wanted a sales level expressed in number of units (for example, number of rooms or number of customers), the equation is

$$\textbf{Required sales revenue units} = \frac{\textbf{Fixed costs + Operating income}}{\textbf{Selling price}_u = \textbf{Variable cost}_u}$$

In both of these equations, the denominator is termed the *contribution margin.* Depending on whether the sales revenue level is wanted in dollars or units, the CVP formula can be changed to include new fixed costs:

$$\text{Required sales (in dollars or units)} = \frac{\text{Fixed costs} + \text{Operating income (BT)} + \text{New fixed costs}}{\text{Contribution margin percentage or units}}$$

With the CVP equation, any of the variables (fixed costs, profit, variable costs) can be changed individually, or they can all be changed together, and the required sales revenue level can be calculated. A special equation is required if unit selling prices are to be changed and variable costs are to be expressed as a percentage of sales revenue:

$$\begin{matrix}\text{Required} \\ \text{sales} \\ \text{revenue}\end{matrix} = \frac{\text{Fixed costs} + \text{Operating income}}{100\% - \left(\dfrac{\text{Present variable cost }\%}{100\% \pm \text{Proposed percentage change in prices}}\right)}$$

The CVP formula can also be used where there are two or more departments even if they have joint fixed costs as long as the variable costs can be identified for each department, and a contribution margin percentage can be calculated for each department:

$$\begin{matrix}\text{Required} \\ \text{sales} \\ \text{revenue}\end{matrix} = \frac{\text{Fixed costs} + \text{Operating income}}{\left(\dfrac{\text{Dept. A }\% \text{ of Total}}{\text{Sales revenue} \times \text{Dept. } CM\%}\right) + \left(\dfrac{\text{Dept. B }\% \text{ of Total}}{\text{Sales revenue} \times \text{Dept. } CM\%}\right)}$$

Although the equation shown is for two departments, it can be extended for as many departments as an establishment may have.

Finally, the CVP analysis equation can be amended to take income tax rates into consideration. The equation for converting an after-tax profit into a before-tax profit follows:

$$\text{Operating income} = \frac{\text{Net income (AT)}}{1 - \text{Tax rate}}$$

$$\text{Operating income} - \text{Net income (AT)} = \text{Tax}$$

To calculate the required sales revenue for an operating income increase, the equation is

$$\frac{\text{Operating income increase}}{1 - VC\%} = \text{Required sales revenue}$$

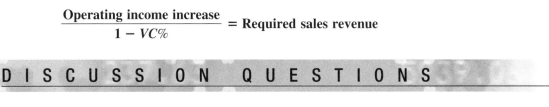

DISCUSSION QUESTIONS

1. Discuss two of the assumptions built into CVP analysis.

2. Discuss two of the limitations built into CVP analysis.

3. Give a brief explanation of how to prepare a breakeven graph or chart to be used in CVP analysis.

4. If one has used a breakeven graph to determine the breakeven level of sales revenue, how can one arithmetically test that the level selected is correct?

5. In an ongoing business, why is a graph not necessarily the best technique to use in CVP analysis?

6. What is the equation for calculating a particular sales revenue level in dollars using CVP analysis?

7. What is the equation for calculating required sales revenue in units using CVP analysis?

8. Define the term *contribution margin*.

9. If management wants to know the sales revenue level it would have to achieve to make a specific profit, how can the required sales level be calculated?

10. In studying the feasibility of a new operation, how can CVP analysis be used to determine the volume of sales revenue required to give a desired return on investment?

11. A restaurant has a food department and a beverage department. Total sales revenue is made up of 80% food and 20% beverages. Food variable costs are 35%, and beverage variable costs are 33%. What is the restaurant's combined contribution margin?

12. State the equation for converting an after-tax profit figure to a before-tax profit amount.

ETHICS SITUATION

A restaurant manager has decided to change the restaurant's contribution margin percentages by lowering it for food and increasing it for beverages. In this way, he hopes to convince the restaurant's owner that a new investment in bar equipment will be rapidly paid for. Discuss the ethics of this situation.

EXERCISES

E8.1 A restaurant has sales revenue of $320,000, fixed costs of $108,000, and variable costs of $128,000. What is breakeven sales revenue?

E8.2 Fixed costs are $137,500 and variable costs are 45%. What is breakeven sales revenue?

E8.3 Fixed costs are $240,000 and the contribution margin is 48%. What is breakeven sales revenue?

E8.4 A restaurant has fixed costs of $53,400 for the month of March 0006. The average check is $12.95, with an average variable cost of $7.38. What is breakeven units of sales revenue for the month of March?

E8.5 A small pub serving only specialty beer has fixed costs of $62,400 per year. The average contribution margin on sales revenue is $2.08. What is the number of units to be sold to reach breakeven?

E8.6 A restaurant has an average check of $12.75, with an average variable cost of $4.85. Fixed costs are $142,200. Calculate the following:

   a. What is the unit contribution margin?

   b. What are breakeven units?

   c. What is the variable cost percentage?

   d. What is the contribution as a percentage?

   e. What is breakeven sales revenue?

E8.7 The owner of a restaurant and bar operation wants a 20% net income after-tax return on his investment of $200,000. The tax rate is 28%. What is the net income before tax and the income tax?

E8.8 A hospitality operation has sales revenue of $462,000 with variable cost averaging 44%. Fixed costs are $188,000. The owner wants a net income after tax of $50,400 based on a tax rate of 28%.

   a. Calculate the total additional sales revenue needed to support the desired net income after tax.

   b. Calculate the total sales revenue required to cover fixed costs, tax, and net income after tax.

E8.9 An operation operates with a variable cost percentage of 72%. The owner wants to increase sales revenue by an amount necessary to provide for an additional operating income of $800 a month, or $9,600 a year. What is the additional increase in sales revenue required?

E8.10 Assume the following information is provided:

$$\frac{\text{Fixed cost} + \text{Added cost} + \text{Increase for OI (AT)}}{1 - VC / SR}$$

$$\frac{\$120,000 + \$22,000 + \$55,000}{1 - (\$186,000 / \$300,000)} = \frac{\$197,000}{1 = 62\%} = \frac{\$197,000}{38\%} = \underline{\underline{\$518,421}}$$

Explain how each numerator item in the CVP equation is an individual item that can be calculated on its own to find the necessary sales revenue to cover that item. Calculate each element in the numerator individually item by item and total the individual calculations to confirm the $518,421 for total sales revenue required is correct.

P R O B L E M S

P8.1 A restaurant with an average check of $14 per guest has the following average monthly figures:

Sales revenue	$700,000
Variable costs	434,000
Fixed costs	168,000

a. What is breakeven sales revenue?

b. If actual sales revenue was $640,000, what would the restaurant's operating income be?

c. If actual sales revenue was $640,000, how many fewer customers per month would be served than at the forecasted sales revenue level of $700,000? The average check remains at $14.

P8.2 A small inn has annual fixed costs of $88,000, variable costs of 68% of sales revenue, and a tax rate of 30%. The owner wants an after-tax net income of $33,600. What sales revenue must be achieved to provide $33,600 net income after tax? Prepare a contribution margin income statement to confirm the calculated required sales revenue.

P8.3 A restaurant is being planned that will require an investment of $150,000 in equipment by the owner. The following shows forecasted variable cost percentages, and identifiable known costs (considered fixed and semi-fixed costs at start-up).

Variable costs will be:
Food cost is 38% of sales revenue
Wage cost is 27% of sales revenue
Other variable costs are 10% of sales revenue

Other known costs will be:

Management salary and wages expense	$48,000
Insurance expense	2,800
Advertising expense	4,500
Utilities and telephone expense	3,000
Rent expense	21,600
Equipment depreciation expense	20%

a. What is the breakeven level of sales revenue for the restaurant? Prepare a contribution margin income statement to confirm the breakeven calculations.

b. What required sales revenue is needed if the owner wants an 18% operating income (before-tax) return on investment? Prepare a contribution margin income statement to confirm the CVP calculations.

P8.4 A cocktail bar is currently doing $582,000 a year in sales revenue. Liquor cost is 38% and other variable costs at this level of sales revenue are 28%. Fixed costs are $150,000.

    a. What is the annual operating income (before tax)?

    b. The owner wants to increase the manager's salary by $12,000 a year. By how much will sales revenue have to increase to provide this additional salary and maintain the current level of operating income? (Any added sales revenue will come from increasing seat turnover by increasing customer service.)

    c. Rather than increasing sales revenue by increasing seat turnover and customer service, the owner decides to increase menu prices by 6%. The owner believes the price increase can be made without losing any customers and without increasing cost of sales or other variable costs. The original variable cost functions and the manager salary increase still apply. What will the bar's operating income (before tax) be?

    d. With the new pricing structure as indicated in part c, how much can sales revenue decrease before operating income falls below $30,000 a year?

P8.5 A motel has 70 rooms it usually rents out, in the following proportions:

45% singles at:	$60 per night
35% doubles at:	$74 per night
20% triples at:	$90 per night

The motel has annual fixed costs of $445,000 and variable costs averages $14 per room occupied.

    a. Calculate the motel's breakeven level and its occupancy percentage.

    b. Calculate the occupancy percentage that will provide operating income (before tax) of $65,000 a year.

    c. Calculate the occupancy percentage necessary to provide an operating income (before tax) of $65,000, if the average room rate were decreased by 20%.

    d. Calculate the occupancy percentage necessary to provide an operating income (before tax) of $65,000, assuming the average room rate will increase by 10%. Variable cost per unit sold will increase to $16.00 and $30,000 per year will be spent on advertising.

P8.6 A 90-room motel has an average room rate of $65.60. Its fixed costs are $300,000 a year, and its variable costs total $476,000 at an average occupancy of 70%.

    a. What is the motel's breakeven occupancy percentage?

    b. What level of sales revenue is required to provide an operating income (before taxes) of $100,000 a year?

c. If the average room rate is increased by $8.00, and operating income of $100,000 a year is wanted, how many fewer rooms per night would need to be sold than was the case in part b?

d. Wage rates for housekeepers are to be increased by $4.00 an hour. It takes a housekeeper half an hour to clean a room. Other cost increases will cause an increase of $1.00 in the variable costs per room occupied. Fixed wages and other fixed costs are expected to increase $4,000 per month. To compensate for the increase in room rate to $73.60 (see part c), $30,000 more per year is to be spent on advertising. Operating income (before tax) is to increase 20% over the present $100,000 per year. What level of sales revenue is required? What is the sales revenue in terms of occupancy percentage?

P8.7 The Relax Inn's rooms department has annual sales revenue of $600,000 and variable costs of $180,000. The inn's food department has annual sales revenue of $200,000 and variable costs of $160,000. The inn's fixed costs are $220,000. The total sales revenue of the inn is $800,000 jointly.

a. Calculate the inn's breakeven point, assuming the ratio of room sales to food sales revenue remains constant at any level of total sales.

b. The owners want to increase their restaurant's sales revenue, and they plan to spend $1,000 on brochures to be displayed in the inn's entry lobby and in the guest rooms. What level of incremental food sales must be achieved to cover the brochure cost? (Assume that room sales remain constant.)

c. If the inn's owners want to increase operating income by $40,000 by increasing rooms occupancy rate, what is the incremental room sales revenue required to support the $40,000 increase to operating income? (Assume no effect on restaurant sales.)

P8.8 A restaurant has a cafe and bar operation. The cafe provides 65% of total sales revenue with a 48% variable cost. The bar provides 35% of total sales revenue with a 38% variable cost. Answer the following:

a. What is the contribution margin of the cafe?

b. What is the contribution margin of the bar?

c. What is the combined contribution margin of the cafe and bar?

d. Assume the owner wants operating income to increase by $50,000, with the increase being provided jointly by the cafe and bar. What is the additional sales revenue required?

P8.9 A motel has a rooms department and a dining room, and total fixed cost of the operation is $335,000. Annual sales revenue and cost figures are as follows:

	Rooms	*Food*	*Totals*
Sales revenue	$440,000	$110,000	$550,000
Variable costs	(132,000)	(66,000)	(198,000)
Contribution margin	$308,000	$ 44,000	$352,000

a. What will be the increase in contribution margin if there is a $20,000 increase in sales revenue only in the rooms department?

b. What will be the increase in contribution margin if there is a $20,000 increase in sales revenue only in the food department?

c. If we want to double the current operating income before tax with variable costs remaining the same and covering fixed costs, what increase in room sales revenue is needed?

d. If we want to double the current total operating income before tax with direct costs remaining the same and covering fixed costs, what increase in food sales revenue is needed?

e. If we want to double the current operating income before tax with direct costs remaining the same, what will increase in sales revenue have to be if the increase is provided jointly by both departments combined? Assume sales revenue ratios stay as originally stated.

f. What would total sales revenue have to be to achieve all of the following:

- Present operating income before tax is doubled
- $5,000 more is spent on advertising
- The sales revenue ratio changes from 80% for rooms and 20% for food to 75% for rooms and 25% for food
- Food variable costs decrease to 55%

P8.10 A neighborhood restaurant opens for lunch only and has a menu limited to five meals. The history of each menu item relative to its percentage of total sales revenue (*SR%*), selling price (*SP*), and variable costs (*VC*) is shown in the following table:

Menu Item	*SP*	*VC*	*SR%*
Food 1	$15.00	$7.75	16%
Food 2	12.95	7.50	20%
Food 3	11.00	5.50	22%
Food 4	8.95	2.85	14%
Food 5	9.95	6.50	8%
Beverages			20%
			100%

Total variable cost of beverages averages 55%. The restaurant has fixed costs of $546,000 a year and wants an operating income (before tax) of at least $25,000 a year.

a. What level of sales revenue will give the desired operating income before tax?

b. Due to the low sales of menu item 5 and its relatively high variable cost percentage, the owner is considering removing this item from the menu. It is anticipated that guests who formerly favored item 5 will split evenly over the remaining four menu items. The owner also believes improved cost control can reduce the beverage variable cost from 55% to 52%. Given these assumptions are valid, what level of sales revenue will be necessary to provide $25,000 of operating income (before tax)?

c. Assuming that $1,200,000 in sales revenue was achieved, what would be the restaurant's operating income (BT) using the information in part b?

P8.11 An owner has $200,000 to invest in a new restaurant. Equipment and furniture are to be purchased for $170,000, and $30,000 will be used for initial working capital. First-year estimates anticipate variable costs as a percentage of sales revenue to be food costs at 35%, variable wage costs at 30%, and other variable costs at 15%. The owner wants an 18% operating income (BT) on his initial investment. Other fixed and semifixed cost estimates are as follows:

Management salaries	$49,200
Rent expense	32,000
Insurance expense	4,800
Depreciation, furniture, and equipment	20%

As an alternative, the owner is considering borrowing $60,000 from a bank at an 8% interest rate instead of using his own money for the investment. Rather than purchasing $40,000 of the needed equipment, it would be rented at a cost of $10,000 per year. Analyze each alternative, (1) using invested capital or (2) borrowing $60,000, and renting some of the equipment. Calculate the annual sales revenue needed to provide an 18% operating income (BT) of the initial investment. Recommend to the owner how to finance the operation.

P8.12 A resort hotel has total annual sales revenue of $1,000,000, variable costs of $350,000, and fixed costs of $570,000. The fixed costs include $80,000 a year for land rental lease.

a. Calculate the hotel's breakeven point.

b. If the owners had an equity investment in the hotel of $1,200,000, what level of sales revenue is required for an operating income (BT) representing a 15% return on their investment?

c. In a renegotiation of the land lease, the landowner has offered management an alternative to the fixed lease currently being paid. The alternative is 10% of the resort's contribution margin.

  i. If management accepts this proposal, what would be the resort hotel's new breakeven point?

  ii. Calculate the indifference point.

  iii. Explain whether management should accept this proposal if next year's total sales revenue is expected to be $1,200,000.

  iv. Should management accept this proposal if next year's total sales revenue is expected to be $1,400,000?

C A S E   8

An analysis of the 4C Company's restaurant costs for the Year 2007 revealed the following:

- Food and beverage: Directly variable with total sales revenue.
- Salary and wages: $156,400 fixed; the remainder are directly variable with total sales revenue.
- Laundry: Directly variable with total sales revenue.
- Kitchen fuel: $3,800 fixed; the remainder are directly variable with total sales revenue.
- China and tableware are directly variable with total sales revenue.
- Glassware is directly variable with total sales revenue.
- Contract cleaning is fixed.
- Licenses is fixed.
- Other operating expenses are directly variable with total sales revenue.
- Administrative and general is fixed.
- Marketing is fixed.
- Utilities costs: $3,100 fixed; the remainder directly variable with total sales revenue.
- Insurance is fixed.
- Rent is fixed.
- Interest is fixed
- Depreciation is fixed.

a. Refer to the income statements in Cases 2 and 3 and calculate the restaurant's total variable costs as a percentage of total sales revenue.

b. Calculate the restaurant's total fixed costs.

c. Calculate the restaurant's breakeven sales revenue and also express the breakeven in terms of the number of guests (using the average check from Case 3).

d. In Year 2007, the restaurant's operating income (before tax) is 6.9% of total sales revenue. To increase the operating income to 10% of Year 2007's sales revenue, how many extra guests are required?

CHAPTER 9

OPERATIONS BUDGETING

INTRODUCTION

This chapter begins by defining budgeting and its purposes. Then it describes various kinds of budgets, such as capital, operating, department, master, fixed, and flexible.

We will examine the responsibility for budget preparation and the advantages and disadvantages of budgeting. We will then go through a five-step cycle of the budgeting process:

1. Establish attainable goals or objectives.
2. Plan to achieve these goals or objectives.
3. Compare actual results with those planned and analyze the differences (variances).
4. Take any corrective action required.
5. Improve the effectiveness of budgeting.

The steps in the preparation of a departmental operating budget are then explained, because it is from these budgets that most of the other kinds of budgets are derived. Budgeting a new operation, which has no information from the past on which to base budgets, is then discussed.

Zero-base budgeting (ZBB) is covered with reference to its value in controlling some types of undistributed cost. The two major aspects of ZBB (decision unit analysis and ranking) are discussed in some detail.

Variance analysis is discussed in this chapter, and the chapter concludes with a section on forecasting methods using techniques such as moving averages and regression analysis.

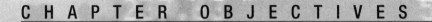

CHAPTER OBJECTIVES

After studying this chapter, the reader should be able to:

1. Explain the concept of budgeting.
2. Define the three purposes of budgeting.
3. Describe some of the types of budgets, such as departmental, capital, fixed, and flexible.

4. Briefly discuss some of the advantages and disadvantages of budgeting.

5. List and briefly discuss each of the five steps in the budget cycle.

6. Briefly explain some of the limiting factors to keep in mind when budgeting.

7. Define the term *derived demand.*

8. Explain what information is required to determine budgeted sales revenue in a restaurant operation and budgeted room sales revenue in the rooms department of a hotel or motel.

9. Prepare budgeted (pro forma) income statements, given appropriate information about estimated sales revenue and costs.

10. Discuss ZBB with reference to decision units and the ranking process.

11. Briefly discuss the pros and cons of ZBB.

12. Use variance analysis to compare budgeted figures with actual results.

13. Use mathematical techniques, such as moving averages and regression analysis, in forecasting.

BUDGETING

A **budget** is a *business plan,* usually expressed in monetary terms. To make meaningful decisions about the future, a manager must look ahead. One way to look ahead is to prepare budgets or forecasts. A forecast may be very simple. For a restaurant owner/operator, the budget might be no more than looking ahead to tomorrow, estimating how many customers will eat in the restaurant, and purchasing food and supplies to accommodate this need. By contrast, in a large organization a budget might entail forecasts up to five years (such as for furniture and equipment purchases), as well as requiring day-to-day budgets (such as staff scheduling). Budgets not expressed in monetary terms could involve numbers of customers to be served, number of rooms to be occupied, number of employees required, or some other unit, as opposed to dollars. The three main purposes of budgeting can be summarized as follows:

1. To provide organized estimates of future unit sales, sales revenues, expenses, net income, staffing requirements, or equipment needs, broken down by operating period and department.

2. To provide management with long-term and short-term goals. These goals can be used to plan future activities.

3. To provide information for control. This is important so that actual results can be evaluated against budget plans and adjustments, if necessary, can be made.

TYPES OF BUDGETS

There are a number of different kinds of budgets. This section describes long-term and short-term budgets, capital budgets, operating budgets, department budgets, and master budgets.

LONG-TERM VERSUS SHORT-TERM BUDGETS

Budgets can generally be considered to be either long-term or short-term. A **long-term budget** would be a plan for anywhere from 1 year to 5 years ahead. Such budgets concern the major plans for the organization (expansion, creation of a new market, financing, and other related matters) and are often called **strategic budgets.** From such long-term plans evolve the policies concerning the day-to-day operations of the business, and thus the short-term budgets.

Short-term budgets could be for a day, a week, a quarter, or a year. Such budgets involve middle management in using its resources to meet the objectives of the long-term plans.

FIXED VERSUS FLEXIBLE BUDGETS

A **fixed budget** is based on a certain level of activity or sales revenue, and expense estimates are based on this level of sales. No attempt is made to introduce greater or lesser levels of sales revenue and, thus, different expense amounts in the budget. The disadvantage of such a budget is that, if the actual sales level differs from the budgeted sales level, there is no plan covering this possibility and expenses can only then be adjusted in the short run by guesswork. For example, suppose the rooms department budget in a hotel is based on the average year-round rooms occupancy of 70%. Operating costs (e.g., payroll, supplies, linen, and laundry) are based on this level of occupancy. If actual occupancy dropped to 60% because of unforeseen economic conditions, it might be difficult for the rooms department manager to know, in the short run, what the new payroll level should be. The same is true for all other expenses.

A **flexible** (or **variable**) **budget** is prepared based on several levels of activity. In our rooms department example, sales revenue could be forecast for 60%, 70%, and 80% occupancy levels (or as many levels as are appropriate). As the actual year progresses, it can be determined at which level the operation is going to fit best, and the appropriate expense levels will have already been determined for this level. In other words, adjustment is easier. The question could be raised, using the rooms department example, as to whether it is truly a flexible (variable) budget or whether it is three (or more, if more occupancy levels are used) fixed budgets at three different occupancy levels. The question is valid, but the practical result is that management is prepared to adjust to the actual situation when adjustment is required.

With a flexible budget, variable expenses will change with the volume of sales revenue, but fixed expenses will remain the same. For example, a budget might be prepared for a restaurant based on a number of levels of sales revenue. Expenses are calculated based on each different revenue level. Variable expenses might be expressed as a percentage of sales revenue or as a dollar amount per unit sold. However, advertising expense might be a fixed expense and will be left the same, regardless of the actual level of sales revenue. In other words, regardless of the volume of sales revenue, a definite, fixed amount is budgeted for this expense. A truly flexible budget will show all expenses that are in fact variable by their nature as percentages for each sales revenue operation (such as restaurant sales revenue and rooms sales revenue). Fixed costs will be shown as a dollar amount.

CAPITAL BUDGETS

A **capital budget** is a plan for the acquisition of new (or replacement of existing) fixed assets. A five-year replacement schedule for hotel room furnishings is a capital budget.

OPERATING BUDGETS

An **operating budget** concerns the ongoing projections of sales revenues and expense items that affect the income statement. For example, a forecast of sales revenue for a restaurant for a month is in an operating budget. Similarly, in a multidepartment hotel the forecast of total payroll expense for the year is an operating budget.

DEPARTMENT BUDGETS

A **department budget** is prepared for a hospitality organization that has multiple sales revenue units (such as a restaurant complex with a dining room, a bar and a banquet area, or hotel or motel with a rooms operation, dining room and a bar). A department budget would therefore be for a specific department and would show the total forecasted sales revenue less operating expenses for that department. Alternatively, if a department does not directly generate any sales revenue (e.g., the maintenance department of a hotel), a department budget could be prepared showing anticipated expenses in detail for an operating period. Generally, such department budgets are prepared annually and broken down month by month.

MASTER BUDGETS

A **master budget** is the most comprehensive of all budgets. Generally, a master budget is prepared for a year and includes a balance sheet for a year hence and all the departmental income and expense statements for the next year.

BUDGET PREPARATION

Who prepares budgets and how often they are prepared varies with the size of the organization and the type of budget being prepared.

WHO PREPARES BUDGETS?

In a small, owner-operated restaurant or motel, the owner would prepare the budget. If it were a formal or written budget, the help of an accountant might be useful. If the budget were an informal one, there might be no written supporting figures. The owner might just have a mental plan about where he or she wants to go and operates from day to day to achieve the objective, or to come as close to it as possible. Budgets are also a record for future budgeting and other planning.

In a larger organization, many individuals might be involved in budget preparation. In such organizations, budgets are prepared from the bottom up. At the very least, the department heads or managers must be involved. If their subsequent performance is evaluated on the plans included in the budget, then they should be involved in preparing their own departmental budgets. They, in turn, might discuss the budget figures with employees in their own departments.

Above the department heads would be a budget committee. Department managers might be members of this committee. Such a committee is required to coordinate the budget to ensure that the final budget package is meaningful. For example, the rooms occupancy of a hotel determines, to a great extent, the breakfast sales revenue for the food department. The budget committee must ensure that the breakfast food sales are not based on an occupancy that differs from the rooms department figure.

The formal preparation of the budget is a function of the accounting department. The organization's comptroller would probably be a member of the budget committee, and his or her task is to prepare final budget information for submission to the general manager for approval.

The worst form of budget preparation is to have budgets imposed from the top down through the accounting department to the operating and other departments. Coordination might be present, but the cooperation of the employees where the activity takes place may be minimal.

WHEN ARE BUDGETS PREPARED?

Each year, top-level management generally prepares long-range budgets for up to 5 years. They may or may not involve department managers. Each year such budgets are revised for the next period (up to 5 years) forward. For coordination, the budget committee would be involved.

Short-term budgets are prepared annually, for the most part, with monthly projections. Each month, budgets for the remaining months of the year should be revised to adjust for any changed circumstances. Department managers should be involved in such revisions and the budget committee should be involved for overall coordination.

The department managers or other supervisory staff usually handle weekly or daily short-range budgets internally. For example, the housekeeping supervisor would schedule housekeepers (which affects the payroll budget) on a daily basis based on anticipated rooms occupancy.

WHAT ARE THE ADVANTAGES OF BUDGETING?

A number of advantages accrues to an organization that uses a budget planning process:

- Since the budgeting process involves department heads and possibly other staff within the department, it encourages their participation and thus improves communication and motivation. Therefore, these operating personnel can better identify with the plans or objectives of the organization.
- In preparing the budget, those involved are required to consider alternative courses of action. For example, should the advertising budget be spent to promote the organization as a whole, or would better results be obtained if emphasis were placed more on a particular department? At the department level, a restaurant manager might consider increasing the number of customers to be served per meal period per server (increased productivity per server) against the possible effects of slower service, reduced seat turnover, and perhaps lower total sales revenue.
- Budgets outline in advance the sales revenue to be achieved and the costs involved in achieving these revenues. After each **budget period** the actual results can be compared with the budget. In other words, a standard for comparison is predetermined, and subsequent evaluation of all those involved in the operation is possible.
- In the case of flexible budgets, the organization as a whole and each department within it are prepared for adjustments to any level of activity between the high and low (minimum and maximum) sales levels.
- Budgeting forces those involved to be forward-looking. For example, do our menu item selling prices need to be changed to take care of anticipated future increases in food, labor, and other operating costs? However, this is not to suggest that what happened in the past is not important and, therefore, ignored in budget preparation.
- Budgeting requires those involved to consider both internal and external factors. Internal factors include such matters as seating capacity, seat turnover, and menu prices in a restaurant; and rooms available, rooms occupancy, and room rates in a hotel. External factors include such mat-

ters as the competition, the local economic environment in which the business operates, and the general inflation rate trend.

WHAT ARE THE DISADVANTAGES OF BUDGETING?

Obviously, just as there are advantages to budgeting, so, too, are there disadvantages:

- The time and cost to prepare budgets can be considerable. Usually, the larger the organization the greater is the amount of time, and thus the cost, of preparing budgets.
- Budgets are based on unknown factors (as well as some known factors) that can have a major impact on what does actually happen. It could be argued that this is not a disadvantage because it forces those involved to look ahead and prepare for the unknown.
- Budget preparation may require that confidential information be included in the budget. However, if confidential information is included, it may not remain confidential.
- The "spending to the budget" approach can be a problem. If an expense budget is overestimated, there can be a tendency to find ways to spend the money still in the budget as the end of the budget period arrives. This tendency can be provoked by a desire to demonstrate that the budget forecast was correct to begin with and to protect the budget from being cut for the next period.

In most cases, the advantages far outweigh the disadvantages.

THE BUDGET CYCLE

The **budget cycle** is a five-part process that can be summarized as follows:

1. Establish attainable goals or objectives.
2. Plan to achieve these goals or objectives.
3. Compare actual results with those planned, and analyze the differences (variances).
4. Take required corrective action.
5. Improve the effectiveness of budgeting.

Each of these five steps will be discussed in turn.

ESTABLISHING ATTAINABLE GOALS OR OBJECTIVES

In setting goals, the most desirable situation must be tempered with realism. In other words, if any factors limit sales revenue to a certain maximum level, these factors must be considered. An obvious example is that a hotel cannot achieve more than 100% room occupancy. In the short run, if a hotel achieves 100% occupancy every night, room rates would have to be increased for sales revenue to increase. But since very few hotels achieve 100% occupancy year-round, it would be unwise, desirable as it might be, to use 100% as the budgeted occupancy on an annual basis.

Similarly, a restaurant is limited to a specific number of seats. If it is running at capacity, sales revenue can only be increased, again in the short run, by increasing menu prices or seat turnover (seat occupancy). But, again, there is a limit to increasing meal prices because customer resistance and competition often dictate upper pricing levels. However, if seat turnover is increased by giving customers rushed service, the end result may be declining sales.

Other limiting factors might be a lack of skilled labor or skilled supervisory personnel. Increased productivity by serving more customers per server would be desirable and would decrease the payroll cost per customer, but well-trained employees, or employees who could be trained, are often not available. Similarly, supervisory personnel who could train others are not always available.

A shortage of capital could limit expansion plans. If financing is not available to add guest rooms or expand dining areas, it would be a useless exercise to include expansion in our long-term budget.

Management's policy concerning the market in which the organization will operate might also limit budgets. For example, a coffee shop department head might propose that catering to bus tour groups would help increase sales revenue. By contrast, the general manager may believe that catering to such large transient groups is too disruptive to the regular clientele.

Another limiting factor might be in the area of increasing costs. An operation might find that it is restricted in its ability to pass on increasing costs by way of higher prices to its customers.

Finally, customer demand and competition must always be kept in mind when budgeting. In the short run, there is usually only so much business to go around. Adding more rooms to a hotel does not automatically increase the demand for rooms in the area. It takes time for demand to catch up with supply, and new hotels or an additional block of rooms added to an existing hotel will usually operate at a lower occupancy than normal until demand increases. A new restaurant or adding facilities to an existing restaurant must compete for its share of business.

PLANNING TO ACHIEVE GOALS OR OBJECTIVES

Once objectives have been determined, plans must be created to achieve them. At the departmental level, a restaurant manager must staff with employees skilled enough to handle the anticipated volume of business. A chef or purchaser must purchase food both in the quantities required to take care of anticipated demand and of a quality that meets the required standards established by management and expected by the customers. Purchases must allow the food operation to match as closely as possible its budgeted food cost. Over the long term, the need to expand the facilities might require top management to make plans for financing and to seek the best terms for repayment to achieve the budgeted additional profit required from the expansion.

COMPARING ACTUAL RESULTS WITH THOSE PLANNED AND ANALYZING THE DIFFERENCES

This is probably the most important and advantageous step in the budget cycle. Comparing actual results with the budget allows one to ask questions:

- Our actual dining room sales revenue for the month of April was $60,000 instead of the budgeted $63,000. Was the $3,000 difference caused by a reduction in number of customers? If so, is there an explanation (e.g., are higher prices keeping customers away, or did a competitive restaurant open nearby)? Is the $3,000 difference a result of reduced seat turnover (is service slowing down)? Are customers spending less (a reduced average check, or customer spending, because of belt tightening by the customer)?

- Yesterday the housekeeping supervisor brought in two more housekeepers than were required to handle the actual number of rooms occupied. Is there a communication problem between the front office and the housekeeping supervisor? Did the front office fail to notify the housekeeping supervisor of reservation cancellations, or did the housekeeping supervisor err in calculating the number of housekeepers actually required?

- The annual cocktail lounge departmental income was greater than the previous year, but still fell short of budgeted income. Did the sales revenue increase reach the budgeted level? Or did costs increase over the year more than in proportion to revenue? If so, which costs? Was there a change in what we sold (change in the sales revenue mix)? In other words, are we now selling less profitable items (such as more beer and wine than liquor) in proportion to total sales revenue?

These are just a few examples of the types of questions that can be asked, and for which answers should be sought, in analyzing differences between budgeted performance and actual performance. Analysis of such differences will be commented upon further in the section on variance analysis later in this chapter. It should be noted that the variances themselves do not offer solutions to possible problems. They only point out that problems may exist.

IF REQUIRED, TAKING CORRECTIVE ACTION

Step 3 in the budget process points to differences and possible causes of the differences. The next step in the budget cycle necessitates deciding if corrective action is required and then acting on the decision. The cause of a difference could be the result of a circumstance that no one could foresee or predict (e.g., weather, a sudden change in economic conditions, or a fire in part of the premises). Or, by contrast, a difference could be caused because selling prices were not increased sufficiently to compensate for an inflationary cost increase; or that the budgeted forecast in occupancy of guest rooms was not sufficiently reduced to compensate for the construction of a new, nearby hotel; or that staff were not as productive in the number of customers served or rooms cleaned as they should have been according to predetermined standards. Whatever the reason, it should be corrected if possible so future budgets can more realistically predict planned operations.

Variances between budget and actual figures should not be an argument in favor of not budgeting. Without a budget, it would not even be apparent that the operation is not running as effectively as it should and could be. If the variance was favorable (e.g., guest room occupancy was higher than budgeted), the cause should also be determined because that information could help in making future budgets more accurate.

Once you have taken corrective action, you should determine the effectiveness of that action in solving the problem. If the corrective action did not solve the problem, the situation needs to be reassessed and a different technique tried to solve the problem.

IMPROVING THE EFFECTIVENESS OF BUDGETING

This is the final step in the five-step budget cycle. All those involved in budgeting should be made aware of the constant need to improve the budgeting process. The information provided from past budgeting cycles and particularly the information provided from analyzing variances between actual and budgeted figures will be helpful. By improving accuracy in budgeting, the effectiveness of the entire organization is increased.

DEPARTMENTAL BUDGETS

The starting point in any complete budgeting process is the departmental income statement. The rest of the budgeting process hinges on the results of these operating departments. For example, a budgeted balance sheet cannot be made up without the budgeted income statements; a cash budget cannot be prepared without knowledge of departmental sales revenue and expenses; long-term budgets for equipment and furniture replacement, for dividend payments, or for future financing arrangements cannot be prepared without a budget showing what income (or funds) is (are) going to be generated from the operation.

The budgeted income statements for each department and the entire operation are probably the most difficult to prepare. However, once this has been done, the preparation of the cash budget and budgeted balance sheet is relatively straightforward. This chapter will therefore deal only with income statement budgets, since they are the prime concern of day-to-day management of a hotel or restaurant. In summary, the procedure is as follows:

1. Estimate sales revenue levels by department.
2. Deduct estimated direct operating expenses for each department.
3. Combine estimated departmental operating incomes and deduct estimated undistributed expenses to arrive at net income.

ESTIMATING SALES REVENUE LEVELS BY DEPARTMENT

Even though departmental income statements are prepared for a year at a time, they should be initially prepared month by month (with revisions, if necessary, during the budget year in question). Monthly income statements are necessary so that comparisons with actual results can be made each month. If the comparison between budget and actual results were made only on a yearly basis, any required corrective action might be 11 months too late. The following should be considered when making monthly sales revenue projections:

- Past actual sales revenue figures and trends
- Current anticipated trends
- Economic factors
- Competitive factors
- Limiting factors

Information about how top management views trends and factors must be communicated to those who prepare departmental budgets. This information must also be put into language that the department managers understand—that is, in specific numeric terms rather than in vague, general language. For example, if an anticipated competitor is due to open nearby during the budget period, top management must state in specific percentage terms how that may influence the operation's sales revenue.

For example, the dining room sales revenue for the past three years for the month of January was as follows:

Year 1	$60,000
Year 2	$65,000
Year 3	$67,000

It is now December in Year 0006, and we are finalizing our budget for Year 0007, beginning with January. The increase in volume for Year 0005 over Year

0004 was about 8% ($5,000 / $60,000). Year 0006 increase over Year 0005 was approximately 3%. These increases were caused entirely by increases in number of customers. The size of the restaurant has not changed and no change in size will occur in Year 0007. Because a new restaurant is opening a block away, we do not anticipate our customer count will increase in January, but neither do we expect to lose any of our current customers. Because of economic trends, we are going to be forced to meet rising costs by increasing our menu prices by 10% commencing in January Year 0007. Our budgeted sales revenue for January Year 0007 would be:

$$\$67,000 + (10\% \times \$67,000) = \underline{\underline{\$73,700}}$$

The same type of reasoning would be applied for each of the 11 other months of Year 0007, and for each of the other operating departments. One other factor that in some situations might need to be considered in sales revenue projections is that of **derived demand.** In other words, what happens in one department might affect what happens to the sales revenue of another. For example, a cocktail bar might generate sales revenue from customers in the bar area as well as from customers in the dining room. In budgeting the bar total sales revenue, the sales revenue would have to be broken down into sales revenue within the lounge area and sales revenue derived from dining room customers. Similarly, in a hotel the occupancy of the guest rooms will affect the sales revenue in the food and beverage areas. The interdependence of departments must, therefore, be kept in mind in the budgeting process.

DEDUCTING ESTIMATED DIRECT OPERATING EXPENSES FOR EACH DEPARTMENT

Since most departmental direct operating costs are specifically related to sales revenue levels, once the sales revenue has been calculated, the major part of the budget has been accomplished. Historic accounting records will generally show that each direct expense varies within narrow limits as a percentage of sales revenue. The appropriate percentage of expense to sales revenue can therefore be applied to the budgeted sales revenue to calculate the dollar amount of the expense. For example, if laundry expense for the rooms department of a hotel varies between 4.5% and 5.5% of sales revenue, and sales revenue in the rooms department for a particular month is expected to be $100,000, then the laundry expense for that same month would be 5% × $100,000, or $5,000. The same is true for all other direct expenses for which cost to sales revenue percentages are obvious. Although this is a convenient method of budgeting, using historical cost percentages assumes that the costs were appropriate. This may not be true.

In certain cases, however, the problem might not be as simple. A good example of this is labor, where much of the cost is fixed and does not vary as sales revenue goes up or down. In a restaurant, the wages of the restaurant manager,

Covers	Monthly Volume in	
	Waitstaff Hours	Bus Help Hours
Up to 5,500	970	485
5,550 to 6,500	1,040	485
6,500 to 7,500	1,210	485
21,500 to 22,500	3,890	990
Over 22,500	4,160	1,040

■ **EXHIBIT 9.1**

Staffing Schedule—Coffee Shop

the chef, the cashier, and the host or hostess are generally fixed. Such people receive a fixed salary regardless of the volume of business. Only the wages of servers and bus help vary in the short run. In such cases, a month-by-month staffing schedule must be prepared, listing the number of variable staff of each category required for the budgeted sales revenue level, calculating the total variable cost, and adding this to the fixed cost element to arrive at total labor cost for that month. It is true that this requires some detailed calculations, but without it the budget might not be as accurate as it could be for effective budgetary control.

Staffing schedules for each department for various levels of sales revenue could be developed. These schedules would be based on past experience and the standards of performance required by the establishment. Then when sales levels are forecast, the appropriate number of labor-hours or staff required for each type of job can be read directly from the staffing schedule. The number of hours of staffing required or the number of employees can then be multiplied by the appropriate rates of pay for each job category. A typical staffing schedule is illustrated in Exhibit 9.1.

Alternatively, if labor (and other costs) have been broken down for use with CVP analysis (see Chapter 8) into their fixed and variable elements, then this information is already available for use in budgeting.

Once all costs have been determined, they can be deducted from total sales revenue to determine each department's operating income.

COMBINING ESTIMATED DEPARTMENTAL OPERATING INCOMES AND DEDUCTING ESTIMATED UNDISTRIBUTED EXPENSES TO ARRIVE AT NET INCOME

The departmental operating incomes determined in steps 1 and 2 can now be added together. At this point, certain undistributed expenses must be calculated and deducted. These expenses are not distributed to the departments because an appropriate allocation is difficult to arrive at. Nor are they, for the most part, controllable by or the responsibility of the department managers.

These unallocated expenses (including fixed charges) usually include the following:

- Administrative and general
- Marketing
- Property operation and maintenance
- Utilities expense
- Property or municipal taxes
- Rent
- Insurance
- Interest
- Depreciation
- Income taxes

Since these expenses are usually primarily fixed, they vary little with sales revenue; historic records will generally indicate the narrow dollar range within which they vary.

Sometimes these expenses will vary at the discretion of the general manager. For example, it might be decided that an extra allocation will be added to the advertising and promotion budget during the coming year or that a particular item of expensive maintenance can be deferred for a year. In such cases, the adjustment to the budget figures can be made at the general manager's level. Usually, these undistributed expenses are calculated initially on an annual basis (unlike departmental sales revenue and direct operating expenses, which are initially calculated monthly). If an overall pro forma (projected or budgeted) income statement, including undistributed expenses, is prepared monthly, then the simplest method is to divide each undistributed expense by 12 and show one-twelfth of the expense for each month of the year. A three-month budget would show one-fourth of the total annual expense. However, only the undistributed expenses are handled this way. Sales revenue and direct expenses (variable and semivariable) should be calculated correctly month by month to take care of monthly or seasonal variations in sales revenue.

For example, Exhibit 9.2 shows how the undistributed expenses could be allocated in a budget prepared on a quarterly basis. Exhibit 9.2 also indicates a budgeted loss in two of the quarters. We would argue that such budgeted losses are misleading, because the quarters with low sales revenue are unfairly burdened with undistributed costs. However, many of the fixed expenses such as the general manager's salary, rent, property taxes, utilities, insurance, and interest will be paid monthly regardless of sales revenue. Another way to distribute such costs would be in a ratio relative to budgeted sales revenue. Such a distribution is calculated in Exhibit 9.3.

	Quarter 1	Quarter 2	Quarter 3	Quarter 4	Totals
Sales revenue	$300,000	$600,000	$800,000	$300,000	$2,000,000
Direct costs*	(250,000)	(450,000)	(550,000)	(250,000)	(1,500,000)
Operating income	$ 50,000	$150,000	$250,000	$ 50,000	$ 500,000
Undistributed expenses	(75,000)	(75,000)	(75,000)	(75,000)	(300,000)
Net income (loss)	($ 25,000)	$ 75,000	$175,000	($ 25,000)	$ 200,000

*Direct costs might include fixed costs.

■ **EXHIBIT 9.2**

Net Income When Undistributed Costs Are Allocated Based on Time

The revised budget, prepared with the new method of allocating undistributed expenses to the various quarters, is shown in Exhibit 9.4. The method illustrated in Exhibit 9.4 may, as it does in our case, ensure that no period has a budgeted loss. Over the year, however, there is no change in total net income.

BUDGETING IN A NEW OPERATION

New hotels and restaurants will find it more difficult to budget in their early years because they have no internal historic information to serve as a base. If a feasibility study had been prepared prior to opening, it should be used as a base for budgeting. Alternatively, forecasts must be based on a combination of known facts and industry or market averages for the type and size of operation. For example, a restaurant could use the following equation for calculating its breakfast sales revenue:

$$\begin{matrix} \text{Number} \\ \text{of seats} \\ \text{available} \end{matrix} \times \begin{matrix} \text{Seat} \\ \text{turnover} \\ \text{expected} \end{matrix} \times \begin{matrix} \text{Average} \\ \text{check per} \\ \text{meal period} \end{matrix} \times \begin{matrix} \text{Operating} \\ \text{days} \end{matrix} = \begin{matrix} \text{Breakfast} \\ \text{total sales} \\ \text{revenue} \end{matrix}$$

Qtr.	Sales Revenue	Sales Revenue (%)	Undistributed Costs Share		
1	$ 300,000	15%	15% × $300,000 =	$ 45,000
2	600,000	30%	30% × $300,000 =	90,000
3	800,000	40%	40% × $300,000 =	120,000
4	300,000	15%	15% × $300,000 =	45,000
Totals	$2,000,000	100%		$300,000

■ **EXHIBIT 9.3**

Calculation of Allocation of Undistributed Costs Using Sales Revenue Volume

	Quarter 1	Quarter 2	Quarter 3	Quarter 4	Totals
Sales revenue	$300,000	$600,000	$800,000	$300,000	$2,000,000
Direct operating costs	(250,000)	(450,000)	(550,000)	(250,000)	(1,500,000)
Operating income	$ 50,000	$150,000	$250,000	$ 50,000	$ 500,000
Undistributed costs	(45,000)	(90,000)	(120,000)	(45,000)	(300,000)
Net income (loss)	($ 5,000)	$ 60,000	$130,000	($ 5,000)	$ 200,000

■ **EXHIBIT 9.4**
Operating Income When Undistributed Costs Are Allocated Using Sales Revenue Volume

This same equation could be used for lunch, dinner, and even for coffee breaks. Meal periods should be separated because seat turnover rates and average check figures can vary considerably from meal period to meal period. The number of seats and days open in the month are known. The seat turnover rates and average check figures can be obtained from published information (generally from a state or city hospitality association) or by observing at competitive restaurants.

In a rooms department, a similar type of equation might look like this:

$$\begin{array}{ccccc} \textbf{Forecasted} & \textbf{Average} & \textbf{Number} & \textbf{Operating} & \textbf{Total} \\ \textbf{occupancy} \times & \textbf{room} & \times \textbf{of rooms} \times & \textbf{days} & = \textbf{rooms sales} \\ \textbf{percentage} & \textbf{rate} & \textbf{available} & \textbf{available} & \textbf{revenue} \end{array}$$

Once monthly sales revenue figures have been calculated for each meal period, they can be added together to give total sales revenue. Direct operating expenses can then be deducted, by applying industry average percentage figures or other projected percentages for each expense to the calculated budgeted sales revenue.

Again, direct operating expenses can then be budgeted using industry percentages for the type of hotel. Note that, to arrive at the average room rate to be used in the equation, one must consider the rooms' revenue sales mix including the rates for different types of rooms, for different market segments, and for discounted rates for weekends and off seasons. Please see Chapter 6 for a comprehensive discussion of room-rate pricing.

Beverage figures are a little more difficult to calculate. There are some industry guidelines, in that a coffee shop serving beer and wine generates alcoholic beverage sales revenue approximating 8% to 18% of food sales revenue. In a dining room, the alcoholic beverage revenue (beer, wine, and liquor) approximates 24% to 34% of food sales revenue. For example, a dining room with $100,000 a month of food sales revenue could expect between $24,000 and $34,000 of total liquor sales revenue. These are only approximate figures, but they might be the only ones that can be used until the operation has its own accounting records.

There is no simple equation for beverage figures in a cocktail lounge. An average check figure can be misleading. On the one hand, one customer could occupy a seat and spend $7.50 to $20.00 on five drinks; average spending for that customer is $13.75. On the other hand, five different customers could occupy the same seat and each spend $7.50 over the same period: average spending, $7.50. Therefore, the equation used for calculating food sales revenue may be difficult to apply in a bar setting. One alternative is to use the current industry average revenue per seat per year in a cocktail bar.

| **Average annual sales revenue per seat** | × | **Number of seats available** | = | **Total annual sales revenue** |

To convert to a monthly figure for budget purposes, this figure can then be divided by 12 and added to the already-calculated monthly beverage sales revenue generated from the food departments. Direct operating expenses can then be allocated by using industry average percentage guidelines.

Although these equations do not cover all possible approaches, they should give the reader some idea of the methods that can be used when budgeting for a new operation.

However, the equations illustrated are not limited to a new operation. They could also be used in an ongoing organization. For example, instead of applying an estimated percentage of sales revenue increase to last year's figure for the current year's budget, it might be better to break down last year's sales revenue figure into its various elements and adjust each of them individually to develop the new budget amount. For example, last year rooms sales revenue was $100,200 for the month of June. This year we want a 5% increase; therefore budgeting sales revenue will be

$$\$100,200 \times 105\% = \underline{\$105,210}$$

A more comprehensive approach would be to analyze last year's figure in the following way:

Actual rooms occupancy percentage		*Average room rate*		*Number of rooms available*		*Operating days available*		*Total rooms sales revenue*
83.5%	×	$80.00	×	50	×	30	=	$100,200

We can then apply the budget year trends and information to last year's detailed figures. In the budget period, because of a new hotel in the area, we expect a slight drop in occupancy—down to 80%. This will be compensated for by an increase in our average room rate by 5% to $84.00 ($80.00 × 105%). The new budgeted sales revenue is computed as follows:

Budgeted occupancy percentage		Budgeted average room rate		Number of rooms available		Operating days available		Budgeted total rooms sales revenue
80%	×	$84.00	×	50	×	30	=	$100,800

This approach to budgeting might require a little more work but will probably give budgeted figures that are more accurate and can be analyzed more meaningfully than would otherwise be the case.

ZERO-BASE BUDGETING

Zero-base budgeting (ZBB) is a useful technique for controlling costs. As its name implies, no expenses can be budgeted for or incurred unless they are justified in advance. ZBB requires each department head to justify in advance the entire annual budget from a zero base. Although ZBB can be used for any cost, this chapter will use an indirect cost as an example.

Since most costs (food, beverage, labor, supplies, and others) are linked to sales revenue levels in a fairly direct way, budgeting for them is relatively easy. However, there are several expenses in the hospitality industry not related as directly to sales revenue levels. These indirect or **undistributed expenses** include the following:

- Administrative and general
- Marketing
- Property operation and maintenance
- Utilities

These undistributed costs are not normally charged to the operating departments but are kept separate. An operation might also have other fixed costs (e.g., property taxes, insurance, interest, and rent) that are not charged to the operating departments. However, the level of these costs is usually partially imposed from outside the operation. Since they are not subject to day-to-day control, or even to monthly or annual control, they will not be included in this discussion of ZBB.

Traditionally, these four undistributed costs have been budgeted for, and are presumably controlled by, **incremental budgeting.** With incremental budgeting, the assumption is made that the level of the last period's cost was correct. For the new period's budget, one adjusts last period's figure upward or downward to take care of the current situation. Management monitors only the changes to the budgeted amounts. Whether last period's total cost was justified is not an issue. The amount of cost is assumed to have been essential to the company's objectives. It is also frequently assumed that, even with no management guidance, the department heads responsible for controlling the undistributed costs are practicing effective cost control, that they are keeping costs in line, and are preventing overspending. No doubt many of the expenses incurred in this category do meet these criteria. But it is likely that the reverse is also true in many establishments that use incremental budgeting.

ZBB can be used by hospitality industry managers to control these undistributed expenses. ZBB, properly implemented, cannot only control costs, but may lead to costs reduction from previous levels. The main reason for this is that it puts previously unjustified expenses on the same basis as requests for increases to the budget—increases that must also be justified.

DECISION UNITS

One of the key elements in successful implementation of ZBB is the decision unit. The number of decision units will vary with the size of each establishment. For example, a small operation with only one employee in its marketing department would probably have only one decision unit for marketing expenses. A larger organization might have several decision units for marketing. These units might be labeled sales, advertising, merchandising, public relations, and research. A very large organization might further break down these units into decision units covering different activities. For example, advertising might be broken down into a print decision unit and a radio and television decision unit.

Each decision unit is competing for the same limited resource dollars. Although it is not mandatory that each decision unit contain only one or two employees and related costs and have about the same total cost, it is easier for the general manager to evaluate each decision unit and to rank it against all other decision units. Once decision units have been established, the next step is for each department head to prepare an analysis of each separate decision unit that is his or her responsibility. This analysis is carried out each year before the new budget period begins. A properly designed form should be used so that each department head will present the data in a standard format. For each decision unit, the department head will document the following:

1. The unit's objective
2. The unit's current activities
3. Justification for continuation of the unit's activities
4. Alternate ways to carry out activities
5. Recommended alternatives
6. Required budget

Unit's Objective

Each decision unit's objective must obviously relate to the organization's overall objectives. For example, the objective of a hotel marketing department's print-advertising decision unit might read as follows:

> To seek out the most appropriate magazines, journals, newspapers, and other periodicals that can be used for advertising in the most effective way at the lowest cost to increase the number of guests using the hotel's facilities.

Current Activities

This statement would include the number of employees, their positions, a description of how the work is carried out, and the resources used. For example, a resource used by the print-advertising decision unit might be an external advertising agency.

The total cost of current activities would be included in this section. Also included would be a statement of how the unit's activities are measured. For example, this might be the number of guests using the hotel's facilities versus the cost of print advertising.

Justification for Continuation of a Unit's Activities

In the case of our print-advertising unit, this might include a statement that it would be advantageous for the unit to continue because the employees are familiar with the marketing strategy of the hotel and with the various operating departments and their special features. They know what special attractions to promote in the advertisements. The explanation should also include a statement of the disadvantages that would accrue if the decision unit's activities were discontinued.

Alternate Ways to Carry Out the Activities

In the example of the print-advertising decision unit, the alternatives might include taking over some of the work now given to the advertising agency, having the agency take over more of the unit's activities, having more of the work centralized in the head office (assuming the hotel is one of a chain), doing more head office work at the local level, or combining the print decision unit's activities with those of the radio and television advertising unit. The list should not be overly long, but it should include as many alternatives as would be practical and that differ from current activities.

Included with the list of alternatives would be the advantages and disadvantages of each alternative, and an estimate of the total annual cost.

Recommended Alternative

The department head responsible must then recommend the alternative that he or she would select for each unit. One alternative would be to stay with the current activities rather than make a change. The selection is based on a consideration of the pros, cons, practicality, and cost of each alternative.

Required Budget

The department head's final responsibility is to state the funding required for each decision unit for the next budget, based on the alternative recommended. This request starts out with a base, or minimum level. This minimum level may be established at a level below which the unit's activities would no longer exist or be worthwhile. Alternatively, the general manager might set the minimum level arbitrarily at, say, 60% of the current budget. Whatever the minimum level is set at becomes the established level; each activity above that level must be shown as an incremental cost. These incremental activities may or may not be subsequently approved.

RANKING PROCESS

Once the decision unit activities have been documented, the general manager begins the review process. To determine how much money will be spent, and in what areas or departments, the general manager must rank all activities in order of importance to the organization. Once this order is established, the activities would be accepted up to the total predetermined budget for all activities.

The major difficulty in ranking is to determine the order of priority for all the operation's activities under review. In a small organization, with the aid of a committee if necessary, this might not be too difficult. In larger operations, each department head might be asked to rank all activities that come within his or her authority. This procedure can then continue through successive levels of middle management until they reach the general manager.

Another approach might be for the general manager to approve automatically, say, the first 50% or 60% of all activities ranked within each department. The next 10% or 20% might then be ranked by middle management and also be automatically approved. Top management might subsequently review all these rankings, then rank the remainder and decide how many of them will be funded, along with any proposed new programs not adopted at lower levels.

The completed ranking process and approved expenditures constitute the new budgets for those areas or departments. This information can then be incorporated into the regular budget process. Theoretically, as a result of ZBB, the activities of that part of the organization have been examined, evaluated, modified, discontinued, or continued as before. This should produce the most effective budget possible. At the least, it should produce a budget that one can have more confidence in than one produced solely on an incremental basis.

ADVANTAGES OF ZBB

There are several advantages of ZBB:

- It concentrates on the dollar cost of each department's activities and budget and not on broad percentage increases.
- Funds can be reallocated to the departments or areas providing the greatest benefit to the organization.
- It provides a quality of information about the organization (because all activities are documented in detail) that would otherwise not be available.
- All levels of management are involved in the budgeting process, which encourages these employees to become familiar with activities that might not normally be under their control.
- Managers are obligated to identify inefficient or obsolete functions within their areas of responsibility.
- It can identify areas of overlap or duplication.

DISADVANTAGES OF ZBB

ZBB also has some possible disadvantages:

- It implies that the budgeting method in use is not adequate. This may or may not be true.
- It requires a great deal more time, effort, paperwork, and cost than traditional budgeting methods.
- It may be unfair to some department heads who, even though they may be very cost-effective in managing their departments, are not as capable as others in documentation and defense of their budgets. They might thus find themselves outranked by other more vocal, but less cost-effective, department heads.

VARIANCES

As each period goes by (day, week, month, quarter), budgeted figures should be compared with actual figures. This can best be done by summarizing the figures on a report by department or by type of cost. For example, one of the major and most difficult costs to control in a hotel or food operation is labor, and an ongoing comparison of actual with budgeted labor cost is useful in controlling this cost. An illustration of a type of report summarizing payroll costs is shown in Exhibit 9.5. The variances each day would require an explanation.

Department	Number of Hours Today Budget	Actual	Labor Cost Today Budget	Actual	Labor Cost to Date Budget	Actual	Labor Cost Variance Today	To Date
Rooms								
Front office	10	10	$ 440	$ 440	$1,320	$1,320		
Housekeeping	42	43	1,280	1,310	3,840	3,900	$+30	$+60
Service	8	8	320	320	960	930		−30
Switchboard	6	6	274	274	822	822		
Food								
Dining room	13	14	$ 456	$ 487	$1,368	$1,399	$+31	$+31
Coffee shop	7	6	245	217	735	707	−28	−28
Banquet	11	11	440	440	1,674	1,674		

Date: September 3

■ **EXHIBIT 9.5**
Sample Payroll Costs Summary and Analysis

VARIANCE ANALYSIS

When we compare budget figures and actual results, it is useful to analyze any difference for sales revenue and each expense item. This is called **variance analysis.** Let us consider the following situation:

Banquet Sales Revenue, March

Budget	Actual	Difference	
$75,000	$69,750	$5,250	(unfavorable)

In determining the amount of the variance, take the absolute value of the difference and then ask the question, "Does this variance increase or decrease operating income?" If it increases operating income, the variance is favorable. If it decreases operating income, the variance is unfavorable. Favorable is often indicated by using *F* and an unfavorable variance is often indicated by using *U*.

In this example, the difference is unfavorable because our actual total sales revenue was less than the amount budgeted and, therefore, will reduce operating income. If we analyze the budget and actual figures for a banquet operation, we might get the following additional information in the form of an overall budget variance:

Budget 5,000 guests × $15.00 average check = $75,000
Actual 4,500 guests × $15.50 average check = 69,750
Variance (unfavorable) $ 5,250

This variance amount is actually composed of two separate figures—a price variance that is the difference between the budgeted and the actual selling price, and a sales volume variance that is the difference between the budgeted number of guests and the actual volume of guests. The sales volume variance is calculated using the standard selling price per guest. These two types of variances are calculated as shown in the following subsections.

Price Variance

The price variance is the difference between the budgeted average check of $15.00 and the actual average check of $15.50. The average price achieved was $0.50 greater than the budgeted price per guest and is considered to be favorable since it will increase operating income:

$$\text{4,500 guests} \times \$0.50 = \underline{\$2,250} \text{ (favorable)}$$

Sales Volume Variance

The sales volume is the difference between the budgeted number of guests as units sold. When the budgeted number of guests is less than anticipated, the sales revenue inflow is also less than anticipated. The 500 fewer guests than was budgeted for is considered unfavorable because it will decrease operating income:

$$\text{500 guests} \times \$15.00 = \underline{\$7,500} \text{ (unfavorable)}$$

If we combine these results, our total budget variance is verified by showing the price and sales volume variances together:

Price variance	**$2,250**	**(favorable)**
Sales volume variance	**7,500**	**(unfavorable)**
Total variance	**$5,250**	**(unfavorable)**

Note that when you add a favorable and unfavorable variance, it is similar to adding a positive and negative number.

A variance analysis matrix can be used to show the budget variance and price and sales volume variances in a simple table format. Actual price and the budgeted or standard price are compared to determine if there is a price variance. As well, the budgeted volume and the actual volume are compared to determine if there is a sales volume variance.

To determine the amount of the variance, begin at the bottom of the total column and subtract each total from the total shown above. If the product is negative, such as ($7,500) below, the variance is unfavorable when dealing with sales revenue inflows since it reduces revenue and, therefore, net income:

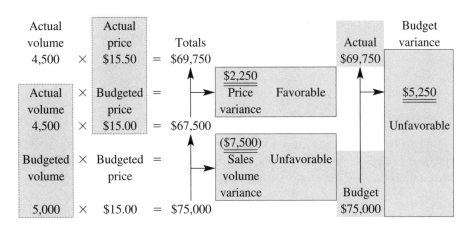

We now have information that tells us that the major reason for our difference between budget and actual sales revenue is a reduction in sales revenue of $7,500 due to serving fewer customers. This has been partly compensated for by $5,250 since the average banquet customer paid $0.50 more than the standard selling price. This tells us that our banquet sales department is probably doing an effective job in selling higher-priced menus to banquet groups, but is failing to bring in as many banquets or guests as anticipated.

Costs can be analyzed in the same way. Let us examine the following situation for the rooms department in a hotel:

Laundry Expense, June		
Budget	*Actual*	*Difference*
$8,250	**$9,300**	**$1,050** (**unfavorable**)

The difference is *unfavorable* because we spent more than we budgeted for and, therefore, *reduced net income*. With the following additional information, we can analyze this variance:

Budget 3,000 rooms sold (occupied) at $2.75 per room = $8,250
Actual 3,100 rooms sold (occupied) at $3.00 per room = 9,300
Budget variance (unfavorable) = $1,050

The $1,050 total variance is made up of two items: a cost variance and a sales volume variance.

Cost Variance

The **cost variance** is similar to the price variance discussed earlier in this chapter. The cost variance is $0.25 over budget for each room sold. This is an *unfavorable* trend:

$$3,100 \text{ rooms} \times \$0.25 = \underline{\$775.00} \text{ (unfavorable)}$$

Sales Volume Variance

The sales volume variance is 100 rooms (or units) over budget, at a budgeted cost of $2.75 per room. From a cost point of view, this is considered unfavorable because it decreases net income.

$$100 \text{ rooms} \times \$2.75 = \underline{\$275.00} \text{ (unfavorable)}$$

If we combine these results, our total variance looks like this:

Cost variance	**$ 775.00**	**(unfavorable)**
Sales volume variance	**275.00**	**(unfavorable)**
Total variance	**$1,050.00**	**(unfavorable)**

The variance analysis matrix shows the cost budget variance and cost and sales volume variances. Actual cost and the budgeted or standard cost are compared to determine the cost variance. The budgeted sales volume, and the actual sales volume are compared to find the amount of the sales volume variance. To determine if the cost variance is favorable or unfavorable, determine if it increases or decreases net income. Since the cost variance decreases net income in our example, it is unfavorable.

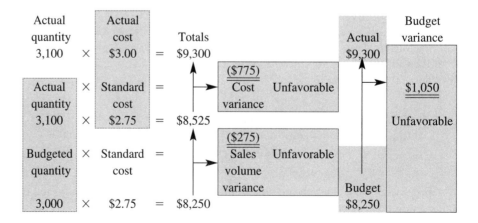

This tells us that, although our total variance was $1,050, or 12.7% [($1,050 / $8,250) × 100] over budget, only $775 is of concern to us. The remaining $275 was inevitable. If we sell more rooms, as we did, we would obviously have to pay the extra $275 for laundry. Even though this is considered unfavorable as a cost increase, we would not necessarily be concerned about it, since the unfavorable difference would be more than offset by the extra sales revenue received from selling the extra rooms. Whether the other $775 overspending is serious would depend on the cause. The cause could be a supplier increasing costs that we may, or may not, be able to do something about; or it could be that we actually sold more twin rooms than budgeted for (which would mean more sheets to be laundered and therefore cause our average laundry cost per room occupied to go up). In the latter case, the additional cost would be more than offset by the extra charge made for double occupancy of a room.

As illustrated, the detailed variance analysis is useful in understanding differences between budgeted and actual sales revenue or cost outflows.

Let us look at another example:

Coffee Shop Variable Wages, for May

Budget 4,350 hrs × $7.50 per hr = $32,625
Actual 4,100 hrs × $7.80 per hr = 31,980
Buget variance $ 645   (favorable)

Actual quantity 4,100	×	Actual cost $7.80	= $31,980					Actual $31,980	Budget variance
					$1,230 Cost variance	Unfavorable			$645
Actual quantity 4,100	×	Standard cost $7.50	= $30,750						Favorable
					($1,875) Sales volume variance	Favorable			
Budgeted quantity 4,350	×	Standard cost $7.50	= $32,625					Budget $32,625	

Note that the net variance is $645 favorable. Variance analysis shows that there was a $1,875 saving on labor due to a reduced number of hours paid, perhaps as a result of less business than budgeted for. However, the saving was reduced by $645 because the actual average hourly rate was $0.30 higher than budgeted for. Was there an increase in the hourly rate paid, or did unanticipated overtime occur because of poor scheduling, which would increase the average hourly rate paid? This would need to be investigated.

Therefore, variance analysis can provide additional information that is helpful in identifying causes of differences between actual and budgeted figures.

The final step in variance analysis is taking corrective action to ensure that procedures are in place to prevent undesirable situations from recurring. For example, investigation of the coffee shop example's increase in actual hourly pay rate may show that it was caused by too much overtime having been paid. To correct this situation, management might initiate new procedures that require the coffee shop manager to have the written approval of his or her supervisor before any overtime is paid.

Note that in this section differences or variances are labeled as favorable or unfavorable only as a matter of accounting convention. In this context, *favorable* is used for a variance that increases net income. Therfore, this is either an increase in sales revenue or a reduction in costs. *Unfavorable* is used for a variance that decreases net income and, therefore, it is either a reduction in sales revenue or an increase in costs.

The words *favorable* and *unfavorable* should not be equated with good or bad, respectively. Indeed, there may be situations in which an unfavorable variance reflects a positive situation, such as a cost increase that is labeled as unfavorable even though it is caused entirely by an increase in sales revenue that automatically necessitates an increase in costs. For example, to produce more food sales without changing prices, there will normally have to be an increase in food sold and, therefore, an increase in food used. In such a case, as long as the cost increase is in proportion to the sales revenue increase, the food cost percentage remains as budgeted, the *unfavorable* dollar food cost increase would be perfectly normal and acceptable.

Thus, the word *unfavorable* should not necessarily be interpreted as having a negative connotation. That judgment cannot be made until the cause of the change has been investigated.

PERCENTAGE VARIANCES

In analyzing variances, it may be useful to calculate **percentage variances.** Percentage variances are calculated by dividing the dollar variance by the budgeted figure for that item and multiplying by 100. For example, if the budgeted figure were $200 and the variance $15, the percentage variance would be as follows:

$$\left(\frac{\text{Variance}}{\text{Budgeted figure}}\right) \times 100 = \frac{\$15}{\$200} \times 100 = 7.5\%$$

It is unlikely that any sales revenue or controllable expense item will not have a variance because, even with comprehensive information available during the budgeting process, budgeted figures are still estimates. The variances to be analyzed are those that show significant differences from budgeted amounts. What is important in this significance test is the amount of the variance in both dollar and percentage terms, not just in one of them. If only one is used, it might not provide information that the other provides. For example, using dollar differences alone does not consider the magnitude of the base or budgeted figure, and the dollar difference might not be significant when compared to the base figure. To illustrate, if the dollar difference in sales revenue is $5,000 (which seems significant) but the budgeted sales revenue is $5,000,000, the percentage variance is

$$\frac{\$\ 5,000}{\$5,000,000} \times 100 = 0.1\%$$

This percentage variance is insignificant. If the actual sales revenue can be this close to the budget sales revenue in percentage terms, this would indicate remarkably effective budgeting. But this is not disclosed if only the dollar difference is considered. If a cost has a 0.1% variance, this variance must be considered along with the sales revenue. If sales revenue was different from budgeted sales revenue but at a cost variance of 0.1%, it is unlikely that the cost was well controlled.

Similarly, considering the percentage difference alone might not be useful. For example, if a particular expense for this same property was budgeted at $500, and the actual expense as $550, the variance of $50 represents 10% of the budget figure. Ten percent seems a large variance but is insignificant when the dollar figure is also considered. In other words, a variance of $50 is insignificant in a business with revenue of $5,000,000, and investigating it would not be worth anybody's time.

What is significant as a dollar and percentage variance depends entirely on the type and size of the establishment. Those responsible for budgets need to establish in advance the acceptable variances in both dollar figures and percentages for each sales revenue and expense item. At the end of each budget period, only those variances that exceed what is allowed in both dollar and percentage terms will be further analyzed and investigated.

FORECASTING

The methods for creating a budget have thus far been somewhat simplistic. However, many hospitality operations use more advanced, quantitatively oriented forecasting techniques, both in budgeting and where other forecasts are required. The ability to accurately forecast is an important aspect of any operation's management. Reliable methods are necessary to help operating department heads forecast sales and plan for the use of resources (e.g., labor and supplies to meet anticipated demand).

Two of the more commonly used techniques are moving averages and regression analysis. Moving averages is sometimes referred to as time-series methods, because it looks at the numbers for a series of past periods to see what patterns and/or relationships may be occurring. Regression analysis is an attempt to find a relation between one event and another.

The number of periods used depends on the forecast you are creating. You need to use enough periods of data so you have reduced the random variation that occurs. However, if you use too many periods of data, you will be using old data that might make the forecast inaccurate. Therefore, the manager must use judgment in deciding how many periods to use. If you want to forecast Sunday's sales revenue, you need to use Sunday's data to create the relationship. Similarly, if you want to forecast November's sales revenue, you need to use November's data. If you use 12 months of data, all the annual cyclical increases and decreases in demand, month-to-month variances, seasonal variations, and unusual external factors that affect such matters as room occupancy or restaurant volume will be included in the numbers. What has happened during the time series is then assumed to be likely to occur in the future and can thus be the basis of the forecast as long as that forecast is adjusted for the current situation by using good judgment.

MOVING AVERAGES

Most forecasts take into consideration past trends. Some trends can be daily ones used for a weekly projection. For example, most transient hotels have high occupancies at the beginning of each week, with a trend to reduced occupancies on Friday, Saturday, or Sunday.

Other trends may be seasonal ones where major changes in demand patterns occur as the climate changes or cyclical or long-run ones caused by economic events, such as a recession. Cyclical patterns are difficult to determine because historic figures are unreliable in indicating when these events are likely to occur again.

Nevertheless, by observation of past trends, a future trend can usually be built into the forecast figures. However, some variables are unpredictable (e.g., events that occur for no particular or observable reason, or sudden and drastic decreases in demand caused by severe and unusual weather conditions), and such random variables are difficult or even impossible to include in forecasts.

Moving averages attempt to remove the random variations that can occur from period to period in the operation of the typical hospitality business. Note that the larger the number of periods used, the less likely it is that any random causes will affect the moving average. To take care of those random variations for a monthly forecast, we can calculate a 12-month moving average. The 12 monthly figures for the past year are added together and then divided by 12. For example, suppose for the past year a small restaurant's monthly guest counts were as follows:

Month	Guest Count
1	2,406
2	2,502
3	1,986
4	1,829
5	2,312
6	2,587
7	2,804
8	3,009
9	3,102
10	2,748
11	2,406
12	2,312
Total	30,003

Rounded, the moving average is **30,003 / 12 = 2,500.**

This figure can be used (modified for the current situation and other variables) as the forecast for the thirteenth month. At the end of the thirteenth month, a new moving average is calculated for the fourteenth month by deleting from the total guest count the first month and including the guest count for the immediately past thirteenth month. As a result, the average is constantly recalculated (thus, the term *moving average*) by including only the most up-to-date figures for the number of periods used.

In calculating the moving average total, it is only necessary to list each of the figures for the number of periods under review when the method is first used. After that, deducting the figure for the earlier period in the series, and adding the figure for the most recent period, will update the total figure. Therefore, keeping the moving average up to date is a simple task.

For example, if the actual guest count in the thirteenth month was 2,296, the new 12-month total would be:

$$30,003 - 2,406 + 2,296 = \underline{\underline{29,893}}$$

and the forecast for the fourteenth month, rounded, is:

$$29,893 / 12 = \underline{\underline{2,491}}$$

In general, the moving average can be expressed by the following equation:

Total for each of the previous *n* periods
$$\frac{}{n}$$

where *n* is the number of periods being used; in our case, 12.

One minor problem with the moving average is that it gives equal weight to each of the periods used in the calculation. For example, in the case of monthly periods, each month is treated like any other. This can be risky in forecasting for the month of February, because the average is based on the typical month having 30.42 days (365 / 12), whereas February has only 28 (or 29) days. However, this is where individual adjustments can be made to the raw moving average produced, using the general equation. As well, if the operation is located in an area with high summer sales revenue, sales in February can be low compared to the rest of the year.

An important question with regard to a moving average is the best number of periods (*n*) to include. On one hand, with a large number, the forecast tends to react slowly to changes in sales volume. On the other hand, a small number provides a forecast that more quickly reflects more recent changes in the time series. A small number of periods might also not reduce the random variation enough to provide an accurate forecast. One solution is to try moving averages of different lengths to determine which one seems to provide the most accurate forecast.

Also, in using a time series of 12 months, the average is influenced by what happened up to a year ago, and the current operating environment might have changed considerably from that time. Again, this is where personal judgment must be used in refining the raw moving average figure to adjust it to today's reality.

REGRESSION ANALYSIS

In some large hospitality operations, the forecast for one department may depend on what happens in another. For example, as the number of guests in a hotel's rooms increases or decreases, there are similar increases and decreases in the sales revenue volume of the restaurants and bars. This is known as a causal relationship (or derived demand) because what happens in the rooms department causes changes in the food and beverage department. Accurate forecasting in the rooms and the food and beverage departments is important because, in many hospitality operations, they provide as much as 80% to 90% of total food and beverage sales revenue.

Regression analysis is a forecasting technique that allows a restaurant to forecast its sales revenue based on the forecast of rooms occupancy. We have already seen regression analysis used in Chapter 7 for separating fixed and variable costs. In our new situation, regression analysis simply uses the independent variable to forecast the numbers for the dependent variable. In regression analysis, restaurant sales revenue in terms of meals served are the dependent variable Y (because food sales depend on the rooms occupancy) and the room sales in terms of number of guest nights are the independent variable X.

Suppose that the following summarizes the room guests and restaurant meals served each month last year:

	Guest Nights (X)	Meals Served (Y)
January	6,102	7,822
February	6,309	7,544
March	6,384	8,021
April	6,501	8,299
May	6,498	8,344
June	6,382	8,245
July	6,450	8,311
August	6,522	8,274
September	6,608	8,328
October	6,502	8,188
November	6,274	7,985
December	5,811	7,502
Totals	$\Sigma X = 76{,}343$	$\Sigma Y = 96{,}863$

Even though we intuitively know that there is a strong relationship between room occupancy and restaurant meals served, we also know that some people who are not hotel guests eat in the restaurant. The regression analysis formula used in Chapter 7 effectively handles the determination of variable and fixed elements of sales revenue. In this situation we will use the alternative regression formula that determines variable and fixed elements on a unit basis. Therefore, we must determine a and b for the following equation:

$$Y = a + bX$$

Where: Y = number of restaurant meals (breakfast, lunch, or dinner)
a = meals served to customers not registered in the hotel
b = average number of meals each hotel guest has per day
X = number of guest nights

The values for a and b are calculated using the following two equations:

$$b = \frac{n\Sigma XY - \Sigma X \Sigma Y}{n(\Sigma X^2) - (\Sigma X)^2}$$

$$a = \text{average of } Y - (b \times \text{average of } X)$$

Using information provided from Exhibit 9.6, the solution to b is calculated as follows:

$$b = \frac{12(616,852,495) - (76,343)(96,863)}{12(486,221,719) - (76,343)(76,343)}$$

$$= \frac{7,402,229,940 - 7,394,812,009}{5,834,660,628 - 5,828,253,649}$$

$$= \frac{7,417,931}{6,406,979} = 1.16$$

To calculate a, we must first calculate the average of Y and the average of X:

$$\text{Average of } Y = \frac{96,863}{12} = \underline{\underline{8,072}}$$

$$\text{Average of } X = \frac{76,343}{12} = 6,362$$

$$a = 8,072 - (1.16 \times 6,362)$$

$$= 8,072 - 7,380 = 692$$

Month	Guest Nights X	Meals Served Y	XY (X × Y)	X² (X × X)
1	6,102	7,822	47,729,844	37,234,404
2	6,309	7,544	47,595,096	39,803,481
3	6,384	8,021	51,206,064	40,755,456
4	6,501	8,299	53,951,799	42,263,001
5	6,498	8,344	54,219,312	42,224,004
6	6,382	8,245	52,619,590	40,729,924
7	6,450	8,311	53,605,950	41,602,500
8	6,522	8,274	53,963,028	42,536,484
9	6,608	8,328	55,031,424	43,665,664
10	6,502	8,188	53,238,376	42,276,004
11	6,274	7,985	50,097,890	39,363,076
12	5,811	7,502	43,594,122	33,767,721
Total	76,343	96,863	616,852,495	486,221,719

■ **EXHIBIT 9.6**

Calculation of Regression Analysis Data

Our result, thus, shows us the following:

$$Y = 692 + 1.16 \ (X)$$

This means the value of (Y) shows that on average, 692 customers who are not registered as hotel guests eat in the restaurant each month and (X) shows that each registered guest room occupant on average eats 1.16 meals each day in the restaurant. We can use this equation to forecast the restaurant's sales revenue volume based on the guest night forecast.

For example, suppose in January the forecast guest night count is 6,200. The restaurant's forecast of meals served will be:

$$692 + (1.16 \times 6,200)$$

$$692 + 7,192 = 7,884$$

Finally, note that regression analysis forecasting relies on the assumption that the past relationship between X and Y remains the same during the forecast period.

LIMITATIONS OF FORECASTING

Limitations of forecasting techniques, such as those illustrated in this section, include:

- Their use provides precise mathematical results that are only as good as the data used. For example, if the guest night forecasts are not very good, then the forecast for restaurant meals served will not be very good.
- The mathematical approaches used in forecasting do not consider variables that can be controlled by management. For example, a forecast of restaurant volume based on historic sales revenue would need to be adjusted for an anticipated increase in demand resulting from an increased advertising campaign that the restaurant manager is planning to implement.
- No mathematical forecasting technique can substitute for experience and individual judgment. Indeed, in some cases (such as opening a new property or expanding an existing one) there may be only limited data available on which to base mathematical forecasting techniques, such as moving averages or regression analysis. In such cases, judgment and other qualitative considerations have to play a greater role.
- Forecasting involves the future, which is always unpredictable. The longer the time between the date the forecast is made and the period of the forecast, the more likely it is that unpredictable events are going to affect the forecasts. As a result, forecasts are bound to be less accurate than the manager would like. However, forecasts can always be revised as time goes by to adjust to changed circumstances.

- Because forecasting deals with the future, it also deals with uncertainty. This should not be a problem for most managers because managers in the hospitality industry typically face many daily uncertainties.

- Most forecasting methods are based on data from the past and use historic information adjusted for the future. Unfortunately, historic data are often not good indicators of the future. Again, a manager can adapt to this by using common sense and good judgment to adjust forecasts based solely on historic information.

- Because of all of these factors, most operations know that forecasts are likely to deviate from the actual and they automatically build in a variance factor of as much as 10%. The actual deviation percentage used can be based on experience. For example, if an analysis of the past shows that actual results invariably differed by 5% from those forecast, then a 5% variance can be built into future forecasts.

CHOOSING A FORECASTING METHOD

Studies show that the lowest forecasting errors result from the use of trend projections, moving averages, and regression analysis rather than judgmental methods. What is important is not the actual forecasting method used, but how effective the forecasts are and their practical value in the operation.

In a small hospitality operation that can adapt quickly to changing circumstances, most forecasting will be done using simple methods, such as adjusting the sales for the coming month by a certain percentage increase or decrease over last year's or last month's, or by using the fairly simple moving average method. Larger enterprises will probably use more complex methods, such as regression analysis.

Even though the regression analysis method requires more work, it does not require tedious manual calculations because most calculators are programmed to perform the arithmetic once each series of X and Y variables have been entered. Spreadsheets can be used for budgeting, forecasting, and variance analysis. Once sales revenue forecasts have been completed, they can be used to help determine the quantities of items such as food and beverages to be purchased and when they should be purchased.

COMPUTER APPLICATIONS

Computer software, such as a spreadsheet program, makes the budgeting process much easier. There are forecasting computer packages available, but a spreadsheet can perform the necessary moving average and regression analysis calculations. Spreadsheets can build in regression analysis formulas. For example, the calculations required in Exhibit 9.6 and all the subsequent calculations were produced using a spreadsheet. A spreadsheet can also compare budgeted figures with actual ones and produce the variances. They can be used to produce graphs that present the forecast, actual, and variance information.

S U M M A R Y

Budgeting is part of the planning process. It can involve decisions concerning the day-to-day management of an operation or involve plans for as far ahead as five years.

The various types of budgets include capital, operating, departmental, master, fixed, and flexible.

Budgeting has three main purposes:

1. To provide estimates of future sales revenues and expenses
2. To provide short- and long-term coordinated management policy
3. To provide control by comparing actual results with budgeted plans and to take corrective action, if necessary

In a small operation, budgets can be prepared by an individual or by a committee in a large organization. In all cases, whether for a day, a year, or some other period, budgets should be prepared in advance of the start of the period. There are several advantages of budgets:

- They involve participation of employees in the planning process, thus improving motivation and communication.
- They necessitate, in budget preparation, consideration of alternative courses of action.
- They provide a goal, and a standard of performance to be accomplished, with subsequent comparison of actual results with that standard.
- If flexible budgets are used, they permit quick adaptation to unforeseen, changed conditions.
- They require those involved to be forward-looking, rather than looking only at past events.

The budgeting cycle is a five-part process:

1. Establish attainable goals (remember the limiting factors).
2. Plan to achieve these goals.
3. Analyze differences between planned and actual results.
4. Take any necessary corrective action.
5. Improve the effectiveness of budgeting.

The starting point in budgeting is to forecast sales revenue. In a large company, department managers would make such forecasts. In forecasting, one must consider past actual sales revenue and trends, current anticipated trends, and the economic, competitive, and limiting factors.

Once sales revenue has been forecast, direct operating expenses can be calculated based on anticipated sales revenue, and, finally, undistributed expenses can be deducted to arrive at the net income for the operation. Once the departmental and general income statement budgets have been prepared, other required budgets such as balance sheets and capital budgets can be made, if required.

If there is no historic information available, which would be the case in a new venture, then forecasting sales revenue and expenses is more difficult. Quite a bit more educated estimating is required.

Zero-base budgeting (ZBB) is another method of forecasting and controlling. With ZBB each category of cost is broken down into decision units that are then analyzed. The department head responsible for the cost prepares the analysis. After each decision unit is analyzed, management ranks all decision units, and the final budget is allocated according to this ranking.

Variance analysis is a useful technique for isolating the causes of differences between budgeted and actual figures. These differences are broken down into price and sales volume variances when analyzing sales revenue figures or cost and quantity variances when analyzing expense figures.

The chapter concluded with a section on forecasting techniques. The moving average and regression analysis methods were illustrated. The limitations of using mathematical techniques in forecasting were summarized.

DISCUSSION QUESTIONS

1. Explain the concept of budgeting.
2. What are some of the purposes of budgeting?
3. List and discuss three advantages of budgeting.
4. Explain the difference between long- and short-term budgeting.
5. Give an example of:
    a. A hotel departmental budget
    b. A capital budget for a restaurant
6. Explain the difference between a fixed and a flexible budget.
7. Two of the steps in the budgeting cycle are establishing attainable goals and planning to achieve these goals. What are the other three steps?
8. Discuss three possible limiting factors to consider in preparing a budget for a hotel or restaurant.
9. A cocktail lounge had sales revenue in May of $40,000. Budgeted revenue was $42,000. List three possible questions that could be asked, the answers to which might explain the $2,000 difference.

10. In projecting sales revenue for breakfast in the coffee shop of a hotel, what factors need to be considered?

11. What is derived demand?

12. List the four items that must be multiplied by each other to forecast total annual food sales revenue for the dinner period of a restaurant.

13. What is a pro forma income statement?

14. List three types of cost that are controllable with ZBB.

15. Give an example of a decision unit in a hotel's accounting office and write a one-sentence objective for that decision unit.

16. Briefly describe the ranking process under ZBB.

17. Give two advantages and two disadvantages of ZBB.

18. Briefly explain how the use of a moving average works as a forecasting method.

19. Using an example, explain what an unfavorable cost variance is.

20. Using an example, explain what a favorable sales volume variance is.

21. Explain the difference between a sales volume variance and a quantity variance.

E T H I C S   S I T U A T I O N

After the hotel general manager and his department heads have produced the budget for next year, the general manager decides to change some of the figures to produce a $10,000 higher profit. The general manager plans to use this changed budget to convince the hotel's owner that the manager's request for a $5,000 increase in salary is justified. Discuss the ethics of this situation.

E X E R C I S E S

E9.1 A restaurant has 100 seats with an average turnover of 2.5, with an average check of $14.75. The restaurant is open 260 days a year. What is the estimated sales revenue for the year?

E9.2 A motel operation has 80 rooms, an occupancy rate of 62%, and an average room rate of $74.00. The owner wants you to give an estimate of sales revenue for the month of April. What is the estimated sales revenue?

E9.3 A motel had budgeted an occupancy of 8,000 rooms with a selling price of $82 per room and a variable housekeeping cost of $4.40 per room. Actual data indicated that a total of 8,480 rooms were sold at an average selling price of $77 per room and the actual cost of housekeeping per room was $4.90 per room. Answer the following about the housekeeping costs:

a. What is the budget variance? Is it favorable or unfavorable?

b. What is the cost variance? Is it favorable or unfavorable?

c. What is the quantity volume variance? Is it favorable or unfavorable?

E9.4 Using the same information in E9.3, answer the following about the sales revenue:

a. What is the budget variance? Is it favorable or unfavorable?

b. What is the price variance? Is it favorable or unfavorable?

c. What is the sales volume variance? Is it favorable or unfavorable?

E9.5 Assume you had a guest count for the first 3 months of the year. In January, the count was 1,670; in February the count was 1,880; and in March the count was 2,882. What was the moving average guest count for the first three months of the year?

E9.6 You manage a small motel that has 45 rooms, with an average room rate of $58 on a 76% occupancy rate. Fixed costs are $480,000 and the *VC* per room sold is $8.00. What do you anticipate your annual operating income (before tax) to be in the coming year?

E9.7 An 80-seat coffee shop is open for all three meals every day of the year. Calculate sales revenue for the coming year. Seat turnover and average check figures are as follows:

	Turnover	*Average Check*
Breakfast	2.50	$ 7.80
Lunch	1.75	8.75
Dinner	2.75	11.25

E9.8 Calculate the room sales revenue for a 50-room motel for the first 3 months of the year. Assume February is not in a leap year and has 28 days. The following information is given:

	Room Rate	*Occupancy*
January	$78.00	65%
February	$87.00	72%
March	$94.00	75%

E9.9 A 70-room motel's average room rate is $125. Its average occupancy is 74%. Fixed costs are $1,056,000 a year and variable costs are $212,704 a year. Calculate the motel's operating income for the year.

E9.10 A restaurant has budgeted sales revenue of $912,000 for the next year. Variable costs are 72% of sales revenue and fixed cost is $102,000. Answer the following questions:

    a. What are the total variable costs in dollars?

    b. What is the restaurant's gross margin expected to be?

    c. What is the amount of operating income (before tax)?

P R O B L E M S

P9.1 A motel has 40 units. During the month of June, its average room rate is expected to be $80, and its room occupancy 74%. In July, the owner is planning to raise room rates by 10%, and occupancy is expected to be 84%. In August no further room rate raises are contemplated, but occupancy is expected to be up to 92%. For each of the three months of June, July, and August, calculate the budgeted rooms sales revenue.

P9.2 As the manager of the 60-room motel, you have the responsibility of preparing next year's budget from the following information:

- Annual occupancy: 74%
- Average room rate: $84
- Variable costs per room occupied: $8
- Annual fixed costs: $825,000

Prepare the Motorway Motel's budget for next year. Assume a 365-day year.

P9.3 A dining room has 66 seats. It is open only for lunch and dinner 6 days a week (closed Sundays). This particular August has four Sundays. Round your calculations to the nearest dollar. Management has forecast the following:

	Seat Turnover	*Average Food Check*
Lunch	1.75	$12.95
Dinner	2.75	$16.95

Beverage sales revenue normally averages 15% of lunch food sales revenue and 32% of dinner food sales revenue. Calculate total budgeted food sales revenue and beverage sales revenue for the month.

P9.4 A hotel coffee shop has 120 seats and is open 7 days a week for all three-meal periods. During the month of January, it anticipates the following seat turnovers and average food checks:

	Turnover	*Average Check*
Breakfast	1.50	$ 7.50
Lunch	2.00	$ 9.50
Dinner	1.50	$12.50

Calculate the budgeted sales revenue for the coffee shop for January.

P9.5 The manager of Buff's Buffet is preparing next year's budget. She wants to prepare a flexible budget for three different annual sales revenue levels using a contribution margin income statement. Three levels of sales revenue are to be used: $800,000, $900,000, $1,000,000. The following information is available to help prepare the flexible budget.

- Food cost averages 38% and variable costs averages 28% of sales revenue.
- Fixed labor cost is $52,000 annually, and other fixed costs are $120,000.
- Other variable costs average 10% of sales revenue.
- Income tax rate is estimated to be 29% on operating income (before tax).

Using the given information, prepare Buff's flexible three-level budget using the contribution margin method. Also calculate the breakeven sales. Comment on the results of each budget level with particular reference to the effect of higher sales revenue on net income (after tax).

P9.6 A resort hotel has a dining room that has no business from street trade; it is dependent solely on the occupancy of its rooms for its sales revenue. It has 150 rooms. During the month of June it expects 80% occupancy of those rooms. Because the resort caters to the family trade, there are, on average, three people per occupied room per night.

From experience, management knows that 95% of the people occupying rooms eat breakfast, 25% eat lunch, and 75% eat dinner in the hotel dining room (some of the units have kitchen facilities, which is why some of the resort's guests do not use the dining room). The dining room opens 7 days a week for all three meals. Its average meal prices are as follows:

Breakfast	$ 7.50
Lunch	$12.50
Dinner	$25.20

Calculate the budgeted dining room revenue for the month of June.

P9.7 A 120-seat family restaurant is open Mondays to Saturdays only for lunch and dinner. On Sundays and holidays, totaling 60 days annually, the restaurant is open for dinner only. During the coming year, the owner anticipates the following:

	Seat Turnover	*Average Check*
Weekday lunch	1.50	$ 8.50
Weekday dinner	1.25	$18.50
Sunday and holiday dinner	2.00	$21.00

In addition, the restaurant has a small private party room and estimates its food sales revenue to be $144,000 next year. Beverage sales revenue is 12% of lunch food sales revenue and 25% of weekday dinner food sales revenue (no beverages are served Sundays and holidays). In addition, beverage sales revenue for private party room averages 40% of its total food sales revenue. Food cost averages 37% of total food revenue, and beverage cost averages 33% of total beverage revenue. Fixed salaries are estimated to be $284,000. The variable wage cost averages 15% of total restaurant revenue. Employee benefits average 12% of total fixed and variable wage cost. Other operating costs are expressed as percentages of total sales revenue from all food and beverage sales:

Cost	*Percentage*
China, glass, silver, linen	1.7%
Laundry	1.5%
Supplies	3.2%
Menus and beverage lists	0.8%
Advertising	2.0%
Repairs and maintenance	1.5%
Miscellaneous expense	1.0%
Total variable operating costs	11.7%

Fixed Operating Overhead Costs	
Administration and general	$48,000
Licenses	15,000
Rent	90,000
Equipment depreciation	73,400

Prepare the restaurant's budgeted income statement for next year using the preceding information. For purposes of this problem, ignore income tax. Also, round figures to the nearest whole dollar where necessary.

P9.8 A restaurant's average monthly income statement is as follows:

Sales Revenue		
Food sales revenue	$40,000	
Beverage sales revenue	10,000	
Total Sales Revenue		$50,000
Cost of Sales		
Food (42% of food revenue)	$16,800	
Beverage (30% of beverage revenue)	3,000	
Total Cost of Sales		(19,800)
Gross Margin		$30,200
Operating Expenses		
Wages expense	$13,600	
Operating supplies expense	4,000	
Administration & general expense	2,600	
Advertising & promotion expense	1,800	
Repairs & maintenance expense	900	
Utilities expense	1,300	
Depreciation expense	700	
Interest expense	600	
Total Operating Expenses		(25,500)
Operating Income		$ 4,700

The owner is considering two possible alternatives for the coming year:

- Alternative 1: By improving purchasing and reducing portions, cutting the food cost from 42% to 37% food sales revenue. There would be no other changes.
- Alternative 2: Cutting the food costs from 42% to 37% of food sales revenue and spending an additional $2,000 a month on advertising. It is estimated that the advertising would bring in extra customers and increase the volume of both food and beverage sales revenue by 20% over current levels. The extra customers would also incur extra costs over current levels as follows:

Wages	$2,000
Supplies	800
Administration	200
Repairs	300
Utilities costs	100

Prepare budgeted average monthly income statements for both alternatives and advise the owner which alternative you consider the best, and why.

P9.9 **a.** Budgeted liquor sales revenue at a banquet were 1,500 drinks at $5.00 each. Actual sales were 1,550 drinks at $4.80 each. Determine the price and sales volume variances.

b. Banquet food sales revenue for a month were estimated to be 20,000 covers at $14.00 each. Actual sales were 21,500 customers at $13.50 each. Determine the price and sales volume variances.

c. Budgeted banquet food cost for a week was 1,000 covers at $6.00 each. Actual covers were 900 at $6.25 each. Determine the cost and sales volume variances.

d. A snack bar budgets 14,000 covers with an average check of $6.45, and an average cost per customer of $2.45. Actual results were 14,800 customers, and an average check of $6.75; average cost per cover was $2.25. Determine the price and sales volume variances for sales revenue, and the cost and sales volume variances for the expense.

e. At a convention buffet, 400 customers are expected, and it is estimated that one waitress will be required for each 20 anticipated guests (for serving beverages). Basic wage rate is $8.00 an hour, and a minimum of 4 hours must be paid each waitress. No overtime is anticipated, but it might occur. Calculate the budgeted payroll cost for this function. After the event, payroll records indicate that a total of 84 hours were actually worked at a total actual labor cost of $714. Analyze total payroll for cost and quantity variances.

P9.10 An 80-room motel forecasts its average room rate to be $68.00 for next year at 75% occupancy. The rooms department has a fixed wage cost of $186,000. Variable wage cost for housekeeping is $9.00 an hour; it takes one-half hour to clean a room. Fringe benefits are 18% of total wages. Linen, laundry, supplies, and other direct costs are $2.75 per occupied room per day.

The motel also has a 50-seat, limited-menu snack bar. Breakfast revenue is derived solely from customers staying overnight in the motel. On average, 40% of occupied rooms are occupied by two persons and, on average, 80% of overnight guests will eat breakfast. Average breakfast check is $6.50. Lunch seat turnover is 1.5, with an average check of $8.95. The average dinner check is $10.95 and there are 2.0 seat turnovers for dinner. The snack bar is open 365 days a year for all three meals. Direct costs for the snack bar are 78% of total snack bar sales revenue. Indirect costs for the motel are estimated at $580,800 for next year.

a. Calculate a budgeted contributory income statement for each department and a consolidated total motel departmental income statement to determine operating income.

b. Assume that at the end of next year, actual sales revenue was based on 21,700 rooms occupied at an average room rate of $68.40. Actual housekeeping wages (before employee fringe benefits) were $108,208. Analyze rooms sales revenue for price and sales volume variances, and housekeeping wages for cost, quantity, and sales volume variances. Assume it took 32 minutes to clean each room occupied (sold).

P9.11 You have been asked to help prepare the operating budget for a proposed new 100-room motel, with a 65-seat coffee shop, 75-seat dining room, and 90-seat cocktail lounge. The operating budget for the first year will be based on the following information:

Rooms Department: Occupancy is 64% with an average room rate of $72. Fixed wages for bellpeople, front-office employees, and other personnel attached to the rooms department are estimated at $326,900. In addition, for every 16 rooms occupied each day, one housekeeper will be required for an eight-hour shift at a rate of $8.50 an hour. Staff fringe benefits will be 12% of total wages. Linen and laundry costs will be 6% of total rooms sales revenue. Supplies and other items will be 3% of total rooms sales revenue.

Food Department: The dining room is open 6 days a week, 52 weeks a year for lunch and dinner only. Lunch seat turnover is 1.5, with an average food check of $8.25. Dinner seat turnover is 1.0, with an average food check of $14.00.

The coffee shop is open 7 days a week for all meal periods. Breakfast seat turnover is 1.0, with an average food check of $5.75. Lunch seat turnover is 1.5 with an average food check of $7.75. Dinner seat turnover is 1.0, with a $9.95 average food check. Coffee shop seat turnover for coffee breaks and snacks is 6.0, with an average check of $1.75.

The cocktail lounge serves an estimated 20 food orders per day, with an $8.50 average check. The lounge is closed on Sundays and certain holidays and only operates for 310 days during the year.

Total payroll costs, including fringe benefits in the food department, will be 45% of total food sales revenue. Other costs, variable as a percentage of total food sales revenue, follow:

Food cost	35%
Laundry and linen	2%
Supplies	5%
Other costs	2%

Beverage Department (310 operating days a year): Each seat in the cocktail lounge is expected to generate $5,250 per year. In addition, the lounge will be credited with any alcoholic beverages served in the coffee shop and dining room. In the coffee shop, beverage sales revenue is estimated to be 15% of combined lunch and dinner food sales revenue, and in the dining room 25% of combined lunch and dinner food sales revenue. The beverage department operating costs are as follows:

- Liquor cost is 32% of total beverage sales revenue.
- Payroll and fringe benefits are 25% of total beverage sales revenue.
- Supplies and other operating costs are 5% of total beverage sales revenue.

From the preceding information, prepare contributory income statements for the first year of operations for each of the three departments. Then combine departmental contributory incomes in a combined departmental operating budget format showing a combined total contributory figure, and deduct the following undistributed, indirect costs to arrive at a budgeted income before depreciation, interest, and income tax. (In this problem, round all final numbers to the nearest dollar.)

Administrative and general	$156,800
Marketing	147,600
Utilities costs	58,900
Property operation & maintenance	52,400
Insurance	15,300
Property taxes	82,100

P9.12 You have the following guest-nights and meals-served figures for the past 12 months for the Inland Inn.

	Guest Nights	*Meals Served*
January	5,509	7,301
February	5,811	7,522
March	5,896	7,555
April	6,022	7,732
May	5,999	7,827
June	5,886	7,752
July	5,973	7,866
August	6,001	7,798
September	6,114	7,851
October	6,027	7,658
November	5,798	7,487
December	5,621	7,009
	70,657	91,358

Use regression analysis to solve the hotel's equation $Y = a + bX$.

P9.13 The manager of the Hospitality Inn has developed regression analysis equations for forecasting the hotel's dining room sales volume based on the hotel's anticipated guest-night count. The monthly equations (where *Y* equals the forecast number of meals to be served, and *X* equals the number of hotel guests) follow:

Breakfast	$Y = 750 + 0.82\,X$
Lunch	$Y = 900 + 1.15\,X$
Dinner	$Y = 1,200 + 0.42\,X$

The hotel has 100 rooms. Its occupancy in November is expected to be 70% and its double occupancy rate is 40%.

The average meal checks follow:

Breakfast	$ 5.25
Lunch	$10.24
Dinner	$15.78

Calculate the dining room's forecast meal period sales, both in number of guests and sales revenue dollars, for the month of November.

CASE 9

a. As a step in preparation of the 4C Company's preliminary budget for Year 2008, calculate the forecast sales revenue based on Year 2007 actual results adjusted as follows: dinner seat turnover figures will not change (see Case 6). Note that at lunch the guest-count figure will increase as a result of the advertising plan (Case 7). The average food check for lunch will increase by $0.60 while the average beverage check for lunch will increase by $0.20. For dinner, the average food check will increase by $0.55 while the average beverage check will increase by $0.40. No additional seats will be added in the restaurant, and operating days will remain the same. Calculate the total forecast sales revenue for food and beverages.

b. Complete the budgeted income statement for Year 2008 with reference to Case 8 (for fixed and variable cost data) and the following additional information:

■ Food and beverage variable cost of sales percentages will remain as in Year 2007 (Case 3).
■ Salaries and wages. First deduct Charlie's salary of $18,000 from the Year 2007 total. Add the cost of the new employee to be hired as the result of the newspaper advertising (see Case 7). Apply a general across-the-board 4% increase for all employees (except Charlie) for Year 2008. Then add on Charlie's salary, which will be $35,000 and is considered as a fixed cost next year.

■ Laundry variable cost percentage to sales revenue will remain unchanged.

■ Kitchen fuel. Fixed amount will increase by $400; the variable portion percentage to sales revenue will remain unchanged (Case 8).

■ China and tableware and glassware variable costs percentages to sales revenue will remain unchanged (Case 8).

■ Contract cleaning. A $600 increase is anticipated in Year 2008.

■ Licenses. No change is anticipated.

■ Other operating variable cost percentages to total sales revenue will not change (Case 8).

■ Administrative and general. A 5% increase should be budgeted for in Year 2008.

■ Marketing. The only increase will be the $3,000 to be spent on newspaper advertising (Case 7).

■ Utilities costs. The fixed cost is expected to rise by $2,000, and the variable portion percentage to sales revenue will be as before (Case 8).

■ Insurance. A 10% increase is expected.

■ Rent. As agreed with the building owner, rental expense is to increase by 10%, as was contracted for after the first year (Case 2).

■ Interest expense will decrease to $19,500.

■ Depreciation will continue to use the straight-line depreciation basis.

■ Income tax will be 22% of operating income (before tax).

c. Assume Charlie achieves the results in the Year 2008 budget. Using the budgeted income statement for Year 2008, compare it to the actual results for Year 2007 (Case 2). Discuss the dollar and percent changes to cost of sales, operating expenses, operating income, and net income. Also use common-size analysis to compare the Year 2008 budget and the Year 2007 actual (Case 3). If Charlie achieves the Year 2008 budget, will the operations be financially successful?

CHAPTER 10

STATEMENT OF CASH FLOWS AND WORKING CAPITAL ANALYSIS

INTRODUCTION

Historically, profit-oriented businesses have used the accrual basis of accounting to create the income statement, balance sheet, statement of ownership equity, and a statement of cash flows. Financial statements serve as a basis for measuring operating performance, financial position, ownership status, and an analysis of cash flows over a given accounting period.

Accrual financial statements indicate profitability (the income statement) and solvency or net worth (the balance sheet). However, these statements include noncash sales revenues and noncash expenses. Therefore, the basic balance sheet and income statement cannot in themselves answer questions regarding cash inflows and cash outflows that have occurred during an operating period.

The primary purpose of the statement of cash flows (SCF) is to identify and report the effects of cash receipts and cash disbursements for three specific areas of business activities. Normally, a business operates within three specific areas of activity that occur over an operating period—operations, investing, and financing.

The day-to-day management of current assets (CA) and current liabilities (CL) is an important aspect of management of any business operation and as such working capital analysis shares the concept of identifying cash inflows and outflows, which increase or decrease working capital ($CA - CL$). Coupled with the SCF, the statement of changes to working capital identifies sources (inflows) and uses (outflows) or working capital.

CHAPTER OBJECTIVES

After studying this chapter, the reader should be able to

1. Define the purpose of the statement of cash flows.
2. Identify the three sections of the statement of cash flows and explain the nature of the types of transactions.
3. Explain the effect that changes in current asset and current liability accounts have on the adjustment of accrual net income or net loss to cash-based net income or net loss.
4. Explain how depreciation expense, amortization expense, and gains or losses on the disposal of noncurrent assets apply in increasing or decreasing the adjustment to net income.
5. Define *working capital*.
6. List and briefly explain some of the sources and uses that change working capital.
7. Prepare a change to working capital accounts and identify the net change to working capital.
8. Explain why cash does not always increase by an amount equal to net income.
9. Explain the common uses of major elements in both the statement of cash flows and the various statements used to analyze working capital.
10. Explain whether the hospitality industry can operate on a relatively low current ratio.

CASH FLOWS

The **statement of cash flows (SCF)** provides a foundation to predict future cash flows. The ability to forecast cash needs and cash availability to purchase capital assets, repay noncurrent debt, and other noncurrent balance sheet items is essential. Owners and creditors assume that if a business generates positive cash flows in the past, the business will likely generate positive cash flows in the future. Since the SCF reports the business's ability to generate cash, it provides this information about cash availability. In addition, SCF can serve as a basis for the evaluation of management's performance regarding cash management.

EVALUATING NET CASH FLOWS

In a hospitality operation, it is possible for an operation to have positive net income and, at the same time, produce a negative cash flow, or to show a net loss and have a positive cash flow. The *operating section* of a statement of cash flows adjusts and reconciles the accural net income or net loss for an operating period to the net cash flow from operations. It is the change in the cash account, which is identified when net cash flow, either positive or negative, is equal to the change in the cash account and the actual cash on hand at the end of the period is confirmed.

Cash includes cash on hand, cash in the bank, and cash equivalents. Cash equivalents typically consist of marketable securities and short-term investments, which can be immediately converted to cash when the need dictates. In this discussion, cash equivalents, marketable securities, and short-term investments will be treated as current asset accounts, not actual cash accounts.

There are two ways of determining net cash flows from operations—the direct and indirect methods. The **direct method** uses cash receipts from operations and cash disbursements to create the income statement on a cash basis. The **indirect method** starts with accural net income and adjusts it for changes in current asset and current liability accounts. The indirect method is generally the easier and more commonly used method, so only the indirect method will be discussed in detail in this chapter. The investing and financing sections are determined the same way regardless of the method used to determine cash flows from operations.

Management must understand the procedures and the necessity to implement effective cash management policies and procedures. The SCF can answer some of the following key questions:

- How much did the cash position increase or decrease from operating activities since the last accounting period?
- Did normal operation activities generate the major portion of cash inflows?
- How much was invested in capital assets, such as new furnishings, equipment, or other long-term physical assets?
- How much cash was recovered from the disposal of furnishings, fixtures, equipment, or other long-lived physical assets?
- How much cash was received from the disposal of long-term investments?
- How much cash was obtained by incurring long-term liabilities?
- How much cash was used to reduce or pay off long-term liabilities?
- How much cash was received through the sale of ownership equity?
- What amount was paid out as dividends?
- What amount of cash did the proprietor or the partners withdraw?

The SCF allows the identification of cash inflows and cash outflows within operating activities, investing activities, and financing activities. The three sections have the objective of identifying cash flows that occurred from the beginning to the end of a period of operations. To prepare a SCF, the reported accrual net income (or loss) is converted from an accrual basis to a cash basis by evaluating the balance sheet accounts that have changed during an operating period. The final result of the SCF is a positive or negative net cash flow, which is equal to the total change in the cash account between the beginning and the end of the year's balance sheets.

In the operating section, each active current asset and current liability accounts except cash is evaluated to determine the change in the accounts for the entire reporting period. The change is identified as an increase or decrease in cash. An increase is called a source of cash and a decrease is called a use of cash. A source of cash is added, and a use of cash is deducted in the process of converting accrual net income, or net loss to a cash basis. The same procedure is used for all sections of the SCF.

VALUE OF STATEMENT OF CASH FLOWS

The SCF is of value to management because it allows an evaluation of the operation's liquidity and provides a basis for analysis of cash management. In addition, it guides management in its decisions regarding cash budgeting, and assists in decisions about its financing and investing requirements. It is also of value to creditors (such as suppliers of goods and services needed by the operation) to assess the operation's ability to meet its payment requirements. These creditors generally like to see that sufficient cash is being generated from operating activities to meet these obligations rather than relying on investing or financing activities to provide that cash.

Lenders of short-term as well as long-term funds can also use a SCF to determine the ability of an organization to continue to meet its debt obligations. Stockholders can use the SCF to assess the operation's ability to pay dividends, or possibly to increase its dividend payments.

The SCF is a historic document showing what has happened in a comparative review, and is an essential document for managers, creditors, lenders, and stockholders for evaluating and forecasting the future.

SEGMENTING CASH FLOW ANALYSIS

Operating activities evaluate and identify cash flow changes that occur within the major operating accounts—current assets and current liabilities. In addition, specific adjustments are considered that, by their nature, are noncash adjustments. The greatest number of transactions affecting cash flows occurs within the major operating accounts during actual operations. The investing and financing sections evaluate noncurrent account transactions affecting cash flows, which typically are not considered normal daily operating transactions. Cash flows are segmented into three specific types of activity: operating, investing, and financing. This segmentation allows the adjustment of accrual net income or loss by adding positive cash flow changes and deducting negative cash flow changes. Each activity is discussed in the sequence that it appears in the SCF.

1. **Operating activities** involve the primary objective of the businesses, the production of sales revenue inflows from the exchange of goods, merchandise, and services creating sales revenue inflows for cash or on credit. Credit card and accounts receivables are the current asset accounts created by sales revenue inflows on credit. In addition to cash, other current assets—such as supplies, inventory for resale, and prepaid expenses—are created and consumed to support sales-revenue-generating operations.

   The generation of sales revenue creates expense outflows, which are recognized when cash is paid or incurred on credit. Accounts payable is the primary current operating liability account. Current liabilities, when paid, represent cash outflows. Ongoing expense outflows occur for payment of cost-of-sales items, employee costs, insurance costs, facilities support, interest, taxes, and other necessary recurring costs of operations. As well, adjustments are made for noncash expenses such as depreciation and the recognition of gains or losses on the sales or disposal of long-term assets.

2. **Investing activities** involve transactions that affect noncurrent accounts. The purchase of a long-term asset creates a cash outflow; the sale of a long-term asset creates a cash inflow. The purchase of a long-term noncash equivalent investment creates a cash outflow; the sale of a noncash equivalent investment creates a cash inflow.

3. **Financing activities** involve transactions that cause changes to ownership equity and the payment or borrowing of long-term debt. Investment or withdrawal of equity capital and operating returns of income (or losses) typically affect financing activities of a proprietorship or partnership. In an incorporated operation, financing activities are affected by the issuance of capital stock, a cash inflow, and the recovery by the corporation's own stock (treasury stock), a cash outflow. The reissue of treasury stock creates a cash inflow. The assumption of long-term debt creates a cash inflow; repayment of long-term debt (principal) creates a cash outflow. The payment of cash dividends to stockholders is a cash outflow.

The accrual income statement reports sales revenue inflows, expense outflows, and the resulting net income or net loss from operations for an entire operating period. The income statement, however, does not allow management to readily see why or how cash changes occurred.

Although the amount of net income or net loss may generally affect the cash account, the reported net income or net loss will not normally equal the increase or decrease in the cash account. The reported net income or loss at the end of an accounting period is normally based on accrual accounting. The accrual method includes recognition of noncash expenses, losses, or gains on the sale of long-term assets and noncash sales revenue transactions.

Typical noncash accrual items deducted in arriving at net income (or loss) are depreciation and amortization expenses and losses on disposal of long-lived assets. These are noncash expense and loss items not requiring cash outflows, and are added back as adjustments in the operating activities section of the SCF. Gains on disposal of long-lived assets are noncash revenues not involving a cash inflow. These noncash gains are deducted as adjustments in the operating activities section since they are included in net income and, therefore, have inflated net income from normal operations.

To prepare an SCF, the following financial statements and information are required:

- Income statement for the current period
- Balance sheet for the current period
- Trial balance of the accounts and balances at the beginning of the period (or the prior period balance sheet and statement of retained earnings or a statement of capital)
- Statement of retained earnings for the current period
- Information relating to noncurrent transactions during the current period

A trial balance of accounts and balances at the beginning of the period, compared to the ending adjusted trial balance of accounts, will isolate changes in the accounts. If preferred, you could compare the prior and current year balance sheets and statements of retained earnings that will provide the same information on changes occurring in the accounts.

Financial statements report key information necessary to complete an analysis of items affecting the conversion of reported accrual net income (or loss) to a cash basis. It is important that you review their structure, components, and sequence, as we discuss the conversion of an accrual income statement to a cash basis.

Each of the three sections of the SCF, indirect method, will be individually discussed, beginning with the net cash flow from operations followed by net cash flow from investing and net cash flow from financing. After all sections have been individually discussed, a completed SCF will be illustrated.

NET CASH FLOW FROM OPERATING ACTIVITIES

The objective of this section is to discuss and describe the procedure to convert reported accrual net income (or net loss) to a cash basis. The accrual nature of reported net income (or net loss) means that sales revenue and expenses are recorded when earned and incurred, not when cash is actually received or paid. The basic format of the accrual income statement is:

Sales revenue − Cost of sales = Gross margin − expenses
= Operating income (or loss)

Sales revenue is made only two ways, for cash or on credit. Expenses are incurred only two ways, paid when incurred or incurred on credit, which creates an accounts payable. The indirect method of determining cash flows from operations starts with reported accrual net income (or net loss). To accomplish the conversion of net income (or loss), each current asset and current liability account must be analyzed to find the change that occurred in the account over the operating period. Once the amount of the change is determined, identify whether the change increased or decreased over the operating period.

For example, the current income statement of a motel reported $800,000 of room sales revenue. Accounts receivable (AR) increased from $10,000 at the beginning of the period to $15,000 at the end of the period. Considering only the $5,000 increase to accounts receivable, reported room sales revenue was converted to a cash basis of $795,000. Since less cash than the sales revenue was received, it is called a use of cash. This adjustment, using the effect of only one current asset account, is determined as follows:

Beginning AR − Ending AR =   Increase to AR
$10,000   − $15,000   = $5,000 increase

Sales revenue − AR increase = Cash basis sales revenue
$800,000   − $5,000   = $795,000

In preparing the operating activities section of the SCF, the $5,000 increase in accounts receivable is treated as a negative number and deducted from net income in the conversion of accrual net income to a cash basis. The actual cash inflow was $795,000 due to the increase in accounts receivable during the period of $5,000. In general, an increase in a current asset account represents a decrease to net income when converted to a cash basis. A decrease in a current asset account has the opposite effect of causing an increase in net income when it is adjusted to a cash basis as it relates to cash sales revenue.

An increase in a current liability account represents an increase in expenses incurred on credit over the operating period. This indicates that actual cash operating expenses were less than the total reported accrual operating expenses. The increases in a current liability account are a source of cash and are treated as a positive number and an increase to net income in the conversion to the cash basis. Thus, the actual cash outflow paid for operating expenses was less than the expenses reported in the accrual income statement.

For example, accrual income reports expenses when they are incurred, not when they are paid. Assume that total reported operating expenses were $280,000, and that accounts payable (AP), a current liability account, increased from $10,000 to $12,000 by the end of the period. The $2,000 change in the account is a source of cash and treated as a positive number, which increases the reported net income in the conversion to the cash basis. Considering only the increase of $2,000 to accounts payable, the cash used for the operating expense was $278,000. The $2,000 was expenses incurred on credit. This adjustment, using only one current liability account, is determined as follows:

Beginning AP − **Ending AP** = **Increase to AP**
$10,000 − **$12,000** = **$2,000 increase**

Operating expenses − **Increase AP** = **Cash basis expenses**
$280,000 − **$2,000** = **$278,000**

This shows an addition to reported net income of $2,000, indicating that actual cash outflow for operating expenses was $278,000; accounts payable increased by $2,000, indicating $2,000 of operating expenses were accrued on credit, thus not requiring the payment of cash.

The net effect of the two basic adjustments on net income based on the foregoing examples involving a $4,000 increase to a current receivable and a $2,000 increase to a current payable follows:

	Accrual Basis	*Cash Basis*	*Effects of Changes*	
Sales revenue	= $800,000	$795,000	Sales revenue (decreased)	$5,000
Operating expenses	= (280,000)	(278,000)	Operating expenses (decreased)	$2,000
Net income	= $520,000	$517,000	Net income (decreased)	$3,000

The foregoing examples show that changes to the primary operating accounts, current assets and current liabilities (with the exception of the cash amount), over an accounting period will cause an increase or decrease to the reported accrual income or loss when it is converted to a cash basis. Changes in each operating account provide a trail to identify accounts that have changed the balance of the cash account over the reported period.

The effect of changes in cash in the current operating accounts (current assets and current liabilities) during the conversion to a cash basis from accrual net income or net loss is shown as follows:

Current assets: **Decreases are sources (inflows), and increases net cash flows**
Increases are uses (outflows), and decreases net cash flows

Current liabilities: **Decreases are uses (outflows), and net cash flows decreases**
Increases are sources (inflows), and net cash flows increases

Some general rules apply to understanding the effect of changes to current assets and current liability accounts within the operating activities section of the SCF. The rules will identify how to treat the changes in current operating accounts and will specify whether the change is an increase in cash or a decrease in cash in determining the effect on accrual net income (or loss).

Current asset increases   = Negative cash outflow = Increase is deducted
Current asset decreases   = Positive cash inflows   = Decrease is added
Current liability increases = Positive cash inflows   = Increase is added
Current liability decreases = Negative cash outflow = Decrease is deducted

After evaluating and adjusting changes to current assets and current liability accounts, the net income figure has to be further adjusted for noncash items that appear on the income statement. These items do not involve a cash inflow or cash outflow. As discussed earlier, the major noncash item typically expensed in most hospitality operations is depreciation. This transaction affects only the depreciation expense and accumulated depreciation (a contra asset account). Since depreciation expense is deducted on the accrual income statement but no cash is involved to arrive at net income, depreciation must be added back to net income to adjust cash from operations. In other words, depreciation expense can be considered a source of cash and is added back to income (or loss).

In addition, if amortization expense was reported on the income statement, it would also be added back to net income because it reduced net income but no cash was involved. Losses or gains on the disposal of long-term assets are reported on the accrual income statement. A gain has increased accrual net income above what it should be from operations and a reported loss has decreased accrual net income below what it should be from operations. Such losses or gains must be adjusted in the conversion of net income from operations to the cash basis. When reported on the income statement, losses will be added back as positive inflows and gains are deducted as negative outflows to adjust reported income (or loss) to the cash basis. The effects of depreciation, amortization, and losses or gains on the disposal of long-term assets should be adjusted automatically in the operating section of the SCF. These adjustments are summarized as follows:

Depreciation expense = Positive effect   =   Add back cash
Amortization expense = Positive effect   =   Add back cash
Loss on the disposal of a long-term asset = Positive effect   =   Add back cash
Gain on the disposal of a long-term asset = Negative effect   =   Deduct cash

Condensed Income Statement, December 31, 0007		
Sales revenue		$7,262,400
Cost of sales		(2,495,300)
Gross margin		$4,767,100
Payroll expense	$2,306,500	
Direct operating expenses	1,609,900	
Total direct operating expenses		(3,916,400)
Contributory income		$ 850,700
Depreciation expense	$ 144,200	
Interest expense	52,900	
Total fixed expenses	488,300	
Total operating expenses		(685,400)
Operating income		$ 165,300
Income tax		(24,200)
Net income		$ 141,000

■ **EXHIBIT 10.1**
Condensed Income Statement

DETERMINING NET CASH FLOW

For the purposes of understanding the net cash flow from operating activities, we will focus on the income statement in Exhibit 10.1 and the comparative balance sheets in Exhibit 10.2 for information to use in conversion of net income (or loss) to a cash basis. The income statement identifies the reported net income (or loss), depreciation and amortization expenses, and losses *and gains* on disposal of long-lived assets. Comparative balance sheets allow the analysis of current asset and current liability accounts to determine their balance changes and how to treat the change as a positive inflow, add adjustment, or a negative outflow, deduct adjustment. The statement of retained earnings in Exhibit 10.3 shows the net income (or loss) and cash dividends paid for the operating period being reported.

CASH FLOW CONVERSION—OPERATING ACTIVITIES

Net income of $141,100 is the first item shown and is the amount being converted to a cash basis through the operations activities section (Exhibit 10.4). If a net loss were reported, it would also be the amount being converted to a cash basis, but would be shown as a negative amount. Net income (or loss) is also reported in the statement of retained earnings.

1. One noncash adjustment, depreciation expense, is identified, which is a positive inflow and is automatically an added-back adjustment.

Comparative Balance Sheets for the Years Ended 0007 and 0008

Assets	12-31-0007	12-31-0008		Change
Current Assets				
Cash	$ 25,200	$ 29,600	+	$ 4,400
Credit card receivables	14,550	12,900	−	1,650
Accounts receivable	4,850	4,100	−	750
Inventories	9,700	8,000	−	1,700
Prepaid expenses	4,100	4,200	+	100
Total Current Assets	$ 58,400	$ 58,800	+	$ 400
Property, Plant and Equipment				
Land	$ 194,000	$ 194,000		-0-
Building	9,800,000	9,800,000		-0-
Equipment	736,400	753,400	+	$ 17,000
Furnishings	184,000	184,000		-0-
Less: Total accumulated depreciation	(2,400,000)	(2,544,200)	+	(144,200)
Net Property, Plant and Equipment	$8,514,400	$8,387,200	−	$127,200
Other assets	509,000	609,000	+	100,000
Total Fixed and Noncurrent Assets	$9,023,400	$8,996,200	−	$ 27,200
Total Assets	$9,081,800	$9,055,000	−	$ 26,800
Liabilities & Stockholders' Equity				
Current Liabilities				
Accounts payable	$ 14,700	$ 16,700	+	$ 2,000
Accrued payroll payable	3,200	4,000	−	800
Taxes payable	5,900	4,700	−	1,200
Current mortgage payable	14,300	14,900	+	600
Total current liabilities	$ 38,100	$ 40,300	+	$ 2,200
Long-Term Liabilities				
Mortgage payable	$7,710,200	$7,704,300	−	$ 5,900
Total Liabilities	$7,748,300	$7,744,600	−	$ 3,700
Stockholders' Equity				
Capital stock	$ 950,000	$ 940,000	−	$ 10,000
Retained earnings	383,500	370,400	−	$ 13,100
Total Stockholders' Equity	$1,333,500	$1,310,400	−	$ 23,100
Total Liabilities & Stockholders' Equity	$9,081,800	$9,055,000	−	$ 26,800

■ **EXHIBIT 10.2**
Comparative Balance Sheets

Statement of Retained Earnings for the Year Ended December 31, 0008	
Retained earnings, December 31, 0007	$383,500
Net income for Year 0008	141,100
Subtotal	$524,600
Cash dividends paid in Year 0007	(154,200)
Retained earnings, December 31, 0008	$370,400

■ **EXHIBIT 10.3**
Statement of Retained Earnings

2. Three of the current asset accounts show a decrease between the beginning and the end of the year and are treated as a positive inflow that increases the cash from operations. The fourth current asset account, prepaid expenses, shows increase and, therefore, is a negative outflow that reduces the cash from operations.

3. Four current liability accounts were identified with changes in their balances. The change in the current mortgage payable is not considered in the operating section of the statement since it is not related to operations. Instead, it is paying off a long-term liability, which is part of the financing activities. Two of the other three had increases in their balances and one had a decrease. The two current liability accounts that increase are treated as positive inflows and are added back; the third showing a decrease in its balance is treated as a

Net Cash Flow from Operating Activities for the Year Ended December 31, 0007		
Adjustments to Reconcile Net Income to		
Net Cash Flow from Operating Activities		
Net Income from Operations		$141,100
Credit card receivables (decreased)	1,650	
Accounts receivable (decreased)	750	
Inventory (decreased)	1,700	
Prepaid expenses (increased)	(100)	
Accounts payable (increased)	2,000	
Accrued payroll payable (increased)	800	
Taxes payable (decreased)	(1,200)	
Depreciation expense	$144,200	
Net Cash Flow Adjustment		149,800
Net Cash Flow from Operating Activities		$290,900

■ **EXHIBIT 10.4**
Net Cash Flow from Operating Activities

negative outflow, and will be deducted in the adjustment. The result of these adjustments is shown in Exhibit 10.4.

NET CASH FLOW FROM INVESTING ACTIVITIES

To determine cash flow adjustments from investing activities, we turn our attention to the comparative balance sheets in Exhibit 10.2. Now we will review the property plant and equipment (fixed assets) section to isolate the purchase and sale of long-lived assets and the purchase or sale of noncurrent investments.

1. No changes occurred in the land or building accounts.
2. The Property, Plant and Equipment (fixed) asset section shows that equipment has increased in Year 0008 by $17,000, which is treated as a negative outflow and deducted. However, an analysis of this account (Exhibit 10.5) shows equipment was sold for $3,000, which is treated as a positive inflow and is added back to cash. In addition, $20,000 of new equipment was purchased during the period, which is treated as a negative outflow and deducted. The only other account in the fixed asset section that changed was accumulated depreciation in the amount of $144,200, which has already been used in the depreciation expense (noncash) adjustment in the operating activities section.
3. The other assets section shows that the investment account increased $100,000, which is treated as a negative outflow and deducted. However, an analysis of this account during this period shows an investment was sold for $25,000, which is treated as a positive inflow and added. In addition, a new investment was purchased for $125,000 during the period that is a negative outflow and is deducted. The result of these adjustments is shown in Exhibit 10.5.

Net Cash Flow from Investing Activities for the Year Ended December 31, 0007	
Cash flow adjustments, investing activities	
Purchase of equipment	$(20,000)
Sale of equipment	3,000
Purchase of investment	(125,000)
Sale of investment	25,000
Net Cash Flow from Investing Activities	($117,000)

■ **EXHIBIT 10.5**

Net Cash Flow from Investing Activities

NET CASH FLOW FROM FINANCING ACTIVITIES

To determine cash flow adjustments from financing activities, we look to the comparative balance sheets in Exhibit 10.2 and the statement of retained earnings, Exhibit 10.3. Our focus now turns to long-term liabilities and stockholders' equity. Determine whether any long-term liability accounts have increased (a positive inflow) or decreased (a negative outflow) during the period. Determine whether any stock equity has been sold, a positive inflow, or repurchased (treasury stock), a negative outflow, and whether cash dividends have been paid, a negative outflow, during the period.

1. The long-term liability section shows the mortgage payable (on a building) account has decreased by $5,900 in Year 0007. However, the amount of cash used was $14,300. This amount is determined from the Year 0007 current mortgage payable. By putting current mortgage payable on the balance sheet, the operation is committing to pay it within the next 12 months or during Year 0008. Therefore, we need to do some additional analysis to determine if we borrowed any additional long-term debt during the year. If we use a T-account, we can see what is happening.

Debit	Credit	Explanation
	$7,710,200	January 1, 0008 balance
$14,900		Transferred to current mortgage payable during Year 0008
	$7,695,300	Balance if there were no other transactions in long-term mortgage
	$ 9,000	Borrowed during Year 0008
	$7,704,300	December 31, 0008 balance

2. The statement of retained earnings reports the payment of cash dividends during Year 0007 of $154,200, which also creates a negative cash flow.
3. The stockholders' equity sections of the comparative balance sheets show that capital stock account has decreased by $10,000 between December 31, 0006, and December 31, 0005. If capital stock account has increased, it would be a positive inflow while a decrease would be a negative outflow. Since the shareholders' equity decreased by $10,000 during the year, stock was repurchased causing a use of cash.
4. The last account to look at is retained earnings, as illustrated in Exhibit 10.3. This shows a beginning balance of $383,500, which was the ending balance at the end of Year 0007. Net income was $141,100, and cash dividends of $154,200 were paid during Year 0008. The Year 0008 ending balance of retained earnings is $370,400. The result of these adjustments is shown in Exhibit 10.6.

Cash Flow from Financing Activities for the Year Ended December 31, 0008	
Cash flow adjustments, financing activities	
Reduction of long-term mortgage	($ 14,300)
Borrow additional long-term debt	9,000
Redeem capital stock	(10,000)
Cash dividends paid	(154,200)
Net Cash Flow from Financing Activities	($169,500)

■ **EXHIBIT 10.6**
Cash Flow from Financing Activities

FINALIZING THE STATEMENT OF CASH FLOWS

A completed SCF using the information discussed in the example is shown in Exhibit 10.7. Note in Exhibit 10.7 the net cash flow increase of $4,400 during Year 0008 is added to Year 0007's cash balance to confirm the cash flow change and the Year 0008 ending cash balance. As discussed earlier, the final net cash flow change reported in the SCF should be equal to the change in the cash account that occurred over the reported period. If the change in the cash account is not the same as the final adjusted cash flow, an error has occurred and should be traced and corrected.

RATIO ANALYSIS USING THE STATEMENT OF CASH FLOWS

The SCF provides additional information that can be used to calculate several useful ratios to analyze liquidity, profitability, and net worth or solvency.

CASH FLOW FROM OPERATING ACTIVITIES TO CURRENT LIABILITIES

The **cash flow from operating activities to current liabilities ratio** is a measure of liquidity and is calculated as follows:

$$\frac{\text{Cash flow from operating activities}}{\text{Average current liabilities}}$$

The cash flow from operating activities in our situation is $290,900 from Exhibit 10.7, and the current liabilities for Year 0007 and Year 0008 are shown in Exhibit 10.2. The result is:

$$\frac{\$290,900}{(\$38,100 + \$40,300)\,/\,2} = \frac{\$290,900}{\$39,200} = 7.42 \text{ times, or } 742\%$$

Statement of Cash Flows for the Year Ended December 31, 0008

Net Income		$141,100
Credit card receivables (decrease)	$ 1,650	
Accounts receivable (decrease)	750	
Inventory (decrease)	1,700	
Prepaid expense (increase)	(100)	
Accounts payable (increase)	2,000	
Accrued payroll (increase)	800	
Tax payable (decrease)	(1,200)	
Depreciation expense	144,200	
Net Cash Flow Adjustments		149,800
Net Cash Flow, Operating Activities		$290,900
Cash flow adjustments investing activities:		
Purchase of equipment	($ 20,000)	
Sale of equipment	3,000	
Purchase of investment	(125,000)	
Sale of investment	25,000	
Net Cash Flow, Investing Activities		(117,000)
Cash flow adjustments financing activities:		
Reduction of mortgage	(14,300)	
Borrow additional long-term debt	9,000	
Redeem capital stock	(10,000)	
Dividends paid	(154,200)	
Net Cash Flow, Financing Activities		(169,500)
Net cash flow increase		$ 4,400
Cash balance, December 31, 0007		25,200
Cash balance, December 31, 0008		$ 29,600

■ **EXHIBIT 10.7**
Statement of Cash Flows

This ratio has advantages over the current and acid test ratios, which are calculated at a single point in time on the balance sheet date. If, on the balance sheet date, the amounts used in the calculations are considerably higher or lower than normal, then distorted ratios will result. The cash flow from operations to current liabilities ratio overcomes this problem because the cash flow is for a year and average current liabilities from two successive balance sheets are used. All users of financial statements like to see this ratio higher rather than lower. It is suggested that a minimum of 200% is desirable, and the more the ratio exceeds that minimum figure, the better will be the operation's liquidity. Our result of 742% is considerably higher than the suggested minimum.

The use of this ratio does not mean that the traditional current and acid test ratios should be discontinued. They still have a value and, indeed, many lenders require that a minimum level of these ratios be maintained.

CASH FLOW FROM OPERATING ACTIVITIES TO TOTAL LIABILITIES

The often-used *solvency* (or net worth) ratio of total assets to total liabilities is calculated at a single point in time, the balance sheet date. As such, the numbers within the balance sheet are static. This ratio considers cash flow from operating activities over a period of time such as a year rather than debt of a specific date. The **cash flow from operating activities to total liabilities ratio** is calculated as follows:

$$\frac{\textbf{Cash flow from operating activities}}{\textbf{Average total liabilities}}$$

In our situation, given the net cash flow from operations of $290,900 in Exhibit 10.7 and the total liabilities for Year 0006 and Year 0007 from Exhibit 10.2, the calculation is:

$$\frac{\$290{,}900}{(\$7{,}748{,}300 + \$7{,}744{,}600)\,/\,2} = \frac{\$290{,}900}{\$7{,}746{,}450} = 0.03755, \text{ or } 3.8\%$$

Further, the **total assets to total liabilities ratio** does not take into account the different liquidities of the various assets used in the equation and the cash flow from operations to average total liabilities ratio overcomes that problem. The total assets to total liabilities ratio is more indicative of the operation's ability to pay its various types of debt. It is suggested that a minimum ratio of 20% is acceptable, and the higher this ratio is, the better the operation's ability to pay off its debts with cash. Our result of 3.8% is significantly lower than the suggested minimum. This low ratio would indicate that the operation has a very high debt and creditors may be concerned about the security of their loans.

CASH FLOW FROM OPERATING ACTIVITIES TO INTEREST

The **cash flow from operating activities to interest ratio** is a *solvency* or net worth ratio and is calculated as follows:

$$\frac{\textbf{Cash flow from operating activities + Interest expense}}{\textbf{Interest expense}}$$

In our case, given the cash flow amount of $290,900, and Exhibit 10.1, the calculation is

$$\frac{\$290,900 + \$52,900}{\$52,900} = \frac{\$343,800}{\$52,900} = 6.5 \text{ times, or } 650\%$$

This ratio is more realistic than the ratio for the number of times interest is earned because interest has to be paid with cash, not with net income. This ratio can provide a more obvious warning that an inability to pay interest may be on the horizon than does the traditional interest coverage ratio. The higher this ratio is, the more comfortable the creditors will be.

CASH FLOW FROM OPERATING ACTIVITIES MARGIN

The cash flow from operating activities margin ratio is a profitability ratio and is calculated as follows:

$$\frac{\textbf{Cash flow from operating activities}}{\textbf{Sales revenue}}$$

In our case, given the cash flow amount of $290,900 and Exhibit 10.1, the calculation is

$$\textbf{Cash flow from operating activities margin} = \frac{\$290,900}{\$7,262,400} = 0.04, \text{ or } 4.0\%$$

The ratio compares the amount of cash generated per dollar of sales. Although this ratio is similar to the profit margin ratio discussed earlier, it is again considered more realistic because it compares sales revenues with cash rather than net income.

In our case, because the cash flow of $290,900 is higher than the net income of $141,100, we know the cash flow from operating activities margin ratio will be higher than the profit margin ratio because both ratios use the same denominator.

ANALYSIS OF CHANGES TO WORKING CAPITAL

The SCF provides additional information needed for effective cash management and budget planning. Working capital analysis is closely related to the SCF and provides another view of information in support of effective management of cash.

Working capital is defined as the excess of current assets compared to current liabilities, and indicates the amount of excess current assets relative to current liabilities available to conduct sales revenue-generating activities. Total current assets minus total current liabilities is the value of working capital ($CA - CL$). These terms are defined as follows:

- *Current assets* consist of cash, marketable securities, notes receivable, credit card receivables, accounts receivable, inventories (for resale), supplies, and prepaid expenses. Current assets are resources that will be consumed in the production of sales revenue in the next operating period.
- *Current liabilities* consist of accounts payable, accrued expenses (e.g., wages and salaries payable, interest payable, taxes payable), and notes payable. Current liabilities represent operating costs that were incurred on credit and will be paid in the next operating period.

The preparation of a **statement of changes in working capital** is similar in many ways to the preparation of an SCF. However, the analysis of working capital differs in a number of ways from the cash flow analysis, and serves different purposes.

Working capital analysis evaluates changes to working capital over an operating period for the following purposes:

- It shows how working capital increased, by identifying the inflows that created the increase.
- It shows how working capital decreased, by identifying the outflow that created the decrease.
- It is used to find the net changes to working capital during the completed operating period.
- It provides management with information related to the effectiveness of working capital controls during the operating period.
- It provides prospective lenders with information so they can evaluate their risk in lending funds to the hospitality organizations.

INFLOWS—SOURCES OF WORKING CAPITAL

The following are the major inflows or sources that will increase working capital.

- *Income from operations.* In general terms, accrued income is sales revenue less all expenses incurred (including income tax) in producing the sales revenue inflow. Sales revenue is generated by cash sales or on credit through receivables that eventually become cash sales revenues. Expenses are incurred by immediate payment of cash or on credit through payables. The payables, accounts payable, and accrued payables will eventually be paid. Net income is expected to increase the organization's cash accounts and increase working capital.

■ *Accrual net income.* This is determined after deducting noncash expenses. Such noncash expenses adjust the book or carrying value of long-term assets through depreciation and/or by recognizing amortization expense. To adjust net income and identify increases in working capital, all capitalized expenses must be added back to net income. This uses the same procedure followed in the operating activities section of the SCF. Other items that are handled in the same way as depreciation and amortization expenses may consist of prepaid franchise fees or the amortization of other intangible assets such as goodwill (see Exhibits 10.8, 10.9, and 10.10).

■ *Sale of long-term or other noncurrent assets.* These include land, building, furniture, equipment, or an investment. Their sale is treated as an inflow, which increases working capital. The sale will create an increase in a current asset, cash, or a current receivable with no corresponding effect to a current liability.

■ *Increase in a long-term liability.* Creating or increasing a loan, mortgage, debenture, or bond achieves this, and is an inflow that increases working capital. Borrowing additional long-term debt will create an increase in a current asset, cash, or current receivable with no corresponding effect to a current liability.

■ *The issuance of stock.* Equity financing creates an inflow that increases working capital. In a proprietorship or partnership (an unincorporated company), stock is not issued; however, any investment by the owner(s) increases their equity capital accounts. The sale of equity or receipt of an owner's investment will create an increase in a current asset, cash, or a current receivable with no corresponding effect on a current liability.

OUTFLOWS—USES OF WORKING CAPITAL

The following are the major outflows or uses that will decrease working capital:

■ *Loss from operations.* Just as accrual net income is an increase in working capital, an accrual net loss is a decrease in working capital. When a loss occurs, operating expenses have exceeded sales revenue, which decreases working capital. Just as net income has to be adjusted for noncash expenditures (depreciation, franchise, goodwill, write-downs, or amortization), the net loss is similarly adjusted. The net loss may be reduced by any noncash expense shown on the income statement.

■ *Purchase of a long-term or other noncurrent asset.* This would include land, building, furniture, equipment, or other investments that are an outflow that decreases working capital. The cost of another noncurrent asset, such as the prepayment of a long-term franchise fee, is also an outflow that decreases working capital.

■ *Payment of long-term liabilities.* Any payment reducing the principal amount owed on a long-term (noncurrent) liability is an outflow that decreases working capital.

■ *Redemption of stock.* Any previously issued stock repurchased by the issuing company is called **treasury stock,** and is an outflow that decreases working capital.

■ *Payment of cash dividends.* Previously declared, these are payable obligations, payment of which is an outflow that decreases working capital. In a non–incorporated company, a partnership, or proprietorship, any cash or other current asset withdrawals made by the owner(s) are reductions of their capital investment and are treated as an outflow, that decrease working capital.

The major activities that create sources that increase working capital (WC) and uses that will decrease working capital are summarized in the following table:

Effect		*Sources*	*Activity*	*Uses*		*Effect*
Increase WC	=	Net income	← Income or loss →	Net loss	=	Decrease WC
Increase WC	=	Sale of assets	← Long-term assets → (or other asset)	Purchase assets	=	Decrease WC
Increase WC	=	Borrowing	← *Long-term liabilities* →	Payment	=	Decrease WC
Increase WC	=	Sold equity	← *Ownership equity* →	Buy back	=	Decrease WC
(No opposite)	=		*Cash dividends* →	Payment	=	Decrease WC

STATEMENT USES

A statement of changes to working capital is discussed first, followed by a statement of changes to individual working capital accounts. Let us consider the following three situations presented in Exhibits 10.8, 10.9, and 10.10, concerning three different restaurants. Each restaurant began the operating year with $88,000 of working capital and ended the year with $100,000 of working capital. In other words, each restaurant increased working capital by $12,000. Each restaurant wants to borrow $15,000 for 3 years with interest from the same bank. Information is readily available from their balance sheets, but it does not clearly identify the causes of the increase to working capital without a statement of working capital inflow sources and outflow uses. The statement, when completed, will clearly identify each source inflow and use outflow of working capital. We will assume the banker compiled the same information.

Restaurant A: Exhibit 10.8

The information for Restaurant A shows it generated sufficient working capital from operations to pay out $8,000 in dividends. If you assume that the restau-

---

Restaurant A Statement of Changes, Working Capital for the Year Ended December 31, 0007

Inflows of Working Capital	
Accrual net income (after tax)	$18,000
Depreciation expense	2,000
Total inflows	$20,000
Outflows of Working Capital	
Cash dividends declared and paid to stockholders	(8,000)
Net Change, Increase to Working Capital	$12,000

■ **EXHIBIT 10.8**

Statement of Changes, Working Capital, Restaurant A

rant's business will stay relatively the same over the next 3 years, it appears there is a low risk to the bank that is lending the restaurant money. The restaurant should be able to pay the interest and repay $5,000 a year to retire the loan.

Restaurant B: Exhibit 10.9

Based on this information, the banker would consider the restaurant to be a moderate to high risk. Although this restaurant also paid out cash dividends of $8,000, it already has an outstanding loan that requires a payment of $5,000 per year plus interest. If a new loan were granted, it might be questionable whether the restaurant could make and sustain total yearly payments of $10,000 per year plus interest. A modest decline in net income over the next few years would decrease the working capital and potentially create difficulties for the restaurant in meeting its debt obligations and paying dividends. If this should occur, the risk involved would grow in proportion to the reduction of net income. Thus, there is high risk to the lender.

Restaurant B Statement of Changes, Working Capital for the Year Ended December 31, 0007

Inflows of Working Capital		
Net income (after tax)	$18,000	
Depreciation expense	2,000	
Loan payable (repayable over 4 years with interest)	20,000	$40,000
Outflows of Working Capital		
Investment in new building	$20,000	
Cash dividends paid	8,000	(28,000)
Net Change, Increase to Working Capital		$12,000

■ **EXHIBIT 10.9**

Statement of Changes, Working Capital, Restaurant B

Restaurant C Statement of Changes, Working Capital for the Year Ended December 31, 0007		
Inflows of Working Capital		
Net income (after tax)	$ 2,000	
Depreciation expense	2,000	
Loans payable (repayable over 4 years with interest)	<u>16,000</u>	$20,000
Outflows of Working Capital		
Dividends paid to stockholders		(8,000)
Net Change, Increase to Working Capital		$12,000

■ **EXHIBIT 10.10**

Statement of Changes, Working Capital, Restaurant C

Restaurant C: Exhibit 10.10

In this last situation, it would be an extremely high risk for the bank to loan this restaurant $15,000. A net income of $2,000 was apparently adequate to meet the current debt payment of $2,000, but not the interest. Payment of the dividend in this situation is in itself questionable. If net income remains at this level, the restaurant will not meet its current debt obligation, let alone be able to pay dividends.

Although the Restaurant C illustration is somewhat extreme, it does point out the way in which information provided by the statement of changes to working capital can be of value in decision making.

▨ TRANSACTIONS AFFECTING ONLY CURRENT ACCOUNTS

Note that all the items discussed and listed earlier under inflows or outflows of working capital affected a current asset or current liability account and a non-current account. Transactions causing inflows and/or outflows of working capital identify the cause of such changes in net working capital. However, it does not show specific details of changes in individual current asset or current liability accounts. Transactions affecting only current asset or current liability accounts will not appear on the statement of changes to working capital. For example, consider the following partial balance sheet information:

Current Assets		*Current Liabilities*	
Cash	$11,000	Accounts payable	$10,800
Credit card receivables	800	Interest payable	200
Accounts receivable	2,500	Bank loan payable	<u>4,800</u>
Inventories (for resale)	<u>8,500</u>		
Total	$22,800		$15,800

The working capital, $CA - CL = \$22,800 - \$15,800 = \$7,000$. If $4,500 cash were paid on accounts payable, only two current accounts would be affected. A new partial balance sheet would be:

Current Assets		Current Liabilities	
Cash	$ 6,500	Accounts payable	$ 6,300
Credit card receivables	800	Interest payable	200
Accounts receivable	2,500	Bank loan payable	4,800
Inventories (for resale)	8,500		
Total	$18,300		$11,300

Since the example transaction affected only two current accounts, current assets and current liabilities, working capital will not change. It is still $7,000 ($18,300 − $11,300). This type of simple transaction affects only two current accounts; both accounts are changed by the same amount. If cash is received in payment of a receivable, a transaction is created that causes an exchange of one current asset for another current asset; no change to total current assets occurs.

The purchase of a current asset on credit affects only two current accounts for the same dollar amount. As a result of these examples, we will not be concerned with changes between individual current asset and current liability accounts.

The statement of changes to working capital views only the effects of transactions that will change total current assets and/or total current liabilities. To complete a statement of changes to working capital, we require the following information:

■ A balance sheet at the close of the previous accounting period
■ A balance sheet at the close of the current accounting period
■ An income statement for the current period
■ A statement of retained earnings at the close of the current period or detailed information about retained earnings on the balance sheet at the close of the current period
■ Any other information not fully disclosed (e.g., information about the purchase or sale of individual long-term assets or details about long-term liabilities or share transactions)

COMPLETION OF A STATEMENT OF CHANGES TO WORKING CAPITAL

To illustrate how a statement of changes to working capital can be developed, we will refer to the comparative balance sheets in Exhibit 10.11, including some information regarding retained earnings. As we move through the dis-

Comparative Balance Sheets for Years 0007 and 0008

Assets	12-31-0007		12-31-0008	
Current Assets				
Cash	$ 10,000		$ 12,000	
Credit card receivables	2,000		2,000	
Accounts receivable	3,000		6,000	
Inventories	3,000		4,000	
Total Current Assets		$ 18,000		$ 24,000
Property, Plant and Equipment				
Land	$ 30,000		$ 30,000	
Building	250,000		250,000	
Equipment	28,000		32,000	
Furniture	7,000		8,000	
Total	$315,000		$320,000	
Less: Accum. Depreciation	(15,000)		(27,000)	
Net Property, Plant and Equipment		300,000		293,000
Total Assets		$318,000		$317,000
Liabilities & Stockholders' Equity				
Current Liabilities				
Accounts payable	$ 4,000		$ 5,000	
Accrued expenses	-0-		4,000	
Bank loan	11,000		8,000	
Total Current Liabilities		$ 15,000		$ 17,000
Long-term Liability				
Mortgage payable		$185,000		$175,000
Stockholders' Equity				
Capital stock	$100,000		$105,000	
Retained earnings	18,000		20,000	
Total Stockholders' Equity		$118,000		$125,000
Total Liabilities & Stockholders' Equity		$318,000		$317,000

■ **EXHIBIT 10.11**

Sample Comparative Balance Sheets

cussion, we will also reference Exhibit 10.12, a condensed income statement and, finally, look at Exhibit 10.13, a statement of retained earnings.

The use of working papers to gather the necessary information defining the changes to working capital is the most accurate proof of working capital evaluation, although working papers are not an absolute requirement. The easiest method is to evaluate the comparative balance sheets, the income statement, and the statement of retained earnings to identify "relevant" items as an inflow (increase) or an outflow (decrease) of working capital.

Condensed Income Statement for the Year Ended December 31, 0008	
Sales revenue	$100,000
Operating expense	(82,000)
Income before depreciation expense	$ 18,000
Depreciation expense	(12,000)
Net Income	$ 6,000

■ **EXHIBIT 10.12**
Sample Condensed Income Statement

▨ CURRENT ACCOUNT INFORMATION, COMPARATIVE BALANCE SHEETS

From Exhibit 10.11, the first step is to find the change in working capital from the previous balance sheet ending date to the current balance sheet ending date $(CA - CL = WC)$:

Year ending 0007:	*Current assets*	−	*Current liabilities*	=	*Working capital*
	$24,000	−	*$17,000*	=	*$7,000*
Year ending 0006:	*Current assets*	−	*Current liabilities*	=	*Working capital*
	$18,000	−	*$15,000*	=	*$3,000*

Working capital 0007	−	Working capital 0006	=	Net change to working capital
$7,000	−	$3,000	=	$4,000 Increase

Working capital increased by $4,000. This figure must agree with the change in working capital that appears as the difference between inflow increases and outflow decreases on the statement of changes to working capital.

Having identified the change in working capital, the current asset and current liability sections of our comparative balance sheets can be ignored. Only

Statement of Retained Earnings for the Year Ended December 31, 0007	
Retained earnings January 1, 0007	$18,000
Add: Net income for year	6,000
Subtotal	$24,000
Less: Dividends declared and paid	(4,000)
Retained earnings December 31, 0007	$20,000

■ **EXHIBIT 10.13**
Sample Statement of Retained Earnings

information from noncurrent sections of the comparative balance sheets in Exhibit 10.11, the income statement in Exhibit 10.12, and the statement of retained earnings in Exhibit 10.13 will be required to complete the changes in working capital.

NONCURRENT BALANCE SHEET INFORMATION

As already stated, we do not need to consider the current balance sheet accounts. The second step is to evaluate the noncurrent assets and noncurrent liabilities.

Noncurrent Assets

The land account remained unchanged at $30,000 and the building account remained unchanged at $250,000 between Year 0007 and Year 0008. The furniture account increased by $1,000, and the equipment account increased $4,000 between Year 0007 and Year 0008. Since additional furniture and equipment were acquired during the Year 0008 operating period, the total $5,000 increase to two noncurrent asset accounts resulted from the use of cash.

Use, outflow, decrease to working capital:
Purchase of furniture, $2,000, and equipment, $3,000
Total decrease to working capital = $5,000

In addition, the contra asset account, accumulated depreciation, increased by $12,000 during the 0008 operating year, because of a noncash depreciation expense transaction. The effect of increasing accumulated depreciation is the reduction of the book value (carrying value) of related long-lived capital assets.

Noncurrent Liabilities

The long-term liability, mortgage payable, decreased during Year 0008 by $10,000. The reduction of the long-term liability was caused by an outflow of current assets, specifically cash.

Use, outflow, decrease to working capital:
Mortgage payable reduction = $10,000

Stockholders' Equity

In the final step, the capital stock account increased during Year 0008 from $100,000 to $105,000. The increase to the capital stock account shows that $5,000 of additional capital stock was issued for cash, which is an inflow of a current asset. Always assume stock is issued for cash unless specifically noted in the accounting records or as a footnote to the balance sheet.

Source, inflow, increase, to working capital:
Capital stock issued (sold) = $5,000

Retained Earnings

Retained earnings changed from Year 0007 to Year 0008. For details concerning this change, we need to refer to the **statement of retained earnings** (Exhibit 10.13). We will do after we have looked at the income statement (Exhibit 10.12).

The income statement reports net income of $6,000, and it is treated as an inflow, increase to working capital. In arriving at net income, depreciation was recognized under the accrual method and did not require a cash expenditure. As discussed earlier, depreciation is a noncash expense and is treated as an inflow, increase to working capital.

Source, inflow, increase to working capital: Net income = $6,000
Source, inflow, increase to working capital:
Depreciation expense = $12,000

The statement of retained earnings identifies the final item remaining to be evaluated from the statement of retained earnings, Exhibit 10.13. Two of the items appearing in the statement of retained earnings have already been evaluated. The first item was net income, which was treated as an inflow, increase to working capital of $6,000. The second item was a noncash expense depreciation, which was treated as an inflow, increase to working capital. The only remaining retained earnings item is cash dividends of $4,000, which is treated as an outflow, decrease to working capital.

Use, outflow, decrease, to working capital, cash dividends = $4,000

Since no other information is given, we have all the data required for compiling our statement of source and use of working capital:

Use, outflow, decreases working capital:	**Purchase furniture**	**$ 2,000**
Use, outflow, decreases working capital:	**Purchase equipment**	**$ 3,000**
Use, outflow, decreases working capital:	**Reduction of mortage payable**	**$10,000**
Source, inflow, increases working capital:	**Additional capital stock issued**	**$ 5,000**
Source, inflows, increases working capital:	**Net income and depreciation**	**$18,000**
Use, outflow, decreases to working capital:	**Payment of cash dividends**	**$ 4,000**

Statement of Changes to Working Capital for the Year Ended December 31, 0008

Inflows, Increases:		
Net income	$18,000	
Capital stock issued	5,000	
Total Inflows, Increases		$23,000
Outflows, Decreases:		
Purchase furniture	$ 2,000	
Purchase equipment	3,000	
Reduction, mortgage payable	10,000	
Payment cash dividends	4,000	
Total Outflows, Increases		(19,000)
Net Working Capital Change, Increase		$ 4,000

■ **EXHIBIT 10.14**

Sample Statement of Changes to Working Capital

This information can now be arranged in an orderly fashion in the form of a statement of changes to working capital as shown in Exhibit 10.14. Note that the net change in working capital shown on this statement, an increase of $4,000, agrees with the amount of the change in working capital previously determined from the Years 0007 to 0008 from Exhibit 10.11.

To clarify specific transactions used in the completion of the statement of changes in working capital, additional information than that shown in the financial statements and statement footnotes is often required. For example, the furniture account shown in Exhibit 10.14 shows that it increased by $2,000, and the equipment account increased by $3,000, for a total of $5,000 from Year 0007 to Year 0008. It was stated earlier that we can assume furniture and equipment had been purchased for a total of $5,000; however, in practice, it is necessary to refer to the actual ledger accounts in the general ledger, and the related invoices. The following situation could have occurred with an item not being shown. To this effect, we will assume that a receipt was located showing old furniture being sold during Year 0008 for $5,500.

Furniture account, December 31, 0007	$7,000
Use, outflow, decrease furniture purchased during Year 0008	6,500
Source, inflow, increase old furniture sold during Year 0008	(5,500)
Furniture account, December 31, 0008	$8,000

The sale of old furniture for $5,500 showing a decrease in the account has occurred but has not been noted. This means that $5,500 of cash received from the sale of the old furniture and $6,500 of cash was paid for new furniture. These two transactions should be recorded separately on the statement of source and use of working capital.

Source, *inflow, increase* to working capital:
Furniture sold $5,500

Use, *outflow, decrease* to working capital:
New furniture purchased $6,500

Any other noncurrent accounts where similar working capital inflow and outflow transactions occurred during the operating period would have to be analyzed in detail. This procedure can ensure that the changes to the working capital statement will provide complete disclosure of working capital changes during the period.

The statement of changes to working capital shows only the net change in total working capital from an outflow decrease and inflow increase basis occurring from noncurrent account transactions in one complete operating time period. It does not show how the individual accounts that are part of working capital have changed. If this information is wanted, or required, it is shown separately in a statement of changes to individual working capital accounts. If we

---

Statement of Changes to Individual Working Capital Accounts for the Year Ended December 31, 0008

Assets	Yr. 0007	Yr. 0008	Increase	Decrease
Current Assets				
Cash	$10,000	$12,000	$2,000	
Accounts receivable	5,000	8,000	3,000	
Inventories (for resale)	3,000	4,000	1,000	
Total Current Assets	$18,000	$24,000	$6,000	
Current Liabilities				
Accounts payable	$ 4,000	$ 5,000		$1,000
Accrued expenses payable	-0-	4,000		4,000
Bank loan payable	11,000	8,000	3,000	
Total Current Liabilities	$15,000	$17,000		
Total Working Capital	$ 3,000	$ 7,000		
			$9,000	$5,000
Net Change, Working Capital				$4,000
Total			$9,000	$9,000

■ **EXHIBIT 10.15**

Sample Statement of Changes to Individual Working Capital

use the current asset and current liability sections of the balance sheet in Exhibit 10.11, we could summarize the changes in individual working capital accounts, as in Exhibit 10.15.

An analysis of individual account changes can be made as a result of preparing a statement of changes in working capital. Questions could then be asked. For example, since the cash account has increased by $2,000, or 20% ($2,000 divided by $10,000), we could ask if we need extra cash on hand, or should the extra cash be used to pay off some of the bank loan to save interest expense? By reducing interest expense, net income may increase. The receivables have gone up by $3,000, or 60%; has our total sales revenue increased 60%, or have we changed our credit policies, or are we not following up effectively on the collection of accounts? The information in the statement of changes in working capital accounts raises these and other questions.

The problem of cash management and the control of individual working capital accounts, such as inventory, accounts receivable, and accounts payable, will be discussed in Chapter 11.

As a point of review, the effects of changes to current assets and current liabilities and their effect on working capital can be summarized using a simple base data set, as follows:

Effects of change in *WC* shown in a symbol format:

↑ = Increased   ↓ = Decreased   NC = No change
CA = Current assets   *CL* = Current liabilities   *WC* = Working capital

↑ *CA* − NC in *CL* = ↑ *WC*   ↓ *CA* − NC in *CL* = ↓ *WC*
NC in *CA* − ↑ *CL* = ↓ *WC*   NC in *CA* − ↓ *CL* = ↑ *WC*

DETERMINING REQUIRED WORKING CAPITAL

How much working capital does a hotel, motel, restaurant, or bar need during an operating period? This question cannot be answered in general terms to identify an absolute dollar amount. For example, suppose it were a rule of thumb that an operation should have working capital of $5,000 available. A small restaurant that maintains small amounts of cash, inventories for resale, credit card and accounts receivables, and other items that are current assets, might find itself with the following working capital:

		Current Ratio
Current assets	$15,000	*CA* $15,000 = 1.5:1
Current liabilities	(10,000)	*CL* $10,000
Working capital	$ 5,000	

A much larger restaurant would need larger amounts of cash, inventories for resale, credit card receivables and accounts receivables, and other items that are current assets. It would also be expected to have larger amounts in its various current liability accounts. Its working capital could look like this:

Current assets	$100,000	Current Ratio
Current liabilities	(95,000)	CA $100,000 = 1.5:1
Working capital	$ 5,000	CL $95,000

The smaller restaurant is in much better financial shape than the larger one. The former has $1.50 of current assets for each $1.00 of current liabilities, a comfortable cushion. The latter has $1.05 of current assets for each dollar of current liabilities, a not-so-comfortable cushion.

As a general rule, a business would prefer to have a 2:1 current ratio, or at least $2.00 of current assets for each $1.00 of current liabilities. This would mean that its working capital (current assets, $2.00, minus $1.00) is equivalent to its current liabilities. However, this rule is primarily for companies that need to carry large inventories that do not turn over very rapidly. Inventories of food and beverages are, in part, perishable, and they are easily and frequently replaced. Thus, a hospitality business can operate with a current ratio of less than 2:1.

Hotels and motels have an inventory that is primarily made up of rooms that appear under fixed, long-lived assets. Relatively speaking, this allows hotels and motels to frequently operate with a very low ratio of current assets to current liabilities, often as low as 1:1. In other words, for each $1.00 of current assets, there is $1.00 of current liabilities. This means that the hotel or motel in fact has no working capital.

At certain times of the year, seasonal hospitality operations may work in a negative working capital position, where current liabilities are greater than current assets. During its peak operating period, such an operation would have current assets in excess of current liabilities. The reverse situation will prevail in the off-season. During the preopening period of a hospitality operation, a negative working capital will normally exist.

COMPUTER APPLICATIONS

Specific hospitality software programs and spreadsheet applications can be used to evaluate cash flows and the statements involved in working capital analysis.

SUMMARY

Two of the most useful documents to support financial statements are the SCF and a statement of changes in working capital. These two statements are related because they both analyze current assets and current liabilities.

The SCF determines the changes that have occurred in the cash account over a specified operating period. The statement is used to convert accrual net income (or net loss) to a cash basis. The conversion process identifies sources and uses of cash, and is commonly used to evaluate the liquidity and solvency (or net worth) of a business entity.

In general, the statement is broken into three separate areas of business activities where net cash flows are shown as an increase or decrease. The first section analyzes net cash flows from operations. Sources of cash include net income and decreases in current asset operating accounts (except cash). An operating net loss and increases in current asset accounts are treated as cash outflows. The operating activities section also recognizes noncash expenses such as depreciation and amortization by adding back such noncash expenses to the reported accrual income or loss. In addition, reported losses on the disposal of long-term assets are added back and gains of the disposal of such items are deducted from the reported accrual income or loss.

The final proof of the correctness of an SCF is to verify that final net cash flow (positive or negative) is, in fact, the same amount that occurred. This amount is shown in the change in the cash account over the operating period.

The general rule to describe the effects of changes in the current accounts that cause increases or decreases in the conversion of the reported net income (or net loss) to the cash basis is as follows:

Symbols Identification

Current asset = *CA*   Current liability = *CL*
Change in account = Increase = ↑ q Decrease = ↓ Q
Deduct = (−)   Add = (+)

Effects of changes to the balances of current accounts:
$$CA \uparrow = (-) \quad CL \uparrow = (+)$$
$$CA \downarrow = (+) \quad CL \downarrow = (-)$$

The first section of the SCF shows the status of the major operating accounts, current assets, and current liabilities; these are also viewed during an analysis of working capital. This analysis shows where cash is coming from and where it is going. From that aspect, the SCF also helps measure the effectiveness of cash management.

The second section of the SCF reviews investing activities, such as the acquisition or sale of long-lived assets and the acquisition or sale of long-lived investments. The acquisitions of such items are treated as cash use outflows, and the sale of such items are treated as cash source inflows.

The third section of the SCF views cash inflows and outflows by reviewing the two primary methods used to acquire capital—the sale of ownership equity and the assumption of long-term debt. If ownership equity (stock) is sold or long-term debt is borrowed, the proceeds are treated as cash inflow source. By contrast, if ownership equity is repurchased (treasury stock) by the business entity or long-term debt is repaid, they are treated as cash use outflows. If a cash dividend is paid during the operating period, the dividend is a cash use outflow.

A statement of source inflows and use outflows of working capital also relies heavily on an effective analysis of the major operating accounts, current assets, and current liabilities. Working capital is defined as current assets minus current liabilities.

In addition to showing how working capital has changed from one operating period to the next, the statement of source inflows and use outflows shows management how effectively working capital is being managed. This statement, along with an SCF, will provide creditors with insight into the use of credit by the business operation.

The major source inflows of working capital follow:

- Income for operations, with noncash expense items of depreciation and amortization added back
- Sales of long-term or other assets
- The borrowing of additional long-term debt
- The sale of stock equity

The major uses of working capital follow:

- Net loss from operations
- Purchase of long-term or other assets
- Payments on the principal of long-term debt
- Repurchase by the business of its own outstanding stock (treasury stock)
- Payment of cash dividends

A transaction that affects only two current asset accounts will not affect working capital. For example, if payment of $100 is received on a receivable, the cash account will increase by $100 and the current receivable will decrease by the same amount; no overall change to current assets has occurred, the $100 of a current receivable has simply been reclassified. If a single current asset account changes, and in the same transaction a single current liability account changes, no change in working capital will occur. The exchange of a current asset for a current asset or the creation of a current asset and a current liability in the same amount in a transaction would not appear on a statement of source inflows and use outflows.

To prepare a statement of source inflows and use outflows of working capital, the following are required:

- Balance sheets for the two latest consecutive periods of operations
- An income statement for the operating period just ended

■ A statement of retained earnings and necessary supporting information for the operating period just ended

■ Other necessary supporting information regarding changes in property plant and equipment (fixed assets) and long-term liability accounts, and other assets not available in the balance sheets

The statement of source (inflows) and use (outflows) of working capital identifies only the change and the cause of the changes that determined net working capital. This statement will not identify changes to individual current asset and current liability working capital accounts. This detail is shown in the SCF indirect method that was discussed in this chapter.

DISCUSSION QUESTIONS

1. What is the purpose of the SCF?

2. What are the major operating accounts by category analyzed in the SCF, indirect method?

3. If a current asset account increases, how is the increase treated in the statement of cash flows?

4. What is the typical noncash item, by name, that is automatically added back in the operating activities section of the SCF?

5. The financing section of an SCF analyzes three different items by category. What are they?

6. What are the primary items by category analyzed in the SCF, investing section?

7. What is working capital?

8. Of what use is the statement of source inflows and use outflows of working capital?

9. List the three major common source inflows and the three major common use outflows of working capital.

10. Explain why depreciation expense is treated as a source inflow of working capital.

11. What is a statement of source inflows and use outflows of working capital?

12. If a business operation has a current ratio of 1.25:1, what does this mean relative to working capital?

ETHICS SITUATION

A motel owner needs to borrow money from the bank. The bank manager has asked for statements of cash flows for the past 3 years to support the loan application. In preparing these statements, the motel owner neglects to show that dividends of $10,000 a year were paid out in each of the last 3 years. Discuss the ethics of this situation.

EXERCISES

E10.1   The following lists current asset and current liability accounts. Identify each account as a current asset (*CA*) or a current liability (*CL*) account. After classifying each account, determine how the change in the account balance is treated in the conversion of accrual net income to the cash basis, indirect method. If cash increases use the word *Source;* if cash decreases, use the word *Use.*

Account Title	*CA or CL*	*Increase*	*or*	*Decrease*
Credit card receivables	_____	_____		_____
Accounts payable	_____	_____		_____
Inventory (for resale)	_____	_____		_____
Accounts receivable	_____	_____		_____
Prepaid expenses	_____	_____		_____
Accrued payroll payable	_____	_____		_____
Interest payable	_____	_____		_____
Marketable securities	_____	_____		_____

E10.2   A monthly income statement reported net income of $180,000. Inventory for resale increased by $12,000. Accounts payable increased by $9,000. Using only these three items, determine the net cash flow from operations, indirect method.

E10.3   Net income is $280,000; Depreciation expense is $38,000; Accounts receivable decreased $2,400; Credit card receivables decreased $2,600; Prepaid insurance increased $2,880; Inventory decreased $3,700; Accounts payable increased $4,700; and other accrued payables decreased $3,600. Complete net cash flow from operations activities, indirect method.

E10.4   Identify how each of the following items would be treated in an analysis of changes to working capital. Answer with the word *Inflow* to show an increase or *Outflow* to show a decrease in working capital.

Net income	_____	Sale of equity stock	_____
Net loss	_____	Purchase of equipment	_____
Depreciation	_____	Repayment of long-term debt	_____
Cash dividends	_____	Increasing long-term debt	_____
Sale of equipment	_____	Redemption of stock	_____

E10.5 A hotel provided the following information for Year 0008: The cash flow from operating activities was $178,200, average current liabilities were $58,800, average total liabilities were $666,500, and total sales revenue for the year was $2,555,450 and interest paid was $59,000. Calculate the following ratios:

    a. The cash flow from operating activities to current liabilities ratio

    b. The cash flow for operating activities to total liabilities ratio

    c. The cash flow from operating activities margin ratio

    d. The cash flow from operating activities to interest ratio

E10.6 Given the following information regarding investing and financing activities of an SCF, evaluate each of the given transactions and identify to which section, investing or financing, the transaction belongs. In addition, identify how the amount is handled. Use *Increase* for positive or *Decrease* for negative for the cash flow adjustment conversion in the SCF.

Invest or Finance	*Increase (+) or Decrease (−)*	
_____	_____	Purchased equipment
_____	_____	Sold shares of equity stock
_____	_____	Sold office furniture
_____	_____	Purchased a long-term investment
_____	_____	Declared and paid a cash dividend
_____	_____	Repurchased equity stock
_____	_____	Increased long-term debt

E10.7 Assume working capital was $87,500 for a given year. During this year, accounts receivable increased by $4,600, inventory decreased by $7,754, and accounts payable increased by $3,737. Determine the amount of cash from operations.

E10.8 Assume a business enterprise reports its total current assets as $42,600 and its total current liabilities as $18,640. Answer the following:

    a. What is the amount of working capital?

    b. What is the current ratio (also called the working capital ratio)?

    c. Will the working capital or its ratio change if a transaction collects $1,892 in cash from its credit card receivables?

E10.9 A review of a balance sheet indicated the beginning and ending totals of current assets and current liabilities for a one-year operating period. Determine the working capital at the beginning and the end of the year.

Calculate the change in current assets (*CA*), current liabilities (*CL*), and working capital (*WC*).

	CA	*CL*	*WC*
January 1, 2008	$137,500	$73,525	$
December 31, 2008	142,240	73,250	
Change, current assets	$		
Change, current liabilities		$	
Change in working capital			$

E10.10 Assume the book value of an item of equipment shows $60,000 in Year 1 and $49,400 in Year 2. Would the $10,600 difference be treated as an inflow source, or a outflow use, or not shown at all with regard to its effect on working capital?

E10.11 A restaurant purchased new kitchen equipment for $44,480. Old kitchen equipment was sold for $1,200. A long-term investment was sold for $50,000. Equity stock was bought back (repurchased) for $18,000, and a cash dividend was paid in the amount of $36,600. The company increased its long-term debt by $60,000.

a. Determine the net cash flow from investing activities.

b. Determine the net cash flow from financing activities.

E10.12 The following are operating transactions that occurred during the current year. Analyze each transaction and explain if the transaction will increase, decrease, or have no effect on working capital.

a. Company purchased inventory on account, $5,800; terms 2/10, n/30.

b. Company borrowed $55,000 on a long-term note.

c. Old equipment with a book value of $2,200 was sold for $1,325.

d. Marketable securities were sold at a gain of $4,800.

e. Company paid $4,200 for insurance covering 1 year from the date of purchase.

P R O B L E M S

P10.1 The following is provided to complete the operating activities section of a statement of cash flows, indirect method.

a. Net income for the year is $43,900.

b. Accounts receivable increased by $10,420.

c. Inventory increased by $1,875.

d. Depreciation expense for the year is $8,000.

e. Accounts payable decreased by $5,782.

f. Other current liabilities increased by $3,500.

g. Taxes payable decreased by $1,970.

P10.2 Balance sheet information for a resort hotel reflects the changes to current accounts that occurred over the annual operating period ended December 31, 0008. Cash account balance at December 31, 0007, was $12,020 and the ending cash balance at December 31, 0008, is $30,840.

Current Asset Accounts	Change	Amount
Cash	Increased	$18,820
Credit card receivables	Increased	680
Accounts receivable	Increased	1,500
Inventories	Increased	1,200
Prepaid expenses	Decreased	800

Current Liability Accounts	Change	Amount
Accounts payable	Decreased	$ 2,100
Accrued payroll payable	Increased	2,400
Taxes payable	Decreased	900

Additional information applying to the current year ending December 31, 0008:

a. Net income for Year 0008 was $112,400.

b. Depreciation expense for Year 2008 was $120,000.

c. Furnishings with a book value of $5,400 were sold for $8,600.

d. Equipment with a book value of $2,800 was sold for $2,000.

e. New furnishings were purchased for $16,800.

f. New equipment was purchased for $24,200.

g. A total of $54,800 was paid to reduce long-term debt.

h. Cash dividends of $122,400 were declared and paid.

Using the information provided, complete an SCF, in good form, using the indirect method.

P10.3 You have the following comparative balance sheets for a restaurant for the years ending December 31, 0007, and December 31, 0008. Calculate the change in working capital and prepare the restaurant's statement of sources and uses of working capital for the year ending December 31, 0008.

	Yr. 0007	Yr. 0008
ASSETS		
Current Assets		
Cash	$14,800	$15,600
Credit card receivables	913	847
Accounts receivable	7,387	6,853
Food inventory	5,925	7,275
Beverage inventory	1,975	2,425
Total Current Assets	$31,000	$33,000
Property, Plant & Equipment		
Furnishings and equipment	15,500	19,500
Accumulated depreciation	(3,500)	(4,500)
Net Property, Plant & Equipment	$12,000	$15,000
Total Assets	$43,000	$48,000
LIABILITIES & STOCKHOLDERS' EQUITY		
Current Liabilities		
Accounts payable	$ 4,800	$ 7,100
Accrued expenses payable	800	700
Taxes payable	1,400	200
Total Current Liabilities	$ 7,000	$ 8,000
Long-term Liabilities		
Long-term note payable	$25,800	$27,800
Total Liabilities	$32,800	$35,800
Common stock	4,200	5,200
Retained earnings	6,000	7,000
Total Stockholders' Equity	$10,200	$12,200
Total Liabilities & Stockholders' Equity	$43,000	$48,000

   a. Net income for Year 0008 $7,000. Annual depreciation of $1,000 was included as an expense to arrive at net income.

   b. New equipment costing $4,000 was purchased.

   c. Dividends of $6,000 were paid out.

   d. New shares (50 at $10 each) were issued.

   e. The long-term loan was increased by $2,500.

P10.4 Refer to information provided in the preceding P10.3 and complete, in good form, an SCF using the indirect method.

P10.5 A motel has the following comparative balance sheets for 2 years:

Assets	*12-31-07*	*12-31-08*
Current Assets		
Cash	$ 4,100	$ 5,200
Credit card receivables	4,700	5,500
Accounts receivable	1,200	700
Inventory	3,000	3,600
Marketable securities	8,000	7,000
Prepaid expenses	1,200	1,500
Total Current Assets	$ 22,200	$ 23,500
Property, Plant & Equipment		
Land	$ 30,000	$ 30,000
Building	150,000	150,000
Accum. depreciation, building	(41,900)	(50,200)
Furniture & equipment	22,700	25,400
Accum. Depreciation, furniture & equipment	(15,400)	(19,100)
Total Property, Plant & Equipment	$145,400	$136,100
Total Assets	$167,600	$159,600
Liabilities & Stockholders' Equity		
Current Liabilities		
Accounts payable	$ 6,900	$ 7,000
Accrued expenses payable	1,400	1,700
Income taxes payable	2,000	1,500
Current portion of mortgage payable	11,500	10,400
Total Current Liabilities	$ 21,800	$ 20,600
Long-term Liabilities		
Long-term mortgage payable	100,000	89,600
Total Liabilities	$121,800	$110,200
Stockholders' Equity		
Capital stock, common	23,000	23,000
Retained earnings	22,800	26,400
Total Stockholders' Equity	$ 45,800	$ 49,400
Total Liabilities & Stockholders' Equity	$167,600	$159,600

From this information, prepare a statement of changes to individual working capital accounts.

P10.6 With the balance sheet information from P10.5, and the additional information from the income statement and statement of retained earnings, prepare the motel's statement of changes to working capital for the year ending December 31, 0008.

Income Statement for Year Ended December 31, 0007

Sales revenue	$204,900
Operating costs	(173,800)
Income before depreciation and interest and tax	31,100
Depreciation, building	(8,300)
Depreciation, furniture and equipment	(3,700)
Income before interest and tax	$ 19,100
Interest	(10,800)
Operating income (before tax)	$ 8,300
Income tax	(1,500)
Net income	$ 6,800

Statement of Retained Earnings
For Year Ended December 31, 0007

Retained earnings, January 1, 0007	$ 22,800
Add: Net income for year	6,800
Subtotal	$ 29,600
Deduct: Dividends paid	(3,200)
Retained earnings, December 31, 0007	$ 26,400

P10.7 Referring to the preceding P10.5 and P10.6 that presented a comparative balance sheet, income statement, and a statement of retained earnings, complete a statement of cash flows in good form using the indirect method.

P10.8 A catering company reported the following financial statements and information for two successive years:

Additional financial information:

1. In Year 0007, the building that was previously rented was purchased for $150,000. The company paid $10,000 cash and assumed a long-term mortgage for $140,000. Depreciation on the building is $7,500 for Year 0007. At the end of Year 0007, $7,100 of the mortgage payable was reclassified as a current liability payable in Year 0008.

2. New stock was issued for cash, 200 shares at $50.00 each.

Statement of Retained Earnings
For the Year Ended December 31, 0007

Retained earnings December 31, 0007	$29,900
Operating loss for Year 0008	(8,100)
Retained earnings December 31, 0008	$21,800

The equipment account, and its accumulated depreciation account, is shown below:

	Equipment	Accumulated Depreciation
Balance December 31, 0006	$31,700	$5,800
Purchased new equipment	6,300	
Disposed of fully depreciated old equipment	(4,100)	(4,100)
Depreciation expense Year 0007		4,500
Balance December 31, 0007	$33,900	$6,200

Comparative Balance Sheet

	12-31-0006	12-31-0007
Assets		
Current Assets		
Cash	$ 8,600	$ 15,000
Accounts receivable	19,800	15,800
Inventory, food	6,100	6,300
Prepaid expenses	1,200	1,700
Total Current Assets	$35,700	$ 38,800
Property, Plant and Equipment		
Building	-0-	150,000
Accumulated depreciation, building	-0-	(7,500)
Equipment	31,700	33,900
Accumulated depreciation, equipment	(5,800)	(6,200)
Net Property, Plant and Equipment	$25,900	$170,200
Total Assets	$61,600	$209,000
Liabilities and Stockholders' Equity		
Current Liabilities		
Accounts payable	$21,200	$ 25,400
Accrued expenses	7,500	8,800
Current portion of mortgage payable	-0-	7,100
Total Current Liabilities	$28,700	$ 41,300
Long-term Liabilities		
Long-term mortgage payable	-0-	$132,900
Total Liabilities	$28,700	$174,200
Stockholders' Equity		
Common stock	$ 3,000	$ 13,000
Retained earnings	29,900	21,800
Total Stockholders' Equity	$32,900	$ 34,800
Total Liabilities and Stockholders' Equity	$61,600	$209,000

Calculate the changes in working capital and prepare the company's statement of sources (inflows) and uses (outflows) for the year ended December 31, 0008.

P10.9 A motel has the following balance sheets at the end of each of its most recent two years of operation.

	12-31-2007	*12-31-2008*
Assets		
Cash	$ 8,800	$ -0-
Accounts receivable	17,200	30,600
Inventory	2,100	5,500
Land	20,000	20,000
Building	50,600	100,600
Accumulated depreciation, building	(30,000)	(40,000)
Total Assets	$68,700	$116,700
Liabilities & Stockholders' Equity		
Accounts payable	$ 6,700	$ 12,800
Bank loan payable	-0-	7,900
Long-term mortgage on building	-0-	30,000
Common stock	2,000	2,000
Retained earnings	60,000	64,000
Total Liabilities & Stockholders' Equity	$68,700	$116,700

The income statements provide the following information:

	12-31-0007	*12-31-0008*
Sales revenue	$100,000	$110,000
Operating costs	90,000	93,200
Net income	$ 10,000	$ 16,800

The statement of retained earnings for 12-31-0008 shows:

Retained earnings, December 31, 0007	$60,000
Net income for Year 0008	16,800
Subtotal	76,800
Cash dividends	(12,800)
Retained earnings, December 31, 0008	$64,000

The owner cannot understand why he has $64,000 of retained earnings and a net income of $16,800 after tax from Year 0008 but has no money in the bank. Give the owner any explanations you can using this information.

C A S E   1 0

Given the following budgeted pro forma balance sheet for 4C Company for Year 0008 and referring to Case 2, Year 2007 information, prepare a budgeted pro forma of cash flows for Year 0008.

4C Company
Pro Forma Balance Sheet as of December 31, 0008

Assets			
Current Assets			
Cash		$ 41,903	
Credit card receivable		17,502	
Accounts receivable		5,834	
Food inventory	$ 6,352		
Beverage inventory	2,195	8,547	
Prepaid expenses		2,176	
Total Current Assets			$ 75,962
Property, Plant & Equipment	$171,524		
Less: Accumulated depreciation	(27,504)		
Net equipment		$144,020	
Furnishings	$ 53,596		
Less: Accumulated depreciation	(12,744)		
Net furnishings		40,852	
Total Property, Plant & Equipment			184,872
Total Assets			$260,834
Liabilities and Stockholders' Equity			
Current Liabilities			
Accounts payable	$ 8,817		
Accrued payroll payable	2,917		
Income taxes payable	13,090		
Current portion, bank loan	42,741		
Total Current Liabilities		$ 67,565	
Long-term Liabilities			
Bank loan payable		82,517	
Total Liabilities			$150,082

Stockholders' Equity

Common stock		$ 30,000
Retained earnings, December 31, 0007	$ 34,342	
Net income, 0008	46,410	
Retained earnings, December 31, 0008		80,752
Total Stockholders' Equity		$110,752
Total Liabilities & Stockholders' Equity		$260,834

CASH MANAGEMENT

I N T R O D U C T I O N

This chapter continues the discussion of cash flows. It illustrates that net income shown on an income statement does not imply that there is an equivalent amount of cash in the bank.

This chapter also demonstrates the method of compiling a cash budget from cash receipts and cash disbursements. Negative cash flow may result at times. Various other nonrecurring transactions that could affect the preparation of a cash budget are also discussed.

Cash conservation and working capital management are covered. Included are such items as cash on hand and in the bank, use of bank float, concentration banking, use of two bank accounts, accounts receivable, use of lockboxes, aging of accounts receivable, marketable securities, inventories, and accounts payable.

Finally, we tackle the topic of long-range cash flow (as opposed to short-term cash budgeting), including the use of CVP analysis (taking income tax into consideration) to convert required cash flow to a sales revenue figure.

C H A P T E R O B J E C T I V E S

After studying this chapter, the reader should be able to

1. Explain why cash planning is necessary, and state the two main purposes of cash budgeting.

2. Explain why net income on an income statement is not necessarily indicative of the amount of cash on hand.

3. List items that would appear under cash receipts and cash disbursements on a cash budget, and with appropriate information prepare a cash budget.

4. Define bank float and discuss the concept of concentration banking.

5. Explain some of the procedures that can be used to minimize outstanding accounts receivable at any given time, including the use of a lockbox.

6. Prepare a schedule of aging of accounts receivable.

7. Discuss the importance of marketable securities with reference to surplus cash funds.

8. Explain long-term cash flow budgeting, and use CVP to calculate the sales revenue required to provide a desired cash flow amount.

CASH MANAGEMENT

Simply stated, cash management is the management of money so that bills and debts are paid when they are due. Money does not always come into a business at the same rate as it goes out. At times there will be excess cash on hand; at other times there will be shortages of cash. Both these events must be anticipated so that surpluses can be used to advantage and shortages can be covered. In this way, the cash balance will be kept at its optimum level.

Although the statement of cash flows discussed in Chapter 10 allows an analysis of inflows and outflows of cash on an annual basis, this chapter mainly discusses inflows and outflows of cash on a monthly basis.

THE CYCLE OF CASH FLOW

The cycle of cash flow through an enterprise is illustrated in Exhibit 11.1. This shows that cash management is not just a problem of making sure that the balance of cash in the bank is correct and that the cashiers have the right amount of money on hand. Rather, it is management of all working capital accounts—cash, inventories, accounts receivable, plus the management of accounts payable and loan payments—and of discretionary spending items, such as purchase of new capital assets and payment of dividends if cash is available.

Control over these various items of cash receipts and cash disbursements can be managed by preparing **cash budgets.** The importance of cash planning, or cash budgets, can best be explained by showing that the net income that a company has on its income statement (the excess of sales revenue over expenditure) is not necessarily indicative of the amount of cash the company has on hand.

Let us consider a simple illustration. An entrepreneur has an opportunity to take over a fully equipped and furnished restaurant for a rental cost of $4,000 a month. The entrepreneur decides that a cash savings of $20,000 should be sufficient working capital to start the business, after which the cash from sales revenue should keep the business going and allow a withdrawal of

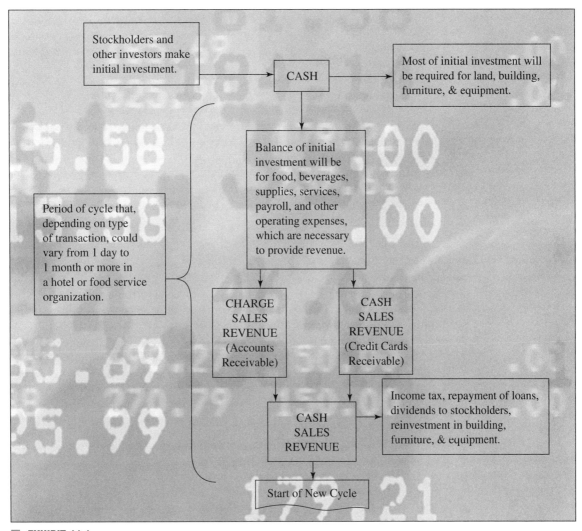

■ **EXHIBIT 11.1**

Illustration of the Cash Flow Cycle

$2,500 a month as a salary. Prior to opening, the proprietor's balance sheet would look like this:

Assets		Liabilities and Equity	
Cash	$20,000	Owner's capital	$20,000

Before the owner can begin operations, some of the available cash was used to purchase of $6,000 of food inventory. Now the balance sheet looks like this:

Assets		Liabilities and Equity	
Cash	$14,000	Owner's capital	$20,000
Inventory	6,000		
Total Assets	$20,000	Total Owner's Equity	$20,000

During the first month the restaurant had the operating results shown in Exhibit 11.2; total sales revenue of $60,000, total expenses of $56,000, and a net income of $4,000. As a result, one might expect to see the bank account increased by $4,000. However, in our case this is not so, although sales revenue was $60,000. To achieve the wanted level of sales revenue, the owner decided to honor national credit cards. In addition, the owner permitted some business customers to sign their bills; it sends them invoices at the end of the month, collecting the accounts receivables by the fifth business day in the following month. As a result, at the end of the month credit cards receivable were $1,350, and accounts receivable were $16,650. The cash sales reveune was only $42,000.

As far as expenses are concerned, the owner used the beginning food inventory that had already been paid for before opening, and purchased additional food inventory totaling $15,000.

The actual cash outlays during the first month were for the additional inventory, the owner's salary, wages, supplies, other expenses, and rent. None of these items were obtainable on credit, so the net cash expenditures totaled $50,000. In summary:

Cash receipts	**$42,000**
Cash disbursements	**(50,000)**
Net change in the bank balance	**($ 8,000)**

Sales revenue		$60,000
Food cost		(21,000)
Gross margin		$39,000
Owner's salary*	$ 2,500	
Other wages	19,500	
Supplies and other expenses	9,000	
Rent expense	4,000	
Total expenses		(35,000)
Net income		$ 4,000

*Since this operation is a proprietorship, the salary would not normally be an expense but would be taken as withdrawals from capital. However, for simplicity, we will assume it is an expense in this example.

■ **EXHIBIT 11.2**

Sample Income Statement

However, since the food inventory has been used, it has to be replaced, and this will require $6,000 cash. Therefore, since at the beginning of the month there was a cash balance (see earlier balance sheet) of $14,000, the month-end cash balance will be zero:

Bank balance beginning of the month	**$14,000**
Change in bank balance from operations	**(8,000)**
Reduction in bank balance for replacement of inventory	**(6,000)**
Bank balance end of month	**0**

The month-end balance sheet will now be:

Assets		**Liabilities and Owner's Equity**	
Cash	$ 0	Owner's capital	$20,000
Credit card receivables	1,350	Net income	4,000
Accounts receivable	16,650		
Inventory	6,000		
Total assets	$24,000	Net owner's capital	$24,000

The balance sheet shows us that despite the positive net income for the first month, there is no cash in the bank to pay any other immediate expenses. Although this illustration is simplified, it is not untypical of what happens to new businesses, and it indicates the danger of assuming that any net income on the income statement is going to be in the form of cash. In this case, the net income of $4,000 was not cash. In fact, the $4,000 of net income and the $14,000 of cash the owner started with at the beginning of the month, are now tied up in credit card and accounts receivables of $18,000 ($1,350 + $16,650).

The same principle applies in an ongoing concern. The net income on the income statement is not generally synonymous with cash. The timing of the cash inflows coming from sales revenue may not parallel the timing of cash outflows being paid for operating expenses. To prevent this difficulty—to see whether a business is going to have excesses or shortages of cash—a cash budget prepared in advance month by month for a year, or at least every quarter, is a useful management tool.

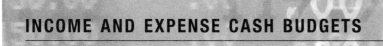

INCOME AND EXPENSE CASH BUDGETS

The starting point in cash budgeting is the forecasted operating income statement showing the budgeted sales revenues and expense expenditures by month for as long a period as is required. In our case, a three-month period will be

	April		May		June	
Sales revenue		$30,000		$35,000		$40,000
Food cost		(12,000)		(14,000)		(16,000)
Gross margin		$18,000		$21,000		$24,000
Payroll and related expense	$9,000		$10,500		$12,000	
Supplies and other expense	1,500		1,750		2,000	
Utilities expense	500		750		1,000	
Rent expense	1,000		1,000		1,000	
Advertising	500	(12,500)	500	(14,500)	500	(16,500)
Income before depreciation		$ 5,500		$ 6,500		$ 7,500
Depreciation		(2,000)		(2,000)		(2,000)
Net income		$ 3,500		$ 4,500		$ 5,500

■ **EXHIBIT 11.3**
Sample Budgeted Income and Expenses

used, and budgeted income statements for a restaurant will be completed for the months of April, May, and June, as shown in Exhibit 11.3.

To prepare our cash budget, we need the following additional information:

1. Accounting records show that each month, approximately 30% of the sales revenue is cash, 65% is on credit cards, and 5% is on accounts receivable. Credit card receivables collected in the month of sales averages 90% and the remaining 10% of credit card receivables are collected in the following month. Accounts receivable sales are collected in the month following the sales. If this restaurant was a new business, a breakdown between cash and credit sales revenue would have to be estimated.

2. March sales revenue was $28,000. This information is needed to calculate the amount of cash that is going to be collected in April from sales receivable made in March.

3. April food purchases were $12,000. Payment of food purchases are paid 25% by cash in the month of purchase and 75% on accounts payable is paid in the month following. The cost of sales–food as shown in Exhibit 11.3 represents food purchases for all three months.

4. March food purchases were $11,000. Again, we need this information so that we can calculate the amount to be paid in cash during April.

5. Payroll, supplies, utilities, and rent are paid 100% cash each month.

6. Advertising of $6,000 was prepaid in the first week of January for the entire year. To show the consumption of the prepaid, prepaid advertising will be expensed at $500 per month over the full year.

7. The cash balance on April 1 is $10,200.

8. The owner repays $2,500 monthly on a bank loan for 12 months beginning in April.

PREPARING THE CASH BUDGET

We can now use the budgeted income statements in Exhibit 11.3, and the previous information to prepare the 3-month cash budget beginning in April. The month of April is used to demonstrate the procedure.

Cash Receipts

Current month cash sales revenue ($30,000 × 30%)	=	**$ 9,000**
Current month credit card receivables, collections ($30,000 × 65% × 90%)	=	**17,550**
Previous month credit card receivables, collections ($28,000 × 65% × 10%)	=	**1,820**
Previous month accounts receivable, collections ($28,000 × 5%)	=	**1,400**
Budgeted cash receipts, April		**$29,770**

Cash Disbursements

Current month cash food inventory purchases, $12,000 × 25%	**$ 3,000**
Accounts payable food purchases, previous month, $11,000 × 75%	**8,250**
Payroll and related expenses, 100% cash	**9,000**
Supplies and other expense, 100% cash	**1,500**
Utilities expense, 100% cash	**500**
Rent expense, 100% cash	**1,000**
Repaid bank loan	**2,500**
Budgeted cash disbursements, April	**$25,750**

Prepaid advertising of $6,000 was a cash disbursement in January. Prepaid expenses are noncash because they are consumed over the period of time they provide benefits. This concept is also valid for depreciation expenses that are noncash expenses and reduce the book value of related depreciable assets.

The completed cash budget for April would then appear as shown in Exhibit 11.4.

The closing cash balance each month is calculated as follows:

Beginning balance + Receipts − Disbursements = Closing cash balance

Each month, the closing cash balance becomes the beginning cash balance of the next month. The completed cash budget for the three-month period is shown in Exhibit 11.5. From Exhibit 11.5, it can be seen that the cash account is expected to increase from the $10,200 on April 1 to $26,070 over the next three months. Continuing the cash budget over the following quarter would show whether the cash balance is going to continue to increase or begin to decline.

Exhibit 11.5 shows that this operation has a good surplus of cash as long as budget projections are reasonably accurate. This cash surplus should not be left to accumulate at no or low interest in a bank account. In this particular case, management might decide to take $15,000 or $20,000 out of the bank and in-

Beginning Cash Balance	$10,200
Cash Receipts	
Current month cash sales revenue	$ 9,000
Current month credit cards receivable, collections	17,550
Previous month credit cards receivable, collections	1,820
Previous month accounts receivables, collections	1,400
Total Cash Available	$39,970
Cash Disbursements	
Cash food purchases	$ 3,000
Accounts payable	8,250
Payroll and related expenses	9,000
Supplies and other expenses	1,500
Utilities expense	500
Rent expense	1,000
Cash disbursements, operating activities	$23,250
Loan repayment, financing activities	2,500
Total Cash Disbursements	$25,750
Ending Cash Balance	$14,220

■ **EXHIBIT 11.4**
Sample Monthly Cash Budget

vest it in high-interest, low-risk, short-term (30-, 60-, or 90-day) marketable securities. Without preparing a cash budget, it would be difficult for management to know that it was going to have surplus funds on hand that could be used to increase net income and subsequently cash receipts. If the cash were taken out of the bank account and invested, the cash budget would have to show this (listed in the financing section). When the marketable securities were cashed in, the amount would be recorded on the cash budget as a receipt in the operating (or financing section, along with interest earned.

As the budget period goes by, the cash budget for the remaining months in that period may need to be adjusted to reflect any changed conditions.

▨ NEGATIVE CASH BUDGET

On occasion some companies, particularly seasonal operations, may find that for some months in the year their disbursements exceed receipts to the point that they have negative cash available. Exhibit 11.6 illustrates such a situation. The operation will be short of cash by an estimated $1,000 in each of Months 4 and 5. However, having prepared a cash budget ahead of time, the company has anticipated the cash shortage and can plan to cover it using a short-term bank loan or by loans from stockholders or owners.

	April	May	June
Beginning Cash Balance	**$10,200**	**$14,220**	**$19,645**
Cash Receipts			
Current month cash sales revenue	$ 9,000	$10,500	$12,000
Current month credit card receivables, collections	17,550	20,475	23,400
Previous month credit card receivables, collections	1,820	1,950	2,275
Previous month accounts receivables, collections	1,400	1,500	1,750
Total Cash Available	**$39,970**	**$48,645**	**$59,070**
Cash Disbursements			
Cash food purchases	$ 3,000	$ 3,500	$ 4,000
Accounts payable	8,250	9,000	10,500
Payroll and related expense	9,000	10,500	12,000
Supplies and other expense	1,500	1,750	2,000
Utilities expense	500	750	1,000
Rent expense	1,000	1,000	1,000
Cash disbursements, operating activities	**$23,250**	**$26,500**	**$30,500**
Loan repayment, financing activities	2,500	2,500	2,500
Total Cash Disbursements	**$25,750**	**$29,000**	**$33,000**
Ending Cash Balance	**$14,220**	**$19,645**	**$26,070**

■ **EXHIBIT 11.5**

Sample Three-Month Cash Budget

OTHER TRANSACTIONS AFFECTING CASH BUDGET: THE FINANCING SECTION

The financing section of the cash budget is used to record all cash receipts and disbursements that are not part of the day-to-day activities of the business.

Just as a cash investment (because of surplus cash) must be recorded on the cash budget, so must cash loans (from banks or stockholders, for example, to cover short-term requirements) be shown as receipts. Repayments of such loans

	Month 1	Month 2	Month 3	Month 4	Month 5	Month 6
Beginning balance	$ 5,000	$ 8,000	$ 9,000	$ 4,000	($ 1,000)	($ 1,000)
Receipts	66,000	72,000	60,000	50,000	48,000	60,000
Total	$71,000	$80,000	$69,000	$54,000	$47,000	$59,000
Disbursements	(63,000)	(71,000)	(65,000)	(55,000)	(48,000)	(55,000)
Ending balance	$ 8,000	$ 9,000	$ 4,000	($ 1,000)	($ 1,000)	$ 4,000

■ **EXHIBIT 11.6**

Sample Negative Cash Flow

are recorded as disbursements. These transactions are recorded in the financing section of the cash budget.

A number of other possible transactions could occur that must be recorded on the cash budget. For example, if any new long-term loans were negotiated, the cash received during a cash budget period must be shown as a receipt in the financing section, as would cash received from any new issues of stock. If any fixed assets were sold for cash, this would also affect the financing section of the cash budget.

By contrast, any repayments of the principal amount of loans, redemption of stock for cash, or purchases of new fixed assets would require disbursements in the financing section of the cash budget.

Finally, any cash dividends paid would further reduce cash on hand, and, therefore, require an entry in the financing section.

The cash budget, particularly if prepared for a year ahead, can not only help management make decisions about investing excess funds and arranging to borrow funds to cover shortages, but also aid in making discretionary decisions concerning such factors as major renovations, replacement of fixed assets, and payment of dividends. The cash budget shows management how much cash is available for these discretionary items.

A cash budget, if carefully prepared, permits management to plan ahead to do or not do certain things, depending on cash availability. If decisions are made and plans are prepared for spending money on items without preparing a cash budget, sudden shortages of cash may develop. These shortages may not be able to be covered quickly with loans because no plans had been made to arrange for loans. As well, if the operation cannot arrange additional financing, the cash budget helps managers plan to change payment and collection schedules to cover the cash shortage. If the cash shortage cannot be covered, the operation could go bankrupt.

CASH CONSERVATION AND WORKING CAPITAL MANAGEMENT

The preparation of a cash budget is an important ingredient to the short-term survival and ultimate success of a business. However, there are certain practices that any hospitality operator should institute as a matter of good business sense to conserve cash, earn interest on it (one possibility), and thus maximize net income. Some of these more common practices of **cash management** are discussed.

CASH ON HAND

Cash on hand, as distinguished from cash in the bank, is the amount of money in circulation in an operation. Cashiers use this cash for change for customers, petty cash, or just general cash in the organization's safe. The amount of cash on hand should be sufficient for normal day-to-day operations only. Any surplus, idle cash should be deposited in savings accounts so it can earn interest. Preferably, each day's net cash receipts should be deposited in the bank as soon as possible on the following day.

CASH IN BANK

Cash in the bank in the current operating account should be sufficient to pay only the employee payroll and current accounts payable due. Any excess funds should be invested in short-term securities (making sure there is a good balance between maximizing the interest rate, security, and liquidity of the investment) or in savings or other special accounts that earn interest. The typical hospitality industry enterprise will probably determine an appropriate level of cash to be held after considering the following:

- Anticipated cash flows indicated by the cash budget
- Unanticipated events causing deviations from the cash budget
- Ability to borrow money for emergencies above the minimal cash requirements, plus any precautionary amounts
- Desire of management to always have more than sufficient cash on hand rather than maintaining a minimum cash level (A minimum cash level may aid in increasing net income, but at the same time it will increase risk.)
- Efficiency of the cash management system (The more efficient a business's system is, the more surplus cash will be available for investment and increased profits.)
- Historical evidence and past experience, which can be a guide to establishing satisfactory levels of cash

USE OF FLOATS

A **bank float** is the difference between the bank balance shown on a company's records and the balance of actual cash in the bank. There is a difference because checks that a company writes are deducted from its record of the bank balance at that time. However, there is a delay between that time (due to mailing and the handling of the check by the recipient and then to the bank) and the time that the check is received by the company's bank and deducted from its records. The use of electronic funds transfer (EFT) is increasing rapidly, and the turn-around time is significantly reduced. If a company can estimate the amount of this *float* and the time involved, it can then invest that amount for that period and increase its net income.

CONCENTRATION BANKING

Concentration banking (also known as **integrated banking**) might be appropriate for chain-operated hotels or restaurants. It is a method of accelerating the flow of funds from the individual units in the chain to the company's head office bank account. The individual units will still have accounts at the bank's local branch in the city where the unit is operated, but arrangements will be made with the local bank to transfer any surplus above a predetermined level in the account to the head office's bank immediately. The use of electronic funds transfers between individual units in a chain organization to and from the company's head office and such transfers are handled almost instantly.

Disbursements for supplies and payroll would be made from the head office account on behalf of the individual units. Only sufficient cash to take care of normal day-to-day disbursements would be held in the local account. Any surplus would be invested in such items as marketable securities (to be discussed later in this chapter). A concentration banking system results in more effective cash management for the entire chain. For example, there might be a temptation for a local unit manager to pay invoices before their due date to keep local suppliers happy. Also, if an individual unit requires cash, the head office can provide it using electronic funds transfers so the local unit manager does not have to negotiate a loan with the local banker at less favorable terms.

In concentration banking, it is important to minimize the cost of funds' transfers, and the use of electronic funds transfers will minimize costs. In certain situations, daily transfers from the individual units to the head office account might not be the most appropriate action. To determine how frequently transfers should be made, the following equation may be used:

$$\text{Transfer frequency} = \frac{2 \times \text{Average bank balance}}{\text{Average daily deposit}}$$

For example, if a restaurant unit were to require an average bank balance of $20,000, and if its average daily deposit was $5,000, the transfer frequency would be calculated as follows:

$$\text{Transfer frequency} = \frac{2 \times \$20,000}{\$5,000} = \frac{\$40,000}{\$5,000} = 8 \text{ days}$$

This means that at the beginning of each 8-day period, the balance in the unit's bank account will be zero. At the end of 8 days it will have accumulated to $40,000, at which time the full $40,000 is transferred, reducing the balance again to zero. Seven transfers are eliminated, thus minimizing transfer costs. In general, the only time that a daily transfer would be profitable for an operation would be if the average bank balance required were less than half the average daily deposit.

TWO BANK ACCOUNTS

In addition to concentration banking, large chain operations can also benefit from the float effect by having one bank account on the East Coast and the other on the West Coast. Collections from the Pacific-side operations would be deposited in the West Coast bank; payments on behalf of these operations would be made from the East Coast bank. The reverse situation would exist for Atlantic-side operations. Electronic funds transfers reduce the time between when the cost payment is made and when the funds are deducted from the bank account, thus reducing the advantage of this technique.

ACCOUNTS RECEIVABLE

Attention to accounts receivable should be focused on two areas: ensuring that invoices are mailed out promptly and following up on delinquent accounts to have them collected. Money tied up in accounts receivable is money not earning a return. Extension of credit to customers is an acknowledged form of business transaction, but it should not be extended to the point of allowing payments to lag two or three months behind the mailing of invoices. In hotels, a special situation arises. Accounts receivable in hotels are made up of city ledger accounts and house accounts. **City ledger** accounts include banquet and convention business, regular credit card charges for individuals using the hotel's food and beverage facilities, and the accounts of people who were staying in the hotel but who have checked out and charged their bills. Normal collection procedures prevail for collecting such accounts. The house accounts are for those registered in the hotel that have not yet checked out. In some cases, such accounts can build up to large amounts in a very short time. A good policy is to establish a ceiling to which the dollar amount of an individual account may rise. Once this ceiling is reached, the night auditor can be instructed to advise the credit manager, or general manager in a smaller hotel, who must then decide whether any action should be taken to request payment, or partial payment, of the account, or to discuss a credit arrangement with the guest. Where guests stay for longer periods without necessarily running up large accounts, a good policy is to give the guest a copy of the bill at least once a week. This serves two purposes. It allows the guest to confirm or question the accuracy of the account, and it suggests that payment should be made or arrangements for credit established.

AGE OF ACCOUNTS RECEIVABLE CHARTS

One of the ways to keep an eye on the accounts receivable is to use **accounts receivable aging**—that is, periodically (at least once a month) prepare a chart showing the age of the accounts outstanding. Exhibit 11.7 illustrates such a chart and shows that the accounts receivable outstanding situation has not improved from March to April. In March, 79.5% of total receivables were less than 30 days old. In April, only 74.2% were less than 30 days outstanding. Similarly,

Age	March 31		April 30	
0–30 days	$59,000	79.5%	$56,400	74.2%
31–60 days	11,800	15.9%	8,800	11.6%
61–90 days	2,400	3.2%	8,600	11.3%
Over 90 days	1,050	1.4%	2,200	2.9%
Totals	$74,250	100.0%	$76,000	100.0%

EXHIBIT 11.7
Analysis (Aging) of Accounts Receivable

the relative percentages in the 31- to 60-day category have worsened from March to April. As well, in the 61- to 90-day bracket, 11.3% percent of receivables are outstanding in April, against only 3.2% in March. This particular aging chart shows that our accounts receivable are getting older. If this trend continued, collection procedures would need to be improved. If, after all possible collection procedures have been explored, an account is deemed to be uncollectable (a bad debt), it would then be removed from accounts receivable. The manager or owner should make the decision as to whether an account is not collectable in a small operation. In a larger operation, the credit manager or comptroller would make the decision if an account is collectable.

LOCKBOXES

The collection of accounts receivable can also be made more efficient by the use of a lockbox. **Lockboxes** are most appropriate for chain operations. When they are used, customers are instructed to mail their checks in payment of accounts to a designated post office mailbox. The hospitality establishment's bank picks up the mail and deposits the receivables' payments into the hospitality operation's bank account and subsequently notifies the establishment of the necessary detail for it to record payments in its accounts receivable. Using electronic funds transfers is rapidly increasing where customers are offered the option of paying their accounts using EFT, rather than paying their accounts by check through the mail; EFT also reduces the cost to the company receiving payment on their account. The main advantages of the lockbox system are that the individual units in the chain are freed from receiving and depositing payment checks and that the collection process is speeded up by one or more days.

There is a cost attached to using a lockbox. To determine whether the added efficiency is profitable, the cost should be compared with the increased income from the cash released for investment elsewhere. If income exceeds cost, the system is profitable; if the reverse is the case, it is not. However, the use of EFT decreases cost significantly and its cost would not normally be anticipated to exceed other investment income.

Alternatively, it may be useful to calculate the minimum level of the average accounts receivable payment that would make a lockbox system profitable. Suppose that the bank charges 20 cents for each payment check handled and that the opportunity cost of the interest the hospitality operation could earn by investing freed-up cash in alternative investments such as marketable securities is 9%. By using a lockbox, the collection of accounts receivable is speeded up by two days. An equation for determining the minimum level of accounts receivable that would make the lockbox system profitable is

$$\frac{\textbf{Bank charge per item}}{\textbf{Opportuntiy cost percentage per day} \times \textbf{Time savings in days}}$$

Using our figures, the minimum accounts receivable amount is:

$$\frac{\$0.20}{(9\% / 365) \times 2} = \frac{\$0.20}{0.00024666 \times 2} = \frac{\$0.20}{0.0004932} = \$405.52$$

Given these assumptions, this means that with a lockbox system, payments in excess of $405 on accounts receivable would be profitable and payments less than $405 would not be profitable. A decision could be made to use a lockbox if the average payment exceeded $405. Alternatively, a more profitable approach might be to handle accounts receivable according to size. For example, when the accounts are mailed out, those in excess of $405 would carry instructions to use the lockbox mailing address, and those less than $405 would be handled in the regular manner.

MARKETABLE SECURITIES

Generally, any surplus cash not needed for immediate and precautionary purposes should be invested in some type of security. Investments could be for as short a period as one day, but are usually for longer periods, although seldom more than a year. If surplus cash were available for periods of a year or more, it might then be wise to seek out long-term investments, such as building a new property or expanding an existing one, because the return on those investments over the long run could be expected to be greater than for investment in short-term securities.

Most hospitality industry enterprises, particularly those that rely for much or all of their trade on seasonal tourists, have peaks and valleys in their cash flows. Surplus cash from peak-season flows should be invested in short-term securities until it is necessary to liquidate them to take care of low, or negative, cash flows during the off-season. Sometimes it is necessary to build up surplus cash to take care of periodic lump-sum payments, such as quarterly tax or dividend payments. These built-up amounts could be invested in marketable securities until they were needed for payment of these liabilities.

In times of high interest rates, many companies find it profitable to invest all cash in excess of day-to-day needs in the most liquid marketable securities, those that can be converted into cash quickly if an unanticipated event requiring cash occurs. In this way, little if any precautionary cash will be carried.

Two important factors need to be considered when investing in marketable securities: risk and maintaining liquidity. A low risk generally goes hand in hand with a low interest rate. A more risky investment would have to offer a higher interest rate to attract investors. Government securities have very low risk and usually guarantee that the security can be cashed at full face value at any time. Their interest rate, however, is also relatively low. On the other hand, investments in long-term corporate bonds may offer a higher interest rate. This type of security is, however, subject to economic factors that make their buy–sell price more volatile. This volatility increases the risk and can reduce the profitability of investing in them if they have to be liquidated, or converted into cash, at an inconvenient time.

Short-term, liquid marketable securities include such items as government treasury bills, bankers' acceptances, short-term notes, bank deposit receipts, and corporate or finance company paper. Long-term, less-liquid investments include corporate bonds, preferred and common stock, equipment trust certificates, and municipal securities.

INVENTORIES

Keeping inventory low is an excellent way to conserve cash. One way to determine if the inventory level is correct is to use the inventory turnover ratio. The inventory turnover ratio was introduced in Chapter 4 when we discussed ratio analysis.

The inventory turnover should be calculated monthly. If the turnover rate at the end of any month is out of line, corrective action can be taken then.

Assuming we had the following figures:

Beginning of the month inventory	$ 7,000
End of the month inventory	8,000
Purchases during month	24,500

Our calculation of the inventory turnover rate is:

$$\frac{\text{Food cost for the month}}{\text{Average food inventory during month}} = \text{Times per month}$$

$$\frac{\$7,000 + \$24,500 - \$8,000}{(\$7,000 + \$8,000) / 2} = \frac{\$23,500}{\$7,500} = 3.1 \text{ times per month}$$

Traditionally, the food industry food inventory turnover ranges between 2 and 4 times a month. However, keeping it close to and even over four is feasible for most operations. On one hand, at this level, the danger of running out of food items is minimal; on the other hand, there is not an over investment in inventory tying up money that could otherwise be put to use earning interest income. However, despite this range of 2 to 4 times a month, there may be exceptions. Perhaps of more importance to an organization is not what its actual turnover rate is, but whether there is a change in this turnover rate over time, and what the cause of the change is. For example, let us assume that the earlier figures of $23,500 for food cost of sales and $7,500 for average inventory, giving a turnover rate of 3.1, were typical of the monthly figures for this operation. If management noticed that the figure for turnover changed to 2, this would mean that more money was being invested in inventory and not producing a return.

$$\frac{\$23,500}{\$11,750} = 2 \text{ times}$$

Alternatively, a change in the turnover rate to 4 could mean that too little was invested in inventory and that some customers may not be able to get certain items listed on the menu.

$$\frac{\$23,500}{\$5,875} = 4 \text{ times}$$

In some establishments, the inventory turnover rate may be extremely low (less than 2). For example, a resort property in a remote location may only be able to get deliveries once a month and is, thus, forced to carry a large inventory. However, a drive-in restaurant that receives daily delivery of its food items from a central commissary and carries little inventory overnight could conceivably have a turnover rate as high as 30 times a month. Each organization should establish its own standards for turnover and then watch for deviations from those standards.

Beverage inventory turnover is calculated using the same formula, but it substitutes beverage inventories and beverage purchases for food. The normal monthly turnover rate for beverages is from 1 to 4 times a month. The volume of beverage business and type of products offered will dictate each operation's beverage inventory turnover.

ACCOUNTS PAYABLE, ACCRUED EXPENSES, AND OTHER CURRENT LIABILITIES

The objective here is to conserve cash in the organization and to delay payment until payment is required. However, this does not mean delaying payment until it is delinquent. A company with a reputation for delinquency may find it has difficulty obtaining food, beverages, supplies, and services on anything other than a cash basis (COD, or cash on delivery). Most business operations will normally take notice of purchase discounts offered and schedule the payment to be made on the last day of the discount period. Most organizations are aware that missing a cash discount results in an implied above-average high interest rate. Generally, a common discount ranges from 2% to 3% off the invoice total if it is paid within 10 days, otherwise it is payable without the discount within 30 days and missing a 2% discount implies a 36.5% rate: [365 days / (Credit period days − Discount period days)] × Cash discount rate = Implied interest rate. The implied interest rate of missing a discount on terms of 3/10, n/30 discount rate (save 10% if paid within 10 days or pay the full amount within 30 days) would be 54.75%. If a cash **discount** for prompt payments is offered, the advantages of taking the discount and paying on the last day of the discount period should be considered. For example, a business made a purchase of $4,400 with terms of 3/10, n/30 and would save $132 if the discount is taken and payment of $4,268 was made by the last day of the discount period. A savings of $132 may not seem to be a significant amount of money, but multiplied numerous times on all similar purchases made during a year, it could amount to a large sum. However, in the example cited, the company might have to borrow the money ($4,268) to make the payment within 10 days. Let's assume the money was borrowed for 20 days at a 10% interest rate:

$$\text{Interest expense} = \frac{\$4{,}268 \times 20 \text{ days} \times 10\%}{365 \text{ days}} = \frac{\$8{,}536}{365} = \$23.39$$

It would still be advantageous to borrow the money since the difference between the discount savings of $132 and the interest expense of $23.39 is $108.61.

OTHER ITEMS

There are other methods of operating with the objective of conserving cash in the business. One example is leasing, rather than purchasing, an asset to take advantage of a tax saving. This and other, more long-range techniques are covered in Chapter 12.

LONG-RANGE CASH FLOW

The **long-range cash flow** budget differs somewhat from day-to-day cash budgeting. The long-range cash flow projections ignore any changes within working capital and assume that the current asset and liability amounts remain relatively constant over the long run. The long-range cash flow budget is usually prepared for yearly periods up to 5 years ahead.

The starting point in the preparation of a long-range cash flow budget is the annual net income figure. Depreciation is added back to determine cash inflow.

	Year 1	Year 2	Year 3	Year 4	Year 5
Net income after tax	$10,000	$21,500	$30,000	$ 35,500	$ 40,000
Add back: depreciation expense	80,000	72,000	65,000	59,000	55,000
	90,000	93,500	95,000	94,500	95,000
Deduct long-term loan payments	(60,000)	(63,000)	(65,000)	(67,000)	(68,000)
Net cash flow	$30,000	$30,500	$30,000	$ 27,500	$ 27,000
Accumulated cash flow		$60,500	$90,500	$118,000	$145,000

■ **EXHIBIT 11.8**

Long-Range Accumulated Cash Flow

Principal payments on long-term borrowings, payment of cash dividends, and equipment purchases make up normal cash outflows. A simple cash flow budget for 5 years appears in Exhibit 11.8.

The long-term cash flow budget serves the following purposes:

- ■ It allows the manager to see whether there will be cash available to meet long-term mortgage, bond, or other loan commitments.
- ■ It indicates a possible need to arrange additional long-term borrowings or the need to issue additional stock to raise cash.
- ■ It allows for planning replacement of or additions to long-term assets (note that if any long-term assets were bought or sold, the cash disbursed or received would be included in the cash flow projections).
- ■ It permits the planning of a dividend payment policy, since it shows whether there will be surplus cash available for dividends.

CASH FLOW AND CVP

CVP analysis (discussed in Chapter 8) can also be applied to cash flow. It can answer the question: How much sales revenue is needed to produce various levels of cash flow? For example, suppose the management of the operation illustrated in Exhibit 11.8 wanted a cash flow of $38,000 in Year 1, rather than the $30,000 illustrated. What would this require in terms of total sales revenue?

First, the desired cash flow has to be converted to an after-tax profit figure by adding to the desired cash flow the long-term loan payments and deducting depreciation, given in Exhibit 11.8:

$$\frac{\text{Required}}{\text{cash}} = \frac{\text{Required}}{\text{net income}} + \frac{\text{Depreciation}}{\text{expense}} - \frac{\text{Loan}}{\text{payment}}$$

This equation can be rearranged so the required net income is isolated and provides the information we need.

$$\underset{\text{cash}}{\text{Required}} + \underset{\text{payment}}{\text{Loan}} - \underset{\text{expense}}{\text{Depreciation}} = \underset{\text{net income}}{\text{Required}}$$

$$\$38,000 + \$60,000 - \$80,000 = \underline{\underline{\$18,000}}$$

The after-tax figure then has to be converted to a before-tax amount by the following equation:

$$\text{Operating income} = \frac{\text{After-tax profit}}{1 - \text{Tax rate}}$$

If the company's tax rate were 25%, this would be:

$$\frac{\$18,000}{1 - 25\%} = \frac{\$18,000}{75\%} = \$24,000$$

The following CVP equation can then be used to convert the operating income before-tax desired to a sales revenue figure:

$$\frac{\text{Fixed costs} + \text{Operating income}}{\text{Contribution margin}}$$

If fixed costs (including depreciation) were $180,000, and contribution margin was 60% of sales, sales revenue required would be:

$$\frac{\$180,000 + \$24,000}{60\%} = \frac{\$204,000}{60\%} = \$340,000$$

This is proved as follows:

Sales revenue		$340,000
Variable costs (40% × $340,000)	$136,000	
Fixed costs	180,000	(316,000)
Operating income		$ 24,000
Tax @ 25%		(6,000)
Net income		$ 18,000
Add-back depreciation		80,000
Cash available		$ 98,000
Deduct loan payments		(60,000)
Net cash flow		$ 38,000

COMPUTER APPLICATIONS

If operating budgets are computerized using a spreadsheet, the same spreadsheet can take the budgeted figures and produce a cash budget. This cash budget can be produced so rapidly that it can indicate cash needs not only on a monthly basis but also on a weekly or even daily basis. This is particularly true when things like the ratio of cash to charge sales revenue remains relatively constant. Because a computerized budget can be constantly updated, it allows management to readily anticipate cash surpluses so the excess cash can be invested or to allow the surpluses to be used for discretionary expenditures.

A spreadsheet program can also handle all the necessary calculations for preparing a long-range cash flow budget, as illustrated in Exhibit 11.8.

SUMMARY

Excesses and deficiencies of cash can occur in any business. This is particularly true of the cyclical hospitality industry. Therefore, cash management becomes most important.

Net income and cash are not synonymous. An organization may have a net income but no cash available to pay bills. Alternatively, the income statement may show a loss, yet there will be cash available to pay dividends.

To project surpluses and shortages of cash, cash budgets for up to a year can be useful. The cash budget converts the budgeted income statements to a cash position. Sales revenue for a particular month is not always received in cash during that month. If some sales revenue are made on a charge basis, that cash may not be received until 30 or more days later. Similarly, expenses recorded on the income statement do not always involve an outlay of cash during that month. Payments can often be deferred. Finally, there are some items of cash revenue (the sale of a fixed asset) or cash outlay (principal payments on a loan) that do not appear on an income statement. These items can be incorporated into the financing section of the cash budget so excess funds can be foreseen and used profitably by, for example, investing, and so cash shortages can be forecast and covered by arranging, in advance, for short-term financing.

Cash management involves a process of cash conservation. This simply means that the good manager will control the amount of cash on hand and in the bank, inventory levels, accounts receivable, and accounts payable. Doing so will allow the business to maintain its most liquid cash position at all times.

Cash budgets require careful day-to-day observation of the various current asset and liability accounts to maximize the day-to-day cash position of the organization.

Long-range cash flow budgets differ somewhat from day-to-day cash budgets in that they ignore changes in the working capital accounts. Long-range cash flow budgets assume that the net income an enterprise makes will, over the long run, be converted into cash. Long-range cash flow budgets, prepared up to 5 years ahead, permit management to see whether long-term mortgage and other loan commitments can be met, or whether further mortgages and/or loans need to be arranged. They also allow management to make plans for capital asset purchases and replacements and to plan dividend payment policies.

DISCUSSION QUESTIONS

1. What is the meaning of cash management or cash planning?
2. What two main purposes are served by preparing a cash budget?
3. Why is net income shown on an income statement not necessarily the same as cash?
4. List two items that could appear on a cash budget under the receipts section.
5. List three items that could appear on a cash budget under the disbursements section.
6. List three items that could appear in the financing section of a cash budget.
7. Define the term *bank float* and explain how it can be used.
8. Explain concentration banking and give the equation for funds transfer frequency when concentration banking is used.
9. What two procedures will help ensure that the total accounts receivable amount is kept to a minimum?
10. Differentiate between city ledger accounts receivable and house accounts receivable in a hotel.
11. What two procedures can be instituted in a hotel to minimize the dollar amount of house accounts?
12. Explain the procedure of aging accounts receivable.
13. Explain how a lockbox is used to minimize funds outstanding in accounts receivable.
14. Discuss the use of marketable securities with reference to temporary surplus cash.
15. Explain why it is important to manage food or beverage inventory turnover.
16. Differentiate between an operating cash budget and a long-term cash flow budget.

ETHICS SITUATION

In reviewing actual cash flows for the past three months and the cash budgets for the next three, a hotel manager notices that the cash sales revenue from the hotel's bar operation has been slowly declining each month. The manager suspects that not all cash sales are being recorded and that bar employees may be pocketing the cash. He has approached a private security firm to have one of its representatives pose as a customer at the bar and observe if his suspicions are in fact true. Discuss the ethics of this situation.

EXERCISES

E11.1 A restaurant purchased $7,500 of food inventory on credit with terms of 3/5, net 30. Calculate the cash discount and determine if the discount should or should not be taken and discuss your decision.

E11.2 The following information is available regarding sales revenue for March and April, Year 0007: What is the vertical common-sized analysis (percentages) of all items based on sales revenue? Discuss any significant findings.

	March	*April*
Sales revenue	$48,200	$50,400
Cash sales	14,460	14,112
Credit card sales	31,330	34,272
Accounts receivable sales	2,410	2,016

E11.3 A restaurant provides the following regarding food inventories for the month of March.

Beginning food inventories	$14,800
Purchases during the current month	74,200
Ending food inventories, current month	12,700

a. Calculate the food inventory turnover for the month.

b. Calculate the days of inventory available for the month of March.

E11.4 A small hotel provided you with the following information for a three-month period showing, at each month-end, the length of time its accounts receivable were outstanding at that time:

	January	*February*	*March*
0–30 days	$21,100	$21,500	$22,100
31–60 days	4,900	7,500	8,500
61–90 days	1,000	900	1,400
over 90 days	500	400	600

During this period, the sales revenue was approximately the same for each of the three months. Carry out any further calculations necessary so that you can then comment about or discuss the results.

E11.5 A motel chain uses a system of concentration banking. Calculate the transfer frequency for each of the following individual motels:

	Average Bank Balance	*Average Daily Deposit*
Motel A	$3,200	$1,600
Motel B	5,700	1,900
Motel C	6,500	6,500
Motel D	2,600	5,800

P11.6 For each of the following alternatives, calculate the minimum account receivable payment (to the closest dollar) that would make a lockbox system profitable:

	Bank Charge per Item	*Opportunity Cost*	*Days Saved*
a.	$0.20	10.0%	2
b.	$0.18	8.0%	3
c.	$0.25	8.5%	4

E11.7 The following information is available regarding sales revenue for March, April, and May, Year 0008: Credit card sales revenue is collected on the average of every three days and the amount remaining uncollected at the end of the month represents 6% of the month's credit card sales revenue. Accounts receivable sales are collected in the month following the sales. Using the following information regarding sales, calculate the cash inflow for the months of April and May, Year 0008.

	March	*April*	*May*
Sales revenue	$46,100	$49,200	$52,800
Cash sales (32% of sales)	14,752	15,744	16,896
Credit card sales (64% of sales)	29,504	31,488	33,792
Accounts receivable sales (4% of sales)	1,844	1,968	2,112

E11.8 A restaurant reported the following information for the months of August, September, and October, Year 0008. Of the cost of sales, 75% is paid in the current month and the remainder is paid in the following month. Of the operating expenses, 98% is paid in the current month and the remainder in the following month.

	August	*September*	*October*
Sales revenue	$48,400	$49,880	$51,200
Cost of sales	(18,392)	(18,954)	(19,456)
Operating expenses	(24,684)	(25,439)	(26,112)
Operating income	$ 5,324	$ 5,487	$ 5,632

Calculate the total cash payments for the months of September and October, Year 0008.

E11.9 The following is income statement information of a restaurant for the first two months of operation. Of the sales revenue, 86% is collected in cash with the remainder collected in the following month. Of cost of sales, 75% is paid in the current month and the remainder is paid in the next month. Wages and operating expenses are paid in the month incurred. The January ending cash balance was $4,448. Using a cash budget format, calculate the ending cash balance for the month of February.

		January		*February*
Sales revenue		$38,400		$39,300
Cost of sales		(14,208)		(14,541)
Gross margin		$24,192		$24,759
Wages expense	$13,056		$13,362	
Other operating expenses	5,760		5,895	
Depreciation expense	768		768	
Total operating expenses		(19,584)		(20,025)
Operating income		$ 4,608		$ 4,734

P R O B L E M S

P11.1 You have the following information about a restaurant in Year 0007:

- Actual sales revenue in November was $80,000.
- Actual purchases (cost of sales) in November was $30,000.

Sales revenue will be 40% cash. Credit card sales revenue is 60% of sales, of which 96% is collected in the month of sales; the remaining 4% is collected early in the following month. Purchases of inventory, 20% is paid in the month of purchase and the remaing 80% is paid in the month following the purchases. The condensed budgeted income statement for December, Year 0007, follows:

Sales revenue		$75,000
Cost of sales	$29,000	
Wages expense	21,000	
Operating expenses	14,000	
Rent expense	5,500	
Depreciation expense	2,500	
Total expenses		(72,000)
Operating income		$ 3,000

The wages and operating expenses included in the budgeted income statement will be paid in December, Year 0007. Rent was prepaid in January for the entire year. Prepare a cash budget for the month of December, Year 0007. November ending cash is $4,800.

P11.2 On December 31, 0007, a small motel has a bank balance of $7,100. On that same date its balance sheet showed that it had a bank loan payable of $73,900. The motel's budgeted income statement is as follows for 0008:

Sales Revenue		$403,900
Operating costs		(302,300)
Total Sales Revenue		$101,600
Other Expenses		
Management salary expense	$23,000	
Building rent expense	18,500	
Insurance expense	2,400	
Interest expense	7,600	
Furniture depreciation expense	9,700	(61,200)
Operating income		$ 40,400
Income tax		(10,100)
Net Income		$ 30,300

Total sales 367,900 from January through October 0008 was $333,391. Sales are 42% cash and 58% on credit cards. Credit card sales collections are 92% in the month of sales and 8% in the following month. Sales for October, November, and December of 0008 are:

	Year 007	Year 0008
October	$32,500	$32,500
November	$34,500	$34,500
December	$36,000	$36,000

The owner pays all expenses at the time they occur so they do not carry any accounts payable. The income tax for 0008 income will not be paid until March 0009. However, $9,800 for 0007 income tax was paid in March 0008.

The motel owner plans to buy new furniture in May 0008 at an estimated cost of $15,600. By the end of December 31, 0008, the bank loan payable will have been reduced to $49,200. Calculate the motel's ending bank balance at December 31, 0008.

P11.3 You have the following information about a restaurant:

	Budgeted Cash Revenue	*Budgeted Credit Revenue*
August	$30,300	$16,000
September	29,500	14,000
October	27,900	13,000
November	25,100	12,000
December	32,400	15,800

Collections on credit revenue average 90% in the month following the sales and the remaining 10% in the month following. Cost of sales (purchases) averages 38% of total sales revenue. Forty percent of cost of sales is on a cash basis, and 60% is paid in the month following purchase. Payroll costs (which are paid on a cash basis) are forecast to be $13,100 for October; $12,700 for November; and $12,200 for December.

Other budgeted expenses according to the forecast income statements follow:

	October	*November*	*December*
Rent expense	$2,500	$2,500	$2,500
Insurance expense	300	300	300
Utilities expense	500	450	550
Other operating costs	1,100	900	1,300
Depreciation (equipment)	4,600	4,600	4,600
Interest expense	400	400	400

Note that the rent, utilities, other operating costs, and interest are paid in cash each month as the expense is incurred. The insurance expense is paid in January each year in advance for the whole year ($3,600). The restaurant financed its equipment and makes monthly payments on the balance owing (principal amount) of $1,000. In December, the restaurant plans to sell off some old equipment and estimates it will receive $1,500 from the sale. At the same time, it must spend $5,400 on new equipment. If there is sufficient cash on hand, the owner plans to pay a bonus to the staff. This bonus will amount to $3,600 and will be paid in December.

Prepare the restaurant's cash budget for each of the three months: October, November, and December. The beginning cash balance October 1 is $2,410.

P11.4 You own a new restaurant that is due to open on June 1, 0008. The restaurant expects to take in $1,500 a day in sales revenue and is open seven days a week. Sales revenue is estimated to be 40% cash and 60%

on credit card receivables; it is estimated that 88% of credit card receivables will be collected in the current month of sales and the balance will be collected in first part of the following month.

Wages and salaries expense is expected to be 37% and cost of sales is 38% of sales revenue. Both these expenses will be on a cash basis.

Other operating costs are estimated to be 10% of sales revenue. These costs will not have to be paid until the month following the incurrence of the cost.

Depreciation is $1,800 a month. Rent is $2,000 a month, payable in advance on the first of each month.

Principal payments on a loan you made to get into business are $3,000 a month. The first payment is due on June 15. Interest expense of $300 will be paid each month. You have only $1,000 cash on hand on June 1. You will not be able to borrow any more money, and you have no income of your own other than the money generated by your new restaurant venture.

a. Produce the budgeted income statement for the restaurant for the month of June.

b. Prepare the restaurant's cash budget for the month of June.

c. Comment about the results shown by these two statements, with particular reference to any possible financial difficulties you might have.

P11.5 A small motel with a small dining room has the following estimates for Year 0007:

Sales Revenue

Rooms sales revenue	$350,000
Dining room sales revenue	$150,000
Cost of sales: dining room	35% of sales revenue

Direct expenses

Wages expense	25% of rooms sales revenue
	40% of dining sales revenue
Rooms expense	25% of rooms sales revenue
Dining room expenses	40% of dining room sales revenue
Cost of sales: food	35% of dining room sales revenue

Other operating expenses

Rooms expense	5% of rooms revenue
Dining room expense	10% of dining room revenue
Other income	$5,500
(vending machines)	

Indirect Expenses

Administrative & general expenses	$25,600
Marketing expenses	$15,400
Property operation & maint. expense	$16,700
Utilities expense	$12,500
Land rental expense	$28,300
Interest expense	$11,500

Depreciation Expenses

Building	$50,200
Furniture and equipment	$24,800

In July of 0007, the owner plans to buy $30,000 of new equipment (for cash), less a $5,400 trade-in of used equipment. The vending machines contractor will continue to pay the same commission rate in Year 0007.

During 0007, principal payments on a mortgage on the building will be $30,300, and principal payments on a bank loan will be $25,300.

The owner, who is also the only shareholder in the company, plans to pay herself dividends of $42,000 during Year 0007.

a. Prepare a budgeted income statement for Year 0007.

b. Calculate the motel's cash flow for Year 0007.

P11.6 From the information following for Cato's Catering, prepare a cash budget for 6 months commencing April 1:

	Sales Revenue		Purchases		Other	
	Food	*Beverage*	*Food*	*Beverage*	*Wages*	*Expenses*
February	$30,000	$ 9,000	$12,000	$4,400	$12,000	$10,300
March	31,000	9,600	12,500	4,800	12,400	10,400
April	34,000	10,800	13,600	5,400	13,000	10,800
May	35,600	12,600	14,000	6,400	13,800	11,200
June	46,000	13,800	14,600	6,800	15,000	11,600
July	50,000	16,200	16,600	8,200	14,800	11,400
August	45,000	14,200	14,600	7,200	13,400	10,600
September	40,800	13,000	14,200	6,400	12,200	10,200

■ Assume that all sales are cash sales.
■ The annual interest of $1,600 on the restaurant's marketable securities will be received in July.

- The time delay in paying suppliers for food and beverage purchases is two months. For example, February purchases are paid in April.
- Wages are paid without any time delay.
- Other expenses are paid with a one-month delay.
- In May, new kitchen equipment will be purchased for $10,000. Payment for this will be made in the following month.
- The restaurant's cash available on April 1 is $30,000.

P11.7 A new restaurant was incorporated on January 1, 0008. Forty thousand shares of stock were issued for $6.00 cash per share. The cash received from the sale of shares was used, in part, as follows:

Construction of building, estimated life 20 years	$120,000
Kitchen equipment and restaurant furniture, estimated life 10 years	90,000
China, silverware, etc., estimated life 5 years	18,000
Food and beverage inventories	7,000

The remaining cash was deposited in a bank account.

The following estimates were made about the volume of business and operating expenses for the first three months:

a. Sales revenue: January $30,200, February $60,800, and March $90,400.

b. Sales revenue will be 55% cash and 45% credit; maximum credit to be allowed is 30 days.

c. Food cost and liquor cost will average 38% of total sales revenue. Forty percent of this cost each month will be cash; the balance will be paid in the month following purchase.

d. Wages and salaries: the fixed portion of wages will be $5,200 a month; the variable portion will be 30% of any sales revenue in excess of $25,000 a month. Total wages and salaries is the sum of the fixed and variable portions. Wages and salaries will be paid in the current month.

e. Other operating costs will be $3,800 a month, to be paid in the month following incurrence of the cost.

f. Depreciation for building, equipment and furniture, and china and silverware is to be calculated on a straight-line basis (no residual values). The annual depreciation amount must be prorated monthly to the income statements.

Note that, because of increasing sales revenue, a further cash investment in food and beverage inventories of $2,000 will have to be made in February, with another increase of $2,000 in March. This will increase total inventory investment to $11,000 by the end of March.

Required

1. A budgeted income statement for the three months ending March 31, 0008.

2. A cash budget for each of the first three months of 0008.

3. A balance sheet as of March 31, 0008.

P11.8 Stew and Brew have decided to lease a new restaurant. Rent for the building will be $3,000 a month to be paid on the first day of each month. They initially invested $225,000 of their own money, which was used in part to purchase:

Furniture and equipment	$180,000
China, glass, and silverware	25,200
Food inventory	9,000

Use straight-line depreciation over 5 years for furniture and equipment (no residual value). China, glass, and silverware are to be fully depreciated in Year 1.

Sales are forecasted as follows for the first three months after opening:

Month 1: $48,000   Month 2: $66,000   Month 3: $84,000

Sales revenue will be 80% cash and 20% accounts receivable with the maximum credit period allowed of 30 days. Food cost of sales is expected to average 30% and all purchases will be cash. Wages and salaries will be $15,000 a month. However, in any month when sales exceed $60,000, additional staff will have to be hired, and the extra wage cost is estimated to be 20% of any excess sales. All salaries and wages will be paid in the month during which they were earned. Other operating costs are expected to be 10% of sales and will be paid in the following month. At the end of Month 3, Stew and Brew plan to pay themselves back part of their initial investment. This payment will be from any cash in excess of $15,000 at that time. In other words, they wish to leave only $15,000 in the restaurant's cash account at the end of each three-month operating quarter.

Prepare

a. A budgeted income statement for each of the three months.

b. A cash budget for each of the three months.

c. A condensed balance sheet for the first quarter at the end of Month 3.

P11.9 Fritz, the owner of the Ritz Cafe, needs an after-tax cash flow of $27,000 next year. Principal payments on loans are $42,000 a year, and depreciation is $21,000. Tax rate for the Ritz Cafe is 25%. Fixed costs (including depreciation) are $55,000, and variable costs are 30% of sales revenue.

a. What level of sales revenue will provide Fritz with his desired cash flow next year?

b. Prove your answer.

P11.10 Cece Saw, a carpenter who has saved some money, has decided to build and operate, with his wife, a 10-unit highway budget motel. Cece invests $50,000 of his own money in the company ($10,000 by way of common stock and $40,000 as a long-term loan). He also obtained a long-term mortgage on the land and building for $240,000 at an 8% interest rate. Interest is estimated to be $1,600 per month for the first few months of the new business, and principal payments are expected to be $1,000 per month.

Land was purchased for $50,000 cash and $200,000 cash was used to construct a building (estimated life of the building is 30 years, no residual value). Furniture and equipment was purchased for $24,000 (estimated life of the furniture and equipment is 10 years, no residual value). Linen was also purchased with cash for $6,000, and the owner decided to write off the linen (depreciated, no residual value) over a 5-year period before the business opened. Cece's company also committed advertising costs of $2,400 for brochures and other items; this cost will be expensed during the first year of business. The first year's insurance premium of $3,600 was prepaid before the business started.

For the first three months of business, rooms occupancy is forcasted to be 60%, 65%, and 70%, respectively. To increase room sales volume, a low average room rate of $65 is to be offered. When calculating sales revenue, use a 30-day month. All sales revenue will be on a cash basis.

Since the motel is relatively small, Cece and his wife will run it themselves but expect to hire some part-time help at a cash cost of $400 per month. Cece and his wife will each be paid $2,500 a month by the company for their services. However, for each of the first six months, they will each only take $750 cash out of the business for living expenses, until they are sure the company has sufficient cash resources to pay them the balance. Cece hired casual labor for $853 which will not be paid when the job is completed and will pay the landscaper on April 1.

Laundry and supplies are estimated to be 10% of monthly sales revenue. This will be paid in cash. Utility costs are forecast to be $300, $325, and $350 for the first three months of operations, respectively; however, each month utility costs will not be paid until the following month. Office expenses are expected to be $100 per month in cash.

For each of the first three months of the motel's operation, prepare an income statement and a cash budget. Also, prepare the balance sheet for the end of Month 3.

C A S E   1 1

In the preceding chapter and case, the compilation of a statement of cash flows was covered.

Using Charlie's budgeted income statement for Year 2008 (Case 9) and the December 31, 2007, actual balance sheet (Case 2), prepare operating and cash budgets for the first six months of Year 2008.

Sales revenue are distributed as follows over the first six months of Year 2008:

Month	Monthly Percentage of Annual Sales Revenue	Food Ending Inventory	Beverage Ending Inventory
January	6.0%	$6,128	$2,378
February	6.0%	$6,352	$2,265
March	7.0%	$6,521	$2,155
April	8.0%	$6,785	$2,855
May	9.0%	$6,985	$2,645
June	10.0%	$7,325	$2,595

Sales revenue will be 60% cash, 36% credit cards, and 4% accounts receivable. Within the month of sale, 90% of credit card sales are collected while 10% is collected in the following month. Accounts receivable sales are collected in the month following the sale.

Fixed expenses will be charged evenly over the 12 months. Food and beverage purchases will be 55% cash in the month of the purchase and 45% on accounts payable. Accounts payable will be paid in the next month. Accrued expenses payable will be paid in the next month and are for administrative, general, and marketing expenses. Accrued payroll payable are for Charlie's salary and will be paid in January 2008. In addition, Charlie will be paid in the next month. Charlie expects a bonus of $5,000 quarterly in the months of March, June, September, in December of 2008.

The annual insurance premium will be paid in January 2008. The loan principal will be paid in 12 equal installments. Years 2007's income tax payable will be paid in two equal installments, one in January and the other in April 2008. All other expenses will be paid in the month they are incurred.

CHAPTER 12

CAPITAL BUDGETING AND THE INVESTMENT DECISION

I N T R O D U C T I O N

This chapter begins by discussing some of the problems associated with capital asset decisions, such as the long life of the assets, the initial high cost, and the unknown future costs and benefits.

Two fairly simple methods of measuring proposed investments—the *accounting rate of return* and the *payback period*—are then illustrated and explained.

The concept of the time value of money is then discussed, and discounted cash flow is illustrated in conjunction with time value.

Discounted cash flow is then used in conjunction with two other investment measurement methods: *net present value* and *internal rate of return*. Net present value and internal rate of return are then contrasted, and capital investment control is discussed.

The chapter concludes by demonstrating how discounted cash flow can be used to help make leasing versus buying decisions.

C H A P T E R   O B J E C T I V E S

After studying this chapter, the reader should be able to:

1. Discuss the ways in which long-term asset management differs from day-to-day budgeting.

2. Explain how the accounting rate of return is calculated, use the equation, and explain the major disadvantage of this method.

3. Give the equation for the payback period, use the equation, and state the pros and cons of this method.

4. Discuss the concept of the time value of money and explain the term *discounted cash flows.*

5. Use discounted cash flow tables in conjunction with the net present value method to make investment decisions.

6. Use discounted cash flow tables in conjunction with the internal rate of return method to make investment decisions.

7. Contrast the net present value and internal rate of return methods and explain how they can give conflicting rankings of investment proposals.

8. Solve problems relating to the purchase versus the leasing of fixed assets.

THE INVESTMENT DECISION

This chapter discusses methods of evaluating which long-term asset to select. This is frequently referred to as **capital budgeting.** We are not so much concerned with the budgeting process as we are with the decision about whether to make a specific investment, or which of two or more investments would be best. The largest investment that a hotel or food service business has to make is in its land and buildings, which is an infrequent investment decision for each separate property. This chapter is primarily about more frequent investment decisions, for items such as equipment, furniture purchases, and replacements. Investment decision making, or capital budgeting, differs from day-to-day decision making and ongoing budgeting for a number of reasons. Some of these will be discussed.

LONG LIFE OF ASSETS

Capital investment decisions concern assets that have a relatively long life. Day-to-day decisions concerning current assets are decisions about items such as inventories that are turning over frequently. A wrong decision about the purchase of a food item does not have a long-term effect. But a wrong decision about a piece of equipment (a long-term asset) can involve a time span stretching over many years. This long life of a capital asset creates another problem—that of estimating the life span of an asset to determine how far into the future the benefits of its purchase are going to be spread. Life span can be affected by both physical wear and tear on the equipment and by obsolescence—invention of a newer, better, and possibly more profitable piece of equipment.

COSTS OF ASSETS

Day-to-day purchasing decisions do not usually involve large amounts of money for any individual purchase. But the purchase of a capital asset or assets normally requires the outlay of large sums of money, and one has to be sure that the initial investment outlay can be recovered over time by the net income generated by the investment.

FUTURE COSTS AND BENEFITS

As will be demonstrated, analysis techniques to aid in investment decision making involve future costs and benefits. On one hand, the future is always uncertain; on the other hand, if we make a decision based solely on historic costs and net income, we may be no better off, since they might not be representative of future costs and net income. For example, one factor to consider is the recovery (scrap) value of the asset at the end of its economic life. If two comparable items of equipment were being evaluated and the only difference from all points of view was that one was estimated to have a higher scrap value than the other at the end of their equal economic lives, the decision would probably be made in favor of the item with the highest future trade-in value. However, because of technological change, that decision could eventually be the wrong one.

TOOLS TO GUIDE INVESTMENT DECISIONS

These, then, are some of the hazards of making decisions about capital investments. The hazards can seldom be eliminated, but there are techniques available that will allow the manager to reduce some of the guesswork. Although a variety of techniques are available, only four will be discussed in this chapter:

1. Accounting rate of return
2. Payback period
3. Net present value
4. Internal rate of return

To set the scene for the accounting rate of return and the payback period methods, consider a restaurant that is using an inefficient dishwasher. The part-time wages of the employee who runs the dishwasher are $4,000 a year. The restaurant is investigating the value of installing a new dishwasher that will eliminate the need for the part-time employee, since the servers can operate the machine. Two machines are being considered. Exhibit 12.1 compares the two options.

	Machine A	*Machine B*
Cash cost		
Installation	$5,000	$4,700
Economic life	5 years	5 years
Trade-in (residual) value	$1,000	$200
Depreciation	$\dfrac{\$5,000 - \$1,000}{5} = \$800 \text{ per year}$	$\dfrac{\$4,700 - \$200}{5} = \$900 \text{ per year}$
Savings, wages of cashier	$4,000	$4,000
Expenses		
Maintenance	$ 350	$ 300
Supplies	650	1,000
Depreciation	800	900
Total Expenses	$1,800	$2,200
Net saving [before income tax]	$2,200	$1,800
Income tax [30%]	(660)	(540)
Net Annual Savings	$1,540	$1,260

■ **EXHIBIT 12.1**
Data Concerning Two Alternative Machines

ACCOUNTING RATE OF RETURN

The **accounting rate of return (ARR)** is sometimes called the **average rate of return.** It compares the average annual net income (after taxes) resulting from the investment with the average investment.

$$\text{ARR} = \frac{\textbf{Net annual saving}}{\textbf{Average investment}}$$

Using the information from Exhibit 12.1, the ARR for each machine is as follows.

$$\text{Machine A: ARR} = \frac{\$1,000}{[(\$5,000 + \$1,000) / 2]} = \frac{\$1,540}{\$3,000} = \underline{51.3\%}$$

$$\text{Machine B: ARR} = \frac{\$880}{[(\$4,700 + \$200)/ 2]} = \frac{\$1,260}{\$2,450} = \underline{51.4\%}$$

Note that average investment is the initial investment plus the trade-in value divided by 2:

$$\text{Average investment} = \frac{\textbf{(Initial investment + Trade-in value)}}{2}$$

In the example given, the assumption was made that net annual savings is the same for each of the 5 years. In reality, this might not always be the case. For example, there might be expenses in Year 0001 (or in any of the other years) that are nonrecurring—for example, training costs or a major overhaul. Alternatively, the amount of an expense might change over the period—for example, depreciation computed using double declining balance. If the amounts are different each year, we project total savings and total costs for each year for the entire period under review. We add up the annual net savings to give us the total net savings figure for the entire period. This net savings figure for the entire period is then divided by the number of years of the project to give an average annual net savings figure to be used in the ARR equation.

Let us illustrate this for Machine A only. Savings and expenses are as in Exhibit 12.1, except that in Year 0003 there will be a special overhaul cost of $1,000, and the double-declining balance method of depreciation (rather than straight line) will be used. Since the asset has a five-year life, the depreciation rate is 40%. Exhibit 12.2 shows the results.

Total net savings over the 5-year period will be the sum of the individual years' savings. This amounts to $7,000. The average annual net savings will be $7,000 divided by 5 = $1,400.

$$\text{ARR} = \frac{\$1,400}{\$3,000} = 46.7\%$$

The same approach should be carried out for Machine B, and then a comparison can be made. Note that in Exhibit 12.2 the change in the method

	Machine A				
	Year 1	Year 2	Year 3	Year 4	Year 5
Wage savings	$4,000	$4,000	$4,000	$4,000	$4,000
Maintenance	350	350	350	350	350
Supplies	650	650	650	650	650
Depreciation	2,000	1,200	720	800	-0-
Total expenses	$3,000	$2,200	$2,720	$1,080	$1,000
Net savings (before income tax)	$1,000	$1,800	$1,280	$2,920	$3,000
Income tax	(300)	(540)	(384)	(876)	(900)
Net Savings	$ 700	$1,260	$ 896	$2,044	$2,100

■ **EXHIBIT 12.2**

Net Savings for Machine A after Special Overhaul and Double-Declining Balance Depreciation

of depreciation, by itself, did not affect the change in the ARR since average depreciation is still $800 per year, and average tax and average net savings are the same. In this particular case, the only factor that caused our ARR to decrease from 51.3% to 46.7% for Machine A was the $1,000 overhaul expense.

The advantage of the accounting rate of return method is its simplicity. It is used to compare the anticipated return from a proposal with a minimum desired return. If the proposal's return is less than desired, it is rejected. If the proposal's ARR is greater than the desired rate of return, a more in-depth analysis using other investment techniques might then be used. The major disadvantage of the accounting rate of return method is that it is based on net income or net savings rather than on cash flow.

▨ PAYBACK PERIOD

The **payback period** method overcomes the cash flow shortcoming of the accounting rate of return method. The payback method compares the initial investment with the annual cash inflows:

$$\text{Payback period (years)} = \frac{\textbf{Initial investment}}{\textbf{Net annual cash savings}}$$

Since Exhibit 12.1 only gives us net annual savings and not net annual cash savings, we must first convert the figures to a cash basis. This is accomplished by adding back the depreciation, an expense that does not require an outlay of cash.

	Machine A	*Machine B*
Net annual savings	$1,540	$1,260
Add depreciation	800	900
Net annual cash savings	$2,340	$2,160

Therefore, our payback period for each machine is:

Machine A	*Machine B*
$\dfrac{\$5,000}{\$2,340} = 2.14$ years	$\dfrac{\$4,700}{\$2,160} = 2.18$ years

Despite its higher initial cost, Machine A recovers its initial investment in a slightly shorter period than does Machine B. This confirms the results of the accounting rate of return calculation made earlier. However, the payback method only considers the cash flows until the cost of the asset has been recovered. Since the ARR calculation takes into account all of the benefit flows from an investment and not just those during the payback period, the ARR method could be considered more realistic. However, the payback method considers cash flows while the ARR method only considers net savings.

Note that in this illustration, straight-line depreciation was used and it was assumed the net annual cash savings figure was the same for each year. This might not be the case in reality. For example, the use of an accelerated method of depreciation, such as double declining balance, will increase the depreciation expense in the early years. This, in turn, will reduce income taxes and increase cash flow in those years, making the calculation of the payback period a little more difficult. To illustrate, consider an initial $6,000 investment and the following annual cash flows resulting from that investment:

Year 1	$2,500
Year 2	1,800
Year 3	1,400
Year 4	900
Year 5	700

By the end of Year 3, $5,700 ($2,500 + $1,800 + $1,400) will have been recovered, with the remaining $300 to be recovered in Year 4. This remaining amount will be recovered in one-third of Year 4 ($300 divided by $900). Total payback time will, therefore, be 3.33 years.

The payback period analysis method, although simple, does not really measure the merits of investments, but only the speed with which the investment might be recovered. It has a use in evaluating a number of proposals so that only those that fall within a predetermined payback period will be considered for further evaluation using other investment techniques.

However, both the payback period and the ARR methods still suffer from a common fault: They ignore the time value of cash flows, or the concept that money now is worth more than the same amount of money at some time in the future. This concept will be discussed in the next section, after which we will explore the use of the net present value and internal rate of return methods.

DISCOUNTED CASH FLOW

The concept of **discounted cash flow** can probably best be understood by looking first at an example of compound interest. Exhibit 12.3 shows, year by year, what happens to $200 invested at a 10% compound interest rate. At the end of 4 years, the investment would be worth $292.82.

	Jan. 1 0001	Dec. 31 0001	Dec. 31 0002	Dec. 31 0003	Dec. 31 0004
Balance forward	$200.00	$200.00	$220.00	$242.00	$266.20
Interest 10%		20.00	22.00	24.20	26.62
Investment value, end of year		$220.00	$242.00	$266.20	$292.82

■ **EXHIBIT 12.3**

Compound Interest, Calculation

Discounting is simply the reverse of compounding interest. In other words, at a 10% interest rate, what is $292.82 4 years from now worth to me today? The solution could be worked out manually using the following equation:

$$P = F \times \frac{1}{(1 + i)^n}$$

Where P is the present value, F is the future amount, I is the interest rate used as a decimal, and n is the number of years ahead for the future amount. For example, using the already illustrated figures, we have:

$$P = \$292.82 \times \frac{1}{(1 + 0.10)^4}$$

$$= \$292.82 \times \frac{1}{1.4641}$$

$$= \$292.82 \times 0.683$$

$$= \$200$$

Although a calculation can be made for any amount, any interest rate, and for any number of years into the future with this formula, it is much easier to use a table of discount factors.

Exhibit 12.4 illustrates such a table. If we go to the number called a factor that is opposite Year 4 and under the 10% column, we will see that it is 0.6830. This factor tells us that $1.00 received at the end of Year 4 is worth only $1.00 × $0.683, or $0.683 right now. In fact, this factor tells us that any amount of money at the end of four years from now at a 10% interest (discount) rate is worth only 68.3% of that amount right now. Let us prove this by taking our $292.84 amount at the end of Year 0004 from Exhibit 12.3 and discounting it back to the present:

$$\$292.82 \times 0.683 = \underline{\$200.00}$$

Period	5%	6%	7%	8%	9%	10%	11%	12%	13%	14%	15%	16%	17%	18%	19%	20%	25%	30%
1	0.9524	0.9434	0.9546	0.9259	0.9174	0.9091	0.9009	0.8929	0.8850	0.8772	0.8696	0.8621	0.8547	0.8475	0.8403	0.8333	0.8000	0.7692
2	0.9070	0.8900	0.8734	0.8573	0.8417	0.8264	0.8116	0.7972	0.7831	0.7695	0.7561	0.7432	0.7305	0.7182	0.7062	0.6944	0.6400	0.5917
3	0.8638	0.8396	0.8163	0.7938	0.7722	0.7513	0.7312	0.7118	0.6931	0.6750	0.6575	0.6407	0.6244	0.6086	0.5934	0.5787	0.5120	0.4552
4	0.8227	0.7921	0.7629	0.7350	0.7084	0.6830	0.6587	0.6355	0.6133	0.5921	0.5718	0.5523	0.5337	0.5158	0.4987	0.4823	0.4096	0.3501
5	0.7835	0.7473	0.7130	0.6806	0.6499	0.6209	0.5935	0.5674	0.5428	0.5194	0.4972	0.4761	0.4561	0.4371	0.4191	0.4019	0.3277	0.2693
6	0.7462	0.7050	0.6663	0.6302	0.5963	0.5645	0.5346	0.5066	0.4803	0.4556	0.4323	0.4104	0.3898	0.3704	0.3521	0.3349	0.2621	0.2072
7	0.7107	0.6651	0.6228	0.5835	0.5470	0.5132	0.4817	0.4524	0.4251	0.3996	0.3759	0.3538	0.3332	0.3139	0.2959	0.2791	0.2097	0.1594
8	0.6768	0.6274	0.5820	0.5403	0.5019	0.4665	0.4339	0.4039	0.3762	0.3506	0.3269	0.3050	0.2848	0.2660	0.2487	0.2326	0.1678	0.1226
9	0.6446	0.5919	0.5439	0.5003	0.4604	0.4241	0.3909	0.3606	0.3329	0.3075	0.2843	0.2630	0.2434	0.2255	0.2090	0.1938	0.1342	0.0943
10	0.6139	0.5584	0.5084	0.4632	0.4224	0.3855	0.3522	0.3220	0.2946	0.2697	0.2472	0.2267	0.2080	0.1911	0.1756	0.1615	0.1074	0.0725
11	0.5847	0.5298	0.4751	0.4289	0.3875	0.3505	0.3173	0.2875	0.2607	0.2366	0.2149	0.1954	0.1778	0.1619	0.1476	0.1346	0.0859	0.0558
12	0.5568	0.4970	0.4440	0.3971	0.3555	0.3186	0.2858	0.2567	0.2307	0.2076	0.1869	0.1685	0.1520	0.1372	0.1240	0.1122	0.0687	0.0429
13	0.5303	0.4688	0.4150	0.3677	0.3262	0.2897	0.2575	0.2292	0.2042	0.1821	0.1625	0.1452	0.1299	0.1163	0.1042	0.0935	0.0550	0.0330
14	0.5051	0.4423	0.3878	0.3405	0.2993	0.2633	0.2320	0.2046	0.1807	0.1597	0.1413	0.1252	0.1110	0.0986	0.0876	0.0779	0.0440	0.0254
15	0.4810	0.4173	0.3625	0.3152	0.2745	0.2394	0.2090	0.1827	0.1599	0.1401	0.1229	0.1079	0.0949	0.0835	0.0736	0.0649	0.0352	0.0195
16	0.4581	0.3937	0.3387	0.2919	0.2519	0.2176	0.1883	0.1631	0.1415	0.1229	0.1069	0.0930	0.0811	0.0708	0.0618	0.0541	0.0281	0.0150
17	0.4363	0.3714	0.3166	0.2703	0.2311	0.1978	0.1696	0.1456	0.1252	0.1078	0.0929	0.0802	0.0693	0.0600	0.0520	0.0451	0.0225	0.0116
18	0.4155	0.3503	0.2959	0.2503	0.2120	0.1799	0.1528	0.1300	0.1108	0.0946	0.0808	0.0691	0.0592	0.0508	0.0437	0.0376	0.0180	0.0089
19	0.3957	0.3305	0.2765	0.2317	0.1945	0.1635	0.1377	0.1161	0.0981	0.0829	0.0703	0.0596	0.0506	0.0431	0.0367	0.0313	0.0144	0.0068
20	0.3769	0.3118	0.2584	0.2146	0.1784	0.1486	0.1240	0.1037	0.0868	0.0728	0.0611	0.0514	0.0433	0.0365	0.0308	0.0261	0.0115	0.0053

EXHIBIT 12.4

Table of Discounted Cash Flows

We know $200 is the right answer because it is the amount we started with in our illustration of compounding interest in Exhibit 12.3. To illustrate with another example, assume we have a piece of equipment that a supplier suggests will probably have a trade-in value of $1,200 five years from now. At a 12% interest rate, what is the present value of $1,200?

$$\$1,200 \times 0.5674 = \underline{\underline{\$680.88}}$$

The factor (multiplier) of 0.5674 was obtained from Exhibit 12.4 on the Year-5 line under the 12% column. The factors in Exhibit 12.4 are based on the assumption that all money is all received in a lump sum on the last day of the year. This is not normally the case in reality, since outflows of cash for expenses (e.g., wages, supplies, and maintenance) occur continuously or periodically throughout its life and not just at the end of each year. Although continuous discounting is feasible, for most practical purposes the year-end assumption, using the factors from Exhibit 12.4, will give us solutions that are acceptable for decision making.

For a series of annual cash flows, one simply applies the related annual discount factor for that year to the cash inflow for that year. For example, a cash inflow of $1,000 a year for each of 3 years using a 10% factor will give us the following total discounted cash flow:

Year	Factor	Amount	Total
1	0.9091	$1,000	$ 909.10
2	0.8264	1,000	826.40
3	0.7513	1,000	751.30
			$2,486.80

In this illustration, the cash flows are the same each year. Alternatively, in the case of equal annual cash flows, one can total the individual discount factors (in our case, this would be $0.909 + 10.8264 + 0.7513 = 2.4868$) and multiply this total by the annual cash flow:

$$2.4868 \times \$1,000 = \underline{\underline{\$2,486.80}}$$

Special tables have been developed from which one can directly read the combined discount factor to be used in the case of equal annual cash flows, but they are not included in this chapter because Exhibit 12.4 will be sufficient for our needs.

NET PRESENT VALUE

The equation for calculating the **net present value (NPV)** of an investment is

$$NPV = A_0 + \frac{A_1}{1+i} + \frac{A_2}{(1+i)^2} + \cdots + \frac{A_n}{(1+i)^n}$$

where A_1 through A_n are the individual annual cash flows for the life of the investment, and i is the interest or discount rate being used. A_0 is the initial investment. Although it is possible with this formula to arrive at an NPV investment decision, it is much easier to use the table of discount factors illustrated in Exhibit 12.4. For example, Exhibit 12.5 gives projections of savings and costs for two machines. Machine A has an investment cost of $10,000; Machine B has an investment cost of $9,400. Estimating the future savings and costs is the most difficult part of the exercise. In our case, we are forecasting for five years. We have to assume the figures are as accurate as they can be. Obviously, the longer the period, the less accurate the estimates are likely to be.

Note that depreciation for each machine is calculated as follows:

	Machine A	Machine B
Initial cost	$10,000	$9,400
Residual (trade-in, scrap) value	(1,000)	(200)
	$ 9,000	$9,200
Depreciation, straight line	$\dfrac{\$9,000}{5} = \$1,800$ per year	$\dfrac{\$9,200}{5} = \$1,840$ per year

The **trade-in**, or **scrap, value** is a partial recovery of our initial investment and is, therefore, added in as a positive cash flow at the end of Year 5 in Exhibit 12.5. Note that depreciation is deductible as an expense for the calculation of income tax, but this expense does not require an outlay of cash year by year. Therefore, to convert our annual additional net income (savings) from the investment to a cash situation, the depreciation is added back each year.

The data we are interested in from Exhibit 12.5 are the initial investment figures and the annual net cash flow figures for each machine. These figures have been transferred to Exhibit 12.6 and, using the relevant 10% discount factors from Exhibit 12.4, have been converted to a net present value basis.

Exhibit 12.6 shows that from a purely cash point of view, Machine A is a better investment than Machine B: $5,703 net present value against $5,107. In this example, both net present value figures were positive. It is possible for a net present value figure to be negative if the initial investment exceeds the sum of the individual years' present values. If the NPV is negative, the investment should not be undertaken because, assuming the figures are accurate, the investment will not produce the rate of return desired.

Finally, the discount rate actually used should be realistic. It is frequently the rate that owners and/or investors expect the company to earn, after taxes, on investments.

Machine A (Investment Cost $10,000)					
	Year 1	Year 2	Year 3	Year 4	Year 5
Savings (wages)	$8,000	$8,000	$8,000	$8,000	$8,000
Operating Expenses					
Initial training cost	$3,500				
Maintenance contract	900	$ 900	$ 900	$ 900	$ 900
Special overhaul			750		
Supplies	1,200	1,200	1,200	1,200	1,200
Depreciation	1,800	1,800	1,800	1,800	1,800
Total expenses	$7,400	$3,900	$4,650	$3,900	$3,900
Savings less expenses	$ 600	$4,100	$3,350	$4,100	$4,100
Income tax (30%)	(180)	(1,230)	(1,005)	(1,230)	(1,230)
Net Income	$ 420	$2,870	$2,345	$2,870	$2,870
Add back depreciation	1,800	1,800	1,800	1,800	1,800
					$4,670
Add scrap value					1,000
Net Cash Flows	$2,220	$4,670	$4,145	$4,670	$5,670

Machine B (Investment Cost $9,400)					
	Year 1	Year 2	Year 3	Year 4	Year 5
Savings (wages)	$8,000	$8,000	$8,000	$8,000	$8,000
Operating Expenses					
Initial training cost	$3,000				
Maintenance contract	850	$ 850	$ 850	$ 850	$ 850
Special overhaul			500		
Supplies	1,700	1,700	1,700	1,700	1,700
Depreciation	1,840	1,840	1,840	1,840	1,840
Total Expenses	$7,390	$4,390	$4,890	$4,390	$4,390
Savings less expenses	$ 610	$3,610	$3,110	$3,610	$3,610
Income tax	(183)	(1,083)	(933)	(1,083)	(1,083)
Net Income	$ 427	$2,527	$2,177	$2,527	$2,527
Add back depreciation	1,840	1,840	1,840	1,840	1,840
					$4,367
Add scrap value					200
Net Cash Flow	$2,267	$4,367	$4,017	$4,367	$4,567

■ **EXHIBIT 12.5**

Calculation of Annual Net Cash Flows for Each Machine

INTERNAL RATE OF RETURN

As we have seen, the NPV method uses a specific discount rate to determine if proposals result in a net present value greater than zero. Those that do not exceed zero are rejected.

| | Machine A | | | | Machine B | | |
Year	Net Cash Flow	× Discount Factor	= Present Value	Cash Flow	× Discount Factor	=	Net Present Value
1	$2,220	× 0.9091	= $ 2,018	$2,267	× 0.9091	=	$ 2,061
2	4,670	× 0.8264	= 3,859	4,367	× 0.8264	=	3,609
3	4,145	× 0.7513	= 3,114	4,017	× 0.7513	=	3,018
4	4,670	× 0.6830	= 3,190	4,367	× 0.6830	=	2,983
5	5,670	× 0.6209	= 3,521	4,567	× 0.6209	=	2,836
Total present value			$15,073				$14,507
Less: Initial investment			(10,000)				(9,400)
Net Present Value			$ 5,703				$ 5,107

EXHIBIT 12.6
Conversion of Annual Cash Flows to Net Present Values

The **internal rate of return (IRR)** method also uses the discounted cash flow concept. However, this method's approach determines the interest (discount) rate that will equate total discounted cash inflows with the initial investment:

$$IC = \frac{A_1}{1+i} + \frac{A_2}{(1+i)^2} + \frac{A_n}{(1+i)^n}$$

where A_1 through A_n are the individual annual cash flows for the life of the investment, i is the interest or discount rate being used, and IC is the investment cost. Although it is possible with this formula to arrive at an IRR investment decision, it is usually easier to use the table of discount factors in Exhibit 12.4.

For example, suppose a motel owner decided to investigate renting a building adjacent to the motel in order to run it as a coffee shop. It will cost $100,000 to redecorate, furnish, and equip the building with a guaranteed 5-year lease. The projected cash flow (net income after tax, with depreciation added back) for each of the 5 years is as follows:

Projected Annual Cash Flow	
Year 1	$ 18,000
Year 2	20,000
Year 3	22,000
Year 4	25,000
Year 5	30,000
	$115,000

In addition to the total of $115,000 cash recovery over the five years, it is estimated that the equipment and furnishings could be sold for $10,000 at the end of the lease period. The total cash recovery is therefore $125,000, which is $25,000 more than the initial investment required of $100,000. On the face of it, the motel owner seems to be ahead of the game. If the annual cash flows are discounted back to their net present value, a different picture emerges, as illustrated in Exhibit 12.7.

Exhibit 12.7 shows that the future stream of cash flows discounted back to today's values using a 12% rate is less than the initial investment by almost $14,000. Thus, we know that if the projections about the motel restaurant are correct, there will not be a 12% cash return on the investment. The IRR method determines the rate to be earned if the investment is made. From Exhibit 12.7, we know that 12% is too high. By moving to a lower rate of interest, we will eventually, by trial and error, arrive at one where the net present value (the difference between total present value and initial investment) is virtually zero. This is illustrated in Exhibit 12.8 with a 7% interest (discount) rate.

Exhibit 12.8 tells us that the initial $100,000 investment will return the initial cash outlay except for $203 ($100,203 – $100,000) and earn 7% on the investment. Or, stated slightly differently, the motel operator would recover the full $100,000, but earn slightly less than 7% interest. If the motel owner is satisfied with a 7% cash return on the investment (note, this is 7% after income tax), then they could go ahead with the project.

A mathematical technique known as *interpolation* could be used for determining a more exact rate of interest, but since our cash flow figures are estimates to begin with, the value of knowing the exact interest rate is question-

Year	Annual Flow	×	Discount Factor 12%	=	Present Value
1	$18,000	×	0.8929	=	$ 16,072
2	20,000	×	0.7972	=	15,944
3	22,000	×	0.7118	=	15,660
4	25,000	×	0.6355	=	15,888
5	30,000	×	0.5674	=	17,022
Sale of equipment and furniture	10,000	×	0.5674	=	5,674
Total present value					$ 86,260
Less: Initial investment					(100,000)
Net Present Value (negative)					$(13,740)

■ **EXHIBIT 12.7**

Annual Cash Flows Converted to Net Present Value

Year	Annual Flow	×	Discount Factor 7%	=	Present Value
1	$18,000	×	0.9546	=	$17,183
2	20,000	×	0.8734	=	17,468
3	22,000	×	0.8163	=	17,959
4	25,000	×	0.7629	=	19,073
5	30,000	×	0.7130	=	21,390
Sale of equipment and furniture	10,000	×	0.7130	=	7,130
Total present value					$100,203
Less: Initial investment					(100,000)
Net Present Value					203

■ **EXHIBIT 12.8**

Discount Factor Arrived at by Trial and Error

able. In most practical situations, knowing the expected interest rate to the nearest whole number is probably good enough for decision-making purposes.

NET PRESENT VALUE VERSUS INTERNAL RATE OF RETURN

Despite the difference in approach used by the NPV and IRR methods, they will usually give the same accept or reject decision for any single project. However, if a number of proposals that were mutually exclusive were being evaluated and were being ranked, the rankings from NPV might differ from the rankings from IRR. A mutually exclusive alternative means that, if only one of a number of proposals is accepted, the others will be rejected. For example, if a restaurant were assessing a number of different point-of-sales systems and only one was to be selected, it would want to select the most profitable one and reject all others, even if the others were profitable. In this sense, *profitable* could mean reduction in costs from current levels.

Another situation where profitable proposals are rejected is when the company is faced with capital rationing. **Capital rationing** means that there is only sufficient capital to accept a limited number of investments for the budget period. Once the money available for the capital budget has been exhausted, all other proposals, even if they are profitable, are postponed for reconsideration during some future budget period.

Therefore, at times, the ranking of projects in order of potential profitability is important if a company wishes to maximize the profitability from its investment. Unfortunately, the NPV and IRR results can indicate a conflict in the ranking of profitability because of differences in the cost of, and/or differences in the timing of, cash flows from alternative investments.

Net Present Value	Alternative A			Alternative B		
	Annual Cash Flow	Discount Factor 10%	Present Value	Annual Cash Flow	Discount Factor 10%	Present Value
Year 1	$ 3,000	0.9091	$ 2,727	$7,000	0.9091	$ 6,364
Year 2	3,000	0.8264	2,479	4,000	0.8264	3,306
Year 3	3,000	0.7513	2,254	3,000	0.7513	2,254
Year 4	10,000	0.6830	6,830	3,000	0.6830	2,049
Total present value			$14,290			$13,973
Less: Initial cost			(10,000)			(10,000)
Net Present Value		(positive)	$ 4,290		(positive)	$ 3,973

Internal Rate of Return	Annual Cash Flow	Discount Factor 25%	Present Value	Annual Cash Flow	Discount Factor 31%	Present Value
Year 1	$ 3,000	0.8000	$ 2,400	$7,000	0.7634	$ 5,344
Year 2	3,000	0.6400	1,920	4,000	0.5827	2,331
Year 3	3,000	0.5120	1,536	3,000	0.4448	1,334
Year 4	10,000	0.4096	4,096	3,000	0.3396	1,019
Total present value			$ 9,952			$10,028
Initial cost			$10,000			$10,000
Net Present Value		(negative)	$ 48		(positive)	$ 48

■ **EXHIBIT 12.9**

Two Investment Alternatives and Their Respective NPV and IRR Ranking Results

To illustrate this, refer to Exhibit 12.9, which shows two alternative investments, each with the same initial cost, but different amounts of cash flow, differences in the timing of cash flow amounts, and differences in total cash flow amounts. Using the NPV method at 10% and the IRR method, the ranking decision is contradictory. Alternative A is preferable from an NPV point of view ($4,290 to $3,973), whereas Alternative B is preferable using IRR (31% to 25%).

The reason for this is that the NPV method assumes annual cash inflows are reinvested at the rate used, in our case 10%, for the balance of the life of the project. The IRR method assumes that the cash inflows are reinvested at the rate resulting from the IRR analysis (in our case, 25% and 31% for Alternatives A and B, respectively) for the balance of the life of the project, an assumption that may not be realistic.

Theoretically, the NPV method is considered the better method because it uses the same discount rate for alternative proposals, and that rate would normally represent the minimum rate acceptable for investments to be made by the company. However, proponents of the IRR method contend that it is easier to interpret, does not require the predetermination of a discount rate, and allows a more meaningful comparison of alternatives.

CAPITAL INVESTMENT CONTROL

One of the major difficulties in capital investment decision making is that it is only possible to approximate the investment rate to be achieved. Investment proposals are based on estimated cash flows, and the decisions based on those cash flows can only be judged as good or otherwise after actual cash flows are known. A review of all investment proposals is, thus, recommended at the end of each project's life. In this way, among other benefits, the process of forecasting cash flows can be reviewed and refined so future investment decisions can be based on potentially more accurate figures.

INVESTMENT AND UNCERTAINTY

In this chapter, we ignored the risk factor in investments, or we assumed that the risk of alternative investments was equal and was built into the discount or investment rates used. **Risk** is defined as the possible deviation of actual cash flows from those forecast. Also, in the illustrations, only short periods were used: 5 years or less. As the time grows longer for more major investments (e.g., hotel or restaurant buildings that may have an economic life of 25 years or more), the risk factor must play a more important role. Forecasting cash flows for periods of 5 years or less is difficult enough. Forecasting for periods in excess of that is increasingly more difficult, and the risks, thus, become much greater.

Although there are techniques, such as the use of probabilities, that can be used to deal with risk, they are quite theoretical and might be difficult to use in practice. Thus, we will not discuss them in this text. However, this does not imply that the business manager should ignore risk, since it does exist. The interested reader wishing to gain more insight into techniques available to encompass risks, or uncertainty, is referred to any of the excellent textbooks available on general managerial finance.

NONQUANTIFIABLE BENEFITS

The results obtained using investment decision techniques may not be the only information needed to make decisions. Some information is not easily quantifiable but is still relevant to decision making. One should not ignore such factors as prestige, goodwill, reputation, employee acceptability, and the social or environmental implications. For example, if a hotel redecorates its lobby, what are the cash benefits? They may be difficult to quantify, but to retain customer goodwill, the lobby may need to be redecorated. Similarly, how are the relative benefits to be assessed in spending $50,000 on improvements to the staff cafeteria or using the $50,000 for Christmas bonuses? Personal judgment must then come into play in such investment decisions.

CHOOSING WHETHER TO OWN OR LEASE

Until this point, the discussion concerning long-term, or fixed assets has been based on purchasing, and owning them. However, there may be situations where renting or leasing is favorable from a cost point of view. For example, income tax is a consideration. On one hand, lease payments are generally tax deductible, so there can be an advantage in leasing. On the other hand, ownership permits deduction for tax purposes of both depreciation and the interest expense on any debt financing of the purchase. What may be advantageous in one situation may be disadvantageous in another. Each case must be investigated on its own merits. Let us look at a method by which a comparison between the two alternatives can be made. Assume that we are considering whether to buy or rent new furnishings for a motel.

Purchase of the furniture will require a $125,000 loan from the bank. Cost of the furniture is $125,000. The bank loan has an 8% interest rate and the principal will be repayable in four equal annual installments of principal ($31,250 per year). The furniture will be depreciated over 5 years at $25,000 per year. It is assumed to have no trade-in value at the end of that period. The income tax rate is 30%. Alternatively, the furniture can be leased for 5 years at a rental of $30,000 per year.

First, with the purchase plan, we must prepare a bank repayment schedule showing principal and interest payments for each of the 4 years (see Exhibit 12.10).

Year	Interest at 8%	Principal Amount	Balance
1	$10,000	$31,250	$93,750
2	7,500	31,250	62,500
3	5,000	31,250	31,250
4	2,500	31,250	-0-

■ **EXHIBIT 12.10**
Bank Repayment Schedule for $125,000

	Year 1	Year 2	Year 3	Year 4	Year 5
Interest expense (from Exhibit 12.10)	$10,000	$ 7,500	$ 5,000	$ 2,500	-0-
Depreciation expense	25,000	25,000	25,000	25,000	25,000
Total tax deductible expense	$35,000	$32,500	$30,000	$27,500	$25,500
Income tax saving (30%)	(10,500)	(9,750)	(9,000)	(8,250)	(7,650)
After-tax cost	$24,500	$22,750	$21,000	$19,250	$17,850
Add: principal payments	31,250	31,250	31,250	31,250	-0-
Deduct: depreciation expense	(25,000)	(25,000)	(25,000)	(25,000)	(25,000)
Net annual cash outflow (inflow)	$30,750	$29,000	$27,750	$25,500	($ 7,150)

■ **EXHIBIT 12.11**
Annual Net Cash Outflows with a Purchase

Next, under the purchase plan we must calculate the net cash outflow for each of the 5 years. This is shown in Exhibit 12.11. In Exhibit 12.11, note that since depreciation and interest expense are tax deductible and since the motel is in a 30% tax bracket, there is an income tax saving equal to 70% of these expenses. Thus, in year 1, the expenses of $35,000 are offset by the $10,500 tax saving. The net cost, after tax, is therefore only $24,500. This $10,500 has to be increased by the principal repayment of $31,250 on the bank loan and reduced by the depreciation expense of $25,000, since depreciation does not require an outlay of cash. In Year 1, the net cash outflow is thus $30,750. Figures for the other years are calculated similarly. Note that in Year 5, since there is no interest expense and bank loan payment to be made, the cash flow is positive rather than negative.

Exhibit 12.12 shows the calculation of annual net cash outflows under the rental plan. Note that under the rental option there is no depreciation expense (since the motel does not own the furnishings) and no interest or principal payments (since no money is borrowed).

	Year 1	Year 2	Year 3	Year 4	Year 5
Rental expense	$30,000	$30,000	$30,000	$30,000	$30,000
Income tax saving 50%	(9,000)	(9,000)	(9,000)	(9,000)	(9,000)
Net cash outflow	$21,000	$21,000	$21,000	$21,000	$21,000

■ **EXHIBIT 12.12**
Annual Cash Outflows with a Rental

Year	Annual Cash Outflow (Inflow)	×	Discount Factor 8%	=	Present Value	Annual Cash Outflow	×	Discount Factor 8%	=	Present Value
1	$30,750	×	0.9259	=	$28,471	$21,000	×	0.9259	=	$19,444
2	29,000	×	0.8573	=	24,862	21,000	×	0.8573	=	18,003
3	27,250	×	0.7938	=	21,631	21,000	×	0.7938	=	16,670
4	25,500	×	0.7350	=	18,743	21,000	×	0.7350	=	15,435
5	(7,150)	×	0.6806	=	(4,866)	21,000	×	0.6806	=	14,293
Total present value					**$88,841**	**Total present value**				**$83,845**

■ **EXHIBIT 12.13**
Total Present Values Converted from Exhibits 12.11 and 12.12

Finally, the net cash flow figures from Exhibits 12.11 and 12.12 have been transferred to Exhibit 12.13 and discounted, using the appropriate discount factor from Exhibit 12.4. The discount rate used is 8%. This rate was selected because it is the current cost of borrowing money from the bank. Exhibit 12.13 shows that from a present value point of view it would be better to rent in this particular case, since total present value of cash outflows is lower by $4,995 ($88,841 − $83,845).

In any buy-or-lease situation, other factors could be taken into the calculations. For example, in the purchase option, a firm might use some of its own cash as a down payment and borrow less than the full purchase amount required. In such a case, the down payment is an additional cash outflow at the beginning of the first year. Under a purchase plan, there might also be a trade-in value at the end of the period. This trade-in amount would be handled in the calculations as a cash inflow at the end of the period. In a rental plan, the annual payment might be required at the beginning of each year, rather than at the end, as was assumed in our illustration. This means that the first rental payment is at time zero, and each of the remaining annual payments is advanced by 1 year. Under a rental plan, there might also be a purchase option to the lessee at the end of the period. If the purchase is exercised, it will create an additional cash outflow.

Furthermore, terms on borrowed money can change from one situation to another, and different depreciation rates and methods can be used. For example, the use of an accelerated depreciation method will give higher depreciation expense in the earlier years, thus reducing income tax and increasing the cash flow in those years.

Because of all these and other possibilities, each buy-or-lease situation must be investigated on its own merits, taking all the known variables into consideration before a decision is made.

COMPUTER APPLICATIONS

Computers can readily handle the calculations necessary for investment decisions. For example, spreadsheet programs can be used to handle all of the calculations required for the ARR, NPV, and IRR investment methods, and can indicate the preferable investment option. Once the spreadsheet has been programmed with the correct formulas, it can be used repeatedly to eliminate the time it takes to perform the calculations manually. Spreadsheets have built in functions to calculate NPV and IRR.

A spreadsheet program can also be used to perform all the calculations necessary in a buy or lease situation.

SUMMARY

Capital asset management involves decision making about whether to make a specific investment or which alternative investments would be best. Capital assets are assets with a long life that have a relatively high cost and about which future costs and benefits are uncertain.

Four methods of analyzing capital asset investments were illustrated: accounting rate of return (ARR), payback period, net present value (NPV), and internal rate of return (IRR).

$$\text{ARR} = \frac{\textbf{Net annual saving}}{0.5 \times (\textbf{Initial investment} + \textbf{Salvage})}$$

The disadvantage of this method is that it is based on accounting income rather than on cash flow.

The payback period method is based on cash flow:

$$\text{Payback period} = \frac{\textbf{Initial investment}}{\textbf{Net annual cash savings}}$$

The disadvantage of the payback period method is that it ignores what happens beyond the payback period. Both the ARR and the payback period methods share a common fault. They do not take into consideration the time value of money. Discounted cash flow tables (the reverse of compound interest tables) have been developed so that flows of future cash can be readily discounted back to today's values. The NPV and IRR methods make use of these tables.

With NPV, the initial investment is deducted from the total present value of future cash flows to obtain NPV. If the NPV is positive, the investment should be considered; if negative, the investment should not be made.

With IRR, one simply uses the tables to determine the rate of interest (rate of return) that will equate the total future discounted cash inflows with the initial investment. If the rate of return is higher than the company has established as a minimum desired return, then the investment should proceed; otherwise, it should not.

Both the NPV and IRR methods will usually give the same accept or reject decision for any specific investment. However, if several alternative projects were being evaluated, the rankings might differ.

Regardless of the investment method used, subsequent to each investment, the results should be reviewed so the investment process can be refined and improved.

Finally, one should not ignore the potential nonquantifiable benefits of each particular investment. There may be situations where it is preferable to rent or lease rather than purchase long-term assets. Cash flows under both alternatives can be discounted back to their present values to make a comparison. In each situation, all the known variables must be taken into consideration so the final decision can be made on its own merits.

D I S C U S S I O N   Q U E S T I O N S

1. Discuss the ways in which long-term asset management differs from day-to-day budgeting.

2. How is the accounting rate of return calculated? What is the major disadvantage of using this method?

3. What is the equation for calculating the payback period? What are the pros and cons of this method?

4. Under what conditions might a hotel consider buying an item of equipment with a rapid payback rather than one with a high accounting rate of return?

5. Discuss the concept that money is worth more now than that same amount of money a year from now.

6. How would you explain discounted cash flow to someone who had not heard the term before?

7. In Exhibit 12.4, in the 11% column opposite Year 5, is the number 0.5935. Explain in your own words what this number or factor means.

8. If an investment requires an outlay today of $10,000 cash and, over the 5-year life of the investment, total cash returns were $12,000, and the $12,000 had a present value of $9,500, would you make the investment? Explain.

9. Contrast the NPV and the IRR methods of evaluating investment proposals.

10. Under what circumstances might NPV and IRR give conflicting decisions in the ranking of proposed investments?

11. Landscaping for a resort hotel is an investment for which the benefits might be difficult to quantify. In what ways might you be able to quantify them? Even if investment analysis (for example, NPV) proved negative, what other considerations might dictate that the investment be made?

12. What factors, other than purely monetary factors, might one want to consider in a buy-versus-rent decision?

E T H I C S   S I T U A T I O N

The manager of a hotel has the permission of the owner to have a new swimming pool built. The manager contacts three companies for bids to do this construction work. The highest bidder has told the manager that if his bid is accepted he will also install a swimming pool at the manager's house at a 25% discount. The manager agrees to accept this offer and justifies the decision by believing that the higher swimming pool cost to the hotel will provide a larger depreciation expense amount. This, in turn, will reduce the income tax that the hotel has to pay and therefore provide the hotel with more working capital. Discuss the ethics of this situation.

E X E R C I S E S

E12.1 Assume you are given the following information regarding a point-of-sale computer terminal: The net annual savings was calculated to be $1,400 on an average investment cost of $5,620. What is the accounting rate of return (ARR) on the terminal?

E12.2 Information is provided on two machines, which had an original cost of $28,400 for Machine X and $26,200 for Machine Y.

	Machine X	*Machine Y*
Net annual savings	$1,440	$3,560
Add: Depreciation	$4,840	5,240
Net annual cash savings	$6,280	$8,800

a. Which is the best investment using the payback period method?

b. Will either of the machines provide the cash investment back in less than 4 years?

E12.3 Investment in an item of equipment is $22,000. It has a five-year life and no salvage value and straight-line depreciation is used. The equipment is expected to provide an annual savings of $2,900, which does not include depreciation. What is the payback period?

E12.4 What is the net present value of $4,285 for each year of 2 years with a discount factor of 0.9009 in Year 1 and 0.8166 in Year 2?

E12.5 Assume an item of equipment is purchased at a cost of $22,800 to be paid for over 5 years, requiring a payment on principal of 20% per year at an annual interest rate of 12%. Complete a repayment schedule for each of the 5 years.

E12.6 Dinah, the operator of Dinah's Diner, wishes to choose between two alternative investments providing the following annual net cash inflows over the five-year investment period:

Year	Alternative 1	Alternative 2
1	$8,000	$ 4,200
2	8,600	5,800
3	8,800	8,500
4	8,200	11,500
5	4,100	12,100

Calculate the payback time for each alternative, assuming an initial investment of $33,000 under each alternative.

E12.7 Using information from E12.6, complete an evaluation using NPV at 12% for both of the alternatives. Would either of the alternatives be a good investment for Dinah?

P R O B L E M S

P12.1 You have the following information about three electronic sales registers that are in the market. The owner of a restaurant asks for your help in deciding which of the three machines to buy.

	Register A	Register B	Register C
Cash investment required	$6,300	$6,000	$6,700
Estimated machine life	5 years	5 years	5 years
Estimated residual trade-in value (at the end of 5 years)	$ 500	-0-	$ 300
Annual operating costs (excluding depreciation)	$ 400	$ 300	$ 300
Annual savings before deduction of costs	$2,000	$2,000	$2,000

Assume a 30% income tax rate and straight-line depreciation.

a. Use the ARR method to decide which of the three machines would be the best investment.

b. If the restaurant owner wants a return on investment of at least 10%, what would you advise?

P12.2 Using the information provided in P12.1, which would be the best investment using the payback period method? If the owner wanted her cash back in less than 4 years, should she invest in any of the machines?

P12.3 An investor is planning to open a new fast-food restaurant. He has a 5-year lease on a property that would require an investment estimated at $205,000 for redecorating and furnishing. He would use his own cash. The present cost of capital (borrowed money) is 13%; use this percentage to determine the discount rate each of the 5 years.

Calculation of net cash flow from the restaurant for the 5 years of operation shows:

Year	Cash Flow
1	$37,500
2	43,800
3	46,300
4	50,000
5	60,000

At the end of the lease, the furniture and equipment would have a cash value of $18,500. Should he make the investment? What IRR comes closest to giving him a complete return on his $205,000 investment?

P12.4 A hotel manager wishes to choose between two alternative investments giving the following annual net cash inflows over a 5-year period:

Year	Alternative 1	Alternative 2
1	$ 8,400	$24,200
2	11,600	19,800
3	17,000	17,200
4	23,000	10,800
5	24,000	8,000

The amount of the investment under either alternative will be $70,000.

a. Using the payback period method, in which year, under both alternatives, will she have recovered the initial investment?

b. Using NPV at 10%, would either alternative be a good investment?

P12.5 A restaurant operator wishes to choose between two alternative roll-in storage units. Machine A will cost $9,000 and have a residual value at the end of its 5-year life of $1,500. Machine B will cost $8,500 and at the end of its 5-year life will have a residual value of $700. Assume straight-line depreciation.

Investment in the machine will mean that a part-time kitchen worker will not be required and there will be an annual wage savings of $9,600. The following will be the operating costs, excluding depreciation, for each machine, for each of the 5 years.

Year	Machine A 1	2	3	4	5	Machine B 1	2	3	4	5
Training	$800					$700				
Maintenance	750	$750	$750	$750	$750	650	$650	$650	$650	$650
Overhaul			550					400		
Supplies	300	300	300	300	300	500	500	500	500	500
Electricity	100	100	100	100	100	100	100	100	100	100

Assume a 30% income tax rate. For each machine, calculate the NPV by using a 12% rate. Ignoring any other considerations, which machine would be the preferable investment?

P12.6 Pete's Pizza is planning to purchase a new type of oven that cooks pizza much faster than the conventional oven now used. The new oven is estimated to cost $20,000 (use straight-line depreciation) and will have a 5-year life, after which it will be traded in for $4,000. Pete has calculated that the new oven will allow him to increase his sales revenue by $30,000 a year. His food cost is 30%, labor cost is 40%, and other variable costs are 10% of sales revenue. Assume a 35% income tax rate. For any new investment, Pete wants a minimum 12% return. Use IRR to help him decide if he should purchase the new oven.

P12.7 You have to make a decision either to buy or to rent the equipment for your restaurant. Purchase cost would be $30,000. Of this amount, $7,500 would be paid in cash now, and the balance would be owed to the equipment supplier. The owner agrees to accept $4,500 a year for 5 years as payment toward the principal, plus interest at 11%. The equipment will have a 5-year life and a residual value of $4,000. The residual value can be recovered by trade-in or selling the equipment. Straight-line depreciation basis will be used over the 5 years. Alternatively, the equipment can be rented for the 5 years at a rental cost of $7,000 a year. Assume a 28% income tax rate. Discount rate to be used is 11%.

a. Using discounted cash flow, which would be the better investment?

b. What other factors might you want to consider that would change your decision?

P12.8 Pizza Restaurant provides a delivery service and is considering purchasing a new compact vehicle or leasing it. Purchase price would be $13,500 (cash), which the restaurant has. Estimated life is 5 years. Residual (trade-in) value is $2,500.

Under the purchase plan, the additional net cash income (increased sales revenue less additional costs such as vehicle maintenance and driver's wages) before deducting depreciation and income tax would be as follows:

Year	Cash Revenue Less Cash Costs
1	$38,000
2	47,000
3	55,000
4	60,000
5	65,000

Depreciation will be straight-line. Income tax rate is 30%. Under the rental plan the cash income will be the same as under the purchase plan, except vehicle maintenance will not be required (the leasor pays for this). Therefore, the given net cash income figures will have to be increased by the following maintenance amount savings:

Year	Amount
1	$1,000
2	2,500
3	2,500
4	4,000
5	5,000

However, under the rental plan, there is a rental cost based on mileage. Estimated mileage figures follow:

Year	Mileage
1	30,000
2	45,000
3	50,000
4	55,000
5	60,000

Rental cost is $0.30 per mile. Income tax rate will be 30%.

a. On a net present value basis using an 11% rate, would it be better to rent or buy?

b. Would your answer change if the rental cost were $1,000 a year plus $0.30 a mile? Explain your decision.

P12.9 For many years, a motor hotel has been providing its room guests with room service of soft drinks and ice using the services of a part-time bell-hop to deliver to the rooms. Typically, the service has been losing money. The average figures for each of the past few years are as follows:

Sales revenue:	Soft drinks	$25,550	
	Ice	2,400	$27,950
Expenses:	Cost of sales	$12,200	
	Labor	17,900	(30,100)
Loss			($ 2,150)

The motor hotel has an offer from a soft drink vending company to install vending machines at no cost to the motor hotel. The vending company would collect the sales revenue (forecast to be as above for the next several years) from the soft drink machines, paying the motor hotel a commission of 10% on that sales revenue. Customers would help themselves to both soft drinks (by inserting cash in the machine) and ice (which would be free), thus eliminating the labor cost.

An ice machine would have to be purchased by the motor hotel at a cost of $7,000. It would have a 5-year life and a residual value at the end of that time of $1,000. Use straight-line depreciation. Annual maintenance and operating costs of the ice machine are estimated to be $100 per year. The motor hotel is in a 30% tax bracket.

a. Calculate the payback period.

b. Calculate the ARR.

c. Calculate the NPV of the investment using a 12% discount factor and state whether the investment should be made.

P12.10 A motel leases out its 1,000-square-foot coffee shop, although it continues to own the equipment. The lease is due for renewal. The motel could continue to rent the space for $2 a square foot per month for the next 3 years, and then $2.50 a square foot for the following 2 years.

Alternatively, the motel could cancel this lease and take over the operation of the restaurant. If this occurs, the motel's management estimates that sales revenue in the first year would be $700,000 and that it would increase by $50,000 per year for each of the following 4 years. Variable operating costs of running the restaurant (food cost, wages, supplies) would be 90% of sales revenue. The motel would also have to assume certain other costs currently paid by the lessee for such items as supervision, advertising, and utilities. These are estimated to be $32,000 in Year 1, increasing by $2,000 per year for each of the following 4 years, so that by Year 5 the costs will be $40,000.

If the motel resumes operation of the restaurant, it will trade in some of the old equipment, for which it will get $5,000, and buy $40,000 of new equipment (this will not happen if the lease is renewed). The new equipment will have a 5-year life and would be depreciated on a straight-line basis with no scrap value.

The motel is in a 25% tax bracket. Use NPV to decide whether the motel should operate the coffee shop itself or continue to lease it out. Use a 10% discount rate.

C A S E   1 2

a. Early in Year 2009, the owner of the building made Charlie an offer. The lease contract has 4 more years to run and, as you will recall from Case 2, the rent is to be increased by 10% a year each year over the preceding year. The rent expense was calculated in Case 9 in Year 2008. The rent is payable in equal monthly installments but, for the sake of simplicity, assume it is all paid at year-end. The building owner's offer is that a lump-sum payment now (early in January 2009 before the January rent check had been prepared) of $80,000 would be considered as prepaid rent for the remaining 4 years of the contract. If the offer is accepted, Charlie would borrow $80,000 from the bank. The arrangement with the bank is that $20,000 of the principal will be repaid on December 31 of Years 2009 through 2011, with interest at 12% on the amount owed at the beginning of each year. Use the interest rate as the discount rate (see Exhibit 12.4). Should the offer be accepted?

b. You will note in part a that year-end discount tables were used, even though the annual rent was paid each month. Discount tickets (Exhibit 12.4) are available to you, and you recalculate the present value with those tables; do you think your decision would change?

FEASIBILITY STUDIES— AN INTRODUCTION

INTRODUCTION

This chapter explains what a feasibility study is designed to do and covers the highlights of the two major parts of such a study.

Part one includes the introduction to the study (front matter), general market characteristics, site evaluation, supply and demand information, and supply and demand analysis. This chapter illustrates a detailed approach to supply and demand analysis for a hotel and covers the four steps involved.

Part two of a feasibility study covers the financial analysis. A financial analysis generally requires four major sections: (1) calculation of the capital investment required and tentative financing plan; (2) preparation of pro forma statements; (3) preparation of cash flow projections from the net income forecasts; and (4) evaluation of the projections.

CHAPTER OBJECTIVES

After studying this chapter, the reader should be able to:

1. Discuss the value of a feasibility study and the information included in its nonfinancial sections.
2. List and briefly discuss the four steps in hotel room supply and demand analysis.
3. Calculate forecast rooms required from given demand information.
4. Prepare pro forma income statements for rooms, food, and beverages from given information.
5. Convert pro forma income statements to cash flow from given information.
6. Evaluate the financial analysis projections of a feasibility study.

FEASIBILITY STUDIES DEFINED

A **feasibility study** is an in-depth analysis of the financial situation of a property development, rather than a promoter's guess that a new idea will be economically successful. A feasibility study is not designed to prove that a new venture will be profitable. An independent feasibility study that is professionally prepared by an impartial third party could result in either a positive or a negative recommendation. If it is negative, both the borrower and the lender should be happy that the proposal is not developed. However, if it is positive, this should not be taken as a guarantee of success. A feasibility study can only consider what is known at present and what may happen in the future. But, since the future is impossible to forecast accurately and so many unforeseen factors can come into play, there can be no guarantees. In other words, a feasibility study may reduce the risk of a particular investment but does not eliminate it.

Some feasibility studies seek out the most appropriate location for a new property and continue with the study from there. Others consider one location without considering alternatives.

FEASIBILITY STUDY FORMAT

Although the scope of a feasibility study for a suburban restaurant differs considerably from one for a major downtown hotel complex, the basic format of any feasibility study is the same. Most feasibility studies conclude with a financial analysis of the proposal. This will be covered in more depth later in this chapter. However, the other parts of a feasibility study that precede the financial analysis will be briefly discussed here. In this discussion, we will assume that the feasibility study is for a hotel with food and beverage facilities. In a feasibility study for a motel with only rooms, facilities data relevant to only guest rooms would be included. In a study for a restaurant without a hotel or motel, room data would be irrelevant.

A suggested format for a hotel feasibility study would generally cover the front matter, general market characteristics, site evaluation, supply and demand information, and supply and demand analysis. Sometimes, the format includes space recommendations. Let's look at these segments in further detail.

FRONT MATTER

This includes an introduction exploring why the study was carried out, what property is being evaluated and how this evaluation was conducted, when the study was conducted and by whom, and a summary highlighting the findings, conclusions, and recommendations.

GENERAL MARKET CHARACTERISTICS

This section covers such items as site location and the general area's population growth trends, industrial diversification and growth, building permit activity, employment and economic trends, disposable incomes, housing, transportation, attractions, convention facilities, and special factors. For example, is the area's economy highly dependent on its local university population? Only those items relevant to the proposed new hotel should be discussed. Both descriptive and statistical data should be included. The information should be concise and primarily related to the demand for rooms (since other services offered by a hotel are generally derived directly from rooms' usage).

SITE EVALUATION

If an in-depth section on the site location is included in the study, that section should include detailed maps of the location. Wherever possible, those maps should show important subcenters of activity related to the proposal, such as industrial areas, shopping malls, and convention and support center locations. Transportation routes, including, for example, routes to and from the airport, should be shown. If access by automobile is important (as it frequently is), these auto routes should be indicated.

Physical information about the site should be included, such as dimensions, existing improvements to buildings on the site, and adequacy of the site for possible future expansion.

Cost of the site, site preparation costs prior to construction, and property taxes should be covered. Finally, any other important matters such as zoning restrictions, height restrictions, parking space requirements, future traffic flow changes, and availability of utility services should be part of this section.

SUPPLY AND DEMAND INFORMATION

There are three possible reasons for a new hotel. One is that the demand for rooms is greater than the supply; another is that there is a demand from a new market that is not being served with the existing supply; and the third is that the supply is inferior in quality to the needs of the demand or market. It is, therefore, important that the study analyze the supply/demand situation to identify the market for the proposed new property. This is preferably done by looking at the current situation for the entire local market and then adjusting for anticipated future changes.

Certain basic information should be included as follows:

- *Occupancy trends in the local area for the past 5 years.* Occupancy trends should be broken down by hotel classification if possible (see next item).
- *A list of hotels currently serving the local market.* The hotels should be listed by type. Three classes are normally listed: those that would be the most competitive properties, those that would be somewhat competitive,

and those that would be less competitive. The list should include each hotel by name, the number of rooms it has, and its current room rates. Any hotels in this list that were built in the past 5 years should be highlighted with added information, such as the facilities they have other than rooms (e.g., number of seats in their restaurants) and the quality of those facilities.

- *Competitive information.* In addition, the most competitive hotels should be further highlighted by including additional information (if available) about their occupancy rates, food and beverage facilities' usage (e.g., seat turnovers and average checks), and the composition of their market for rooms, food, and beverages.
- *The principle sources of demand.* Generally, for a city hotel, the sources of room demand are classified into three major types of customers: the traveling businessperson, the convention delegate, and the general tourist or vacationer. For each category, relevant data should be provided that could indicate demand for rooms.

For the business traveler, relevant data might include growth in local airport traffic, and/or growth in local office space occupancies for the past five years, since there is frequently a high correlation between these items and demand for hotel rooms.

Data concerning the convention or business meeting would include the number of conventions held each year in the area, types of conventions, their size, total number of delegates, average length of delegates' stay, and average conventioneers' daily spending.

Data concerning vacationer arrivals would include number of tourists, average length of stay, average daily spending on hotel accommodations and meals, and any change in or extension of the tourist season over the past several years.

If there is any significant demand for hotel accommodations from any special source, this should be included. For example, sporting events can often be a major source of demand for hotel rooms close to the sporting event location.

Much of the information necessary for this section of the study can be obtained from local chambers of commerce, convention and visitor bureaus, hotel and motel associations, airport authorities, government agencies, and, in the case of office space occupancies, the local office building owners' association. Each individual situation will require contact with other possible sources of relevant information.

SUPPLY AND DEMAND ANALYSIS

Once the supply and demand information has been assembled and tabulated, it must then be analyzed to determine if additional hotel rooms in the area can be justified. This requires four steps:

1. Calculate the most recent 12-month average occupancy rate of the most competitive hotels.

2. Calculate the composite growth rate of demand from various sources.

3. Calculate the additional rooms required year by year.

4. Calculate the future supply of rooms required.

Step 1: Calculate the Most Recent 12-month Average Occupancy of the Most Competitive Hotels

Let us assume there are five competitive hotels and their number of rooms and occupancies are as follows for the most recent year:

Hotel	Average Rooms in Hotel	Average Occupancy (%)	Current Nightly Demand
1	320	70%	224
2	108	75%	81
3	246	85%	209
4	170	70%	119
5	312	85%	265
Total	1,156		898

For each hotel, the number of rooms has been multiplied by that hotel's average occupancy percentage to arrive at average nightly demand. We use these figures to calculate the total average nightly demand of 898 rooms.

The average annual occupancy of the most competitive hotels is then calculated using the following equation:

$$\frac{\textbf{Average nightly demand}}{\textbf{Rooms available}} = \textbf{Average annual occupancy} = \frac{898}{1,156} = 77.7\%$$

Step 2: Calculate the Composite Growth Rate of Demand from the Various Sources

Let us assume that our demand information gave the breakdown figures in percentages for each source, as well as annual compound growth rates for that source, as follows:

Source	Source of Demand (%)	Annual Compound Growth (%)	Composite Growth (%)
Business travelers	75%	8%	6.0%
Convention delegates	10%	5%	0.5%
Vacationers	15%	10%	1.5%
Total	100%		8.0%

Source-of-demand percentages (sales mix) have been multiplied by the annual compound growth rate percentages in the next column to provide the composite growth rate figures in the right-hand column (e.g., 75% $\times$ 8% = 6.0%). The annual compound growth rate figures can be estimated from historic growth rate figures projected into the future. The total overall composite growth rate figure is 8.0% as already indicated.

Step 3: Calculate Future Rooms Demand Year by Year

This calculation is shown as follows:

Year	Composite Demand	Future Growth (%)	Rooms Demand
1	898	108%	970
2	970	108%	1,048
3	1,048	108%	1,132
4	1,132	108%	1,223
5	1,223	108%	1,321

In Year 1, the current average nightly demand for rooms figure of 898 (calculated in step 1) is multiplied by the composite growth rate figure of 108% (100% + 8% composite growth rate figure calculated in step 2) to arrive at the future demand figure of 970 rooms in Year 1. The 970 figure is carried forward into Year 2, and is itself multiplied by 108%. Similar calculations are made for each of the remaining 3 years.

Step 4: Calculate the Future Supply of Rooms Required

We know from step 1 that the current occupancy rate in the competitive area is 77.7%. Let us now assume that a 70% occupancy of hotel rooms is normal for our competitive area. Normal means that, at that occupancy, a hotel should be profitable. We, therefore, know that the local market could support additional rooms right now, since current occupancy is averaging 77.7%. We can calculate the total needed to maintain rooms at a 70% occupancy rate by dividing current nightly demand by 70%:

$$\frac{\textbf{Average nightly demand}}{\textbf{Average occupancy \%}} = \textbf{Rooms required} = \frac{\textbf{898}}{\textbf{70\%}} = \underline{\underline{\textbf{1,283}}}$$

From this we can conclude that in Year 1 there is currently a shortage of 127 rooms (1,283 that the market could support less than the 1,156 that the market currently offers). Stated another way, if a new 127-room hotel were built today, given the current demand for rooms, the new overall average occupancy rate would be 70%:

$$\frac{\text{Average nightly demand}}{\text{Rooms shortage + Rooms available}} = \frac{\text{Average}}{\text{occupancy}} = \frac{898}{127 + 1{,}156} = 70\%$$

Next, the future demand for additional hotel rooms is projected for the next five years, as follows:

$$\frac{\text{Rooms demand}}{\text{Normal occupancy \%}} = \frac{\text{Supply}}{\text{required}} - \frac{\text{Current}}{\text{supply}} = \text{New rooms required}$$

Year	Rooms Demand	Normal Occupancy (%)	Supply Required	Current Supply	New Rooms Required
Current	898	70%	1,283	1,156	127
1	970	70%	1,386	1,156	230
2	1,048	70%	1,497	1,156	341
3	1,132	70%	1,617	1,156	461
4	1,223	70%	1,747	1,156	591
5	1,321	70%	1,887	1,156	731

In this tabulation, the future demand figures from step 3 have each been divided by a 70% occupancy rate (as was demonstrated earlier for the current year) to arrive at the figures in the supply-required column. From each year's supply-required figure, the current supply of rooms (1,156) has been deducted. The end result is a forecast of the number of new rooms that could be supported over each of the next 5 years, given all these assumptions. We see that, at the end of 5 years, 731 additional rooms could be supported at an average occupancy of 70%. Note, also, that the rooms-required figures in the right-hand column are cumulative.

To reduce risk we might want to assume that a 75%, rather than a 70%, occupancy should be used. In that case, the year-by-year demand figures would be divided by 75%, resulting in a reduced number of additional rooms per year that the market could support.

However, before the supply/demand analysis is finalized and a recommendation is made about the size of the property to be planned, some other factors might need to be considered. For example, if any of the existing competitive facilities are expected to be removed from the market (demolished or converted to some other use), the supply figures should be adjusted accordingly. Similarly, if any information is available about other proposed competitive hotels in the area, this should be adjusted for in the future supply figures. Finally, the decision about whether to build should not be based on numbers alone. Frequently, two adjacent, competitive hotels, motels, or restaurants will have vastly different demands for their products. There are many nonquantifiable factors that cause this to be so, such as atmosphere, quality of decor, management, and staff training, to name only a few.

SPACE RECOMMENDATIONS

The feasibility study at this point could include information that the architect might require to prepare more detailed plans. This should include not only such items as the number of rooms and the proportion of rooms of various types (singles, doubles, twins), but also the proportion of space and number of seats recommended for food, beverage, and related facilities, such as meeting rooms and public spaces (lobbies), and possibly even suggested themes for bars and restaurants. Back-of-the-house facilities and space requirements (kitchens, storerooms, offices) should be included, as should parking space requirements. Finally, any recommendations concerning recreation facilities should be covered in this section.

FINANCIAL ANALYSIS

A major part of any feasibility study is the financial analysis section. This section is normally broken down into four subsections, such as the capital investment required and a tentative financing plan, pro forma income statements, projected cash flow, and evaluation of projections.

Each of these subsections will be discussed in relation to the financial feasibility of a hypothetical new 100-room motor hotel that will have a 65-seat coffee shop, 75-seat dining room, and 90-seat cocktail lounge. Any income received other than from these operating departments will be incidental.

CAPITAL INVESTMENT REQUIRED
AND TENTATIVE FINANCING PLAN

Estimates based on professional advice from architects, contractors, and other useful sources indicate that the investment required in the proposed property will be as follows:

Land	$ 300,000
Building (including all professional fees for architects, designers, and lawyers)	2,100,000
Furniture and equipment	600,000
Interest on construction financing	220,000
Pre-opening operating expenses	100,000
Initial working capital	50,000
Total	$3,370,000

The total estimated investment required of $3,370,000 is tentatively broken down into the following possible financing plan:

	Debt	Equity	Total
Land and building (75% debt / 25% equity)	$1,800,000	$ 600,000	$2,400,000
Furniture and equipment (80% debt / 20% equity)	480,000	120,000	600,000
Interest on construction financing		220,000	220,000
Pre-opening expenses		100,000	100,000
Initial working capital		50,000	50,000
Totals	$2,280,000	$1,090,000	$3,370,000

Assumptions and other information:

1. Interim, or bridge financing of $1,800,000 will be required for partial payment of the land and for construction financing. This amount, advanced by the lender month by month as required, will carry a 12% interest rate, or 1% per month. Interest will be paid monthly out of equity funds available. The full amount of the advance ($1,800,000) will be refunded, just prior to opening, out of the proceeds of a permanent first mortgage to be taken out on the land and building. Total pre-opening interest cost will be $220,000 as calculated in Exhibit 13.1. This interest expense is the amount the developer has to pay the lender at the prevailing rate on the total amount of money advanced to that date.

2. The permanent first mortgage of $1,800,000 will have a 20-year term and will carry a 10% interest rate for the first five years. A schedule showing the combined annual installments broken down between interest and principal for the first 5 years following the hotel's opening is illustrated next.

Year	Annual Payment	Interest	Principal	Balance
				$1,800,000
1	$211,000	$180,000	$31,000	1,769,000
2	211,000	177,000	34,000	1,735,000
3	211,000	173,000	38,000	1,697,000
4	211,000	170,000	41,000	1,656,000
5	211,000	165,000	46,000	1,610,000

In these calculations, figures have been rounded to the nearest $1,000. Note that payments on such a mortgage would normally be made monthly and the schedule of repayments calculated on this basis. However, for the sake of simplicity, annual payments have been assumed.

Months Before Opening	Equity Amount	Land and Building	Furniture and Equipment	Interim Loan Financing	Prepaid Expenses	Working Capital
19	$ 216,500	$215,000		$ 1,500		
18	15,000	10,000		5,000		
17	15,500	10,000		5,500		
16	16,000	10,000		6,000		
15	32,000	25,000		7,000		
14	33,000	25,000		8,000		
13	34,000	25,000		9,000		
12	35,000	25,000		10,000		
11	36,000	25,000		11,000		
10	37,000	25,000		12,000		
9	38,000	25,000		13,000		
8	39,000	25,000		14,000		
7	40,000	25,000		15,000		
6	41,000	25,000		16,000		
5	61,500	25,000	$ 20,000	16,500		
4	82,000	20,000	20,000	17,000	$ 25,000	
3	102,500	20,000	40,000	17,500	25,000	
2	103,000	20,000	40,000	18,000	25,000	
1	113,000	20,000		18,000	25,000	$50,000
Totals	$1,090,000	$600,000	$120,000	$220,000	$100,000	$50,000

■ **EXHIBIT 13.1**
Equity Investment Schedule

3. The equipment and furniture will be financed using a chattel mortgage (the chattels being the equipment and furniture) over 5 years at a 12% interest rate. Repayment will be made with combined equal annual installments of principal and interest. A schedule showing these repayment amounts, broken down into principal and interest, is illustrated as follows. (Again, all figures are rounded to the nearest $1,000.)

Year	Annual Payment	Interest	Principal	Balance
				$480,000
1	$133,000	$58,000	$ 75,000	405,000
2	133,000	49,000	84,000	321,000
3	133,000	39,000	94,000	227,000
4	133,000	27,000	106,000	121,000
5	136,000	15,000	121,000	-0-

*The final year is increased due to rounding.

4. The total initial equity investment is forecast to be $1,090,000. It is useful to prepare a schedule showing the timing of this investment, by month, prior to opening, so the equity investors know when they have to put up the money and what it is for. This is illustrated in Exhibit 13.1 for our proposed hotel.

5. The interest expense of $220,000 on the interim financing will be capitalized and expensed as part of the depreciation expense of the building.

6. The pre-opening expenses of $100,000 (for such items as insurance, property taxes, wages and staff training, advertising, and other operating costs incurred prior to opening) will be amortized (shown as an expense) over the first 2 years of operation.

7. For the building, as well as the furniture and equipment, declining balance depreciation will be used. Building depreciation will be 3.75% per year, and furniture and equipment, 20% per year. Depreciation schedules are as follows:

Year			*Building Depreciation Expense*			*Balance*
						$2,100,000
1	3.75%	×	$2,100,000	=	$79,000	$2,021,000
2	3.75%	×	$2,021,000	=	$76,000	$1,945,000
3	3.75%	×	$1,945,000	=	$73,000	$1,872,000
4	3.75%	×	$1,872,000	=	$70,000	$1,802,000
5	3.75%	×	$1,802,000	=	$68,000	$1,734,000

Year			*Furniture and Equipment Depreciation Expense*			*Balance*
						$ 600,000
1	20%	×	$600,000	=	$120,000	$ 480,000
2	20%	×	$480,000	=	$ 96,000	$ 384,000
3	20%	×	$384,000	=	$ 77,000	$ 307,000
4	20%	×	$307,000	=	$ 61,000	$ 246,000
5	20%	×	$246,000	=	$ 49,000	$ 197,000

PRO-FORMA INCOME STATEMENTS

The next step is the preparation of pro forma income statements by the two departments (rooms and food and beverage).

Rooms

Rooms sales revenue is based on the assumption that, in the first year, occupancy of the 100 rooms will be 60% and that the average room rate will be

$52. This rate would be competitive with what other motor hotels in the area are charging. In Year 2, and for the remaining 3 years of our 5-year projections, occupancy is expected to climb to 70%, and average room rate will be increased to $56. Year 1 room sales revenue is therefore

$$\textbf{100 rooms} \times \textbf{60\%} \times \textbf{\$52} \times \textbf{365 nights} = \underline{\textbf{\$1,138,800}}$$

and for each of the next 4 years room sales revenue will be

$$\textbf{100 rooms} \times \textbf{70\%} \times \textbf{\$56} \times \textbf{365 nights} = \underline{\textbf{\$1,430,800}}$$

The operating costs for the room department are estimated as follows for Year 1:

Payroll and related expenses	**$244,000**
Other direct operating costs	**54,000**
Total	**$298,000**

These estimated operating costs will generally be based on a percentage of sales revenue, using national averages for that size and type of operation, adjusting for local conditions if necessary. In Year 2 and the remaining years of our forecast, these costs are increased in total by $74,000 a year to take care of the increased occupancy. Our rooms department income condensed statements would now be as follows, with figures rounded to the closest $1,000:

	Year 1	*Years 2 to 5*
Sales revenue	$1,139,000	$1,431,000
Operating costs	(298,000)	(372,000)
Net department operating income	$ 841,000	$1,059,000

Food and Beverage

Food and beverage, insofar as sales revenue and cost of sales are concerned, should be broken down into two separate components: food and alcoholic beverages. Food sales should, in turn, be broken down by sales area (coffee shop and dining room) and then, in turn, by meal periods within each sales area. Sales are then calculated by using the basic equation given in Chapter 9.

$$\textbf{Food sales} = \frac{\textbf{Number}}{\textbf{of seats}} \times \frac{\textbf{Seat}}{\substack{\textbf{turnover} \\ \textbf{rate}}} \times \frac{\textbf{Average}}{\textbf{check}} \times \frac{\textbf{Days}}{\substack{\textbf{open in} \\ \textbf{year}}}$$

For example, in our 65-seat coffee shop, assuming it will be open every day of the year, breakfast sales revenue are calculated as follows, assuming one seat turnover and a $5.25 average check:

$$65 \times 1 \times \$5.25 \times 365 = \text{Total sales } \$124,556$$

Similar calculations would have to be made for the other meal periods, and, possibly, for coffee break periods if these coffee breaks expected to generate significant amounts of sales revenue. Seat turnover figures and average check amounts normally vary enough from one meal period to another to require separate calculations. Turnover rates and average checks can often be based on an assessment of what local competitive hotel restaurant operations are doing, combined with an evaluation of the type of clientele the guest rooms will be catering to.

In the calculation of total food sales revenue, it might be necessary to consider sales revenue generated in areas such as room service. In room service, the rooms occupancy figure will give an indication of the number of guests per day who might require some type of food service. This would give total daily sales revenue, which should then be multiplied by 365.

In addition, the derived demand from nonfood areas might add to total food sales revenue. For example, if food service is offered to customers in the cocktail lounge, an estimate of the number of daily orders that could be expected, multiplied by an assumed average check, would give a forecast of daily sales revenue. This daily sales revenue figure can then be multiplied by the days in the year that the lounge will be open.

Let us assume that this work has been completed and that total annual food sales revenue is estimated at $1,570,000. To this food figure must be added the alcoholic beverage sales in the coffee shop and dining room, as well as in the lounge. You are referred to the relevant section in Chapter 9 for forecasting beverage sales revenue. Assume that total annual beverage sales for the proposed hotel have been calculated and are estimated to be $1,038,000. Combined food and beverage sales revenue will be $2,608,000.

From the combined food and beverage sales figures, the direct operating costs must be deducted. As was the case with the rooms department, these costs can be estimated as a percentage of sales revenue, using national restaurant industry figures for this size and type of operation, adjusting if necessary for local conditions. The departmental income statement can now be prepared.

	Food	*Beverage*		*Total*
Sales revenue	$1,570,000	$1,038,000		$2,608,000
Cost of sales	(628,000)	(261,000)		(889,000)
Gross profit	$ 942,000	$ 777,000		$1,719,000
Payroll and related expenses			$921,000	
Other direct operating expenses			519,000	(1,440,000)
Net departmental operating income				$ 279,000

Once the forecast departmental income statements have been finalized, total departmental operating income can be calculated. From this can be deducted the undistributed expenses (administrative and general, marketing, property operation and maintenance, and energy costs). These expenses are generally primarily fixed in nature and can usually be estimated with some accuracy. In this case, the figure is estimated to be $480,000 annually.

The forecasted departmental operating income figures, less undistributed expenses, have been transferred to Exhibit 13.2 for each of the first 5 years of operation. It should be noted that these figures are constant for each of the years (except for changes in Year 2 for the rooms departmental income, due to the anticipated increase in occupancy percentage, room rate, and direct expenses, as explained earlier). In all other cases, the possibility of increasing costs has been ignored on the assumption that any increased costs will be passed on in the form of higher room rates or food and beverage prices. Thus, net operating income will not change significantly. Also, for Years 2 through 5, no upward adjustment has been made for any additional sales revenue that the food and beverage areas would derive from the additional rooms occupancy. At this point, the sales revenue figures should be kept as conservative as possible.

In Exhibit 13.2, in Years 1 and 2, the $100,000 pre-opening operating costs have been deducted: $50,000 in each of the years. For tax purposes in the United States (as well as some other countries), the interest expense on interim financing of $220,000 cannot be deducted to arrive at operating income (before tax). Instead, the interest has to be capitalized—that is, added to the total cost of building construction. Some of the interest expense is, thus, included each year as

	Year 1	Year 2	Year 3	Year 4	Year 5
Departmental operating income					
Rooms	$ 841,000	$ 1,059,000	$ 1,059,000	$ 1,059,000	$ 1,059,000
Food and beverage	279,000	279,000	279,000	279,000	279,000
	$ 1,120,000	$ 1,338,000	$ 1,338,000	$ 1,338,000	$ 1,338,000
Less: undistributed expenses	(480,000)	(480,000)	(480,000)	(480,000)	(480,000)
Pre-opening expenses	(50,000)	(50,000)			
Income before interest & depr:	$ 590,000	$ 808,000	$ 858,000	$ 858,000	$ 858,000
Interest	(238,000)	(226,000)	(213,000)	(197,000)	(181,000)
Depreciation	(199,000)	(172,000)	(150,000)	(131,000)	(117,000)
Operating income (before tax)	$ 153,000	$ 410,000	$ 495,000	$ 530,000	$ 560,000
Income tax (40%)	(61,000)	(164,000)	(198,000)	(212,000)	(224,000)
Net Income	$ 92,000	$ 246,000	$ 297,000	$ 318,000	$ 336,000

■ **EXHIBIT 13.2**

Pro Forma Income Statements

part of the building's depreciation expense. The following table shows the depreciation of the interest expense.

		Construction Interest Depreciation				
Year		*Depreciation Expense*				*Balance*
						$220,000
1	3.75%	×	$220,000	=	$8,000	212,000
2	3.75%	×	212,000	=	8,000	204,000
3	3.75%	×	204,000	=	8,000	196,000
4	3.75%	×	196,000	=	8,000	190,000
5	3.75%	×	189,000	=	7,000	183,000

To arrive at the proposed hotel's overall net income (or loss), permanent and chattel mortgage interest, as well as building, furniture, and equipment depreciation, have been deducted for each of the five years. Finally, income tax has been deducted. If there had been an operating loss before income tax in Year 1, there would be no income tax. Also, that loss would be carried forward into Year 2 and deducted from the pretax income before applying the 40% tax rate on the taxable income.

PROJECTED CASH FLOW

The next step in our financial feasibility is to convert the hotel's annual net income to an annual cash flow. This is illustrated in Exhibit 13.3.

First, the non-cash expenses of depreciation and amortization of the pre-opening expenses are added back to net income to determine net cash flows from operations.

	Year 1	*Year 2*	*Year 3*	*Year 4*	*Year 5*
Net income	$ 92,000	$246,000	$297,000	$318,000	$336,000
Add: Depreciation	199,000	172,000	150,000	131,000	117,000
Preopening expenses	50,000	50,000			
Cash available	341,000	468,000	447,000	449,000	453,000
Deduct: Principal payments	(106,000)	(118,000)	(131,000)	(133,000)	(166,000)
Net Cash Flow	$235,000	$350,000	$316,000	$302,000	$287,000

■ **EXHIBIT 13.3**
Budgeted Cash Flows

Finally, the principal portions of the permanent and chattel mortgage payments have been deducted, since these require an outlay of cash that is not an expense is not deducted to arrive at net income. The resulting figure for each year is the net cash flow. See Exhibit 13.3.

The cash flow is positive each year, indicating that with the proposed financing plan, there will be no problem in meeting both the interest and principal payments on the debt.

EVALUATION OF PROJECTIONS

At this point in the analysis, it might be useful to determine the return on the equity investment that would be achieved with the given estimates of revenue and expenses. Over the first five years, the total net income from Exhibit 13.2 is as follows:

Year 1	$ 92,000
Year 2	246,000
Year 3	297,000
Year 4	318,000
Year 5	336,000
Total	$1,289,000

This is an average return of less than $257,800 a year ($1,289,000 divided by 5), or an average return on the initial $1,090,000 equity investment of about 23.7%, which, although not high for the risk involved, could be considered reasonable after income tax. However, as seen in Chapter 12, the accounting rate of return on investment might not be the best criterion to use in evaluating an investment proposal. The net present value (NPV) and/or internal rate of return (IRR) methods discussed and illustrated in that chapter are frequently more valid measures for project evaluation.

Also, the forecasts used were based on only one level of occupancy, set of room rates, and food and beverage prices. It is normal practice to prepare a flexible budget and determine estimated net income from a level of sales revenue higher than expected (thus providing a higher return on investment), as well as a level of sales revenue lower than expected.

If a satisfactory return could not be anticipated, the project might be terminated at this point. Alternatively, a different financing arrangement might be attempted, using more or less financial leverage and/or different terms and interest rates. To do this manually may require considerable work, but spreadsheets can be easily programmed to handle changes in a number of variables, individually or at the same time, to produce new net income and cash flow figures based on the changes.

If a plan were to be arranged that seemed to produce net income and cash flow figures that were, in the initial years acceptable, then the cash flow projections should be continued beyond the five-year period to extend them for the entire life of the project. Finally, the lifetime cash flow figures could then be evaluated, using the NPV or IRR investment analysis methods, before a final decision is made to proceed with the development.

FEASIBILITY OF EXPANDING EXISTING OPERATION

Although this chapter has discussed a financial feasibility study for a new operation, the same techniques can be applied equally well to the feasibility of expanding an existing hotel, motel, restaurant, or similar business. In that case, only the marginal or incremental sales revenues and expenses, as well as debt and equity financing costs associated with the expansion, would be considered in the net income and cash flow projections. In fact, these projections are much easier to make for an existing business, since it has its current operation's historic accounting data to use as a basis for forecasting.

COMPUTER APPLICATIONS

A spreadsheet can be used for all the calculations necessary for a feasibility study pro forma income statement and budgeted cash flows for as many years into the future as desired. It will also allow rapid results to be produced in what-if situations—for example, by changing forecast room rates and/or occupancy percentages. Finally, it will allow NPV or IRR to be applied to the forecasts to provide a more valid measure of a proposed project's viability.

SUMMARY

A feasibility study is an in-depth analysis of the financial feasibility of a property expansion or a new property development. A feasibility study cannot guarantee financial success, but it does reduce much of the guesswork and risk of a new venture.

A feasibility study for a hotel can usually be broken down into two major parts. The first part includes such items as the front matter (including conclusions and recommendations), general market characteristics (location, population and industrial growth, employment, incomes, economic trends), site evaluation (including maps, transportation routes, and physical information about the site), and supply-and-demand information (market to be served, information about competitive properties, and the likely sources of demand for the facilities to be offered). The next section in the first part of the study would be a supply-and-demand analysis for guest rooms (in a hotel situation).

The supply-and-demand analysis has four steps:

1. Calculate the most recent 12-month average occupancy of the most competitive hotels.
2. Calculate the composite growth rate of demand from the various sources.
3. Calculate the additional rooms required year by year.
4. Calculate the future supply of rooms required.

Once these steps have been completed, the first part of the study can be concluded with recommendations about the number and types of rooms proposed and about other facilities proposed, such as number of seats and themes for food and beverage areas.

The second part of a feasibility study is a financial analysis of the proposal based on the facilities recommended. This part is composed of four major sections:

1. Calculation of the capital investment required and tentative financing plan. The investment required is broken down into such items as land, building, furniture and equipment, construction loan interest, other pre-opening expenses, and working capital. The financing plan is then broken down into its debt and equity elements.
2. Preparation of pro forma income statements. These are usually initially prepared for a minimum 5-year period. Sales revenue for each department is first forecast, and from this are deducted estimated direct expenses (usually based on a percentage of sales revenue). Next are deducted the indirect expenses and other pre-opening expenses. Finally, mortgage interest and depreciation are deducted, as well as income tax, where relevant, to arrive at net income.
3. Preparation of cash flow projections from the net income forecasts. Net income is adjusted for depreciation and principal payments on debt financing to arrive at cash flow.
4. Evaluation of the projections to date is made at this point. If necessary, sales revenue levels and/or other variables can be changed to see how this might affect the results. Finally, if the proposal appears feasible, a complete evaluation of the project's entire life, using NPV or IRR (see Chapter 12) should be carried out before making the final decision on the investment.

DISCUSSION QUESTIONS

1. Since a feasibility study for a proposed new venture cannot guarantee that the venture will be successful, of what value is such a study?

2. In a feasibility study for a restaurant in a downtown office building, what general market characteristics do you think would be relevant?

3. In preparing a feasibility study for a motor hotel to be located in an area where there are several other motor hotels, what factors would you consider to determine which of the other operations are the most competitive?

4. A resort hotel is to be located in a mountain area near a major highway about 150 miles from the closest town or city. What sources of demand might you consider in a feasibility study for this property?

5. Briefly describe how a composite growth rate of demand for hotel rooms can be calculated.

6. Two similar competitive restaurants have quite different levels of demand (average total number of customers per day). What factors could cause this to be so?

7. In preparing the pro forma income statement for a rooms department, how do you think the average room rate and occupancy figures could be established?

8. In estimating total sales revenue for a coffee shop in a proposed new hotel, why is it important to begin by estimating sales revenue by meal period?

9. What adjustments generally have to be made to the net income figures to convert them to a cash flow basis?

10. In what way might a change in the depreciation method used affect the projected cash flow figures in a feasibility study?

11. If the initial feasibility of a proposed new hotel does not appear good from a financial point of view, what variables might one try to change to improve the result?

ETHICS SITUATION

The owner of a proposed new motel has received a feasibility study from a consultant that shows that, at best, the operation would be only marginally profitable. The owner knows that this report will not convince possible investors to advance the funds for this proposed project, so the owner changes the feasibility study figures to improve the profitability of the operation. Discuss the ethics of this situation.

PROBLEMS

P13.1 There are five competitive motels in a resort area with the following number of rooms and current occupancy rates:

Motel	Rooms	Occupancy
A	74	82%
B	45	73%
C	58	85%
D	48	70%
E	52	75%

Demand for rooms in the area is broken down into the following sources and growth rates:

Source	Percentage	Growth Rate
Business traveler	10	5%
Vacation traveler	80	8%
Other travelers	10	1%

a. Calculate the current average occupancy of the five motels.

b. Calculate the composite rate of growth in demand.

c. Apply the composite growth rate to the demand figures to obtain projected demand for each of the next 4 years.

d. Assume that a 70% average room occupancy for the motels in this resort would be profitable. Calculate the future supply of rooms that could be supported for each of the next 4 years.

P13.2 Six competitive motor hotels have the following number of rooms and current occupancy rates.

Motor Hotel	Rooms	Occupancy
1	150	80%
2	140	90%
3	90	70%
4	110	80%
5	66	75%
6	120	75%

Demand for rooms in the area where the motor hotels are located is broken down into the following sources and growth rates:

Source	Percentage	Growth Rate
Business traveler	60%	6%
Vacation traveler	30%	5%
Other travelers	10%	4%

a. Calculate the current average occupancy of the six motor hotels.

b. Calculate the composite rate of growth in demand.

c. Apply the composite growth rate to the demand figures to obtain projected demand for each of the next four years.

d. Assume the average room occupancy is 75% for the motor hotels in this area and is considered profitable. Assume also that Motor Hotel 3 is due to be demolished in Year 2 to make way for a new highway. Calculate the future supply of rooms that could be supported for each of the next four years.

P13.3 A financial feasibility study is being carried out for a proposed new 120-seat restaurant. It will be open for both lunch and dinner from Monday through Saturday and for dinner only on Sunday. For the sake of simplicity, assume a 52-week year. Seat turnover and average food check figures are estimated as follows:

	Turnover	*Average Food Check*
Weekday lunch	1.50	$ 5.60
Weekday dinner	1.25	$10.50
Sunday dinner	1.75	$13.00

In addition, the restaurant has a small banquet room, and food sales revenue in this area is estimated at $14,000 a month. Alcoholic beverage revenue is estimated to be 12% of lunch food sales revenue and 30% of all food sales revenue. In the banquet room, alcoholic beverage revenue is forecast to be 40% of food sales revenue in that area. Food cost is estimated at 40% of total food sales revenue, and beverage cost is 28% of total beverage sales revenue.

Wage cost for salaried personnel (manager, chef, hostess, head server, and cashier) is estimated at $300,000 per year. Wages for all other employees will be 15% of total annual restaurant sales revenue.

Employee benefits (vacations, meals, etc.) are estimated to be 10% of total annual wages. Other operating costs are estimated at 12% of total annual wages and salaries. Undistributed costs are forecast to be $130,000 per year.

Prepare the restaurant's pro forma income statement for the first year. Ignore income tax.

P13.4 A new 50-room budget motel is being planned. Total cost will be $1,450,000, of which land will be $150,000, building $900,000, furniture and equipment $300,000, and the balance for pre-opening interest and other expenses. The building will be financed 70% by an 8% mortgage for 21 years. The annual payment to amortize (pay back principal and interest) this mortgage will be $63,000. The furniture and equipment will be financed 75% by a mortgage at 11%, repayable in five equal installments of $61,000 principal and interest. Apart from the mortgage and chattel mortgage amounts, the balance of the total investment required will be from equity.

a. Calculate the amount of the equity investment.

b. Prepare the building mortgage repayment schedule for the first five years. Round calculated figures to the nearest $1,000.

c. Prepare the chattel mortgage repayment schedule. Round calculated figures to the nearest $1,000.

P13.5 Given the facts in P13.4, assume the building will be depreciated at 6% double declining balance, and that furniture and equipment will be depreciated at 25% double declining balance. Prepare depreciation schedules for the first 5 years. (Round calculated figures to the nearest $1,000.)

P13.6 Given the facts in Problems 13.4 and 13.5 and the following additional information, prepare the pro forma income statements for each of the first five years:

Year	Average Room Rate	Occupancy (%)
1	$30.00	70%
2	$30.00	75%
3	$33.00	75%
4	$35.00	75%
5	$35.00	80%

Rooms operating costs average 60% of total room sales revenue. Indirect expenses will be $40,000 in Year 1, and will increase by $4,000 a year for each of the next 4 years. The pre-opening interest and other expenses total $100,000 and will be amortized equally over each of the first 5 years. Income tax, if any, will be 25% of earnings before income tax. Note, however, that if there are any losses, they may be carried forward and deducted from earnings before income tax, before the 25% tax rate is applied. (Round all calculated figures to the nearest $1,000.)

P13.7 Given the facts in Problems 13.4, 13.5, and 13.6, calculate the net annual cash flow figures for each of the 5 years. What would be your evaluation of the financial feasibility of this proposed motel?

C A S E   1 3

Although Charlie (4C) has been in business for only a short time, he is thinking about opening a second restaurant similar to his current operation—a relatively medium-priced operation catering to the local neighborhood's family and small business trade.

Assume that he has asked you to do some preliminary work on a feasibility study for this second restaurant. Select a specific geographic location in your town with which you are familiar and which you think would be suitable for this new operation. Prepare a two- or three-page report for Charlie describing this location (include a map if you think it will help), explaining why that location might be suitable and briefly discussing the economic and demographic factors (about which you would eventually need more detailed information) that would support the need for a restaurant in this location.

CHAPTER 14

FINANCIAL GOALS AND INFORMATION SYSTEMS

INTRODUCTION

This chapter has two major parts: the first part is about financial goals and the second is about information systems. The section on financial goals discusses mission statements and the objectives and purposes of financial statements. Two financial management goals are then explored: profit maximization and maximization of return on investment, neither of which is a commonly used goal.

Some time is spent on the most commonly used goal, maximization of stockholder wealth. Secondary goals are then discussed, as is management by objectives (MBO). This section of the chapter also includes comments

about other goals, such as social goals, and concludes with developing an action plan to achieve goals.

The second section of the chapter covers information systems. The four levels of an information system are introduced: data production, data sorting, information production, and decision making. Most of this section concentrates on the last two of the four levels, since these are the keys for a company to establish an information system that will allow it to meet its financial goals.

This chapter concludes with comments about the effectiveness of a management information system.

CHAPTER OBJECTIVES

After studying this chapter, the reader should be able to:

1. Discuss the role of mission statements with reference to financial goals.
2. Discuss the general concept of financial management and list the types of financial and other goals that a company might have.
3. Discuss the pros and cons of profit wealth maximization as a financial goal.

4. Define *MBO,* explain how it is used to measure performance, and define the term *goal congruence.*

5. Discuss social goals.

6. Discuss the role of strategies and tactics in developing an action plan to achieve financial goals.

7. List the four levels in the decision-making process.

8. Explain the ways in which information is obtained in an organization, list the main criteria for information to be useful in the decision-making process, and state how an information system should be judged for quality.

9. Define management by exception.

FINANCIAL GOALS

Regardless of the type and size of an enterprise in the hospitality industry, financial management will be an ongoing aspect of the overall management of the business. This financial management may be quite unsophisticated in a small, owner-operated establishment and considerably more complex in a large, multi-unit organization. Despite the vast range of sizes and types of establishments in the industry, any operation can benefit from an understanding of the value and importance of financial management. Even nonprofit organizations, such as hospitals, must be able to obtain funds and then invest them to maximize benefits; stated another way, they must be able to provide the most benefits at the least possible cost. The concepts of financial management are, therefore, the same for both nonprofit and for-profit organizations; the only difference is how the operating or financial results are measured against the objectives.

MISSION STATEMENT

Before developing financial goals, some large hospitality corporations first prepare the organization's mission, or purpose, in a statement. A **mission statement** is sometimes referred to as a statement of business purpose. This statement should be definable and measurable and should consider customer needs. For example, a mission statement for a **resort hotel**—one with extensive recreational facilities—might read as follows:

> The Redwood Resort will position itself as the dominant luxury hotel in its area. Its prime weekday market will be corporate meetings and conference groups who will patronize both its guest rooms and food and beverage facilities. The hotel will offer a combination of first-class meeting, guest room, food

and beverage, and recreational facilities in a relaxing resort environment. The major sales strategy will be to seek out meeting planners and organizers and use a personal sales approach to obtain their business.

At weekends and during holiday periods, its market will include the upper end of the social scale. To satisfy the entertainment needs of both the corporate and society markets there will be nightly live entertainment.

Its pricing strategy will be to establish high prices that reflect the quality of its facilities and that the market segments selected can afford to pay. Prices will be set to yield an average minimum year-round guest room occupancy of 75% and allow overnight guests free use of all the resort's recreational amenities.

In comparison, vision statements are what the organization strives to achieve. The following is the one from Domino's Pizza, Inc., a major chain.

Exceptional people on a mission to be the best pizza delivery company in the world utilizing the company's guiding principles, which are:

At the moment of choice . . .

1. We demand integrity.
2. Our people come first.
3. We take great care of our customers.
4. We make pizzas every day.
5. We operate with smart hustle and positive energy.

As well as being the focus for developing financial goals, the mission statement establishes a sense of direction for an organization by defining what the organization is, what it does, how it does it, and for whom it is being done. In other words, a mission statement is a philosophy for doing business. Mission statements for an organization can do any or all of the following:

- Provide a brief statement of its current market position.
- Show which customer groups will be its targets for the marketing plan.
- Provide guidelines for allocation of its resources.
- Indicate where its future growth will occur.
- Give an indication of how its products differ from its competitors' products.
- Focus management's attention on marketing opportunities that conform to its mission.
- Serve as a basis for internal communication.
- Provide a direction to all its employees by alerting them to a common goal.
- Provide a basis for its control and evaluation.

OBJECTIVES OF FINANCIAL MANAGEMENT

Any business, at any particular time, must have funds available to conduct its operations. These funds come from creditors who lend the company money, from owners or stockholders who invest in the company or who own shares in it, and from earnings (profits) retained in the business. These funds may be kept in the business in a very liquid form, such as cash or marketable securities. They can also be tied up in food, beverage, and other inventories or in accounts receivable, or they can be invested in long-term assets, such as land, buildings, and furniture and fixtures.

At any particular point, the balance sheet will give a picture of the business's financial position. At a later date, another balance sheet will probably indicate a different financial position, because the position is never static. Funds are constantly flowing into and out of the business. The mix between the various sources of funds and the various uses of funds is constantly charging. The mix of sources and mix of uses, according to some overall plan, are what financial management is all about.

In large organizations, this plan is usually coordinated by a financial manager, who works closely with the general manager. In a smaller operation, the general manager and financial manager are the same person.

Generally, financial management has three objectives:

1. To establish goals, such as how large the company will be, how rapidly it will expand, and how it will measure its success in meeting these goals.
2. To decide on the sources of needed capital and to obtain the funds required by the firm to meet its goals.
3. To allocate these funds effectively to the various assets of the company, again with the company's goals in mind.

Only with clearly stated goals can an organization effectively manage its finances. Without them, a business operates without a plan. In a small owner-operated enterprise, a goal may be expressed in simple terms, such as that the owner wishes to make enough net income in the first 11 months of the year to take a vacation in the twelfth month. In a large or chain operation, goals would be established in a much more formal way by the board of directors. Goals are frequently expressed in monetary terms. Some of these financially measurable goals are discussed next.

PROFIT MAXIMIZATION

Profit maximization, or making the most amount of money in the shortest possible time, is one of the commonly considered objectives or goals of a company. It is argued that the total amount of profit or net income is not a realistic measure, since one can always sell more shares and invest the proceeds in marketable securities, thus increasing total net income. Because of this, maximization of earnings per share may be a better way to measure net income. In either case, however, the time element is important because of the time value of money. Most people would agree that $100,000 net income in the first year and nothing in each of the following 9 years is preferable to $10,000 per year for each of 10 years. The reason is that the entire $100,000 could be invested in the first year and continues to accumulate interest until the end of the tenth year, thus maximizing net income.

However, one of the problems with profit maximization as a goal is that it may ignore the possible risks of an investment. An international hotel corporation could open new, profitable hotels in countries with politically unstable governments, ignoring the threat of future government expropriation of the investment. Is the immediate potential net income worth the risk?

The profit maximization goal also ignores investment financing risks. A company might become highly financially levered by borrowing large amounts of debt money at high interest rates in pursuit of some extra net income. Owners of shares, perceiving the risk, might begin selling their shares, thus reducing the market value of the shares. Alternatively, the company might issue new shares to obtain the financing (considerably reducing debt leverage), thereby diluting the value of present stockholders' shares. In other words, profit maximization as an objective might tend to ignore the company's commitment to its stockholders and create a rift between them and the company's management.

Profit can also be maximized by not paying dividends or by making dividend policy a less important goal. This, too, would probably engender a negative reaction from stockholders.

Finally, if management is being measured by profit maximization, it might tend to emphasize very profitable but short-run investments while ignoring long-run, more consistently profitable investments.

Thus, while a business must have profits, profit maximization as a sole goal is generally shortsighted, particularly if the company has many stockholders.

MAXIMIZATION OF RETURN ON INVESTMENT

The maximization of percentage return on investment is a variation of the profit maximization goal. To meet this goal, the company's management attempts to use its funds so that each dollar invested returns the most dollars of net income, or the higher return on investment.

Obviously, no investment would be made if the return was less than the cost of financing. Frequently, a minimum return on investment will be established for the company as a whole, and no individual investment will be made unless it is expected to yield at least this minimum. The return on investment goal, although it has its place, also has many of the disadvantages of the profit maximization goal.

MAXIMIZATION OF STOCKHOLDERS' WEALTH

Generally speaking, most successful larger companies try, over time, to maximize stockholder wealth because this will make stockholders happier than if the wealth were not maximized. One could ask why a company attempts to maximize stockholder wealth and not the wealth of its debt lenders, or the tax department, or employees, or the company's management. The reason is that stockholders are, legally, the owners of the company. All the other groups mentioned must be given their due before the stockholders who, as residual claimants, get what is left over.

Maximization of stockholder wealth has as its objective the highest combination of dividend payouts by the company and increase in the market value of the price of the company's shares. With this goal, net income is not as important as earnings per share. The time value of earnings, mentioned earlier, must be a consideration, as must the relative risks of alternative investments and alternative methods of financing those investments. In emphasizing earnings per share, dividend policy and its effect on market price per share must also be considered. Note that maximizing earnings per share may not be the same as maximizing market price per share. The market price shows how well management is doing for stockholders. Dissatisfied stockholders will sell their shares and invest their money elsewhere. If enough of them do this, the market price of the shares will drop.

A company can maximize its retained earnings by never paying dividends, but this would please neither the individual stockholder nor the market for stockholders generally. The market comprises all current and prospective stockholders who assess the risk of ownership of the shares of the company, including potential future earnings, the timing and risk of these earnings, the company's dividend policy, and other factors that are deemed important to establish the price of a share. The individual in the market buys or sells shares according to his or her perception of the firm. The market price is influenced upward by those wishing to buy shares and downward by those selling. It thus serves as a barometer of how well management is doing on behalf of the stockholders.

Management's policies and plans will therefore be established, under the maximization of stockholders' wealth goal, to ensure that wise investments are made, that they are sensibly financed, and that an appropriate dividend policy is established.

One of the disadvantages of this goal is that the market price of the company's shares may be influenced by factors beyond the control of the company's management, such as a general recession. Management could also be so concerned with the goal of maximizing stockholder wealth that it forgets about the business's day-to-day operations, and in the interest of its own short-run survival, management might be unwilling to take reasonable risks, even though the investments would be to the stockholders' advantage. Further, where the company is large and share ownership is separate from control of the company, management might not always operate in the best interest of stockholders, although in the long run this is unlikely to occur. Sometimes managers may attempt to maximize their own wealth at the expense of stockholders, but again, in the long run, if management does not appear to maximize stockholders' wealth, the board can fire it. Note again, however, that the board may be less responsive if stockholders are widely dispersed, and the absence of effective stockholder representation on the board may decrease the pressure on management to maximize stockholder wealth.

Finally, earnings per share in the hospitality industry might not fully reflect the company's true wealth. In the hospitality industry, a company's value can increase considerably through appreciation of its real estate assets, but it may not be reflected in earnings per share. Nor is it apparent on balance sheets that typically show assets at cost less accumulated depreciation (net book value). For a successful hospitality industry enterprise that has been in business for some years, those cost or net book value figures will not be very meaningful.

SECONDARY GOALS

Even though a favorite goal of many organizations is maximization of stockholder wealth, some consider this goal too broad. For that reason, it is often supported with secondary goals that will help the overall organization reach its objective, something that department heads can relate to. These secondary goals are often translated into such objectives as achieving a certain minimum rooms occupancy or restaurant seat turnover or aiming for a specific minimum level of sales revenue dollars within a budget period. If these secondary goals are achieved, this should ensure that the overall corporate financial goal is also achieved. In some cases, the secondary goals are not even expressed in monetary terms. For example, a restaurant may only emphasize quality, service, cleanliness, and value for money and achieve its overall financial goal by conforming to those secondary goals.

One problem that secondary goals create is that there may have to be a trade-off between a decision in one department and a decision in another, or a conflict between short-run and long-term earnings. An example is reducing prices to gain a larger share of the market. This may lower short-run profits. Another example is the reduction in housekeeping quality standards, which might improve short-run profits but may cause occupancies to drop over the long run. The general manager's role is to maintain a balance between short-run secondary goals and the long-term financial objectives of the company.

It is important to rank objectives and secondary goals in order of priority and implement only those from the top of the list that are achievable. If too many objectives and secondary objectives are established and all are tackled, both financial and other resources might be spread too thin for any of them to be achieved.

MANAGEMENT BY OBJECTIVES

Achievement of goals in an organization has to be carried out by people. Therefore, an important aspect of secondary goal setting is to have the employees involved in the whole process of setting those goals. This basic concept is known as **management by objectives (MBO).** MBO is based on the assumption that employees can be committed to their work and allows for maximum involvement and participation in setting secondary goals, personal goals, and performance standards for judging employees' work. The term **goal congruence** is often used in this regard. Goal congruence is the alignment of organizational goals with the personal and group goals of subordinates and superiors.

For example, a hotel might establish as an objective increasing total sales revenue by 10% for the coming year. The rooms department manager of that hotel might then set as two of its goals increasing its average room rate by 5% and increasing rooms occupancy by 3% to help achieve the hotel's overall goal. Goal congruence provides direction so that the activities of each department are working toward achievement of the organization's overall objectives and mission.

There are four important characteristics of MBO:

1. The department head, or department manager, participates in establishing the criteria by which he or she will be judged.
2. The criteria, once established, are known by the person and his or her supervisor before the period begins.
3. Criteria are established in absolute or quantitative terms (i.e., dollars, percentages, or other units), so that results can be measured.
4. Goals should also be expressed relative to desired results to be achieved within a specified time frame.

For example, a restaurant manager might state that her objective is to increase sales revenue by adding a special entrée to the menu each day. This is not an objective because no results have been stated in quantitative terms and no time frame has been established. Instead, the restaurant manager has stated how she is going to achieve something. Stating how something is to be achieved is not an objective. The restaurant manager in this situation would not find it difficult to implement what she says the objective is, but there is no way to measure the results. A more comprehensive objective for this restaurant might be to increase sales revenue by increasing customer average check by $1 by the end of a 90-day period.

Research has shown that the more objective a performance measure is, the more likely it is that supervisors and those they supervise will work with effort. Accounting systems play a key role in this because they can provide relatively objective performance evaluations. Research further shows that unless those being measured think that their behavior can influence the performance measure, they are unlikely to invest effort to achieve goals.

The measurement criteria, or standards, motivate the individuals to perform according to a clear understanding of expectations. An important aspect of MBO is that the department heads are not judged on a personal basis, but rather, against the mutually agreed upon standards.

If standards are not achieved, the employee is not penalized, but, rather, is assisted by the supervisor in locating problem areas and identifying the cause of the problem. This investigation is then used to assist the department head in future performance or, if necessary, in reestablishing performance standards if the standards are the fault.

OTHER GOALS

The financial goals mentioned to this point, were discussed under the assumption that an individual company will decide on one goal or a combination of goals, clearly spell out the objective(s), and operate toward that objective(s). This is probably true of very large operations in the hospitality industry, and particularly of those whose shares are publicly traded and for whom the goal of maximizing shareholders' wealth would be most appropriate.

However, many smaller hospitality corporations do not operate with many shareholders. Indeed, they may operate with as few as two. Such companies operate under quite different circumstances. They might find it inappropriate to have as a goal maximization of stockholders' wealth as indicated by market price of the shares, since the shares are not publicly traded. The majority of smaller hospitality industry companies would probably find themselves in this category. They may not even have clearly defined financial goals, and such matters as maximization of profit or stockholders' wealth are not relevant in their decision making. Internal operating decisions may be made without reference to financial objectives. For example, a hotel sales department might be convinced that accommodating bus tour groups could considerably increase sales revenue. The rooms department manager might think this type of business is too disruptive to normal operations and might cause some regular customers to be denied accommodation when the hotel is full with tour groups. If this hotel had as one of its objectives the maximization of sales revenue (and many companies do establish sales revenue targets as goals), then management would side with the sales department. Management could also decide the issue on a compromise basis, however, agreeing to accept a limited number of tours. This would increase sales revenue and net income, but not necessarily maximize them. It would keep regular customers—and the two departments involved—happy. Management and the stockholders (who in many cases will be one and the same) will still be satisfied with the net income. In fact, this method of operating a business is frequently known as *satisficing*.

Even though companies may not have clear-cut financial goals to rely on for decision making, this should not preclude them from operating toward the other two objectives of financial management: deciding on the sources of funds required by the company and allocating those funds effectively to the various assets of the company to provide a satisfactory net income.

SOCIAL GOALS

Even though the goals discussed so far have been of a financial nature, **social goals** cannot be ignored. Social responsibility embraces such things as protecting the consumer who buys the hotel's or restaurant's goods or services, maintaining equitable hiring practices, and paying fair wages, supporting further education and training of employees, and being concerned about environmental factors.

A resort hotel that owns beachfront property would act in a socially mature way by giving access to the beach to persons other than registered hotel guests. A take-out fast-food restaurant that uses disposable paper or plastic supplies would be socially responsible if it were to hire someone to ensure that the neighboring streets were kept free of litter discarded by customers. Obviously, since they have a cost, many social goals conflict with financial goals. However, some social goals, even with a cost attached, may improve financial results. For example, in the restaurant situation just cited, the restaurant might find that its business improves considerably as a result of its litter-cleaning decision. More customers might patronize the restaurant because they appreciate its socially responsible action or because they want to visit a restaurant that is in a clean neighborhood. To the extent that the increased net income exceeds the cost of clearing litter, a benefit will accrue.

DEVELOP AN ACTION PLAN

After an organization has developed a suitable mission statement and established financial objectives to conform to that, it must prepare an action plan. An organization's overall mission statement and objectives define what the organization wants to achieve. The action plan shows how it is going to get there. Normally, this plan covers all functional areas of an organization, such as managerial, financial, operational, and marketing. It includes matters such as the way the premises are furnished, the theme it wishes to establish, and the types of customers it wishes to attract. At the same time, it requires an understanding of the limitations that any business has. These limitations include the physical size and condition of the property, competition, funding available, economic environment, and many similar factors.

STRATEGIES

An action plan first requires the establishment of strategies to achieve objectives. Objectives and strategies should not be confused. Objectives are simply generally fixed statements that, by themselves, cause no changes. *Strategies* are stated plans of action that will cause changes in order to meet objectives. Strategies can also be flexible, whereas objectives are often not, at least in the short run. For example, a restaurant might have as an objective to increase sales revenue by a certain percentage over the next 12 months. Strategies to achieve this might include increasing menu prices, increasing seat turnover, selling more wine with meals, or using any combination of these and other approaches. If the chosen strategy or strategies do not work, then they can be replaced or combined in some other way.

It is also important to ensure that a strategy is not implemented while ignoring other strategic alternatives. For example, it is possible for a strategy to be based on an inappropriate or biased management style that has too narrow a focus. Note also that strategies have a life cycle, just as products and mission statements have. And even where a mission statement may still be appropriate for a particular organization, strategies that were appropriate to that mission statement in early years may no longer be practical for achieving that mission.

TACTICS

Tactics to supplement strategies may need to be developed. Strategies are often long-term (a year or more) in nature, whereas tactics (of which there may be several for each strategy) are short-run because they often have to be adjusted to circumstances that are constantly changing. This does not imply that strategies do not also need to be changed in the short run. Extraordinary, unanticipated events that require both altered strategies and altered tactics may occur.

INFORMATION SYSTEMS

To achieve the objectives established for a company, it is necessary for managers to make decisions constantly. To make rational decisions, they must have information and a system that provides this information.

For example, consider a hotel that is contemplating offering its room guests a "free" continental breakfast as a new marketing tactic. This seems like a relatively simple matter. What information is needed? First, the decision maker must have information about the type of guest that is the hotel's market. Is it the vacationer or the businessperson? Predominantly male or female? If the hotel is an international one, is the nationality of the guest important? Is age relevant? What about average length of stay? Obviously, guest registration cards must be designed to provide these data, and someone must be delegated to sort through these cards to summarize the data into meaningful information.

However, the manager needs further data from suppliers concerning the type of bakery products available, types of packages and their sizes, and information about costs as well as availability of any quantity purchase discounts. Finally, the manager must have information about the added costs of storage and distribution of the food without a kitchen.

For many day-to-day decisions, much of the necessary information already exists in most hospitality enterprises. Some of it is required by the law (e.g., the requirement to keep accounting records for income tax filing purposes). Other information exists as a byproduct of carrying out normal business transactions (such as purchasing records and sales invoices). Further information exists as a result of transactions between departments (e.g., requisitions given to the storeroom for needed supplies). But quite a lot of information is available that is not formalized (such as the chef's knowledge about the best way to tackle each day's production of food requirements).

FOUR LEVELS OF DECISION MAKING

Four levels can be identified in the decision-making process, and these can be viewed as a pyramid. These four are data production, data sorting, information production, and decision making.

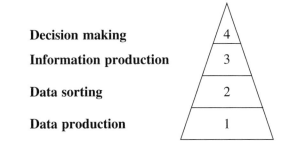

Decision making — 4

Information production — 3

Data sorting — 2

Data production — 1

Level 1: Data Production

The base of the pyramid is the production of data. These data are often a byproduct of a regular business activity (e.g., cash register tapes, guest checks, guest registration cards). It is important to establish what is to be stored and for how long, and what is to be discarded immediately. For example, are dining room guest checks to be kept for a week, a month, a year, or for five years? Although some of these decisions are management's responsibility, the government will have requirements on how long some of these documents must be kept.

Level 2: Data Sorting

The second level of the pyramid is the management of the data where they are sorted, converted, combined, or manipulated into more useful sets of data. In other words, the data need to be classified so specific items can be recalled or retrieved without processing the entire batch. For example, while registration cards can be stored by day and then by month, you may need a system that segregates registration cards for all VIPs so that they can be accessed without having to go through all registration cards for an entire month.

Level 3: Information Production

These converted sets of data in turn provide the information for the third level in the pyramid, the information level. Data are converted into information when they acquire meaning. For example, Exhibit 7.7 in Chapter 7 is a columnar table of two sets of data, one column showing rooms sold month by month and the second showing wage cost month by month. In Exhibit 7.9, these data have been plotted on a graph and have taken on meaning, since the graph indicates information concerning the fixed wage cost.

Normally, the collection and conversion of data to provide information is a routine process that can often be done by mechanical or computerized means. It is not the manager's job to do this. The manager's task is the interpretation of the information and the actual decision making. Nevertheless, it is the manager's task to be involved in establishing the information-gathering system so it will provide the information that he or she needs to make the kinds of decisions necessary so the company can meet its goals.

As organizations grow, the information system becomes more structured. For example, in a small restaurant, the one and only cook may have the recipes stored in his or her head, but in a large restaurant, recipes need to be formalized so that all cooks follow the same food preparation formulas and procedures. In other words, which system is most desirable really depends on the specific organization of the business and its needs. As the organization changes over time, so will the information system. What is good today might not be of value in five years.

Computerized information systems more readily allow the linking of data from different areas of an operation. For example, a room service department manager could constantly access forecasts of guest room occupancies in order to staff the department more adequately from day to day.

Some sets of data can be compared to provide information (e.g., relating last year's sales revenue to this year's, or this year's sales revenue to a budget). At the very elementary level, such comparisons are not too helpful, since they do not allow for conditions that have changed between last year and this year, or this year and its budget. Also, if, for example, August last year had five Sundays and this year only four, comparisons can be distorted. Comparisons made based on indices or percentages are an improvement over nominal dollars, as is a comparison based on a standard, such as the standard food cost system described in Chapter 5 (Exhibits 5.15 and 5.16).

Further improvement in information occurs when variances between actual and standard are broken down into differences in quantity, sales volume, and cost or price variances (see Chapter 9 for a discussion of variance analysis). This breakdown indicates how much of the variance is the fault of poor planning (sales volume variances) and how much is a failure to achieve standards (for example, quantity and cost or price variances in a food cost control system). At this point, the information system has reached the stage of providing a guide to solving problems and making decisions.

What prevents many managers from producing more sophisticated information, and in particular from implementing a computerized system, is that costs of implementing a system are often considered, but value is put on the benefits.

In fact, some managers consider that there is, and should be, no cost for information gathering; in other words, there is no cost to compiling a daily food cost or for producing a manager's daily report. These are simply byproducts of the accounting and/or control system, and to spend money to provide more and better information makes no sense. For many managers the concept that information is not free creates a dilemma that is difficult to resolve.

An information system should be judged by how well it facilitates the achieving of a given goal or set of goals. The main criterion for judging one system against another is costs versus benefits. Systems cost money and benefit an organization by helping decision making. If two systems cost the same, the one that provides the most useful information about operating decision making is preferable. For example, when choosing between two computerized accounting systems that cost approximately the same, this might be the deciding factor.

Level 4: Decision Making

The information that is provided by the system is used to identify and help solve problems that are resolved at the top of the pyramid, or the fourth level (which is the decision-making level). The types of decisions that have to be made dictate the information that needs to be collected; the information indicates the data that are needed, and this, in turn, regulates the data collection system.

Any manager is constantly faced with decisions. These can be routine and simple, often requiring no action, or more complex and important. Most decisions require the use of information and frequently the use of judgment.

In problem solving, four decision-making steps can be identified:

1. *Define the problem.* Without doing this, information cannot be properly analyzed and alternatives cannot be identified. If the problem is not defined, or is incorrectly defined, time and effort will be wasted.
2. *List alternative solutions.* Creativity is a requirement for this, but that creativity should not be limited to the decision maker's bias or prior experience.
3. *Gather all necessary information about the problem and its alternative solutions.* The information gathered must be relevant, since that increases knowledge, reduces uncertainty, and minimizes the risk of making the wrong decision. It must also be presented in a format that is understood and must be received in good time to affect any decisions made. Note, also, that decision making is often a matter of judgment based on the best information available.

   Obviously, the more accurate the information available, the more value it has for planning, control, and decision making. Speed of information and the risk of incomplete information are also factors to be considered. On the one hand, it is sometimes better to have a rough idea of the daily food cost without taking inventory than to have a more accurate food cost 24 hours after taking inventory. On the other hand, in a feasibility study for expanding the business, risk is so high that the extra time involved in preparing an informative study is well spent. In any decision-making situation, the manager, given the constraints of time and availability of data, must have enough information to consider alternative decisions or solutions. Obviously, however, the more time that is spent on collecting information and data, the greater the cost.

For many decisions, accounting records, forms, and reports are a major source of information. This type of information is verifiable, objective, and quantitative and can provide specific data about an activity, event, or problem. The three most important aspects of accounting information are that it is relevant and appropriate for the problem at hand, that it is current, and that it is accurate within the measurement standards imposed by the needs of the problem.

4. *Make the decision.* Even though the foregoing three steps may be followed, decision making may still be difficult, since important variables of the problem may affect one another.

In some situations, the information can provide its own solution. For example, perpetual inventory cards as an aid to inventory control were described in Chapter 2. These perpetual inventory cards can show, for each storeroom item, the minimum and maximum inventory levels. If the minimum stock level for a specific product is 5, and inventory has dropped to that point, and maximum is 15, then 10 more of that item need to be ordered. However, in such a situation, no attempt is made to relate the purchase to current conditions. What if the consumption for that product is no longer as high as it used to be? Perhaps the maximum inventory of 15 should be reduced to 10 and the reorder point to 2 until conditions change again.

To make such decisions from manual information might be difficult, but computerized inventory systems can be programmed to provide information concerning such matters as rate of consumption of inventory products, as well as quantity discounts and inventory holding costs. In a really intelligent computerized system, the idea of fixed reorder points for any items might be completely abandoned, and the computer will consider all the relevant factors item by item and only print a list of items to be ordered and in what quantities.

One type of decision making is known as management by exception. With management by exception, small deviations from normal, which do not require any management action, are not drawn to its attention. For example, the standard food cost is established at 40%. As long as the food cost variance is only 1% point above or below 40% (i.e., from 39% to 41%), it is considered acceptable. Only if food cost is below 39% or above 41% is the change drawn to management's attention.

The question of establishing an item's exception level has to be established on a situation-by-situation basis and company by company. There are no rules, or even guidelines, because of the many variables that differ from business to business.

Although management by exception has the advantage of relieving higher-level management of spending a lot of time on information when there is no problem, it can also prevent management from noticing worsening trends (e.g., a cost item that is slowly increasing) until that item of information has reached or exceeded its exception level. In other words, if the manager had been made aware of the worsening trend, some corrective action could have been taken before the exception level was reached.

A further refinement in decision making is to examine the assumptions that were made when earlier plans were formulated and then compare not only actual and planned results, but also actual with possible results. Those possible results are opportunity costs. Earlier in this chapter the possibility of a hotel increasing its sales by accommodating bus tour groups was discussed. If bus tour groups are not accommodated, or only a limited number of them are accepted, the sales revenue from those not accommodated is an opportunity cost, and this opportunity cost (lost sales revenue) could be built into the information system for management comparison with actual results. One difficulty with building opportunity costs into the information/decision-making system is that some bus tour groups who were turned down may have eventually canceled their reservations anyway, even if they had been accepted. But, if effective decisions are to be made, a well-designed information system must be able to respond to some incompleteness of information and possibly suggest where additional data might be collected to make the information more complete. Obviously, at this level of sophistication, information manipulation would be exceedingly complex without the aid of a computerized system.

The way in which an information system is designed and integrated into a hospitality enterprise is a challenge for any manager. The more appropriately it is designed to support decision making, the more effectively will the enterprise be able to compete in the marketplace and achieve its already established financial objectives.

MIS SYSTEM EFFECTIVENESS

A management information system (MIS) must have stated objectives so that its effectiveness can be measured by how it meets those objectives. Management should also be concerned with whether the system is doing everything it could to be effective. There are three ways of determining this.

One way is to review the reports provided by the system to see if employees using them have made notations or calculations on them. If any of the information had to be recalculated or redrafted in some way to make it meaningful to the user, or if information has had to be added from some other source, this could indicate that the system is not doing everything it could.

A second method is to use test observations to see whether the information system is used for decision making. If information is required for a decision before the formal MIS can provide it or if the formal MIS has to be supported by information from informal sources, then perhaps the MIS is not doing the job it was designed to do. For example, suppose a hotel has a computerized guest room system that is intended to provide housekeeping and front-office personnel with information about the status of each guest room at any time. If the computer system is so slow that housekeeping and front-office employees pass this information back and forth by telephone, then the formal computer information system is not performing effectively.

The third method is to have those who review the system's reports list or state which items on a report are relevant and which ones are irrelevant. If there is consensus that there is a great deal of irrelevant information that is of no use in decision making, then the system is not doing its job. A dramatic test is to temporarily stop producing a report for a while. If there is no protest from those who are supposed to use the report, its permanent discontinuance will simplify but not reduce the effectiveness of the information system. However, removal of a report can have unexpected repercussions. For example, department heads might be receiving the same report as the general manager, even though they make little direct use of it. If the report is discontinued, department heads might think they have lost status because they are no longer deemed important enough to receive it.

SYSTEM EFFECTIVENESS VERSUS EFFICIENCY

Management must also be aware of the difference between MIS effectiveness and efficiency. The two terms are not synonymous. With reference to gross profit analysis (see Chapter 6) of menu items, a computerized information system might show that a different set of menu offerings will improve gross profit per guest. However, after the new menu is implemented, total gross profit declines because customers do not like the new menu. The information system was efficient but not effective because it did not consider potential customers' menu preferences.

S U M M A R Y

Before developing financial goals, some large hospitality operations prepare a mission statement. Regardless of the type and size of enterprise in the hospitality industry, financial management will be an ongoing part of the business. Generally, financial management has three objectives:

1. To establish certain goals, such as how large the company will be, how rapidly it will expand, and how it will measure its success in meeting these goals.

2. To decide on the sources of needed capital and to obtain the funds required by the firm to meet its goals.

3. To allocate these funds effectively to the various assets of the company, again with the company's goals in mind.

Profit maximization is one type of goal. This means making the most money in the shortest possible time. Profit maximization emphasizes the short run over the long run and ignores any risks involved.

Maximization of return on investment is a goal that eliminates any investment that does not yield at least a minimum return on investment. The disadvantages of this goal are similar to those for the profit maximization goal.

The goal most commonly used by business is that of maximization of stockholder wealth. Under this goal, management plans to ensure that wise investments are made, that they are sensibly financed, and that an appropriate dividend policy is established.

Secondary goals are also often established. These could be for individual operations within a chain and/or for individual departments within an operation. With secondary goals, management by objectives (MBO) is a useful managerial technique. With MBO, managers are involved in establishing their own goals and standards against which their performance is subsequently measured. Goal congruence is an alignment of organizational goals with the personal and group goals of subordinates and superiors. With any form of goal setting, social goals must not be ignored.

An organization's overall mission statement and objectives define what the organization wants to achieve. The action plan, through strategies and tactics, shows how it is going to get there.

To achieve its financial goals, an organization must have a reliable information system that allows the best decisions to be made. Four levels can be identified in an information system: data production, data sorting, information production, and decision making. The larger the organization, the more structured is this information system.

A well-defined information system is also invaluable in problem solving. Four steps can be identified in problem solving: Defining the problem, listing alternative solutions, gathering all necessary relevant information, and making decisions.

Information is a resource that costs money. When comparing different information systems, a cost/benefit analysis is required. An information system should be judged by how well it facilitates achieving a given goal or set of goals.

The way an information system is designed and integrated into a hospitality enterprise is a challenge for any manager. The more appropriately it is designed to support decision making, the more effectively will the enterprise be able to compete and achieve its already established financial objectives.

Finally, management also needs to be sure (and determine from time to time) that its information system is effective and must be aware that there is a difference between efficiency and effectiveness.

DISCUSSION QUESTIONS

1. Explain your understanding of a mission statement and state four purposes that it can serve.

2. Briefly describe your understanding of the meaning of financial management.

3. Explain how you think a small restaurant operation can practice good financial management.

4. What is your understanding of the term *satisficing*?

5. In what way might a policy to pay no dividends affect a hotel corporation's market price of shares? If the policy were to pay out all net income in dividends, how might this affect the company's future net income? How might this affect the future share price?

6. Explain why wealth maximization, as indicated by market price of shares, may not be achieved by profit maximization.

7. Would the objective of no net income for a certain period (e.g., three years) be consistent with the goal of wealth maximization? Explain.

8. What is a secondary goal? Give an example that might be appropriate for the housekeeping department of a hotel.

9. Define *MBO* and explain how it is used in an organization. What is goal congruence, and how does it fit in with MBO?

10. Explain why a resort hotel that is the only one in the area would or would not be likely to practice social responsibility. Do you think such a resort hotel might act differently if it were only one of a number of competitive hotels in that area? Explain.

11. Discuss the need for an action plan to achieve goals and differentiate between strategies and tactics.

12. What are the four steps in the decision-making process?

13. Discuss how you think an information system should be judged for quality.

14. What are the main criteria for information so it is useful in the decision-making process?

15. Define management by exception and give an example of a circumstance where it might be used.

16. Briefly discuss two ways in which the effectiveness of a management information system can be determined.

PROBLEMS

P14.1 Some hospitality enterprise entrepreneurs, even with limited education, have successfully operated their businesses for many years. They have probably never heard of management by objectives (MBO). Their only goal is to work hard and make an adequate profit. In your opinion, and given examples from your own experience and/or observations where this might be helpful, explain why they are successful. If they are successful, why should they bother using managerial techniques such as MBO?

P14.2 The following paragraph appeared in a chain motel's monthly in-house newsletter announcing the creation of a trophy that will be awarded to the motel with the most outstanding performance each year:

> The trophy will be given to the motel with the best combination of sales revenue percentage increase and net income percentage increase. The actual calculation will be to take the sales revenue percentage increase, add the net income percentage increase, and divide that total by 2, with equal weight given to both sales revenue and net income growth. Only motels achieving a minimum 15% sales revenue increase will be eligible.

What is your evaluation of the way performance is to be measured in this motel chain? Use two or three examples to demonstrate your opinion.

P14.3 Following are performance objectives for three different organizations:

  a. A restaurant's manager: "To establish a position in the market by providing top-quality menu items created from the freshest locally grown produce."

  b. Year-round recreational resort hotel's marketing manager: "To establish an image for the resort as an exclusive one providing a luxurious atmosphere and environment."

  c. A hotel's nightclub manager: "To considerably increase visits to the nightclub by residents of the area living within driving distance."

  Evaluate each of these objectives. Comment about how each of them does, or does not, satisfy the criteria for a good objective. Rewrite each objective in your own words in such a way that it meets the criteria for a well-stated objective.

P14.4 You are the manager of the maintenance department of a hotel. You are paid a basic salary, plus a bonus. The bonus consists of another $1,000 each time your expenses are under budget, plus 2% of the amount you are able to save. For the past six budget periods, the following are the results. Note that U stands for unfavorable, or over budget, and F for favorable, or under budget.

Period	Budget	Actual	Variance
1	$80,000	$82,000	$2,000 *U*
2	80,000	79,000	1,000 *F*
3	78,000	74,000	4,000 *F*
4	72,000	74,000	2,000 *U*
5	72,000	73,000	1,000 *U*
6	72,500	72,000	500 *F*

a. Using this information, as a rational person what would you do if you were the department manager running the maintenance department over again from period one? Use a numerical example to prove your point.

b. If you were the hotel's general manager, what would you recommend be done, if anything, to this hotel's maintenance department's bonus system?

P14.5 A small resort hotel that caters primarily to the family trade set as an objective an increase of 5% in its rooms occupancy over the next 12 months. Its strategy for achieving this was to convert some unused ground-floor storage space into a conference room that could seat about 30 people. It then marketed the resort property to businesses and organizations that agreed to hold two- or three-day meetings and use the guest rooms overnight. During the first conference that the hotel booked, the conference organizer complained severely about noise from children using the outdoor swimming pool and recreation facilities immediately outside the window area of the conference room. Furthermore, the conference room delegates found there was no provision to have an evening meal served to them in the meeting room so that they could continue their discussions in private. Conference delegates were obliged to use the resort's regular dining room, where other residents were also seated. When subsequent conference groups arrived, they made the same complaints, and the resort found that negative word-of-mouth publicity had created difficulties for them in booking further conference groups. As a result, they did not achieve the desired increase in occupancy. Discuss the resort's problem with specific reference to the strategy it used to achieve its objective.

P14.6 The concierge's department of a large hotel normally has a head concierge and nine concierges on duty during the day shift for the peak tourist months. During the past peak month, there have been far more than the normal number of guest complaints about the slow service received, creating a problem for the rooms department manager.

The following are descriptions of several situations or events pertaining to the concierge service department. For each separate item, state in which of the four areas of the problem-solving process the item belongs. The four areas are defining the problem, identifying alternatives, gathering information, and making the decision.

a. Several guests have complained to the front office manager that they are experiencing a longer than usual wait for service or that they are receiving poor service.

b. The bell service department has priorities for jobs. The check-out baggage of guests is handled first. Second is guest check-in baggage. Third is delivery of other items to guest rooms. Fourth is the sale of airport limousine, bus tour, and theater tickets. Fifth is other requests for service.

c. One guest complained that the theater tickets were for the wrong night.

d. One guest suggested replacing the head concierge with a better organizer.

e. One guest complained that a request to have flowers purchased and delivered to another guest's room was never carried out.

f. The paging system that allows the head concierge to signal to concierges when they are away from the service area has malfunctioned three times in the last month and has taken as long as 24 hours to repair.

g. One of the desk clerks suggests that the sale of theater and bus tour tickets be handled by a new person who will operate strictly on a commission basis.

h. The rooms department manager will consider having a commission arrangement for next summer, since it is too late to do anything about it this year.

i. The head concierge suggests hiring one more concierge.

j. One concierge has been away sick for the past two weeks.

k. A sick concierge was replaced by a temporary employee who was not familiar with the hotel and its operating procedures. The replacement's work was marginal.

l. Guests who complain are advised of the concierge desk's order of priorities.

m. During the past month, the hotel's occupancy has been 10% above normal for that month, creating extra demands by guests for service.

n. The rooms department manager has approved the hiring of one extra temporary concierge for as long as occupancy stays above normal.

o. A new paging system will be purchased with a maintenance contract guaranteeing instant service.

P14.7 In late January 0008, George Ray, president of Restoration Resort Ltd., is concerned about how he could finance the more than $200,000 he estimates he needs to convert, improve, and expand the company's resort facilities. The resort has very little cash, and George and his wife have about $20,000 in savings. The land on which the resort is located has been in the Ray family for 40 years. The 12-unit motel was constructed 25 years ago. The motel is open year-round. Occupancy of rooms in the peak summer months (mid-June to mid-September) is 100%, but a lower occupancy during the shoulder and winter months reduces overall annual occupancy to 60%. In the winter months, the rooms are rented on a monthly basis.

About 20 years ago, a swimming pool was added along with a change house, snack bar/souvenir shop, and a 20-space trailer park. The trailer park is only open during the summer months (approximately 150 days), and, during that period, spaces are 90% occupied.

Although losses occurred in earlier years, the resort is now reasonably profitable. However, the resort has not until now been considered the main business of the Ray family, since both George (who inherited the resort from his parents 10 years ago) and his wife work at other jobs and look at the resort as a part-time business. It has become increasingly apparent to them that, because of the economic times, they will have to make changes to the resort and work at it full time if it is to remain successful.

After considerable thought and discussion, the Rays decided that the following changes would have to be made to bring the resort up to a standard acceptable to today's traveling public:

a. Add eight fully furnished 400-square-foot cabins with a potential of 32 additional overnight guests.

b. Fill in the pool, which has become badly corroded from minerals in the water. This pool has been fully depreciated.

c. Construct a new 3,300-square-foot swimming pool.

d. Renovate and modernize the combined frame change house and snack bar.

e. Add an extension to the change house that includes shower rooms for trailer park guests and houses the resort's office.

f. Expand the trailer park area from 20 to 50 stalls and provide electrical and sewer hookup to all stalls.

In addition to the Restoration Resort land, George personally owns land that includes a hill at the back of the property, which has potential for skiing. This piece of land is estimated to be worth about $50,000 at today's prices. However, George thinks that the investment required to develop it for skiing would not make the project currently feasible, even though it might considerably improve the winter rooms occupancy.

The investment costs for the proposed changes to the property are estimated as follows:

Construction/renovation of buildings	$128,000
Swimming pool	27,000
Furniture, equipment and fixtures	16,000
Trailer park site improvements	21,000
Contingency	10,000
Total	$202,000

A balance sheet for the year ending December 31, 0007, follows, as do income statements for the Years 0006 and 0007.

Restoration Resort Balance Sheet as of December 31, 0007

Assets

Current Assets

Cash	$ 8,700	
Inventory	3,000	$ 11,700
Property Plant & Equipment		
Land	$ 70,200	
Buildings	83,800	
Furniture & equipment	14,600	
Swimming pool	15,400	
Stationwagon	5,600	
	$189,600	
Accumulated depreciation	(64,200)	125,400
Total Net Assets		$137,100

Liabilities and Stockholders' Equity

Current Liabilities

Bank loan	$ 4,300	
Accounts payable	2,100	
Current mortgage	12,800	$ 19,200
Long-term Liabilities		
Mortgage	$ 24,600	
Loan from shareholder	8,700	$ 33,300
Stockholders' Equity		
Capital—shares issued	$ 40,000	
Retained earnings	44,600	84,600
Total Liabilities & Stockholders' Equity		$137,000

Restoration Resort income statements:

	Year Ending Dec. 31, 0006		Year Ending Dec. 31, 0007	
Sales Revenue				
Rooms and trailer rentals	$65,100		$74,400	
Snack bar/souvenir shop	23,900	$89,000	26,700	$101,100
Operating Expenses				
Salaries & wages	$36,700		$40,100	
Maintenance & repairs	14,100		16,200	
Supplies and other expenses	9,000		9,900	
Interest	3,200		2,800	
Depreciation	6,900	(69,900)	6,300	(75,300)
Operating Income (before tax)		$19,100		$ 25,800
Income tax		(4,800)		(6,400)
Net Income		$14,300		$ 19,400

Restoration Resort retained earnings statement:

	Year Ending Dec. 31, 0006	Year Ending Dec. 31, 0007
Retained earnings, beginning of year	$10,900	$25,200
Add: net income for year	14,300	19,400
Retained earnings, end of year	$25,200	$44,600

Sales revenue for the Year 0008 is estimated to be about 5% above Year 0007, primarily as a result of a price increase, rather than an occupancy increase. Operating expenses are estimated in total to be about 5% higher than in 0007.

a. Given the balance sheet and income statements, calculate whatever financial ratios (see Chapter 4) you think are appropriate that will indicate the financial health of the Restoration Resort.

b. List the information that you would like to have that is not shown on the financial statements, but would make it easier to carry out some financial projections as a preliminary step before going ahead with a complete feasibility study (see Chapter 13) for expansion.

With the possibility of branching out into a second restaurant, Charlie is concerned that he does not have any formal financial objectives, although he does understand that most successful companies do need to have financial, as well as other, objectives. Write a report to Charlie summarizing possible financial objectives that he might wish to consider. Include an explanation of MBO and how it differs from conventional management (where the employee is judged by personal traits such as initiative and integrity) typically used by small businesses. What specific recommendations do you have for Charlie? Support these recommendations with reasons.

GLOSSARY

The technical words and terms used in this text are briefly explained in this glossary. For more expanded definitions and discussions, the reader should refer to the text itself.

Accelerated depreciation: a method of depreciation that gives greater amounts of depreciation expenses in the earlier years of an asset's life. See also *Depreciation.*

Account: a record in which the current status (or balance) of each type of asset, liability, owners' equity, sales revenue, and expense is kept.

Accounting cycle: a recurring series of steps that occurs during each accounting period.

Accounting equation: assets = liabilities + owners' equity. Sometimes referred to as the *balance sheet equation.*

Accounting period: the time period covered by the financial statements.

Accounting rate of return (ARR): See *average rate of return method.*

Accounts payable: amounts due to suppliers (creditors); a debt or a liability.

Accounts receivable: amounts due from customers or guests (debtors); an asset.

Accounts receivable aging: preparing a schedule classifying receivables in terms of time left unpaid.

Accounts receivable average collection period: the number of days the average receivable remains unpaid.

Accounts receivable turnover: annual sales revenue divided by average accounts receivable.

Accrual basis: as opposed to cash accounting, a method of accounting whereby transactions are recorded as they occur and not when cash is exchanged; the matching of sales revenue and expenses on periodic income statements regardless of when cash is received or disbursed.

Accrued expenses: expenses that have been incurred but not paid at balance sheet date; a liability.

Accumulated depreciation: the total depreciation that has been shown as an expense on the income statements since the related assets were purchased. See also *Depreciation.*

Acid test ratio: see *Quick ratio.*

Activity ratios: see *Turnover ratios.*

Adjusted trial balance: a trial balance of accounts after period-end adjustments have been made. See also *Trial balance.*

Adjustments: entries made at the end of each accounting period in journals and then in the accounts so that the accounts have correct balances under the accrual accounting method.

Advance cash deposits: advance money received for room reservations or banquet bookings, which should be shown on financial statements as liabilities because the money is due to the guests until it has been earned.

Allowance for uncollectable accounts: an amount established to cover the likelihood that not all accounts receivable outstanding at balance sheet date will be collected.

Amortization: a method of writing down the cost of certain intangible assets (such as franchises or goodwill) in the same way that depreciation is used to write down the cost of tangible fixed, or long-term assets.

Asset: a property or resource owned by a business.

Asset shrinkage: the decline in value of assets during bankruptcy.

Audit: a verification of accounting procedures and records. See *external audit; internal audit.*

Audit tape: a continuous chronological record of each transaction recorded in a cash or sales register. The tape can usually only be removed at the end of each day by authorized accounting office personnel.

Audit trail: an internal control method that allows each business transaction to be traced back from its initial source document through each step of the recording process.

Average check: sales revenue divided by number of people served during a certain period of time. Sometimes called average cover or average spending.

Average cover: see *Average checks.*

Average rate of return (ARR) method: a method of measuring the value of a long-term investment. The equation is net annual saving divided by average investment.

Average room rate: room revenue divided by number of rooms used during a certain period of time.

Average spending: see *Average checks.*

Bad debt: an account receivable considered or known to be uncollectible.

Bad debts allowance: see *Allowance for uncollectible accounts.*

Balance: the amount of an account at a point in time.

Balance sheet: a statement showing that assets = liabilities + owners' equity. A balance sheet shows the financial position of a company at a point in time.

Bank float: the difference between the bank balance shown on a company's records and the actual balance of cash in the bank.

Bank reconciliation: a monthly or periodic procedure to ensure that the company's bank account balance amount agrees with the bank's statement figure.

Beverage cost: see *Cost of sales.*

Bond: a form of financing by a company. A bond is a debt or long-term liability to be repaid with interest over time.

Book value: initial cost of an asset or assets less related accumulated depreciation.

Breakeven equation or formula: an equation useful in making business decisions concerning sales levels and fixed and variable costs.

Breakeven: the level of sales at which a company will make neither an income nor a loss.

Bridge financing: see *Interim financing.*

Budget: a business plan, usually expressed in monetary terms. See also *Incremental budgeting* and *Zero-base budgeting.*

Budget cycle: the sequence of events covered by a budget period from initial budget preparation through comparison of actual results with budgeted estimates.

Budget period: the specific amount of time over which a budget is determined.

Business cycle: a sales revenue cycle that exists during recessionary inflationary cycles, in which hospitality operations experience a major decline in sales revenue.

Business entity: the concept that a business, and business transactions, should be kept separate from personal transactions of the business's owners.

Capital asset: see *Fixed asset.*

Capital budget: a budget concerning long-term, or fixed, assets.

Capital rationing: occurs when only a limited amount of funds is available for long-term investments during a budget period, and even profitable investment proposals are deferred to future budget periods.

Capital stock: the amount of money raised by a company from issuing shares.

Capital surplus: the amount of money raised by a company in excess of any par or stated value of the shares.

Cash basis: a method of accounting (as opposed to accrual accounting) whereby transactions are only recorded at the time cash is received or disbursed.

Cash budget: a budget concerned with cash inflows and cash outflows.

Cash disbursements: money paid by cash or by check for the purchase of goods or services.

Cash flow from operating activities margin ratio: cash flow from operating activities divided by sales revenue.

Cash flow from operating activities to current liabilities ratio: cash flow from operating activities divided by average current liabilities.

Cash flow from operating activities to interest ratio: cash flow from operating activities plus interest divided by interest.

Cash flow from operating activities to total liabilities ratio: cash flow from operating activities divided by average total liabilities.

Cash management: cash conservation and the management of other working capital accounts to maximize effectiveness of the company's use of cash.

Cash receipts: cash or checks received in payment for sale of merchandise or services.

Chattel mortgage: a long-term debt or mortgage secured by the chattels (e.g., equipment and furniture) of the business. See also *Mortgage.*

City ledger: in a hotel, the accounts receivable for guests who have charge privileges in food and beverage areas, and the accounts of room occupants who have left and have charged their accounts.

Closing entries: the last entries posted from the closing journal entry to the ledger.

Collateral: assets pledged by a company as security for a loan.

Collusion: two or more people working together for fraudulent purposes.

Common-size vertical statement: one financial statement presented with all data in both dollar and percentage figures.

Common stock: a form of stock or shares issued by a company to raise money.

Comparative horizontal analysis: comparing financial statements for two or more periods presented so that the change in each account balance from one period to the next is shown in both dollar and percentage terms.

Concentration banking: a method of accelerating the flow of funds from individual units in a chain operation to the company's head office bank account.

Conservatism: a principle of accounting to help ensure sales revenue and assets are not overstated or expenses and liabilities understated.

Consistency principle: a principle of accounting to help ensure that financial statements are comparable from one period to the next.

Consumer price index (CPI): one of the most commonly used and widely understood indexes available; trend index numbers are calculated for each year by dividing the average check for each year by the average check for Year 1 and multiplying by 100.

Contra asset account: accounts with a balance that is shown on the "wrong" side of the balance sheet as a reduction of a related account, for example, allowance for bad debts shown as a reduction of accounts receivable.

Contribution margin: the difference between sales revenue and cost of sales.

Contribution margin income statement: a form of income statement presentation whereby variable costs are deducted from sales revenue to show contribution margin, and then fixed costs are deducted from contribution margin to arrive at net income.

Contributory income: see *Departmental income.*

Controllable cost or expense: a cost that is controllable by an individual (such as a department head) in a company.

Corporation: An incorporated business regarded as an artificial person. It has three defining characteristics: limited liability, easy transfer of ownership through stock sale, and continuity of existence.

Cost: the price paid to purchase an asset or to pay for the purchase of goods or services. Also frequently used as a synonym for *expense.*

Cost center: a department (such as maintenance) in a hospitality operation that generates no sales revenue.

Cost management: an awareness of the various types of cost and the effect that the relevant ones have on individual business decisions.

Cost of sales: generally referred to simply as food cost or beverage cost. Calculated by adding beginning of the accounting period inventory to purchases during the period, and deducting end of the period inventory, adjusting where necessary for items such as employee meals and/or interdepartmental transfers.

Cost principle: Accounting for assets at their *original* cost to the current owner.

Cost variance: the difference between budgeted cost and actual cost.

Cost–volume–profit analysis: an analysis of fixed and variable costs in relation to sales as an aid in decision making. Abbreviated as CVP analysis. See also *Breakeven equation.*

Credit: 1. an entry on the right-hand side of an account; 2. to extend credit or to allow a person to consume goods or services and pay at a later date.

Credit card receivables: Amounts due from credit card companies based on credit card sales.

Credit card receivables turnover ratio: the average number of times during an annual operating period that the repetitive cycle of earning credit card sales revenue and their reimbursement occurred.

Credit invoice: an invoice prepared by a supplier showing, for example, that goods delivered to a company have been returned as unacceptable.

Credit memorandum: a dummy credit invoice made out by a company prior to receipt of a credit invoice from the supplier.

Creditor: a person, or company, to whom a firm owes money.

Current assets: cash or other assets likely to be turned into cash within a year.

Current dollars: historic (previous periods') dollars converted to terms of today's dollars for purposes of comparison.

Current liabilities: debts that are due to be paid within one year.

Current liquidity ratios: ratios that indicate a company's ability to meet its short-term debts.

Current ratio: the ratio of current assets to current liabilities.

Day rate: the rate charged by a hotel or motel for the use of a room for a portion of the day and not overnight.

Daily operating cycle: sales revenue cycle in which restaurant operations depend on meal periods for sales revenue

Debenture: a form of financing by a company. A debenture is a debt or long-term liability to be repaid with interest over time.

Debit: an entry in the left-hand side of an account.

Debt: money owed to a person or organization; an obligation.

Debt to equity ratio: the amount of debt (liabilities) expressed as a ratio of stockholders' equity.

Declining balance depreciation: a method of accelerated depreciation whereby higher amounts of depreciation expense are recorded in the earlier years of an asset's life.

Deferred expense: an expense that has been incurred that is going to be written off over a period of time greater than one year.

Deficit: a deficit situation exists when losses accumulated since a business began exceed accumulated net incomes.

Demand, elasticity of: see *Elasticity of demand.*

Department budget: an operating budget prepared for an individual department in a multidepartment organization.

Departmental contributory income: the income of an individual operating department after direct expenses have been deducted from sales revenue; sometimes referred to as contributory income.

Dependent variable: an item that is affected by what happens to another item. For example, labor cost is affected by level of sales; labor is the dependent variable.

Depreciation: a method of allocating the cost of a fixed asset over the anticipated life of the asset, showing a portion of the cost, for each accounting period of the life, as an expense on the income statement.

Derived demand: the business that one department has as a result of business in another department—for example, cocktail lounge revenue resulting from customers having drinks while eating in the dining room.

Direct cost or expense: an expense that can be distributed directly to an operating department and generally controllable by that department.

Direct method:

Discount: a reduction of the amount paid on a purchase because of prompt payment.

Discounted cash flow: a method of converting future inflows and/or outflows of cash to terms of today's dollars.

Discount grid: a table that shows the additional hotel room occupancy required to compensate when rack rates are discounted at various percentages.

Discretionary cost or expense: one that could be incurred but does not have to be at the present time.

Dividend: an amount paid out of net income, after tax, to stockholders as a return on their investment in the company.

Double-declining balance depreciation: A method of accelerated depreciation that allocates a larger amount of depreciation expense in the earlier years of the life of an asset.

Double-entry accrual accounting: an accounting procedure that requires equal debit and credit entries in the accounts for every business transaction. This ensures the accounting equation is kept in balance.

Double-occupancy rate: the percentage of rooms occupied in a hotel or motel that are occupied by more than one person.

Drawings: see *Withdrawals.*

Earnings per share: net income for the year divided by average shares outstanding during the year.

Elasticity of demand: the effect that a change in price has on demand for a product or service.

Electronic funds transfer: any transfer of funds done by electronic means, such as by telephone, computer, magnetic tape, or automatic teller machine.

Expenditure: payment in cash for purchase of a good or service, or incurrence of a liability for purchase of a good or service.

Expense: goods or services consumed or used in operating a business.

Expense outflows: outflows of assets consumed to generate sales revenue.

External audit: audit conducted by an objective, outside firm of auditors who are certified public accountants.

Feasibility study: a study prepared prior to starting a new business or expanding an existing one, to indicate whether the proposal seems feasible and will provide an adequate return on the investment.

First-in, first-out (FIFO) inventory costing: a method of inventory costing where the earliest items purchased are assumed to be the first ones used.

Financial accounting: information provided to users outside of a business that are in some way concerned or affected by the performance of the business.

Financial position: the financial condition of a business as indicated by its balance sheet.

Financial leverage: ratio analysis term used to describe the use of debt, rather than equity, financing to increase the return on ownership equity.

Financial statements: a balance sheet and an income statement and, where appropriate, a statement of retained earnings, a statement of source and use of working capital, and other supporting information.

Financing activities: raising money by debt (liability) or equity (owners).

Financing, interim: see *Interim financing.*

Fiscal year: an annual accounting period that is 12 months.

Fixed asset: asset of a long-term or capital nature that will be depreciated over a number of years.

Fixed asset turnover: annual sales revenue divided by average fixed assets.

Fixed budget: one that is not flexible or variable; one that is not adjusted to compensate for various possible levels of sales or revenue.

Fixed charges: indirect costs such as property taxes, insurance, interest, and depreciation. Sometimes referred to as indirect costs. See also *Direct cost* and *Undistributed operating cost.*

Fixed cost or expense: a cost that does not change, in the short run, with changes in volume of business.

Flexible budget: a budget based on more than one level of possible sales revenue.

Float (or bank): an amount of money advanced to an employee for change-making purposes. See also *Bank float.*

Folio: the account of a guest staying in a hotel or motel. Usually kept in the front office until paid.

Food cost percentage: see *Cost of sales.*

Franchise cost: the cost to purchase the right to use the name and/or services of another organization.

Full-cost accounting: The manager of a sales revenue operation knows the minimum sales revenue to be generated to cover all costs, even though control of some costs is not their responsibility.

Full disclosure principle: a principle of accounting whereby financial statements provide all the relevant information that a reader of them should have.

General ledger: a book of accounts holding those accounts from which the financial statements are prepared.

Generally accepted accounting principles (GAAP): Accounting principles developed over time and accepted as accounting rules, methods, and procedures used as a uniform basis to be used as a guide in the preparation of financial statements.

Goal congruence: the alignment of organizational goals with the personal and group goals of subordinates and superiors.

Going concern principle: an accounting assumption that a business entity is to remain in business indefinitely.

Goodwill: the value of an established business, based on its name or reputation, above the value of its tangible assets.

Graph: a method of illustrating accounting information in pictorial form.

Gross margin: sales revenue less cost of sales. Also called *gross profit.*

Gross return on assets: income before interest and income tax divided by total average assets for the period.

Guest account: see *Folio.*

High–low method: three-step method of separating costs into fixed and variable elements: first, the low figure is deducted from the high figure of each unit; then, the change in wage costs is divided by the change in units sold; finally, the variable cost per unit answer is used to calculate the fixed cost element. Also known as the *maximum–minimum method.*

Historic cost: the cost of something at the same time it was paid for, not adjusted to current cost.

Hospitality managerial accounting: specialized internal information to a business's managers responsible for directing and controlling operations within the hospitality industry.

House accounts: the accounts of guests staying in a hotel. See also *City ledger.*

Hubbart formula: a method of calculating required average room rate so that at a particular level of occupancy all costs will be covered and a desired return on investment achieved.

Income statement: a financial statement showing money earned from sales of goods and services, less expenses incurred to earn that income, for a period of time; sometimes referred to as the profit and loss statement.

Income summary: An account that receives the sums of all sales revenue and expense accounts when they are closed to a zero balance. The final balance of the income summary account will represent net income or net loss which is transferred to the capital account(s) or the retained earnings account.

Incremental budgeting: a method of budgeting whereby an increase, generally on a percentage basis, is automatically applied to last year's budget. See also *Zero-base budgeting.*

Independent variable: an item that is not affected by what happens to another item. For example, guest room sales are not affected by the number of maids on duty; room sales are the independent variable.

Indirect cost or expense: a cost not allocated directly to an operating department. See also *Direct cost, Fixed charges,* and *Undistributed operating cost.*

Indirect method: determining net cash flows from operations by starting with accrual net income and adjusting it for changes in current asset and current liability accounts.

Integrated banking: see *Concentration banking.*

Integrated pricing: a method of reviewing prices in two or more departments to ensure products are not priced independently of each other.

Interim financing: financing that is required for a new project from the time that construction is started until the project is completed. Sometimes referred to as bridge financing.

Internal audit: an appraisal of the operating and accounting controls of an establishment to ensure that internal control procedures are being followed and assets are adequately safeguarded.

Internal control: a system of procedures and forms established in a business to safeguard its assets and help ensure the accuracy of the information provided by its accounting system.

Internal rate of return (IRR): a method of measuring the value of a long-term investment using discounted cash flow. See also *Discounted cash flow.*

Inventory: merchandise (generally food and beverages) purchased but not yet used to generate sales revenue. See also *Physical inventory.*

Inventory turnover: cost of sales for a period of time divided by the average inventory for that period.

Investing activities: a type of cash flow activity involving transactions that affect noncurrent accounts. The purchase of a long-term asset creates a cash outflow; the sale of a long-term asset creates a cash inflow. The purchase of a long-term noncash equivalent investment creates a cash outflow; the sale of a noncash equivalent investment creates a cash inflow.

Investment: money loaned to a company either by way of a debt (liability) or equity (stock).

Invoice: document prepared to record the sale of goods or services and giving details about the transaction and total value of the sale.

Invoice approval form: a form or stamp showing that all necessary control steps have been carried out to ensure that an invoice is correct and can be paid.

Joint cost or expense: one that is shared by more than one department.

Journal: accounting record summarizing business transactions as they occur prior to posting the information to the individual accounts.

Journal entry: the recording of a business transaction in a journal.

Kiting: writing a check on one bank, failing to record it as a disbursement, and depositing it in another bank for fraudulent purposes.

Lapping: a method of fraud that can occur when an employee has complete control of accounts receivable and payments received on these accounts.

Last-in, first-out (LIFO) inventory costing: a method of inventory costing where the most recently purchased items are assumed to be the first ones used.

Lease: the renting of a building and/or equipment, usually in lieu of a purchase.

Leasehold improvements: architectural and interior design changes made to rented (leased) premises.

Ledger: a book of accounts in which business transactions are entered after having been recorded in journals.

Leverage: a method of financing whereby more debt (liabilities) is used than equity (owners' investment) to finance an operation.

Liability: a debt; an obligation.

Liquidation: the closing of a business by selling its assets and paying off the liabilities.

Liquidity ratio: the financial strength of a business in terms of its ability to pay off its short-term or current liabilities without difficulty; a healthy working capital position; a good current ratio.

Loan: an amount borrowed; a debt; a liability.

Loan principal: the repayment of the initial amount borrowed on a loan is a principal payment as distinct from interest that is in addition to principal payments.

Lockboxes: a special bank service to speed up the collection of accounts receivable.

Long-range cash flow: a cash flow budget for periods of time generally in excess of one year.

Long-term asset: see *Fixed asset.*

Long-term budget: a budget for a period of time generally in excess of one year.

Long-term investment: on a balance sheet, the value of leases, future employee benefits, deferred taxes, and other obligations not requiring interest payments during the next year.

Long-term liability: a debt or obligation to be paid off more than one year hence.

Long-term solvency ratio: ratio that indicates a company's ability to meet its long-term liabilities as they fall due; an example is the debt to equity ratio.

Loss: an excess of expenses over sales revenue.

Management by objectives (MBO): a concept based on the assumption that employees can be committed to their work, allowing for maximum involvement and participation in setting subgoals, personal goals, and performance standards for judging employees' work.

Manager's daily report: a report prepared daily, generally by the accounting office, to indicate each day's key business operating statistics, such as room occupancy percentage and average food check by meal period.

Marginal cost or expense: see *Variable cost or expense.*

Marketable securities: investments in notes or similar securities that can be readily converted into cash.

Market segment: a type of customer (such as business travelers) with whom an operation does business.

Market segment profit analysis (MSPA): a method of analyzing both sales and expenses (including indirect expenses) by market segment to determine the most profitable segments.

Market value: the current value of an asset, sometimes known as replacement value.

Markup: the difference between the cost of an item and its selling price.

Master budget: the overall budget for an establishment embracing all other budgets.

Matching principle: a principle of accrual accounting relating expenses to the sales revenue earned during a period regardless of when the cash was received or the expenses paid.

Materiality concept: the significance of an item in relation to the total business. If an item is not significant, other accounting principles may be ignored for reasons of practicality.

Memorandum invoice: a temporary, dummy invoice prepared in the absence of a proper invoice.

Menu engineering: a method of menu analysis that combines each menu item's contribution margin (gross profit) with its popularity, or the demand for that item by the restaurant's customers.

Mission statement: a statement detailing the purpose of a business.

Modified T account: a basic skeleton of a general ledger account used in an academic setting for beginning accounting students. The T account format focuses directly on the debit or credit posting of the account by showing how a posting affects the balance of the account. The modified T account identifies the account by name and the name of the account identifies the account as normally being either a debit or credit balanced account.

Monetary unit principle: the primary national monetary unit is used for recording numerical values of business exchanges and operating transactions.

Mortgage: a long-term debt or liability generally secured by using long-term assets (such as land and/or building) as collateral. See also *Chattel mortgage.*

Moving average: a method of forecasting that takes an average of the previous *n* periods of business and uses that average as the basis for the next period's forecast.

Mutual exclusivity: a mutually exclusive alternative requires that if only one of a number of proposals (such as a long-term investment) is accepted, all others will be rejected.

Net assets: see *Net worth.*

Net book value: see *Book value.*

Net income: total sales revenue from sales and other income less total expenses.

Net income to sales revenue ratio: net income divided by sales revenue and multiplied by 100.

Net present value (NPV): a method of measuring the value of a long-term investment using discounted cash flow. See also *Discounted cash flow.*

Net return on assets: net income after income taxes divided by total average assets for the period.

Net worth ratio: total assets less total liabilities; it equals owners' equity.

Noncontrollable costs or expenses: costs or expenses that are generally fixed in nature and a manager cannot influence the amount spent in the short run, such as rent or interest.

Notes payable: a liability documented by a written promise to pay at a specified time.

Note receivable: an asset documented by a written promise from the borrower to pay it.

Objectivity principle: a principle of accounting requiring all business transactions to be documented in writing.

Obligation: see *Debt.*

Occupancy percentage: the ratio of rooms occupied to rooms available expressed in percentage terms.

Operating activities: type of cash flow activity involving the primary objective of the business's production of sales revenue inflows from the exchange of good, merchandise, and services creating sales revenue inflows for cash or on credit.

Operating budget: a budget concerned with sales revenue and/or expenses.

Operating cost: see *Expense.*

Operating department: a department concerned with a particular segment of a business such as rooms or food.

Operating leverage: the relationship between fixed and variable expenses; high fixed expenses compared to variable expenses indicate high operating leverage.

Operating ratios: key business ratios (such as restaurant seat turnover and guest room occupancy percentage) that are often calculated daily.

Operating time period: period of time for which a business reports the financial condition and profitability of its business operation (e.g., a fiscal year, a month).

Opportunity cost: the cost of not doing something. If a company does not invest surplus cash, the interest income not gained by this is the opportunity cost.

Organization chart: a document showing levels of responsibility and authority, and lines of communication for an establishment.

Outstanding check: a check issued in payment of a debt that has not yet been cashed by the payee or that has been cashed in but has not yet been deducted from the payer's bank account.

Overhead: operating expenses of a business includes the cost of rent, utilities, interior decorations, music, property taxes, and insurance. The cost of labor, inventory, and materials are excluded.

Ownership equity: total assets minus total liabilities; net worth.

Paid-in capital, excess of par: the amount received by incorporated companies when their stock has sold for more than its par value; formerly referred to as *capital surplus.*

Partnership: an unincorporated business owned by two or more persons.

Payback period method: the time it takes to recover an investment; initial investment divided by net annual cash saving.

Percentage variance: the dollar variance from budget divided by the budgeted figure for that item, multiplied by 100.

Periodic inventory: a method of inventory control where the quantity of each item in stock is not known until an actual physical count of storeroom quantities is taken, usually at each month-end.

Periodic method: inventory control method that relies on an actual physical count and costing of the inventory over a specific period of time to determine the cost of sales.

Periodicity: an accounting principle that states that the operating results of a business should be monitored by preparing financial statements for periods of time.

Perpetual inventory: a method of inventory control where a continuous record is maintained for each item in stock on a perpetual inventory card of items received and items issued and a running balance of the quantity of each item in stock is constantly updated.

Perpetual inventory card: a form that is used to record the movement of all items in and out of storage rooms. One card is used for each item.

Perpetual method: inventory control method requiring a greater number of records for continuous updating of inventory showing the receipt and sale of each inventory item, and maintaining a running balance of inventory available.

Petty cash: a fund of money controlled by an individual from which minor purchases of goods or services can be paid.

Physical inventory: the actual counting, recording, and pricing of assets.

Post-closing trial balance: A balance done after preparing and posting closing entries.

Posting: recording of business transactions in accounts, or from journals to accounts.

Preferred stock or shares: a form of stock or share issued by a company to raise money, generally ranking before common stock with reference to dividends.

Prepaid expense: an expense paid for and shown as an asset until it is matched up with related sales revenue and shown as an expense. See *Matching principle.*

Present value: see *Discounted cash flow.*

Price/earnings ratio: for a company whose shares are publicly traded, market price per share divided by earnings per share.

Price variance: difference between budgeted price and actual price.

Product differentiation: a method of presenting a product or service in a different way from competitors, for example, by creating a unique ambience or providing superior service.

Profit: see *Net income.*

Profit and loss statement: see *Income statement.*

Profit center: a department (such as the rooms department) that generates profit or net income while controlling costs.

Profit margin: see *Net income to revenue ratio.*

Profit maximization: making the most amount of money in the shortest possible time.

Profit to sales ratio: see *Net income to revenue ratio.*

Profitability: the net income of a company related to the value of its assets, to the owners' equity, and to sales revenue.

Profitability ratios: ratios that measure profitability such as return on assets, return on investment, and net income to sales revenue.

Pro forma: forecast or tentative figures; a budgeted income statement is a pro forma statement.

Prorate: to allocate an amount on a logical basis; for example, to allocate overall company rent expenses to the operating departments on a basis of square footage occupied by each department.

Purchase order: a form prepared by the purchasing department authorizing a supplier to deliver needed goods and services to the establishment.

Purchase requisition: a form, usually prepared by a department head, requesting the purchasing department to buy required goods or services. See also *Requisition.*

Purchasing department: the department responsible for ensuring that supplies, equipment, and services are available to the establishment as required.

Quantity variance: the difference between budgeted and actual quantity.

Quick assets: cash and readily convertible securities and/or receivables.

Quick ratio: the ratio of quick assets to current liabilities.

Rack rate: the normal maximum rate charged for a hotel guest room.

Ratio: the relationship of one item to another. For example, $2,000 of current assets to $1,000 of current liabilities would be a 2:1 ratio.

Ratio analysis: the use of various ratios to monitor the ongoing progress of a business.

Receiving report: a form, completed daily, listing all goods received for the day.

Regression analysis: a statistical method that can be used in such areas as breaking down semifixed or semivariable expenses into their fixed and variable components and that can also be used in forecasting the sales revenue in one department (such as food) based on the sales revenue in another (such as rooms).

Relevant cost or expense: one that is important and to be considered in a particular business decision.

Replacement value: see *Market value.*

Requisition: a form, completed by an authorized person, requesting that needed items be issued from the storeroom.

Residual value: This is the estimated value of a physical long-lived asset at the end of its estimated useful life for depreciation purposes. The term also applies to the estimated value of a leased asset at the end of its leased life.

Resort hotel: generally one that has extensive recreational facilities.

Responsibility accounting: a method of accounting in which department heads or managers are made responsible for the departmental profit achieved.

Retained earnings: accumulated net income less accumulated losses less any dividends paid since the business began.

Return on assets: see *Gross return on assets.*

Return on investment: net income after income tax divided by average owners' equity for the period.

Revenue center: Revenue is generated but has little or no direct costs associated with its operation, such as the leasing of floor space within a major operation to a separate entity provides revenue to the major operation, all of which is profit.

Revenue management: a flexible pricing policy for rooms that adjusts quickly to supply and demand, with the objective of selling all rooms at all times.

Revenue mix: the ratio of sales revenue among various departments in a multidepartment establishment. See also *Sales mix.*

Revenue per available room (REVPAR): calculated by dividing total room revenue by available rooms or by multiplying occupancy percentage by average room rate.

Risk: possible deviation of actual cash flows from forecasted cash flows.

Room rate: the price charged for a guest room in a hotel or motel.

Room rate ratio: a hotel's actual average room rate for a period of time expressed as a percentage of the potential or maximum average room rate.

Sales revenue: money earned from sales and/or income received in exchange for goods or services.

Sales check: a document used in food and/or beverage operations to record the sales of goods.

Sales mix: the ratio of what people select from various menu items offered. See also *Revenue mix.*

Scrap value: see *Trade-in value.*

Seat turnover: number of seats available in a food and/or beverage operation divided into the number of seats used or occupied during a particular period.

Seasonal cycle: sales revenue cycle in which hospitality operations depend on vacationers to provide sales revenue during vacation months.

Semifixed or semivariable cost or expense: one that has both fixed and variable elements and is neither entirely fixed nor entirely variable in relation to sales.

Share: see *Common stock* and *Preferred stock.*

Short-term budget: a budget prepared for a period of time generally less than a year.

Skip: a person who has consumed goods or services in an establishment and has left without paying the bill.

Social goals: goals that are generally nonfinancial in nature but that may have an effect, positive or negative, on financial results.

Sole proprietorship: an unincorporated business owned by a single individual.

Solvency: the ability of a company to meet its debts as they become due.

Specific identification: inventory valuation method that records the actual cost of each item.

Standard cost or expense: what the cost should be for a particular level of sales or revenue.

Statement of business purpose: see *Mission statement.*

Statement of capital: ownership equity section of a financial statement for a sole proprietorship or partnership.

Statement of cash flows: a financial statement, produced at least annually, that uses the income statement, beginning and end of the year balance sheets, the statement of retained earnings, and other information to show all sources and uses of cash for the year.

Statement of changes in working capital: a statement showing in dollars the amount of change from one period to the next in each individual current asset and current liability account.

Statement of retained earnings: a statement showing previous balance sheet figures, plus net income for the period, less any dividends paid during the period, to arrive at current period-end retained earnings.

Statement of source and use of working capital: a statement showing previous period working capital balance plus funds received during the period (sources) less funds paid out during the period (uses) to arrive at current period-end working capital.

Stock: see *Common stock* and *Preferred stock.*

Stockholder: an investor who owns shares in a company by way of common and/or preferred stock.

Stockholders' equity: see *Ownership equity.*

Stock redemption: the purchase by a company of shares that it had originally sold to investors or stockholders.

Straight-line depreciation: a method of depreciation whereby equal portions of the amount paid for an asset are shown as an expense during each accounting period of the life of the asset.

Strategic budget: a long-term budget for periods of time generally in excess of one year.

Sum-of-the-years'-digits depreciation: a method of accelerated depreciation that allocates larger amounts of depreciation as an expense during the earlier years of the life of an asset.

Sunk cost or expense: a cost incurred that is no longer relevant and cannot affect any future decisions.

T account: a simplified form of account in the shape of a T, with account title on top, debit on the left, and credit on the right.

Total assets: all assets of a company added together, or the total resources available to it.

Trade-in value: the scrap or cash value of an asset at the time its useful life is over or when it is exchanged with cash for a new asset.

Transaction: a business event requiring an entry in the accounting records.

Treasury stock: Stock reacquired by a corporation; it can be resold to the public or retired.

Trend index: in a series of periods of operating results, the result for the first (base) period is given the value of one hundred. Subsequent period results are then given a number higher or lower than one hundred to better reflect each period's change relative to the base year.

Trend percentages: analysis method that results when the dollar amount between two periods is divided by the dollar amount of the first period to find the percentage of change.

Trend results: business operating results compared for a number of sequential periods.

Trial balance: a totaling of all debit balances and credit balances in accounts to ensure that total debits equal total credits.

Turnover ratios: ratios that measure the activity of an asset during an accounting period, such as inventory turnover.

Unadjusted trial balance: this trial balance shows each general ledger account and its balance before any adjusting entries are made to the accounts to correct sales revenue and expenses.

Undistributed operating cost or expense: one that is not normally controlled by or the responsibility of an operating department. See also *Direct cost* and *Fixed charges.*

Uniform System of Accounts: a method of presenting financial statement information so that comparison is made easier between establishments or with hospitality industry averages.

Units-of-production depreciation: method of depreciation basing expense on number of units used or produced by the asset during an accounting period to total estimated units to be used or produced during the life of the asset.

Variable budget: see *Flexible budget.*

Variable cost or expense: one that increases or decreases in direct, or linear, fashion with increases or decreases in related sales or revenue.

Variance analysis: a method of comparing budgeted figures with actual results, breaking differences down into quantity variance and price or cost variance.

Volume: level of sales expressed in dollars or units.

Voucher: a document supporting a business transaction.

Voucher system: a method of preparing special documents (vouchers) to support each purchase transaction to help control disbursements.

Weekly cycle: a sales revenue cycle for a 7-day period.

Weighted average inventory cost: a method of inventory costing where the average cost of each item in stock is recalculated each time more of that item is purchased and received.

Window dressing: a method of adjusting current asset and current liability accounts to improve the current ratio.

Withdrawals: monies taken out of a business by individual owners in a proprietorship or partnership (similar to dividends in an incorporated company).

Working capital: current assets less current liabilities.

Working capital management: see *Cash management.*

Working capital turnover: sales revenue divided by average working capital for the period.

Working papers: informal accounting records prepared as an aid to completion of the formal accounting records.

Worksheet: document prepared at the end of an accounting period to ensure that all the accounts are in balance and to show all information needed to journalize adjusting and closing entries, and to prepare major financial statements.

Yield management: a method in a hotel of matching customers' rooms purchase patterns and their demand for rooms to derive more precise occupancy forecasts and develop appropriate room rates to maximize revenue.

Yield management: practice in which managers seek to maximize sales revenue by using calculated yield statistics and basic principles of supply and demand to allocate services to patrons.

Yield statistics: actual total room revenue for a period of time divided by potential sales revenue for that period and multiplied by 100.

Zero-base budgeting: a method of budgeting that starts from a zero base and requires budget managers to justify each element of the present budget as well as any requested additions to it. See also *Incremental budgeting.*

INDEX